THE PRAIRIE WEST AS PROMISED LAND

THE PRAIRIE WEST AS PROMISED LAND

EDITED BY

R. DOUGLAS FRANCIS
& CHRIS KITZAN

UNIVERSITY OF CALGARY PRESS

University of Calgary Press
2500 University Drive NW
Calgary, Alberta
Canada T2N 1N4
www.uofcpress.com

LIBRARY AND ARCHIVES CANADA CATALOGUING IN PUBLICATION

The Prairie West as promised land / edited by R. Douglas Francis & Chris Kitzan.

Includes bibliographical references and index.
ISBN 978-1-55238-230-1

1. Prairie Provinces–History–Textbooks. I. Francis, R. D. (R. Douglas), 1944- II. Kitzan, Chris, 1970- III. Title: Promised land.

FC3237.P734 2007 971.2 C2007-903173-0

The University of Calgary Press acknowledges the support of the Alberta Foundation for the Arts for our publications. We acknowledge the financial support of the Government of Canada through the Book Publishing Industry Development Program (BPIDP) for our publishing activities. We acknowledge the financial support of the Canada Council for the Arts for our publishing program.

Canada Council for the Arts
Conseil des Arts du Canada

Printed and bound in Canada by Houghton Boston
♾ This book is printed on Enviro 100 Edition acid-free paper

Cover design, page design and typesetting by Melina Cusano

TABLE OF CONTENTS

SECTION II: SETTLING THE PROMISED LAND

SECTION III: ENVISIONING THE PRAIRIE WEST AS A PERFECT SOCIETY

SECTION IV:
A PROMISED LAND FOR THE "CHOSEN PEOPLE"

SECTION V:
READJUSTING THE VISION OF THE PROMISED LAND IN THE MODERN ERA

INTRODUCTION

R. Douglas Francis and Chris Kitzan

So the emblem of the West
Our bright Maple Leaf is bless'd
To its children of the goodly open hand;
All the nations of the earth
Are now learning of its worth
And are flocking to this wealthy, promised land.[1]

So concluded the final verse of "The Sugar Maple Tree," subtitled the "New National Song" and published in 1906 with various other songs, poems, letters, and testimonials in *The Last West: The Latest Gift of the Lady Bountiful*. While the song never amounted to anything, it did capture a popular image at the time of the Prairie West as the Promised Land. Thousands of others around the turn of the twentieth century could be found singing a similar tune. Winnipeg, one itinerant traveller rhapsodized, was the "gate to the promised land – the bourn to which flock men from all parts of the world who desire to convert into gold the infinite capabilities of a rich, virgin soil."[2] Boosters of Swan River, Manitoba, described their West as "God's good gift to a tired, teeming world; the new promised land running with peace and plenty,"[3] while the railways depicted it as "une veritable terre promise où la fortune attend l'homme laborieux, l'homme d'initiative."[4]

These quotations provide but a small sample of the countless ways in which the Prairie West was identified and depicted as a Promised Land in the late nineteenth and early twentieth centuries. Indeed, this image became *the* dominant perception of the region during the formative years of agricultural settlement from the mid-nineteenth century to the First World War. It motivated a group of Canadian expansionists in the mid-nineteenth century to pressure the newly created Canadian government to purchase the North West from the Hudson's Bay Company in 1869 so as to enable Canada to rival the United States as a great transcontinental nation. The Canadian government, in turn, drew on the same vision to inspire a transformation of the region from a fur trade domain into a vast agricultural homeland. Along with the railways and other prairie boosters, it further developed and propagated the image within the widely distributed promotional literature that was used to attract millions of immigrants from the four corners of the world. Like the biblical Promised Land, the Prairie West was described as a land "flowing with milk and honey" where those worthy of living there – the "Chosen People" – would enjoy happiness, prosperity, and contentment, free from the servitude that they experienced in the Old World. Whether escaping indentured labour, unproductive land, intolerable working and living conditions in industrial cities, religious persecution, or simply blocked opportunities, the Prairie West offered prospective immigrants the promise of something new and better.

While the specific desires and dreams of those who sought their future in the Canadian West were various, the image of the region as a prairie Promised Land was shaped and promoted in three broad forms. The first was that of an Arcadian paradise, a natural, simple, and peaceful retreat where individuals could escape from the stresses of urban and industrial society in Europe, the United States, or Eastern Canada to find solace and peace. As one poet-pamphleteer proclaimed:

Has ever the smoke of your factories
Obscured any longing ye had
For a life that gave promise of freedom
From all the unwholesome and bad,
The smoke, and the din, and the squalor –
The crowding that God never meant?
If not, ye may listen to Nature –
For to you has her message been sent.[5]

This myth pictured the Prairie West as an Edenic paradise. It was a region of natural beauty where one could commune with God, but equally a land of abundance, full of God's bountiful riches that were bestowed upon those worthy of living here. In *Prairie Agriculture*, George Bryce, a longtime resident of Manitoba and one of its early historians, captured these two images when he reminded immigrants that in the Prairie West the farmer could engage in the "purest of human pleasures," by remaining "in close touch with nature, watching over the sprouting seeds, tending the opening flowers, cultivating the useful herbs and grains, and gathering from the fruitful soil what the Great Creator supplies as the reward of our industry."[6]

The second version of the Prairie West as Promised Land image envisioned a region where, more than anywhere else, the perfect society could be created. This version was most strongly espoused by social gospellers, those who maintained that religion should be concerned principally with social issues not personal concerns. Social gospellers believed that the Prairie West was destined to be a New Jerusalem, or the Kingdom of God on Earth. Here only the virtuous and morally upright would reside because the region itself had the ability to transform its inhabitants into perfect individuals. The sentiment was colourfully captured by one pamphlet aimed at attracting British settlers to the Canadian West; its author predicted that "the time will come when the farmers of the North-West will form a peculiar class which never before had an existence. They will possess a national character decidedly their own – an agricultural aristocracy – strong in body, clear in understanding, honorable in business, moral in their lives, and determined in their conduct."[7] Once transformed, these inhabitants would live harmoniously and co-operatively, sharing moral and ethical values premised on the good of the community over that of the individual. William Lyon Mackenzie King, an ardent social gospeller and Canada's longest serving prime minister, held such an image of the Prairie West in his younger days. As King embarked on his political career, he saw his divine mission as "a true servant of God helping to make the Kingdom of Heaven prevail on Earth. This is what I love politics for."[8] King envisioned the Prairie West as being in the vanguard of social reform and of a rejuvenated Canadian nation.

The third perspective was a secular one, geared to the individual as opposed to society as a whole. This version posited the Prairie West as a *tabula rasa* – a blank sheet – upon which each individual could write his or her own destiny of success, wealth, and happiness. This myth depicted the region as being free of the limitations of privilege and tradition that hampered advancement in the East and in the Old World. It was a "land of opportunity" where almost anyone and everyone could succeed because the conditions for success were intrinsic to the region. Western newspapers promoted this perspective. Historian Paul Rutherford notes that the West they depicted was:

> ... a better society, free from the mistakes of other lands. By "better," they meant more simple, more individualistic. They took great pride in the democratic, egalitarian spirit of the west. They claimed that the prairies offered immigrants new opportunities, since elsewhere farms were poor and channels of advancement clogged by too many people. In the west the individual was released from the restrictions of privilege which interfered with his life even in eastern Canada. Wealth had to be earned, not inherited; success depended upon hard work, not birth.[9]

Whether drawn by descriptions of an Arcadian, societal, or a personal Promised Land, hundreds of thousands of immigrants flocked to the Canadian West near the turn of the century in search of utopia. Those who stayed rarely acknowledged the fact that many soon abandoned the region impoverished and disillusioned. It was simply assumed that those who failed suffered from a "lack of intelligence or perseverance," had "some other defect of character," or were simply not industrious enough.[10] This El Dorado, after all, was no place for the lazy. "No matter how milk and honey may abound, no matter how large and luscious are the grapes of Eschol," one early pamphleteer wrote, "all intending emigrants should remember, that a new country like this, is not the idlers paradise, that all its mines of wealth are surrounded by bustling difficulties.... Its great superiority is, that it is a land of opportunities."[11] The type of optimists that would pack up a family and head off to a new, largely undeveloped, land would rarely identify themselves as idlers or potential failures. Maintaining their optimism in the face of hardship and disappointment, those who stuck it out often blamed their failures on external interests, rarely on themselves or on the land. For here, according to W. L. Morton, the dean of prairie history, they faithfully continued to believe that they could author a "practical, really viable, utopia." Without such conviction, he concluded, those who stayed would never have "toiled and ventured as they did."[12]

Although their images, their experiences, and their reactions were ultimately unique, those promoting, seeking, and, occasionally, even realizing their visions of a prairie Promised Land drew some of their utopian inspiration from a well-established tradition that had long viewed North America as the New World of promise. Rooted in the Old World, this tradition was transplanted by early European adventurers and settlers. Shortly after Christopher Columbus "discovered" America, an image of that distant frontier as a Promised Land was already taking hold in the minds of Europeans. According to Ray Allen Billington, renowned for his histories of the American frontier, this image was " based not on what they knew but on what they hoped to be there."[13] They envisioned a veritable Garden of Eden, overflowing with Nature's bounties, only waiting for the right occupants – the "Chosen People" – to fulfill its destiny. Columbus himself had contributed to this positive image by proclaiming his discovered land to be "fertile to a limitless degree" and its native inhabitants "free of avarice because they claimed no property but held all things in common."[14]

As Britain secured a foothold in the New World, British imperialists added their own twist to this vision of America as the Promised Land. Seeking justification for their imperial expansion, and desirous of arousing enthusiasm for the Empire among the British public, British imperialists painted rosy pictures of exotic lands in the distant corners of the Empire.[15] They depicted America as an ideal land awaiting the British people – the master race – whose mission it was to bring the promise of the continent to fruition by populating the region and bringing the benefits of "civilization" to the "infidels" already there.

As settlement spread across the continent after the American War of Independence, so too did the vision of the Promised Land. Only now the vision took on an American quality. Frederick Jackson Turner, author of the Frontier Thesis, concluded that the American Promised Land was developed at the point where civilization met the wilderness – on the American frontier. As this point of contact kept repeating itself as settlement moved westward, it created a newer, purer America in the Great West. The American West became for Turner and his followers a mythical "region of the mind" that was more "real" than the "real West," that physical area west of the Mississippi Valley. It was here that America's promise would be fulfilled. Billington notes that: "the tendency of the image makers was to glorify western America as a land of beauty and rejuvenation, where Nature played a larger role in the purification of man than in decadent Europe."[16]

When America's westward expansion reached its outer limits, the Canadian West replaced it as both the practical and mythical "last best West." Although underpinned by the long-established North American Promised Land vision, the new promise of the Canadian West was acknowledged as something different. It was to be a gentler, milder west. Here the ideals of "peace, order, and good government" would be placed above that of the "inalienable rights of the individual," and British culture and British law and order above American frontier culture and vigilante rule. According to Carl Berger, the leading historian of English-Canadian imperialism, the ideal would be realized by transplanting only the best of Britain in the Canadian West. This sentiment was captured by imperialists like William Kirby, the popular Canadian novelist and poet, who portrayed the West as "an agrarian paradise to which the essence of British freedom was transferred and where it would flourish in isolation from those sinister forces that were destroying it in Britain."[17] The Canadian Prairie West as Promised Land would uphold values of harmony, co-operation, and the good of society as a whole. It was a different – and superior, Canadians believed – utopian vision of the Promised Land than that of the American West.

W. L. Morton was the first historian to identify Western Canada's unique strain of utopianism. While he speculated on its roots, and on the ways that it had impacted upon the history of the region in his essay "The Bias of Prairie Politics," he left it to a later generation to pursue the subject in depth.[18] In *Promise of Eden: The Canadian Expansionist Movement and the Idea of the West, 1856–1900*, Doug Owram explores the origins of the utopian image of the West in the minds of eastern Canadian expansionists and nationalists in the mid- to late-nineteenth century.[19] Paul Rutherford examines the role of Western Canadian newspaper editors in promoting the West as a utopia in "The Western Press and Regionalism." Rutherford notes that the newspaper editors "presented the settlers with a simple but attractive vision of a new rich land, an open society, and a great destiny."[20] Anthony Rasporich has studied specific utopian communities in the West, showing the diversity of approaches yet united effort to achieve the perfect society.[21] He has also taken up Morton's challenge to study the idea of utopianism in Western Canadian thought by at least highlighting the various strains of utopian thought that existed prior to the Second World War in his article "Utopia, Sect and Millennium, 1870–1940."[22] Douglas Francis has analyzed the utopian strain in the immigration literature sent out to lure immigrants to the West as well as in the artistic and literary works of the early settlement period in one of the chapters in his *Images of the West: Changing Perceptions of the Prairies, 1690–1960*.[23] In his essay "The Western Canadian Identity," Gerald Friesen has noted the "myths" that underlay prairie utopianism in the formative years of the West from environmentalism to pastoral and agrarian myths, physiocratic beliefs, and elements now associated with the "frontier thesis" – "democracy, egalitarianism, individualism, co-operation, virility, opportunity, innovation."[24] More recently, Brad Rennie has identified a utopian strain in the ideology of the Alberta farm movement in its formative years, which he analyzes in *The Rise of Agrarian Democracy: The United Farmers and Farm Women of Alberta, 1909–1921*.[25]

Most major studies that deal with some aspect of utopianism in Western Canada focus on the pre-First World War period. No attempt has been made to identify or trace utopian strains in Western thought after the Great War. The reason may be posited from the work of George Melnyk, an historian who has grappled with an understanding of the mythology of the West. In his essay "Western Myths: Beyond Alienation," Melnyk argues that the utopian spirit failed to survive beyond the settlement era. Realizing that they had been sold a false bill of goods, and that the West did not in fact offer an agricultural paradise or a society of equality, the settlers "denounced the utopian West as a mirage." Thus the utopian myth, he concludes, "floundered on its own exaggerated claims."[26]

Melnyk goes on to draw an important distinction between two different types of myths, those that are externally constructed from images that may or may not have any correlation with the reality of the region, and those coming out of indigenous movements from within the region itself.[27] While the latter have come closer to capturing the true spirit of the West, they have not necessarily been any more realistic. They also tend to dwell on what is wrong with the West, often laying the blame for the region's limitations on external forces, a trend that led to radicalism in the interwar years and alienation in the post-Second World War period. Of the latter, Melnyk writes: "It is a destructive interpretation and a negative image."[28]

While Melnyk has noted a positive utopian strain in the interwar years and has even suggested the need for an anti-alienation myth in the current West to get beyond the negativism associated with the contemporary image,[29] his writings tend to focus on the negative side of Western radicalism and alienation in the twentieth century. Francis likewise offers an ambivalent perspective on Western utopianism after the Great War. While he suggests that the utopian ideal that was so evident in the settlement era may have survived the war years "to fuel the agrarian protest movements,"[30] he too, like Melnyk, dwells on the negative side of agrarian protest. His chapter in *Images of the West* on "The Promised Land: The Utopian West" is followed by a chapter on "Western Realism." Thus even these two historians, while acknowledging a utopian strain in twentieth-century Western Canadian thought, have failed to pursue the topic further.

The decision by Francis and Melnyk to focus on disillusionment and realism in the interwar and postwar years is understandable. The bitter divisions within the country and the widespread loss of life on the battlefields of Europe belied the pre-war optimism that fuelled the image of the Promised Land. So too did the severe climatic conditions and the dramatic economic downturn that arrived during the 1930s. Recognizing the devastating psychological impact these events had on many Western Canadians, historians and political scientists have tended to interpret the agrarian revolt as a form of protest and widespread discontent. They have consequently focused on the grievances that fuelled these protest movements. What most have failed to emphasize or explore in any depth was the idealism and utopian spirit that also underlay this prairie protest. Political scientist Walter D. Young perceptively notes in *Democracy and Discontent*, his study of prairie protest, that the Canadian west spurred more protest movements than any other region in North America because they were optimistically aimed at creating a better society. He attributes this optimism to the "difference of expectation" among prairie settlers. As he explains: "The settlers had gone to the west filled with high hopes of a prosperous, independent, self-sufficient existence. Like many men before and after, they believed implicitly in the agrarian myth of solid honesty, purity and rewarding nature of rural life. Life was supposed to be good in the West."[31]

Young realized that Western protest is a double-edged sword. While it has been used to hack away at the existing society (and often at the outside forces believed to be responsible for limiting the potential of the region), it has also been invoked to realize a "better" or "new" West in the future – a prairie utopia. Such a perspective is in keeping with the nature of utopian thought throughout history. In his reflective study of utopianism, *Utopia and Critical Thinking*, Martin Plattel notes: "every utopia, which wishes to open new perspectives for society, at the same time, assumes a negative attitude toward the existing situation which it endeavours to change.... It offers both a destructive image of the present and a constructive image of the future."[32] The same can be said of optimism, a necessary utopian ingredient. Although joking that preaching on optimism in the West was like bringing coal to Newcastle, University of Toronto professor Reverend Robert Law, in a speech delivered in

Winnipeg in 1918, contended that optimists did not let failure deter them. In fact, they learned from it; if their dreams had not taken root, they had only to seek deeper soil in which to plant them. For optimism, he concluded is "not only a temperament or an attitude toward life; it is a philosophy, a creed."[33]

What Walter Young and Martin Plattel both observe is a healthy tension within utopian thought: a discontent with the present combined with a vision of something better for the future. The one feeds on the other. The aim of this volume and the focus of its articles is on the tension revealed by those in the past who have reflected on the concept of the Prairie West as Promised Land. We have included articles on individuals and groups who promoted the image, but equally on those who challenged that image or denied its validity. As well, we have attracted authors who have noted these tensions within the writings and artistic depictions of the Prairie West as Promised Land. Those who accepted the image often tempered it with a discussion of the existing obstacles that, once removed, would allow for the realization of the ideal. Equally, those who focused on the existing limitations of the region did so because they also had a vision of how the region could be better in the future, a vision that could only be realized by attacking those elements that impeded its realization. Both discontent with the present and hope for the future, pessimism and optimism in the Prairie West, are premised on a utopian faith in region as Promised Land, an enduring theme throughout Prairie history. It is the richly nuanced study of the theme of the Prairie West as Promised Land in these essays that makes this collection new and exciting.

We as editors realize the limitations of this volume. As a series of articles, it cannot tackle the subject of Promised Land holistically or comprehensively. We are also aware of gaps that remain unfilled, and aspects of the topic that need to be studied in greater detail. We would like to have had a better representation of those "usurped" or displaced by the dominant group within the West with their exclusionary image of the Promised Land. Likewise, we would like to see the significance of the Promised Land theme further explored in relationship to other groups such as Blacks, Asians, Jews, or Arabs, as well as other individuals and groups whose voices were muffled by advocates and boosters within the region. It is our hope that these essays will stimulate further research on the topic, fill in gaps, and provide greater depth on this important theme in prairie history. Still, the articles in this volume offer a fresh, new perspective on the important theme of the Prairie West as Promised Land, a theme that prevailed from the mid-nineteenth century when the concept first took hold to the present.

The articles are arranged under five sections. In Section I: Visions of the Promised Land are articles that look at various individuals or groups that promoted the image in the mid- to late-nineteenth century. In "The Promise of the West as Settlement Frontier," a revision of Chapter 3 of his ground-breaking study, *A Promise of Eden*, Doug Owram shows how the Canadian expansionists succeeded in shaping an image of the prairies as an agricultural paradise – a veritable Promised Land – for millions of potential homesteaders, and as the linchpin of a great Canadian nation. In "Adventurers in the Promised Land: British Writers in the Canadian North West, 1841–1913," Laurence Kitzan compares British writers in the North West in the years 1841 to 1913 to British imperial writers in other parts of the Empire in terms of the theme of Promised Land, thus reminding us that the British envisioned many of their colonial possessions as being promised lands. He also notes that the image of the Prairie West as Promised Land changed from that of an area of adventure in the fur trade era to that of a region of solitude where one could commune with God and Nature on the eve of settlement to a place of bounty for potential settlers during the settlement era. In "Canada's Rocky Mountain Parks: Rationality, Romanticism, and a Modern Canada," Matthew Wangler examines the conflicting views of three groups who were united in their vision of the Rocky Mountains as the Promised Land. First Nations saw the mountains as their "sacred place," while Euro-Canadian romantics saw them as a "natural sanctuary" in which to find solace and peace from the hectic pace of modern life. In contrast, park advocates viewed the Rockies as "exploitable resources," used to attract tourists by transforming them into a controlled and "sanitized" wilderness. In "Clifford Sifton's Vision of the Prairie West," David Hall examines the views of the man who masterminded the settlement of the West as minister of the interior from 1896 to 1905. Hall argues that Sifton was one of the great boosters of the region who believed that it was a "land of opportunity" for anyone willing to come and take advantage of all that the region had to offer. Accepting the West's potential as the Promised Land, Sifton used his boundless energy, superb organizational skills, and sheer determination to bring his vision into reality. It was these visions of the Prairie West as Promised Land that attracted visitors and settlers to the region.

The articles in Section II: Settling the Promised Land show the influence of the vision of the Promised Land on the settlement experience as well as on the adjustments that had to be made to bring the vision in line with reality. Sarah Carter's article, "'We Must Farm to Enable Us to Live': The Plains Cree and Agriculture to 1900," reinforces the fact that Aboriginal people were made "promises" by the federal government that were not kept. What might have been their "promised era" never materialized through no fault of their own. They were ready to embrace the vision of the Prairie West as a land of agricultural promise for themselves, but a series of factors, including a series of punitive measures instituted by the federal government, made it well nigh impossible for Aboriginals to fulfill their vision. In "Utopian Ideals and Community Settlements in Western Canada, 1880–1914," Anthony W. Rasporich examines the wide variety of utopian communities in Western Canada that emerged in the settlement period, all united in envisioning the region as a Promised Land. Few of the settlements realized their aspirations, yet their failures did not deter later utopian settlement experiments but rather, ironically, provided inspiration to those who believed they could learn from these mistakes in their own quest for the Promised Land in the Prairie West. In "'Land I Can Own': Settling in the Promised Land," Bill Waiser uses first-hand accounts of immigrants who homesteaded in Saskatchewan to show how they attempted to turn their dreams – and the promise of the immigration propaganda – of the Prairie West as a Promised Land into reality. He shows how pervasive the image of the West as a land of opportunity was for immigrants, and thus how difficult it was for many settlers to adjust to the realization that their vision of a Promised Land was a mirage.

As settlement proceeded apace and a prairie society took shape, some social reformers worried about the type of immigrants entering the region, the nature of the society emerging, and the shape of the prairie cities. They offered their advice as to how to create the perfect city, the ideal society, and a regional Promised Land. Section III: Envisioning the Prairie West as a Perfect Society examines the views of some prairie reformers. Anthony W. Rasporich examines the vision of prairie urban reformers in "The City Yes, The City No: Perfection by Design in the Western City." He notes how prairie urban reformers drew inspiration from urban reformers in Europe, Britain, and the United States in envisioning the perfect prairie city, while having to adjust to the environmental, social, and economic realities of the Canadian prairies. In "Land of the Second Chance: Nellie McClung's Vision of the Prairie West as Promised Land," Randi Warne argues that for this popular prairie social reformer the concept of "promise" in the Prairie West had to do with the opportunity the region afforded new immigrants to start life anew. Lacking precedents and without the restraints of tradition, this new region of Canada, McClung believed, could become the Promised Land. Warne, however, notes a darker side to McClung's later life vision of the West, a result of the impact of the Great War and the relative failure of reformers to achieve their objectives. Ultimately, however, her disillusionment was with the people, not with the land. In "The Kingdom of God on the Prairies: J. S. Woodsworth's Vision of the Prairie West as Promised Land," Douglas Francis argues that this noted prairie social gospeller believed that the Prairie West in the early twentieth century held the potential to become the veritable Kingdom of God on Earth. Woodsworth's vision of that earthly kingdom came closer to his social gospel ideals, Francis argues, only after he distanced himself from the views of the Methodist Church, especially with regard to the contribution of "foreigners" in transforming the Prairie West into the Promised Land. Brad Rennie examines the roots and the nature of the utopian spirit that inspired the agrarian reform movement in Alberta in "'A Far Green Country Unto a Swift Sunrise': The Utopianism of the Alberta Farm Movement, 1909–1923." The utopianism of the movement found practical expression in the establishment of the United Farmers of Alberta (UFA) government in 1921 and in the formation of the Alberta Wheat Pools of 1923.

Section IV: A Promised Land for the "Chosen People" examines the attitudes and actions of those individuals and groups on the prairies who wanted to shape the region into an ideal society for a select group only – the "Chosen People." They fought to restrict or to control certain ethnic or gendered groups in the West in an effort to achieve their vision of the Prairie West as Promised Land. In "'No Place for a Woman': Engendering Western Canadian Settlement," Catherine A. Cavanaugh argues that, from the outset of agricultural settlement on the prairies, the region was conceived as a "manly" space where women did not belong, or at least were not valued for their contribution. Depicting women as "civilizers" and "gentle tamers" in a West that was imagined to be rough, wild, and fiercely independent – all considered to be masculine traits – insinuated that the Prairie West as Promised Land was "no place for a woman." In "Preaching Purity in the Promised Land: Bishop Lloyd and the Immigration Debate," Chris Kitzan outlines Lloyd's attitudes and actions towards non-British immigrants within the context of his personal vision of the Promised Land – a prairie society wholly British in ethnic composition and culture. Lloyd believed that the Railways Agreement of 1925, which allowed Canadian railway companies to recruit agricultural labourers from central and eastern Europe, was undermining the British and Christian nature of the Prairie West. In response, he spearheaded a vociferous, and ultimately successful, national campaign aimed at abrogating the Agreement. In "Policing the Promised Land: The RCMP and Negative Nation Building in Alberta and Saskatchewan in the Interwar Period," Steve Hewitt examines the role of the Royal Canadian Mounted Police (RCMP) in restricting and controlling those immigrants who, according to the dominant Anglo-Celtic group in the West, did not qualify as "Chosen People." Particularly targeted were the Chinese, considered to be unassimilable and a threat to the safety of "white women," and Ukrainians, whose desire to maintain their ethnic identity was seen as a threat to a Canadian identity. Hewitt argues that the attempt to "purify" the West was particularly strong in the aftermath of the First World War as part of a concerted effort at nation-building.

A "New West" emerged in the post-World War II period in which the traditional image of the Prairie West as Promised Land appeared incongruent and thus came under critical review. The articles in Section V: Readjusting the Vision of the Promised Land in the Modern Era examine the transformation of the region and, along with it, the vision of the Prairie West as Promised Land. The image does not so much disappear as take on a new meaning more in line with the changed reality of the modern West. In "Uncertain Promise: The Prairie Farmer and the Post-War Era," Doug Owram chronicles the de-mythologizing of three basic tenets underlying the traditional vision of the Prairie West as Promised Land: that the Prairie West was the arch region in constructing a strong Canadian nation; that agriculture was the backbone of the prairie economy; and that prairie farmers were God's chosen people, setting the moral standards for the nation. Coming to terms with the reality that these myths no longer applied created a psychological trauma in the region as prairie inhabitants searched for new symbols of prairie identity. George Melnyk constructs the images of the Prairie West as Promised Land in the agrarian period (1880 to 1969) and then deconstructs that image in the post-agrarian period (since 1969) through a comparison of modern and post-modern prairie art in "The Artist's Eye: Modernist and

Postmodernist Visualizations of the Prairie West." He argues that artists of the modern period celebrated the overt achievements of agrarianism, while post-modern artists used the symbols and trappings of modern art in an ironic and irreverent way to de-mythologize the highly romantic and uncritical image of the Prairie West as Promised Land. Michael Fedyk deconstructs Saskatchewan's Golden Jubilee celebrations in 1955 in "The Dream Still Lives: Promised Land Narratives during the Saskatchewan Golden Jubilee." He argues that organizers of the event drew on the successes of past settlers but equally on the adversities they had faced, especially during the Great Depression, to construct a future for the province as the Promised Land. Like the biblical Promised Land, the Saskatchewan vision was premised on the belief that it would only come about through adversity and fortitude – after a time in the "wilderness." In "From Farm to Community: Co-operatives in Alberta and Saskatchewan, 1905–2005," Brett Fairbairn examines the changing nature and alternate roles of prairie co-operatives over the century since the creation of these two prairie provinces. He argues that co-operatives began as highly politicized rural organizations for agrarian interests but have since transformed into large urban organizations serving the consumer society. What has not changed over time is their attachment to the local community and their vision of the Promised Land as one where individuals banded together for the good of the community as a whole.

Even today the rhetoric of the West as Promised Land is used by the Alberta politicians to present the province as a free enterprise conduit and ideological mecca, while the government of Saskatchewan touts its socially progressive approach as an outcome of utopianism. These essays allow an analysis of the binary of discontent and hope, pessimism and optimism, as a symbiotic one. Image and myth are always in a dance with an evolving reality. It is a partnership made in history that westerners cannot seem to tear asunder.

NOTES

1 Final verse of "The Sugar Maple Tree Song," in George Livingston Dodds, *The Last West: The Latest Gift of the Lady Bountiful* (Winnipeg: Winnipeg Printing and Engraving, 1906), 30.

2 Herbert Grange, *An English Farmer in Canada and a Visit to the States: Being Notes and Observations by a Practical Farmer and Commercial Man on Canada as a Field for British Capital and Labour* (London: Blackie, 1904), 32.

3 Swan River Valley Board of Trade, *Swan River Valley: The Garden of the Canadian West* (Swan River, MB: Swan River Valley Board of Trade, 1907), 7.

4 Canadian Pacific Railway, *La laiterie, la culture, l'élevage du bétail et les mines dans le grand ouest du Canada* (Winnipeg: Compagnie du chemin de fer canadien du Pacifique, 1891?), 3.

5 "The Call of the Land," in Robert Thompson Anderson, *Canadian Born, and other Western Poems* (Edmonton: Esdale Press, 1913), 13.

6 George Bryce, *Prairie Agriculture: Containing a List of Chemical Experiments, a Series of Experiments on the Growth of Seeds, ... Advantages of Mixed Farming* (Winnipeg: Consolidated Stationery Company, ca. 1900), 1.

7 Thomas Spence, *The Question of the Hour! 1883: Where to Emigrate: Advice to Intending Emigrants from Great Britain with Important Facts for their Information Illustrating the Superiority of the Soil and Climate and the Advantages of the Great Canadian North-West as a Future Home, in Comparison with the Western States of America: Together with Other Valuable Information of Interest to the Capitalist and Settler* (Montreal, 1883), 16.

8 Quoted in Ramsay Cook, *The Regenerators: Social Criticism in Late Victorian English Canada* (Toronto: University of Toronto Press, 1985), 213. For a discussion of Mackenzie King's early vision of the Prairie West, see Robert A. Wardhaugh, *Mackenzie King and the Prairie West* (Toronto: University of Toronto Press, 2000), chap. 1.

9 Paul Rutherford, "The Western Press and Regionalism," *Canadian Historical Review* 53 (September 1971): 291–92.

10 Howard Angus Kennedy, *Canada: The Prairie Provinces in 1912* (Ottawa: Department of the Interior, 1913), 34.

11 Spence, *The Question of the Hour!*, 32, 21.

12 W. L. Morton, "A Century of Plain and Parkland," in *A Region of the Mind: Interpreting the Western Canadian Plains*, ed. Richard Allen (Regina: Canadian Plains Studies Centre, 1973), 174.

13 Ray Allen Billington, *Land of Savagery, Land of Promise: The European Image of the American Frontier in the Nineteenth Century* (New York: W.W. Norton, 1981), 1.

14 Quoted in ibid., 2–3.

15 See Laurence Kitzan, *Victorian Writers and the Image of Empire: The Rose-Colored Vision* (Westport, CT: Greenwood Press, 2001).

16 Billington, *Land of Savagery, Land of Promise*, 79–80.

17 Carl Berger, *The Sense of Power: Studies in the Ideas of Canadian Imperialism, 1867–1914* (Toronto: University of Toronto Press, 1970), 179.

18 W. L. Morton, "The Bias of Prairie Politics," in *Transactions of the Royal Society of Canada*, Series III, Vol. XLIX (June 1955): 57–66.

19 Doug Owram, *Promise of Eden: The Canadian Expansionist Movement and the Idea of the West, 1856–1900* (Toronto: University of Toronto Press, 1980).

20 Rutherford, "The Western Press and Regionalism," 291.

21 See A. W. Rasporich, "Utopian Ideals and Community Settlements in Western Canada, 1880–1914" (1977). Reprinted in this volume.

22 A. W. Rasporich, "Utopia, Sect and Millennium in Western Canada, 1870–1940," *Prairie Forum* 12, no. 2 (Fall 1987): 217–43.

23 R. Douglas Francis, *Images of the West: Changing Perceptions of the Prairies, 1690–1960* (Saskatoon: Western Producer Prairie Books, 1989).

24 Gerald Friesen, "The Western Canadian Identity," Canadian Historical Association Annual *Report* (1973): 15.

25 Bradford Rennie, *The Rise of Agrarian Democracy: The United Farmers and Farm Women of Alberta, 1900–1921* (Toronto: University of Toronto Press, 2000).

26 George Melnyk, "Western Myths: Beyond Alienation," in *Beyond Alienation: Political Essays on the West* (Calgary: Detselig Enterprises, 1993), 117. See as well George Melnyk, "The West as Protest: The Cycles of Regional Discontent," in *Riel to Reform: A History of Protest in Western Canada*, ed. George Melnyk (Saskatoon: Fifth House, 1992), 1–9.

27 Robert Irwin makes a similar distinction in "Breaking the Shackles of the Metropolitan Thesis: Prairie History, the Environment and Layered Identities," *Journal of Canadian Studies* 32 (Fall 1997): 100.

28 Melnyk, "Western Myths: Beyond Alienation," 120.

29 Ibid., 118–19.

30 Francis, *Images of the West*, 123.

31 Walter D. Young, *Democracy and Discontent: Progressivism, Socialism and Social Credit in the Canadian West* (Toronto: Ryerson Press, 1969), 109.

32 Martin G. Plattel, *Utopian and Critical Thinking* (Pittsburgh: Duquesne University Press, 1972), 44.

33 Rev. Professor Robert Law, *Optimism: An Address Delivered at the Annual Convocation of the University, May 10, 1918* (Winnipeg: University of Manitoba, 1918), 8.

I

VISIONS OF THE PROMISED LAND

1

THE PROMISE OF THE WEST AS SETTLEMENT FRONTIER

Doug Owram

By the mid-nineteenth century, the colony of the United Canadas had reached a critical stage.[1] In the years since the 1837 rebellions, new immigration and considerable construction in canals and then railways had transformed it from a straggling frontier colony to an entity that had begun to dream of a new and more glorious future. Yet that future was far from certain. French-English tensions and political deadlock frustrated governments. Railway construction was both a powerful tonic to the economy and a dangerous temptation to those who would build now and pay later. Most of all, the key ingredient to growth, an open frontier of high quality agricultural land, was filling up. New available lands in the province were both more inaccessible and marginal in quality. Toronto, in particular, was conscious of the need for room to grow if its business and political aspirations were to be fulfilled. As one report put it, Canada had to decide whether "this country shall ultimately become a Petty State or one of the Great Powers of the earth."[2]

At the same time, far to the west, the sprawling trade area of the Hudson's Bay Company was also changing. The growth of settlement created instability between the complex network of native tribes, Métis, Europeans, and newly enthusiastic Canadians in the area of Red River. The inability of the Company to enforce its fur trade monopoly after 1849 added to that instability, while growing criticism in Britain placed additional pressure on the venerable company. The future of the West seemed unlikely to remain in the hands of the great Company.

Dreams of growth on the part of the colony of the United Canadas and crisis in governance in the West spawned a group of expansionary enthusiasts. Centred in Toronto and along the Ottawa valley, these individuals were a loose collection of people who began to look westward in their search for the destiny of the United Canadas. Some, like George Brown, the editor of the Toronto *Globe*, were well-known public figures. Others, like sometime businessman and politician Alexander Macdonnell, had long associations with the West and endless business schemes for the region. Still others were politicians or civil servants whose interest arose from their links to provincial issues. They tended to be young, though not all of them were. There were probably more who were politically affiliated with the Reformers than with the Conservatives, though the issue was not a partisan one. What linked them was the cause itself. A new nationalism seemed to be fuelled by visions of a Canadian empire of the West within a grand imperial context.

The West was thus to be settled and civilized within the grand traditions of the British Empire, but outside of the domain of the Hudson's Bay Company. Earlier missionary writings had expressed concern about the Hudson's Bay Company's treatment of the native population. Expansionists relied on this rhetoric when it was convenient. The reality was, though, that the vision for the future of the West rested firmly upon a British dominated agricultural and commercial society. If asked about the native population in the region, the expansionists would have argued that the natives would benefit from the exposure to the benign civilizing forces of British culture. The reality, however, was that the existing population of the West was not central to the expansionists' vision for the future.

Initially, these expansionists seemed more romantic than realistic. Between them and this potential Promised Land lay a number of seemingly insurmountable obstacles. The inhospitable shield made gradual expansion of agriculture impossible. There would have to be a leap of nearly a thousand miles to carry agriculture to the prairies. Issues of transportation, governance, and the place of the native tribes all had to be considered. Nonetheless, throughout the years 1856 and 1857, in newspaper columns, parliamentary hearings, and pamphlets, this group of expansionists wrote enthusiastically that the challenges were incomparable to the benefits that would be gained. In the North West, Canada would find its future assured.

But how real were those supposed benefits? One of the most fundamental problems for those who would promote western development was the image of the West itself. For decades it had been seen as a remote, semi-arctic wilderness suitable only for the fur trade. If the North West was really a barren tract, forever destined by its soil and climate to remain a wilderness, then Canada, if it could be roused to action at all, would find its acquisition of limited use. The fur trade was hardly the means on which to build the new power base of the British Empire.

Enthusiastic expansionists, with a vision of the North West as a Promised Land, had raised the question of the possibilities of the North West as an agricultural frontier. In an attempt to convince themselves and the rest of Canada, expansionists soon began to make optimistic estimates as to the value of the land and climate. As early as December 16, 1856, the Toronto *Globe* stated hopefully that "there is a stretch of country" between Lake Superior and the Rocky Mountains "containing probably over two hundred million acres of cultivable land." Others, re-reading earlier works on the Hudson's Bay territories, began to find evidence to show, as James Fitzgerald had said years before, that the North West was not a barren land but that its resources had been hidden from the world by the Hudson's Bay Company.[3] Canadian expansionists had to find good land in the West if their visions were to come to anything. In response to their needs, the existing sources began to yield new, optimistic information on the region.

One of the best examples of the changing perspective on the land came in a map drawn up in one of the central institutions of expansionism, the Crown Lands Department. The new map of the North West, which Thomas Devine created in 1857, was based on the great works of Arrowsmith. Unlike Arrowsmith, however, Devine did not content himself with a delineation of the major physical features of the vast territory. His map was, in fact, as much a product of the expansionist impulse as was any editorial in the *Globe*. Even its title, "Map of the North West Part of Canada," reflected the new possessive attitude of the province to the Hudson's Bay territories. More basic to his purpose, however, was the running commentary, drawn largely from American sources, on the resources and capabilities of the region. The map was covered with such comments as the one placed between the North and South Saskatchewan rivers, which described "the scenery of these fertile valleys as magnificent, and the banks of the rivers on either side luxuriant beyond description." Even that area that would soon be described as an extension of the Great American Desert was termed "fine land."[4] Devine's ability to reshape the map of the North West without any new evidence revealed the power that man's perspective has on his conclusions.

All the enthusiastic estimates by the *Globe* and descriptions on Devine's map could not hide the fact that Canadians were largely ignorant of the resources of the North West. Expansionists were all too aware that little was known of the region and that, outside of Red River, agricultural experiments had been spotty and inconclusive. Even Red River had a far from perfect record, and 1857, at the very time when the region's agricultural capabilities were being extolled in Canada, brought the destruction of crops by the perennial pest, the grasshopper. Expansionists therefore could use those works that did praise the West with only limited effect. There was not enough evidence to conclude firmly that the West was capable of supporting agriculture.

If anything, all the hard evidence pointed in the opposite direction. When Hudson's Bay Company Governor Sir George Simpson testified negatively on the resources of the West before a British select committee, his comments could be dismissed as coming from a man with an obvious bias. Simpson, however, was not the only man to make a pessimistic assessment of the region. The famous British scientist, J. H. Lefroy, concluded that "agricultural settlement can make very slender progress in any portion of that region." Sir John Richardson, equally well known and respected for his knowledge of the territory, testified that, though "the alluvial points on the Saskatchewan might be productive," the prairie itself, "although fit, probably for sheep pasture, is not a soil that I think would be productive for cereal cultivation." Lefroy and Richardson were joined by Canadian John Ross and even by that original crusader, Alexander Isbister.[5] While few in 1857 would deny Canada the right in principle to open the North West, there were still many who felt that right to be of questionable value.

The Canadian government, although it had laid formal claim to the North West, was especially uncertain as to the actual value of the region. William Draper's testimony before the select committee clearly indicated that the position taken by the government in 1857 was essentially a holding action. It was a manifestation of the desire expressed some time earlier by the Montreal *Gazette* to "see that the way is cleared," should Canada decide it wanted to expand.[6] No legal or financial commitments had been made, nor were they likely to be until the government ascertained the nature of the resources and population of the region.

While the Canadian government's position in 1857 annoyed expansionists, it was, in spite of its limitation, a victory for their movement. The Canadian public and the Canadian and British governments had been made aware of the possibilities, and their interest guaranteed that further investigations would be undertaken. Over the next decade dozens of individuals would go west to look at this newly important region and would write of what they saw. Together they would dispel the ignorance of the North West that existed in 1857 and end for all time the negative assessments of the land and climate that had characterized the testimony of people like Lefroy and Richardson.

Those who went west over the next few years ranged from settlers in search of new land to merchants, adventurers, and tourists. Though there were probably as many reasons for going as there were people who went, it is possible to divide them into three general types. The first group to go, in times as well as classification, did so as a direct result of the claim that had been laid by the Canadian government in 1857. Canada had made a commitment and this, no matter how limited or hesitant, resulted, as Draper put it, in "a desire to survey and explore before we do anything."[7] Even as Draper presented the Canadian case in London, preparations were underway to follow up this resolution.

In July 1857 an expedition formed under the auspices of the Canadian government left Toronto for the North West. This group was formally under the charge of George Gladman, a retired fur trader whose primary qualification seems to have been his knowledge of the Hudson's Bay territories. Gladman had testified before the Canadian select committee on the Hudson's Bay Company and his stated opposition to the organization may have been seen by the government as additional qualification.[8] Gladman, however, proved to be only the nominal head of the party, a fact made clear when he was let go in 1858 as the expedition prepared for the second stage of its investigations.[9] The real charge of the Canadian scientific party rested in the hands of a professor from the University of Toronto, Henry Youle Hind.

Hind had been born in England and educated at Cambridge, emigrating to Canada in 1846. At the time the expedition was formed, he was a professor of chemistry and geology at Trinity College. Hind was only thirty-four years old in 1857, but in spite of his relatively youthful age, he was well known in Canadian scientific circles. He was one of the earliest members of the Canadian Institute and had edited that organization's periodical, the *Canadian Journal*, from 1852 to 1855. He was the author of several articles and had firmly established himself as a leading figure in the Toronto scientific community. His work had brought him to the attention of the head of the Canadian Geological Survey, Sir

William Logan, and Logan's recommendation had helped secure him a position on the North West party.[10] The expeditions of 1857 and 1858 were to make Hind's name familiar throughout Canada. At the same time, although he lived until 1908, these expeditions also marked the peak of his career. Hind seemed unable to refrain from attacking those whom he felt did not recognize his talents, and this inevitably had repercussions.[11] Most of his later years were spent as secretary of a women's school in Nova Scotia where, with one exception, he had little to do with the North West.

Another member of the Canadian expedition was to become almost as well known as Hind. Simon James Dawson was hired by the government to assess the potential of the territory between Lake Superior and the Red River as a line of communication. Dawson, a thirty-seven-year-old native of Scotland and brother of William Dawson, had emigrated to Canada and settled near Richmond in the expansionist Ottawa Valley. His position with the expedition marked his first senior appointment and began a connection with the region west of Lake Superior that was to last more than twenty years. On Dawson's shoulders fell the immense task of developing an initial transportation link between Canada and Red River.[12]

The Canadian expedition was not the only one to survey the West in 1857. The British government was also interested in the region over which it had ultimate, if remote, control. When a private exploration party was proposed by the prestigious Royal Geographical Society, the government picked up the idea and provided support. Midway through the hearings of the British select committee, authority was given to Captain John Palliser to proceed to the Hudson's Bay territories in order to make a scientific exploration of the country.

John Palliser was a member of the Irish gentry. At the age of forty, the only claim he could make to relevant experience was a hunting expedition he had made to the western United States a few years before.[13] No doubt he had learned something on that trip of the problems of wilderness travel and the necessity for tactful dealings with the Indians. The choice of Palliser as head of the expedition, however, can be most easily explained in terms of the inter-relationships of upper-class British society. In his initial support from the Royal Geographical Society and, eventually, from the British government, a string of influential people furthered Palliser's cause. It was influence that raised the Palliser expedition from the status of a private adventure to a major, official exploration under the auspices of the British government. Hudson's Bay magnate Edward Ellice commented caustically of the whole affair that Palliser simply had enough influence to allow him to indulge in his taste for buffalo hunting at government expense.[14] Ellice was too cynical, but only in his assessment of Palliser's motive, not in the degree to which the efforts of others played a role in the formation of the expedition.

Even Ellice could not challenge the credentials of the others who made up the party. A well-known botanist, Eugene Borgeau, was added to the group early in the planning stage and provided a high degree of expertise and enthusiasm throughout the exploration. Thomas Wright Blakiston, a British army officer, joined the group on the recommendation of Lefroy to act as magnetic observer; his scientific dedication and rigid personality soon brought him into conflict with Palliser. James Hector, only twenty-three years old and a recent graduate of the medical faculty of the University of Edinburgh, was perhaps the most important addition to the expedition; he worked closely with Palliser throughout and more than made up for his superior's lack of scientific training.[15]

The two scientific expeditions were perhaps the most important immediate consequence of the expansionist campaign. Others, however, had their interest aroused by expansionist writings and went west for very different reasons. In the years after 1857 the North West became almost fashionable as a destination for the young and adventurous tourist. With increasing frequency between 1857 and 1869, well-to-do young men from Britain headed to the far west in search of new game and new adventures. The purpose and attitudes of these men were in marked contrast to those of the members of the official expeditions. As one of them said, "it was no definite purpose of mine to gather notes, nor closely record the geographical features of the country."[16] Their aim was to experience the excitement of a wilderness before it succumbed to the forces of civilization. Many did not leave any records of their experiences and only the odd letter or other scrap of information indicates that they went west at all. Nevertheless, those who did write of their travels often provided some of the most acute and sensitive observations of a region in transition.

A third group had motives for going west and an attitude towards the region that distinguished them from both the scientists and the tourists. This group comprised those Canadians whose interest in the North West had been so aroused by expansionism that they emigrated to Red River, perhaps hoping to establish themselves before the rush began.

Typical of them was a nineteen-year-old doctor, John Christian Schultz, who set up practice in Red River in 1859. Schultz hoped that the move would enable him to combine an interesting life with a successful career.[17] His hopes were to be abundantly fulfilled. While others were not always as successful as Schultz, they did resemble him in other ways. They were also well-educated, young, and from middle-class Canadian families.[18] Like him they had accepted the promises of expansionism and based their lives on it. Their outlook and their published works reflected this fact.

Members of these three groups were, of course, far from homogeneous in their character or outlook. At the one extreme was the relatively high degree of scientific objectivity that Palliser brought to his examination of the region. Less swept up than others by the rhetoric of expansionism, Palliser refused to minimize those difficulties, particularly in the area of transportation, that would confront a transcontinental Canada.[19] At the other end of the spectrum were people like the young poet from Lanark, Charles Mair. When Mair visited the West in 1868 and 1869, he was already a complete convert to expansionism.[20] As a result he interpreted what he saw within the framework of expansionist ideals. On discovering, for instance, that the "utopia" of Red River was experiencing famine, he tried to dismiss it. "The half-breeds are the only people here who are starving," he wrote, and "it is their own fault – they won't farm."[21] Though Mair's ideas on the famine were later to change, his initial attempt to minimize a major economic crisis indicates the way in which expansionist hopes biased his views of the West.

In spite of their differences, all these people did have one thing in common: they viewed the West in the light of the expansionist campaign. Even those like Palliser who did not completely accept the expansionist image of the West were influenced by it. The events of 1856 and 1857 made it apparent that the region was on the eve of a major change and this alone was sufficient to alter perceptions of the North West. Previously, the West had been viewed in the context of its existent wilderness state; as a result, the land and climate had been judged within the perspective imposed by the fur trade. The expansionist campaign of 1856 and 1857, however, challenged all of the traditional premises and brought a new perspective to bear on the North West, seeing it as a Promised Land in terms of its agricultural potential.

The difference can be clearly seen in the writings and in the very travels of the men who went to the country after 1857. First, the focus of interest in the Hudson's Bay territories shifted to the south. Until 1857, as has been argued, the majority of scientific expeditions and a large proportion of the writings on the region had been concerned with the Arctic and Subarctic; the region that was to become the agricultural heartland of the West had generally been traversed only in a perfunctory manner on the way to more northerly regions. This changed as questions of settlement and commerce came to the fore. Setting the new pattern were the two official scientific expeditions. Neither Hind nor Palliser went north of the fifty-fourth degree of latitude and both spent most of their time within two hundred miles of the American border.[22] As a result, the years after 1857 saw the North West become progressively less associated with the Arctic.

Secondly, and even more important in determining the image that was formed of the region, travellers after 1857 began with the assumption not of an economy based on the wilderness but of the potential of an economy based on agriculture. Once again the two official expeditions set the pattern for later observers. Both were instructed to look specifically at those economic questions raised by the idea of expansion. Hind, for example, was told that the "character of the timber and soil [should be observed] and the general fitness of the latter for agricultural purposes ascertained."[23] The instructions led to an examination of the potential of the region rather than its present state.

The questions asked altered the conclusions that were reached. The West was no longer seen through the eyes of the fur trader or the missionary but through those of the potential farmer. The possibility of agriculture was not only no longer ignored, as it had been in the past, but became the first priority of those who would make observations on the West. Once again man's tendency to find what he expected or wanted to find was revealed. This time, however, all the circumstances oriented the observer towards agriculture rather than the fur trade. None of the travellers after 1857 could really claim to be journeying through unexplored territory. Even the expeditions of Palliser and Hind travelled through regions that had been known to fur traders and buffalo hunters for generations. Nevertheless, their purpose in going over these routes and their perspective on the country around them made those who went west original observers of the land.

The investigations of the North West that began in 1857 redefined the geographical and climatological structure of the prairie region between Red River and the Rocky Mountains. Newly acquired masses of detail made possible a type of description that had previously existed only for those well-travelled areas adjacent to fur trade posts. This additional information, set out by the Hind and Palliser expeditions, provided the basis for the redefinition of the geography of the North West. The work of Palliser and Hind, to which might be added the writings of the American, Lorin Blodgett, reshaped nineteenth-century geographical understanding of the region. Old generalizations concerning the hostile nature of the land were broken down. Such loose definitions and descriptions as had been circulated by fur traders and missionaries were given a new accuracy. The works of Blodgett, Hind, and Palliser became the new standard references for anyone who sought information on the North West.

The first of these men to come before the public was Lorin Blodgett. In 1857 he published his massive book, *The Climatology of the United States and the Temperate Latitudes of the North American Continent.* Blodgett offered little new hard evidence on the resources of the North West; he had only six sets of observations from all of British North America and not one of these was from the Hudson's Bay territories.[24] Nevertheless his work made a significant impact on both the scientific and popular mind. He was one of the first people to look at the West in terms of its agricultural possibilities, and his scientific method, no matter how limited his evidence, contributed to the expansionist campaign.

Blodgett appealed to those who would picture the North West as habitable because he challenged the assumption that latitude determined climate. As long as that belief was widely held, the North West could be viewed as suitable for settlement only with great difficulty. Canadians were aware of the harsh climate north of Lake Superior. The North West was just as far north and, it could be asked, even if the soil improved, was there any indication that climate would not prove an insurmountable barrier to settlement? Blodgett's answer was a resounding affirmative. Basing his work on the concept of the isotherm as developed by Alexander Humboldt, he concluded that such fears were groundless. Climate varies for reasons independent of latitude and any real understanding of a region has to come from following the isothermic temperature line rather than the degree of latitude. Specifically, in this case, the isothermic lines of the North West indicated "the increase of temperature westward is quite as rapid as it is southward to New Mexico." It was not the climate of Lake Superior that was analogous to the North West but another and much more favourable region in the same latitude: "The west and north of Europe are there reproduced."[25]

Blodgett's work was especially significant because it appeared in time to influence those Canadians who were about to undertake their own investigations of the North West. *Climatology* included in its subscription list the University of Toronto, the Canadian Institute, and the Magnetic and Metropolitan Observatory of Toronto.[26] It was thus well known in scientific circles in Canada from the beginning and, by 1858, if not before, both Henry Youle Hind and Simon Dawson were aware of Blodgett's conclusions.[27] His optimism and the sense of destiny his style conveyed may have remained with them as they viewed the vast new territory that Canada claimed as its own: "it is demonstrable that an area, not inferior in size to the whole of the United States east of the Mississippi, now almost wholly unoccupied, lies west of the 98th meridian and north of the 43rd parallel, which is perfectly adapted to the fullest occupation by cultivated nations."[28]

For obvious reasons Blodgett's work had a great deal of prestige in expansionist circles and it was to be quoted repeatedly in the future. It was, however, hardly the detailed set of observations that were needed to counter years of skepticism as to the value of the North West. Blodgett's work was inspirational, but it was the evidence accumulated by the expeditions under Palliser, Hind, and Dawson that was to reshape the North West in a new image.

The initial contribution made by Hind and Palliser was their division of the region into identifiable sub-regions.[29] The three "steppes" or levels described by others were confirmed and delineated and the resources of particular areas such as the valleys of the Swan River, the Assiniboine, and the Saskatchewan were recorded. Even the seemingly homogeneous prairie was found to contain very different conditions of soil and climate from place to place. The work of Palliser and Hind was influenced by the biases of their age, but this does not in any way depreciate the significant contribution to knowledge that resulted from their work in the North West.

What gave the work of Hind and Palliser such impact was the fact that, once they had torn apart old generalizations into more detailed observation, they reassembled the geographical picture of the North West into a clear and dramatic outline. Moreover, as suited their instructions, it was an outline based on the potential of the region rather than its actual state. The two terms that their expeditions made a standard part of geographical description in the West – "the fertile belt" and "Palliser's triangle" – were definitions that made sense only in terms of agriculture and settlement.

"Palliser's triangle" was an area of land "forming a triangle, having as its base the 49th parallel from the longitude 100 degrees to 114 degrees W., with its apex reaching the 52 parallel of latitude." It was a region characterized by the man who gave it its name as one of "arid plains" and "extensive sandy wastes," unfitted in all probability for agriculture.[30] Hind was in full agreement, describing the region as "not, in its present condition, fitted for the permanent habitation of civilized man."[31] Both men thus virtually dismissed over 16,000 square miles of the North West. The lands of the Sioux and the Blackfoot, so long avoided by the Hudson's Bay Company, were now seemingly destined to be avoided by the settler and farmer.

Both Palliser and Hind believed this triangle to be but a sub-region of a much vaster area of poor land and climate. Beginning with the accepted premise that there existed in the United States "a more or less arid desert," Palliser concluded that the area of bad land in the North West was in fact a northerly extension of that phenomenon. Hind, using American sources, came to the same conclusion, stating that "this vast treeless prairie forms in fact the northern limit of the great arid region of the eastern flank of the Rocky Mountains."[32] Whole areas, including the upper Qu'Appelle Valley, the South Saskatchewan, and the prairies between them and the border, thus became identified with the enormous wasteland that for more than a generation had been accepted as the heritage of the United States.

In such conclusions there was certainly nothing of great inspiration for the ardent expansionist. The identification of the prairie with the Great American Desert had existed long before Palliser and Hind made their trek west. If, however, the triangle did little to encourage the expansionists, the same can not be said of "the fertile belt." It was this term that gave the expansionists what they needed, and ultimately it dominated the image of the sterile triangle in determining the Canadian assessment of the value of the North West. The concept of "the fertile belt" was essential to those who wanted to annex the North West. Presented most dramatically by Hind in a map in his 1860 *Narrative*, the area of fertility was depicted as a vast band of yellow sweeping in a giant arc from the American border at Red River northwest to the forks of the Saskatchewan and from there along the North Saskatchewan to the Rocky Mountains. As it approached the foothills of the Rockies it turned southward until it reached the border at 114 degrees west.[33] Here was scientific and dramatic support for those who would extend the proven fertility of the Red River valley to the west. The settlement was no longer an oasis in a desert but simply the small, easternmost portion of a vast area of land suitable for settlement.

Interestingly, neither the existence of the triangle nor the fertile belt challenged the older traditional relation between the absence of trees and aridity. The line between the fertile belt and the triangle was the region that Palliser and Hind felt divided the natural prairie from those areas that would support trees. Hind, in fact, began his definition of the area that he thought was an extension of the American desert by describing it as a "vast treeless region."[34] Equally, both parties went out of their way to explain the absence of trees in some portions in the fertile belt. Palliser dismissed the absence of trees in the Battle River area as artificial, pointing to the "debris of large trees" as proof that the area could support vegetation. The lack of trees, both felt, was due to prairie fires, often set by Indians.[35] It was still felt necessary, then, to explain why trees did not exist in a supposedly fertile land.

Given the definition of Palliser's triangle and the caution with which both Hind and Palliser approached the prairie, it is perhaps surprising that they played such an important role in changing the image of the West. Their impact came from the fact that, having accepted an extension of the Great American Desert, they then imposed definite limits on it. Furthermore, they inserted between that area and the other region that had tainted the image of the West, the Arctic, an extensive band of fertile land and appropriate climate. The fertile belt provided the agricultural hinterland and path to the Pacific that the expansionists sought. Hind was acutely aware of this and thought it of sufficient importance to set it down in block letters.

> IT IS A PHYSICAL REALITY OF THE HIGHEST IMPORTANCE TO THE INTERESTS OF BRITISH NORTH AMERICA THAT THIS CONTINUOUS BELT CAN BE SETTLED AND CULTIVATED FROM A FEW MILES WEST OF THE LAKE OF THE WOODS TO THE PASSES OF THE ROCKY MOUNTAINS, AND ANY LINE OF COMMUNICATION, WHETHER BY WAGGON ROAD OR RAILROAD, PASSING THROUGH IT, WILL EVENTUALLY ENJOY THE GREAT ADVANTAGE OF

BEING FED BY AN AGRICULTURAL POPULATION FROM ONE EXTREMITY TO ANOTHER.[36]

This fact was what mattered to Canadians. The implications of the fertile belt made all the qualifications of both Hind and Palliser seem largely irrelevant. The point had been made that the North West was not a barrier to the Pacific and that it had resources that would allow it to become a valuable hinterland for Canada.

The importance of the two scientific expeditions was probably best summed up by Hind himself when he commented that "the North-West Territory is no longer a *terra incognita*."[37] The weakest link in the chain of expansionist arguments had been the lack of knowledge concerning the region in which they placed so much faith. Now, with the results of the expeditions, the expansionist could state with certainty that these reports "have established the immediate availability for the purposes of Colonization," of vast portions of the Hudson's Bay territory.[38]

The expansionists had not needed much convincing, of course. They simply found in the efforts of the scientific expeditions confirmation of what they had believed all along. The real importance of the two expeditions lay in the influence they had on those less committed. These people had needed proof, and in the seemingly objective assessments of Palliser and Hind they found strong evidence of the validity of the expansionist position. The work of these two parties provided sufficient material on the potential of the North West to shift the weight of evidence in favour of the expansionist argument. Over the next years it became standard in Canada to accept the conclusion that the North West was suitable for settlement rather than the reverse. By the time the Canadian government, in 1864, talked of the region as being "fertile and capable of sustaining a vast population," the comment was so commonplace as to be almost a cliché.[39]

Scientific reports alone were not responsible for the dramatic change in the image of the North West. While the volumes published on the two expeditions provided an essential basis of evidence, they were hardly the sort of material that could, by themselves, have wrought the transformation that took place in the public mind. Toronto scientist, Daniel Wilson, summed up their limitations when he commented: "it is an old saying that Parliament can print blue books, but it is beyond its power to make people read them."[40] In order to understand the change that occurred, it is necessary to consider all those writings, whether by scientist or layman, that appealed, as one expansionist later put it, to the "mind and emotion of the great agricultural community."[41] The experience of the West after 1857 was as much an emotional process as it was intellectual.

Anyone who went west in the later 1850s or 1860s could not escape the feeling that he was entering a distinct environment. The Hudson's Bay territories were still isolated from the rest of British North America in terms of both trade and transportation. Most who journeyed to Red River had to go by way of the United States to St. Paul in Minnesota and then northward. By the time they approached Fort Garry, they had left behind such symbols of civilization as the railroad and the telegraph. Those who made the journey saw their own movement from civilization to wilderness as significant. Travellers gloried in their ability to return to a basic, primitive mode of existence and to thrive on it. The travellers of the 1860s, especially those tourists who had come to the West specifically for a wilderness adventure, recreated the sense of romance that had long been apparent in the writings of R. M. Ballantyne. The Earl of Southesk, on leaving Crow Wing, Minnesota, in May 1859, exulted: "at last, I thought, at last the prisoner of civilization is free." British tourist Doctor William Cheadle was in a long-standing tradition when he concluded after his own trip on the prairies that "truly the pleasures of eating are utterly unknown in civilized life."[42]

In spite of the timelessness of such comments, the reaction to the wilderness was changing. In the wake of the expansionist campaign, explorers and travellers approached the wilderness in a manner that differentiated them from both the romantics and those earlier missionaries who had reacted so adversely to a heathen land. Gradually the very idea of the wilderness began to soften and change until it too conformed to the requirements of progress.

The changing approach was typified by the reaction of Henry Youle Hind, one of the first to reconcile the romance of the wilderness with the implications of expansionism. As had many before him, Hind found certain aspects of the wilderness life to be charming. His lengthy description of a camp scene early in the morning, where "the stars are slightly paling," and "the cold yellow light begins to show itself in the east," reveals that his sensitivity was not constricted by his scientific purpose. It was a description, more than anything else, of a peace inherent in nature, where "no sound at this season of the year disturbs the silence of the early dawn."[43] Such scenes and experiences of "boundless prairies, sweet scented breezes, and gorgeous sunset," made a trip to the North West an emotional as well as an intellectual experience for Hind.[44]

If the beauty and peace of the wilderness were impressive, so was its power. The incredible forces that often shattered the peace of nature were awesome to Hind. "The grandeur of a prairie on fire belongs to itself," he wrote. Only unchecked nature was capable of creating such an impressive sight, since "like a volcano in full activity, you cannot imitate it, because it is impossible to obtain those gigantic elements from which it derives its awful splendour." Even the tiny grasshoppers, massed in quantities appropriate to the vastness of the West, became an awe-inspiring, if destructive, manifestation of the power of the wilderness: "Lying on my back and looking upwards as near the sun as the light would permit, I saw the sky continually changing colour from blue to silver to white, ash grey and lead colours, according to the numbers in the passing cloud of insects ... the aspect of the heavens during the greatest flight was singularly striking. It produced a feeling of uneasiness, amazement and awe in our minds, as if some terrible, unforeseen calamity were about to happen."[45]

While Hind was awed by the wilderness, he felt no temptation to ascribe to it moral attributes superior to civilization. His enthusiasm, for instance, did not extend to the men who lived in the wilderness. His attitude to the Indian, in fact, resembled the disdain and pity of the missionary more that it did the praises of the romantic. The native, he felt, was not in harmony with nature but degraded by it. When Hind visited an Indian village he thought of the comparison "between the humanizing influence of civilization and the degraded, brutal condition of a barbarous heathen race." The power and beauty of the wilderness was indeed impressive, but it was too powerful for man to accept unaltered without becoming dominated by it.

Hind's whole reaction to the wilderness and to the North West rested on his awareness and acceptance of Canadian expansionism. The power and beauty of the wilderness were, for him, inseparable from his hopes for the movement. In fact, it simply demonstrated the importance of expansion: "the vast ocean of level prairie which lies to the West of Red River must be seen in its extraordinary aspects, before it can be rightly valued and understood in reference to its future occupation by an energetic and civilized race, able to improve on its vast capabilities and appreciate its marvelous beauties."[46] Hind felt none of the conflicts of

Alexander Ross, because for him the romance of the wilderness was not in its own intrinsic beauty but in its potential.

In the wake of the expansionist crusade, the land began to be viewed in terms of agricultural potential not only in the scientific but in the aesthetic sense. Descriptions of present scenes of beauty became prophecies of future development. "I stood upon the summit of the bluff" near the Qu'Appelle, wrote James Dickinson, a member of the Hind expedition, "looking down upon the glittering lake 300 feet below, and across the boundless plains, no living thing in view, no sound of life anywhere." It was a romantic scene in itself, but for Dickinson the romance was as much in the mind as in the scene, for he "thought of the time to come when will be seen passing swiftly along the distant horizon the white cloud of the locomotive on its way from Atlantic to Pacific, and when the valley will not resound from the merry voices of those who have come from the busy city on the banks of the Red River to see the beautiful lakes of the Qu'Appelle."[47] Similarly, while traversing a series of hills, the English tourists, Milton and Cheadle, "remarked to one another what a magnificent site for a house one of the promontories would be, and how happy many a poor farmer who tilled unkindly soil at home would feel in possession of the rich land which lay before us."[48]

In the later 1850s and 1860s man's reaction to the North West began increasingly to be determined by his sense of its potential, in the same way that, in previous years, the missionary's reaction had been conditioned by the fact that it was a heathen wilderness. The prairie took on a new beauty because of the resources it contained. As S. J. Dawson said of Red River, "if the scenic beauty which characterizes the region so near it to the eastward is wanting, this country is incomparably superior in all that can minister to the wants of man."[49] Charles Mair said almost the same thing a decade later when he enthused that "there is, in truth, a prospective poetry in the soil here – the poetry of comfort and independence."[50] It is not surprising that expansionists paid little heed to the costs that civilization would impose on the North West, for to them the charm of the wilderness lay mainly in its potential for development.

The expansionists' belief that civilization was, unquestionably, preferable to wilderness placed them closer to the missionary than to the romantic. Even the rhetoric of expansionism often resembled the earlier missionary tracts. Both groups looked forward continually to a time when "the deserts of the North-West shall blossom as a rose where now a few thousand savages drag out a miserable existence."[51] The views of the two groups were, however, far from identical. The missionary had found little beauty or romance in the wilderness. Landscape had, for him, been viewed against the heathen and miserable condition of the Indian. The expansionists, on the other hand, enthused over the land and scenery even as they looked to the time when it would be transformed. Whereas the missionary had found the wilderness a reproof to the moral sensibilities of man, the expansionist saw as positive the very fact that the land was still a wilderness.

The fact that vast areas of good and habitable land still existed was in fact providential. The region had been kept isolated from the rest of the world until Canada had been prepared to occupy it.[52] Now, however, its potential was becoming known. As George Brown pointed out, it involved an area "greater in extent than the whole soil of Russia," and that vast resource would be "opened up to civilization under the auspices of the British American Confederation."[53] The millions of acres available for the farmer were valuable precisely because even after centuries of expansion and settlement they lay "free and unoccupied."[54] The missionary had felt blocked and frustrated by the isolation, emptiness, and seeming permanence of the wilderness in which he worked. In contrast, the wilderness state added to the expansionist's estimate of the region. "Man is a grasshopper here," wrote Charles Mair, "making his way between the enormous discs of heaven and earth. And yet man is master of all this."[55]

This reaction to the wilderness was reinforced by the fact that the North West was in a state of flux. The wilderness, as if preparing for things to come, already seemed to be receding. "The days when it was possible to live in plenty by the gun and the net alone, have already gone by on the North Saskatchewan," wrote Milton and Cheadle. While the disappearance of game signalled the end of the wilderness, other developments predicted the coming of civilization. "The river communication has been opened up," Bishop Anderson noted in 1860; "the road over the prairie has been traversed; and the appliances of modern science have rendered more easy the production of some necessities of modern life."[56]

Observations such as these, and the continued orientation towards the potential of the region, began to diminish the image of the wilderness in the minds of those who observed the North West. Wilderness, by definition, implied a region where the natural dominated the works of man, whether those works be put in technological, legal, or spiritual terms. This view was common to Hind, Ross, and early missionaries.

Where earlier observers differed from the expansionists, however, was in the implication they drew from this fact. In various ways both the missionaries and Ross had tended to see the wilderness as irreconcilable with civilization; there was, in a sense, an adversary relationship between the two states. To Hind and the expansionists, no such implication was thought to be necessary; rather, civilization, the works of man, was a superstructure to be imposed on nature. The only necessary question, therefore, was whether the natural environment was suitable as a base for European society. The re-evaluation of the climate of the North West had, seemingly, answered that question, and thus in a very real sense the distinction between wilderness and civilization was reduced to matter of time. The only difference between the resident of the North West and that of Europe was, "if the greatness of his country is past or passing, ours is yet to come."[57]

The more that men viewed the North West in terms of its potential, the more they began to concentrate, either inadvertently or deliberately, on those attributes of the region that reinforced the new image. Those facets of the North West that had previously been used to emphasize its wilderness state – isolation, savagery, harshness – were downplayed and replaced with quite different attributes. Ruggedness of land and climate was scarcely mentioned; instead, the North West began to be described in terms more appropriate to the estate of a well-to-do landowner than to a vast unpeopled land: "There are many delightful spots in the belts, the herbage is clean as well shaven lawn, the clumps of aspen are neatly rounded as if by art, and where little lakes alive with waterfowl abound, the scenery is very charming, and appears to be artificial, the result of taste and skill, rather than the natural features of a wild, almost uninhabited country."[58] While the harsh and wild aspects of the North West were not ignored, there was an increased tendency, from the time of Hind on, to look on the North West as a rather tame wilderness.

Man's work in this vast land was not overlooked in the process. The expansionists turned to Red River as proof that men could live in the North West; even in the midst of an empty land, it was possible to develop a comfortable and civilized way of life. By its very nature the expansionist approach challenged Ross's argument that this isolated settlement was in danger of being overwhelmed by the wilderness that surrounded it. Rather, Red River was viewed as a somewhat quiet place with all the basic attributes of a civilized community: the people were "hardy, industrious, and thrifty," living in a settlement with "churches many; and educational advantages which will endure comparison with those of more pretentious communities."[59] In going to Red River, the Canadian was not entering the howling waste that had been imagined. Comfort was not just a thing of the East for, as Charles Mair wrote of Red River, "they live like Princes here." Houses were "all snug and respectable" and there was even "an hotel with two billiard tables."[60]

Canadians wished to see Red River as a civilized community and every opportunity that allowed them to do so was given great play. Typical of this was the attention given to the formation of the "Institute of Rupert's Land," a western version of the Canadian Institute. The *Nor'Wester*, that western voice of Canadian expansion, devoted columns to the event, while the meeting itself attracted most of the leading members of the community. In Toronto the *Canadian Journal* noted the event and well-respected Daniel Wilson wrote a long and laudatory article on its importance.[61]

The significance attached to the formation of the institute was very much a by-product of the Canadian expansionist outlook. The expansionist perspective had altered the social image of the region; in the most basic sense it can be said that those interested in or affected by expansionism had ceased to see the region as a true wilderness at all and were, instead, judging it as the outpost of an expanding and powerful civilization. Events that reinforced this image became, in themselves, further proof of the expansionist argument. As Daniel Wilson pointed out, the importance of the formation of the institute lay as much in the principle as in any contribution that might actually be made in the field of science. Its very existence was proof "of the changes which are slowly but surely revolutionizing this vast continent; and giving evidence of an intellectual dawn which heralds the period when states and empires of the great northwest are to claim their place in the world's commonwealth of nations." Given the historical significance of the occasion, it was somewhat unfortunate that the *Nor'Wester* referred to a number of stuffed animal specimens presented to the institute as "tastily arranged."[62]

If civilization triumphed over savagery in Red River, it was in part because that settlement was no longer an oasis in a dangerous and hostile wilderness. If one accepted the existence of the fertile belt, it was simply the eastern point of a vast region suited for the settlement of man. In social and political terms, it was no longer viewed as an island of civilization in the midst of barbarism, but simply the first of many centres of civilization. In fact, it came to be seen as the natural staging ground for other communities in the North West. As the *Globe* suggested as early as December 13, 1856, it could be made "the *point d'appui* for the Canadian government's operations in opening up the Hudson's Bay Territories for settlement." The more evidence that accumulated on the resources of the West, the more common this idea became. Expansionists began to realize that the presence of the settlement would make their task all that much easier. As S. J. Dawson argued in 1859: "There is already a nucleus where the wants of settlers may be supplied in the first instance, and the population of ten thousand ready to welcome them and give them the advantage of their experience."[63]

The new role that expansionists envisaged for Red River also meant that that community ceased to be seen in terms of its own history or society. Instead it came to be viewed, in the same manner as the wilderness, in terms of its future potential and in relation to Canadian expansion. "This settlement," wrote one George Le Vaux in 1869, "now surrounded by a vast wilderness, and far removed from the civilized world, is nevertheless destined to become the nucleus of a new empire."[64] That empire was to be the product of Canadian expansion, and, from at least 1860 on, Red River was viewed as the outpost of Canadian-Britannic civilization. Such an image not only had no place in it for the concept of an oasis but equally made impossible Alexander Ross's hope that it might serve as a link between the wilderness and civilization. Red River was to represent the force of civilization and the wilderness was to be subjugated.

Cumulatively, the writings on the West in this period shifted the tone of the expansionist campaign. Previously, the expansionist image of the settlement frontier had always been left ill-defined. In the wake of the exploring expeditions and the increasingly optimistic reports of the region, however, more attention began to be paid to the potential benefits of agricultural settlement. The populating of the prairies, rather than a hazy by-product of expansion, became an immediate and major reason for it. As early as 1865 George Brown talked ambitiously of the North West as the key factor in a scheme to establish "a government that will seek to turn the tide of European emigration into this northern half of the continent."[65] Such statements revealed that by the mid-1860s the idea of the West as an agricultural empire was becoming an important part of expansionism. Minerals, furs, and even the route to Asia began to be subordinated to the hope that the North West would become "the seat of an industrious, prosperous and powerful people."[66]

As agriculture assumed greater importance, expansionists began to appeal not only to those in the east who would benefit from annexation but to those who would go west to take up farms. The land began to be talked of as a place where "millions yet unborn may dwell in peace and prosperity."[67] Once it was ascertained that the North West did have resources to offer "temptation to the emigrant nowhere excelled," that fact became central to the expansionist campaign.[68] At the same time, this emphasis on the farmer did not alter the commercial orientation of the movement. The farm, rather than the fur trade or Asia, was now seen as the primary source of trade, but it was still trade that was discussed. There would be a "joint extension of settlement and commerce."[69] The future farmer of the North West was to be a man who bought and sold goods, not one leading a self-sufficient existence.

The idea of an agricultural empire significantly reinforced and extended the importance of the North West in the Canadian mind. More and more, in a time of uncertainty, it was looked to as the most important single guarantee of Canada's future existence. In terms of external relations, it would permit the development of a British North American nation with enough power to withstand any hostile pressures from the south. As one anonymous writer put it, the possession of the North West would make Canada "an almost impregnable military post in an enemy's country" and would be "the best possible barrier against aggression."[70] Charles Mair's friend, the formidable George Denison of Toronto, agreed. "I am very glad to hear such good accounts of the resources and fertility of the great North West," he wrote Mair in 1869, for "I have every confidence in time it will prove a great source of strength to the Dominion and together we men of the North (as Haliburton says) will be able to teach the Yankees that we will be as our ancestors have always been[,] a dominant race."[71]

Denison's interest in the whole question reveals the broadening appeal of the expansionist movement by the later 1860s. As estimates of the importance of the North West increased, the idea of expansion became a sort of umbrella solution for all of Canada's problems. As such, it appealed increasingly to all those Canadians who considered themselves ardent nationalists. Denison saw the region as the means by which his particular phobia, American annexation, could be avoided, but others, with different concerns, also looked to expansion as a solution. The response of the Canada First group, formed in Ottawa in 1868, was typical. Its members included, initially, Denison, Mair, R. G. Haliburton,

W. A. Foster, and H. J. Morgan.[72] Of all these men only Mair could be considered an expansionist; the others had different causes to keep them occupied. Yet all of them seem to have felt that the annexation of the North West was a necessary corollary to the preservation of the Canadian nation.

By the later 1860s, expansionism had become intertwined with nationalism. The very definition of the young Dominion of Canada and its hopes for the future were increasingly thought to be inseparable from the opening of the West. An editorial entitled "Patriotism" in the Toronto *Globe*, on February 16, 1869, summed up the relationship. In order to build a great country, Canadians had first to understand that their nation, while just emerging, was inferior to none, and the *Globe* argued, there was no reason to feel ashamed: "There are few countries, indeed, on the face of the earth of which the inhabitants have more reason to be proud." The source of that pride was the "mighty resources of the North West." Thomas D'Arcy McGee, Canada's most eloquent nationalist, put it even more succinctly when he concluded in 1868 that "the future of the Dominion depends on our early occupation of the rich prairie land."[73]

In the 1850s Canadians had sensed, or hoped, that they were on the threshold of some new stage in their evolution as a people. In their efforts to assure that this new stage would be attained, a number of them turned to the North West. By 1869 these expansionists had determined that future development to their own satisfaction. For them, the years between 1857 and 1869 simply brought confirmation of the belief that Canada's route to greatness was through the opening and settlement of the North West. The next stage had been defined, and in that definition the expansionist saw, as Mair put it, "the significance and inevitable grandeur of his country." "Far behind him are his glorious and old native province, the unsullied freedom of the North, the generous and untiring breed of men. Before him stretches through immeasurable distance the large and lovelier Canada." Mair's description of man's movement onto the prairies contained within it the expansionist vision of Canadian development. It was an image of history and destiny, for by imposing the traditions and energy of Canada's past to the potential for the future that existed in the North West lay "the path of empire and the garden of the world."[74] The image of the Prairie West as a Promised Land was established, to be projected in later writings on the region, and then, by the mid-twentieth century, challenged.

NOTES

1 This article is essentially a reprint of Chapter 3 of Doug Owram, *Promise of Eden: The Canadian Expansionist Movement and the Idea of the West, 1856–1900* (Toronto: University of Toronto Press, 1980).

2 Province of Canada. *Journals of the Legislative Assembly*, 1857, app. 17, "General Remarks."

3 See comments by William Kennedy in the *Globe*, Toronto, August 21, 1857; and report of meeting in Hamilton, ibid., September 25, 1857. See also Province of Canada, *Journals of the Legislative Assembly*, 1857, app. 17.

4 Library and Archives Canada (LAC), Devine, "North West Part of Canada," vi-11000-57, Toronto, March 1857.

5 *Select Committee*, "Minutes of Evidence," 13, 152, and 124–25.

6 *Gazette*, January 8, 1856.

7 *Select Committee*, "Minutes of Evidence," 212.

8 Ibid., app. 8, contains Gladman's testimony.

9 Henry Youle Hind, *Narrative of the Canadian Red River Exploring Expedition of 1857 and of the Assiniboine and Saskatchewan Exploring Expedition of 1858* (1860), I, 267.

10 Morris Zaslow, *Reading the Rocks* (Toronto: Macmillan, 1975), 78, and W. L. Morton, *Henry Youle Hind 1823–1908* (Toronto: University of Toronto Press, 1980).

11 Ibid., 96.

12 J. K. Johnson, ed., *The Canadian Directory of Parliament* (Ottawa: sn, 1968), 155–56.

13 Palliser, *Solitary Rambles and Adventures of a Hunter in the Prairies* (London, 1853).

14 Irene Spry, ed., *The Papers of the Palliser Expedition, 1857–1860* (Toronto: Champlain Society, 1968), "Introduction," xxiii, xxi.

15 Ibid., xxi.

16 Earl of Southesk, *Saskatchewan and the Rocky Mountains* (London, 1875), xxxii.

17 Public Archives of Manitoba, Winnipeg, Schultz Papers, vol. 16, Henry McKenney to Schultz, March 22, 1859.

18 The relative youthfulness of this group is easy to demonstrate: William Buckingham was 26 when he moved to Red River; William Colldwell, 24; Alexander Begg, 30; Thomas Spence, 34; Charles Mair, 31.

19 United Kingdom, *Further Papers Relative to the Exploration of British North America* (London, 1860), 5.

20 See Schultz Papers, vol. 16, Mair to Schultz, May 14, 1866, for an indication of his earlier interest in the West.

21 *Globe*, January 4, 1869; letter from Mair.

22 Hind, *Narrative*, contains the route map; LAC, "Route of the Exploring Expedition under Command of Captain Palliser," VI/701, 1857–58, shows the route taken by that expedition.

23 T.J.J. Loranger to Hind, April 27, 1858; cited in Henry Youle Hind, *North-West Territory: Report on the Assiniboine and Saskatchewan Exploring Expedition* (Toronto, 1859), 2.

24 G. S. Dunbar, "Isotherms and Politics," in *Prairie Perspectives 2*, eds. A. W. Rasporich and H. C. Klassen (Toronto: Holt, Rinehart and Winston, 1973), 89.

25 L. Blodgett, *Climatology* (Philadelphia, 1857), 533, 529.

26 Ibid., "Introduction."

27 Dawson cites Blodgett in his 1859 report; *Journals of the Legislative Assembly*, 1859, app. 36. "The Great North-West," The *Canadian Almanac and Repository of Useful Knowledge*, 1858, also cites Blodgett and is attributed to Hind in John Warkentin, "Steppe, Desert and Empire," in Rasporich and Klassen, *Prairie Perspectives 2*, 132–33, n. 40.

28 Blodgett, *Climatology*, 529.

29 Warkentin, "Steppe, Desert and Empire," 116–21.

30 United Kingdom, *The Journals, Detailed Reports and Observations Relative to the Exploration by Captain Palliser*, 1859, "The General Report," 7, 10–11.
31 Hind, *North-West Territory*, 31.
32 *Journals ... by Captain Palliser*, "General Report," 7; Hind, ibid., 123.
33 Hind, *Narrative*, I, "Map of the Country from Lake Superior to the Pacific Ocean."
34 Hind, *North-West Territory*, 124.
35 *Journals ... by Captain Palliser*, 86; Palliser, *Papers Relative to the Exploration of British North America* (London, 1859), 30; Hind, ibid., 53.
36 Hind, *Narrative*, II, 234.
37 [Hind], "North-West British America," *British American Magazine*, May 1863, 3.
38 *Nor'Wester*, "Prospectus," 1859.
39 "Report of the Committee of the Executive Council," approved November 11, 1864; *Documents Relating to the Opening up of the North West Territories to Settlement and Colonisation* (n.p., 1865), 4.
40 *Canadian Journal* (March 1861), 175.
41 Charles Mair, "The New Canada: Its Natural Features and Climate [Part 1]," *Canadian Monthly and National Review* 8 (July 1875): 1–8, 1.
42 Southesk, *Saskatchewan and the Rocky Mountains*, 13; Viscount Milton and W. B. Cheadle, *The North-West Passage by Land* (London, 1865), 98.
43 Hind, *Narrative*, I, 70–2.
44 Hind, T. C. Keefer, J. G. Hodgins, Charles Robb, M. H. Perley, and Rev. W. Murray, *Eighty Years' Progress of British North America* (Toronto, 1863), 88.
45 Hind, *North-West Territory*, 52, 44.
46 Hind, *Narrative*, I, 124, 134.
47 Ibid., 373.
48 Milton and Cheadle, *North-West Passage by Land*, 72.
49 *Journals of the Legislative Assembly*, 1859, app. 36.
50 *Globe*, January 20, 1869; letter from Mair.
51 George V. Le Vaux, "The Great North West – No. II," *New Dominion Monthly*, January 1869, 226.
52 Alexander Morris, *The Hudson's Bay and Pacific Territories* (Montreal, 1859), 7–10.
53 Province of Canada, *Parliamentary Debates on the Subject of the Confederation of the British North American Provinces* (Quebec, 1865), 86.
54 Hind, *Narrative*, I, 191.
55 *Globe*, May 28, 1869; letter from Mair.
56 Milton and Cheadle, *North-West Passage by Land*, 160; David Anderson, *A Charge Delivered to the Clergy of the Diocese of Rupert's Land at his Triennial Visitation, January 6, 1860* (London, 1860), 8.
57 *Nor'Wester*, February 14, 1860.
58 Hind, *North-West Territory*, 68.
59 *Nor'Wester*, "Prospectus."
60 *Globe*, 14 and December 27, 1868; letters from Mair.
61 *Nor'Wester*, March 5, April 16, 1862; Wilson, "Science in Rupert's Land," *Canadian Journal* (July 1862): 336–47.
62 Wilson, ibid., 336; *Nor'wester*, April 16, 1862.
63 *Journals of the Legislative Assembly*, 1859, app. 62 and 36.
64 Le Vaux, "The Great North West – No. II," 222.
65 *Confederation Debates*, 86.
66 Hind et al., *Eighty Years' Progress*, 80.
67 W.H.W., "The Red River Settlement," *New Dominion Monthly* (May 1868), 101.
68 *Nor'Wester*, "Prospectus."
69 Alexander Russell, *The Red River Country, Hudson's Bay and the North-West Territories Considered in Relation to Canada* (Ottawa, 1869), 5.

70 *The Interests of the British Empire in North America* (Ottawa, 1868), 5.

71 Queen's University Library, Kingston, Mair Papers, vol. 1, Denison to Mair, March 10, 1869.

72 Carl Berger, *The Sense of Power: Studies in the Ideas of Canadian Imperialism, 1867–1914* (Toronto: University of Toronto Press, 1970), 49–51.

73 Speech read before the Montreal Mechanics' Institute; cited in *Nor'Wester*, April 15, 1868.

74 *Globe*, May 28, 1869; letter from Mair.

2

ADVENTURERS IN THE PROMISED LAND: BRITISH WRITERS IN THE CANADIAN NORTH WEST, 1841–1913

Laurence Kitzan

Since the formation of the Hudson's Bay Company in 1670, there has been a constant stream of individuals from Britain who have come out to what became the Canadian North West, later called the Prairie West, either to stay long periods, even lifetimes, or for relatively short visits. Many wrote books about their experiences, books for which there was a ready market, as, indeed, there was for much of what was written about all parts of the world where British men and women increasingly travelled. Their books about the North West helped to create powerful images of this area, particularly of the prairies. Because the writers came at different times and brought with them different preconceptions, the images they created were "moving images," changing with the times and the needs of the image makers. By the middle of the nineteenth century, the fur trader's image of a land of a bountiful economic resource had begun to shift to wider images of a Promised Land, images that held the promise of adventure, of freedom, of meeting the challenges of the wild and overcoming barriers, whether physical or psychological. From the late nineteenth century up to the First World War, the image of an agricultural frontier dominated, holding out the promise of a better life for the discontented and restless inhabitants of the industrialized societies of Britain and Western Europe, and later, for the stratified and oppressed populations of Eastern Europe.

This paper deals with a number of British writers in the period 1841–1913 whose works illustrate the differing versions of the North West as Promised Land.[1] Robert Ballantyne, especially in his fiction, emphasized freedom and exhilarating, sometimes heart-stopping, adventure. The Earl of Southesk, who initially appeared to be one of the popular breed of great white hunters, like Frederick C. Selous,[2] found in the North West the solution to a number of his dilemmas. William Francis Butler discovered his personal Promised Land in an area that was best described in the titles of his first two books, *The Great Lone Land*, which went through many editions and impacted a generation, and the poetic *The Wild North Land*. In the settlement era from 1880 to 1914, Catherine Laura Johnstone, John Foster Fraser, James Lumsden, and Mrs. George Cran found in the North West a land that was not a ready-made utopia, but a true Promised Land for those British settlers who had earned the right to it.

Earlier periods of British history certainly had their travellers and explorers[3] who wrote books about their adventures. Prior to the nineteenth century, most exploration had an economic purpose, such as the search for riches, or a route to areas of great trading potential, which motivated the numerous voyages seeking a viable North West Passage and North East Passage to the Orient.[4] In the eighteenth century, the Age of Enlightenment, economic motives were partially modified by a search for knowledge. Perhaps the most notable example of this mixture was Captain James Cook, who undertook three voyages of exploration that covered vast areas of the Pacific.[5] The same mixture prevailed in the nineteenth century and was behind the various expeditions to Africa, which set the stage for later imperial acquisitions in that continent by a number of European states.

By the middle of the nineteenth century, while explorations continued in areas such as Central Africa, in British North America most exploratory travels were to fill in the blanks of the maps of the far northern regions of the continent, to find routes for railways through the mountainous areas into British Columbia, and to map the agricultural potential of the Great Plains. Increasingly, the British who travelled in the Canadian North West came for information, experience, and the fulfillment of personal goals and desires.

British travels and explorations in the nineteenth century coincided with the development of a popular imperialism that stretched well into the twentieth century. To a large extent this popular imperialism was fuelled by the increasing number of adventure stories set in various areas of the world, many parts of which were to become, in the course of the nineteenth century, part of Britain's formal and informal empire.[6] While certain individuals might equate this imperialism with jingoism, or the desire for the acquisition of new territories, for the majority of the British people who bothered to think about empire, imperialism was a sentiment celebrating what to them was so obviously true. The British had reached the height of achievement, directed either by natural evolution or divine plan. This belief shaped their attitudes to life and their relationships to other peoples and parts of the world, generally in a passive way. For British travellers in the Canadian West, the acquisition of further territory was irrelevant; they were fully aware that the North West had been claimed by Britain since the seventeenth century, and that they were travelling in a British colony. They came to enjoy the region's bounty and to ensure its continuance as part of the great British Empire.

Except for Robert Ballantyne, whose experience was, mainly, not in Canadian territory but in a land claimed by a trading company that exercised only a rudimentary control in the lands where it operated, the writers included in this study were writing about a self-governing colony. Self-governing status meant that the British government to a large extent was only peripherally involved in the internal affairs of Canada. The historian J. A. Froude, writing in 1885,[7] felt that the self-governing dominions of the empire, if properly treated by Britain and not foolishly pushed away, would be a strength to Britain because the colonists "prize their privileges as British subjects. They are proud of belonging to a nationality on whose flag the sun never sets."[8] The writers in this paper who investigated the North West in the 1890s and in the pre-1914 twentieth century operated on the assumption that Canada was, and would continue to be, a contented part of the British Empire, and, while not a spectacular "jewel in the crown" like India, would strengthen the empire through the "bread basket" development of its Great Plains.

The published works of many explorers and travellers in many parts of the world made known to their readers various elements of a "promised land."[9] Most writers emphasized the "promise" involved. A fur trader crisscrossing the Canadian North West, for example, always pursued the promise of maintaining or increasing a profitable enterprise, while a hunter saw in the same territory the promise of an almost unlimited supply of animals, mostly large, and some dangerous, which he could shoot. The curious traveller was attracted by the promise of new and exotic sights and experiences; in this there was often an element of self-testing. For many of the newcomers, the Promised Land as a land "flowing with milk and honey" also had a strong element of attraction. This was especially true of those who, in rapidly increasing numbers,[10] uprooted themselves, to settle in a new land. Now that the outer reaches of the American frontier had been reached, the Dominion of Canada offered large quantities of arable land, and the advantage of being nearer to Britain than the other settlement colonies.

Adventurers who travelled and then wrote books about their travels helped to create images of the lands through which they had adventured, images that often took strong hold on generations of their readers.[11] The images could, and often did, create romantic expectations and ideals, and such images characterized much of the literature of travel in the Canadian North West.[12] At the same time the writers often included powerful images that were not so romantic, that presented the Canadian North West as less than the ideal Promised Land. In many ways these images appeared to contradict both the romance and the promise. Such books certainly portrayed the North West as a land of opportunity, not for the faint-hearted, but for those who were willing to take up the challenges that would bring out the best in British character.

Robert Michael Ballantyne, best known as a writer of a large number of boys' adventure novels in the last half of the nineteenth century, started his adventures in the adult world as an employee of the Hudson's Bay Company. When he received his letter of appointment as apprentice clerk in May of 1841, he "was thrown into a state of exstatic [*sic*] joy."[13] Such a statement by a sixteen-year-old boy suggests a surge of romantic images about the life of a fur trader, but Ballantyne went on to add that "from that moment I fancied myself a complete man-of-business and treated my old companions with the condescending suavity of one who knows that he is talking to his inferiors."[14] Young Ballantyne came from a Scottish middle-class family in severe enough economic difficulties that his formal education was cut short, and he was consequently home-schooled;[15] now he had a job and prospects such as had sent many Scots into the service of the Hudson's Bay Company, most for a life-long career. For Robert Ballantyne, it did not lead to a lifetime of fur trading in the Canadian North West, but it did point him in the direction of a successful career as a writer of adventure stories when a relative persuaded him to publish a re-written version of his letters home, *Hudson's*

Bay. While the book itself was not a financial success,[16] it provided him with the material for a novel, *The Young Fur-Traders: Snowflakes and Sunbeams*,[17] which was to launch him as an increasingly successful writer of adventure stories for boys.

For Ballantyne the voyage to Hudson Bay was not the stuff of romantic sea tales. No raging storms disturbed the voyage, no exciting encounters at sea, no greater danger than pushing through increasingly thick ice packs, which, however, hindered the ship very little. Similarly, when Ballantyne first saw the shores of Hudson Bay, near York Factory, he noted: "truly their appearance was any thing but prepossessing."[18] As he was coming ashore "a small bark canoe, with an Indian and his wife in it, glided swiftly past us, and this was the first Indian, and the first of those slender craft, I had seen," a romantic thrill, no doubt, especially since he had earlier expressed his disappointment at not seeing any "Esqimaux." This image of romance was quickly dispelled, however, by his next statement: "Afterwards, I became more intimately acquainted with them than was altogether agreeable."[19]

Ballantyne's descriptions of his life in the North West were couched in romantic terms, but in an easy, almost somnolent romanticism. He did not take part in any wild or dangerous adventures; when such romantic tales appear, they are in stories told by other people. He hunted, but mainly for ducks, geese, partridges, and ptarmigan. His clerkly duties quickly become routine and did not appear to distress him. He socialized in a largely male society much given to practical jokes, occasional parties, and hunting and fishing. Ballantyne's most telling adjective about an experience was that it was "agreeable." He did rhapsodize mildly about the scenery, which struck him as being "pretty and romantic."[20] Low-keyed descriptions of life in the North West might be mandated in letters home to his mother; any real danger needed to be downplayed, but under Ballantyne's placid prose ran a current of the excitement and sense of adventure, which he was to cultivate in his later years.

Robert Ballantyne's impact on the evolving mythology of the West came not from his relating of his personal experiences of that country, but from the use he made of them in his fictional writings. When he was making his way through the system of rivers and lakes from York Factory to Fort Garry, where he was to be assigned to another post, he began

> ... to speculate as to what part of the country I might be sent to. The whole wide continent of North America was now open to the

> excursive flights of my imagination, as there was a possibility of my being sent to any one of the myriads of stations in the extensive territories of the Hudson's Bay Company. Sometimes I fancied myself ranging through the wild district of Mackenzie's River, admiring the scenery described by Franklin and Back in their travels of discovery; and anon, as the tales of my companions occurred to me, I was bounding over the prairies of the Saskatchewan in chase of the buffalo, or descending the rapid water of the Columbia to the Pacific ocean. Again my fancy wandered, and I imagined myself hunting the grizzly bear in the woods of Athabasca.[21]

This was the full-blown romantic adventure myth of the North West for the first time expounded by Ballantyne. He was sent instead to Montreal. A few years later, his knowledge of the West and his romantic idyll were given free reign in *The Young Fur-Traders*. Here his principal hero was Charley Kennedy, the son of a Scots employee of the Hudson's Bay Company and a half-breed woman.[22] Charley at fifteen was destined by his father for the type of clerical career at Fort Garry that Ballantyne had known, but this young man rebelled against being cooped up this way, and was set free to live the life of an adventurous fur trader in the regions Ballantyne had only dreamed of.

Four years later, Ballantyne completed another western adventure, *The Dog Crusoe*,[23] which was set in the regions of his imagination – but further south. Dick Varley started his adventures from an American settlement on the prairies of the Missouri River area, and then travelled west through the prairies into the mountains. Ballantyne now was drawing much more on the stories told to him by his comrades in the posts he had occupied, and also on research. Here were the detailed descriptions of the running of buffalo and dangerous encounters with the grizzlies that appeared to thickly populate Varley's routes of travel. Also here were a number of dangerous confrontations with Indian bands. Ballantyne was incorporating much of the stereotype of the West that was to be the staple of the fictional West presented by a great many writers and was to survive into the twentieth century. It is quite possible as well that the emphasis in his own memories of the North West had shifted from the reality of his own experiences to the romanticism of the many stories he had heard.

Despite the Americanization of Ballantyne's image of the West, a number of differences remained throughout the remainder of his writing career. Most noticeable was Ballantyne's treatment of the Indians. While

Ballantyne's heroes had very dangerous confrontations with the Indians, they always managed to escape by some stratagem, and never killed their opponents. This is in complete contrast to another popular contemporary British writer of boys' adventure stories, G. A. Henty; in *Redskins and Cowboys* and *In the Heart of the Rockies*, both set in American territory, the British adventurers and their American allies had very bloody encounters with the Indians.[24] Ballantyne's relatively mild attitude to the Indians found in *Hudson's Bay* continued in his fiction of the Canadian West.[25] Each book contained at least one example of a Noble Savage, brave and good and true. In the preface to *The Prairie Chief*, Ballantyne defended such portrayals: "If the reader should be tempted, while perusing the extraordinary incidents of this Tale, to think the hero thereof too good, too wise, too absurd, too romantic – too anything, let it be borne in mind that there are exceptional characters among North American Indians, as among other savages and ourselves."[26] Condescending perhaps, but Ballantyne's noble savages were no servants to the white men, but their equals.

The treatment of the "savages" was not the only contrast between the stories of Ballantyne and G. A. Henty, the two premier writers of British boy's adventure novels of the Victorian period. Both writers wrote primarily stories of wild, often reckless, deeds of adventure; Ballantyne's stories came mainly from his imagination; Henty's were fictionalized versions of historical events. To Ballantyne the free-wheeling adventures were illustrations both of freedom and of the bravery, resourcefulness, and moral fibre of British boyhood. Henty's adventures were equally free-wheeling and revealing of the character possessed by his young heroes, but they portrayed less of an escape into exhilarating freedom. Henty's heroes always laboured under the burden of some misfortune, usually family-related, and, having successfully dispelled at least some of this misfortune by proving their worth as examples of the best qualities of British youth, received their reward in the shape of substantial financial gains and a return to Britain to live the pleasant lives of country gentlemen. For Ballantyne's heroes, the adventure was the real incentive, and the successful mastering of all challenges was the reward.

Robert Ballantyne was a popular author, writing adventure novels and adventure stories aimed at the boys' market. This undoubtedly was another factor in the shift in his image of the North American North West. A combination of stirring deeds and exotic locales sold books; no doubt it also turned the attention of many young British males, made restless for one reason or another, to the possibility of adventure in various parts of the world. Very likely it played a role in attracting many of these to the supposed wilds of the Canadian North West, as so effectively described in Patrick Dunae's *Gentleman Emigrants*.[27] These young gentlemen would not have been as much impressed by the ubiquitous moralizing and religious tone of almost all of Ballantyne's books[28] as by the assurances, often expressed in prefaces, such as in *The Buffalo Runners*, that: "Nearly all the incidents in this tale are either facts, or founded on fact. The region in which the scenes were enacted, although now within the fringe of civilization with the large and populous city of Winnipeg as its centre, formed – at the time I write of and still later when I sojourned there – part of the almost unknown wilderness of Rupert's Land." Here was the stamp of authenticity, and if "the large and populous city of Winnipeg" was at the fringes of civilization, rousing and romantic adventure surely must still be found in the Promised Land – further west.

One of Robert Ballantyne's chief interests was hunting. He progressed from shooting sparrows as a young boy in Scotland to ducks and geese and other birds in the North West. In his novels his heroes hunted bigger game – buffalo, grizzlies, and fierce wolves. The North West was a hunters' paradise, at least in common image, and it is this that attracted another Scot, James Carnegie, Earl of Southesk, to go adventuring to this territory in 1859.

The Earl of Southesk travelled to the British North West in 1859, and published a book, based on his diaries, about his experiences in 1875.[29] Being of indifferent health and in need of distraction following the death of his first wife, and thinking that "an active open-air life in a healthy climate" in which "good sport could be met with among the larger animals" would do him a lot of good, he set off on his grand adventure. His visit to the North West overlapped with the Palliser expedition, sent out from Britain by the Royal Geographical Society, and financed by the British government, in 1857–60.[30] Captain John Palliser had wanted to return to North America on a hunting expedition; he had travelled and hunted in the American West in 1847 and 1848, had published a book about his adventures, and now wanted to repeat the experience. Seeking finances, he suggested some exploration and information gathering, and this blossomed into a full-fledged expedition, which included several scientists.[31] Many of the experiences of the Palliser and

Southesk expeditions were similar, though Palliser and his colleagues appeared to be more successful in their hunting.

There are in Southesk's diaries many romantic passages, as he rhapsodized over the singing of birds, the exhilaration of racing his horse after a buffalo bull, the feeling of freedom within the vastness of the landscape, and the beauty of sunsets: "on one side all was orange and gold, beneath a black cloud which melted into misty gray as it met the bright tints of the sunlight, and on the opposite side moved the dark departing thunder-cloud with a perfect rainbow enameled on its face."[32] His description of the frontiersmen that he employed was picturesque and affectionate.[33] So were his descriptions of individual Indian males; Indian women he repeatedly characterized as being too "flat." He climbed mountains to try to find the perfect view, and often returned to vistas that he had discovered in order to make detailed sketches. But for all that, his narrative was often tinged with disappointment.

The running of buffalo could be exhausting and he did not always manage to make a kill. A buffalo bull or a mountain sheep ram successfully slain did not always yield the perfect trophy head that he could take back to Scotland. A wounded animal frequently managed to escape – the wolves were especially notorious for this – leaving behind disappointment tinged with humanitarian concern. Southesk had come to hunt large animals, but the buffalo for long periods of time were difficult to find, the grizzlies rare, the mountain goats too high, and the wolves usually too distant. Very frequently the hunt became a desperate search for food for the expedition, and in the course of events Southesk dined and breakfasted on skunk and marmots and porcupines; interesting experiences, but they were not the juicy buffalo or venison steaks that the romantic image could conjure up. Worse still, the meat from some of the big game was scarcely palatable, since the animals were in poor condition or past their prime. If game was often scarce, mosquitoes were not, and they and various vicious biting flies seemed to exist only to torment man and beast.

Even more distressing, though Southesk occasionally felt the stimulus to his health of the fresh air and primitive nature, there were often passages from his diary that gave a contrary picture: "Never did I feel more utterly prostrated. From various causes – my long journey on horseback, bad sleep owing to the cold at night, indifferent food of late, no drink stronger than tea, sudden hard work on foot since we came to the mountains, … I was now very weak, and able to climb steep places slowly, and with constant rests."[34] Eventually, he was asking himself "Why am I enduring this? For pleasure – was the only reply, and the idea seemed so absurd that I laughed myself warm. Then as circulation returned, I remembered that I was taking a lesson in that most valuable of human studies – the art of Endurance."[35] It was valuable, perhaps, but not the romantic vision of the North West to be found in Ballantyne's books. Still, the endurance of great hardship can be viewed as romantic, and this might account for the preponderantly romantic view of his adventure Southesk portrayed in his book published in 1875. He had met great challenges and ultimately passed every test to his own satisfaction; the hardships and the disappointments had been an essential element in the adventure. He returned to Britain in better health, remarried, and settled down to a long career as poet and antiquary.

The satisfaction that can be gained from an adventure free from the conventions of life in the British Isles and the avid pursuit of challenges were the dominant characteristics of better known adventurer William Francis Butler. Butler was Irish, born to a small and poor landholder, and received his commission in 1858 through influence, and not by the purchase which was the surer path through officer ranks in those days.[36] This meant that his only way to earn promotion was to attract the attention of his superiors, and in times when battle experience was scarce, it could necessitate volunteering for difficult and adventurous experiences. So it was that Lieutenant Butler, upon hearing of the 1870 expedition from Canada to the Red River country to quell a disturbance that had developed there, wired Colonel Garnet Wolseley, the commander of the expedition, "Please remember me,"[37] and promptly booked passage for North America without waiting for a reply.

There is no doubt that William Butler was a romantic and that he had a romantic view of the North American West and its inhabitants. His favourite boyhood author had been James Fenimore Cooper, and he had earlier, while briefly posted to Canada, seized the opportunity and three months leave to travel in the United States to Fort Kearney in Indian territory, and to spend two weeks living the life of his imagination, during which he shot a buffalo, and formed a strong attachment to the West.

Butler's presumption in heading for North America without an appointment was rewarded when Colonel Wolseley made him intelligence officer and sent him to enter Red River by way of the United States. It was, in his own words, an assignment that he performed with considerable dash. He made his way to Fort Garry, met and talked to the local Indians as well as the English settlers, and finally had a conversation with Louis Riel. He then headed east, by canoe, accompanied by four local men, to meet the Wolseley expedition still painfully making its way across the wilderness of North Western Ontario. Twelve days later he met Wolseley and returned to the Red River to find that the Métis resistance had collapsed. It was all dashing and invigorating, even though the Battle of Red River that many in the expedition had anticipated had not materialized.

The establishment of Canadian civil government at Red River and the withdrawal of the troops to the east left Butler in something of a dilemma. His career had not been advanced, and he faced returning to garrison duty. At this point, the newly appointed Lieutenant Governor Archibald of the Red River colony offered him a commission to go on a mission further west, as far as at least Edmonton, and report on the "state of affairs" and make recommendations concerning the establishment of "peace and order" in the North West. He was also expected to report on the outbreak of smallpox, the number and condition of the Indians, and the trade of the area and who was conducting it.[38]

Butler accepted the offer instantly. He left on October 24, 1870, accompanied by a Hudson's Bay Company officer and a French half-breed, on a more than four thousand kilometre trek that took him to Fort Carleton, Edmonton House, and Rocky Mountain House. He started back from Edmonton on December 20th; from Fort Carleton he followed the Saskatchewan River northeast, and then travelled south to Fort Garry by way of Lakes Winnipegosis and Manitoba. He arrived back at Fort Garry on February 20th. Butler started the journey on horseback and came back by dog team. It was a journey, given the conditions of travel in the winter months, which certainly tested his powers of endurance. Most of all, it gave him the kind of freedom and independence he was to relish for the rest of his career.

Butler's report to Lieutenant Governor Archibald was warmly received, but the looked-for rewards were slow in coming, and Butler returned to his regiment in England. The following year, *The Great Lone Land* was published, and Butler also cleared a large sum of money from a speculation in American oil lands. He promptly invested in a return to the Canadian North West, jumping off from the Red River on October 4th on an even longer expedition, which took him to the Peace River country and then across the mountains to Hope and Victoria. From here he travelled to San Francisco, and across the United States on his way home. It was another epic of endurance, since so much of the expedition in Canadian territory took place in winter, or, later, in the rugged terrain of the British Columbia. His homage to the North West was found in the lyrical *The Wild North Land*, published in 1873.[39]

William Butler's two books on the North West were well-written, being not only easy to read, but a pleasurable read. While they did not hide the fact that winters could be brutally cold, and that smallpox ravaged the Indian tribes, as did their conflicts, they managed to submerge much of the unpleasantness in the romantic glow that always shone when Butler thought of the North West.[40] On his second trip, after he had lived for two months, December and January, in a cabin built for him at the Forks of the Saskatchewan River, as he set out for the Peace River country, he enthused: "The day was bright and beautiful, the dogs climbed defiantly the steep high point, and we paused a moment on the summit; beneath lay hut and pine wood and precipitous bank, all sparkling with snow and sunshine; and beyond, standing motionless and silent, rose the Great Sub-Arctic Forest."[41] It was melancholy and grand, this land, and in Butler's mind, a land certainly fit for adventurers. Butler had the knack possessed by Rudyard Kipling, the great writer of imperial fiction, of suggesting that there was much more present than he could possibly say, and it was wondrous. And, like Kipling in his descriptions of India, he appeared to be seeing the North West with his heart rather than with his eyes – a heart that had been well informed by the novels he had read in his youth.

However, Butler's eyes were not always blinded to what he saw, and the implications of what he saw. His report to Lieutenant-Governor Archibald[42] was factual and prosaic, though it was also full of his impressions – of the Indians, the French half-breeds whom he saw to be as unhappy as the Manitoba population had been in 1869–70, the missionaries and the impact of their sectarian disagreements on the Indians, and the impact of miners, especially Americans, also on the Indian population. He described the devastation caused by the smallpox. He recommended more government, and especially the recruitment of a small military force to help maintain order and support the officials of civil government. Very realistically, he pointed out that there could not be an influx of settlement into the region of the Saskatchewan without the establishment of law and order and some decent promise of security.

That the Canadian government was interested in the settlement of the territory it had purchased from the Hudson's Bay Company in 1869 was perfectly obvious to Butler, and he did see settlement as inevitable. The way of life of his "great lone land" would be changed, though he hoped it would be with fairness to the current inhabitants. He was not reluctant to state his opinion about the suitability of the land for settlers:

> Like all things in this world, the Saskatchewan has its poles of opinion; there are those who paint it a paradise, and those who picture it a hell. It is unfit for habitation, it is to be the garden spot of America – it is too cold, it is too dry – it is too beautiful; and, in reality, what is it? I answer in a few words. It is rich; it is fertile; it is fair to the eye. Man lives long in it, and the children of his body are cast in manly mould. The cold winter is intense; the strongest heat of summer is not excessive. The autumn days are bright and beautiful; the snow is seldom deep, the frosts are early to come and late to go. All crops flourish, though primitive and rude are the means by which they are tilled; timber is in places plentiful, in other places scarce; grass grows high, thick, and rich.[43]

All this Butler had to perceive in a winter's journey of investigation, his imagination and his conversations with inhabitants supplying what his eyes could not see. In essence, his passage set out the parameters of this new Promised Land – all that was right and wrong with the promises and images that were to be so much promoted in the decades to come.

Butler returned to his beloved North West briefly in 1883.[44] His love for the land remained constant, as did his regard for the people he had known during his previous journeys. He also saw and lamented what were the consequences of the process of development that he had had a hand in setting into motion. It was not so much the settlers that he objected to, but the vulgar promoters that he encountered that caused him dismay.[45] This journey to the region of the Saskatchewan River, like his previous two, started out on the cusp of autumn turning into winter, as always apparently the least favourable time to travel this region. Despite this, Butler's reaction to the land and most of its people remained overwhelmingly romantic. It was as if the sheer exhilaration of testing his limits again contributed to the romance and enhanced his appreciation of his experiences. In a different age he might have climbed Mt. Everest.

The settlers that Butler foresaw did come, and in increasing numbers as the railroads crossed the prairies. They were a new form of adventurers, responding to the challenge of a new land, and the opportunity to remake themselves. A great many of those settlers came from the British Isles, and in their wake came adventurers of a different sort who came for limited periods of time to observe their countrymen in the promised land, and to report back to those left behind just what was happening in this much-hyped North West. Their books remain as snapshots of the settler adventurers, but also as impartial judgment of this corner of the British Empire.

A number of well-known British intellectual, literary, and political figures made trips to British colonial possessions in the nineteenth century and wrote books about their experiences. The novelist Anthony Trollope and the politician Charles Dilke visited Ontario and Quebec as brief adjuncts to their travels in the United States. The historian James Anthony Froude crossed the United States but avoided Canada because he felt it would be too cold in May. None appeared interested in the North West, though Dilke did speculate that its ultimate fate would be absorption into the United States, as had happened to Texas and California. Froude, had he thought about it, would have judged the Canadian North West as dreary as he judged the American plains to be.[46] All three writers wrote extensively about other parts of the settlement empire, Dilke and Froude about Australia and New Zealand.[47] Trollope wrote extensively about Australia, where one of his sons had settled, New Zealand, and South Africa.[48]

Many other British inhabitants, far less known, made trips to distant parts of the Empire and published their impressions for an eager audience back in England.[49] Generally, they were very favourable to what they saw; if there were drawbacks, they were usually caused by man rather than by nature. In a sense, what they all described were Promised Lands in that they were lands that held the promise of opportunity to those who had the stamina and character to be able to seize it. The lands they described were not paradise, and they did not hide the drawbacks; it would have been unwise, considering the numbers of people who had first-hand experience of all the colonies and had written books about them. Painting their promised lands in unrealistic colours could only have discredited what they had written.

In the Canadian North West, when the railways began to cross and crisscross the prairies, the settlers came in increasing numbers. It is difficult to tell just how many had read anything about the Canadian West, apart from, perhaps, the promotional literature of the railway companies and the emigration agents, but it is unlikely that the migrants from Britain did not already have a perception of the North West. Enough books had been written, both fiction and non-fiction, in which the images of cold winters and immense distances were featured prominently, and enough people had relatives that lived in North America to ensure that these images had common circulation. The immigrants from the American Midwest and the Canadian East would have had first-hand experience of such matters, and the Eastern Europeans, even if they were ignorant of the existing written sources of image-making, should not have been surprised to find that such conditions existed. The images might have been a deterrent to some but obviously not to all. Many factors are involved in the decision to migrate to another land, but the availability of land clearly ranks high on the list. Now land was available on a vast scale, and this proved to be a magnet to a great many settlers. With them eventually came the writers willing to examine a version of the Promised Land. Two writers in this study were women and presented a feminine view of what they saw. Male or female, all these writers included in their books a sense of the adventure of the North West, as well as the beauty, the distant vistas, and the challenges of this country. Their readers were receptive to such messages to a large extent because of the widely read works of Ballantyne and Butler, which indelibly imprinted in the minds of the British reading public, young and old, the images of an exciting, even enticing, frontier land.

C. L. Johnstone published her *Winter and Summer Excursions in Canada*[50] in 1894, after her second excursion, which included the Prairie West. She spent considerable periods of time there, and more than one winter, visiting, travelling, and talking to the settlers, with special interest in those who came from Britain. The book contains little in the way of her itinerary, though she does describe a railway journey from Qu'appelle to Regina, from Regina to Duck Lake, and later to Prince Albert. Most of her book is her discussion of life on the prairies, and the experiences of young emigrants to that area. The Promised Land, though always present, sometimes emerged as a somewhat dubious proposition.

Johnstone was determined that her readers not be unaware of the climate in Western Canada, especially in the winter. It could be bitterly cold, and for extended periods of time. Winter settled in by November, if not earlier, and stayed until April, if not later. Frost could come with disastrous consequences during the summer growing season. The severity and length of the cold weather, she pointed out, often came as an unexpected shock to naïve or unprepared immigrants. She was also careful to note other drawbacks, including the isolation that was still a part of the great lone land.

Despite pointing out all the drawbacks, Johnstone did insist that for the right young man the prairies were a good place to settle. Many told her that they were now in good health, even if they had suffered in Britain.[51] So the climate need not be a deterrent to migration. The best preparation for settlement in Canada would be for a family to send out a boy at the age of twelve or thirteen, to acclimatize and to learn how Canadians did things. Barring that, a young man could enroll in a reputable training farm to give him necessary experience, or he could work as a hired hand on an existing well-managed farm to learn proper techniques before going out on his own.[52] It would help if he had some capital, but a less fortunate individual could manage by hard work both on his own lands and for neighbours, and by keeping out of debt, to build up the stock, machinery, and cleared land that he needed. He must be realistic; success would only come gradually, and even a better-endowed farmer had to count on several years of losses before he could rely, almost, on a profitable season. The young farmer must also be prepared to take on all kinds of labour, even to the extent of doing what he would consider to be menial back in Britain.[53] Johnstone gave a lot of anecdotal evidence that young men who were prepared to be seriously industrious could be and often were successful in this new land.[54] This was the Promised Land, but dilettantes need not apply.

Johnstone's travels were not a luxury tour. If she spoke of the hardships of the settler life, she had direct experience of sleeping in small and often crowded houses or primitive hotels, and of travelling by sleigh on cold and uncomfortable excursions. To some extent the lady's travels were closer to those of Butler than were the more luxurious journeys of Britons travelling only a decade later, and there is an undertone of pride in her endurance. All this helped to give a curiously uneven tone to her book. Positive descriptions of the development of religious and educational structures in the territories alternated with discouraging passages on the difficulties of achieving anything in the circumstances that existed. Pictures of success in establishing viable farms vied with discouraging descriptions of how difficult it was to get there. Quite clearly she was struggling to maintain a positive image of the Prairie West as

Promised Land, but unlike some of the male writers, was unable to hide what to her were the grim prices that needed to be paid in order to arrive at such a blissful state. Still, it was always clear that the deserving would succeed.

Almost a complete contrast to Johnstone's *Winter and Summer Excursions in Canada* is John Foster Fraser's *Canada As It Is*.[55] Fraser's book was reprinted five times after its first printing in April, 1905, and then appeared in a new edition in 1911. It is easy to see why. It is a "feel good" book, despite its mild caveats. "The wheat lands are the core of Canada," he claimed,[56] strengthening the pride of prairie inhabitants. He had established earlier "the fact that men with scant agricultural knowledge can raise good crops and make a satisfactory living, is not so much proof of ability as of the munificence of the Almighty in giving Canada a soil which has only to be scratched to bring forth dollars."[57] To many, the munificence of the Almighty would have seemed obvious. Many of Fraser's interviews with farmers in the West were with men who had arrived with little or nothing and had achieved comfort and, sometimes, considerable wealth. But, he was careful to point out, very much depended on hard work, the short summers of intense, crop-ripening heat, and the "good luck" that brought the Canadian Pacific Railway into being.

Fraser created compelling images of the West. He pointed out that from a hilltop on the prairies one could see "the top of the world … robed in wheat, where the wheat patches are fifty, a hundred, five hundred acres without a break; then … a sea full of oats … then more wheat, and on like this, till the eye can follow no further.… The immensity of it impresses you. Then comes a weary feeling at the sameness of it all.… After that comes the wonder, and this is abiding."[58] Here was the Prairie West as Promised Land in its splendour and glory. Fraser's book complemented the colourful posters put out by the companies seeking settlers to come to the North West to buy the lands that they had to sell.[59]

Shortly before Fraser's book appeared, James Lumsden published *Through Canada in Harvest Time*.[60] He was one of a party of British journalists travelling through Canada during the harvest of 1902. The purpose of the journey, he explained, was to gather information about the "present state of the Canadian West, to describe its agricultural and mineral resources, and to explain the far-reaching consequences" to Canada and the United Kingdom of the prairie grain lands.[61] He also noted "the attractions which Canada holds out to emigrants from the

British Isles."[62] Throughout the journey, Lumsden mentioned the attention his party received from "public men" everywhere, and the knowledge they made available. The party gained a great deal of statistical information from these sources, but he insisted that the major part of his book was based on his own observations. His impressions may have been somewhat influenced by the fact that the Canadian Pacific Railway placed a luxurious private railway car with its own porter at the disposal of the party from Fort William westward.

The summation of Lumsden's image of the Prairie West could be found in the title of his tenth chapter, "The 'Granary of the British Empire'." While he was obviously acting as an agent of the Canadian government in its effort to promote the prairie region, he was also motivated by a desire to bring as many British settlers as possible to this Promised Land. He dedicated his book "to the workers of England, Scotland, and Ireland, hoping that it might inspire many to seek homes in a land which, though it may not 'flow with milk and honey,' assuredly offers to all who are not impatient of toil better opportunities of attaining comfort, independence, and fullness of life, than are to be found in any of the Old World states."[63]

Mrs. George Cran's book on Canada was published in 1912.[64] It recorded her second trip to Canada, taken under the auspices of the Canadian government, with travel passes from the Canadian Pacific Railway and the Canadian Northern Railway. She was asked to see "the country from a woman's standpoint as much as possible; to study the lives of Englishwomen settled there; to form my own opinion as to their happiness, their usefulness, their success or failure as settlers and wives of settlers."[65] The Canadian government knew that there was a surplus of women in England, and a serious shortage of them on the prairies.

Virtually all those who wrote about the Prairie West commented on the climate. Mrs. Cran began by recounting her image of Canada prior to her first trip: "Canada was an ugly, cold, icebergy place."[66] She quickly learned that her preconceptions were wrong, and in her book she stoutly maintained: "The climate of Canada is magnificent, extremer in heat and cold than England, but dry and bracing."[67] In her two trips, she spent a total of six and a half months in Canada, in the summer and fall, though on her return from British Columbia, her train was "snowed up" in Maple Creek.[68]

Mrs. Cran quickly became an enthusiast for the country, its natural resources, its fish and game (she shot gophers from a buckboard in

Saskatchewan and went fishing in British Columbia), the forest and the black soil, and, in British Columbia, "gold in all its rivers and fruit orchards in its valleys."[69] But she did find some problems from the woman's viewpoint, especially among the settlers on the prairies. A shortage of female labour prevailed because single women who came out as servants quickly got married; the farm wives were, therefore, kept so busy at their tasks that they could not maximize the productivity of the areas of the farm under their supervision, with more chickens, eggs, pigs, milk, and butter sent to market. Farms far away from railway lines suffered from isolation because of sparse settlement in those areas, which could lead to loneliness for women, but mainly meant difficulty of access to midwives, doctors, and nursing care. Still, the shortage of women also provided an opportunity: single English women could come out and buy land near the major cities of the West and set up market gardens and poultry farms. The more women that settled in the West, the better would be the conditions under which all women in the West would live, she argued. But, she cautioned, they needed to be women of the middle class, with their education, their refinement, and their sense of what made life comfortable and enjoyable. Mrs. Cran's last words were: "If I had to earn my living I would go to Canada."[70]

The works of Ballantyne, Butler, Cran, and Johnstone often contained contradictions within them that appeared to send mixed messages about the images they were intended to portray. There were similarities between the works of Ballantyne and Butler, on one hand, and those of Johnstone and Cran, on the other, despite the generation of time that separated them, and the gender differences. They all conveyed a feeling for the vastness of the country; Cran's drivers especially were constantly getting lost, thereby emphasizing that even in the settlement era, a residue of the trackless wilderness still remained. All placed an emphasis on the courage of the inhabitants of the land, who were both challenging nature and working within it. All were aware that the price of challenging nature could be hardship and even disaster. Success in the Promised Land was not guaranteed, and even Ballantyne in his fiction expressed his awareness of this. In *The Dog Crusoe*, the protagonist Dick Varley and his friends were sent out to negotiate with the Indians about the right of passage through native lands and almost paid with their lives when the Indians proved unreceptive.

Despite such reservations, all of the writers worked within the premise that their adventures were occurring in the context of a Promised

Land and that their mission was to convey such promise. They were not only reacting to what they saw, but also, more importantly, to what they expected to see. If their views appeared to be contradictory, they were not aware of it. The emotional response to what they saw allowed them to fit everything within the promises that they expected, whether they were the promises of adventure in a land of wilderness, of romance in a land of beauty and grandeur, or bounty in a land of milk and honey.

All of these authors in this study were writing primarily for British readers. They did so in the context of the popular imperialism prevalent in the second half of the nineteenth century and the early twentieth, which held that any area ruled or advised by the British was bound to flourish. What they did and wrote was not unique to the Canadian North West; similar books, including works of fiction, were written in the same period about the other settlement colonies, in Australia, New Zealand, and Southern Africa.[71] Colonies in South Asia and Central Africa also had their enthusiasts, not for the agricultural promised lands that could beckon large numbers of British settlers, but for adventures in hunting, or for business opportunities, such as in mining, tea planting, or commercial ventures.[72]

In Canada, Ballantyne, Southesk, and Butler portrayed the North West as a type of paradise promising excitement, adventure, and some place to test their limits; the other writers discussed here presented an image of the North West as an area full of potential, already underway, but to be achieved in the future, perhaps by some of their readers who were taken by their image of the Prairie West as a Promised Land. With all the reservations they might directly or indirectly express, the writers analyzed here were imperialists, and their versions of the Promised Land were tinged with the optimism of Victorian imperialism, which painted the prospects of the British Empire in bright colours, an optimism which only turned sour as the events of the twentieth century progressed.

NOTES

1 Modern and scholarly analyses of why the various images have emerged and changed can vary as much as the images themselves. See R. Douglas Francis, "Regionalism, Landscape, and Identity in the Prairie West," in *Challenging Frontiers: The Canadian West*, eds. Lorry Felske and Beverly Rasporich (Calgary: University of Calgary Press, 2004), 29–49.

2 Selous wrote books about his hunting exploits, such as *A Hunter's Wandering in Africa* (London: Macmillan, 1907 [1881]), and *Recent Hunting Trips in British North America* (London: Witherby, 1907).

3 The term "explorer" can be troublesome. In the context of European history in the last few centuries, an explorer was a traveller who travelled through regions seldom if ever travelled by other Europeans.

4 See Derek Hayes, *Historical Atlas of the Arctic* (Seattle: University of Washington Press, 2003).

5 Cook has attracted a great deal of biographical attention, with recent excellent additions, such as J. C. Beaglehole, *The Life of Captain James Cook* (London: Adam & Charles Black, 1974), Richard Hough, *Captain James Cook* (New York: W.W. Norton, 1994), and Anne Salmond, *The Trial of the Cannibal Dog: The Remarkable Story of Captain Cook's Encounters in the South Seas* (New Haven, CT: Yale University Press, 2003).

6 See Laurence Kitzan, *Victorian Writers and the Image of Empire: The Rose-Colored Vision* (Westport, CT: Greenwood Press, 2001).

7 *Oceana: or England and her Colonies* (London: Longmans, Green, and Co., 1886).

8 Ibid., 335.

9 "Promised land" has its religious connotations, from the Christian Bible, Book of Exodus, Chapter 33, where the land promised to the Israelites is spoken of as " a land flowing with milk and honey." However, this is not to be confused with "paradise." Canaan came with a multitude of challenges for the Israelites.

10 In 1895, fewer than 1,500 new homesteads were granted in Saskatchewan and Alberta. This number rose to more than 40,000 in 1911. Bill Waiser, *Saskatchewan: A New History* (Calgary: Fifth House, 2005), Appendix, 494.

11 See Kitzan, *Victorian Writers and the Image of Empire*, Chapter 2.

12 R. Douglas Francis, *Images of the West: Responses to the Canadian Prairies, 1690–1960* (Saskatoon: Western Producer Prairie Books, 1989); R. G. Moyles and Doug Owram, *Imperial Dreams and Colonial Realities: British Views of Canada, 1880–1914* (Toronto: University of Toronto Press, 1988).

13 Robert M. Ballantyne, *Hudson's Bay or Every-Day Life in the Wilds of North America During Six Years Residence in its Territories of the Honourable Hudson's Bay Company* (Rutland, VT: Charles E. Tuttle, 1972 [1848]), 2.

14 Ibid.

15 Eric Quayle, *Ballantyne the Brave: A Victorian Writer and His Family* (Chester Springs, PA: Dufour Editions, 1967), 27–28.

16 Ibid., 83–87.

17 *The Young Fur-Traders: Snowflakes and Sunbeams* (London: Ward, Lock & Co., n.d. [1856]).

18 Ibid., 18.

19 Ibid., 22.

20 Ballantyne, *Hudson's Bay*, 81.

21 Ibid., 183.

22 Frank Kennedy, sixty years in the North West, and now retired to Red River, was a comical and slightly preposterous character. Perhaps Ballantyne was expressing relief

that the collapse of his romantic idyll had brought him back to Scotland after only six years' service.

23 *The Dog Crusoe* (London: Abbey Classics, 1970 [1861]). A later book, *The Buffalo Runners: A Tale of the Red River Plains* (London: James Nisbet, n.d. [1891]), brought him back to familiar territory, and *The Prairie Chief: A Tale* (London: James Nisbet, 1886), was set, vaguely, in the North American prairies. Like *The Dog Crusoe*, they incorporate more dramatic and romantic encounters with nature and with the Indians. These books represent just a few of the books that Ballantyne wrote about this region.

24 G. A. Henty, *Redskins and Cowboys* (London: Blackie & Sons, n.d. [1892]), and *In the Heart of the Rockies: A Story of Adventure in Colorado* (London: Blackie & Son, n.d. [1895]). The body count was also high in most of Henty's books set in different parts of the world.

25 It also is mirrored in his treatment of aboriginals in other part of the world; for example, in the South Pacific in *The Coral Island* (London: T. Nelson & Son, n.d. [1857]), and in East Africa in *Black Ivory: A Tale of Adventure Among the Slavers of East Africa* (London: James Nisbet, n.d. [1873]).

26 Ballantyne, *Prairie Chief*, 7.

27 Patrick A. Dunae, *Gentlemen Emigrants: From the British Public Schools to the Canadian Frontiers* (Vancouver: Douglas & McIntyre, 1981).

28 They most likely completely missed the religious messages. Ballantyne's unfailing good humour and boyish sense of fun revealed in his books more than compensated for the intrusion of more serious matters.

29 The Earl of Southesk, *Saskatchewan and the Rocky Mountains. A Diary and Narrative of Travel, Sport, and Adventure, During a Journey Through the Hudson's Bay Company's Territories, in 1859 and 1860* (Edinburgh: Edmonston and Douglas, 1875).

30 Irene M. Spry, *The Palliser Expedition: An Account of John Palliser's British North American Exploring Expedition 1857–60* (Toronto: Macmillan, 1963).

31 Ibid., Chapters 1 and 2. Unfortunately, Palliser never published a book about this expedition, but his report was published in a Blue Book.

32 Southesk, *Saskatchewan and the Rocky Mountains*, 146.

33 Ibid., 205.

34 Ibid., 241.

35 Ibid., 283.

36 Edward McCourt, *Remember Butler: The Story of Sir William Butler* (Toronto: McClelland and Stewart, 1967), 8–9.

37 Capt. W. F. Butler, *The Great Lone Land: A Narrative of Travel and Adventure in the North-West of America* (London: Sampson Low, Marston, Low, & Searle, 1873), 8. Much of Butler's successful military career was to owe a great deal to the connection he now made with Wolseley, who summoned him to service in West Africa, South Africa, and the Sudan.

38 Ibid., Appendix, 353–54.

39 *The Wild Northland: Being the story of a winter journey, with dogs, across Northern North America* (New York: Allerton, 1922 [1873]).

40 In *Remember Butler*, 248, McCourt says that Butler, retired and in his seventies, was "unable to suppress entirely the longing, never to be satisfied, to see again the great open prairies of the Canadian West from which the passage of time had removed all imperfections and left only memories of sunlight and distance and the passionate response of life at high noon to the challenge of a new world."

41 *The Wild Northland*, 79.

42 *The Great Lone Land*, Appendix, 355–86.

43 Ibid., 231.

44 Sir William Butler, *Sir William Butler: An Autobiography* (London: Constable and Co., 1911), 249–73.

45 Francis, "Regionalism," 41–47, discusses the apparent contradictions in Butler's reactions to the North West.

46 Anthony Trollope, *North America* (London: Chapman & Hall, 1862); Charles Dilke, *Greater Britain: A Record of Travel in English Speaking Counties During 1866 and 1867* (London: Macmillan, 1869); and James Anthony Froude, *Oceana.*

47 In Dilke, *Greater Britain,* and Froude, *Oceana.*

48 Trollope, *Australia and New Zealand* (Leipzig: Tauchnitz, 1873), and *South Africa*, 2 vols. (London: Chapman & Hall, 1878).

49 For example, Rosamond and Florence Hill, *What we saw in Australia* (London: Macmillan, 1875), and Julius M. Price, *The Land of Gold: the Narrative of a Journey Through the West Australian Goldfields in the Autumn of 1895* (Victoria Park: Hesperian Press, 1981).

50 Catherine Laura Johnstone, *Winter and Summer Excursions in Canada* (London: Digby, Long & Co., n.d. [1894]).

51 Ibid., 155.

52 Young Edward ffolkes came to Canada in 1880, studied at the Ontario Agricultural College in Guelph, Ontario, worked two months on a farm in Ontario, and then went west to Manitoba. Here he bought an existing farm that already had some broken land and worked hard to achieve a fair amount of success. Ronald A Wells, ed., *Letters from a young emigrant in Manitoba* (Winnipeg: University of Manitoba Press, 1981).

53 *Winter and Summer Excursions*, 51.

54 Johnstone illustrates this point of view in *The Young Immigrants: A Story for Boys* (London: Thomas Nelson and Sons, n.d.), in which several boys in their teen years travel to western Canada, undergo hardships and setbacks, and eventually emerge happy and successful. She points out that the "moral is, that many a young emigrant does not fit at once into the right place. But neither he nor his friends should despair," 171.

55 *Canada As It Is* (London: Cassell, 1911 [1905]).

56 Ibid., 194.

57 Ibid., 5.

58 Ibid., 131.

59 Fraser was a professional traveller and writer who travelled to various parts of the word and wrote lively books about them. There is no indication that he was "bought" by the Canadian government. He was writing what the market wanted to read.

60 *Through Canada in Harvest Time: A Study of Life and Labour in the Golden West* (London: T. Fisher Unwin, 1903).

61 Ibid., xii.

62 Ibid., xiii.

63 Ibid., 1.

64 Mrs. George Cran [a.k.a. Marion Dudley], *A Woman in Canada* (Toronto: Musson, n.d. [1912]).

65 Ibid., 17, 21–22.

66 Ibid., 9.

67 Ibid., 24.

68 Ibid.

69 Ibid.

70 Ibid., 283.

71 See, for example, J. Ewing Ritchie, *An Australian Ramble: or a Summer in Australia* (London: T. Fisher Unwin, 1890). Ritchie had earlier written *To Canada with Emigrants: A Record of Actual Experiences* (London: T. Fisher Unwin, 1885).

72 See Isabella L. Bird, *The Golden Chersonese and the Way Thither* (Kuala Lumpur: Oxford University Press, 1967 [1883]), and Mary Kingsley, *West African Studies* (London: Frank Cass, 1964 [1899]).

3

CANADA'S ROCKY MOUNTAIN PARKS: RATIONALITY, ROMANTICISM, AND A MODERN CANADA

Matthew Wangler

Wilderness occupies a privileged place in the Canadian imagination. The continuing importance of wilderness symbols such as the beaver, the maple leaf, and the vast emptiness of the Great White North testify to the power of this idea in the historical development of the Canadian identity. Wilderness is, as one scholar puts it, the "*sine qua non* of what we have chosen to identify as Canadian culture."[1] One of the primary manifestations of this sensibility is a robust pride in our national parks and a romantic attachment to the iconic landscapes – like the Rocky Mountains – that they contain. The early history of the parks, however, bears witness to a more complicated perspective on our relationship to nature. The creation of the first parks embodied a seeming contradiction between an affinity for nature's wild beauties on the one hand, and a desire to domesticate that wildness in order that the natural world could be accessed, enjoyed, and consumed on the other. A similar tension was manifest in Canadian perspectives upon the Natives who inhabited the lands destined to become parks, where a romantic attachment to the simple dignity of "the noble savage" co-existed with a conviction in the superiority of Euro-Canadian cultural beliefs and practices.

These seeming paradoxes were evident in the establishment of the Rocky Mountain parks, where rationalist and romantic ideals of the human relationship with nature competed with one another and with the pre-modern Native vision of the natural world of the mountains as a sacred cosmos. The history of these three distinct, though often interrelated, cultural visions in imagining the Rockies possesses in microcosm many of the influential intellectual, economic, social, political, and spiritual impulses and institutions that animated post-Confederation Canada and that would dictate the manner in which the nascent West would be developed and viewed. Each of these perspectives was rooted in a view of the Rockies as a kind of Promised Land. For the Natives in the vicinity of the Rocky Mountains, prior to the arrival of the white man, the mountains were a domain they had long dreamed of and that had been divinely revealed to them, an elemental place in their spiritual economy linking individual, society, and cosmos. For the Euro-Canadians, the mountains were a place that had the potential to be transformed from "wasted wilderness" into a promised land, a garden of delights. Once transformed, the Rockies could offer pragmatists a seemingly inexhaustible source of economic riches, and for those more romantically inclined, a wealth of sublime beauty. This essay explores how the Rocky Mountain parks region – and particularly the Banff area – was transformed by these impulses, being figured and refigured as sacred site, a constellation of exploitable resources, and a sanctuary from the numbing excesses of modernity.

By the early nineteenth century – and perhaps much earlier – the Stoney tribe was frequenting the eastern slopes of the Rocky Mountains. Branched off from the Sioux nation, the Stoneys (also called the Assiniboine) gradually moved west from their original haunts north of Lake Superior in the seventeenth century. Stoney legend has it that a spirit man, White Light, "led the Mountain People the rest of the way to the land they had dreamed of – the *Yahey Yamneska*, the Cliff Rocks of Alberta."[2] During their westward trek, the Stoney separated into a number of bands. Those living near the foothills and mountains hunted big game in the region and ventured onto the plains in the spring and autumn to pursue the buffalo.

The Stoneys' journey to western Canada brought them into frequent contact with Euro-Canadian traders, explorers, and missionaries. They were experienced trappers and traders and carried on commerce with the Hudson's Bay Company employees at Fort Edmonton and Rocky Mountain House. They were also indispensable for explorers and entrepreneurs as guides and hunters. Nimrod, James Hector's remarkably skilled hunter, was merely one among the many who shepherded

Euro-Canadian men through the wilds of western Canada. In addition to their familiarity with Euro-Canadian economic life, the Stoneys were also deeply attuned to the rhythms of the newcomers' spiritual vision. Members of Stoney tribes were some of the earliest Native converts to Christianity in the area; a Methodist mission site was built at Morleyville in 1873 to accommodate converts.[3]

Prior to, and, indeed, to a large extent after, the arrival of Christian missionaries, the Stoney religious vision was rooted in a profound, reverential, and dialogical relationship with nature. The missionaries who came brought with them a sensibility about nature that differed fundamentally from the Stoneys'. Whereas in the Christian religious tradition, "the earth itself is not sacred; it is created by the sacred, by God," in the Stoney religious vision, "the landscape is sacred; it is deity."[4] The Stoney's pre-modern consciousness of the natural world perceived an environment suffused with the divine presence; the sacred was manifest in land forms, plants, and animals. As Catherine Albanese notes in Nature Religion in America: "For native North Americans the numinous world of nature beings was always very close, and the land itself expressed their presence. Indian peoples created religious geographies in which specific sites were inhabited by sacred powers and persons."[5]

These sites held a privileged place in Native mythic consciousness. Loci of ultimate reality, pervaded with mystery and power, such sites become existential centres for the religious individual and culture, offering both a physical and spiritual orientation point. This consciousness of the sacred, manifest in certain places that bridged the divide between human and divine, created the spiritual geography within which pre-modern individuals lived and moved and had their being.

There were numerous sites in the territorial range of the Stoneys that were viewed as sacred, places of theophany in which the divine was more fully manifest than in other locales. The places associated with a vivid, robust sacrality were sites of spiritual encounter and were often unpredictable, capable of both beneficent dispensations and terrifying revelations. Several sacred sites had a markedly disturbing character, equally evoking fascination and terror. Lake Minnewanka – literally the "Water of the Spirits" – , for example, was viewed with deep trepidation as a place associated with strange, half-human, half-fish beings and the sounds of drum songs and spirit voices.[6] A cave near Ghost Lake evoked similar seduction and horror as the culturally understood burial place and home of the cannibalistic spectre Pretty Feathers.[7] The hot springs at Sulphur Mountain and elsewhere had a no less profound, yet exceedingly more positive, hold of the Stoneys' cultural understanding. Chief John Snow writes: "the sacred waters of the mountains – the mineral hot springs – were also important to maintaining our health and curing illness. A person would journey to the sacred waters at the direction of a medicine man or woman and use them with suitable preparation and prayer."[8] After bathing in the waters of the hot springs, the Stoneys "would drop something in the water as a sacrifice, as a thank-you to the spirits for the use of their water or the use of their paint, the yellow ochre."[9] It is perhaps not surprising that Chief Walking Buffalo, one of the great Stoney medicine men, received his life's vocation from a spirit buffalo just after bathing in the springs. After his vision, the chief became mystically identified with the buffalo spirit and was transformed into a being capable of moving across the fluid boundaries between the human and the animal, the divine and the mundane.[10]

Although the natural world in general was filled with embodiments of the divine for the Native people, the Rocky Mountains were particularly significant in the Stoneys' sacred consciousness. As Stoney elder Jonas Dixon puts it: "[I]t is said that the great Shining Rocky Mountains are the Stoney ancestors turned into stone and boulder and rock. And that is why these mountains are places that are sacred."[11]

Chief John Snow of the Stoney tribe identifies the Rocky Mountains as "a place of hope, a place of vision, a place of refuge, a very special and holy place where the Great Spirit speaks with us."[12] An integral dimension of the Stoney's physical and symbolic environment, the mountains both participated in the tribe's vision of the sacred cosmos and represented a crown jewel of that vision, a place uniquely favoured for the ancestral spirits that resided there.[13] The centrality of the mountains in the Stoney's sacred imagination is vividly embodied in the life history of one of the tribe's greatest medicine men and healers, Hector Crawler. Crawler is reputed to have had numerous profound and mystical experiences in the mountains. One account of his life suggests that, after a deep depression of two years, Crawler was compelled by a dream vision to visit the peak of Rock Mountain, near Lake Minnewanka, where he fasted, meditated, and prayed, and was gifted with spiritual insight and the gift of healing.[14] Crawler himself spoke of a mystical experience in which he was transported to the "top of the very highest mountain, Tcasehtinda (Falling-timber-Plane-Mountain), Kananaskis," in which he experienced the "Son of God" and was gifted with healing powers.[15]

Those who encountered Hector Crawler after his transformational experience "say that the emaciated creature who came down the mountain barely resembled the Calf Child [another name for Crawler] who had set out."[16] His vision and the gift of healing had essentially changed Crawler's outer aspect and inner being.

Thus for the Stoneys, the Rockies were an integral part of their experience of the sacred cosmos. As dwelling place of their ancestors, a bridge between the divine and the human, a ritual site for the hallowing of time, and the place of communion and reconciliation with the spirits, the mountains held a profound existential and communal significance for the tribe.

The general character of the Euro-Canadian cultural perception of the Rockies that would challenge the Stoneys' view and come to dominate after Confederation differed dramatically. In post-Confederate Canada, views of nature were rooted in two closely related, yet in many ways contradictory, intellectual streams. The scientific and political communities of Canada gave voice to a view of nature as the dominion of humankind, to be catalogued, analyzed, and ultimately exploited to satisfy human desire and need. This perspective contrasted with that of Canadian thinkers – particularly artists and social critics – who perceived this rational, exploitative mentality as a kind of modern disease, thoroughly embodied in the metropolitan world and inimical to the true nature of human freedom and virtue. For these women and men, nature provided a refuge from the atomism and enervation of modern life.

Drawn from rationalist and romantic streams of thought in Europe and America, these two intellectual currents, it could be argued, constitute the heart of modern identity. Though often conflicting, rationalist and romantic ideals of nature would dramatically reshape the predominant cultural vision of the Banff area, overthrowing the pre-modern Native notions of humanity's ecological relationship to nature from a more anthropocentric perspective and replacing it with a perspective of nature as a storehouse of illimitable physical and spiritual resources to be exploited for human purposes. Ideas of a sacred cosmos were replaced with notions of exploitable or romantic nature; conceptions of mountains as the sites of an "eternal present" would be succeeded by images of the Rockies as an integral part of the inexorable march of Canadian society into a progressive future, while a perspective of the Rockies as a place for a solitary religious encounter was supplanted by one that emphasized the comforts and cacophony of mass tourism.

The rationalist, utilitarian view of nature was evident in Victorian English Canada in the intellectual hybrid known as natural theology.[17] Anchored in the belief that one could trace the "footprints" of God in His material world, those who espoused national theology asserted that meticulous study of "the book of nature" would reveal to the patient mind the order and interconnectedness of the natural world – tangible authentication of God's wisdom and creative power. But natural theology was more than simply a conceptual matrix for studying the arrangement and interrelations of the natural world. It also stressed man's unique place in that world. For natural theologians, man was the crown jewel of creation. As Carl Berger notes in Science, God and Nature in Victorian Canada, natural theology was "not so much about nature as about man's special place above and beyond nature."[18] Human supremacy over nature implied human dominion over nature. This figuring of the relationship between humanity and the natural world reflects the influence of Baconian ideals and represents a fundamental challenge to the Native-Canadian vision of a reverent relationship of humans with nature.

The belief in humanity's dominion over nature would be an essential intellectual and spiritual current in the claiming and remaking of the Canadian West, including the Rocky Mountains. Confronted by what was perceived to be an "unknown, unrealized, and humanly undigested"[19] region of Western Canada, the Canadian government endeavoured to assert its authority over this extensive wilderness through instrumental reason. The conversion of wilderness to rationalized space "advanced geometrically across the country," according to literary critic Northrop Frye, "throwing down the long parallel lines of the railways, dividing up the farmlands into chessboards of square-mile sections and concession-line roads."[20] Extensive scientific surveys of the landscape, life forms, and geology of the West were undertaken. Resembling on a much larger scale the inventory taking of amateur natural theologians, such surveys reinforced the belief in the progressive utility of the scientific enterprise. As historian Suzanne Zeller notes:

> Of crucial importance in justifying inventory science was the doctrine of utilitarianism. Victorian science in British North America both reflected and reinforced the criterion of practical value or usefulness.... With roots set deep in the British experience, utilitarianism lent a sense of purpose and meaning to the arduous task of settling British North America. It drew science into a value system which had emerged out of the industrial and agricultural changes of late

> eighteenth-century Britain. Utilitarianism encouraged the belief that even social problems were manageable through quantification and the statistical accumulation of facts. Science in the utilitarian sense was a tool, not merely to locate sources of material wealth but also to construct an ordered society. Victorians saw science emerge from a peripheral leisure-class activity to become the fundamental basis of industrial society.[21]

Canada's scientific and political communities' response to the western wilderness was often practical, viewing the natural world through the utilitarian lenses of "quantification" and "the statistical accumulation of facts" in order to locate sources of material wealth and to establish peace, order, and good government in the territory.[22]

Once the inventory had been taken, once epistemological dominion over nature had been to some extent achieved, technology offered ontological dominion through railways, ploughs, and industrial machinery. In Victorian Canada, the seemingly inexorable march of steel and settlement across the nation inspired a belief that Canada was a progressive nation. The "Idea of Progress" was ubiquitous and essential: "all the evidence of daily life – the forests felled, the fields cleared, the roads made and the canals dug – lay before men's eyes as emphatic evidence of progress. Moral progress and material, none could doubt, advanced together."[23] Thus, expansion of the Dominion into the Canadian West "had social and moral overtones that imparted to the secular idea of potential wealth a sense of mission."[24] That mission bore witness to a European concept of the human relationship to nature – first articulated centuries ago and manifested in Baconian science and Canadian natural theology – that asserted that "man was chosen by the Creator to possess and dominate the rest of creation ... for the land to be fully possessed, it must be cultivated: tilled, improved, developed. The result: a promised land, a paradise, a garden of delights."[25] As settlement and government extended westward, the pre-modern sensibilities of tribal peoples – with their sacred cosmos, their "eternal present," their sense of the Holy suffusing their experiences – would be largely overtaken by an ideology that emphasized a progressive future to be secured through an inventory, analysis, and exploitation of natural resources.

Once the Banff region was viewed in terms of its potential profitability to the fledging Canadian nation, it ceased to be seen simply as part of Canada's vast geographical space and instead became a "place" in utilitarian consciousness to be exploited. In 1883, coal was discovered in the Cascade Basin east of Banff and the copper ore mining community of Silver City, at the base of Mount Castle, was born. In the same year, three young railway workers, Franklin McCabe, William McCardell, and William's younger brother, Thomas, "discovered" several hot springs in Sulphur Mountain (then known as Terrace Mountain). Sid Marty, a historian of the national parks and a former park warden, offers us a perspective of what this meant to the men at the time:

> It was not sulphur the three men smelled as they stripped and plunged into the crystal pool for the first swim. Their nostrils flared to the invigorating scent of dollar bills. The stalactites gleamed like bars of silver and gold, the roof glittered as if studded with diamonds. There were thousands of navvies due to start work next spring, and hot water bathing was a luxury item along the CPR right-of-way. More importantly, the railroad would bring the wealthier set, and the hot springs would draw them like honey draws bees.[26]

The young railway workers immediately recognized their good fortune. In response to this serendipitous gift, the men erected a fence around the site and built a shanty to stake their claim.[27] Their action places in sharp relief the differences between Stoney and Euro-Canadian sensibilities about the springs. The first thought of these young Canadians was to claim ownership of the waters and to profit by them in contrast to the Stoney bathers who made an offering to the sovereign and beneficent spirit which had blessed them with the healing waters.

John A. Macdonald, Canada's prime minister, and William Cornelius Van Horne, general manager of the Canadian Pacific Railway, were captivated by the discovery of the springs. In 1883, the year that the three railway workers came across the hot springs, the CPR, whose interests were so intimately wed to those of Macdonald's government, "floundered toward bankruptcy. The immigrant flow had stopped. Land sales had not provided the promised revenue."[28] Banff's spectacular scenery and thermal waters augured well for the development of a tourist industry in the region. Similar springs, after all, had been developed into profitable endeavours in Britain and other parts of Europe through thoughtful landscaping and clever marketing of the water's health-giving effects.[29] Why not in Canada too? Macdonald envisioned waves of upper-class tourists flocking to the springs and spending their leisure in villas to be built around the site. Van Horne saw a way to induce passengers to travel to the West on his CPR and spend lavishly on refined accommodation and entertainment.

Before tapping into the seemingly inexhaustible wealth of minerals, timber and, above all, the springs of the Banff area, the government felt the need to make its claim on the land. After dealing with the three individuals who had been the first to stake their claim to the springs, the government set aside the area as a reserve in 1885. Two years later, it created Rocky Mountains Park, Canada's first national park. The first provision of the *Rocky Mountain Parks Act* of 1887 entailed defining the precise space that made up the park:

> The tract of land comprised within the limits hereinafter set forth … commencing at the easterly end of Castle Mountain Station grounds, on the Canadian Pacific Railway … thence on a course about south thirty-five degrees east, ten miles more or less to a point in latitude seven minutes, six seconds and ninety-six hundredths of a second south of the point of commencement, and in longitude seven minutes, fifty-four seconds and ninety-eighth hundredths of a second east of the point of commencement.

Everything within the park – from "shrubbery" to "natural curiosities," from mineral waters to mines, traffic to timber, pasturage to protection of wildlife – came under the "control and management of the Minister of the Interior."[30] All forms of industry within the park – and there was to be industry – were to be controlled by the government.

Here was the creation of a managerial jurisdiction in the wilderness, precisely delineated spatially and administratively. Through the *Rocky Mountains National Park Act* of 1887, the Canadian government asserted its claim of sovereignty over the "Empire of Nature." This claim encompassed, in the words of historian Robert Craig Brown, "the great untapped sources of wealth of the Rocky Mountains" – a seemingly limitless "supply of timber, myriad mineral deposits, and, most of all, boundless varied scenery."[31] The ideology of largely unrestrained exploitation of the area rendered sublime scenery a commodity, differing from coal or timber only in its inexhaustibility. In order to profit from this sublime scenery, however, both the government and the CPR believed it necessary to transform the untamed environs of the Banff area. With abstract, rational control now established and the area's resources fully inventoried and assessed, the makers of the park turned to the task of further asserting their supremacy over nature through an aggressive campaign of subduing and improving the natural world.

Such improvements were seen as essential to generate revenue from tourism in the parks. As Brown explains: "the term 'wilderness' was scarcely used in discussion of parks policy and then only to suggest a primitive condition demanding 'improvement' in order to 'make a park.'"[32] Clifford Sifton, the minister of the interior in the Laurier government, referred to the area as a "wasted wilderness" in need of redemption by scientific and technological remaking. Much of the rhetoric around the creation of the park centred on how to convert the area to "usefulness." Contrary to the Stoney view of nature as holy in itself, being the sovereign realm of the Great Spirit, the architects of the parks saw wilderness as a kind of raw material in need of transformation and improvement. Thus, in the decades following the establishment of Rocky Mountains National Park, the Banff area would be thoroughly "improved" with a host of new facilities and natural features that would offer Canadians a new "promised land" and "garden of delights."

"Improvement" had two aspects, the human and the natural. Human improvement entailed the removal of the Stoney tribe from the area. Despite having entered into a treaty in 1877 and being granted a reserve around the Morleyville mission, the Stoneys continued to travel to the mountains to hunt and pray, continuing to see the region as their sacred territory. Their presence disturbed parks officials. Park Superintendent George A. Stewart argued in 1887 that "if possible the Indians should be excluded from the Park. Their destruction of the game and depredations among the ornamental trees make their too frequent visits to the Park a matter of great concern."[33] W. F. Whitcher asserted: "Exceptions of no kind whatever should be made in favor of Indians. Those who now invade that territory are stragglers and deserters from their own reserves, where they are well cared for in food and clothing at the public expense."[34] The fear that the Stoneys would damage the "ornamental trees" and, more importantly, deplete game stocks that would attract hunters from around the world led the government to restrict tribal access to their traditional hunting grounds in the park.[35]

The process of dislocating Native peoples from their traditional haunts was re-enacted throughout the expansion of settlement and government in the West. Rationale for their removal often tapped into the powerful currents of utilitarianism and its progressive ideology. Historian Daniel Francis describes this ideology succinctly in regards to

Native people: "Because they did nothing with the resources of the land – built no cities, tilled no fields, dug no mines – Indians deserved to be superseded by a civilization that recognized the potential for material progress."[36] Parks officials viewed Stoney hunting as a wanton waste of a valuable natural resource. Within this conceptual system, the Stoneys' lack of a progressive vision of material progress rooted in the rational exploitation of the natural world would necessarily consign them, like the wilderness they once inhabited, to history. Improvement through civilization – meaning settlement, agriculture, and Euro-Canadian cultural assimilation – was the national prescription. It is intriguing that the Stoneys' removal from the Banff area and its consequences – development and tourist inundation – seem to have stripped the Stoneys' sacred springs of their power. As Chief Walking Buffalo put it: "since the white people came, the strength has gone out of the water. That mysterious power that comes from the spirits is there no more. Probably the white people do not pray to get well."[37] Stoney god-man Iktomni's prophecy, related by tribal elders, seemed fulfilled in the dramatic transformation of Banff after the arrival of Euro-Canadians:

> When [the long whiskers] arrive, the hoop will be broken ... and our sun spirits will have fled and hid in the deepest mountain canyon.... And these will take as many hills for one man as a nation cannot fill. For these do not hear our wise ones who say that too many things brings delirium and much sickness for any man.... They will bring leaves-with-a-power [documents, treaties] to take our sacred mountains.... These will measure and mark every stone.[38]

This displacement of the living memory of the springs, re-enacted throughout Canada, is symbolic of the erasure of the pre-modern vision of the natural world throughout western Canada by a progressive utilitarianism.

Just as the Native people were seen as needing civilization, so too the natural world was seen as requiring massive reform as well. From the creation of the park in 1885 to 1911, the Banff region underwent a dramatic change with the establishment of an extensive tourist infrastructure. Roads were built to transport visitors to this rapidly developing area, which eventually included a boat house, animal paddock, zoo, aviary, and Museum of Natural History. In 1888, the CPR completed construction on the majesterial Banff Springs Hotel. A sulphur pipeline brought thermal water from the springs to the hotel, as well as to Dr. R.

G. Brett's Sanitorium.[39] Claiming that "the want of variety in our foliage has been constantly remarked," Park Superintendent George A. Stewart promptly imported forty thousand trees from the "North-Western States" in 1888 to diversify the variety of tress in the park.[40] Earlier, in 1886, W. F. Whitcher had proposed drastic changes to the fauna of the park to improve its attractiveness to tourists:

> [Bears] need not be wantonly killed nor dealt with as we should do with the lupine, vulpine and feline vermin that prey upon furred and feathered game with savage impartiality … countless innocent and gay plumaged birds it is extremely desirable to let alone for the present at least. They form part and parcel of living ornaments interesting to visitors on every public reservation.… Wolves, coyotes, foxes, lynxes, skunks, weasels, wild cats, porcupines and badgers should be destroyed.… The same may be said of eagles, falcons, owls, hawks and other inferior rapaces, if too numerous; including also piscivirous specimens such as loons, mergansers, kingfishers, and cormorants.[41]

He also suggested the importation of certain animals, like quail and pheasants, to further enhance and diversify the park's "living ornaments." Though Whitcher's remarkable directives were not zealously followed, the idea of eliminating "noxious beasts and birds" – particularly those that preyed on the valuable game in the park – and bringing in more "desirable animals" remained a practice in the park.

With the appointment of J. B. Harkin as the first commissioner of the National Parks in 1911, the rate of improvement accelerated. Possessing an unusual intellectual perspective that combined natural mysticism and bureaucratic deftness, Harkin employed the calculating logic of utilitarianism to secure funds for his ambitious projects to open the parks up to the Canadian public. He noted the profitability of similar tourist parks in Europe and the United States, and even went so far as to determine the relative economic value of picturesque park land to that of the wheat field – $13.88 to $4.91, in favour of the mountain scenery![42] With the money received, Harkin developed in Banff an effective game protective service, a more efficient fire protection service, new trails, telephone lines, and more and better roads. In the wake of these innovations came changes to waterways, construction of a golf course, more roads, more hotels, more stores, and more people, not to mention the introduction of new animal and plant species, while annihilating some natural species in the park. Now mass tourism became the defining feature of the Banff area.

Here was the apotheosis of John A. Macdonald's desire to turn the uncivilized lands of the West to "usefulness," and of the Baconian ideal of reasserting man's dominion over nature through science and technology. Variations on this pattern were repeated in all the other new parks in the Rocky Mountain area – Yoho and Glacier (1886), Waterton (1895), Jasper (1907), and Kootenay (1920). The change in the perception of the landscape from the Stoney vision is marked. Considering the meaning of Jasper's sublime mountain peaks within this new context, now serving, essentially, as backdrop for a golf course, literary historian Ian MacLaren notes: "the mountain is prior to the human, but it exists in this rendition to identify, enhance, and complement human recreation. That is, the mountain serves as *setting*."[43] Here is a landscape utterly domesticated; this is nature remade to accord with the economic purposes of the nation and the pleasures of its individual citizens. This is a nature in which sublimity is not granted by the Great Spirit but created by men.

The Euro-Canadian vision of Western Canada's national parks was not strictly defined by the pragmatic ideals of government and railway officials. Though a utilitarian ethic may have driven the supply side of the parks' creation, there can be little doubt that a very different mentality informed the demand side of many of the people who visited the parks. Many of those who responded to the "Call of the Rockies" were drawn by romantic ideas that saw nature not as a constellation of material resources to be exploited, but rather, ironically, as a necessary counterbalance to the very materialist, utilitarian ideology that drove the developers of the park and that informed so many of the soul-destroying dimensions of modern urban life.

During the Laurier years, concerns about industrialization, urbanization, and materialism fed the anti-modernist critique of Canadian life. Drawing upon the American transcendentalist movement and the intellectual currents of European romanticism, these critiques challenged the scientific, utilitarian vision of nature and society in post-Confederation Canada and hailed wilderness experiences as a necessary corrective to the diseases of the metropolis. As historian George Altmeyer points out:

> Indeed, as a reaction against certain distressing tendencies in their society, many Canadians wanted to get "back to nature," to better manage her resources and to use her as an instrument of religious expression.... This positive perception involved the ideas of Nature as a Benevolent Mother capable of soothing city-worn nerves and restoring health, of rejuvenating a physically deteriorating race and of teaching

> lessons no book learning could give; as a Limited Storehouse whose treasures must in the future be treated with greater respect; and as a Temple where one could again find and communicate with Deity.[44]

In central Canada, these impulses were expressed in numerous ways – through the animal stories of Ernest Thompson Seton, the emergence of publications focussing on the outdoors, the push for outdoor education for youth, the formation of boy scout packs, the poetry of Archibald Lampman, and the Nature study movement. Cottaging culture also became more widespread. The "back to nature" movement envisioned the natural world as an integral – indeed essential – dimension of a whole human life. Cultivating a proper relationship with this vital aspect of the human soul was believed to lead to a happier, healthier, more virtuous and fulfilling existence.

In the West, this impulse to contemplate Nature was evident in the promotional material for the Rocky Mountain parks. CPR advertisements for their resorts, for example, urged Canadians to flee the city to save their sanity. As one advertisement read: "Day by day it is becoming more and more apparent that some holiday of rest and relaxation – call it by the good old-fashioned name of holiday if you like – is rapidly becoming one of the essentials of our exciting twentieth century existence. What was once a question of caprice and luxury is now a necessity, if the danger of a breakdown is to be avoided."[45] Such textual imperatives were supplemented by artistic visions of the sublime beauty and contemplative solitude that the CPR offered to prospective tourists in the Rockies. The railway offered incentives to artists to ride the rails and document the dramatic evidence of national expansion and the majestic wilderness being unveiled in western Canada. In this early period of the parks, when access was largely limited to those with the resources necessary to visit the Rockies, the hope was that such cultured representations of the landscape would compel the urban élites of central and eastern Canada to head west. CPR promoters believed that the advertisements would resonate with urbane Canadians burdened by the malaises of modern, industrial society and compel them to seek adventure and renewal in the "CPR Rockies."[46]

Though the emergence of the automobile in Canada would alter the method of conveyance to the parks, the romantic vision of those parks as capable of restoring urbanites' mental and spiritual health would persist. Harkin secured funds and orchestrated development in the parks from 1911 until 1936, years in which the automobile was rapidly transforming Banff into a mass tourism destination. As both "The Father of National Parks" and "The Father of Tourist Travel," Harkin initiated road-building projects throughout the Rocky Mountain parks to open this profound source of human betterment to Canadians, including the Banff–Windermere Highway, opened in 1923. Other developments in Banff during his tenure include the Banff Springs Golf Course (1911), the Mount Rundle Campground (1914), the Banff Recreation Ground (1914), the Administration Building Gardens (1930s), the Banff Airfield (1930s), and the Mount Norquay ski area (1930s).[47] He viewed making such developments as a kind of patriotic duty, offering the inestimable spiritual riches of the mountain parks to Canadians.

Harkin left the task of cultivating the romantic sensibility to Mabel B. Williams, his appointed author of Rocky Mountain guide books. Like the railway marketers before her, Williams employed florid language to extol the natural world as a vital antidote to the soul-numbing excesses of urban life. She set out her romantic perspective on the parks in her *Through the Heart of the Rockies and the Selkirks*:

> They [national parks] exist in order that every citizen of Canada may satisfy his soul-craving for Nature and Nature's beauty; that he may absorb the poise and restfulness of the forests; that he may steep his soul in the brilliance of the wild flowers and the sublimity of the mountain peaks; that he may develop in himself the buoyancy, the joy, and the activity he sees in the wild animals; that he may stock his brain and his mind as he would a warehouse with the raw materials of intelligent optimism, great thoughts, noble ideals; that he may be made better, happier, and healthier.[48]

On another occasion, she wrote:

> Here, in these vast playgrounds, among the great mountains and primeval forests, thousands are re-discovering the pure pleasure of simple and strenuous life in the open. In these sanctuaries of the primitive and the wild, they are recovering with a strange thrill their ancient companionship with Nature, and finding room again for that old sense of wonder in the mystery and miracle of her ways for which our mechanical and material civilization has often little room.[49]

For those more inclined to a spiritual or aesthetic appreciation for Nature, she compared the journey to the mountains to another famous pilgrim's voyage: "The sordid cares and anxieties brought from an outside competitive world drop away like Christian's burden at the sight of the Delectable Mountains. One gives himself up to the spirit of the place realizing that after all 'living, not getting a living' is the true end of life."[50]

Her works were filled with similar encomiums to a wild, primeval Nature and its capacity to save us from the "Seven Devils of our modern life – the little demons of Fear, Worry, Over-Haste, and Over-work, Indigestion, Unrest, and Abysmal Boredom."[51] Williams presents Nature as a primeval presence capable of saving us from the endless getting and spending, the enervating rationalism that constituted metropolitan malaise in the modern, industrial cities of Canada.

This celebration of the romantic ideals of a wild nature was not unproblematic; co-existing with this vision of nature was a panegyric to the very utilitarian, civilizing tendencies that were rendering so much of the "virginal" wilderness developed. The core of Williams' eloquent advertising of the Rocky Mountain parks was a vision of progressive anthropology, imagining the area as a wild haunt of chaotic nature, superstitious Indians, and terrified animals subdued and made "sacred" by civilization, science, and rational administration. The purpose of such reformations of culture and environment in the Rocky Mountains was, as Williams put it in a particularly telling phrase, to "make some of 'the wild places of the land sacred.'"[52] Sacred places, Williams asserts, are *made*; the human reshaping of the natural world within the parks is envisioned here as a necessity in developing the "shrines of the earth."[53]

Her narratives rebound with romantic evocations of nation-building, nationalist heroism, and scientific conquest. She writes of some of the region's early European visitors: "While the quest of the fur traders was commercial gain still its best officers were actuated, not by this lure only but by that undying spirit of adventure, that impulse to dare the most intractable wilds, which has carried the British flag into so many of the remote places of the earth."[54] That same spirit of adventure and civilized daring would be manifest in the gradual conquest of those "most intractable wilds":

> [T]he final conquering of the Rockies in so short a period of time constitutes a victory over the opposing forces of Nature of which any century might well be proud.... It seems strange that fifty years ago the Canadian Rockies were still an unknown wilderness, a tangled

chaos of peaks, thrusting their terrifying barrier of four hundred miles between the prairies and the sea.[55]

In the wake of this scientific and technological conquest, the "tangled chaos of peaks" was domesticated: "Nowhere else, they will tell you, can a man feel so at home with the mountains. Here the great peaks do not threaten or oppress a man with the sense of his own littleness. There is something about the very atmosphere that is friendly and benign."[56] Williams forcefully reiterated the notion that human subduing and reshaping of the wilderness – the domestication of the primeval and awful – had established a "Promise Land, a garden of delights." Rational governance ensured the continuing beauty of this paradise: "The Government … [protects] them by eternal vigilance from the ever-threatening menace of fire, guarding the rich heritage of wild life, preserving and enhancing the natural beauty of the landscape, opening the many attractions by roads and trails and making provisions … for the convenience and comfort of visitors."[57] Williams thus trumpeted the ability of park visitors to revel in the comfort of the "primeval" and the "wild" while marvelling at man's continuing subjugation of a terrifying, chaotic nature.

A similarly paradoxical perspective is evident in the writings of both Harkin and Williams on the Native peoples. Both suggested that the Native people lived in harmony with their natural surroundings. In his preface to Williams' *Through the Heart of the Rockies and Selkirks*, Harkin told readers of the Indian legend of Ah-ka-noosta:

> Each spring he would disappear from the tribe, returning in the autumn with renewed vigour as if he had recovered the spirit of his youth. At last his brothers, wondering, begged him to tell what secret magic he had discovered. Ah-ka-noosta, however, declared he had no magic; he had only been away in the mountains, living like the wild goat and the eagle among the peaks, sleeping in the tepee of the pine forest and drinking the clear waters of the mountain springs … a legend grew up among them [his brothers] that Ah-ka-noosta had discovered in the mountains a magic lake whose waters were the Elixir of Life.[58]

Throughout her books, Williams also portrayed pre-contact Native life as uniquely wed to both nature and a heroic ethic. She invited her readers to witness the Stoneys in all "their old time glory" at Banff Indian

Days, an annual event at which tribe members would dress in full Native regalia and perform in a rodeo.

But just as Williams touted primeval nature while also lauding development within the parks, so too she spoke of the glories of Stoney culture while simultaneously encouraging park visitors to consider the way in which the Euro-Canadian, progressive vision of the Rockies had superceded the antiquated, superstitious worldview of the Native peoples. Williams wrote of how the Cree Indians "were apparently ignorant of their [the Banff hot springs] medicinal qualities, regarding them with superstitious dread." This "irrational fear" existed in pointed contrast to the Euro-Canadian scientific appreciation for the therapeutic value of the springs – "artificially prepared radioactive waters ... [which] were found to cause a multiplication of the red blood cells, stimulation of the digestive processes and increased elimination of uric acid."[59] Similarly, Williams suggested that for many years in the Rockies, "the inroads of Indian hunters prevented the wild life from increasing to any appreciable extent."[60] In another passage, she juxtaposed Native "wastefulness" with rationalized wildlife administration, linking the former with the expulsion from the Garden of Eden and the latter with a return to Eden: "It is a paradise for wild life, guarded on all sides not by flaming swords, but by the eternal vigilance of an administration which loves and is determined to protect the wild life heritage of this beautiful domain."[61] The Natives' inability to perceive the medicinal benefits of the springs or the aesthetic value of wildlife is paralleled, Williams suggested, by an almost sub-human incapacity to master, scientifically and technologically, the nature that surrounded them: "the Shuswaps ... built their half-buried dwellings at the base of Mount Rundle where now the tourist plays golf, but the Indians left few more marks of their habitation than the wild animals."[62] Her logic provided a justification – more or less explicit – for dispossessing Natives of the land and creating golf courses, wildlife wardens, and hot springs' resorts.

In Williams' writings, nature and the Native people in their "wild" state were consigned to the past by the ideals and practices of progressive rationality at the same time that they were bathed in a nostalgic romanticism. Not surprisingly, the "wilderness" she describes and the Stoneys' display of their "old time glory" at Banff Indian Days bore little relation to the contemporary realities of the natural and human worlds in the rapidly developing Rocky Mountain parks. Williams' "wild and solitary and beautiful"[63] nature was fast becoming a highly developed mass tourist destination. And the "Indianness" on display at Banff Indian Days – including painted tepees and the slaughtering of buffalo – had little to do with the lifestyle of the Stoneys in either the past or the present. The painting of tepees had been a break from Stoney tradition designed to cater to tourist aesthetic sensibilities, and the slaughtered meat was rarely eaten, being exchanged with park officials for beef in the days following the event.[64] In the Rocky Mountain parks, domesticated nature and the "civilized savage" were cloaked with the now safely colonized aura of a wild past. What historian Patricia Jasen observes to be the tourist vision of Native cultures in Canada in general equally applies to the vision of the wilderness in the West:

> Virtually all tourists visiting the Canadian wilderness, whether European, American, or urban Canadian, saw themselves as agents of, or temporary refugees from, the civilized world. The relentless march of progress, they believed, would inevitably triumph in all parts of North America, but in the meantime they looked to the Native inhabitants to satisfy their curiosity about humanity and its wild state and to confirm their confidence in their own civilization. Regardless of whether Native people were seen as good or bad, noble or ignoble, innocent or demonic, they were cast in the role of a race in decline. Tourists might idealize or condemn them, but the belief that Native people belonged to the past and were without a future supplied a powerful, unifying theme. Confining 'Indians' to the past had a particular advantage for tourists, for it allowed them to see Native people as 'authentic' and yet ineffectual and unthreatening at the same time.[65]

Herein lies one of the great paradoxes of the parks experience, namely that the romantic current of park tourism, so often touted as a return to the wild and the primitive, in fact supported the essentially progressive vision of modern civilization.

This tension between utilitarian political logic, on the one hand, and the romantic tourist vision, on the other, seems to have been reconciled in the idea of natural beauty as a consumable product. As historian John Wadland explains: "Although modern Canadians tend to consider wilderness and culture antithetical notions, as consumers they unite in identifying both with their leisure time – with their recreation."[66] Thus, the seeming contradictions between the celebration of the wild and the developed along with the savage and the civilized in the writings of Williams are resolved by binding these threads together in a modern consumptive package, premised on a vital difference between pre-modern and modern visions of nature. Willliams' idea of the sacred holiness involves a sacrality the element of awfulness and dread that religious scholar Rudolf Otto saw as an essential component of the idea of the holy.[67] Indeed, she seems to view such dread as a dimension of the "opposing forces of Nature" – the terrifying and chaotic wilderness – to be subdued through instrumental reason. Thus, the Stoneys' profound existential encounter with the terror and majesty of the mountains is rendered safe, predictable by the remaking of human and natural worlds in the interest of romantic consumption. Denuded of their terrible power, the mountains now become "safe" for tourists of any taste or sensibility. Williams explained: "Perhaps one of the reasons why so many people love Banff is because they find there such a number of things to interest and amuse. Banff has an infinite variety of attractions and she knows how to please each of her lovers in his own way."[68] Whether scientist, mystic, climber, aesthete, or motorist, Banff – the ever-seductive mistress – offered her paramours whatever they might desire. In satisfying the romantic yearnings of her lovers, of course, Banff also helped to fill the federal treasury, thus fulfilling dimensions of both the utilitarian and the romantic ideals.

The early history of the national parks bears witness to several prominent trends in the history of the Canadian West. The establishment of the parks represents both the symbolic and quite literal overthrow of a pre-modern sensibility of place to be replaced by a modern conception. The utilitarian logic that reimagined and ultimately refigured the wasted wilderness as profitable scenery and hot springs testifies to the significance of rational, scientific traditions in the Canadian imagination. The romantic vision of nature challenged the utilitarian and metropolitan ethos but also supported that vision by participating in the commodification of nature and the consignment of wilderness and Native peoples to a nostalgic past. Taken together, the many strands of cultural sensibilities evident in the early history of the parks – Christian ideas of natural theology, utilitarian arguments about political and economic efficacy, romantic visions of the restorative powers of nature – all speak to the burgeoning of a modern vision in Canada.

One of the central elements of modernity is the opening of multiple sources of moral meaning, multiple reservoirs of value and sensibility. Philosopher Charles Taylor, an authoritative voice on the modern identity, writes: "Our forebears were generally unruffled in their belief, because the sources they could envisage made unbelief incredible. The big thing that has happened since is the opening of other possible sources."[69]

The challenging of God and religious orthodoxy – largely the sole moral source in pre-modern culture – was a significant feature of Victorian Canada. As historian David Marshall notes:

> By the 1890s churchmen had become conscious of the fact that Canadian society was increasingly pluralistic and secular. There were organized and competitive sports, recreational sports such as cycling, amusement parks, Mechanics' Institutes, trade unions, social clubs, political organizations, libraries, theatre, and music-halls, which could assume some of the functions that the church and religion traditionally held. Moreover, these institutions and activities competed directly with religion and the churches for the attention of the masses.[70]

The early history of the parks thus embodies an axial moment in Canadian – and Western – history: the moment when a singular moral source becomes more complex and contested. In the decades since, we have witnessed a process of disentangling some of these threads, so that utilitarianism and romanticism, divorced from the Christian forms that often sustained them, become moral sources in themselves.

The Canadian perspective upon nature evident in the establishment of the early national parks in the Rocky Mountains is complex and contested. Rooted in three distinct visions of the mountains as a promised land – the Stoney belief in the Rockies as a divinely revealed sacred site, and the Euro-Canadian conceptions of the area as both a treasury of natural resources and a sublime antidote to rational, industrial society – the Rocky Mountain parks manifested many of the essential spiritual and cultural currents that defined the remaking of Western Canada in the post-Confederation period. These currents continue to inform and animate the Canadian perspective upon nature today in the emergence of questions about Native rights to hunt and fish, ideas about "sustainable development" and the rise of a generalized, often quite romanticized, form of spirituality with sources in nature. Such ideas about nature define our own cultural vision, because, as I. S. MacLaren observes: "Wilderness is us."[71] To understand the continual unfolding of these images and ideals of Canadians' relationship to the natural world is to gain vital insights into our national vision.

NOTES

1 John Wadland, "Wilderness and Culture," in *Consuming Canada: Readings in Environmental History*, eds. Chad Gaffield and Pam Gaffield (Toronto: Copp Clark, 1995), 14.

2 Sebastian Chumak, *The Stonies of Alberta: An Illustrated Heritage of Genesis, Myths, Legends, Folklore and Wisdom of Yahey Wichastabi, the People-Who-Cook-With-Hot-Stones*, trans. Alfred Dixon, Jr. (Calgary: The Alberta Foundation, 1983), 64.

3 Hugh A. Dempsey, *Indian Tribes of Alberta* (Calgary: Glenbow Museum, 1997), 49–55.

4 Jordan Paper, "Landscape and Sacred Space in Native American Religion," *Perspectives of Canadian Landscape: Native Traditions*, ed. Joan M. Vastokas (North York, ON: Robarts Centre for Canadian Studies, York University, 1990), 44.

5 Catherine L. Albanese, *Nature Religion in America: From the Algonkian Indians to the New Age* (Chicago: University of Chicago Press, 1990), 21.

6 Ella Elizabeth Clark, *Indian Legends of Canada* (Toronto: McClelland and Stewart, 1971), 97–98.

7 Chumak, *The Stonies of Alberta*, 174.

8 Chief John Snow, *These Mountains Are Our Sacred Places* (Toronto: Samuel Stevens, 1977), 6.

9 Clark, *Indian Legends of Canada*, 96.

10 Ibid., 132–33.

11 Chumak, *The Stonies of Alberta*, 136.

12 Snow, *These Mountains*, 13.

13 Mountains feature prominently in the consciousness of premodern peoples. The great religious scholar Mircea Eliade explains that "since the sacred mountain is an *axis mundi* connecting earth with heaven … [it] is holy ground, *because it is the place nearest to heaven*, because from here, from our abode, it is possible to reach heaven." Mircea Eliade, *The Sacred and the Profane: The Nature of Religion*, trans. Willard R. Trask (New York: Harcourt, 1957), 38–39.

14 John Laurie, *The Stony Indians of Alberta: Volume I*, unpublished manuscript, 1957–59, 109–116. Glenbow Archives 4390. Norman Luxton offers another account of Crawler's conversion, claiming that it was a secluded, visionary encounter with the mountains' elfish beings that began him on the path to being a healer. See Marius Barbeau, *Indian Days on the Western Prairies* (Ottawa : Dept. of Northern Affairs and National Resources, National Museum of Canada, 1960), 115–16.

15 Barbeau, *Indian Days*, 113–14.

16 Laurie, *The Stony Indians*, 113.

17 For an extensive discussions of natural theology, see Carl Berger, *Science, God, and Nature in Victorian Canada* (Toronto: University of Toronto Press, 1983) and A. B. McKillop, *A Disciplined Intelligence: Critical Inquiry and Canadian Thought in the Victorian Era* (Montreal and Kingston: McGill-Queen's University Press, 2001).

18 Berger, *Science, God, and Nature in Victorian Canada*, 45.

19 Northrop Frye, *The Bush Garden: Essays on the Canadian Imagination* (Toronto: House of Anansi Press, 1971), 220.

20 Ibid., 224.

21 Suzanne Zeller, *Inventing Canada: Early Victorian Science and the Idea of a Transcontinental Nation* (Toronto: University of Toronto Press, 1987), 5–6.

22 It bears mentioning that the link between Victorian science and utilitarianism was not always obvious or direct. Some scientists during this period viewed themselves as engaged in a "pure science" inspired by a religious sensibility. Their intentions notwithstanding, their work was often put to utilitarian ends. See, for example, Nancy Christie, "Sir William Logan's Geological Empire and the 'Humbug' of Economic Utility," *Canadian Historical Review* 75, no. 2 (June 1994): 161–204.

23 W. L. Morton, "Victorian Canada," in *The Shield of Achilles*, ed. W. L. Morton (Toronto: McClelland and Stewart, 1968), 319.

24 Doug Owram, *Promise of Eden: The Canadian Expansionist Movement and the Idea of the West, 1856–1900* (Toronto: University of Toronto Press, 1980), 125.

25 Ramsay Cook, "1492 and All That: Making a Garden out of Wilderness," in *Consuming Canada*, 62–63.

26 Sid Marty, *A Grand and Fabulous Notion: The First Century of Canada's Parks* (Toronto: NC Press, 1984), 34–35.

27 Their response recalls Rousseau's description of humanity's emergence from its natural (premodern?) state: "The first man who, having enclosed a piece of ground, to whom it occurred to say *this is mine*, and found people sufficiently simple to believe him, was the true founder of civil society.... Beware of listening to this imposter; You are lost if you forget that the fruits are everyone's and the Earth no one's." *The Discourses and Other Early Political Writings*, ed. and trans. Victor Gourevitch (Cambridge: Cambridge University Press, 1997), 161.

28 Desmond Morton, *A Short History of Canada* (Toronto: McClelland and Stewart, 2001), 121.

29 See, for instance, Joseph R. Skoski's review of Phyllis Hembry's book *British Spas from 1815 to the Present: A Social History* in *Victorian Studies* 42, no. 1 (Autumn 1998/99): 158–61. Interestingly, the vogue of profitable spas frequented by the rich seemed to have ebbed in Britain by 1850, well before the discovery of the Banff hot springs, and have been replaced by the seaside resort. The clientele of springs changed to invalids seeking recuperation.

30 "Rocky Mountain Parks Act, 1887," *Documenting Canada: A History of Modern Canada in Document*, ed. Dave De Brou and Bill Waiser (Saskatoon: Fifth House, 1992), 155.

31 Robert Craig Brown, "The Doctrine of Usefulness: Natural Resource and the National Park Policy in Canada, 1887–1914," in *The Canadian National Parks: Today and Tomorrow*, eds. J. G. Nelson and R. C. Scace (Montreal: Harvest House, 1969), 48.

32 Ibid., 58.

33 George A. Stewart, *Annual Report of the Department of the Interior for the Year 1887* (Ottawa: Roger & Co., 1888), Part VI, 10.

34 W. F. Whitcher, *Annual Report of the Department of the Interior for the Year 1886* (Ottawa: Maclean, Roger, & Co., 1887), Part I, 92.

35 A similar process took place in Jasper, where utilitarian logic – the greatest good for the greatest number – removed Métis from the region through a decree that made their presence within the park boundaries illegal. As I. S. Maclaren puts it, "Sovereign in right of the Crown, the valley becomes the site of a disturbing paradox in which the impersonal national collectivity dispossesses its personal predecessors by abjectly and summarily identifying them as criminals." I. S. MacLaren, "Cultured Wilderness in Jasper National Park," *Journal of Canadian Studies* 34, no. 3 (Fall 1999): 17.

36 Daniel Francis, *The Imaginary Indian: The Image of the Indian in Canadian Culture* (Vancouver: Arsenal Pulp Press, 1992), 25.

37 Clark, *Indian Legends of Canada*, 96.

38 Chumak, *The Stonies of Alberta*, 66.

39 Robert C. Scace, *Banff: A Cultural-Historical Study of Land Use and Management in a National Park Community to 1945* (Calgary, Dept. of Geography, University of Calgary, 1968), 40–42.

40 George A. Stewart, *Annual Report of the Department of the Interior for the Year 1888* (Ottawa: Queen's Printer, 1889), Part VI, 5.

41 Whitcher, *Annual Report*, 87.

42 Marty, *A Grand and Fabulous Notion*, 98.

43 MacLaren, "Cultured Wilderness," 26.

44 George Altmeyer, "Three Ideas of Nature in Canada, 1893–1914," in *Consuming Canada*, 97–98.

45 E. J. Hart, *The Selling of Canada: The CPR and the Beginnings of Canadian Tourism* (Banff: Altitude, 1983), back cover.

46 See Lynda Jessup, "The Group of Seven and the Tourist Landscape in Western Canada, or The More Things Change …", *Journal of Canadian Studies* 37, no. 1 (Spring 2002): 144–79.

47 Scace, *Banff*, 105.

48 Mabel B. Williams, *Through the Heart of the Rockies and the Selkirks* (Ottawa: Department of the Interior, 1924), foreword.

49 Mabel B. Williams, *Waterton Lakes National Park* (Ottawa: National Parks Branch, 1927), 5.

50 Williams, *Through the Heart of the Rockies and the Selkirks* (Ottawa: Department of the Interior, 1924), 16.

51 Williams, *Waterton Lakes National Park*, 7.

52 Mabel B. Williams, *Jasper National Park* (Ottawa: F. A. Acland, 1928), 2.

53 Williams, *Through the Heart of the Rockies and the Selkirks*, 51.

54 Williams, *Jasper National Park* (1928), 10.

55 Mabel B. Williams, *Kootenay National Park and The Banff Windermere Highway* (Ottawa: F. A. Acland, 1929), 8.

56 Mabel B. Williams, *Jasper National Park: A Descriptive Guide* (Hamilton: H. R. Larson, 1949), 2.

57 Williams, *Through the Heart of the Rockies and the Selkirks*, 2.

58 Ibid., foreword.

59 Ibid., 21.

60 Williams, *Jasper National Park* (1928), 133.

61 Ibid., 83.

62 Williams, *Through the Heart of the Rockies and the Selkirks*, 7.

63 Ibid., 1.

64 Laurie Meijer Drees, "'Indians' Bygone Past:' The Banff Indian Days, 1902-1945", *Past Imperfect* 2 (1993), 13.

65 Patricia Jasen, *Wild Things: Nature, Culture, and Tourism in Ontario, 1790–1914* (Toronto: University of Toronto Press, 1995), 17.

66 Wadland, "Wilderness and Culture," 12.

67 Rudolf Otto, *The Idea of the Holy*, trans. John W. Harvey (New York: Oxford University Press, 1969).

68 Williams, *Through the Heart of the Rockies and the Selkirks*, 16.

69 Charles Taylor, *Sources of the Self: The Making of the Modern Identity* (Cambridge, MA: Harvard University Press, 1989), 312–13.

70 David B. Marshall, *Secularizing the Faith: Canadian Protestant Clergy and the Crisis of Belief, 1850–1940* (Toronto: University of Toronto Press, 1992), 127.

71 MacLaren, "Cultured Wilderness," 38.

4

CLIFFORD SIFTON'S VISION OF THE PRAIRIE WEST

David Hall

Clifford Sifton, Minister of the Interior in the Liberal government of Sir Wilfrid Laurier, enthused about the future of western Canada when, in November 1902, he addressed the General Assembly of the Methodist Church in Toronto:

> Doubtless you have for a good many years looked upon [the West] as a land of large promise but somewhat slow and poor performance, as a land of illimitable possibility but limited realities, a land generally described, indeed, with a fine flow of rhetoric, but which has so far failed to realise the hopes which had been entertained of it. But a change has come, and all in a very short time. Stagnation has given way to abounding activity, production is now reckoned by tens of millions instead of by hundreds of thousands. Where we counted our incoming settlers by hundreds we now count them by thousands, and the whole situation has undergone an alteration that is little short of phenomenal.[1]

Settlers were flooding into the West in unprecedented numbers; Sifton predicted that the population of the prairie region would triple, to 750,000, within three years. Many of these settlers would help to create "one of the richest and most independent agricultural communities in the world," and soon they would "constitute a most potent factor in the national life of Canada."[2]

Although he would have considered himself a hard-nosed realist, Sifton was in fact an optimist about the future of the Prairie West. Indeed he fitted readily into the group of promoters of the West known as "boosters."[3] He shared their roseate image of a region populated by productive homesteaders who would enrich the entire country both as producers and consumers.

They also would contribute to shaping the character of the Dominion, and be shaped as citizens in turn by their experience on the land. Just as the settlers would transform the region, so they would be transformed by it. And just as Sifton shared and popularized Westerners' optimism about the future of their region, so he, through his powerful advocacy and successful recruitment of settlers, helped to reshape Canadians' image of the West.

Notions of the prairie provinces as constituting a region now are broadly categorized as formal, functional, or imagined.[4] The idea of a formal region derives from the distinctive geography and climate of the prairies. The idea of the imagined region, which now tends to be associated mainly with literary studies, contends that the notion of region is a product of the mind or, in the words of Gerald Friesen, "that a place must be imagined before it can exist." The functional region derives from certain purposes – often economic – or human characteristics associated with a particular geographical area. It is this last definition – the functional region – that best suits Clifford Sifton's vision of the Prairie West. At the same time, he imagined or envisaged aspects of the region's future character in many ways that went beyond the normal limits of "functional."

A vision entails anticipation of what might or will occur. It is a product of past experience and of the projection of hopes (or fears) into the future. It usually is dynamic, changing over time. It cannot be argued that Sifton's vision for the West was in any sense original. Its importance derives from at least two general points: first, it encapsulated well the opinions and wishes of many people in his era; second, he had the opportunity and capability as a powerful and influential politician to realize a significant portion of his vision.

Sifton's vision of the West first derived from Ontario roots. His father was an active Reformer or Clear Grit in the age of George Brown and Alexander Mackenzie. This was the party that first pushed to annex Rupert's Land from the Hudson's Bay Company. The intent was both to provide a "British" frontier of settlement as an alternative to the American western frontier, which was attracting many young men from British North America, and to be a field of expansion for central Canadian business. When young Clifford Sifton entered his teens, his father,

John Wright Sifton, won some early contracts to build the telegraph and some initial stages of the Pacific railway between Lake Superior and Red River in Manitoba. The elder Sifton relocated his family to Winnipeg in 1875. There was no doubt that the small province of Manitoba was being annexed to Canada, and that the railroad and telegraph symbolized the new order.[5] By these means of communication and transportation, settlers were to come to exploit the land and send their produce to market. Also by these means, central Canada was to bring this region under its economic and political suzerainty. That is, it was to be a region that was integrated into the larger Canadian society, economy, and polity. It would be, for the foreseeable future, a region dependent upon the centre, a hinterland of the metropolis.

That said, Ontarians like the Siftons brought with them ideas about the desirable shape of the future Western society, ideas which often conflicted with the reality of what they actually found in Manitoba. The *Manitoba Act*, 1870, attempted to realize a compromise between the desire of Ottawa to have a free hand in the future development of the region, and the desire of the local, mostly mixed-blood, population to preserve and protect their society and way of life. Put simply, Ottawa retained control of public lands, the better to facilitate settlement and railway development. At the same time, the *Act* made both English and French official languages; it provided for an appointed Legislative Council, which would be dominated by "old-timers" who were expected to curb the elected Legislative Assembly's enthusiasm for change as new settlers became dominant electors; and it provided guarantees for the educational rights of Catholics and Protestants.[6] Newcomers like the Siftons envisaged, among other things, a future dominated by settlers from Ontario, with a government-run school system like that of Ontario, no bilingualism, and unfettered freedom for the majority to control the government.[7] The Legislative Council was abolished in 1877, but not until 1888 did the newcomers dominate the government, and only in 1890 did they succeed in changing the school system and (illegally, as it turned out) the language law.[8]

The struggle to achieve a society similar in principle to that of Ontario was, at first, largely internal, within Manitoba. Another struggle was necessary to assert provincial rights within the Dominion. Ontario Reformers were imbued with provincial rights sentiment,[9] and it is not surprising that they soon would find themselves fighting Ottawa for the rights of their new province. During the 1870s, the tiny province of

Manitoba was very much at the mercy of Ottawa, and tended to vote for the government party in order to ensure federal favour. By the 1880s, however, at least two serious areas of conflict emerged, both resulting from Ottawa's contract with the Canadian Pacific Railway. The federally guaranteed monopoly ensured that the CPR could charge whatever the traffic would bear, and that it would face no competition. When the federal government in 1881 disallowed several Manitoba railway bills intended to provide competition for the CPR, a storm of provincial rights agitation convulsed the province, aided and abetted by the Liberal/Reformers, including Clifford Sifton. Many Manitobans also resented federal control of revenues from public lands, and – to be frank – the subordinate relationship created by provincial dependency upon the annual federal grant. When the Liberals triumphed provincially in 1888 under Thomas Greenway, one of their first successful and enormously popular actions was to force the federal government to abandon the CPR monopoly.[10]

Premier Greenway named Clifford Sifton attorney-general of Manitoba in 1891. By this time the province was embroiled on both legal and political fronts in defending its national school legislation of 1890. The French-Catholic minority engaged the support of their confrères in Quebec, as well as the federal government, in seeking restoration of their lost educational rights. Sifton became the principal defender of Manitoba's right to determine its own school legislation, and of the broader view of the nature of Western society that underlay that legislation. It was not a multicultural society that Sifton and his supporters had in mind, but an assimilationist society. It was not to be a replication of the English-Protestant and French-Catholic cultures of central Canada, but a distinctively Western society with British values and little ethnic or religious diversity.

Appointed minister of the interior by Sir Wilfrid Laurier in 1896, Sifton arrived in Ottawa with fairly complex and sometimes contradictory views of the Prairie West's place in Confederation. Like many Westerners, he had attacked the National Policy, a highly protective tariff, imposed in 1879 by the federal government, the CPR monopoly, high freight rates, and generally Ottawa's ignorance of, or lack of interest in, Western needs. But Sifton was not anti-Ottawa. He believed that the federal power could and must be used in the interest of the West to stimulate growth and assist the farmers. The West was, after all, still a dependent region within Confederation. Its material growth and prosperity was important, but not as an end in itself. The prairie region must be an integral part of a strengthening nation. Sifton also was a realist. In order to accomplish what he wanted for the West and Canada, the Liberal government had to remain in power, and this meant making necessary political arrangements and compromises along the way.

His father, among other things, had been a farmer, and like a majority of Canadians of his day, Sifton believed that a stable, progressive society was rooted in agriculture. The moral nature of the country was created and continually regenerated by those who lived on the land and struggled with nature to make a livelihood. As he said in 1910:

> Agriculture is the foundation of all real and enduring progress on the part of Canada. It is one of the striking facts of the present social condition in the United States and Canada that, with a few exceptions, those men who, by reason of strength of character and intellectual pre-eminence, take the lead in public affairs, in professional life and in scholarship are, as a rule, removed not more than one or, at most, two generations from ancestors who tilled the soil.
>
> The possession of a preponderating rural population having the virtues and strength of character bred only among those who follow agricultural life, is the only sure guarantee of our national future.[11]

Sifton's most immediate goal was to get the West settled with a productive agricultural population. He accepted, in other words, the prevailing view of the West as a vast under-utilized resource which awaited development of its economic potential. Since the Confederation era, the West had been expected to be a producer of agricultural, timber, and mineral resources for the domestic and international markets, and a consumer of manufactured goods in a protected domestic market. The dream had been slow in becoming reality. The rate of settlement over the previous twenty years had been disappointing, especially after the completion of the Canadian Pacific Railway in 1885. The new minister of the interior believed that the reasons were essentially two: impediments to settlement and successful farming created by Ottawa, and poor promotion of the region by government and private agencies. He was determined to rectify problems in both areas.[12]

Native peoples were, in Sifton's view, more an impediment to economic development of the region than a potential partner in its growth.[13] He believed that Canada had an obligation to assist the aboriginal population in transition, but it was a transition to assimilation that he had in mind. He also hoped that the natives would become sufficiently independent economically to be free of the necessity of government support. The long-standing goal of the Canadian government, he told Parliament in 1901, was "to bring the Indians into a state of civilization or comparative civilization, [rather] than to take any chance of their becoming a disturbing factor in the community."[14] The emphasis in educating native children was to prepare them for farming and domestic life on the reserves, rather than on skills necessary to compete with whites in life off the reserve. Natives were pressured to become self-sufficient farmers. Yet the government took every opportunity to maintain its paternal supervision of native life, which did not encourage the development of an independent spirit.[15]

Sifton's vision for the West was, as noted, not much different from that which had been held by many Canadians for fifteen or twenty years. It was expected to be essentially a region populated by hard-working yeoman farmers, supported by an extensive communication, transportation, and urban infrastructure. He even continued to use many of the same techniques as his predecessors to attract immigrants and get them settled on their homesteads. What was different about Sifton was his energy, organization, and range in seeking agricultural settlers.

Aggressive salesmanship was crucial. "In my judgment," he told the House of Commons, "the immigration work has to be carried on in the same manner as the sale of any commodity; just as soon as you stop advertising and missionary work, the movement is going to stop."[16] Under his direction, the department of the interior produced dozens of pamphlets in tens of thousands of copies and a variety of languages to advertise the advantages of settling in the Canadian Prairie West.[17] These, in turn, are quite revealing of the vision of the West that Sifton wished to convey. Many of the pamphlets were heavily illustrated with photographs of prosperous prairie farms, often well-treed with gently rolling hills and well-watered; or there were maps, charts, and graphs, all outlining the remarkable growth and productivity of agriculture, transportation, and other economic activities in the West. The pamphlets fairly bristled with facts and figures to give them an aura of authenticity, and to try to answer the many questions that any prospective settler might have. Almost all the pamphlets contained testimonials from successful farmers or from journalists (usually from the United States or Britain) who had been sent through the country to report on its virtues; indeed, some pamphlets consisted entirely of this sort of material.

Certain themes emerged consistently. One was climate, which was represented as invariably salubrious: "Malarial diseases are totally unknown, and contagious complaints are rarely heard of." Winters were admittedly cold, but clear and with lower humidity than other countries. Manitoba, intending settlers were informed, was not subject in summer to "those hot, parching winds" that prevail "in that portion of the United States known as the American desert."[18] The climate in Alberta likewise was held to be beneficial to "invalids suffering from pulmonary weakness," and to "nervous, overtaxed men and women."[19] As time went on, the reports provided more detail and even greater enthusiasm. In 1904 one pamphlet reported that the water in northern Alberta (around Edmonton) was "ample and wholesome from a sanitary point of view," while the air was found to be "clear, pure, and aseptic, containing a large proportion of ozone – the natural air purifier." The soil "does not breed malaria [a subject that arose often enough to suggest some ongoing concern on the part of prospective settlers], which is the cause of ague in its many forms." Not only was the climate healthful for adults, "but it seems to have a special influence in developing strong and healthy children." Moreover, "sufferers from consumption, asthma, chest and throat affections, and many other diseases are always greatly benefited and frequently cured by a residence here."[20] Those concerned about the Edmonton district's northern location were reminded that it lay on the same latitude as Dublin, Liverpool, and Hamburg, farther south than Scotland, or anywhere in Scandinavia, and 455 miles farther south than St. Petersburg.[21] That it did not share the modifying influences of a maritime location was, of course, omitted.

Another theme was physical geography, topography, soil quality, rainfall, and ready accessibility of water and fuel. Copious quantities of high quality land were said to be available, and the Department was at pains to maintain that the land in Manitoba, for example, was not monotonously flat, but "is everywhere more or less undulating, dotted here and there with hills and valleys" that afford "good pasturage for all domestic animals." The very rich soil "stands more cropping without manure, than any other surface known to agriculture."[22] No one could deny statistical evidence that the region had much less rainfall than, say, eastern Canada or Europe, but a spin still could be applied: "it rains very little in winter, most of the precipitation being in spring and autumn, when needed for agricultural purposes, [so that] the difference is not so marked after all." The coolness of prairie nights after hot summer days apparently had a special benefit, producing heavy dews, which, "to a certain extent, protect the grain from the effects of drouth, even in the driest seasons." Moreover, the dews "produce a rich growth of prairie grass," aiding the stock farmer. The literature admitted that across the vast Prairie West there were "many different conditions of climate, soil, and topography," but "all parts offer inducements, according to the desire of the settler."[23]

No image of the West was more powerful than that of a grain-growing region:

> Reaching Manitoba and the Territories in the latter part of August, you realize the force of the designation, 'the Granary of the Empire,' the motto on the Canadian coronation arch in London [in 1902]. It is harvest time, and the wheat fields are like a sea of gold. This 'Granary' extends east and west for 1,000 miles to the foot of the Rocky Mountains, and about five hundred miles from south to north.[24]

This image of an unbroken sea of wheat fields nevertheless conflicted with much else in the promotional literature, which portrayed the West as having vast areas of unsettled, potentially productive land, and which also encouraged mixed farming in Manitoba, eastern Assiniboia, Saskatchewan, and northern Alberta, and ranching in the dry areas of western Assiniboia and southern Alberta: "some of the best farming land on the continent of America is to be had almost for the asking, by anyone who wishes to cultivate it. The settlement of these lands is heartily encouraged by the government, because a fertile soil and great natural resources are of no service unless people are there to cultivate and develop them."[25] In the pamphlets, urban centres – cities and towns – existed simply to service the agricultural industry, and immigration to these centres was actively discouraged: "Clerks, shop assistants, and persons desiring such situations are advised not to emigrate unless proceeding to appointments already secured or to join friends. Encouragement is not held out to professional men, especially in cases where immediate employment is desired."[26]

Another myth that had to be constantly dispelled was that of the prairies as forbidding wilderness. The pamphlets admitted that the Territories once had been viewed as inhospitable to settlement, only good for the fur trade, exploring, and big game hunting. Now, however, they emphasized the agricultural potential of the region: "large districts await only the transforming influence of the industrious husbandman to be converted into happy and prosperous homes."[27] Sometimes the wilderness image was still promoted, with the region said to provide "fish and wild fowl, affording amusement and supplying valuable articles of diet."[28] A touch of the exotic was, perhaps, appealing to some, but the main message was that this was a properly civilized society. "As an evidence of the growth of intelligence in the country there are sixty-three newspapers published in it [Manitoba, 1897], one for every 4,000 people, showing that many read three or four newspapers," noted one pamphlet. Moreover, "there are no castes or classes in this country, all are equal." One American observer was said to have reported in 1898 after a tour of the Alameda, NWT, district: "It is far from being the wilderness we had pictured it to be; it is, instead, a land having all the facilities required by modern civilization, such as railroads, markets, stores, churches, schools, &c., in fact, an ideal home for those having the future welfare of themselves and families at heart."[29] By 1904 the writers of the pamphlets were almost waxing poetic as they contemplated the happy state of the western farmer-settler:

> With a farm free from debt, his fields of ripening grain ready for harvest; with herds of cattle on his pasture lands, and flocks of sheep feeding on the hillside; dairy and poultry providing the household with groceries and many other comforts; schools for his children in the immediate neighborhood; churches close at hand, and such other social advantages as he desires within easy reach – what more is required for a wholesome existence? And that is the condition of the average Manitoba farmer to-day.[30]

The Prairie West was also depicted as a society of wholesome, law-abiding people. As one pamphlet noted: "the strict observance of the Sabbath is commented upon by visitors from districts where greater laxity is the rule." The schools, said to be "equal to any on the continent," were non-sectarian and "national in character," teaching both secular subjects and "general public morality." If desired, religion could be taught "during hours set apart for that purpose." Furthermore, "all religious denominations, whether Christian or otherwise, enjoy equal rights." Not only was it a high-quality, educated society, but, in addition to hospitals, it had institutions for those with visual, hearing, and mental disabilities. It also had fraternal lodges such as the Masons.[31]

It also was a masculine audience to whom the writers appealed; the assumption clearly was that men were making the decisions about settling in the West. "Canada," declared one pamphlet, "is a man's country, from the fact that all new countries first attract men, who are more adventurous and better fitted for pioneer life than women." The writer noted the excess of men over women in Manitoba and the Territories, and added, perhaps inconsistently with the previous statement, that "there is an increasing demand for woman's help, and especially for servant girls." Yet the demand was also for wives. One couple, Mr. and Mrs. Willliam Garrison, wrote a testimonial about how happy they were on their farm at Egg Lake, Alberta, but added: "We have but one great need – young women. For marrying, our settlement offers unparalleled advantages, as there are at least fifty unmarried young men, nearly all of them young and in every way suitable."[32]

To judge from the literature, settlement in the West almost guaranteed a life of comfort with the possibility of wealth for the industrious young man. Not much was needed to begin. "We can say this for Alberta," wrote four American emigrants from Edmonton in 1898: "it is the best poor man's country between the Atlantic and the Pacific oceans. We are getting two homesteads seven miles from Edmonton – timbered land, easily cleared, and will move on them this fall. Would not go back to the United States nowhere. No taxes but school taxes."[33] Others reported from Assiniboia: "Any man with a good team and money enough to buy provisions and seed for six months can become rich there in five years."[34] Farmers would be able to settle close to railways, towns, villages, grain elevators, and services such as flour mills, blacksmithing, woodworking, and carpentry, and farm implement repair shops. The Department did concede, however, that "Capital Means Opportunity," and explained how men could get work and experience while saving money to purchase a farm. It set out how a man possessing $250, $500, or $1,000 could best plan to begin farming, noting that "the first great demand is for persons with some capital at their disposal."[35]

Of course many prospective settlers still had doubts about taking the leap and investing so heavily in the risk of prairie farming. The Department was at great pains to make the investment appear to be a "sure thing." Bad news, such as a poor crop in 1896, must be directly countered – a typical Sifton tactic. A table purported to show, for example, that a ten-year average of wheat crops in Manitoba yielded 21.7 bushels per acre, compared to averages between 11 and 14 bushels in the wheat-growing areas of the United States; the Territories were said to have yields equal to or superior to those of Manitoba. Another way of calculating potential profits was provided, using 1902 (an unusually good year) as an example:

> Areas under wheat in 1902 gave a clear profit of over $6 an acre. The average yield was 26 bushels, which at 55 cents per bushel gave a return of $14.30 per acre. It is conceded that all the labor of ploughing, seeding, harvesting, and marketing can be hired, done at $7.50 per acre. Even allowing $8, there is a balance of $6.30 clear profit. This means a revenue of 7 per cent on land worth $90 per acre. Farmers who make this profit can rest assured that their lands will rise in value from year to year, a fact which sets a premium on farsightedness and enterprise as well as upon industry.[36]

This sort of specificity, however dubious or unreliable in practice, was the sort of evidence that was persuasive to prospective immigrants who considered themselves hard-nosed realists. And, of course, for a variety of reasons a greater proportion of farmers *were* succeeding after 1896 than had been able to do so previously, which helped to lend credibility to at least some of the Department's statements. Still, much of the literature amounted to shameless boosterism, for which Sifton would not have been apologetic.

The fact remains that none of this promotion would have much meaning if Sifton could not first reduce or eliminate barriers to homesteaders. The West had to be welcoming to agriculturalists, and the government needed to be seen to facilitate settlement. This involved a number of fronts. Although formally he respected the right of native peoples to approve land surrenders deemed to be in their interest by the Department, he also increased pressure on them to surrender land that it was thought homesteaders would exploit more efficiently. He simplified homestead regulations and made them more flexible. He had little sympathy with land companies whose owners were not aggressively seeking settlers and instead preferred to sit back and speculate on the rising value of western lands. The most important of these speculators, of course, were the railway companies, most notably the CPR. Vast tracts of western lands were withheld from settlement in railway reserves from which the railways would eventually select the lands to which their contracts entitled them. By its contract, the CPR did not have to pay taxes on its lands for twenty years after selecting them, though the value of the railway lands was rising rapidly as nearby areas were settled. The courts upheld the validity of the railway's interpretation of its contract, but Sifton at least forced the companies to make their selection of lands.[37]

That said, he also was prepared to use railway lands for the purpose of constructing railway lines needed to open up new areas. He supported the creation of the Saskatchewan Valley Land Company to settle a large tract of dry lands between Regina and Saskatoon; it was very successful in attracting immigrants – and controversial because it was highly profitable for the entrepreneurs.[38] He promoted irrigation schemes in dry areas of southern Alberta, and – more problematically – encouraged homesteading in semi-desert areas of southeastern Alberta and southwestern Saskatchewan, where drought later would take an appalling human toll.[39]

Sifton also believed that capitalists should be encouraged to develop the natural resources of the region, not only for profit but also to facilitate settlement. He directed the geological survey, which fell under his jurisdiction, to put less emphasis on pure science and instead to provide information that would be useful to "men who are practical miners and prospectors."[40] Coal and timber lands were more systematically exploited, even in the national parks where conservation meant efficient management, not preservation.[41]

The West had long resented the means Ottawa used to integrate the region into the nation. Westerners believed that they paid excessive profits to central Canadian businesses protected by the tariff. Farmers operated on slender margins, had little of the tariff protection enjoyed by central Canadian businesses and the railways, and had to deal with the vagaries both of international pricing for their product and of the weather. Westerners note that their freight rates were much higher than those in Ontario for shipping goods comparable distances, a situation that they attributed to the lack of competition for the CPR in the West, while they blamed the CPR for reaping enormous revenues and hindering settlement through its land monopoly and exemption from taxation. To some extent, the competition issue had been resolved by the beginning of the 1890s, but reductions in freight rates had been disappointingly modest. Sifton had supported these complaints only to a limited extent while in Manitoba politics.[42] The question was: how would he address them once in Ottawa? Would he, as the sole western representative in the Laurier government after 1896, carry sufficient weight in the national government to bring about serious change? Indeed, would he even wish to do so?

Sifton, Westerners soon discovered, was no ideologue. "I have a profound distrust of the wholesale application of theories to business," he told a surprised supporter, James Fleming, in March 1897.[43] In part this stemmed from political realities: the Liberals had persuaded the business community prior to 1896 that a Liberal government would not radically change the tariff, and they had gained an unprecedented level of business support as a result. To many grass-roots Liberals who had anticipated a serious assault on the tariff wall, the first Liberal budget in 1897 was a major disappointment, making only relatively minor changes. "I not only would not retire from the Government because they refused to eliminate the principle of protection from the tariff," he informed Fleming, "but I would not remain in the Government if they did eliminate the principle of protection entirely from the tariff." He did fight for some politically essential tariff reductions, but he also fought to retain certain tariffs that benefited western producers. Moreover, he believed that American protectionism required Canada to have its own protective tariff. Westerners would have to accept that their interests could not always prevail: "I do not intend to insist that the business of other Provinces shall be destroyed and thousands of good Canadian people turned out of employment for the sake of carrying out a theory."[44]

This reflected an important part of Sifton's view of Canada, and of the West's position within the larger nation. "Canada," he told a Winnipeg audience in 1904, "is a national entity. Canada is an organism, and you cannot develop a single part of an organism satisfactorily. Each and all parts must contribute to the vitality of the whole."[45] The growth of the West would infuse new energy into the country as a whole. At the same time, the West needed to appreciate that development elsewhere could benefit the prairie region as well. An integrated national transportation system was, in Sifton's opinion, badly needed, one having in mind not only railway requirements, but efficient ports and imperial and other international trade. Once the requirements were determined, "I would then proceed to expend whatever amount of money was necessary to bring about the result that we have in view."[46] Although the money might not all be spent in the West, the West nevertheless would benefit.

Transportation and national economic integration were properly the roles of the federal government. The provinces had charge of education, necessary to ensure that "we shall be certain of a new generation which will furnish intelligent and progressive citizens." The churches also had a vital role to play through home missions in the West, making certain that "in the new Canada we are to have a population animated by the same motives, actuated by the same ideas and governed by the same principles as obtain among the rest of our people."[47]

These comments were in part intended to respond to concerns raised by many Canadians about Sifton's own policy with respect to immigration. What sort of vision of the future underlay his policy? Many feared that his policies threatened, intentionally or inadvertently, the essential nature of Canadian, and especially western Canadian, society.[48]

Writing in *MacLean's* magazine in 1922, Sifton made his most famous statement on what would be a desirable immigration policy.

> When I speak of quality, I have in mind, I think, something that is quite different from what is in the mind of the average writer or speaker upon the question of immigration. I think a stalwart peasant in a sheep-skin coat, born on the soil, whose forefathers have been farmers for ten generations, with a stout wife and a half-dozen children is good quality.

He demonstrated that his ideas had changed little in the seventeen years since he had left the Laurier cabinet. He was critical of policies since 1905 that had focused more on ethnic compatibility in immigrants and on sheer numbers, rather than on the sort of immigrants who could succeed in settling new and challenging agricultural frontier. Britain would not be a significant source of such immigrants. Instead he urged the government to look to Scandinavia, Belgium, Bohemia, Hungary, and Galicia [Ukraine]. "These men are workers. They have been bred for generations to work from daylight to dark. They have never done anything else and never expect to do anything else."[49]

Because these remarks seem to encapsulate so well the essence of Sifton's policy while minister of the interior, and because it was during his time in office that large numbers of immigrants from Scandinavia and eastern Europe began to arrive in Canada, they have been endlessly repeated. How well do they really reflect his policy and vision as minister of the interior? As with any historical document, one needs to remember that this statement was the product of particular circumstances. Among other things, this includes his experience as minister, his dissatisfaction with immigration policy in intervening years, and his optimism that a renewed flood of immigrants would help to reinvigorate the Canadian economy from its post-war doldrums. He was speaking out in hope of influencing government policy in the 1920s. Sifton's boosterish comments were criticized at the time for being out of touch with the reality of what was possible in the post-war context.[50] Also, it is fair to note that they only partially reflect his policies while in office.

Sifton, when minister of the interior, focussed on agricultural immigrants for the prairie region. Most Canadians believed that their country should have an essentially British character, and Sifton continued and expanded past practice of encouraging agricultural immigration from the mother country. Attracting British immigrants was politically essential. However, Sifton was not entirely enamoured of the efforts of some officials to promote non-agricultural workers who would end up competing with many underemployed Canadians in the cities and towns. Some of these newcomers, he complained, were "perfectly helpless, that is to say, people who neither know how to take care of themselves nor want to do it." Such people "are hopelessly incapable of going on farms and succeeding."[51]

The minister of the interior greatly expanded operations in the United States. With the era of free land on the American settlement frontiers rapidly drawing to a close, Canada became an attractive alternative for settlers. Canada encouraged the migration of ethnic groups deemed desirable – that is, assimilable – from those areas of the American West where the people had practical experience of farming in conditions similar to those found on the Canadian prairies. They came with education, goods, and wealth that gave them a good chance of success. Because opportunities to expand farms and settle children or ethnically compatible friends and relatives were limited for many American farmers in their home districts, the Canadian West was attractive because land could be purchased relatively cheaply. For example, the first significant immigration of Scandinavian settlers to the Canadian West since the Icelanders came to Manitoba in the 1870s came from Scandinavian settlements in the United States, and not directly from Europe.[52]

Sifton also sought to attract large numbers of agricultural settlers from central and eastern Europe, as well as Scandinavia. These people came with a willingness to begin farming areas of the West that had been passed over by others, often in the wooded parkland and clay soil areas on the northern fringes of previous settlement. When a critic pointed out in a statement of 1922 that the areas that Sifton claimed were readily available for settlement included lands "quite unsuited to any form of agricultural settlement," the former minister of the interior snorted: "People's ideas of what kind of land is fit for settlement undergo radical changes." Most of the "foreign settlers" on the prairies were occupying lands that had been thought unfit for settlement when he had taken office in 1896.[53] In addition, Sifton would have pointed out what he viewed as the success of settlement in dryland areas, especially the region settled by the Saskatchewan Valley Land Company and large stretches of southern Alberta. The essential message – again, that of the booster – was that the land would respond to the right kind of settlers.

Many of these settlers came, as noted, from Europe. They were criticized by nativists and xenophobes as having nothing in common with the traditions of the country, and denounced as "European freaks and hoboes."[54] There was much fear that these people would undermine the British race and traditions. The *Winnipeg Telegram* claimed that the Galicians were barely human, "herding with cattle" and "in the habit of selling their wives." Fears abounded that crime was rampant amongst the newcomers from eastern Europe. Hugh John Macdonald, son of the great Sir John A. Macdonald and leader of the Conservative opposition in Manitoba in 1899, reportedly stated that "he did not want to have a mongrel breed in this portion of Canada. He did not want Slavs introduced among us, whether from Austria, Poland or Russia, men who are practically serfs and slaves. He wanted white men.... [They] do not know what free government is. They are not free men and they will simply be up for sale.... They will be influenced by the Church; they are Roman Catholics."[55]

Sifton did not disagree with his critics about one principle: "that immigration is desirable which can be assimilated." Neither multiculturalism nor the notion of a mosaic of cultures was an accepted concept. Most people agreed that British, French, Scandinavian, and Germanic peoples had similar values and would be assimilated to the benefit of all. The major disagreement occurred over whether Slavs, Hungarians, and others from central and eastern Europe could be assimilated because of their very different languages, religions, and customs. Sifton was optimistic that they could be, and indeed that they came with a commitment to hard work and success in their new environment. They mostly settled on the land, not in cities. This, along with British institutions, would have a transforming effect on the immigrant, according to Sifton's newspaper, the *Manitoba Free Press*: "in Canada if you get the immigrant on the land he becomes at once naturalized and nationalized."[56]

Some of Sifton's critics also feared that the large flow of immigrants from the United States would bring with them tendencies that might undermine Canadians' loyalty to the British empire and British institutions. Indeed, Canadians tended to look down on Americans as avaricious, inclined to flout the law, and possessed of a looser set of morals than Canadians.[57] The *Free Press* claimed, in response, that the Americans would find that in Canada "the will of the people rules." They would discover

> ... a greater freedom, a better administration of justice and greater respect for the law, guaranteeing the equal rights of all, in Canada than there is in the United States. The security of life and property is greater. The accessions to our population which we are now receiving from the United States are very largely of British origin. They are of our own stock. Their interests, once they make their homes on Canadian soil, become Canadian. So it has always been; and that it will continue so is not to be doubted.[58]

Thus a mutually transformative process was going on: the people would transform the land, and the land would transform the settlers into a loyal *British* population. Yet, despite these public assertions, Sifton privately had his own reservations about "foreigners ... from Continental Europe." He thought that the naturalization period for them should be five years instead of three, and that "the privileges which we grant to the settlers in the way of affording them free grants of land ought not to be accompanied by the rights of citizenship until they have resided in the country sufficiently long to become thoroughly acquainted with the language and institutions of the country."[59] One of the reasons that he had so strongly supported the idea of national schools in Manitoba was their power to aid in assimilation of immigrant communities. Yet, whether it was by working the land, by attending school, or by experiencing British laws and institutions, he never doubted that the immigrants would all be assimilated. A great civilization would emerge from this process of struggle for material wealth and independence on the land. Canada was developing a distinctively Canadian sentiment, he told an English audience in 1903: "we are engaged in overcoming a great many natural difficulties for the purpose of building up what we believe will be outside of England, perhaps, the greatest British community in the world." In this community, a poor man who was diligent and frugal could find prosperity and social advancement in a community that exhibited respect for law and cultural and intellectual development.[60]

At the same time, Sifton believed that settlers ought to make it on their own, with little or no assistance from the government. "Once a man is taken hold of by the Government and treated as a ward," he declared, "he seems to acquire the sentiments of a pauper, and forever after will not stand on his own feet or try to help himself."[61] The liberal state should provide opportunity, not assistance beyond getting the settler on the land. The new West would be populated with "self-made men."

In theory, Canada was a country of mostly open doors, and most people who could reach it had ready entry. "Any man," declared the *Manitoba Free Press*, "no matter what his nationality, so long as he desires to earn an honest living and is willing to till the soil, is a welcome addition to this western country, and his arrival is a national blessing."[62] Not everyone would have the opportunity, however. A head tax to discourage Chinese immigration had been implemented in 1885; because of anti-Oriental agitation in British Columbia, it was increased – with Sifton's approval – in 1900 from $50 to $100 and to $500 in 1903. The general consensus of the day was that Orientals were not assimilable.[63] Canadian legislation also included prohibitions common in the era, including those with criminal records, those who were diseased, the insane, and those guilty of moral turpitude. Furthermore, in 1897 the Laurier government passed the *Alien Labour Act*, mainly in retaliation to American legislation and to please Canadian labour organizations who were concerned about transient workers taking jobs and undercutting wages. This *Act*, despite its stated intentions, was never rigidly enforced.[64]

If the vision of prairie society excluded most orientals formally, the government also sought to exclude others deemed unsuitable by less formal means. The government's contract with the North Atlantic Trading Company, the main agent in recruiting settlers from continental Europe, excluded the Iberian peninsula, southern Italy, Greece, and most of the Balkans. Jewish immigrants were also discouraged. Initially Sifton supported a proposed settlement of Romanian Jews, but prime minister Laurier, sensitive to anti-Semitism in Quebec, opposed the movement, ordering a memorandum "to make it clear, that whilst the doors of the country are open to all, we favour only agricultural immigration." Sifton complied, producing a statement that efforts "to induce [Jewish people] to remain upon the land and become cultivators of the soil" had failed, and that the Jewish population of both Canada and the United States was "to be found entirely in the cities and towns." He continued:

> It is admitted that additions to the population of our cities and towns by immigration is undesirable from every standpoint and such additions do not in any way whatever contribute to the object which is constantly kept in view by the Government of Canada in encouraging immigration or the development of natural resources and the increase of the production of wealth from those resources.[65]

Sifton also opposed any encouragement of Blacks from the United States or, indeed, people of colour from anywhere. The stated rationale was much the same: that they would not make good farmers. The reality was that Canadians of the day believed that people of colour were inferior and that assimilation was undesirable.[66]

Another aspect of Sifton's vision for the Prairie West may be seen in his relations with the government of the North-West Territories, and in his role in the provincial autonomy process that ultimately led to his resignation from the government in 1905.[67] From the late 1880s a movement to promote provincial autonomy for the Territories had begun to grow intermittently. Residents of the region between Manitoba and British Columbia chafed under federal control and regulations, dependency upon Ottawa, and insufficient federal funding to meet the requirements of the local government, which did not have the same powers and taxing authority as provincial governments. Sifton appeared to support these demands when he announced, shortly before going to Ottawa to assume his new ministerial duties in 1896, that "the swaddling clothes plan of treating the North-West had come to an end." He claimed to believe that "there would be no longer any attempt made to prevent the people of the North-West from doing business which can be done better by themselves than by people at Ottawa."[68]

Less than a year later, Sifton appeared to deliver on this promise, though only in part. A system of responsible government was instituted for the territories. As Sifton said, the territorial government would "not have the full powers of a provincial government, but in so far as they have power to deal with subjects, they shall do it in the same way as the other provinces." Nevertheless, the provision fell well short of full provincial status, and the accompanying increase in the annual grant for the territories was far less than the local government anticipated.[69]

Ensuing years exacerbated the difficulty. The success of Sifton's immigration policy placed enormous pressures on the local government to provide schools, roads, bridges, and other local services, but its revenues increased far too slowly to enable it to cope with the people's expectations.

The provincial autonomy movement simply exploded, aided and abetted by the territorial government of F.W.G. Haultain. The Laurier government put off the demands as long as it could. Finally, during the 1904 general election, the prime minister announced that, if re-elected, he would proceed to create provincial status for the territories.

Introduced in February 1905, the government's autonomy bills created the new provinces of Saskatchewan and Alberta. They also produced a ministerial crisis which led to Sifton's resignation.[70] Sifton was, nonetheless, influential in shaping the settlement, and certain aspects of it say much about his view of the West and its place in Confederation. First, he opposed turning over to the new provinces control of public lands and natural resources. He told Laurier that "the mere report that the lands had been handed over and that there might be a change in the policy of administering them would cost us tens of thousands of settlers in the next two years to say nothing of the more distant future. The continued progress of Canada for the next five years depends almost entirely on the flow of immigration." Similarly, with respect to western waterways, interprovincial and international complications were bound to arise: "By retaining the plenary power at Ottawa you ensure the fact that a central body which for its own interest is bound to try and do justice to all parties will be able to adjust difficulties as they arise."[71] Clearly Sifton, after over eight years administering the West from Ottawa, had acquired a view of the primacy of national interests that had much in common with the view of the Macdonald government, which had denied control of lands and resources to Manitoba in 1870. Western interests must continue to be subordinated to the national interest of controlling western settlement and development.

Second, the crisis over the school question in 1905 highlighted Sifton's view of what prairie society ought to be. He believed that the ideal would be provincial control over the schools. There were those, especially in Quebec and amongst the Roman Catholic community, who wanted the federal government to restore rights to the Catholic minority, which had been gradually but significantly reduced over the previous two decades. Sifton thought that continuing the existing territorial education system would be the best compromise, and he believed that the proposal put forth by Laurier would go farther and open the door to restoration of at least some Catholic rights. He and Laurier had two quite different views about the essential nature of Canada, and on this issue he resigned. It was important, in Sifton's view, that western schools be empowered to play a role in assimilating newcomers to a common education and set of values, if a strong and united society was to emerge from the mix of cultures that was settling the West. Special privileges for one minority – French and Catholic – struck him as wrong in principle. Laurier's view was that, at bottom, Canada was a compromise between two cultures: French Catholic and English Protestant. Whatever the applicability of that view for central Canada, Sifton believed it was as inappropriate in the new provinces as he had thought it to be in Manitoba when he was in the local government.

The Prairie West, as conceived by Sifton and many of his contemporaries, was a distinct region within Canada. It was to be populated by an industrious, self-motivated, independent, and ambitious agricultural population; cities and towns, railways and other infrastructure, existed to serve the farming communities. The population was to be overwhelmingly white, educated to at least a basic level of literacy, sharing common values of what it meant to be a British subject and a Canadian. Ideally, the West would be free of the disputes between French and English that had so troubled central Canada. It would be a region that would serve Canada through the production of agricultural and natural products, and consumption of domestically produced manufactured products. It would be part of an integrated national economy. At the same time, Canada would serve the West, providing the means (for example, railways, ports, terminal elevators) to ship goods to and from the region. The process would be mutually strengthening.

Sifton's was an optimistic stance. It was grounded in faith that abundant prosperity would accrue to those who persevered to make the West productive economically and united in values and purpose. Those who failed were somehow deficient in character because with sufficient will the land itself could be transformed and utilized. Those deemed likely to fail or to assimilate were discouraged, if not formally excluded. While it is fair to acknowledge that Sifton encouraged some to settle on unsuitable or marginally suitable land with eventual serious human cost, many others did succeed where failure would have been predicted only a few years previously.

The cost to Canadian taxpayers of attracting and settling immigrants, of building railways and other infrastructure to open new districts in the West and to provide support and markets, was high. The expenditure on the CPR had seemed to produce limited benefits, and some Canadians were unsure that continued heavy expenditure on the

West was wise. It perhaps should be acknowledged that Sifton's able and aggressive leadership while minister of the interior helped to persuade Canadians that the expenditure was worth it, an investment in the long-term prosperity of their country. It certainly helped to convince them that the West could be an integrated and valuable partner in Confederation, and, over time, a Promised Land.

NOTES

1 *Toronto Globe*, November 18, 1902.

2 Ibid. Material for this article is drawn largely from my biography of Sifton: *Clifford Sifton*, vol. I, *The Young Napoleon, 1861–1900*; and vol. II, *A Lonely Eminence, 1901–1929* (Vancouver: UBC Press, 1981, 1985).

3 Alan F. J. Artibise, "Boosterism and the Development of Prairie Cities, 1871–1913," in *Town and City: Aspects of Western Canadian Urban Development*, ed. A. Artibise (Regina: Canadian Plains Research Center, University of Regina, 1981), 209–35; Paul Voisey, *High River and the Times: An Alberta Community and Its Weekly Newspaper, 1905–1966* (Edmonton: University of Alberta Press, 2004), chaps. 3 and 4.

4 The following discussion derives mainly from Gerald Friesen, "Defining the Prairies: or, why the prairies don't exist," in *Toward Defining the Prairies: Region, Culture, and History*, ed. Robert Wardhaugh (Winnipeg: University of Manitoba Press, 2001), 13–28, and esp. 14–15. Also helpful is R. Douglas Francis, *Images of the West: Changing Perceptions of the Prairies, 1690–1960* (Saskatoon: Western Producer Prairie Books, 1989).

5 See Hall, *Clifford Sifton*, vol. I, chap. 1.

6 *The Manitoba Act*, 33 Victoriae, c. 3. This is conveniently reprinted in W. L. Morton, ed., *Manitoba: The Birth of a Province*, vol. 1, Manitoba Record Society Publications (Altona, MB: D. W. Friesen, 1965), 251–59.

7 Like their Ontario brethren, they also were heavily involved in promoting the Methodist church and Sunday School, and temperance.

8 On the language issue, see Gerald Friesen, "Bilingualism in Manitoba: The Historical Context," in *River Road: Essays on Manitoba and Prairie History*, ed. G. Friesen (Winnipeg: University of Manitoba Press, 1996), 23–28.

9 See Paul Romney, *Getting It Wrong: How Canadians Forgot Their Past and Imperilled Confederation* (Toronto: University of Toronto Press, 1999).

10 See Hall, *Clifford Sifton*, vol. I, chaps. 2 and 3; and T. D. Regehr, "The National Policy and Manitoba Railway Legislation 1879–1888," Master's thesis, Carleton University, 1963.

11 D. J. Hall, "Clifford Sifton: Immigration and Settlement Policy, 1896–1905," in *The Settlement of the West*, ed. Howard Palmer (Calgary: University of Calgary, Comprint Publishing, 1977), 84.

12 See ibid., 60–65.

13 D. J. Hall, "Clifford Sifton and Canadian Indian Administration 1896–1905," *Prairie Forum* 2, no. 2 (November 1977): 127–51.

14 This was, of course, only sixteen years after the Northwest Rebellion, the memory of which was still fresh to many Canadians.

15 Hall, "Clifford Sifton and Canadian Indian Administration," 141–45, and 151 n. 77. His policy appears moderate compared to the aggressive approach of his successor, Frank Oliver.

16 Canada. House of Commons. *Debates, 1899*, cols. 8654–5, July 27, 1899.

17 The most complete list is found in Ernie B. Ingles and N. Merrill Distad, eds. and comps., *Peel's Bibliography of the Canadian Prairies to 1953*, revised and enlarged,

Based upon the Work of Bruce Braden Peel (Toronto: University of Toronto Press, 2003). Many of the pamphlets are available on-line at <http://peel.library.ualberta.ca>. See also R. Douglas Francis, *Images of the West*, 109–12.

18 Canada. Department of the Interior. *Manitoba and the North-West Territories. Assiniboia, Alberta, Saskatchewan: In which are included the newly discovered gold fields of the Yukon: Information as to the resources and climates of these countries for intending farmers, ranchers and miners, 1897* (Ottawa: Government Printing Bureau, 1897), 46 pp., illus. (Peel #2324), 6.

19 Canada. Department of the Interior. *The Wonders of Western Canada: A U.S. Press Correspondent's Graphic Description* (Ottawa: Government Printing Bureau, 1898; Peel #2389), 6, 22.

20 Canada. Department of the Interior. *Geography of the Dominion of Canada and Atlas of Western Canada. Setting forth for use in schools and for the guidance of intending settlers, an account of its resources and development, with maps of Ontario, Quebec and the Maritime Provinces, Manitoba, British Columbia, Assiniboia, Alberta and Saskatchewan, besides general maps and numerous diagrams* (Ottawa: Department of the Interior 1904), 64 pp. (Peel #2750), 51.

21 *Geography of the Dominion of Canada*, 51.

22 *Manitoba and the North-West Territories ... 1897*, 6; Canada, Department of the Interior. *Reports of United States Delegates on Western Canada* (Ottawa: Government Printing Bureau, 1898; Peel #32387), 6.

23 *Geography of the Dominion of Canada*, 7, 36.

24 *Geography of the Dominion of Canada*, 10. The coronation was for Edward VII.

25 *Geography of the Dominion of Canada*, 9. On ranching, see for example pp. 41, 51.

26 *Geography of the Dominion of Canada*, 57; R. Douglas Francis, *Images of the West*, 111.

27 *Manitoba and the North-West Territories ... 1897*, 25.

28 *Manitoba and the North-West Territories ... 1897*, 6; *Geography of the Dominion of Canada*, 51.

29 *Manitoba and the North-West Territories ... 1897*, 17; *Reports of United States Delegates*, 9.

30 *Geography of the Dominion of Canada*, 40.

31 *Manitoba and the North-West Territories ... 1897*, 7, 9; *Geography of the Dominion of Canada*, 36.

32 *Geography of the Dominion of Canada*, 55, 57.

33 *The Wonders of Western Canada*, 12.

34 *Reports of United States Delegates*, 5.

35 *Manitoba and the North-West Territories ... 1897*, 7; *Geography of the Dominion of Canada*, 56.

36 *Manitoba and the North-West Territories ... 1897*, 10–12, 15; *Geography of the Dominion of Canada*, 37, 40.

37 Hall, *Clifford Sifton*, vol. I, 129–31, 183–84, 252–56; vol. II, 57–63.

38 Ibid., vol. II, 61–62, 184, 186–87.

39 David C. Jones, *Empire of Dust: Settling and Abandoning the Prairie Dry Belt* (Calgary: University of Calgary Press, 2002), 20–21; and Jones, "The Toll of Two Images," in *Harm's Way: Disasters in Western Canada*, eds. Anthony Rasporich and Max Foran (Calgary: University of Calgary Press, 2004), 223.

40 Hall, *Clifford Sifton*, vol. II, 49–51.

41 Ibid., 51–52.

42 Hall, *Clifford Sifton*, vol. I, 36–38, 58–59, 101–4.

43 Library and Archives Canada (LAC), Sir Clifford Sifton Papers, vol. 218, 244–46, Sifton to James Fleming, March 13, 1897.

44 Ibid.; and Hall, *Clifford Sifton*, vol. I, 144–50; vol. II, 90–97.

45 *Manitoba Free Press*, July 27, 1904.

46 Hall, *Clifford Sifton*, vol. II, 79.

47 Ibid. On the subject more broadly, see George Emery, *The Methodist Church on the Prairies, 1896–1914* (Montreal and Kingston: McGill-Queen's University Press, 2001), esp. chap. 7.

48 A good introduction to the topic is Howard Palmer, *Patterns of Prejudice: A History of Nativism in Alberta* (Toronto: McClelland and Stewart, 1982), chap. 1.

49 Sir Clifford Sifton, "The Immigrants Canada Wants," *MacLean's Magazine*, April 1, 1921: 16, 22–24. Sifton also addressed the Canadian Club in the same vein: Sifton, "Immigration," *Proceedings of the Canadian Club, Toronto, for the Years 1921–22* 19 (April 3, 1922): 182–91.

50 Hall, *Clifford Sifton*, vol. II, 299–302.

51 Hall, "Clifford Sifton: Immigration and Settlement Policy," 69–70, 76.

52 Ibid., 70–71; Howard Palmer, *Land of the Second Chance: A History of Ethnic Groups in Southern Alberta* (Lethbridge: Lethbridge Herald, 1972), 166–69.

53 LAC, Sifton Papers, vol. 209, 163075-77, E. J. Ashton to Sifton, March 13, 1922, and reply, March 14, 1922.

54 Hall, "Clifford Sifton: Immigration and Settlement Policy," 79, 83.

55 Hall, *Clifford Sifton*, vol. I, 264.

56 *Manitoba Free Press*, May 13, 1899.

57 S. F. Wise and Robert Craig Brown, *Canada Views the United States: Nineteenth-Century Political Attitudes* (Toronto: Macmillan, 1967); J. L. Granatstein, *Yankee Go Home: Canadians and Anti-Americanism* (Toronto: Harper Collins, 1996), chs. 1–2.

58 *Manitoba Free Press*, April 1, 9 and 14, and June 12, 1902.

59 LAC, Sifton Papers, vol. 230, 86–88, Sifton to David Mills, January 6, 1899.

60 Hall, "Clifford Sifton: Immigration and Settlement Policy," 81–82.

61 LAC, Sifton Papers, vol. 230, 787–89, 859–60, Sifton to W. W. Buchanan, February 11 and 15, 1899.

62 *Manitoba Free Press*, July 8, 1898, May 13, 1899.

63 Patricia E. Roy, *A White Man's Province: British Columbia Politicians and Chinese and Japanese Immigrants, 1858–1914* (Vancouver: UBC Press, 1989), esp. chap. 5, and 155–57; Hall, *Clifford Sifton*, vol. I, 263. This legislation did not fall under the jurisdiction of the Department of the Interior, so Sifton had no direct responsibility for it.

64 Hall, *Clifford Sifton*, vol. I, 155–56, 267.

65 Hall, "Clifford Sifton: Immigration and Settlement Policy," 78.

66 Harold M. Troper, *Only Farmers Need Apply: Official Canadian Government Encouragement of Immigration from the United States 1896–1911* (Toronto: Griffin House, 1972), esp. chap. 7.

67 Background on this matter is covered in Lewis Herbert Thomas, *The Struggle for Responsible Government in the North-West Territories, 1870–97*, 2nd ed. (Toronto: University of Toronto Press, 1978 [1956]). The standard treatment for the Sifton years is C. Cecil Lingard, *Territorial Government in Canada: The Autonomy Question in the Old North-West Territories* (Toronto: University of Toronto Press, 1946).

68 Thomas, *Struggle for Responsible Government*, 259.

69 Ibid., 259–60.

70 D. J. Hall, "A Divergence of Principle: Clifford Sifton, Sir Wilfrid Laurier and the North-West Autonomy Bills, 1905," *Laurentian University Review* 7, no. 1 (November 1974): 3–24; Hall, *Clifford Sifton*, vol. II, chap. 8; J. Willliam Brennan, "The 'Autonomy Question' and the Creation of Alberta and Saskatchewan," in *The New Provinces: Alberta and Saskatchewan, 1905–1980*, ed. Howard Palmer (Vancouver: Tantalus Research, 1980), 43–63; Peter A. Russell, "Rhetorics of Identity: The Debate over Division of the North-West Territories, 1890–1905," *Journal of Canadian Studies* 20, no. 4 (Winter 1985–86): 99–114.

71 LAC, Sir Wilfrid Laurier Papers, vol. 352, 93969-73, Sifton to Laurier, January 22, 1905.

II

SETTLING THE PROMISED LAND

5

"WE MUST FARM TO ENABLE US TO LIVE": THE PLAINS CREE AND AGRICULTURE TO 1900

Sarah Carter

For Aboriginal people, especially those who entered into treaty negotiations, the Canadian West of the late nineteenth century was the "Promised Land." But the promises were not kept. In the treaties, they were promised that they would share the wealth to be created from their land and resources, but instead, the late nineteenth century began an era of profound dispossession and deprivation. The infinite riches described by boosters of the Canadian West to entice newcomers from all over the world were the resources and the land of First Nations, the peoples' sacred gifts from the Creator, or in Cree "*iyiniw saweyihtakosiwin*"[1] The "promised land" for immigrants, or "God's good gift to a teeming world," was the homeland of First Nations, where they were restricted to small and scattered reserves, their former mobility sharply curtailed.

The promotional literature used to entice immigrants by extolling the "countless thousands of leagues of territory,"[2] and the "wealth of commerce, agriculture, mining, lumbering, and fishing" to be found there, rarely mentioned Aboriginal people.[3] The bountiful riches were not for them, nor was there a place for them in the superior society to be created. There was no role for them but to disappear quietly. They were represented as invisible, non-threatening, and as a "dying race," as in other British settler colonies. To legitimize and justify possession and exploitation of their territory, their land was depicted as "tenantless and silent." Aboriginal people were cast as unworthy custodians of the land, as they lacked the "energy, industry and capital" to develop the natural riches.

Yet at the treaty negotiations, Aboriginal people insisted that they must be part of the vision of a bountiful and prosperous West that was to be based on a new foundation of agriculture. They agreed to share their resources with newcomers, to live harmoniously and cooperatively with them, and in turn they sought the assistance they required to establish a new livelihood and economy based on agriculture. They sought, and in their view achieved, guarantees of economic self-sufficiency and independence in a living, evolving treaty relationship.[4] But as this article demonstrates, the land of promise did not materialize for them.

This article explores the topic of agriculture on Plains Cree reserves in the late nineteenth century, addressing the question of why farming failed to form the basis of a viable economy in these communities by 1900. The answer to this question is complex but has little to do with the prevailing explanation that Plains people had no inclination or ability to farm. The Plains Cree made sustained, determined efforts to establish an economy based on agriculture, but they faced many obstacles. There were environmental and technological challenges shared by all farmers at this time. Aboriginal farmers laboured under particular disadvantages because of their unique relationship with the federal government that ought to have assisted them in this enterprise but ultimately functioned to undermine their efforts. A "peasant" farming policy imposed from 1889 to 1896 was especially damaging to Plains Cree agriculture. It is also argued that non-Aboriginal people have persistently found it useful to insist that Aboriginal people and agriculture were incompatible, despite obvious evidence to the contrary. It was a convenient myth to sustain because it could be claimed that people who did not farm were not in need of much land and that economic underdevelopment of the reserves was due to the indifference and neglect, not of the government, but of Aboriginal people.

Early in September 1879, at Fort Carlton, North-West Territories, Plains Cree chiefs Ahtahkakoop, Mistawasis, and Kitowehaw, with five councillors, met with Edgar Dewdney, the recently appointed Commissioner of Indian Affairs. The chiefs were frustrated that promises of agricultural assistance, made to them three years earlier in Treaty No. 6, were "not carried out in their spirit."[5] They stated that they intended to live by the cultivation of the soil, as "the buffalo were our only dependence before the transfer of the country, and this and other wild animals are disappearing, and we must farm to enable us to live." They insisted that government had not fulfilled its part of the treaty in assisting them to make a living by agriculture and that what had been given them made a mockery of the promises made in 1876. This was by no means the first effort of these chiefs to place their concerns before government officials, and there were similar expressions of dissatisfaction and disappointment throughout Manitoba and the North-West Territories.[6]

Such evidence of the strong commitment of the Plains Cree to agriculture seemed startling to me when I set out to explore why agriculture failed to provide a living for residents of arable Indian reserves in western Canada. The standard explanation, one firmly embedded in the non-Aboriginal prairie mentality, seemed compelling: that Aboriginal people of the Plains never had any inclination to settle down and farm despite concerted government efforts and assistance. I originally approached the topic with the argument in mind that agriculture was the wrong policy, for the wrong people, at the wrong time. Before I was too far along in my research, however, I found that there was little evidence of agriculture floundering because of the apathy and indifference of Aboriginal people, although it was certainly the case that this view was consistently maintained and promoted by the Department of Indian Affairs and later by many historians. Yet from the time of the treaties of the 1870s and well before, Aboriginal people were anxious to explore agriculture as an alternate economy when they began to realize the buffalo were failing them. It was not government negotiators but the Aboriginal spokesmen who insisted that terms be included in the treaties that would permit agricultural development. Aboriginal people of the western Plains were among the earliest and largest groups to attempt agriculture west of the Red River Settlement. Like most other "sodbusters," Aboriginal farmers were inclined to become commercial farmers specializing in grain. The fact that they did not had to do with government policy and intent, not with Aboriginal choice and inability.

My topic and approach are the product of a number of influences, including the work of "new" social historians who, beginning in the 1960s, argued that history should be not only the study of elites but of ordinary people as well, and of the day-to-day as well as the dramatic events. The new social history stressed that non-elites – ethnic minorities, women, the working class, and non-literate peoples – sought in various ways to transcend the limitations placed on them and were not hopeless victims of forces beyond their control but rather coped creatively with changing conditions. While Arthur J. Ray, Sylvia Van Kirk, and John Milloy cast Native people in a central role as active participants in the history of the pre-1870 West, the same could not be said of the more modern era. In the dominant narrative histories of the West in the post-1870 era, Aboriginal people all but disappeared after they made treaties and settled on reserves. The story of the establishment of the rural core of the Prairie West was inevitably told from the point of view of the new arrivals, with little mention of the host society, and generally a record of positive achievement was stressed and the casualties of development were downplayed. Studies of late nineteenth-century imperialisms, which increasingly drew regions into a transcontinental network, provided context for understanding that what happened in western Canada was not unique, but was part of a global pattern of western expansion.

The Plains culture that evolved over centuries in western Canada seemed far removed from the sedentary lifestyle of farms, fields, and fences that began to alter forever the prairie landscape in the late nineteenth century. The Plains Cree, the northernmost people of the Great Plains of North America and one of the last Aboriginal groups to adopt Plains culture, developed a lifestyle that was well suited to the predominantly flat, treeless landscape and to the northern Plains climate of extremes and uncertainties. Particular habits of movement and dispersal suited the limited and specialized nature of the resources of the northern Plains. The Natives exploited the seasonal diversity of their environment by practising mobility. Plains people moved their settlements from habitat to habitat, depending on where they expected to find the greatest natural food supply. All aspects of life hinged on this mobility; their tepees, for example, were easily taken apart and moved, and their other property was kept to a strict minimum so that they would be unencumbered. As homesteaders were later to learn, basic necessities such as good soil, water, game, and fuel rarely came together in many Plains areas, and this combined with the great variability and uncertainty of the climate to make mobility central to the survival of the indigenous peoples of the Plains. Many of the earliest homesteaders on the Plains found that they could not stay put either, certainly not at first; they sought off-farm jobs, especially during the "start-up" years, or they were obliged to try several localities in their search for basic necessities. External inputs in the way of seed-grain relief, subsidies, or rations were often necessary as the resources of a fixed locality could not always sustain the inhabitants.

The buffalo was the foundation of the Plains economy, providing people not only with a crucial source of protein and vitamins but with many other necessities, including shelter, clothing, containers, and tools. Aboriginal life on the Plains followed a pattern of concentration and dispersal that to a great extend paralleled that of the buffalo. But Plains people were not solely hunters of buffalo. To rely on one staple resource alone was risky in the Plains environment, as there were periodic shortages of buffalo, and it was mainly the gathering and preserving work of women, based on their intimate understanding of the Plains environment, that varied the subsistence base and contributed to "risk reduction," a role the immigrant women to the Plains would also acquire. Mid-summer camp movements were determined not only by the buffalo but by considerations such as the ripeness and location of saskatoon berries, the prairie turnip, and other fruits and tubers. Many of the foodstuffs women gathered were dried, pounded, or otherwise preserved and stored for the scarce times of winter. Women fished, snared small game, caught prairie chickens and migratory birds, and gathered their eggs. A high degree of mobility was essential for people effectively to draw on the varied resources of the Plains.

Nineteenth-century European observers tended to see the Great Plains as a timeless land, as a place without history, its people unaffected by any outside forces and leaving no mark of their presence upon the land. Captain William Butler, who described the Plains in 1870 as a great ocean of grass, wrote that "This ocean has no past – time has been nought to it; and men have come and gone, leaving behind them no track, no vestige of their presence."[7] European observers saw Plains people as living at the mercy of natural forces and failed to appreciate the sophisticated adaptations to the environment and the many ways in which resources were altered, managed, and controlled. Methods such as the buffalo pound, like the Huron enclosures and Beothuk drivelines for capturing deer, have been described as a form of animal management. There is evidence that people of the northern Plains were concerned with keeping up buffalo herd numbers as they periodically burned the grasslands in the autumn to keep forage levels high. This burning increased yields, encouraged spring grass growth earlier, and induced buffalo into favoured areas of fresh, young grass. Fire was used to influence buffalo movement – to direct a herd to a kill site and to keep buffalo away from fur trade posts so that Europeans could not provision themselves. Fire was also used to protect valuable stands of timber.

Well before the treaties of the 1870s, some Plains people, particularly the Cree and Saulteaux, had begun to raise small crops and to keep cattle to smooth out the seasonal scarcities that were increasing as the buffalo receded westward. As the homesteaders were later to learn, however, especially those who attempted farming before the development of dry-land farming techniques and early-maturing varieties of grain, yields from cultivated plants were highly unpredictable, and a more flexible economy that combined agriculture with hunting and gathering was the most feasible until the disappearance of the buffalo in the late 1870s. Agriculture was a far more ancient and indigenous tradition on the Plains than the horse culture, which was a much more fleeting episode. Cree were acquainted with cultivated plant food and techniques of agriculture through several of their contacts, most notably the Mandan, Arikara, and Hidatsa, who maintained a flourishing agricultural economy on the upper Missouri. There is evidence of an agricultural village on the banks of the Red River near the present-day town of Lockport, Manitoba, that dates from between AD 1300 and AD 1500.[8] Blackfoot were found by the earliest of European fur traders to be growing tobacco.

Aboriginal people of the Plains were not as "passive" as the landscape; their world was not static and timeless. The archaeological and historical records suggest that on the Plains learning new ways took place regularly, that there was much adaptation and borrowing among people, and that changes occurred constantly. The Plains Cree, for example, had a history of making dramatic adjustments to new economic and ecological circumstances, modifying the ways in which they obtained their livelihood. With the establishment of fur trade posts on Hudson Bay after 1670, the Cree, along with their allies the Assiniboine, quickly seized the opportunity to function as middlemen to the trade. With the expansion of European fur trade posts inland in the late eighteenth century, the Cree took advantage of a new economic opportunity and worked as provisioners of buffalo meat to the trading companies. They showed themselves to be remarkably flexible in rapidly adjusting to the rewards and demands of different environments – the forest, parklands, and Plains. The branch that became the Plains Cree readily adopted many of the characteristics, techniques, and traits of Plains buffalo and horse culture. Aboriginal people such as the Cree were accustomed to making dramatic adjustments to new ecological and economic circumstances, and there is no inherent reason to believe that they could not have made adjustments to the new order of the post-1870 era by becoming full participants in the agricultural economy. The fact that they did not was due not to their own choice; rather, there was a refusal to let them do so as they were denied access to the opportunities and resources that would have allowed them a more independent existence.

While Aboriginal people of the Plains required assistance and instruction to establish a farming economy, they had certain advantages that new arrivals did not enjoy. They had an intimate knowledge of the resources and climate of the West. They were much better informed on rainfall and frost patterns, on the availability of water and timber, and on soil varieties. They had experience with locusts, fires, and droughts. Aboriginal farmers might have had a better chance than many of the settlers from the humid East. Many of these never could accept the discomforts and conditions, and they departed, and even for those who remained acclimatization could take several years. Settlers from elsewhere might well have benefited from the knowledge Aboriginal people of the Plains had to offer. One settler in Saskatchewan, who had previously worked as a trader, consulted an Aboriginal friend named South Wind when he wanted to locate his homestead in the 1880s, and learned, for example, how to use fire to protect stands of timber and how to replenish the hay swamps. He later found local legislation regarding fire to be a "positive evil" and wrote that "our legislators should have had old South Wind at their Councils."[9] Accounts of such consultation are, however, very rare.

As early as the 1850s European travellers to the Plains reported that the Cree were concerned about the scarcity of buffalo, that many were anxious to try agriculture and wanted assistance in the ways of instruction and technology. They were well aware that the buffalo hunt was no longer going to sustain them. With the demise of the fur trade, agriculture appeared to be the only option. During the treaty negotiations of the 1870s, Plains people sought government aid to make the transition to an agricultural economy. In return for their offer of an opportunity for peaceful expansion, Aboriginal people asked that they be given the instruction and technology that would allow them to farm. Aboriginal spokesmen did not see any inherent conflict between their distinctive identity and active participation in an agricultural economy. Circumstances obliged them to cease living as their ancestors had done, but they did not therefore cease to be Aboriginals. Like the Natives of the older provinces of Canada, they were in favour of agriculture, resource development, and education that would assist them to survive, but they did not, for example, intend to abandon their religious ceremonies and beliefs. Euro-Canadian observers consistently insisted on seeing Plains people as hunters, gatherers, and warriors incapable of adopting agriculture.

The main focus of this study is those people of the Treaty No. 4 district of southeastern Saskatchewan who settled on reserves in the Touchwood Hills, File Hills, and along the Qu'Appelle River. Most were Plains Cree, collectively known as the *mamihkiyiniwak*, the Downstream People, although Assiniboine, mixed Cree-Assiniboine (Young Dogs), and Saulteaux also settled here and were intermingled with Plains Cree bands. Although these people form the main focus, evidence was also drawn from the Treaty No. 6 district, settled primarily by Plains Cree known as the Upstream People. In the later 1870s, the earliest years of Indian reserve settlement in present-day Saskatchewan, farming proved nearly impossible despite concerted efforts. For some bands, farming was never to be successful because of the nature of the reserve site itself. Other bands received high-quality agricultural land that was later to excite the envy of other settlers. The earliest instructions to surveyors were that care should be taken to ensure reserve lands "should not interfere with the possible requirement of future settlement, or of land for railway purposes." At that time what was seen as the "fertile belt," and the proposed route for the Canadian Pacific Railway, ran northwest along the Assiniboine and North Saskatchewan rivers. Land further south was considered arid and unlikely ever to be wanted by settlers, so many reserves, such as those along the Qu'Appelle River, were surveyed there. But when the CPR route was changed in 1881 and rerouted through the south, many of these reserves were located near or on the railway route, in the midst of what was hoped would become the settlement belt and the heart of a prosperous agricultural economy.

Farming in the 1870s proved to be nearly impossible because the implements and livestock promised in the treaties were inadequate. Ten families, for example, were to share one plough. Bands varied in size, numbering between seventeen and fifty families, but regardless of size, each was offered only one yoke of oxen, one bull, and four cows. To earn a living from the soil, a yoke of oxen was required by every farming family. As one Plains Cree chief pointed out in 1879, it was perfectly ridiculous to expect them to get on with so few oxen, that every farmer in the Northwest, however poor, had his own yoke of oxen, that "We are new at the kind of work, but even white men cannot get on with so few oxen."[10] In addition to the overall inadequacy of the agricultural assistance promised in the treaties, government officials were reluctant and tentative about distributing what was promised. The people prepared to farm expected their supply of implements, cattle, and seed immediately, but officials were determined to adhere strictly to the exact wording of the treaty, which stated that implements, cattle, and seed would be given to "any band … now actually cultivating the soil, or who shall hereafter settle on these reserves and commence to break up the land." Aboriginal people could not settle until the surveys were complete, and in some cases this took many years. They could not cultivate until they had implements to break the land, yet these were not to be distributed until they were settled and cultivating. Government officials shared the belief that the distribution even of those items promised in the treaties could "encourage idleness," and there was concern that the implements and cattle would not be used for the purposes for which they were intended.

There were also problems with the quality and distribution of seed grain. In the earliest years the seed arrived in a damaged state and was received in midsummer when the season was far too advanced for planting. Acres sometimes lay idle because there was no seed available, and more land might have been broken had there been seed to sow. It was also learned after a number of years that people cultivating the reserves had to be supplied with some provisions in the spring during ploughing and sowing. The people of Treaty No. 6 had successfully bargained for this during their negotiations, but no such promise had been made to the people of Treaty No. 4. Although David Laird, Lieutenant-Governor and Indian superintendent for the North-West Superintendency, recommended in 1877 that some provisions be distributed in the spring to Treaty No. 4 bands, this request was struck from the estimates in Ottawa. It proved impossible for more than a few to remain on their reserves and cultivate as the others were obliged to hunt and gather provisions for the group to survive. Once seeding was finished, and sometimes even before, many residents of the reserves were out on the Plains, leaving behind only a few to tend the crops.

Aboriginal farmers were hampered in their earliest efforts by the kind of ploughs they were issued. By the late 1870s, Manitoba farmers had learned that American ploughs, especially the John Deere, with its chilled-steel mouldboard, were far superior for western conditions than the Ontario models. The Indian Department, however, continued until 1882 to purchase only Canadian-manufactured ploughs, which proved to be unsatisfactory. There were problems keeping in good repair the implements and wagons that were distributed, as they frequently broke down, crippling operations. Wooden parts were sometimes replaced by the farmer, but the breakage of metal parts was much more serious, as reserve farmers did not have access to blacksmiths, who were also required to point, or sharpen, plough-shares. Other equipment and livestock supplied by contractors under the terms of the treaties were clearly inferior, and Aboriginal people simply refused to accept some of it. An 1878 commission of investigation found Winnipeg Indian commissioner J.A.N. Provencher guilty of fraud in the awarding of contracts and it was discovered, among other things, that it was standard practice to furnish the Indian Department with "the most inferior articles."[11] In 1879 one observer described the carts and wagons supplied to but refused by Treaty No. 6 people near Fort Carlton as "the poorest description of Red River carts, which have been used by freighters up to this point, and are really unfit for further use; while the wagons are literally falling to pieces." The axes, "miserably small," were also refused.[12]

Perhaps the most scandalous example of corruption was in the cattle sent to a great many reserves in the late 1870s. They received wild Montana cattle, which were unaccustomed to work and could not be hitched to the plough. The milk cows given out were of the same description. The Fort Carlton bands were astounded when these cattle were brought to them from Montana, when tame cattle could have been purchased at Prince Albert or Red River. Most of them died over the first winter of 1878–79. Some choked themselves when tied in stables; others could not be fed because they did not take to the food. As one Plains Cree chief stated: "We know why these Montana cattle were given us; because they were cheaper, and the Government, thinking us a simple people, thought we would take them."[13] He was correct. It became clear during the 1878 investigation that individuals in Winnipeg had profited by purchasing these creatures from Montana at about half the rate that they actually charged the Indian Department.

Aboriginal farmers laboured under other disadvantages as well. In these earliest years there were no grist mills located near reserves, and the wheat they raised was of no use to them without milling facilities. With the disappearance of the buffalo, the main source for all their apparel also vanished. They lacked clothing and footwear, which one official described as the greatest drawback to their work. To cover their feet they cut up old leather lodges, but these too rapidly diminished. Often hungry, weak, and ill, people could not work no matter how willing.

There was little progress in agriculture in the years immediately following the treaties of the 1870s. Early on, government officials insisted that this had to do with the indifference and apathy of Aboriginal people, who willfully rejected an agricultural way of life and inflexibly and stubbornly insisted on pursuing hunting and gathering. Through idleness they were creating their own problems. An explanation that belittled and deprecated the abilities of Aboriginal farmers absolved the government of any responsibility in the matter, and it was to be the favoured explanation of department officials well into the twentieth century. During these initial years of government parsimony, indifference, and outright corruption, an opportunity was lost. Many of those who wished to farm found it impossible and became disheartened and discouraged. Had the government shown a genuine interest, some steps towards the creation of an agricultural economy might have been taken during the years before 1878–79, when the food crisis, brought on by the total disappearance of the buffalo, became severe. There was much distress, suffering, and death throughout the Northwest by 1878, although reports of starvation were systematically denied by government officials and the western press, as such news could damage the reputation of the region as a prospective home for thousands of immigrants. Once again, Aboriginal people were portrayed as chronic complainers with imaginary grievances, and they were blamed for having "not made the usual effort to help themselves."[14]

The other legacy of the years immediately following the treaties was the sense of betrayal felt by Aboriginal people who had expected government assistance in the difficult transition to an agricultural economy. As Chief Ahtahkakoop stated in 1879: "On the transfer of the country we were told that the Queen would do us all the good in the world, and that the Indians would see her bounty. With this message came presents of tobacco, and I took it at once; and I pray now that the bounty then promised may be extended to us." Three years after the treaty, the chief was convinced that the "policy of the Government has been directed to its own advantage, and the Indians have not been considered so much." These chiefs had made several representations to government authorities, "but they were as if they were thrown into water."[15]

Chief Pasquah, from the Pasquah Reserve in southeastern Saskatchewan, had presented Joseph Cauchon, Lieutenant-Governor of

Manitoba, with similar grievances and concerns a year earlier.[16] His people, though willing to farm and diversify their subsistence base, had no cattle to break and work the land, no seed to sow, and no provisions to sustain them while at work. Aboriginal people had reason to feel that they had been deceived and led along a path that ended in betrayal, that their treatment constituted a breach of faith. They were getting the clear impression that the treaties were made simply as a means of getting peaceable possession of the country without any regard to their welfare. As Aboriginal spokesmen grasped every opportunity to implore the government to assist them to make a living by agriculture, department officials increasingly reacted by blaming the Natives for their misfortunes and portraying them as troublemakers and chronic complainers, incapable of telling the truth.

In the wake of alarming reports from the Northwest of destitution and starvation, an ambitious plan to both feed and instruct Aboriginal people in farming was hastily contrived in Ottawa in the fall and winter of 1878–79. A squad of farm instructors, mainly from Ontario, was sent west in the summer of 1879. They were to establish "home farms" at fifteen sites in the Northwest: six in the Treaty No. 4 district and nine in the Treaty No. 6 district. At these farms, located on or near the reserves, the instructors were to raise large quantities of provisions to support not only themselves, their families, and employees but also the neighbouring Aboriginal population. Their farms were to serve as "model farms" for Aboriginal observers, and in addition the instructors were to visit the reserve farmers from time to time to assist them in breaking, seeding, and harvesting and in building their houses, barns, and root houses. At two "supply farms" in the Treaty No. 7 district, large quantities of produce were to be raised, but the farmers at these sites were not given the additional responsibility of instructing Aboriginal farmers.

The home farm plan was hastily and poorly conceived in Ottawa by people without any knowledge of Aboriginal people or of the region's soil and climate. The men chosen as instructors were unfamiliar with conditions of life in the West and knew nothing about Aboriginal people. They had to be provided with both guides and interpreters. As one Aboriginal spokesman stated, it only made sense that a farm instructor be a man "from the country, who understands the language, and with whom I could speak face to face, without an interpreter."[17] The official rationale for not choosing local people was that "strangers" were likely to carry out their duties more efficiently, would not have their favourites, and would treat all fairly and alike. It is also clear, however, that the position of farm instructor was a patronage appointment, and all were chosen by Sir John A. Macdonald, the Canadian prime minister, from a list furnished by Laurence Vankoughnet, deputy superintendent-general of Indian Affairs. In addition, the tasks assigned the instructors were beyond the resources and capabilities of any individual, however well acquainted he might be with conditions in the Northwest. It soon proved that the instructors had great difficulty establishing even the most modest farms. The government found itself responsible for the support of instructors, their families, and employees, who ran farms with such dismal returns that they contributed almost nothing to the expense of running them. It was also soon discovered that the farmers simply could not attend both to their own farms and to assisting on reserve farms. The instructors seldom visited the reserves and lacked even basic knowledge about the people they were to instruct. The program turned out to be an administrative nightmare. Difficulties with personnel arose early, and the program was characterized by resignations and dismissals. The instructors were angered by government decisions to charge them for the board of themselves and family, and also to charge them for food they consumed that they had raised themselves.

Beset with all of these difficulties, the home farm program floundered. In the House of Commons, government critics hammered away at the plan. They claimed that the instructors were incompetent carpetbaggers, but the central criticism was that there should be no such expenditure on the Aboriginal people of the Northwest, as this was encouraging idleness when they should be made to rely solely on their own resources. One member of Parliament argued that the program was an enormous waste of money because efforts to "civilize Indians" were inevitably doomed to failure.[18] Government defenders of the program argued that the essential problem lay with Aboriginal people, who were "idlers by nature and uncivilized." In the opinion of Prime Minister Macdonald, they were not suited to agriculture, as they "have not the ox-like quality of the Anglo-Saxon; they will not put their neck to the yoke."[19]

There were many vocal critics of the home farm program in the Northwest as well. Non-Aboriginal residents viewed the program as unfair because too much was being done to equip Aboriginal people to farm, more than was available to the true "homesteaders," upon whom it was felt the prosperity of the region depended. The home farm program ingrained the idea that Aboriginal farmers were being lavishly provided with farm equipment and other assistance that was "conducive to the destruction of self-reliance, and calculated to give them a false impression of what the Government owed them." In the wake of the food crisis in the Northwest, the government had begun to provide modest rations to reserve residents. Indeed, some of the farm instructors found much of their time taken up issuing relief in the form of "musty and rusty" salt pork in exchange for assigned work. Many non-Native residents were critical of the distribution of rations, which they saw as a reward for idleness and as unfair because it gave Aboriginal farmers an advantage over other struggling farmers.

The home farm program had a very brief life in its original form. By 1884 the department had officially retired the policy, which had already undergone much modification. Farm instructors remained and their numbers increased, but their own farms were to consist of no more than a few acres and they were to concentrate on instruction. New recruits were no longer brought from Ontario at great expense but were men from the Northwest.

All who attempted farming on the Plains in the 1880s experienced frustration and failure. Crops during this decade were damaged year after year by drought and early frosts. Prairie fires became a serious hazard, consuming haystacks as well as houses, stables, and fences, and hampering the abilities of farmers not only to winter cattle but to carry out the whole cycle of arming operations. There was a high rate of homestead cancellation, and many of the community experiments of ethnic, religious, working-class, and aristocratic groups did not survive the decade.

A major difference between the Aboriginal farmer and his neighbours was that, while newcomers had the option to leave and try their luck elsewhere, reserve residents had little choice but to persevere, as under the *Indian Act* they were excluded from taking homesteads. Aboriginal farmers could not obtain loans because they were not regarded as the actual owners of any property, however extensive and valuable their improvements might be, and they had difficulty obtaining credit from merchants. Because of many of the technicalities and prohibitions of the *Indian Act*, Natives were prevented from doing business or transacting even the most ordinary daily affair. They were deprived of the right to do what they chose with nearly everything they acquired by their own personal industry. People who came under the *Indian Act* were prevented by a permit system from selling, exchanging, bartering, or giving away any produce grown on their reserves without the permission of department officials. A pass system, imposed initially during the 1885 Rebellion but continued well into the twentieth century, controlled and confined the movements of people off their reserves. Those who wished to leave the reserve were obliged to acquire a pass from the farm instructor or Indian agent declaring the length of and reason for absence. The most recent arrivals to the country had far more rights, privileges, and freedom than the original inhabitants.

Despite these restrictions and the drought, frost, and prairie fires of these years, reserve farmers in some localities made significant advances in the 1880s. Several of the problems that had hampered reserve farming in the past had to some extent been ameliorated. Through a "cattle on loan" policy, for example, many bands had considerably increased their numbers of work oxen, cows, steers, heifers, and bulls. Under this system, the department "loaned" a cow to an individual who was to raise a heifer, either of which had to be returned to the Indian agent. The animal became the property of the individual, although the agent's permission was required to sell or slaughter. Reserve farmers also had increased access to grist mills in the 1880s as the department initiated a program of granting bonuses to individuals who would establish mills in the Northwest. Recipients of the bonus were obliged to charge Aboriginal customers a little less than ordinary customers for a ten-year period. The department also displayed greater concern to supply the services of blacksmiths, which bolstered agricultural operations.

Reserve farmers began to acquire some of the up-to-date machinery necessary to facilitate their operations. Mowers and rakes were the most common purchases. Some reserves were fortunate in their abundant hay supplies, and a number of bands sold hay on contract to other reserves, to settlers, and to the North-West Mounted Police. Selling hay was one of the very few opportunities for outside employment available to reserve residents. These machines were purchased with their own earnings or through pooled annuities. They were not purchased for them by the department. Agents and farm instructors in the 1880s felt that access to mowers and rakes was essential for all bands, not only those that sold hay. As stock increased on the reserves, mowers and rakes were necessary to provide enough hay. Reapers and self-binders were also acquired during this period. The self-binder lessened the danger of being caught by frost during a protracted harvest and it also reduced the waste experienced in binding with short straw. Such machinery permitted farmers to cultivate larger areas. By the late 1880s on some reserves in the districts of Treaty No. 4 and Treaty No. 6, farmers were beginning to see some significant results of their labour, and they had produce that they wished to sell: predominantly cattle, grain, and hay.

Like other prairie women of this period, Aboriginal women helped in the fields during peak seasons such as haying and harvest, but otherwise the business of grain farming was predominantly a male activity. Women continued to harvest wild resources such as berries, wild rhubarb, prairie turnip, and birch sap, and they hunted rabbits, gophers, and ducks. Because of increased settlement, the pass system, and calls for the restriction of Aboriginal hunting rights, these opportunities became increasingly constricted. Aboriginal women were eager to learn new skills and to adopt new technology. By the late 1880s the wives of many farm instructors acquired the title of "instructress" and they, as well as the wives of missionaries, taught skills such as milking, butter-making, bread-making, and knitting. Women adapted readily to these activities, but a chronic shortage of raw materials made it difficult to apply what they had learned. While the women knew how to make loaf bread, for example, they did not have the proper ovens, yeast, or baking tins, so they continued to make bannock, despite government attempts to abolish it from the diet as it required more flour than loaf bread. They seldom had yarn with which to knit. There were no buttons for the dresses the women made. They were often short of milk pans, although they made their own using birchbark. One instructress reported in 1891 that the greatest drawback was "their extreme poverty, their lack of almost every article of domestic comfort in their houses, and no material to work upon."[20] They lacked basic necessities such as soap, towels, wash basins, and wash pails, and had no means with which to acquire these.

The log dwelling on reserves in this era and well into the twentieth century were invariably described as "huts" or "shacks" that were one storey and one room. The roofs were constructed with logs or poles over which rows of straw or grass were laid. They were chinked inside and out with a mixture of mud and hay and had clay stoves but no flooring, and tanned hide was used for window covering. It was impossible to apply lessons of "housewifery" in such shacks. In publications of the Department of Indian Affairs, however, Aboriginal women were often depicted as poor housekeepers who willfully ignored instruction in modern methods. They were blamed for the poor living and health conditions on the reserves. Explanations that stressed the incapacity of Aboriginal women to change, like those that disparaged the farming abilities of the men, absolved the government of any responsibility for the poverty of the reserves.

As Aboriginal farmers acquired the technology required by western conditions and as they began to increase their acreages and their herds, they also began to pose a threat as competitors in the marketplace. By the late 1880s, farmers in parts of the Northwest were complaining loudly about "unfair" competition from Aboriginal people. It was widely believed that government assistance gave Aboriginal farmers an unfair advantage. Non-Aboriginal settlers had the misconception that reserve farmers were lavishly provided with livestock, equipment, government labour, and rations, and did not have to worry about the price at which their products were sold. There was absolutely no appreciation of the disadvantages they laboured under, or of how government regulation and Canadian laws acted to stymie their efforts. Editorials in the *Fort Macleod Gazette* regularly lamented "Indian competition," which was injuring the "true" settlers of the country. If the Siksika (Blackfoot), Kainai (Blood), Pikuni (Peigan), and Tsuu T'ina (Sarcee) were "cut loose" from the treaty, support could be given to their industries, according to the *Gazette*, but it was "pretty hard to ask the people of the country to contribute toward the support of a lot of idle paupers, and then allow them to use this very support for the purpose of taking the bread out of the settler's month [*sic*]."[21]

It was argued in the *Gazette* throughout the 1880s and 1890s that Aboriginal people should not be permitted to compete with the settlers in the sale of hay, potatoes, or grain. Any evidence that they were successful in securing contracts was used as proof that they had underbid non-Natives. There was no consideration that their product might be superior, as was certainly the case with the hay purchased by the North-West Mounted Police, who often noted in their reports that the best hay was bought from reserve farmers.[22] In a letter to the editor in July 1895, one local resident claimed that "it is altogether unfair to allow these Indians to enter into competition with white men who, even with hard work, find it difficult to make both ends meet and provide for their families." Evidence of unfair competition was used by the editors of the *Gazette* to bolster their larger campaign of the later 1880s to have Aboriginal people moved to one big reserve, an "Indian territory" out of the way of the Euro-Canadian settlements. It was argued that Indian policy had been a failure as Aboriginal people "had not made a single step toward becoming self-supporting."[23] There was apparently no recognition of the fact that it was impossible to become self-supporting to any degree unless they were allowed to sell their products.

Concerns about unfair "Indian competition" were echoed in other parts of the Northwest as well. The residents of Battleford and district were particularly strident in their objections to the competition of the Plains Cree in the grain, hay, and wood markets. Here, as well as in the district of southern Alberta, there was concern that reserve residents not become successful stockraisers as the supply of cattle to the Indian Department for rations was a vital source of revenue for many settlers. On October 13, 1888, the editor of the *Saskatchewan Herald* of Battleford denounced any plan to "set the Indians up as cattle breeders, encouraging them to supply the beef that is now put in by white contractors."

Here, as in other districts, Aboriginal farmers were in competition with new settlers for hay land. Because of the predominantly dry years of the 1880s, hay was very scarce some seasons. Off-reserve areas where reserve farmers had customarily cut hay became the subject of heated disputes. Non-Aboriginal residents of the Battleford district successfully petitioned the minister of the interior in 1889 to limit the hay land available to Aboriginal farmers off the reserves, despite the fact that the Battleford agent had warned that there would be no alternative but to decrease stock on the reserves. Many influential people in the West had a direct interest in the continuation of rations and in seeing that Aboriginal people were not self-supporting. Large operations like the W. F. Cochrane Ranch in southern Alberta found a sizable market for their beef on the neighbouring reserves. In his correspondence to department officials, Cochrane naturally objected to any reduction in rations, arguing that this meant that their lives, as well as their property and cattle operation, would be in danger.[24]

In 1889, Hayter Reed, Commissioner of Indian Affairs in Regina, announced that a new "approved system of farming" was to be applied to Indian reserves in western Canada. Reserve farmers were to reduce their area under cultivation to a single acre of wheat and a garden of roots and vegetables. Along with a cow or two, this would sufficiently provide for a farmer and his family. They were to use rudimentary implements alone: to broadcast seed by hand, harvest with scythes, bind by hand with straw, thresh with flails, and grind their grain with hand mills. They were to manufacture at home any items they required, such as harrows, hayforks, carts, and yokes. This policy complemented government intentions to subdivide the reserves into small holdings of forty acres each. Publicly, the subdivision of the reserves and the peasant farming policy were justified as an approach intended to render reserve residents self-supporting. Individual tenure, it was claimed, would implant a spirit of self-reliance and individualism, thus eroding "tribalism." Hayter Reed argued that the use of labour-saving machinery might be necessary and suitable for settlers, but Indians first had to experience farming with crude and simple implements. To do otherwise defied immutable laws of evolution and would be an "unnatural leap." In Reed's view, Aboriginal people had not reached the stage at which they were in a position to compete with white settlers.[25] Another argument forwarded against the use of labour-saving machinery was that rudimentary implements afforded useful employment for all.

Clearly, however, there were other reasons for the peasant farming formula and for allotment in severalty, reasons that were understood and appreciated by non-Aboriginal settlers. The *Saskatchewan Herald* applauded the policy for the Aboriginal farmer:

> Thrown thus on himself and left to work his farm without the aid of expensive machinery, he will content himself with raising just what he needs himself, and thus, while meeting the Government's intention of becoming self-sustaining, they at the same time would come into competition with the white settler only to the extent of their own labour, and thus remove all grounds for the complaint being made in some quarters against Government aided Indians entering into competition with white settlers.[26]

This was a policy of deliberate arrested development. The allotment of land in severalty was viewed by officials, as well as by Prime Minister Macdonald himself, as a means of defining surplus land that might be sold.[27] Severalty would confine people within circumscribed boundaries, and their "surplus" land could be fined and sold. Arrested development was a certain means of ensuring that much reserve land would appear to be vacant and unused.

Despite the protests of Aboriginal farmers, Indian agents, farm instructors, and inspectors of the agencies, the peasant farming policy was implemented on Plains reserves beginning in 1889. Officials were not to authorize the purchase, hire, or use of any machinery. Even if people had purchased machinery before the policy was adopted, they were still to use hand implements. Farmers with larger holdings were to use the labour of others rather than revert to the use of machinery, or they were to restrict their acreages to what they could handle with hand implements alone. Officials in the field were dismayed by the policy that robbed the farmers of any potential source of revenue. They argued that the seasons in the Northwest were simply too short for the use of hand implements, which meant a loss in yield at harvest time and resulted in a much reduced supply of hay. Agent W. S. Grant of the Assiniboine Reserve protested that "the seasons in this country are too short to harvest any quantity of grain, without much waste, with only old fashioned, and hand implements to do the work with." In his view the amount of grain lost in his agency through harvesting with hand implements would be of sufficient quantity to pay for a binder in two years.[28]

Aboriginal farmers were profoundly discouraged by the new rules. It was widely reported that many refused to work with the hand implements and gave up farming altogether. One farmer from Moose Mountain declared he would let his grain stand and never plough another acre, while another gave up his oxen, his wheat, and the reserve.[29] Other aspects of the program, such as the home manufactures idea, were unrealistic and unworkable. Homemade wooden forks, for example, were simply not strong enough for loading hay, grain, or manure. They were to make their own lanterns, but agents protested that people could not look after their cattle at night without proper lanterns. At headquarters in Ottawa, it proved impossible even to acquire some of the old-fashioned implements, such as hand mills, destined for the Aboriginal farmers. But Reed was not sympathetic to or moved by the objections and complaints, and he refused to give in to the "whims of farmers and Indians." He advised that losing some of the crop or growing less grain was preferable to the use of machinery. If grain was being lost, the solution was for farmers to confine their acreage to what they could handle. Department employees were not to convene or be present at meetings with Aboriginal farmers, as this would give "an exaggerated importance" to their request for machinery. They risked dismissal if they refused to comply with peasant farming policy.

The policy of deliberate discouragement of reserve agriculture worked well. By the mid-1890s, per capita acreage under cultivation had fallen to about half of the 1889 level and many serious farmers had given up farming altogether. In 1899 a resident of Prince Albert, William Miller Sr., wrote to the minister of the interior that in passing through the Duck Lake and Carlton reserves, he noted "no less than five fields [which can] be seen from the trail now without a bushel of grain sown in them ... that previously used to be an example to the settlers around."[30] Peasant farming, severalty, and measures such as the permit system combined to undermine and atrophy agricultural development on reserves. The Canadian government acted not to promote the agriculture of the indigenous population but to provide an optimum environment for the immigrant settler. Whatever Canada did for its "wards" was subordinate to the interests of the non-Aboriginal population. Government policy was determined by the need to maintain the viability of the immigrant community.

Aboriginal people protested policies that affected them adversely, as they had from the 1870s. They raised objections to government officials, petitioned the House of Commons, sent letters to newspapers, and visited Ottawa. But the outlets for protest were increasingly restricted. Grievances related to instructors and agents rarely went further. Agency inspectors were, as mentioned, not allowed to hold audiences with reserve residents. The published reports of agents and inspectors were to divulge only that "which it was desired the public should believe."[31] Visiting officials such as the governor-general, who were usually accompanied by journalists, were taken only to select agencies that would leave the best impression. Department officials, particularly those in the central office, shared the view that Aboriginal people were chronic complainers not to be believed and a people who would go to extraordinary lengths to avoid diligent work.

Hayter Reed and the peasant farming formula were disposed of the year after Wilfrid Laurier and the Liberals came to power in 1896, but the damaging legacy of the policy was to be felt for years to come. Laurier was fortunate in coming to power just at a time when a constellation of factors, including rising world wheat prices, increased rainfall on the prairies, innovations in dry-land farming techniques, and massive immigration allowed a wheat economy to prosper in western Canada. Aboriginal farmers, however, had little place in this new age of prosperity. By the turn of the century, agriculture did not form the basis of a stable reserve economy, and after that date the likelihood faded even further as the new administrators of Indian Affairs promoted land surrenders that further limited the agricultural capacity of reserves. The fact that there was "vacant" and "idle" land on many reserves, to a great extent the result of the peasant farming years, conveniently played into the hands of those who argued that Aboriginal people had land far in excess of their needs and capabilities. Government policy was that it was in the best interests of all concerned to encourage reserve residents to divest themselves of land they held "beyond their possible requirements" and the policy received widespread support in the western press and from farmers and townspeople. Residents of towns near Indian reserves regularly submitted petitions claiming that these tracts retarded the development and progress of their districts. Such pressure resulted in the alienation of many thousands of acres of reserve land, often the best land, in the years shortly after the turn of the century. The economic viability of reserve communities was deliberately eroded by the dominant society, mainly through government policies.

In the post-treaty era to 1900, the Plains Cree were resolved to establish a new economy based on agriculture. They faced many impediments and frustrations in these efforts. Implements and livestock promised under treaty were inadequate, and government officials proved reluctant to distribute these. These officials insisted that people were to be settled on their reserves *and cultivating* in advance of their receiving the implements and cattle promised to them, although that which had been promised was necessary for cultivation. Seed grain arrived too late or in a damaged state and wild Montana cattle were distributed instead of domestic oxen. Workers on reserves lacked proper clothing and footwear, and they were weak because of hunger and illness. Many reserves were distant from markets and transportation, and there were no milling facilities in the earliest years of reserve life.

The government attempted to address some of these problems and the food crisis in the Northwest through a "home farm" policy that was hastily devised and implemented in 1879. The plan was to have farm instructors establish model farms, raise large quantities of food for rations, and teach agriculture. It was a poorly conceived policy as these tasks were beyond the capabilities of the men appointed, most of whom had no acquaintance with Aboriginal people or with conditions in the Northwest. This policy was shelved by 1884, but farm instructors remained on many reserves, indicating an important measure of government commitment to the establishment of farming at that time, and some advances in agriculture were made in the mid- to late 1880s. But environmental conditions were grim for all farmers at that time. There were early frosts, and drought and prairie fires caused enormous damage. Aboriginal farmers laboured under particular disadvantages. Because of the prohibitions of the *Indian Act*, they could not expand their land base or try their luck elsewhere by taking out homesteads, and they could not take out loans or transact their own business affairs.

Despite all of the challenges of the 1880s, Plains Cree farmers in some localities made significant advances, raising a surplus for sale and acquiring necessary machinery by the end of that decade. Non-Aboriginal residents of the West expressed concern about this success and the threat of competition in the limited markets. In 1889, in response to these concerns, the government introduced a "peasant" farming policy. Reserve farmers were to cultivate no more than an acre or two using only rudimentary hand implements. The central argument of this article is that this policy, combined with the other disadvantages and conditions that beset Plains Cree farmers, impaired the establishment of a viable economy.

NOTES

1 Harold Cardinal and Walter Hildebrandt, *Treaty Elders of Saskatchewan: Our Dream Is That Our Peoples Will One Day Be Clearly Recognized as Nations* (Calgary: University of Calgary Press, 2000), 10.

2 Patrick Wolfe, *Settler Colonialism and the Transformation of Anthropology: The Politics and Poetics of an Ethnographic Event* (London: Cassell, 1999): 1–3.

3 See, for example, Anonymous, *The New West: Extending from the Great Lakes Across Plain and Mountain to the Golden Shores of the Pacific* (Winnipeg: Canadian Historical Publishing Co., 1888), preface, n.p. Although not mentioned in this passage, Aboriginal people are there between the lines, or at least a jumble of ideas about them are there: "… although the strides in the march of progress, keeping pace with the advancement of nineteenth century civilization, have been marvelously rapid in this fair land, there are countless thousands of leagues of territory on which the foot of man has never trod, lying tenantless and silent, only awaiting the advent of the Anglo-Saxon race to be transformed into a prosperous and thriving country. The wealth of commerce, agriculture, mining, lumbering and fishing, latently exists in untold measure. The virgin soil, the primeval forest and the teeming lakes and rivers all possess undeveloped riches. Man alone is apparently the missing quantity, and his energy, industry and capital are the required elements in developing this young, but sturdy Dominion into the great Britain of the West."

4 Cardinal and Hildebrandt, *Treaty Elders of Saskatchewan*, 61.

5 Anonymous, *Chronicles by the Way: A Series of Letters Addressed to the Montreal Gazette Descriptive of a Trip Through Manitoba and the North-West* (Montreal: Montreal Gazette, 1879), 26.

6 "North-West Territories" was the form used until 1912, when it became the present "Northwest Territories."

7 William F. Butler, *The Great Lone Land* [1872] (Edmonton: Hurtig, 1968), 317–18.

8 Neal Putt, *Place Where the Spirit Lives: Stories from the Archaeology and History of Manitoba* (Winnipeg: Pemmican, 1991), 64.

9 Library and Archives Canada (LAC), Saskatchewan Homesteading Experiences, MG 30 C16, Vol. 3, 790.

10 Anon., *Chronicles by the Way*, 28.
11 E. Brian Titley, "Unsteady Debut: J.-A.-N. Provencher and the Beginnings of Indian Administration in Manitoba," *Prairie Forum* 22, no. 1, 1997: 21–46.
12 Anon., *Chronicles by the Way*, 29.
13 Ibid., 28.
14 *Saskatchewan Herald* (Battleford), April 26, 1879.
15 Ibid.
16 LAC, RG10, Vol. 3665, file 10094, Interpreter to Joseph Cauchon, June 1, 1878.
17 Ibid.
18 *House of Commons Debates*, 1884, 2: 1105 (Philipe Casgrain).
19 Ibid., 1107 (John A. Macdonald).
20 LAC, RG 10, Vol. 3845, File 73406-7, T. P. Wadsworth to Hayter Reed, February 17, 1891.
21 *Macleod Gazette*, December 7, 1886.
22 Annual Report of Commissioner L. W. Herchmer for 1889, in *The New West: Being the Official Reports to Parliament of the Activities of the Royal* [*sic*] *North-West Mounted Police Force from 1888–89* (Toronto: Coles, 1973), 6.
23 *Macleod Gazette*, December 7, 1886.
24 LAC, Hayter Reed Papers, W. F. Cochrane to L. Vankoughnet, September 6, 1893, file W. F. Cochrane.
25 LAC, RG 10, vol. 3964, File 148285, Hayter Reed to A. Forget, August 24, 1896.
26 *Saskatchewan Herald*, August 20, 1887.
27 Kenneth J. Tyler, "A Tax-Eating Proposition: The History of the Passpasschase Indian Reserve," Master's thesis, University of Alberta, 1979, 114.
28 LAC, RG 10, Vol. 3964, File 148285, W. S. Grant to Reed, October 1, 1896.
29 Ibid., J. J. Campbell to Reed, Oct. 8, 1896, and Grant to Reed, October 1, 1896.
30 LAC, RG 10, Vol. 3993, File 187812, William Miller Sr. to the Minister of the Interior, July 21, 1899.
31 LAC, RG 10, Deputy-Superintendent letterbooks, Vol. 1115, Reed to J. Wilson, August 3, 1894.

6

UTOPIAN IDEALS AND COMMUNITY SETTLEMENTS IN WESTERN CANADA, 1880–1914

Anthony W. Rasporich

Utopia is a term of many definitions and dimensions. Broadly considered, the utopian tradition is based upon the optimistic assumption that harmony, co-operation, and mutual trust are more natural to humanity than competition, exploitation, and social alienation. Spiritually, utopia also represents a refuge or escape from the existing evils of society and projects a new social order based upon communitarian ideals. The literary expression of these ideals may be expressed in extraordinary voyages to lost islands, planets, or cities out of time, or more practically in platonic speculations upon ideal constitutions in social reorganization of family relationships or a radical re-ordering of economic production and work. The social forms that utopian ideals take have also varied widely, from static to dynamic, from aristocratic to democratic, and from collectivist to individualist in their aims and structure.[1]

But, despite its elasticity and universality, utopia is still not a term that has been treated widely in Canadian or western Canadian historical literature. Suggestive allusions have been made by W. L. Morton to the utopian element in the ideology of Henry Wise Wood, and later in the Social Credit movement. Direct examination of the utopian concepts expressed in E. A. Partridge's "co-operative commonwealth" has been made in a brief but penetrating essay by Carl Berger. And George Woodcock, among others, has examined the imperfect realization of utopianism in the radical Finnish social experimental Sojntula (Harmony) on Malcolm Island in British Columbia.[2]

Such studies, including modern sociological analyses of communal societies in western Canada, tend, however, to ignore the broader role that utopian and quasi-utopian idealism played in the social and intellectual development of the West prior to the First World War. At Confederation, the prairies were in essence little more than a literary projection, a garden (or a desert) in the eyes of eastern beholders such as Palliser, Hind, or Dawson.[3] But, shortly after the completion of the railway, the image of the West in central Canada and Great Britain progressed rapidly from the *outopia*, "nowhere" or *terra incognita*, to *eutopia*, a "somewhere" or "good place" of unlimited progress, enterprise, and development.[4] Indeed, not only the garden west of the farm, but also the city, became the literary paradise of the boosters and pamphleteers who conjured mirages of industrial and commercial progress in the West.

The colonization land company and community settlement were the vehicle by which the prairies were to be settled. The central Canadian government in fact extended a familiar technique of land settlement derived from the romantic schemes of systematic colonization such as the Canada Land Company, which had peopled the western peninsula of Upper Canada. The central difference was that most of the colonization companies of the 1880s were in fact paper schemes generated in the capital markets of England and the United States, and calculated to reap short-term gains.[5] Very few of these empire settlement schemes actually placed settlers on the land, with their mixture of motives, which lingered in Stephen Leacock's satire *My Discovery of the West*, halfway between "philanthropy and rapacity."[6]

The ideology of the English land settlement schemes was, however, a persuasive one, as Leacock himself suggests in his inverted utopian satire of the company's operations. As he describes it, the appeal to the prospective settler was both "patriotic as well as pecuniary," since the company was pledged to all-British settlement, to an annual dividend, and to the eventual prospect of land-ownership in "The Valley of Hope." The English village system that was promised by many of these co-operative land schemes was the central focus of their inspiration. Its appeal was recaptured in another literary reconstruction of the land company utopia rendered later in 1920 by the CPR colonization agent Robert Stead, in his novel *Dennison Grant*. His central character's "Big Idea" was a carefully planned co-operative venture that substituted group settlement in villages for the rectangular survey. Such a large joint-stock venture would, in Grant's view, provide centralized urban services in a rural context and allow centralized direction of all economic and social activity "to the betterment of humanity."[7]

The point of these literary digressions is simply to establish that group-settlement ideology combined with a moral projection of a new order was a continuing theme in early western Canada. Indeed, if some of the early examples of actual settlements were to be examined closely for their social ideals and aspirations, and in their economic and social organization, there are parallels to the late nineteenth-century utopian visions of Ruskin, Bellamy, Hudson, and Morris. Either as social experiments or as arcadian refuges, they generally failed within a generation to achieve either the intrinsic perfection of their ideals, or the anticipated benefits of social escape from the industrial ills of urban England, continental Europe, and central Canada. Most resulted in settlement abandonment within a generation, as had their counterparts in England and America, but they reveal at least something of the idealistic roots of prairie society prior to the First World War.

The Qu'Appelle Valley of Saskatchewan was the focus of several such community experiments in the 1880s, and became a promised land to a wide variety of social classes and ethnic groups. These ranged from the Scottish crofter colony at Benbecula and the East London Artisans' Colony near Moosomin to a welter of ethnic colonies such as Esterhazy, New Sweden, and Thingvalla.[8] Perhaps the two most obvious utopian projections from among the English-speaking settlements were the aristocratic society at Cannington Manor south of Moosomin, and the democratic social experiment at Harmony, near Tantallon, on the Qu'Appelle River. They were bi-polar opposites as expressions of the utopist outlook, the first emanating from the urban middle-classes of England, and the latter from the western Ontario agrarian tradition, and briefly co-existed less than seventy-five miles apart before their common failure at the turn of the century.

Cannington Manor anticipates in ideal terms what Lewis Mumford describes as the utopia of the "Country House," or in literary terms is expressed in the medieval visions of William Morris's *News from Nowhere* (1891) and W. H. Hudson's *Crystal Age* (1905). Past, present, and future are fused in the latter about a self-sufficient little feudal community centred around a magnificent country house, peopled by beautiful, cultured inhabitants. Life in nature is idealized, and the inhabitants happily engage themselves in agriculture, in artisan handicrafts, or in the leisure activities of art, music, and cultured conversation.[9]

The real Cannington Manor was established in 1882 by Captain Edward Mitchell Pierce, a British "gentleman and soldier" ruined by a London bank failure. The Canadian Northwest and the prospect of homesteads for himself and his four sons represented a social escape, as it apparently did also for those who followed. Shortly after his arrival, Pierce wrote a letter to an English newspaper offering to take on "young men of good birth and education" under his superintendence for $500–$1,000 per year, and instruct them in the art of farming. The collection of remittance men who were attracted by the advertisement is described in the colourful prose of one of Cannington's early founders:

> It is well known that oft times a wild son was shipped off to Canada and allowed enough to live on so long as he stayed there; there were and still are others who have left their native shores because they deemed it expedient to beat a hasty retreat; then there are the failures, the misfits, the men who fail in some examination for the Army, Navy, Civil Service, for the Bar, for the Church, or other calls in life; the colonies as they were once called, now the Dominions, offer a home and a fresh start to all of those who wish to embrace it; as a rule this class of Englishman has been well educated, he has been taught how to comport himself as a gentleman, he has been taught how to idle, how to spend money, and how to get amusement out of life. As a rule he is sport and natural, devil-me-care and often loveable, but he has never been taught how to work, that important part of a modern education has been omitted.[10]

The village society that was reconstructed at Cannington consciously defied the individualistic precepts of homestead farming and the rectangular survey. Its co-operative economic nexus was the Moose Mountain Trading Company centrally placed on the Pierce land by its several trading partners. The company planned, built, and owned the community services, which included a grist-mill, blacksmith's and woodworker's shop, co-operative cheese factory, hotel, and post-office. In addition it built a village church and a community assembly hall, which operated as a school, and co-operatively hired the services of a doctor from England.[11]

Community life for the English group at Cannington revolved about two poles: work and leisure. James Humphrys, a marine engineer from Barrow-in-Furness, was the leader of the "worker" or artisan faction in the colony, and marshalled pork production for export back to the mother country. His spacious home, built in 1888, was an impressive reflection of his utilitarian personality – its capacious attic was built large enough to quarter two hundred troops in anticipation of another uprising such as the recent Northwest Rebellion. In direct contrast was the domicile of the sporting faction represented by the Beckton brothers, who inherited their wealth from Sir John Curtis, the ex-Lord Mayor of Manchester. Their palatial manor house, "Didsbury," completed in 1889, contained twenty rooms, a bachelor wing of another five rooms, and a large billiard parlour. Even the livestock quarters were an elaborate complex of stone barns, kennels, and sheds designed to segregate species as well as the sexes.

The community of leisure that played in and around the Beckton establishment was the preserve of the "drones," who occupied themselves with an elaborate ritual of indoor and outdoor pastimes. The former were comprised of equally refined parlour activities, from choral music and painting to poetry readings and "scientific" discussions of agriculture and politics. The latter included the outdoor class sports of the English aristocracy, from cricket and tennis to sailing and fox-hunting. A typical summer day in the life of Canningtonians is described by one of the residents, who first explained that during the winter they would often return home overseas or to other warmer climes in the tropics:

> Tea was served on the Tennis Courts by the Ladies, and indeed it was a bright and happy scene intermingling with the pretty summer frocks of the ladies could be seen young men in flannels wearing the blazers and colours of all the best known English and Scottish public schools and even varsity blues. Eton, Harrow, Fettes, Loretto, Cheltenham, Clifton, Rugby, Marlborough, Wellington, Shrewsbury were all represented, to mention only a few of the best known schools. Then back usually in a buckboard home to dress for dinner, to dine with friends or attend some public or private dance, card party, midnight frolic, drive or ride to the lake.[12]

Political enthusiasm also ran high, and imperial events such as the relief of Mafeking during the South African War occasioned the entire settlement to take to their "ponies" and to ride to Cannington Hall, where one of the bluebloods, Cecil LeMesurier, impersonated Queen Victoria presenting medals to the returned soldiers.[13]

Ultimately this sporting culture declined, notably because of its failure to establish a sustained economic base beyond its elaborate first phase of construction. The bachelor society gradually disbanded, some by the gentle attrition of intermarriage with the Ontario and English women on the nearby homesteads, and others by the sudden patriotic fever engendered by the Boer War and the speculative excitement of the Klondike gold rush. Certain economic decline was ensured to Cannington when the CPR built its spur line ten miles to the south in 1900, and the village store was forced to relocate in the new village of Manor. Only a few of the original English settlers remained in old Cannington, clustered about their tennis courts, village church, and manor house.[14]

A sobering Calvinist contrast was offered by the radical utopian experiment entitled the Harmony Industrial Association, located at the centre of a bloc of free homesteads near Tantallon. In 1895 a group of western Manitoba farmers of radical Protestant denominational roots in western Ontario met at Beulah, Manitoba, to project a new social order of "Hamona" further to the west. Directly inspired by the writings of John Ruskin, William Morris, and Edward Bellamy, they drafted a constitution and by-laws for a co-operative community based upon the ideal of brotherhood.[15] The preamble to the constitution fused evangelical and universalist precepts with co-operative economic ideals and common ownership:

> Feeling that the present competitive social system is one of injustice and fraud directly opposed to the precepts laid down by "Our Saviour" for the guidance of mankind in subduing all the forces of nature and evils springing from selfishness in the human heart, we do write under the name of the "Harmony Industrial Association" for the purpose of acquiring land to build homes for its members, to produce from nature sufficient to insure its members against want or fear of want.
>
> To own and operate factories, mills, stores, etc. To provide educational and recreative facilities of the highest order and to promote and maintain harmonious social relations on the basis of co-operation for the benefit of its members and mankind in general.[16]

The economic organization of Hamona followed the joint-stock formula, established upon a common stock of $100,000 divided into 500 shares of $200 each. To ensure social equality, the constitution provided that each member could hold no more than five shares and that profits would be divided annually upon the basis of the number of days of labour given in work to the colony.

Economic activity would be closely prescribed and regulated, despite legal guarantees that individuals could be fully employed at whatever activity they performed best. Day labour would be limited to ten hours, and rates of hourly or daily compensation were to be equal. But the problem of productivity was clearly one that concerned the founders, who also provided for penalties to those of greater ability who under-produced and required that work foremen be obeyed at all times. On the other hand, they feared that enterprise might be under-rewarded, and provided for special incentives "to call out the best endeavour of employees" and "a system of preferment subject to the approval of a majority of the membership and designed to best promote the interests of the Commonwealth."[17]

Its puritanical and totalitarian control of its membership was further apparent in the rigorous qualifications for entry and for expulsion beyond its pale. Applicants were strictly enjoined to possess "good moral character," and also to pass an examination in the principles of social co-operation. After receiving two-thirds of the colony's support for entry, the novice was reminded upon entry that he surrendered his natural freedom for the freedoms of right and justice conferred by the civil or social contract. And despite disclaimers protecting the free exercise of individual rights, majority rule obtained in matters of public discipline. Arraignment would be determined after inquisition, and the question of innocence or guilt voted in public meeting, with the offending member being expelled from the association payroll.

Despite the considerable number of social services in the way of health care, education, and child allowances that the Harmony Industrial Association offered, the colony did not attract widespread interest. At most, fifty persons joined the village settlement. Economic failure soon overtook the community, which, like Cannington, failed to develop a staple export base to sustain the expensive services it offered to its members. The anticipated railway link failed to revive its economic fortunes, and by 1900 the association disbanded after less than two full years of operation.[18]

Hamona came closest then in conception and actuality to the literary utopias later articulated by Robert Stead in *Dennison Grant* and E. A. Partridge's *War on Poverty*.[19] The autocratic methods of social control that Stead's protagonist places in the hands of the board of directors are clearly intended to substitute community control for the State. Equally, the thought-control and government by experts in Partridge's co-operative commonwealth of virtue are anticipated in miniature by the Harmony Industrial Association a generation earlier, and only a few miles to the east of Partridge's Sintaluta. While Partridge's High Court of Control may have owed more intellectually to H. G. Wells' *A Modern Utopia* than to Hamona, its totalitarian and plebiscitarian paradoxes are probably explained better by the agrarian populism of eastern Saskatchewan and its grass-root adaptations of nineteenth-century English utopianism.

Significantly, it was to be the utopia of calm, pastoral felicity that was to hold greater attraction for later British experiments in the developing Northwest. While none would match Cannington Manor in the refinements of leisure, they would nevertheless attempt a more modest recreation of British society and ideals on the prairies. Among such group settlements, communitarian ideology was poorly developed or absent, and depended in the main upon the shared assumptions of Anglo-Saxon race and imperial ideals. Their economic objectives were more individualistic than collective, and a group identity and community focus served only as a transitional vehicle to individual survival. In this sense, the pastoral vision is the primary object of the quest for self-fulfillment in nature, much as in Thoreau's *Walden*, or in the English romantic poets, and the secondary objective the survival of communitarian values.[20]

The Edenic quest for paradise is clearly evident in the story of the Parry Sound colonists, who travelled from their homesteads near Georgian Bay to Fort Saskatchewan in 1894. At least insofar as related by their main chronicler, W. C. Pollard, in *Life on the Frontier*, the opening of the West by the CPR excited the romantic imaginations of the predominantly Anglican farming village of Magnetawan, who sensed that their present lives were "erring and aimless."[21] From Pollard's perspective, two main ideals spurred them on to the West: the prospect of entering "the Promised Land," and the realization of the landed heritage of the British people on the 160-acre homestead. And, despite the considerable hardships endured in the process of settlement along the North Saskatchewan, he could relate in retrospect at least his enthusiasm for the pioneering experience in lyrical poems addressed to the "Prince of Nature," and ecstatic pastoral prose upon his early years in the Northwest:

> Did humanity ever set for itself a nobler task than that of pioneering in a new and virgin country, there the work of Nature can be seen on every side, and there avarice and selfishness are unknown, and all

> are engaged in Man's primitive occupations: tilling the soil, guarding the flocks and herds, fishing in the waters, hunting in the wilderness and mining under the ground.
>
> There the brotherhood of man is amplified and common interests cement together social ties and friendships and there the works of the Creator are seen before man makes any contributions or contaminations.[22]

Not untypically, "the building of Jerusalem in this pleasant land" proved more an individual than a collective enterprise, and the Parry Sound Colony prospered and gradually moved on. Pollard himself studied law with the prominent Calgary firm of Lougheed and Bennett and then at Osgoode Hall, and moved back to Uxbridge, Ontario, after World War I.

A rather more familiar form of British Israelitism and pastoral capitalism in the Northwest was the Barr Colony in western Saskatchewan. Its founder, the Anglican curate of Tollington Park, Rev. Isaac M. Barr, drafted a prospectus for the Canadian Northwest designed to appeal to urban clerks, artisans, and professional men intent on seeking a rural life in the New World. In common with a vast amount of literature then being generated to popularize the Canadian Northwest among British youth,[23] Barr rang the imperial changes with such masculine appeals as: "Britons have ever been the great colonizers. Let it not be said that we are the degenerate sons of brave and masterful sires." His second prospectus to intending members of the colony in 1903 was even more explicit in its clarion call: "Let us take possession of Canada. Let our cry be 'CANADA FOR THE BRITISH.'"[24]

The projected settlement was either a naive rendering or a calculating exploitation of English middle-class perceptions of prairie life. Barr assured the prospective settler that "this is to be no village or communistic settlement. Everyone will live on his own land; that is, it will be a settlement of the ordinary kind." Companionship, social co-operation, and mutual help would naturally spring forth from the community values of the British population. Indeed, prospective settlers were urged to leave behind all but the basic household items and a few garden seeds, and perhaps bring along a gun or an English saddle if they possessed one. Since any form of labour could be reasonably bought in this land of felicity, no implements or horses were required of the small homesteader. But everyone should "own a cow or two, and perhaps a pony with a light waggon, and some hens and pigs." This pastoral vision of happy farm life was completed with a recitation of the great natural benefits that the land possessed, from temperate climate, abundant fuel, and accessible transportation, to good markets for everything that the farmer would want to produce. Vague mention was even made of a product for export, since British Columbia was "a good and growing market" for the total production of a community creamery.[25]

Despite the understandable failure of Barr's enterprise, the British ideals that inspired community life were sustained after his replacement by Rev. George Exton Lloyd. According to the latter, the British colony was very much alive, although the Barr Colony was dead; he officially renamed it "Britannia," and the first town he modestly named after himself, Lloydminster. The sense of British election among the survivors of the Barr disaster increased as communitarianism dissolved into the community of the surviving elect. One Cockney took pride in his ability to clear up his debts and win a prize for his wheat in 1911, despite his complete lack of experience in farming before coming to Canada. And another fantastic success story followed Jimmy Bruce, who inherited a fortune from a rich aunt in Manchester, thus enabling him to build a $150,000 mansion in nearby Lashburn, which contained thirty-five rooms, including reception rooms, conservatory, and billiard room.[26] Such was the stuff that pioneers were made of in North America, and the sight of Lord Jimmy parading with coach and livery down the streets of Lashburn confirmed the great myth of progress that other immigrant bachelor societies depicted in the symbolic return to "The Mountain of Gold."[27] But in the case of the Britannia colonists, the pioneering myth was more ideally cast in the brave new world of Walt Whitman's *Pioneers* (as quoted by one of the colonists, J. Hanna McCormick):

> All the past we leave behind:
> We debouch upon a newer mightier world, varied world,
> Fresh and strong the world we seize, world of labour and the march,
> Pioneers, O Pioneers.[28]

Nowhere was the pastoral theme of economic self-realization in nature so eloquently stated as in the promotional literature for the fruit lands of British Columbia intended for the overcrowded urbanites of Great Britain. Following closely upon the late nineteenth-century promotion of the ranchlands of Alberta, this literature, which circulated in the decade prior to World War I, was calculated to persuade the scions of wealthy British families to settle in the interior valleys of southern British Columbia.

The Canadian Pacific Railway, various trust companies, and government agencies in British Columbia assiduously peddled the theme of the fruit farmer as "nature's gentleman," toiling in the idyllic climate of the dry interior. Three themes stand out strongly in the promotional advertising of B.C. "fruit ranching": the myth of the garden and a neo-Rousseauistic idyll of natural man at work and play in paradise; the racial nostrums of Anglo-Saxon imperialism in the late nineteenth century; and the idea of social and economic co-operation as an evolved characteristic of the British upper class.[29]

A typical piece of "booster" literature of this genre was that produced by the British American Trust Company in 1907, entitled "The Potential Riches of British Columbia."[30] Contained within its frothy contents was an article by the Anglo-American traveller and journalist Agnes Deans Cameron, entitled "England's Last Vedette: The New British Columbia." The garden myth was amply orchestrated in such hollow clichés as: "Great is the power of environment. In her giant mountains, lone lakes, deep rushing rivers and lush valleys, Nature intended this Pacific province to cradle a people big, broad and unselfish." More specifically, Cameron hoped that the British immigrants' children would be counselled in the natural beauties of British Columbia. This birthright of nature was of course the natural right of Englishmen, and Canada was unequivocally declared the outpost of the Anglo-Saxon race and its historic traditions. More important to Cameron than the citation of those paradigms of English values from King Alfred to Florence Nightingale was the emphasis upon co-operative ideals among the refined classes, who should be encouraged to take up their birthright in western Canada. To this purpose, she cited a poem exemplifying a Ruskinian spirit of brotherhood which was in the air of the far west:

> There shall come from out this noise of strife and groaning
> A broader and a juster brotherhood
> A deep equality of aim postponing
> All selfish seeking to the general good
> There shall come a time when knowledge wide extended
> Sinks each man's pleasure in the general health
> And all shall hold irrevocably blended
> The individual and the commonwealth.

More detailed brochures and personal testimonials spelled out the practical applications of these social ideals to "fruit ranching" in the interior.

J. S. Redmayne's *Fruit Farming in the "Dry Belt"* and J. T. Bealby's *Fruit Ranching in B.C.* were both published in London in 1909 to encourage both young people and families to emigrate from English cities.[31] Public school boys were enticed to leave their school desks and to continue their school-ties in British Columbia, "with joint sporting expeditions as happy interludes to lucrative fruit-farming operations." Further to this, they were cautioned to beware of "land sharks" (usually Americans), but to trust in the larger "Land Development Corporations" for sale and counsel in the science of fruit culture in arid regions. Intending farmers were also advised to join the fruit-growers' associations, since these were practical expressions of the principle of social co-operation. Through co-operative distribution and marketing techniques, the individual member would be secured the best prices for the least possible costs in transport. In fact, the destination of the apples themselves had an imperial mission, for this western "Orchard of the Empire" would provide apples for the hungry consumers in British cities and thus contribute to the dual benefit of colony and empire.

The most conspicuous of the community experiments that was inspired by this spate of imperial boosterism was the settlement of Walhachin, established between Kamloops and Lytton in 1910. The excellent research article by Nelson A. Riis, "The Walhachin Myth: A Study in Settlement Abandonment," has described in detail the nature and duration of this precarious experiment in irrigated apple-growing.[32] In brief, his research demonstrates the same intellectual and social factors at play as were previously revealed in the Cannington experiment twenty years earlier. A similar bachelor society of remittance men made up of the graduates of English public schools and the Army Service formed the core of this community of nearly two hundred. Their passion for sumptuous residences and an endless round of games and activities was the equal of those at Cannington. And the ultimate abandonment of the settlement followed the prescribed formulae of earlier abortive experiments. The outbreak of war in 1914 attracted many of the army men back to their regiments, and careers in the imperial civil service beckoned for others. Also, the negative attitude of Oliver's Liberal government in British Columbia destroyed the conservative ties that had linked the community's largest landowner, the Marquis of Anglesey, to the previous administration of Sir Richard McBride. And in common with other similar ventures in British idealism there was the fatal economic flaw, an export-oriented mentality that sought the magic commodity, whether apples or tobacco, but which failed to develop a sufficiently diversified agricultural base. Walhachin probably outdid all others, however, for the sheer magnitude of its capital debt structure, for it bequeathed a costly irrigation system of wooden water flumes that would require a quarter of a million dollars to be made operable if the orchards were to be revived after the Great War.

The aristocratic and democratic utopias of social escape and the pastoral ideal were not confined solely to English-speaking groups. A high degree of fragmentation along ideological and class lines occurred among French settlers in western Canada at fin de siècle. Increasing cleavages in old-world French society created similar social fragments that sought refuge in an idealistic re-creation of a declining class-order, or in the projection of a democratic social order in the new world. Increasingly, the impulse to establish community settlements on the Canadian prairies devolved from optimistic adventures on the part of the French aristocracy, resembling the utopias of commerce and leisure at Cannington manor, to negatively-inspired political escape from the polarization of French political life in the Third French Republic.

The French settlement at Whitewood, near Moose Mountain, Assiniboia, was a replica of the Cannington experiment some forty miles away. A community of French counts and noblemen took up several homesteads in 1885 and concentrated their settlement about the chateau of *La Rolanderie*, which became the focal point of the ranching venture later headed by the Comte de Roffignac. Other noblemen established homes in the valley, importing various types of livestock for breeding, a labour force to do their menial work, and the accoutrements necessary for the fine life to which they were accustomed. Their "Race Days" rivalled and often surpassed the horse races of Cannington for their opulent parade of wealth and Parisian fashions. And the "Frenchmen's Ball" held in the Commercial Hotel in Whitewood was the outstanding social event of the Pipestone Valley in the late 1880s, complete with white shirt fronts, white kid gloves, and the *politesse* of French aristocratic society.[33]

The co-operative economic ventures of the French counts suffered the common fate of nearly every other trading company established in the Qu'Appelle region. Cattle and sheep ranching were tried, and the Rolanderie Stock Society underwent two reorganizations of capital funding by 1890. Several ventures were then launched by the Society to process agricultural products for export, ranging from Gruyère cheese to chicory and sugar beets. The Gruyère cheese failed because of dry prairie pastures;

the chicory scheme flourished all too well and glutted for years to come markets in the Northwest; and the sugar beets were frustrated by the government's ban on the sale of alcoholic by-products, thus precluding the manufacture of rum. The French noblemen also proved singularly cavalier in approaching their losses in livestock, for they occasionally abandoned their sheep to prairie blizzards or threw their excess Berkshire hogs into Pipestone Creek. The community soon lost its social cohesion as economic failure dogged its capital ventures, and the noblemen gradually returned to France. Occasionally their journey was punctuated by a diversion to the Klondike or to the South African War, and sometimes even a return to the Northwest.[34] The quixotic spirit of the colony was summed up by the return of the Comte Henri de Soras, who returned after the turn of the century to the village of Whitewood in the middle of winter because he preferred prairie snowstorms to the perpetual rain in Paris!

An element of continuity was established between the Whitewood experiment and one further to the west in Alberta at Trochu by the Comte Paul de Beaudrap. Originally a secondary member in the first community, he emerged with Armand Trochu as one of the founders of the French ranching company at Trochu in 1905.[35] Composed partially of army officers disillusioned by the Dreyfus affair and the consequent expulsion of the Catholic religious orders, and of urban *bourgeois* seeking economic opportunity in Canada, the group formed the St. Ann Ranch Trading Company and the Jeanne d'Arc Ranch. Its pastoral vision was pre-eminently stated by its major stockholder, Joseph Devilder, the son of a banker in Lille, who noted that the group "devient un modèle d'installation pratique qui va nous permettre de nous livrer tranquillement à l'élevage des chevaux et à l'engraissement du bétail – par conséquent de gagner de l'argent, but de nos efforts."[36]

The bachelor communal society that briefly flowered on the St. Ann Ranch from 1905 to 1907 was a romantic exercise in co-operative capitalism and urban customs transferred to a rural context. The men rose with military precision to their tasks at 5 a,m. from May 1 to November 1, and at a more indulgent 5:30 in the winter months. Bookkeeping and accounting were a passion; meticulous records were kept of livestock and poultry production, and egg counts were documented with some excitement in the personal diaries of Paul de Beaudrap: "(January 8, 1906) aujourd'hui deux oeufs!!! (January 11, 1906) aujourd'hui, trios oeufs! (February 25, 1906) Huit oeufs!!"[37] Other ventures such as a co-operative creamery, which was established in 1907 for export, also gave the company a common element of failure that united it with the previous French business experiments in Saskatchewan. On the other hand, its success as a social experiment was equally resounding. The camaraderie of social life in "Bachelors' Hall," the merrymaking that followed monthly mass, and the passionate pursuit of leisure activities such as rabbit-hunting, swimming, and horse-racing established Trochu Valley as a masculine refuge *par excellence* in the far west.

Ironically, the coming of the railway disrupted the tranquillity of this pastoral idyll, for it brought a new townsite and all of the other trappings of civilization common to the urban frontier. Women arrived from France to join their husbands; general stores and other essential services, such as schools and churches, were established at Trochu; and even sports became institutionalized in the Sports Days after 1907. The community ultimately lost its French homogeneity as it was opened to the outer world with the arrival of the Grand Trunk Pacific in 1911, which resulted in the gradual departure of the French settlers. The coming of World War I in 1914 spelled the final end to the officer class that had formed the backbone of the Trochu colony, for most returned to serve in their former regiments, and their sons often enlisted in the British or American armed services.

A contrast in abortive French communities prior to 1914 was the democratic-socialist experiment attempted not far from Red Deer, at Sylvan Lake, in 1906. Although little is known of this community, it was apparently inspired by the abortive coal miners' strikes in the Lille-Vieux Condé region of northern France in 1905. Routed by Belgian strike breakers and French regiments of *cuirassiers*, several of these miners and other townspeople banded together under the direction of one Dr. Tanche of Lille to project a socialist colony in the new world. Attracted by the ubiquitous advertising of the CPR land advertisements and the possibility of coalescing a few homesteads into a village settlement, they set out in the winter of 1906–07 to establish a model community that would consist initially of machinists, carpenters, a blacksmith, baker, butcher, seamstress, cook, musician, poet, doctor, and druggist.[38]

Economic difficulties beset the colony almost as soon as it began. The intermediary sent to secure homesteads failed in his mission , and the cattle that he purchased froze to death in the winter of 1907. Farming on a collective basis proved impossible on the marshy land of Burnt Lake, and gradually its members began to desert to homesteads of their own, or to return gradually to France. Co-operative business ventures such as the sawmill proved unworkable when the Sylvan colony failed to secure a stable external market and lost much of its stockpile in floods along the Red Deer River. Finally the leader of the colony, Dr. Tanche, suffered a stroke in 1911 while trying to break the unyielding prairie sod, and died back in France while visiting his brother in 1917. The query that his son, the chronicler of the colony, raised concerning the lack of communitarian ideals by the membership of the colony speaks volumes for the curious admixture of motives that destroyed this socialist commonwealth: "It seems rather than trying to develop a socialist colony, they tried to become rich overnight, the riches of communal lives, of getting along together, of understanding one another as a steppingstone to future greater endeavours, seemed to have been marked by an insane desire to get rich quick, something alien to the country. Does an intellectual produce the best leadership?"[39]

Another common social impulse to nineteenth-century reform utopias was alcoholic temperance, which inspired at least one industrial utopia in England founded in the 1850s by Titus Salt near Leeds. The model community of "Saltaire" warned at its boundary that "ALL BEER ABANDON YE THAT ENTER HERE," since its founders believed that drink and lust were at the root of all urban social evil. And others such as the "Cosme" colony of English workingmen in Paraguay were clearly founded in the early 1890s by William Lane in the anticipation that it would be a dry workingman's paradise in the new world.[40] American frontier utopianism was similarly inspired by the prospect of a temperate haven in the wilderness for the degraded masses of the industrial city. Part of Horace Greeley's fascination for Fourier's socialist phalanasteries was inspired by his strong teetotalling convictions, and the prohibition of alcoholic beverages became a central feature of many American frontier communes.

It is in this context that the short-lived Temperance Colony of Saskatoon can be seen as a form of frontier social escape prompted by the temperance movement of late nineteenth-century Toronto. As Bruce Peel has noted in *Saskatoon Story*: "The idea of a colony founded for moral or religious reasons was not unique in the history of the North American frontier: cheap land and isolation had always beckoned reformers seeking sites for their utopias. However, Saskatoon was probably the only frontier colony founded on temperance principles alone."[41] Spurred by a massive publicity campaign endorsed by Toronto merchants, the Sons of

Temperance, the Odd Fellows, and the Methodist Church, the organizers attracted Principal Grant of Queen's University as their speaker at the Toronto Exhibition and Stampede in September, 1881. The Temperance Colonization Society subsequently received over three thousand signatures in support of their application for nearly two million acres of prairie land. The inevitable joint-stock company was formed with a grandiose capitalization of two million dollars, divided into twenty thousand shares valued at one hundred dollars each, to take advantage of the recent order-in-council permitting large land sales to such colonization companies.

A classic pioneer trek to the promised land was in the making, complete with the trying prelude of a wagon-journey of 150 miles out of Moose Jaw, which was the end of steel in the fall of 1883. The founding of a village of virtue in the wilderness was enshrined in the constitution of the Temperance Colony Pioneer Society, the preamble of which declared its communal purpose as "the discussion of matters pertaining to the welfare of settlers, mutual counsel, the dissemination of useful knowledge, and social intercourse." Among some of its first discussions were the establishment of essential services, but also included were some cosmopolitan digressions into climate, tariffs, socialism, and physiology. Indicative of the community penetration of decision-making was the successful passage of a resolution in March of 1885 that the settlers should not flee to Moose Jaw because of the impending Métis rebellion but should calmly attend to their "usual avocations." It appeared to win popular favour, for the sporting diversions planned for Dominion Day appeared more important than either agriculture or the rebellion, and one veteran of Middleton's army later reminisced that the last time he had seen cricket played was in July, 1885 in Saskatoon!

Ultimate abandonment of the settlement did not follow, as was the norm with many similar utopian experiments, but only because the Temperance Colony was saved from extinction by the Qu'Appelle Long Lake and Saskatchewan Railway, completed in 1890. All told it had only attracted 101 settlers, for which the society received 100,000 acres from the Dominion government. In common with most other communitarian joint-stock ventures, its successes were in community and cultural services such as schools and recreation or the community-owned ferry and telephone service, and its failures were in such business ventures as the steamboat and sawmill enterprises. Even its efforts at community social discipline proved less viable on the frontier than in urban Toronto, for internal factional disputes soon wracked the colony and called the enforcement of the temperance pledges by the society into question. The prospect of moral compulsion even upon an issue that united most of the colonists proved impossible of success with the availability of economic and social opportunity in the nearby frontier.

Other efforts at establishing temperance-oriented co-operatives among the Scandinavian groups in the West were more successful initially, although they too eventually suffered a similar fate. British Columbia appeared to attract a wide variety of such temperance-inspired experiments, particularly among the Norwegians and the Finns, although several co-operative Scandinavian settlements such as New Finland and Thingvalla (Icelandic) sprang up in the late 1880s in the Qu'Appelle Valley of Saskatchewan.[42] As a recent study of the Scandinavians in British Columbia has indicated, the banning of spirituous liquor was "a theme which was to be perpetuated in the temperance societies which were an important feature of the community life of all Scandinavian groups."[43] The membership of the Bella Coola colony of Norwegians, founded in the 1890s by Reverend Christian Saugstad, demanded that its members give evidence of "good moral character and working ability." The prospect of a dry haven in the wilderness seemed particularly appealing to a group of well-to-do Norwegians of Minneapolis, as indeed it seemed to many other Scandinavian groups, who were being evangelized against the demon drink throughout the urban frontiers of Wisconsin and Minnesota.[44] Another group of Norwegians from Minneapolis was attracted to nearby Quatsino Narrows with the prospect of establishing a logging co-operative, but it grew to only 125 settlers and gradually declined after the turn of the century. The Bella Coola settlement proved more self-sufficient and economically successful, probably because it had more capital to begin with, but the co-operative ideal dissipated there as well, and it soon hived off into other colonies. Their main distinguishing feature was their Norwegian ancestry and success at free-enterprise occupations such as fishing, construction, the skilled trades, and professions.

The much-discussed radical-socialist features of the Finnish utopia "Sojntula" on Malcolm Island need only be discussed in general here. As J. Donald Wilson has noted, Sojntula, in common with other Scandinavian settlements "was characterized by virtual isolation, a homogeneous ethnic population, a desire to escape from 'civilization' and government supervision, and a determination to control the education of their children."[45] Thus social escape, particularly from the precarious existence in the mines of Vancouver Island, operated as a primary impulse to this Finnish island commune. The founders invited the Finnish socialist intellectual Matti Kurikka from Australia, where he had founded a similar utopian colony in Queensland. Convinced that drunkenness had ruined the Queensland experiment, he married temperance to his radical anti-clericalism as the twin ideals of the British Columbia colony. Thus, neither churches nor liquor were to be allowed in Sojntula. Otherwise the colony was organized along similar lines to other co-operative colonization companies, with common shares, and communal business undertakings based upon a common wage-labour rate of a dollar a day plus board.[46]

In brief, the company collapsed within four years of its inception in 1901. In common with other utopian ventures, the Kalevan Kansan Colonization Association proved highly successful as a cultural arm but uncommonly poor in pursuing its business undertakings. Its initial lumbering and fishing operations yielded little revenue, and the colony experienced several subsequent disasters such as the fire of 1903 that caused $10,000 in damages. As a result, the colony declined rapidly in numbers, approaching 250 in 1903 when Kurikka himself departed, and fought desperately to liquidate its mounting debts, which were finally too great to overcome when a $3,000 bridge-building contract in 1904 failed to recoup even its equipment costs. There were also strong challenges within the community to Kurikka's peculiar views on marriage and free love, much as there had been in 1879 with John Humphrey Noyes, the leader of the utopian colony at Oneida, New York. No doubt Kurikka's premature departure had as much to do with suspicion of his mismanagement of the colony's funds as with the moral outrage he had created by challenging traditional Victorian shibboleths surrounding monogamy. Intellectual schism also emerged from the Marxian left-wing elements in the colony, led by A. B. Makela, which regarded Kurikka and his faction as hopelessly utopian "windbags and fanatics" incapable of realizing their ideals. Ultimately the schismatics left to establish their own colony in the Fraser Valley, which also ended, as the Island colony did, in settlement dispersal and reversion to a series of individual family farms.

Elements of utopianism may also be seen in the early history of sectarian religious groups that established community experiments designed to achieve social perfection. In this respect, the early history of the Mormon experiment in southern Alberta, and the early Doukhobor settlements in eastern Saskatchewan were atypical to those abortive utopias described above in that they ultimately survived, although in somewhat altered forms of social and economic organization. Their survival was, however, connected more to the commitment mechanisms usually found in the communitarian religious sects, the most successful of which in western Canada were the Hutterites and Mennonites. Strong restrictions on membership, powerful ideological commitment, asceticism, and charismatic leadership were all characteristic of such sectarian movements. Indeed, their pre-adaptation to rural life and agriculture made them distinctly unlike their urban utopian counterparts in their capacity to survive economically as well as culturally. Yet despite their ultimate success at group survival, early elements in their economic and social organization and group ideology had certain overtones of utopian idealism, which were subsequently altered by the successful adaptation of the sect to frontier life.

The Mormon experience in the western United States has in fact been described by Leonard J. Arrington as inspired by communitarian ideals and a pragmatic and open concept of membership. As he explains: "Group economic self-sufficiency was the hallmark of Mormon policy on the Great Basin frontier. Above all, co-operative economic endeavour, which played such an important role through the history of the church, was to a large extent an outgrowth of this ideal economic system, or of the same ethic which produced it."[47] What is perhaps doubly important from the point of view of the Canadian Mormon experience was that it became a social fragment of the American experience during a phase of conscious de-theocratization occasioned by the *Edmunds Act* of 1882, which established heavy penalties against polygamy.[48] That year also conformed with the end of the Mormon boycott of Gentile stores, thus creating a boom period of business formation outside of ecclesiastically sponsored co-operatives. The diaspora to Canada thus occurred in a period of forceful assimilation of American economic and social values, and the flight northward may be seen as a form of conservative social escape to preserve the integral socio-economic features of their culture.

Several distinctive aspects of early community settlement in the Cardston area mark the Mormon settlements as an attempt to restore a past state of social perfection. First was the appeal in 1887 to Edgar Dewdney, minister of the interior, by Francis Lyman, John Taylor, and Charles Ora Card, to recognize polygamous marriages to that point.[49] Failing this, polygamous practices were defended by the Mormon convert from British Columbia, A. Maitland Stenhouse, when he came to

Cardston in 1888. Urging the citizens of Lethbridge and Fort Macleod to adopt polygamy, he noted with sociological precision: "Polygamy secures a husband for every woman that wants one, giving her a large stock to select from, and by division of labour, it also ensures better supervision and kinder treatment for the rising generation."[50] Other aspects of conscious ideological design on social organization were more visible than the clandestine polygamy that followed in the nineties. The nuclear farming village modelled roughly on the millennialist Plat of Zion with centrally located public buildings, temple, and storehouses was consciously favoured by C. O. Card and John Taylor. The square-grid pattern of block settlement became the standard form of community plan in the first ten years of Mormon settlement, thus imposing the town plan of settlement used in eighteenth-century New England.

The co-operative economic organizations sponsored by the Cardston Company, which applied for a charter from the governor of the North-West Territories in 1890, was a central economic feature of early Mormon settlement in southern Alberta.[51] A number of successful economic institutions in Cardston were financed by the Cardston Company and organized and supervised by the leaders of the church. The degree of their commitment in this early co-operative phase was apparent in times of depression and monetary scarcity in the early nineties, when C. O. Card signed his name to paper scrip that circulated freely among the Saints. And, when prosperity returned in 1895, the Cardston Company paid a forty-percent dividend, half in cash and half in goods.[52]

It was only after 1895 and the organization of the Alberta Stake and the sale of 600,000 acres of land by Card and Taylor to the Church in Salt Lake City that the economic self-sufficiency of this pioneer co-operative enterprise began to break down. Further signs of economic and institutional integration appeared with the first issue of the Cardston *Record* in 1898, and the creation of the first branch of the Bank of Montreal in the same year. With the inception of the large-scale irrigation project in 1898, the community became even more dependent upon its larger economic connections with Salt Lake City, which sponsored the labour costs in building the St. Mary's canal and found capital in England to back the large-scale project. Further capital penetration followed in 1901 with the investments of Jesse Knight, a wealthy Utah industrialist who began sugar beet production and invested widely in milling and elevator companies near Raymond and Lethbridge. Whether coincidental or not, community plans for the new farming villages after 1898 also reflected greater deviation from the square-grid Plat of Zion, reaching their most unorthodox with Apostle John Taylor's radial street plan for the town of Raymond, which he reputedly borrowed from Paris![53] Taylor's openly avowed practice of polygamy and his excommunication by Salt Lake City in 1904 was also an index of the increased direct control exercised by orthodox elements in the American church over this small Canadian fragment of Mormonism. The community itself was submerged demographically with the wave of American migration into southern Alberta after 1898, and the small community of Cardston, which numbered about a thousand, was rapidly absorbed by the new farming villages such as Caldwell, Stirling, Raymond, and Taber, which mushroomed around it.[54] A common Canadian-American frontier had by 1905 absorbed this small pocket of sectarian utopianism and its brief attempt to establish a self-sufficient community of Saints in southern Alberta.

Several sects and cults would follow into southern Alberta in the next decade, such as the Dreamers, the latter of which visited their peculiar notions of charismatic occultism, inspirational dreams, and occasional pyromania upon the farmers of the Medicine Hat region in 1907–08. The American "Sharpites" or "Adamites" who followed next in the summer of 1908 were subsequently denied entry to Alberta by immigration agents. They must have wondered at the claim of their leader James Sharpe, who claimed to be Christ and had personally led his band of twelve on a special mission to the Saskatchewan Doukhobors only to be rejected by Peter Verigin, who had his own claims in that direction. Subsequent vigilance at Alberta border crossings militated against further incursions of any other charismatic sects of this kind, which might disturb the fragile social peace of southern Alberta.[55]

The Doukhobors themselves present a fascinating case study in sectarian utopianism. While their movement has attracted much historical interest and voluminous scholarship, several salient utopian features in their group ideology might be mentioned. In the first instance, the communitarian outlook of the Doukhobors was the extrinsic object of admiration among late-nineteenth-century British idealists, utopians, and anarchists who came to sponsor their migration to Canada. The role of J. C. Kenworthy and the anarchist colony at Purleigh is occasionally neglected in the Doukhobor chronicle. Kenworthy was a conscious disciple of Carlyle, Ruskin, and Henry George (and critic of Marxian socialism), and a strong exponent of the utopian rural communes that had been established in nineteenth-century America. He promoted similar ventures in England such as the English Land Colonization Society in 1893 for middle and lower-class people seeking escape from the city. In 1894 he formed a Brotherhood Church in Croydon, which was economically based on fruit-growing, and socially centred about five o'clock tea. Kenworthy's magazine, the *New Order*, printed by the Brotherhood Publishing Company, soon reported on communitarian experiments across the world, and it was this venture that brought him in 1896 to Russia and into contact with Leo Tolstoy and the Doukhobors.[56] In fact, it was from Kenworthy's visit that Peter Verigin, the Doukhobor teacher, borrowed the concept of the "Brotherhood Church" for his own putative sect "The Christian Community of Universal Brotherhood."[57] And it was Kenworthy and other Tolstoyans, such as J. Bruce Wallace, Aylmer Maude, Vladimir Tchertkoff (Chertkov), and Prince D. A. Hilkoff, who lent the moral and material support of the Purleigh garden colony in Essex to the migration of the Doukhobors to Cyprus and to Canada in 1899. Over one thousand pounds was raised for their transportation to western Canada, and a young Tolstoyan teacher from the Purleigh colony, Herbert Archer, was sent to instruct the Doukhobor colony at Swan River in Saskatchewan.

Once in Canada, the Doukhobors established highly successful communal colonies in eastern Saskatchewan, which have been described at length in the rich historical literature on such settlements at Thunder Hill, Swan River, and Yorkton. Perhaps these village communities on the prairies, which were broadly based and ideologically pluralistic, might be considered less consciously utopian in character than the communities established by Verigin and the CCUB in southern British Columbia from 1908 to 1917. An analysis of the spatial structure of Doukhobor communal architecture by F. M. Mealing at Brilliant demonstrates a sharp departure from the traditional Russian *mir* characteristic of the Saskatchewan colonies and the appearance "of a wholly novel material expression of the social ideal of Communalism … drawing equally upon Russian and North American traditions, and upon an innovative complex, the Community Village."[58] More insular and tightly organized, they combined large dormitories with industrial and administrative buildings such as saw mills, canning works, office, and warehouse buildings, and a community meeting hall. It is this unique village life-style that Woodcock and Avakumovic also describe as a utopian spatial organization and material culture most consciously resembling the Phalansterian and Icarian colonies of mid-nineteenth-century America.[59]

But the Doukhobor experiments probably succeeded more because of their social character as charismatic millenarian movements and less because of their utopian-anarchist ideology, and because they were rural not city people. Classic resistance mechanisms of the sect also made them ultimately impervious to social leadership from the outside, as is indicated by the failure of Herbert Archer and the persistent Quaker teachers to penetrate the communities in Saskatchewan. Verigin himself conformed more to the ideal type of messianic-charismatic leader typical of millenarian movements – at least in Saskatchewan – although he appeared to mute somewhat the oriental deference he demanded in the Second Community. But his claims to miraculous birth and near divinity separated Verigin's universal Christianity from the utopian tradition that usually outlines a plan of what is possible through human effort rather than dependence on divine plan and revelation.[60]

The abortive utopia was thus a common mirage in the vanishing landscape of the pioneering West. This first generation of early western settlement was inspired by a common desire to escape the social confines of the late-nineteenth-century city and the broader national and imperial controls that characterized European and North American polity. In classical utopian terms, their common urge appeared to be rooted in a desire for a pastoral social condition in which work and leisure would be equally complemented in nature. The term "pastoral capitalism," which Soviet historians pejoratively applied to the Doukhobor experiment in universal brotherhood, might profitably be applied to the abortive utopias above, for their ideological derivation was more often in liberal-anarchism than in utopian socialism.[61] The persistent acknowledgment of their intellectual debt to the pastoral ideals of Ruskin, Carlyle, and Morris reveal common roots in nineteenth-century British idealism. The ideals of social co-operation and of work as a creative act of self-fulfilment, and the concept of the garden city were all essential components of these strains of late-century liberal-imperial thought, which shaped the Anglo-Canadian mentality of the early Northwest before World War I.

Northrop Frye's interesting analysis of literary utopias makes an observation that also helps explain the significant role of the Scandinavians as perhaps the most prominent of the ethnic groups to establish utopian community experiments. He notes that William Morris's concept of artisan manufacture came close to a Scandinavian ideal of craftsmanship and the simplification of human wants.[62] Indeed, it appears that the short-lived utopias established on the Pacific coast were attempts by the Danes, Norwegians, and Finns to recapture that simplified rural life as a response to the first contacts with North American cities in the midwestern United States. In this respect, the Kalevan Kansan Association's identification of the Finnish settlement as "Sojntula," literally translates as the "People of Kaleva." They were the ancient Finns as described in the national epic poem the *Kalevala*. Archaism was a central theme in recapturing pastoral innocence and readily derived from the utopian literature of Scandinavia as well as Anglo-Saxon folklore. Indeed the common rooting of the co-operative idea in both the political culture of Britain and the Scandinavian countries, particularly Denmark, was to have a profound impact on the later development of the Canadian West in the 1920s and 1930s.

It might be ventured as a closing hypothesis that pastoral utopianism and the theme of economic failure and settlement abandonment was a dominant aspect of the first phase of western settlement. Whether aristocratic or democratic, liberal-anarchist, communist or socialist, the utopian experiments were a necessary pastoral phase in the pioneer development of the West. For if nothing else, the frontier phase of development provided ample mistakes from its misplaced dreams and aspirations of unknown space and indeterminate time. The second generation of settlement that followed the war would develop a collective agrarian ideology that was more comprehensive and totalitarian in its organization of co-operative production and consumption. Ironically, the militaristic social commonwealth that E. A. Partridge would conjure in his *War on Poverty* in 1925 was a far cry from the fervent Ruskinian ethics and co-operative brotherhood that inspired his attacks on the corporate giants in 1905.[63] Perhaps even Partridge would have admitted that the naïve experiments and lost causes of the first generation contributed to the realities of economic co-operation in the second, and may even have been more humane.

NOTES

1 Frank Manuel, ed., *Utopias and Utopian Thought* (Cambridge: Riverside Press, 1966), introduction; Rosabeth Moss Kanter, *Commitment and Community: Communes and Utopias in a Sociological Perspective* (Cambridge, MA: Harvard University Press, 1972).

2 See, for example: W. L. Morton, "A Century of Plain and Parkland," *Alberta Historical Review* 17, no. 2 (Spring 1969): 6; "The Social Philosophy of Henry Wise Wood, The Canadian Agrarian Leader," *Agricultural History* 22 (April 1948): 114–23; Carl Berger, "A Canadian Utopia: The Cooperative Commonwealth of Edward Partridge," in Stephen Clarkson, ed., *Visions 2020* (Edmonton: Hurtig, 1970), 257–62; George Woodcock, "Harmony Island: A Canadian Utopia," in R. E. Walters, *British Columbia: A Centennial Anthology* (Toronto: McClelland and Stewart, 1958), 206–13.

3 See J. Warkentin, "Steppe, Desert and Empire," in A. W. Rasporich and Henry C. Klassen, eds., *Prairie Perspectives 2* (Toronto: Holt, Rinehart and Winston, 1973), 102–36; and for the American West in literature, Henry Nash Smith, *The Virgin Land: The American West as Symbol and Myth* (New York: Vintage, 1950).

4 These terms commonly employed in descriptions of the utopian genre in literature are contained specifically in E. A. Partridge's *War on Poverty: The One War that Can End War* (Winnipeg: Wallingford Press, 1925), 130.

5 Norman Macdonald, *Canada, Immigration and Colonization, 1841–1903* (Toronto: Macmillan, 1970), chap. 5, 235–57; W. A. Corrothers, *Emigration from the British Isles* (London: 1929); Stanley C. Johnson, *A History of Emigration from the United Kingdom to North America, 1763–1912* (London: 1913).

6 Stephen Leacock, *My Discovery of the West* (London: John Lane, 1937), 278–304.

7 Robert Stead, *Dennison Grant: A Novel of To-day* (Toronto: Musson, 1920), 270–77.

8 See J.R.A. Pollard, "Railways and Land Settlement, 1881–91," *Saskatchewan History* 1, no. 2 (May 1948): 16–19.

9 Frederik L. Polak, *The Image of the Future* (Leyden: A. W. Seythoff, 1961), vol. 1, 357–68.

10 *University of Saskatchewan Archives*, Cannington Manor, MSS, C555/2/14.11, no. 20; "Old Cannington Manor," by Irr. W. LXXIII, May 22, 1927, written by Fred Kidd, 2, typescript.

11 A.E.M. Hewlett, "The Manorless Manor of Cannington," *The Producing News*, 1960, 15–22; from clippings file, *University of Saskatchewan Archives*, MSS, C555/2/14.14. Morton, 7pp., *University of Saskatchewan Archives*, MSS, C555/2/14/ll,no. 16.

12 Fred Kidd reminiscence, op. cit., ff. 10. See also C. Evelyn Sheldon-Williams, "Chronicles of Cannington Manor" (Regina, September15, 1938), ms. copy for A. S.

13 *University of Saskatchewan Archives*, A.E.M. Hewlett Collection, MSS, C555/2/14.15, no. 7, "Life of Old Cannington Village," 3.

14 Ibid., A.E.M. Hewlett, "Old Cannington Manor, N.W.T., An Experiment in English Colonization," MSS, C555/2/14.15, no. 15 (b).

15 Gilbert Johnson, "The Harmony Industrial Association: A Pioneer Co-operative," *Saskatchewan History* 4, no. 1 (Winter 1951): 11–21. See also D. S. Spafford, "Independent Politics in Saskatchewan before the Nonpartisan League," *Saskatchewan History* 18, no. 1 (Winter 1965): 4–6.

16 *Saskatchewan Archives, University of Regina*, "Prospectus of the Harmony Industrial Association (Co-operative System)" (Birtle Printing Co., Beulah, Manitoba [1895]), 4.

17 Ibid.

18 Gilbert Johnson, "The Harmony Industrial Association," 15.

19 E. A. Partridge, *A War on Poverty* (Winnipeg: Wallingford Press, 1925).

20 Northrop Frye, "Varieties of Literary Utopias," in F. Manuel, ed., *Utopias and Utopian Thought*, 48–50.

21 W. C. Pollard, *Pioneering in the Prairie West: A Sketch of the Parry Sound Colonies* (Toronto: Thomas Nelson, 1926), 7.

22 W. C. Pollard, *Life on the Frontier: A Sketch of the Parry Sound Colonies That Settled near Edmonton N.W.T. in the Early Nineties* (London: Arthur Stockwell, 1931).

23 Patrick Dunae, "The Popularisation of the Canadian West among British Youth: 1890–1914," unpublished paper delivered to the Canadian Historical Association, Edmonton, June 1975.

24 Eric J. Holmgren, "Isaac M. Barr and the Britannia Colony," Master's thesis, University of Alberta, 1964, 52. Citation from Isaac Barr, *British Settlements in Northwestern Canada on Free Grant Lands* (London: 1902).

25 Barr, *British Settlements*, 18.

26 C. Wetton, *The Promised Land: The Story of the Barr Colonists* (Lloydminster Times, 1953), 48–49.

27 See Betty L. Sung, *Mountain of Gold: The Story of the Chinese in America* (New York: Macmillan, 1967); Kenneth O. Bjork, *West of the Great Divide: Norwegian Migration to the Pacific Coast, 1847–93* (Northfield, MN: Norwegian-American Historical Association, 1958), chap. 2, "Argonauts in California," 22–73.

28 J. Hanna McCormick, *Lloydminster, or 5,000 Miles with the Barr Colonists* (London: Drane's, 1924), 248–49.

29 Typical early examples would include: E. Hepple-Hall, *Lands of Plenty: British North America for Health, Sport and Profit* (London: W. H. Alien, 1879); British Columbia: Its Position, Advantages, Resources and Climate (CPR pamphlet, 1904).

30 *Potential Riches of British Columbia* (British American Trust, 1907), 11–19.

31 J. T. Redmayne, *Fruit Farming on the "Dry Belt" of British Columbia* (London: The Times Book Club, 1909); J. T. Bealby, *Fruit Ranching in B.C.* (London: A. & C. Black, 1909), 2–196.

32 Nelson A. Riis, "The Walhachin Myth: A Study in Settlement Abandonment," *B.C. Studies*, no. 17 (1973): 3–25; "Settlement Abandonment: A Case Study of Walhachin, B.C.," *Urban History Review* no. 2 (June 1972): 19–24. See also Kathleen Munro, "The Tragedy of Walhachin," *Canadian Cattleman* 18, no. 1 (May 1955): 7–31.

33 A.E.M. Hewlett, "France on the Prairies," *The Beaver* (March 1954): 3–8.

34 John Hawkes, *The Story of Saskatchewan and its People* (Chicago: S. J. Clark, 1924), vol. 2, 937–46.

35 Sheilagh S. Jameson, "The Story of Trochu," *Alberta Historical Review* 9, no. 4 (Autumn 1961): 1–10.

36 P. A. Shandro, "The French Settlers at Trochu, 1903–14," Master's thesis, McGill University, 1974, 30.

37 *Glenbow-Alberta Archives, Paul de Beaudrap Diary* (microfilm), entries for January, February, 1906.

38 *Glenbow-Alberta Archives*, John Tanche, "Reminiscences and Biography of Tanche Family, Sylvan Lake, Alberta, 1906–16," 1–2.

39 Ibid., 6.

40 W.H.G. Armytage, *Heavens Below: Utopian Experiments in England, 1560–1960* (Toronto: University of Toronto Press, 1961), 252–54, 359–69.

41 Bruce Peel, *The Saskatoon Story, 1882–1952* (Saskatoon: 1952), 9.

42 See, e.g., W. J. Lindal, *The Saskatchewan Icelanders* (Winnipeg: Columbia Press, 1955), 82–88; Gilbert Johnson, "The New Finland Colony," *Saskatchewan History* 15, no. 2 (Spring 1962): 69–72.

43 John Norris, *Strangers Entertained: A History of the Ethnic Groups of British Columbia* (Vancouver: Evergreen Press, 1971), 127.

44 John Kolehmainen and George Hill, *Haven in the Woods: The Story of the Finns in Wisconsin* (Madison, WI: State Historical Society of Wisconsin, 1965), 113–18, 156–60.

45 J. D. Wilson, "Matti Kurikka: Finnish-Canadian Intellectual," *B.C. Studies* 20 (Winter 1973–74): 65.
46 John Kolehmainen, "Harmony Island: A Finnish Utopian Venture in British Columbia," *B.C. Historical Quarterly* 5, no. 2 (1941): 114.
47 Leonard J. Arrington, "Early Mormon Communitarianism," *Western Humanities Review* 7 (Autumn 1953): 341–69.
48 Leonard J. Arrington, "Crisis in Identity: Mormon Responses in the Nineteenth and Twentieth Centuries," in Marvin S. Hill, *Mormonism and American Culture* (New York: Harper and Row, 1972), 171.
49 Cited in Carlana Bartlett, "Early Mormon Settlement in Alberta," honours thesis, Lakehead University, 1973, 43.
50 Ibid., pp. 46–47. Citation of *Macleod Gazette*, December 26, 1888.
51 Ibid., 58.
52 *A History of the Mormon Church in Canada* (Lethbridge: Stake, 1968), 57.
53 J. Lehr, "Mormon Settlement Morphology in Southern Alberta," *Alberta Geographer*, 8 (1972), pp.6-13.
54 See C. A. Dawson, *Group Settlement: Ethnic Communities in Western Canada*, vol. VII (Toronto: Macmillan, 1936), "Mormon Settlement Process," 205–13.
55 See Howard Palmer, "Responses to Foreign Immigration: Nativism and Ethnic Tolerance, 1880–1920," Master's thesis, University of Alberta, 1971.
56 W.H.G. Armytage, *Heavens Below*, chap. 5, "The Tolstoyan Communities," 342–58.
57 George Woodcock and Ivan Avakumovic, *The Doukhobors* (London: Faber and Faber, 1968), 96.
58 F. M. Mealing, "Canadian Doukhobor Architecture: A Conspectus," unpublished manuscript, paper presented to the Canadian Society for the Study of Architecture, June 1975, Edmonton, 14.
59 Woodcock and Avakumovic, *The Doukhobors*, 234–36.
60 F. Manuel, ed., *Utopias and Utopian Thought*, p. 70; Frederik L. Polak, *Image of the Future*, 407, 437; Michael Barkun, "Law and Social Revolution: Millenarianism and the Legal System," paper delivered to the American Political Science Association, Los Angeles, 1970.
61 Woodcock and Avakumovic, *The Doukhobors*, 275.
62 Northrop Frye, "Varieties of Literary Utopias," in F. Manuel, ed., *Utopias*, 25–50.
63 See W. A. Mackintosh, *Agricultural Co-operation in Western Canada* (Kingston: Queen's University; Toronto: Ryerson Press, 1924), 18–21.

7

"LAND I CAN OWN": SETTLING IN THE PROMISED LAND

Bill Waiser

"There was one good thing – we were all in the same boat."[1] That's how Danish immigrant N. K. Neilson nostalgically summed up his homesteading days in the Robsart area in southwestern Saskatchewan in the early twentieth century. He was not alone in his assessment. One of the more popular myths of Saskatchewan history is that the pioneer story was largely a common experience; settlers not only faced the same challenges, but had to contend with similar problems in the struggle to succeed. The actual homesteading record, however, greatly varied from period to period, from region to region, and from settler to settler. Staying on the land and meeting the homestead requirements came at a terrible human cost that many were not willing to pay, especially those without partners or families. Nor was it an egalitarian frontier. Some settlers were clearly better off than others, while most women were deliberately barred from taking up homestead land. What they all shared, though, was the desire to turn dreams into reality, to become something – if not themselves, then their children. "The real divide," one western historian has argued, "was the line that divided past from future – the line of hope, and ... it seemed to stretch into infinity."[2]

If Canadian immigration literature in the early twentieth century was to be believed, Saskatchewan was the land of opportunity. The new province had two things that gave it an edge over other Canadian destinations: good farmland and lots of it. One popular guide even boasted that "all that is needed is a mere scratching of the soil" to bring the virgin prairie under cultivation.[3] This image of Saskatchewan as an agricultural wonderland captured the popular imagination in much the same way as did the Klondike gold discovery only a few years earlier. Tens of thousands of people, many of them with little or no experience in farming, headed to the province to stake their claim to a new beginning. Kristian Askeland left his Ontario home for the same reason: "It was the alluring news of ... the 'new world' to the west ... that moved me to cut the ties with people, home and mother country."[4] English-born Anthony Tyson travelled to Neidpath in 1912 in search of "land I can own,"[5] while nurse Lena Bacon, a Nebraskan widow with a young daughter, was attracted by "the freedom of a great new country with no fences to hold one in. It was a place to give birth to one's own dreams."[6] Maritimer R. W. Sansom, working as a harvester near Souris, Manitoba, in the fall of 1905, was constantly being told by the other hired hands about the homesteads waiting for them in Saskatchewan. "That's all you could hear morning, noon, and night," he reminisced, "and if that old separator stopped for five minutes (which it didn't very often) they would have a sod shack half built.... After working and sleeping with those men for forty days and nights I began to get infected with the disease myself."[7] Sansom applied for land near Rosetown that December.

What enticed these and other settlers to Saskatchewan was the prospect of owning 160 acres of free land. These homesteads were a central feature of the federal government's Dominion Lands policy. Rejecting the traditional river-lot system that the Métis had used along the Red and Assiniboine rivers in present-day Manitoba for over half a century, Ottawa decided in April 1871 to copy the successful American system and adopted a grid pattern based on six-square-mile townships of thirty-six equal sections (640 acres or one square mile). Teams of Dominion Lands surveyors began working that summer and by the end of 1887 had measured an incredible 70 million acres. The survey crews were able to proceed at a steady and accurate pace because the same uniform grid was employed throughout the region, regardless of local soil and climatic conditions. It was simply assumed that most of the land was suited for agriculture. Their work was also less subject to mistake because the system, based on astronomical observation, completely ignored the natural contours of the land in favour of an artificial, standard checkerboard ordering. The only major adjustments were "correction lines," made necessary by the gradual northern convergence of meridians. Once the system was in place, the location of a homestead anywhere in the North-West proved a relatively straightforward matter.[8]

Dominion Lands policy was designed to satisfy several purposes. Each township contained thirty-six one-square-mile sections, which in turn were subdivided in quarter sections. Most of the even-numbered sections in each township (the numbering commenced in the lower right or southeast corner) were to be used for homesteads. All but two of the odd-numbered sections, on the other hand, were reserved as "railway lands." Sections 11 and 29, designated as school lands, were to support local educational needs, while sections 8 and three-quarters of 26 were turned over to the Hudson's Bay Company as part of the 1869 land transfer agreement that gave Canada control over Rupert's Land. Ottawa intended to use the railway sections to encourage railroad construction in the western interior; railway companies would be offered huge land grants if they built lines to and through the region. But the setting aside of railway reserves in every township served to disperse homestead lands and thereby increase the isolation of the pioneer farmer. Until these land grants were actually taken up by the company, moreover, railway reserves remained closed to settlement. Even though the CPR, for example, signed a deal with the Canadian government in 1881 and completed the transcontinental line just four years later, it was extremely slow to select the 25 million acres specified in its contract with the federal government. Other railway companies and their subsidiaries were equally tardy in choosing their land. This situation rankled Clifford Sifton, especially since the lands would be needed for the expected flood of settlers, and he lost little time after becoming federal minister of the interior in 1896 in seeing that the railways applied for their outstanding land grants. Curiously, Saskatchewan supplied almost half of the 29 million acres claimed by the railways, even though less than 25 per cent of the lines were built in the province. Ontario and British Columbia, by contrast, provided no railway land.[9]

Anyone, excluding Indians, who wanted to file for a homestead in 1905 had to be male, eighteen years old, and prepared to become a British subject, if not one already. Women who were the sole head of a family – in other words, a widow or divorcée with dependants – were also eligible to apply.[10] To secure their land, prospective homesteaders had to visit the nearest Dominion Lands office, choose their 160 acres, or quarter section, and pay a ten-dollar registration fee. This procedure sounds simple but there was no shortage of pandemonium when new areas were opened up to homesteading, especially during the boom years in the early twentieth century. Some even waited outside the office all night to get a particular parcel of land. Settlers could send someone else on their behalf to file for their homestead, but they had to be on their land within six months of application.

To secure title or what was called "patent" to their quarter section, homesteaders had to meet certain basic requirements by the end of three years: they had to live on the land for six months each year, erect a shelter, and cultivate at least fifteen acres. Raising twenty head of cattle and constructing a barn for the animals was an acceptable alternative. These duties might not seem too onerous, but many a settler was defeated by them. Two out of every five homestead applications in the three prairie provinces between 1871 and 1930 were cancelled; the failure rate actually climbed above 50 per cent during the last two decades of the program.[11] Perhaps Englishman W. C. Pollard put it best when he suggested that homesteading was "a gamble in which the entrant bets ten dollars with the Government against 160 acres of land that he can stay on it ... for three years *without starving*."[12] Those who managed to survive and secure their patent could purchase an adjoining quarter section, known as a "preemption," at three dollars per acre; title to the land required an additional three years residence and another fifteen acres under cultivation.[13] Or they could buy railway land. The railway reserves proved an unexpected blessing by providing successful farmers with the opportunity to expand their land holdings. By 1903, an estimated 50 per cent of the homesteaders in Assiniboia had purchased adjoining railway land.[14]

Prospective homesteaders could expect only minimal assistance from the Canadian government, such as temporary accommodation in immigration sheds or help in locating land. Ottawa generally did no more once people were on their homesteads. Certainly there were exceptions to this policy, such as the terrible winter of 1906–07, when the RNWMP were dispatched with food-laden sleighs to check on settlers in some of the worst-hit areas.[15] Clifford Sifton, however, wanted a population of sturdy, independent homesteaders, who placed individual progress and achievement above everything else. This goal was not simply a matter of saving the government money. The interior minister genuinely believed that the best settlers were those who persevered and succeeded on their own. "I have never known anybody," he once remarked, "that was materially assisted by the Government to amount to anything."[16] An official in his department put it more succinctly: what western Canada needed was "men of good muscle who are willing to hustle."[17]

Timing, location, capital, experience, assistance, endurance – and sheer good luck – were consequently all factors in determining a homesteader's success.[18] Future farm leader and Saskatchewan politician W. R. Motherwell, for example, took up prime land in the Abernethy district in the wake of the building of the CPR main line across the prairies. By the time Saskatchewan entered Confederation more than two decades later, he had converted his homestead into Lanark Place, a replica of pastoral Ontario, complete with an ornate, imposing stone farmhouse with separate living quarters for the servants. Although Motherwell's operation was unique – the restored homestead is recognized today as a national historic site – there were other similar fine homes in the area at Balcarres and Sintaluta. Indeed, pioneer days were generally well past in parts of southeastern Saskatchewan by 1905, and settlers moving into the area could expect a range of services and facilities.[19] But unfortunately there were few homesteads available in the region by that time, and only those with enough money could afford to buy land in established districts. Most people who headed to the province in the first decade of the twentieth century had come to make their fortune, enticed by the prospect of 160 acres of free land for a mere ten-dollar entry fee. With little capital, and often even less farming experience, many were forced to apply for land in isolated areas without a rail line or even a nearby town. There was no shortage of takers: in 1905–06 alone, two out of every three homestead applications were in Saskatchewan. Little did this wave of settlers realize, though, that they were not the first occupants of the land in many instances and that many of the homesteads had been abandoned by those who had moved on to another location or had simply given up.[20]

The first crucial decision for homesteaders was choosing their quarter section. Although federal homestead policy was based on the assumption that all the land was equally good throughout the North-West, the quality greatly varied from place to place, even within the same district. Some settlers used local agents to help find good farmland. George Hamilton of Toronto hired a Saskatoon land dealer in the fall of 1904 to take him southwest out along the Old Bone Trail towards Rosetown before making his application. "He had a choice of all the eye surveyed," his daughter Leila recalled, "and selected the best quarter in the district."[21] Others were not so fortunate. Many settlers had no time to inspect their prospective homestead beforehand, made a poor selection because of their inexperience, or were sadly deceived by the government literature, believing that any parcel of land would prove suitable. "We were almost the first people to settle in this part of the country and could have had the best of the land," F. N. Krischke of Baljennie confessed. "Instead we got the worst."[22] A few moved on, unhappy with their original choice. British-born George Shepherd homesteaded first in the Girvin-Stalwart area in 1908 before relocating to Maple Creek five years later.[23]

Upon reaching their quarter section for the first time, homesteaders spent hours tramping over the land, searching for the survey markers and inspecting every acre along the way. It was also when the hard reality of the situation started to sink in, and many had their first doubts about what they were doing. "We reached our homestead at last," recounted one woman. "I'll never forget the desolate feeling that came over me, when, with the contents of the wagon out on the ground, we sat on a box and looked around, not a sign of a human habitation or road leading to one, to be seen, nothing but bluff, water, and grass." She continued: "Then I realized that we were at the end of our journey, that this was to be our home."[24] For many, the prairies were a foreign, if not discomfiting, landscape, completely different from the world they had once known. "Even though I had been told it was prairie land," Helen Shepard of the Consul district remembered, "my first glimpse of the country ... was something of a shock."[25] One Ontario settler regularly walked to two solitary trees more than a mile from his homestead "just to touch them and stand in their shade."[26]

Homesteading was an impoverishing experience for many settlers, especially those living on their own in isolated areas. Not even the favoured British escaped this reality. While the early twentieth century marked the beginning of remarkable technological innovation and steady improvement in Canadian daily life, those in pioneer farm districts seemed to have stepped back in time. Since it often took several years before crops provided a decent income, homesteaders had to become virtually self-sufficient and learn to live a simpler life by making do with little. Hardship and privation were common.[27] "We did not have very much to eat," Dan Thompson described his first year on the family homestead in 1911. "I used to get so hungry I would eat grass."[28] Settlers faced the double challenge of bringing the land under cultivation and trying to survive in the meantime. Survival took valuable time and energy away from other activities, making it difficult for homesteaders to establish themselves, even though they worked incredibly long hours each day. "The ruthless pressure of time ... bears down on the shoulders of every farmer," James Minifie observed of his own father's experience. "There is never enough time on the prairie."[29] Hard work, though, could not guarantee success. Any single calamity during the first few years could prove disastrous, particularly for those with few resources to fall back on. For many, homesteading was a fragile, frustrating existence – a gamble – where many critical factors, such as weather or a rail link, were beyond their control. "In a just world," one historian has noted, "sweat and tears might have counted for something in the rain gauge."[30]

Before breaking a single acre, homesteaders faced three major tasks: finding a reliable source of drinking water, building a shelter, and putting in a garden. Some confidently began to dig a well, only to give up in exasperation after going several feet or starting several times without success. Others pulled water from sloughs, if it was not too brackish, or excavated a pit near the edge of a slough and collected the water that flowed into it. It was not unusual to travel for the better part of a day to retrieve a barrel of water. A couple headed to their homestead in 1906 came across an abandoned, rundown shack on their fourth day on the trail. A poem was faintly scrawled across the weather-beaten door: "I'm twenty miles from water, and forty miles from wood; So I'll leave you now my happy home, I'll leave you now for good."[31]

Homesteaders generally lived in tents until they could erect a more permanent structure. The majority of the first homes were constructed of either milled (dressed) lumber or, more likely, wood from the nearest bush.[32] It could be a daunting assignment for those without any experience. Bob Sansom of Rosetown spent an entire day wandering about his land "trying to figure out how to build the shack."[33] Those on the open, treeless prairie turned to the material at hand and constructed sod homes. But the sod needed adequate root growth to hold together, and the roof would often leak for days after a heavy rain. The Addison sod house, built in 1910–11 in the Oakdale district northeast of Kindersley, and still occupied by Edith (Addison) Gardiner, has recently been designated a national historic site. Most houses were initially one-room, many with earthen floors, and were expanded over time. In 1910, the T. Eaton Company started advertising prefabricated home packages, shipped from British Columbia by rail, in the Winnipeg edition of its catalogue. The blueprints cost $2.50, but the fee was refunded when the house was ordered. Sales were so brisk that the company introduced a separate catalogue of home plans in 1914–15.[34] Shrubs and trees from federal nurseries at Indian Head and Sutherland sheltered the new houses. Almost half of the millions of seedlings distributed were caragana.[35] Today, the shrubs mark the site of former homesteads.

Homesteaders also planted gardens to stave off hunger or add variety to an otherwise monotonous diet. Many did not bring enough provisions, and if they lived in isolated areas or had little money, they often had to make do with what they had – sometimes no more than oatmeal each day. Even a garden was difficult to maintain. "One can hardly grow a garden ... without cats to catch gophers," lamented Lillian Turner, who joined her husband on a homestead west of Saskatoon in 1906. "I hardly know how I shall get on, but will make a desperate effort to manage some way."[36] R. E. Bayles of Glen Adelaide was equally frustrated: "Gophers – it used to be a fight between us who should have the crop."[37] Beginning in 1905, Eaton's shipped canned goods and dried fruit in case lots from its new Winnipeg department store, but these bulk mail orders were generally restricted to settlers who lived near a rail line.[38]

Those best able to meet the homesteading challenge were the thousands of immigrants from the American Midwest, provided they secured decent land. Not only were they well equipped, often arriving with household effects, machinery, and animals, but many had homesteaded south of the line and brought practical experience farming the open plains. Continental Europeans, by contrast, were relatively poor, but no less prepared to create a new livelihood. But they seldom did so on their own, naturally gravitating to areas populated by their own kind, where they found material, as well as spiritual and emotional, support. "We all felt lost," explained Vladimir Wirkowski of Arran. "We wanted to stay together and help one another, just as we did in the Old Country."[39]

By congregating in group settlements, Doukhobors, Mennonites, and Ukrainians settled the land with assistance from their extended family, friends, or the wider community. They were also surrounded by familiar symbols and customs, such as their distinctive homes and traditional village patterns, which served to lessen any feelings of dislocation and isolation.[40] John Letkeman, for example, was one of eight men who investigated the farming potential of the new Mennonite reserve near Swift Current in the late spring of 1904. Before selecting their land, they took turns digging a well to decide where the village, named Schoenfeld, should be located. The group then applied for homesteads in the same area on the understanding that they would work together to establish their farms.[41] These ethnic enclaves, as they were called, intensified the immigrants' sense of separateness from the larger society. They also went against the government ideal of a society of rugged, independent homesteaders, capable of surviving and prospering on their own. But ironically, without this kind of co-operative enterprise, successful settlement of the land would have been difficult at best, if not significantly delayed.

Co-operative activity was not restricted to continental European immigrants. Most homesteaders came to rely on neighbours for help of some kind. One evening in the spring of 1906, Bob Sansom spied a team of oxen waddling along to a small tent about a half mile away from his place and excitedly hurried off to meet Jim McGregor, a moulder by trade, fresh from England. The pair immediately became friends and worked together for the next few months, starting with the building of Bob's house from local poplar. "We managed to get ten acres each broken that summer," Sansom later reported, "built a sod stable, put up some hay, dug a well ... got out a supply of wood for next summer."[42] Some men who were good with a plough did breaking work for neighbours in exchange for other help on their homestead. Often, two homesteaders might simply strike a deal to get supplies; one would go to town, several days' travel away, while the other would remain behind to work on the land so that no time was lost. These partnerships could be rocky, but more often than not proved resilient because of the simple fact that they needed each other. Nor did nationality seem to matter in most instances. Help was help, and a person's ethnic background was less important than their ability to lend a hand when it was needed most. It was only after the land was settled that questions about assimilation and integration became more pronounced.[43] There were exceptions, though. Leslie Nearby vividly remembered how his brothers and sisters singlehandedly had to run their Watrous-area homestead because his English parents refused to associate with their "riffraff" neighbours.[44]

Many homesteaders also turned to off-farm work to make some much-needed money. Bob Sansom and Jim McGregor's partnership ended in October 1906, when Bob headed to Minnesota to do logging for the winter, while Jim went to Winnipeg to work at his trade. Come spring, both were back on their homesteads, where Bob had second thoughts about what he was doing and almost gave up twice. "100 miles from civilization, and a little 12X16 shack that you could throw a cat through any place," he looked back on one of his low points. "I got cold feet and the blues so bad that if I had been offered the whole of Saskatchewan you could not have held me here."[45] Homesteaders also found seasonal work with the railways. Art Wheeler, who took up land in the

Ladstock district in the fall of 1906, spent the following three summers as a labourer on the Grand Trunk Pacific main line at $1.50 to $1.75 per day, excluding board. Men with their own team of horses earned even more. While based at camp five, east of Punnichy, in June 1907, Wheeler noted: "Probably every homesteader from a wide area was employed.... There were over a hundred teams assembled."[46]

This summer employment, albeit temporary, took settlers away from their land when they could least afford to be away. But in helping to build the railways they were doing their part to end isolation and improve their overall prospects, and the extra cash could ultimately mean the difference between success and failure. Some prospective homesteaders even worked for several years as hired hands, gaining valuable experience and sufficient capital, before they applied for their own quarter section. Sometimes the dream was never realized. Hungarian Martin Bremner came to Indian Head in the early twentieth century intent on securing his own land, but his seasonal jobs, alternating between local farms and the railway, provided little support for his growing family, let alone enough money to homestead.[47]

Women were probably more important than any other factor to a homesteader's survival. Without a spouse, many men would have given up before they secured their patent, and many did. It was common practice for husbands to go ahead alone to get established on their homesteads before sending for their wives and children. Thousands of single men were also attracted to Saskatchewan by the promise of free land and planned to get a start before seeking a partner. What many "bachelor" homesteaders quickly learned, though, was that it was next to impossible to work on the land and maintain a household. There was no one to prepare the all-important noon-time dinner, wash sweat-drenched grimy clothes, or make their first home a little more habitable. Something had to be sacrificed, and it was usually the men's diet and hygiene. Many lived in primitive and isolated conditions during their first few weeks and months on their homestead, which only made things worse. Elizabeth Mitchell, who visited western Canada before the Great War, described bachelors as poor, lonely creatures "who need kindness badly."[48]

Homesick husbands consequently sent for their wives earlier than they had planned, but even then their reunion could be delayed because of the isolation of some districts. In the fall of 1906, Mrs. Margaret McManus and her two little boys spent six anxious weeks in the Saskatoon immigration hall until word reached her husband on his homestead that she had arrived from Scotland.[49] Other men sought wives. Bob Sansom decided to return to his Rosetown-area homestead only because of his pending marriage. Percy Maxwell felt the same way about his engagement to his girlfriend, Mabel. "If it wasn't for her I don't think I would stay on my homestead," he wrote his family. "I am thoroughly sick of baching."[50] Finding partners, however, was difficult in Saskatchewan, where in 1906 the ratio of single men to single women was 1.7 to 1. Nor did the situation for prospective suitors get any better. By 1911, there were 3.5 single men for every single woman in the province. Many bachelors persevered as long as they could, but ultimately the lack of companionship took its toll. According to a sampling of pioneer surveys conducted by the Saskatchewan Archives in 1955 in commemoration of the province's fiftieth birthday, loneliness drove many bachelors from their homesteads. Indeed, where ranchers welcomed isolation, farmers hated it.

Women, like their male partners, were excited about Saskatchewan's bright future and joined their husbands on homesteads with a sense of purpose and determination. But it would be a mistake to view them as stoic "helpmates," who simply played a supporting role in wresting a living from the land. Survival on the homestead meant that wives had to learn new skills, do new things that were not normally expected of women at the time. They worked in the fields alongside their husbands, tended animals, ran machinery, and picked up a hammer and nails to repair something. In other words, they did whatever they had to do. At the same time, they were expected to keep their femininity and continue to handle their traditional duties in the home, including the rearing and care of children. This invasion of the so-called male sphere meant that women "hauled a double load" or worked "a second shift" on the homestead. And they performed these never-ending tasks with a flexibility and resourcefulness that seems truly incredible today.[51] Many a man owed his success to his partner's labour and readily acknowledged it. But women were taken for granted far too easily. Nellie McClung, an outspoken advocate of female suffrage, liked to tell the story of Jane, who died three days after giving birth to her seventh child: "The bereaved husband was the most astonished man in the world. He had never known Jane to do a thing like that before, and he could not get over it. In threshing time, too!"[52]

Despite women's many contributions to the homestead, their role and place on the settlement frontier was narrowly proscribed. Although the Laurier government promoted the immigration of women to western Canada as part of the overall plan to boost the population of the region, it regarded farming as a strictly male activity. Ottawa therefore steadfastly refused to extend to women – except in rare circumstances – the right to take up homestead land, even though the United States did so. As Frank Oliver, Sifton's successor as interior minister, informed the House of Commons in 1910, as if it was some well-known fact: "the purpose … in giving free land to homesteaders is that the land may be made productive.… Our experience is entirely against the idea of women homesteading."[53] The federal government's intransigence provoked a "homesteads for women" movement in the years leading up to the Great War. But the intensive lobbying effort, including letters and a petition, failed to sway Ottawa, and the eligibility rules remained the same until the end of the homesteads program in 1930.

One of the leading figures in the campaign was Georgina Binnie-Clark, who had come to Saskatchewan in 1905 to check up on her brother, Lal, a brewer by trade, homesteading near Fort Qu'Appelle. Shocked to discover that he was failing miserably and ready to quit, Georgina bought a half section of land and with her sister Hilaria ran a successful farm operation for the next few decades. But she deeply resented how a woman farmer was disadvantaged by federal homestead policy. "She may be the best farmer in Canada," Binnie-Clark observed in her prairie classic, *Wheat and Woman*, "she may buy land, work it, take prizes for seed and stock, but she is denied the right to claim from the Government the hundred and sixty acres of land held out as a bait to every man."[54]

This failure to see women as legitimate homesteaders effectively made their work on the farm "invisible." They may have helped to fulfill homestead requirements in any countless number of ways, but as long as agriculture was deemed a male enterprise, their crucial role was severely discounted or blindly ignored.[55] Nor did women enjoy any dower rights in the three western provinces. Men could dispose of their land as they saw fit without consulting their wives, while women were not guaranteed any share in the property upon their husband's death. "In no country under the sun," explained Isabel Graham, editor of the women's page of the *Grain Growers' Guide*, in calling for provincial dower laws in 1910, "has woman been more responsible for increased land values ... [but] they do not earn anything at home ... their work is valueless."[56] Women readers agreed. One correspondent suggested that "the universal lot of the farmer's wife is one of ceaseless toil without adequate compensation."[57] Men, on the other hand, were strongly opposed to any legislation, even forming a Farmers' Anti-Dower Law Association in the province. "A Saskatchewan Farmer" claimed in a letter to the *Guide* that "nearly all farmers treat wifey generously."[58] Another admitted: "I have a great respect for the ladies – when they know their place."[59] The dower campaign, though, proved more successful than the homestead issue, largely because these rights were recognized in law in other Canadian provinces. In 1915, the Saskatchewan government provided some initial protection for women's interests in the *Homestead Act*, but it would be another two generations, not until 1979, before women finally secured an equal share in matrimonial property.[60]

Like their husbands, many women found homestead life to be terribly lonely. The isolation and privation weighed heavily upon them because of the lack of female contact and companionship. In fact, historian James Gray half-jokingly quipped that the placement of settlers on individual quarter sections could not have done more "to drive the farm women up the walls of their shacks."[61] Men at least worked with their neighbours or visited town to get supplies or retrieve the mail. Women, meanwhile, were captive to the homestead and its constant demands. It was as if the outside world ceased to exist. "We fared well," remembered a daughter, "but it was hard on mother ... struggling to keep clean and sane in a one-roomed shack. I have heard her say many a time she felt like running out for miles and screaming. Pioneering is hardest on women shut up alone for days and months."[62] Mrs. J. I. Anderson reported she left the homestead so rarely during the first ten years that people in the Gregherd district, except for the local storekeeper, thought her husband was a bachelor.[63] Others had similar stories. Catherine Neil went so long without seeing another woman that when she visited a neighbour with a young baby for the first time, "we ran to each other ... and put our arms around each other's neck and just had a good cry. All the hunger and longing which we had stifled for so long came to the surface."[64]

Some women found the isolation, the primitive conditions, and the constant work to be too much. Barbara Bent remembered being summoned by a neighbour to attend to a homesick woman whose husband was afraid to leave her alone. The couple, no more than in their late teens, had come directly from London, England, to the open Saskatchewan prairie. The woman seemed to be in shock. "Well I stayed with that young couple for three days and nights because I felt so sorry for the little woman," recounted Bent. "I found poor Daisy was just suffering from the intense loneliness ... and I told him [the husband Charlie] plainly he had better take his little wife to some town and try to work at this trade [watch repair]."[65] In another more desperate case, Mrs. Running, a mother of three children, was being sent home to Ontario for a much-needed visit. But the wait was apparently unbearable, and while visiting friends near Eastend one evening, she politely left the dinner table, put on her hat and coat, and drowned herself in the well behind the house.[66]

Children did much to alleviate the loneliness of the homestead, but pregnancy had its own perils. Expectant women often had to make do without the support and advice of other women; first-time mothers, who knew little about pregnancy and childbirth, were particularly vulnerable, especially if they lived in isolated areas far away from trained medical personnel. Babies were usually delivered at home with the assistance of local women who, by necessity, became midwives. Sometimes only husbands were there to help. Mothers and babies often died from complications, especially if a doctor could not be summoned in time. Most infant deaths in Saskatchewan occurred within the first week of birth; in 1914, one-third of all childhood deaths under five were newborns. In fact, it was unusual for a family not to have lost at least one child. In 1910, the Saskatchewan government took steps to deal with infant mortality by introducing a maternity package for newborns and a maternity grant for mothers in remote areas or in financial need. But the other real need, pre- and post-natal care, was virtually non-existent in pioneer districts. Because of the need for labour on the homestead, women commonly had several children, in some cases over a twenty-year period. They also had little time to recuperate before they were back to work or tending to their other children. Difficulties during pregnancy or childbirth, together with the strain of multiple pregnancies and exhaustion, consequently took their toll. In a contradictory vein, it seemed that "women were indispensable to successful settlement yet treated as dispensable."[67]

Children who grew up on homesteads learned from an early age to perform any number of chores under all kinds of conditions. Girls in particular came to believe that women's work included seeding and harvesting, especially if there were no boys in the family.[68] Natalie Forness of Maple Creek proudly boasted: "By the time I was fourteen I worked outside like a man."[69] Eldest daughters often served as a second mother to their brothers and sisters. These years clearly left their mark on a generation. "For us children," Leslie Neatby summed up his days on the family homestead, "it meant toil and suffering beyond our years. But it toughened us and imparted initiative and a capacity for self-help." They also never forgot the weather. Neatby recalled one dreadful winter when "the unending depression of a chill within doors" forced him and his family to spend time in bed in order to keep warm.[70] Wallace Stegner, describing his adolescent years near Eastend in *Wolf Willow*, spoke of "its wind, which blows all the time in a way to stiffen your hair and rattle the eyes in your head."[71] Sickness, too, left a lasting impression. One of the favourite home remedies was goose grease, which was used so liberally that some children worried that they might grow feathers.[72] Somewhat sadly, Nettie Bellows, the eldest of twelve children, looked back upon her bout with scarlet fever with fondness; it was the only time her mother doted on her, because she feared Nettie was going to die.[73]

Settlers enjoyed simple recreational pursuits. Homesteaders arrived with only a few books and magazines and normally shared them with neighbours, especially during the long winter months. The Aberdeen Association, founded by the wife of Canada's governor general in the 1890s, also sent monthly parcels of reading material by rail to pioneer districts. One of the most widely read items, apart from the Bible, was Eaton's mail-order catalogue, which boasted: "If you can't find what you want on our pages, it wasn't made or you didn't need it." Immigrants used the catalogue to learn to read English, while children would cut out figures and other pictures to make playthings.[74] Some districts organized literary societies where participation was more important than talent. "Everyone had to do something," reported Tom Perry of Watson, "even if they could only whistle or tell a story – strange to say those were very enjoyable evenings."[75] Work bees also doubled as social events. The raising of a barn, for example, might be followed by a dance to the music of a fiddle, accordion, harmonica, or spoons. At Leader in 1914, W. T. "Horseshoe" Smith, a Kentuckian with big ranching plans, built the largest barn in North America, measuring 400 feet long, 128 feet wide, and 60 feet high. Thousands attended the opening barn dance. But the astronomical cost of building and maintaining the immense barn proved too much even for Smith's ambition, and the structure was torn down seven years later and the wood and other materials sold to local farmers and businesses.[76]

Religion also brought people together. Before churches were erected, services were held in all kinds of places – from a tent, barn, and box car to a local home and district school – and attracted worshippers from all denominations. As one homesteader remarked: "Sunday was the one day and church the one opportunity in the week to meet neighbours and friends."[77] Church and community picnics, with their games for children and adults, proved extremely popular, as did box socials with men bidding on lunches specially prepared by local women. The big event of the year, though, was the fair. Those in pioneer districts were modest, featuring garden produce, baking, and handicrafts, as well as contests to see who could plough the straightest line and at the right depth. But in older, more settled areas, fairs highlighted country life at its best and the competition for prizes was fierce.[78]

In winter, both men and women skated or played hockey on the nearest frozen slough. Curling was also common since it required only a household broom and frozen, water-filled jam or lard cans for the rocks. Cards, dominoes, crokinole, and other games filled the hours when it was too cold to spend much time outdoors. Come the busy months of summer there was little time for sports, but young, single men, whether homesteaders or hired hands, congregated whenever they could for a pick-up game of soccer or baseball; they also played lacrosse and cricket, depending on the availability of equipment. The same isolation that drove these men to come together, however, prevented the scheduling of regular games or the formation of local leagues. Instead, they had to be content with the annual sports day, normally held in conjunction with the 24 May or 1 July holidays, when they finally got their chance to play against a visiting team or compete in track events.[79] It was only when transportation and communication improved that sports could flourish. Baseball, for example, followed the CPR main line westward, and teams popped up throughout the province as branch lines were pushed into new areas. The village of Liberty, because of the presence of so many Americans, became known as "The Baseball Town," while Oxbow fielded the U.N. squad – the "useless nine."[80]

Until isolation was ended and distances shrunk, homesteaders scratched out an existence as best they could. Many failed, but many more secured title to their land and stayed for the rest of their lives. Those who homesteaded in Saskatchewan in the new century came looking for a better life in a land where one could "see clear through to half past tomorrow."[81] James Minifie sensed this optimism in his father. He spoke with the "ring of triumph," Minifie declared: "Whatever this great North-West might be, he was proud of it, proud to be part of it."[82] In accepting *and* meeting the government challenge, homesteaders turned abstract plans into reality – turned 160 acres of real estate into a new way of life for themselves and their families. Ronald Jickling realized the larger meaning of what he was doing while hauling a load of wood with his neighbour Stanley Doyle one day. Breaking camp after lunch, Stan said they would likely reach home by sundown. "Then the significance of what Stan said at noon struck me," Ron recounted. "Possibly he didn't realize what he said. He said we would be HOME by sundown. That word HOME was the first time we had, either one of us, used it, and we were coming HOME now.... Well, this place so far is not much of a home, that's for certain, but one has to make a start some place and this is as good a place as any."[83]

NOTES

1 *Robsart Pioneers Review the Years* (Robsart, SK: 1957), 49.

2 B. LaDow, *The Medicine Line: Life and Death on a North American Borderland* (New York: Routledge, 2001), 191.

3 Quoted in W. A. Waiser, *The Field Naturalist: John Macoun, the Geological Survey and Natural Science* (Toronto: University of Toronto Press, 1989), 53.

4 *Range Riders and Sodbusters* (Eastend, SK: Eastend History Society, 1984), 251.

5 E. T. Parson, *Land I Can Own* (Ottawa: E. T. Parson, 1981).

6 L. K. Bacon, "Four Years in Saskatchewan," provided by S. Haid (n.d.).

7 R. W. Sansom typescript, provided by D. McKercher (n.d.)

8 W. A. Waiser, "The Government Explorer in Canada, 1870–1914," in *North American Exploration*, vol. 3: *A Continent Comprehended*, ed. J. L. Allen (Lincoln: University of Nebraska Press, 1997), 426–34.

9 B. Waiser, *The New Northwest: The Photographs of the Frank Crean Expeditions, 1908–1909* (Saskatoon: Fifth House, 1993), 6 n. 13; C. Martin, *Dominion Lands Policy* (Toronto: McClelland and Stewart, 1973), 47.

10 The entry application, the first document to be filed, listed the location of the land and the age, place of birth, nationality, citizenship status, previous place of residence, and previous occupation of the homesteader.

11 Martin, *Dominion Lands Policy*, 172–74.

12 W. C. Pollard, *Pioneering in the Prairie West* (London: A. H. Stockwell, n.d.), 51 [emphasis added].

13 Ottawa discontinued the preemption option in 1890, but reintroduced it in 1908.

14 R. Widdis, *With Scarcely a Ripple: Anglo-Canadian Migration into the United States and Western Canada, 1880–1920* (Montreal and Kingston: McGill-Queen's University Press,1998), 326.

15 See J. Cherwinski, "The Rise and Incomplete Fall of a Contemporary Legend: Frozen Englishmen in the Canadian Prairies During the Winter of 1906–07," *Canadian Ethnic Studies* 31, no. 3 (Fall 1999): 20–43.

16 Quoted in D. J. Hall, "Clifford Sifton: Immigration and Settlement Policy, 1896–1905," in *The Settlement of the West*, ed. H. Palmer (Calgary: University of Calgary Press, 1977), 75.

17 Quoted in ibid., 71.

18 See L. Dick, "Estimates of Farm-Making Costs in Saskatchewan, 1882–1914," *Prairie Forum* 6, no. 2 (Fall 1981): 183–201.

19 S. Carter, *A Materials History of the Motherwell Home*, Canada Parks Service manuscript report, no. 320, 1979, 278.
20 Widdis, *With Scarcely a Ripple*, 257, 329.
21 L. Reed, "Pioneer Courage on the Prairie," *Saskatchewan History* 39, no. 3 (Autumn 1986): 108.
22 A. R. Turner, "Pioneer Farming Experiences," *Saskatchewan History* 8, no. 2 (Spring 1955): 44.
23 G. Shepherd, *West of Yesterday* (Toronto: McClelland and Stewart, 1965).
24 "Simple Experiences of Pioneer Days," Women's Canadian Club competition, 1924, A. S. Morton manuscript collection, C555/1/2.29, University of Saskatchewan Libraries Special Collections.
25 Quoted in J. W. Bennett and S. B. Kohl, *Settling the Canadian-American West 1890–1915: Pioneer Adaptation and Community Building* (Lincoln: University of Nebraska Press, 1995), 57.
26 R. Rees, *New and Naked Land: Making the Prairies Home* (Saskatoon: Western Producer Prairie Books, 1988), 107.
27 Bennett and Kohl, *Settling*, 64.
28 *Robsart Pioneers*, 38.
29 J. Minifie, *Homesteader: A Prairie Boyhood Recalled* (Toronto: Macmillan, 1972), 52.
30 LaDow, *The Medicine Line*, 87.
31 "A Reminiscence of a Bigone Day," 1924, Morton manuscript collection, MSDS C555/2.1.
32 K. M. Taggart, "The First Shelter of Early Pioneers," *Saskatchewan History* 11, no. 3 (Autumn 1958): 81.
33 Sansom typescript.
34 L. Henry, *Catalogue Houses: Eatons' and Others* (Saskatoon: Henry Perspectives, 2000).
35 J.A.G. Howe, "One Hundred Years of Prairie Forestry," *Prairie Forum* 11, no. 2 (Fall 1986): 243–51.
36 L. Turner to family, April 29, 1906, Lillian Turner fonds, Glenbow Archives M8244.
37 Quoted in Turner, "Pioneer Farming Experiences," 51.
38 B. M. Barss, *The Pioneer Cook: A Historical View of Canadian Prairie Food* (Calgary: Detselig Enterprises, 1980), 93–94.
39 Quoted in D. P. Fitzgerald, "Pioneer Settlement in Northern Saskatchewan" (PhD diss., University of Minnesota, 1965), 150.
40 Rees, *New and Naked Land*, 50.
41 J. Letkeman, "My Walk in Life," November 26, 1954, provided by S. Thiessen.
42 Sansom typescript.
43 Widdis, *With Scarcely a Ripple*, 306.
44 L. H. Neatby, *Chronicle of a Pioneer Prairie Family* (Saskatoon: Western Producer Prairie Books, 1979), 30.
45 Sansom typescript.
46 A. J. Wheeler, "Helping to Build the G.T.P.," *Saskatchewan History* 4, no. 1 (Spring 1951): 27–28.
47 P. A. Mazzone, "An Immigrant Family in Saskatchewan 1903–1943," *Canadian Ethnic Studies* 12, no. 3 (Fall 1980): 134.
48 E. Mitchell, *In Western Canada before the War* (London: J. Murray, 1915), 47.
49 *Pioneer Surveys*, M. McManus, 1906, Saskatchewan Archives Board, 2110.
50 P. A. Maxwell, *Percy Augustus Maxwell: Letters Home* (Toronto: 1967), 120.
51 S. Rollings-Magnusson, "Canada's Most Wanted: Pioneer Women on the Canadian Prairies," *Canadian Review of Sociology and Anthropology* 37, no. 2 (May 2000): 225–29; S. B. Kohl, *Working Together: Women and Family in Southwestern Saskatchewan* (Toronto: Holt, Rinehart, and Winston, 1976): 32–36; A. C. Moffatt, "Experiencing

Identity: British-Canadian Women in Rural Saskatchewan, 1880–1950" (PhD diss., University of Manitoba, 1996), 111.

52 N. McClung, *In Times Like These* (Toronto: McLeod and Allen, 1915), 191.

53 Canada, House of Commons, *Debates*, April 30, 1910, 8489–90. In the United States, any woman (American-born or naturalized citizen) eighteen or older could claim a homestead.

54 G. Binnie-Clark, *Wheat and Woman* (London: Heinneman, 1914), 395–96.

55 C. A. Cavanaugh, "'No Place for a Woman': Engendering Western Canadian Settlement," *Western Historical Quarterly* 28 (Winter 1997): 505.

56 *Grain Growers' Guide*, July 6, 1910.

57 Ibid., November 3, 1915.

58 Ibid., November 10, 1915.

59 Ibid., August 14, 1909.

60 M. E. McCallum, "Prairie Women and the Struggle for a Dower Law, 1905–1920," *Prairie Forum* 18, no. 1 (Spring 1993): 19–34; S. Rollings-Magnusson, "Hidden Homesteaders: Women, the State, and Patriarchy in the Saskatchewan Wheat Economy, 1870–1930," *Prairie Forum* 24, no. 2 (Fall 1999): 171–83.

61 J. H. Gray, *The Roar of the Twenties* (Toronto: Macmillan, 1975), 45.

62 "Pioneer Days," Morton manuscript collection, C555/1/2.29.

63 *Pioneer Surveys*, Mrs. J. I. Anderson, no. 218, Saskatchewan Archives Board.

64 Quoted in Saskatchewan Women's Division, *Saskatchewan Women, 1905–1980* (Regina: Saskatchewan Labour Women's Division, 1980), 21.

65 B. Bent, "Latter Day Pioneering," Morton manuscript collection, C555/1/1.5.

66 LaDow, *The Medicine Line*, 165.

67 N. Langford, "Childbirth on the Canadian Prairies," in *Telling Tales: Essays in Western Women's History*, ed. C. A. Cavanaugh and R. R. Warne (Vancouver: UBC Press, 2000), 170.

68 Moffatt, "Experiencing Identity," 111.

69 Quoted in LaDow, *The Medicine Line*, 186.

70 Neatby, *Chronicle*, 4, 20.

71 W. Stegner, *Wolf Willow: A History, a Story, and a Memory of the Last Plains Frontier* (New York: Viking, 1962), 3–4.

72 N. L. Lewis, "Goose Grease and Turpentine: Mother Treats the Family's Illnesses," *Prairie Forum* 15, no. 1 (Spring 1990): 67–84.

73 G. Swerhone, e-mail communication to author, June 24, 2003.

74 E. C. Morgan, "Pioneer Recreation and Social Life," *Saskatchewan History* 18, no. 2 (Spring 1965): 41–54; S. Mein, "The Aberdeen Association: An Early Attempt to Provide Library Services to Settlers in Saskatchewan," *Saskatchewan History* 38, no. 1 (Winter 1985): 2–19; C. Tulloch, "Pioneer Reading," *Saskatchewan History* 12, no. 3 (Summer 1959): 97–99.

75 *Pioneer Surveys*, T. E. Perry, no. 219, Saskatchewan Archives Board.

76 J. H. Archer, *Saskatchewan: A History* (Saskatoon: Western Producer Prairie Books, 1980), 163.

77 C. MacDonald, "Pioneer Church Life in Saskatchewan," *Saskatchewan History* 13, no. 1 (Spring 1960): 16.

78 D. C. Jones, *Midways, Judges, and Smooth-Tongued Fakirs: The Illustrated Story of Country Fairs in the Prairie West* (Saskatoon: Western Producer Prairie Books, 1983).

79 D. G. Wetherell, "A Season of Mixed Blessings: Winter and Leisure in Alberta before World War Two," in *Winter Sports in the West*, ed. E. A. Corbet and A. W. Rasporich (Calgary: Historical Society of Alberta, 1990), 42–44; F. R. Holt, *Sharing the Good Times: A History of Prairie Women's Joys and Pleasures* (Calgary: Detselig Enterprises, 2000); R. Ellis and E. Nixon, *Saskatchewan's Recreation Legacy* (Saskatoon: Modern Press, 1986); Morgan, "Pioneer Recreation and Social Life," 47.

80 P. Hack and D. Shury, *Wheat Province Diamonds: A Story of Saskatchewan Baseball* (Regina: Saskatchewan Baseball Association, 1997), 8–10.

81 S. Ellis, *A Prairie as Wide as the Sea: The Immigrant Diary of Ivy Weatherall* (Markham: Scholastic Canada, 2001), 17.

82 Minifie, *Homesteader*, 29.

83 R. Jickling diary, Manuscript Division, Library and Archives Canada.

III

ENVISIONING THE PRAIRIE WEST AS A PERFECT SOCIETY

8

THE CITY YES, THE CITY NO: PERFECTION BY DESIGN IN THE WESTERN CITY

Anthony W. Rasporich

A few years ago in Calgary, I attended a reading by the Ukrainian poet Yevgeny Yevtushenko of his poem, "The City of Yes, the City of No."[1] In essence, the poem passionately affirmed the positive impulse over the negative, of life over death, of creativity over stasis, of beauty over drabness, of optimism over fear. It is those impulses that lie at the core of the visions, both positive and negative, that moved the builders and critics of the rapid development of western Canada at the turn of the twentieth century. On the one side were the idealists, visionaries, and utopians, riding the wave of change, of envisioning a new world order, of "the City Beautiful," of a new society based on new premises of social change, leading to social perfection. On the other were ranged both the realist critics of the new order, and those whose negative vision of the current state of affairs clouded their own prescriptions for development. Complicating both outlooks were the times themselves, which rapidly dissolved from nearly two decades of economic boom from 1896 to 1913 into an uncertain decade of war and postwar slump.

Western European philosophers and thinkers have long been enamoured with ideal systems of social organization, in particular, the city. Plato's *Republic* was perhaps the earliest expression of this ideal state, extending forward to the Italian Renaissance expressions of a similar impulse to Tommaso Campanella's *City of the Sun* (1602), Valentin Andreae's *Christianopolis* (1619), and to its articulation in the English language in Thomas More's *Utopia* (1516), and Francis Bacon's *New Atlantis*

(1627). Thereafter, the notion of a radically re-organized rational utopia spread throughout the English Reformation among the revolutionary sects through to the French Enlightenment philosophes such as Diderot and their nineteenth-century heirs such as Cabet, Saint-Simon, and Fourier. As well, the rush was on to realize dreams of societal reformation, first in Europe but largely in North America, which became the receptacle of co-operative experimentation, notably Fourierist Phalansteries, Owenite communities, and a multitude of communitarian groups seeking the creation of a new social order.[2]

The difficulties inherent in utopian thought, apparent first to critics of theorists, and even more so of the communitarian experiments themselves, were numerous. The tension between authoritarian leadership structures – the rulers and the ruled – tended to favour the absolutist model, particularly in the earlier models, which acknowledged slavery as a given. But, the central tension was between the ruling element, such as H. G. Wells' samurai, "a voluntary nobility" who rule by noblesse oblige in *A Modern Utopia* (1905), and the masses who followed in drone-like submissiveness the dictates of their wiser masters.[3] Indeed, it is this very tension that was so clearly articulated in later critiques of totalitarian state-socialism such as Aldous Huxley's *Brave New World* (1932) and George Orwell's *Nineteen Eighty-Four* (1949). While enlightened despotism on a smaller scale of cults and sects on the fringe of society was somehow more acceptable in the pluralistic social context of the nineteenth-century, libertarian and anarchistic ideals became more suspect in the context of totalitarian regimes of the twentieth century.

There were other inherent difficulties as well. Communal versus private property was a central tension, particularly as the economies of scale increased. So also were traditional social institutions such as marriage, which were challenged by notions of free-love, polygamy, and other social experimentation. The economic dividends of group economic activity were another arena of potential conflict, particularly with successful ventures, which were not the norm. Yet another area of potential conflict was the tendency towards authoritarian social thought aimed at improvement of the masses through schemes of social planning and social controls, followed by social engineering and biological experimentation aimed at the improvement of the racial stock. While a spirit of idealism and optimism persisted among those infused by utopian social theories of the nineteenth and early twentieth century, there were increasing doubts raised by utopianism's realist critics, who challenged its communitarian social theories and decried its track record of failed experiments.

Nineteenth-century Canada became a proving ground, although on a much lesser scale than did the United States, for social experimentation of a communitarian character. Certainly the sectarian groups were well represented in old Ontario, such as the Old Order Mennonites and the Shakers in early Upper Canada. There was even an early failed experiment with Robert Owen's ideas on the shores of Lake Huron in 1826 by Henry Jones, which attempted a colony based on communal property called "Toon o' Maxwell."[4] Other experiments followed the expansion of Canada into the West after Confederation, mostly also of a rural and sectarian character, but some also with an ethnic socialist dimension, such as the Sojntula, the Harmony Island experiment at the turn of the century, and the Harmony Industrial Association at Teulon in western Manitoba.[5] In sum, western Canada was the scene of several abortive rural settlements based upon the social ideal of co-operation and harmony, some inspired by the Rochdale experiments of Robert Owen in early nineteenth-century Scotland as well as by other diverse European and American sources.

From an urban perspective, the city itself became the subject of idealistic reform in the late nineteenth-century transatlantic world. Urban space – public architecture and its design in the new urban landscape – city planning, and urban reform all became the subject of holistic change of the city. In particular, the growth of the industrial city with its attendant urban slums had created nightmarish social conditions in the Victorian era, from "Satanic mills" to overcrowded immigrant ghettoes, crime, prostitution, alcoholic degradation, undernourished children, and impoverished families. Various social movements grew to address particular problems, from emigration societies, church-sponsored societies for the remedy of poverty, temperance organizations against alcohol abuse, and dozens of self-help organizations dedicated to particular issues of urban social blight.

An obvious example of social escape to western Canada was the formation in Toronto of the Temperance Colonization Society in 1882 to establish a dry colony in the North West. Its founder was John Lake, a Methodist minister from 1855 to 1870, and its backers included prominent Ontarians such as Principal George Monro Grant of Queen's University, and prominent business leaders who would ensure its "Co-operative, Benevolent, and Christian institutions." Soon a townsite was selected at Saskatoon, and grandiose prospectuses of a dry metropolis on the banks of the North Saskatchewan were circulated to attract temperance escapees from the evils of alcohol in Toronto. Yet another settlement of sectarian/utopian social escape was the establishment of the Mormon village of Cardston in southern Alberta in 1887. Its spatial organization was along the square-grid model of the Plat of Zion. In essence, western Canada had, by the late nineteenth century, begun to be dotted by rural communitarian experiments, as well as non-farm villages and towns, with distinct spatial and social organizations.[6]

In central Canada, the evils of industrialism in the city of Montreal were well documented by the Royal Commission on Labour in 1892. The attendant social problems of overcrowding were later detailed in *The City Below the Hill* (1899) by Herbert Ames,[7] a wealthy industrialist and civic-minded reformer. The study comprised of a series of articles he had done two years earlier in the *Montreal Star*. Ames' searing indictment of working-class living conditions became a classic, as did some of his proposed remedies, which focused upon improved sanitation measures, in particular the wider use of water-closets (indoor toilets), as a first step to improvement of health conditions in the city's west end.

Another fundamental aspect of urban reform was that of urban design and civic planning. Originating in Great Britain with Jeremy Bentham, the utilitarian philosophy of "the greatest good for the greatest number" was developed further by John Stuart Mill and led to the attendant growth of the social sciences and positivistic applications of statistics to ameliorate society along the lines of health, economy, convenience, and order. Such notions were pushed further in their spread to the United States, with notions of greater happiness, the idea of progress, and conservationist ideals that would enable the city to transform itself through the provision of parks and the turning of wilderness into garden cities and decentralized industrial parks. In this way, rural conservation was combined with urban planning. In the insightful observation of P. J. Smith: "Urban decentralization was therefore to proceed in an orderly and controlled manner, and for all its romanticism and utopian idealism, the Garden City concept was firmly rooted in a belief in efficiently planned urban systems."[8] Thus utility and efficiency were added to yet another strand of aesthetic urban planning, the City Beautiful movement, also from the United States, which had caught the imagination of civic planners imbued with progressive ideals for social reorganization of the blighted urban landscape.[9]

These two strands of thought, one British, represented by Ebenezer Howard's *Garden Cities of Tomorrow* (1898), and the other American conservationism, combined to exert powerful influence on the newly formed Commission of Conservation established by the Government of Canada in 1909. The commission would advise all levels of government on issues relating to conservation and utilization of natural resources in Canada.[10] Not long after, in 1914, the Commission hired Thomas Adams, a disciple of Howard, and an inspector of the Local Government Board administering the British urban planning act of 1909. He quickly established himself as an authority in Canada, creating the Civic Improvement League, exerting a powerful influence upon education and legislation, and consulting on urban issues and town planning in Canada over the next decade. William Lyon Mackenzie King, the deputy minister of labour in the Laurier government, who visited the British new townsites, and later praised them in his *Industry and Humanity: A Study in the Principles Underlying Industrial Reconstruction* (1918), became another important receptor and carrier of British town planning ideals to Canada. Also, Lord Grey, Canada's governor-general, had presided over the first Garden City Conference in England in 1901, and later invited Henry Vivian, M.P. and prominent Garden City advocate, to speak in Toronto on the subject in 1910.[11]

Canada had thus become a proving ground for the new wave of urban reform that was sweeping the transatlantic English-speaking world in the first decade of the twentieth century. Anxious to demonstrate their willingness to throw off the bonds of colonialism, Canadian civic leaders and businessmen eagerly embraced these modern principles of urban design and planning. In the words of Byron Walker to the Canadian Club of Toronto: "We want to show the British what our material civilization amounts to.... We do not want to remain a wooden backyards place with provincial ideas."[12] To demonstrate their serious intent, civic leaders in Toronto and Ottawa developed urban plans in 1906 and 1915, respectively, based largely on City Beautiful planning principles.

It was in the heady atmosphere of boom and burgeoning population growth at the turn of the century that Thomas Mawson strode into Canada with seven-league boots. Mawson was born in 1861 in England and evolved from being a gardener to a landscape architect and finally to an urban planner in the late nineteenth and early twentieth century. With offices throughout the British Empire, including one in London and Calcutta, he was also active in Vancouver. Here he designed campus plans for Dalhousie University in Halifax, a university in Calgary, and the University of British Columbia. He therefore became a logical choice for the recently formed City Planning Commission in Calgary that was searching for an internationally renowned city planner to develop a long-term plan for an "Ideal City."[13]

Mawson came to Calgary in April of 1912 and delivered an address to the local Canadian Club.[14] Entitled "The City on the Plain and How to Make it Beautiful," he engaged his audience with a philosophical address on the subject of urban planning, detailing the problems of proceeding without one as in England, or having a poor one such as the gridiron town plans of North America. He then launched into a discourse on the City Beautiful and the proper attention that must be paid to the elements of nature, art, and science in creating the perfect city, all the while flattering Calgarians by noting that its recent buildings showed "you have already a high degree of excellence."

> What if Calgary was not blessed by Naure [*sic*] as many other cities are – still we might have parks and gardens. There are only seven notes on the musical scale, but with these seven tones a master can open the gate of Paradise for a moment or draw the veil from Hades itself.... Calgary must see to it that she has playgrounds for her children and see to it right quickly.... The child without playgrounds is father to the man without a job.

He ended by appealing to the civic elite to develop a plan for all ages and classes in the city and to "awaken in the soul of the citizen a high desire for civic art ... by setting before the people a tangible vision of what your city is capable of becoming." Mawson's proposal was put to a vote of the city council and given a unanimous endorsement to proceed early in 1913. A year later, he presented a finished product for a fee of six thousand dollars.[15]

The Mawson Plan of 1914 provided a monumental and comprehensive vision of the city's future – a radial street design that would cut through the gridiron street design already in place. Anticipating the impact of the motorcar, he advocated diverting the flow of traffic out of the centre of the city on diagonal spokes to the outlying areas. Planned vistas were set forth to accentuate present and future buildings, such as the Armouries at the end of Seventh Avenue, and a proposed university in the Spruce Cliff area overlooking the Bow River. The river itself would be the focal point of a continuous system of parks, playgrounds, and boat reaches. To this end, he advised city council to reserve all riverside areas and land too marshy or steep for building purposes. It was his belief that the river escarpments offered an opportunity for natural park development, not unlike Vienna's Ringstrasse, linked by bridges beginning with one at the junction of the Elbow and Bow rivers and ending at a low-level Centre Street bridge. Other grandiose designs of railway depots, shopping malls, and an open-air city market with glassed-roof sections were all a part of the grand vision of a "Garden City on the Bow." Almost by way of a challenge to potential philistines in Calgary, Mawson chided those who would only see the potential cost of his beautification plan by quoting John Ruskin: "Beware of those … who are always crying 'Utopianism.' It is one of the Devil's pet words. Cast it out of your dictionary altogether, there is no need for it. Things are either possible or impossible, you can determine which in any human or social state."[16]

Mawson's vision, however, was not to be implemented; World War I and a deepening recession heightened other civic priorities. Mawson was forced to close his office in Vancouver. There were design problems as well posed by his preferred low-level Centre Street Bridge, the boating-reach, and open-air market in a climate such as Calgary's with river-flooding and icing problems. But most problematic of all was the astronomical cost his plan would have entailed. It was – and remains – a reminder of the optimism of the Edwardian Age – a superb example of the ideals of Civic Beautiful planners with lavish civic centres and elaborate walkways and parks in a Garden City environment. (The irony is that Mawson's handsome watercolour drawings were found insulating the walls of an inner city garage when fortunately rescued from obscurity, a harshly realistic separation of function from form.)[17]

The second venue for Thomas Mawson's visionary approach to long-term urban planning was the city of Regina. The city fathers wanted a development proposal for Wascana Park in 1913. As a spinoff, the Regina City Planning Association was formed in March of 1913 in direct imitation of the British City Planning Association. Its stated purpose was the "promotion of city planning and garden suburbs … housing and improvement of sanitation."[18] The city was then prompted into piggy-backing onto a provincial initiative to hire Thomas Mawson to prepare a landscaping plan for the new Legislative Building. The civic government would get a comprehensive plan for city development in the long-term, while the landscaping plan for Wascana Lake would be implemented in the short term. Mawson's plan was finished in 1914, but the city refused even to address any of its recommendations, largely on the grounds of cost. It was not even considered until after the war, when the city, under pressure from the province, finally agreed to make the plan public in 1923.[19]

Mawson's Regina plan was in the same spirit of the City Beautiful vision that he had proposed for Calgary. The gridiron North American cityscape was rejected in favour of a more aesthetic circular and radial plan, which would move the city forward "with firmness and zeal towards the realization of your dreams for a Capital at once efficient, commanding and beautiful."[20] He predicted that the city would have a population of 120,000 and would be the centre of government and of marketing, manufacturing, and railway transportation for the province. The circular design of the plan showed the core centre area as being commercial, administrative, and government, surrounded by residential areas of the first- and second-class citizens in the south end. In the north half would be an industrial and third-class residential district. Mawson believed in the segregation of "the foreign elements" and the working class in residential suburbs that would be distinct from the more preferred residential areas to the south.

Mawson consistently integrated aesthetics and form with function. His planned city took into account motor vehicle ingress and egress from centre to periphery along diagonal routes.[21] He also allowed for the integration of the Grand Trunk and Canadian Pacific railway systems in a common station, which would serve "as the Organic traffic Centre." As well, he planned for the "natural evolution of suburban areas" where traffic collected, and frequently developed into "complete community centres – assembly halls, theatres, cinemas, schools, churches, etc." These he would plan for in groupings around open spaces, and control with "some uniformity in the facades of the shops … the alignments of shop fronts and especially their show boards and signs." All should be done as a "properly coordinated artistic conception and each community ought to show in a minor key the dignity and civic consciousness which should govern the great civic centre."[22] He believed that the greatest care and consideration had to be reserved for the city centre. He compared a centre that was badly conceived to "a man suffering from heart trouble." Congestion would block it from achieving a proper state of "civic health." Viewing himself as a sort of "civic doctor" bringing proper arterial connection and blood flow to the road system, Mawson tinkered with the road networks. He envisioned a civic centre at one end of a vista and the Houses of Parliament at the other on 16th Avenue.[23]

The park system was the crowning glory of his plan. He believed it would "raise Regina from its present treeless condition and so adorn it with sylvan beauty that it will become the Garden City of the Prairies, a worthy Capital of a great Province."[24] Its three essential divisions were: protective belts of greenery, the Wascana Creek and Lake parkway, and boulevards and smaller parks to connect the first two. Further to this, he added exhibition grounds and a park, and recreation grounds on the Ponton Reserve with lawns and playing fields, not unlike Hyde Park in London. The jewel in the crown was undoubtedly Wascana Lake, "Regina's aesthetic asset," which simply needed the enhancements suggested above. Then, in a rhetorical flourish designed to curry favour with his Canadian clients, Mawson indulged them with a boosterist epilogue to a "Giant Country," which will assume its place "among the world's most famous and influential nations." And to be sure, he was laying in the "infant present the foundations stones of an uncommonly lusty manhood."[25]

It was the responsibility of the city, under the guidance of the new *Town Planning and Rural Development Act* of 1917, to prepare a development plan out of Mawson's Report by 1921. The city's development plan ignored all of the recommendations but one as being too ambitious and expensive, that one being the enhancement of Wascana Lake. The Rotary Club of Regina began the development of a small park to the west of Albert Street, but not until 1938.[26] Nevertheless, this one small step was one more than had been made in Calgary. The demise of both of Mawson's plans marked a sad end to the glory days of the prewar boom, when all seemed possible in dreams conjured on the banks of the Bow River and Wascana Creek. Once again, the realities of war and depression had triumphed over the urban dreams born of prewar prosperity and optimism.

The Garden City and City Beautiful movements had been inspirations for social progressives in their hope for a complete societal transformation, since modernism relied so heavily on the city as its central element of communication, and its organizing metaphor in the twentieth century. With the roughly equal balance of urban and rural population in the offing, the prospect of a new social order, in secular terms, lay in the city. Its new exemplars, "the modernist pilgrims,"[27] as Ramsay Cook has called them in *The Regenerators*, were the Christian reformers like W. L. Mackenzie King, J. S. Woodsworth, A. E. Smith, and Salem Bland. Their "earthly paradise" – a veritable "Kingdom of God on Earth" – was the modern metropolis, the proving ground of the new man, and the central nervous system of the new nation. The Promised Land had, so to speak, left the country and come to the city.

All now seemed possible in the rarefied air of prosperity in the early twentieth century. An incipient social science for cities was in the works, and it was not long before western Canadians were imbued with the progressive impulse. The rapid peopling of the rural West in the decade prior to 1914 combined with an astonishing population boom in western Canadian cities cried out for planning expertise to deal with issues of sanitation, health, overcrowding of immigrant ghettoes, and attendant social problems such as illiteracy, liquor controls, prostitution, and crime. Winnipeg's north end had already become the stuff of fictional legend with Ralph Connor's depiction of *The Foreigner* in 1909. Other ethnic enclaves, or "foreign quarters," had been identified in the east end of Fort William, the south end of Port Arthur, "Germantowns" in east end Regina and in east Calgary, and an ethnic polyglot in Vancouver's east end. All were identified as "problematic" for the host populations of these cities, which agonized over "the alien problem," with its threats to the health and safety, as well as the cultural well-being, of the dominant class. Civic planning had thus become a must from the point of view of emergent civic elites by the end of the first decade of the new century. They were spurred on by larger national concerns emanating from such organizations as the Commission on Conservation.

Equally, such national organizations as the Protestant churches, service clubs, and the national press added their voice to the chorus of social concern over the impact of "urban evils," which threatened the social fabric of the city. In fact, the most comprehensive studies of the emerging problems of Canadian cities were provided by the churches and their missions in the city, such as the Fred Victor Mission in Toronto, and All Peoples' Mission in north Winnipeg. It was the latter which prompted one of the restive young Methodists, James Shaver Woodsworth, into implementing progressive social thought into social action over his four years as superintendent of All Peoples' from 1907 to 1911. Woodsworth produced two holistic and social scientific studies of the city of Winnipeg: *Strangers within Our Gates* (1908) and *My Neighbor* (1911). Indeed, in his passion for historical facts, social statistics, and multiple citation of impeccable progressive sources, Woodsworth admitted that *Strangers* had "no literary pretensions; its aim is entirely practical."[28] The data and analysis, which followed, was a solid sociological analysis of prewar immigration to Canada, replete with contradictory ethnic stereotypes of the day. Mostly, its religious fervour and social passion was palpable on every page, as he sought to lay out solutions for the social problems ensuing from immigration.

It was in the sequel, *My Neighbor*, that Woodsworth focused on the city of Winnipeg with its problems arising from ethnic ghettos in the north end, from the vantage point of his social laboratory of All Peoples' Mission. While it too was an incipient sociological treatise, it was also a religious jeremiad on poverty, want, and despair. He wrote with a post-millennial conviction in the creation of a heavenly city with a "highly developed social man, [who] will be psychologically, ethically and spiritually far in advance of his ancestors." This conviction was equally rooted in his faith in the progressive application of science, echoing the utopianism of H. G. Wells' *Anticipation of the Reaction of Scientific Progress upon Human Life and Thought* as proof of the efficacy of a scientific social regeneration of the city. Together, religion and science would usher in a new social order, a vision inspired by Revelations 21, verses 2&3: "And I saw a holy city, new Jerusalem, coming down out of heaven from God, made ready as a bride adorned for her husband."[29]

The creation of a new man in a new city required a biological planning of the earthly paradise. The science of eugenics was the vehicle for the creation of this new racial prototype, the "new Canadian" who would populate the Garden City and the City Beautiful. Much as the American was the new man, the Canadian prototype would be the expression of the new-world Eden. In that sense, Woodsworth was the consummate assimilationist, even though he appreciated the diversity of world cultures.[30] Citing Israel Zangwill's *The Melting Pot*, he clearly preferred the disappearance of old-world feuds: "Into the crucible with you all! God is making the American."[31] In the *Manitoba Free Press*, Woodsworth urged the creation of a new and united "Canadian people," free of the racial, national, religious, social, and linguistic prejudices of the past.[32] This "new people" would, for the most part, exclude certain "races" such as Orientals and Blacks, as well as those who were considered medically unfit. And the restrictions extended to the feeble-minded and the insane in his eugenicist ideas, which he later developed during World War I.[33] Perhaps inspired by wartime rhetoric, he became more militant in condemning the arrival of "degenerate stock," which threatened "the vast experiment in race culture" then underway in North America, and further extenuated by the war losses of men "most fit to be the fathers of a virile race."[34]

If careful race selection and eugenics were to solve the problems posed by nature, social planning would resolve issues of nurture and environment. Government by Wellsian experts, or "social physicians," would diagnose and cure the complex social problems inherent in the civic organism.[35] His guiding light was an abiding faith in the natural and social sciences, derived from nineteenth-century positivism. Problems of corruption and machine politics would be resolved by the new progressive political science, exemplified by S. Morley Wickett's *Municipal Government in Canada* (1907), and a whole host of American progressive classics by Lincoln Steffens, Richard Ely, and James Bryce. As a thoroughgoing modernist, Woodsworth saw public education as the premier vehicle of assimilation and uplift in the population as a whole, which he believed, would result in an enlightened and right-thinking citizenry. Similarly, social science, in the form of geography and civic planning, would address the spatial problems of the city through the proper management of civic space to accommodate parks, playgrounds, and industrial parks or "villages" to create a healthy civic environment for working families. Urban sanitation, closely monitored by the municipal council and the department of health, would similarly ensure proper sanitation by-laws, quarantines, and isolation hospitals to control communicable diseases. In short, he presented a comprehensive plan to redress "the seamy side of social pathology" in the city.[36]

Woodsworth's vision of the ideal city widened further after his resignation from All Peoples' in 1911. He was commissioned to do studies of several other Canadian cities via the Methodist and Presbyterian churches. He was assisted in this task by W. A. Riddell for Regina, and by Bryce Stewart for Port Arthur and Fort William. In fact, the reports of the latter were almost a boiler-plate version of the Winnipeg study, despite the social differences in these other cities. The positivistic collection of data in these urban studies – crime and health statistics, overcrowded housing reports, the state of public education, parks and playground studies – had become a formulaic condemnation of the moral economy of the city. "The liquor problem." "the social evil," and "the immigrant problem" were the main subject headers. But there were the minor notes of social disapproval, such as the red-light district's proximity in Fort William to a mattress factory, or the number of occupants of local poolrooms as socially dangerous. For example, it was noted that the Ruthenian poolroom at Westfort "polled 29 persons at 9 p.m." More serious yet were the occupants of two moving picture theatres, the polling of which showed that the Palace Theatre counted 362 patrons, of which "English-speaking [were] 145; Foreign, 217." Worse were the counts for the local bar rooms in Fort William, thirteen of which were counted and contained 229 patrons between nine and ten p.m. on March 11, 1913. The mere existence of foreign dance halls was a lesser cause for concern, since the count showed an average age of 25, with men outnumbering women 2:1, but since there were no alternative community venues other than two skating rinks, there could be "little objection … made."[37]

The heaviest concentration of Bryce Stewart's fire, like that of his mentor Woodsworth, was reserved for the "foreign quarter" as breeding grounds for crime and the consequent safety of the children. Overcrowding of rooming houses led naturally to depravity, which impacted on children, and more broadly upon the morals of future generations. "When we realize the meaning of the facts than can be proven from records, that the average of convictions that those born in America [*sic*] of foreign parents is three times that of the native-born American; that the second generation of those coming to us from other countries is twice as criminal as his father, and three times as criminal as the native-born, we will not rest until a solution has been reached in regard to the living conditions amongst the 'Foreigners.'"[38] The social pathology of the ghetto was all the more dangerous because of its imperviousness to the penetration of majoritarian Canadian values, which would normally lead the children towards assimilation. The institutional completeness of the ethnic east-end of Fort William posed formidable barriers to majority values and assimilation in that regard:

> The social, political and industrial forces of the community have little force in the Canadianization of these peoples in as far as the adults are concerned at least. The children learn English in the schools, but the older members of the immigrant community have little connection with the libraries and opportunities for instruction in English are few. They attend their own churches, and therefore have no opportunity of becoming Canadianized through these institutions. They have their own societies and their own social gatherings. The English papers scarcely reach them at all, each reading as they do generally being in their own native papers. In the industries, they work in their own national groups to a very great extent, this being true of

> the foundries and all the railroad construction work, so that there they come into little contact with Canadian life.[39]

The social cures for these problems had to be drastic, holistic, and draconian in nature, involving legislation for child welfare abuses, and legal controls and enforcement of the liquor trade and of prostitution. But there was massive social intervention required in the building of more and better hospitals, clinics, and isolation hospitals for disease control, and for similar institutions for the mentally feeble and insane. Parks, playgrounds, community centres, all of the amenities later adopted in the twentieth century and widely accepted as inherent to good urban living after World War II, were advocated in these pre-World War I social surveys conducted by the moral reform.

Perhaps the most holistic and idealistic expressions of social regeneration were offered by Salem Bland, an Ontario-educated Methodist divine, who had formulated his theories of a "new Christianity" before coming west in 1903 to teach at Wesley College. He had fused the emerging social thought of Herbert Spencer, Benjamin Kidd, and Henry George, with an activist Christian mission by 1899. In doing so, he chose the metaphor of the "City of Destruction," which expressed the old Christian theology of escapism and passivity, versus "The City of Salvation," which was an activist social faith, expressed in mission churches, college settlements, good government clubs, and municipal reform associations.[40] Soon he had inspired his students at Wesley College in Winnipeg, men such as William Irvine, who went into the secular realm of United Farm politics in Alberta, and William Ivens, who became active in the labour church in Winnipeg.[41] Bland himself became directly involved in the prohibition, single tax, and direct legislation causes, and in July, 1917, was listed on the masthead of *The Single Taxer* newspaper as honorary president. In fact, his extracurricular activities in social causes likely cost him his position at Wesley College in the same year. His loss was lamented by the editor of the newspaper, D. W. Buchanan, because "he made himself offensive to certain interests which exercise a powerful influence in the affairs of the college."[42]

During his tenure in western Canada, Bland further developed his abiding interest in science as the key to social regeneration, particularly in relation to modern urban living. In 1908, at a convocation address at the University of Saskatchewan, he urged the creation of an academic department devoted to the "science of civics," in addition to another devoted to the "science of money-making," or political economy, and another to the "science of man-making," or sociology.[43] Throughout his sermons in this period, Bland continually reconciled his Christian faith with science, such as in his sermon on "Darwin and His Significance to the Christian Church," given in August of 1909, which showed "science triumphing in every case" of controversy from Galileo to evolution.[44] His conviction that science was the key to an "orderly, scientific, and brotherly regeneration" deepened during the war years in his sermons on the labour movement.[45]

All of Salem Bland's convictions on the necessary union of science and a new social Christianity were fused in his final treatise *The New Christianity or the Religion of the New Age,* published in 1920. Here, his Hegelian elaboration on the historic evolution of Christianity culminates in the final Comtean scientific phase of "positive Christianity" in Canada, which was American and continental in character, but Canadian in its "simple, yet free and varied, practical, democratic, brotherly, in a word, truly catholic" nature.[46] This amalgam of humanism and science appeared to have led Mackenzie King to a similar, albeit more secular, intellectual space in *Industry and Humanity*.[47] King's ruminations on the necessary compromises between capital and labour in collective bargaining and his concern for scientific planning in the city were reminiscent of other progressive reformers in search of solutions to a divided world.

The year 1919 was a turning point for another radical Methodist reformer, A. E. Smith, whose experience paralleled that of Salem Bland and J. S. Woodsworth. He too had followed the social gospel reform path in his various ministries in Portage la Prairie, Dauphin, and Brandon in Manitoba, Nelson, B.C., and Calgary, Alberta. By the time of World War I, Smith too had contemplated the potential of an ascendant labour Christianity, and also espoused science as its leading edge. "The duty of the hour," he wrote, "is to discover to ourselves the fact that there is a science of social architecture, and the building resulting therefrom must be founded upon righteousness and fraternity, and reared in the love of God and man."[48] By the end of the Winnipeg General Strike and the repression that followed, Smith devolved quickly towards politics as a provincial labour member for Brandon, and then finally towards scientific socialism and communism by 1925. All the while, he remained convinced that social science would remain the basis for the reconstruction of society.

The postwar denouement of the social gospel with its faith in the establishment of a new order left the city of salvation, the city of yes, in some doubt. The utopian impulse had lost its progressive steam in the aftermath of the war and the Winnipeg General Strike and moved into the wider battleground of secular political and social action in the twenties. The transitions of Woodsworth, Irvine, Smith, and Ivens into what the Marxists later called "praxis" in the class struggle was also exemplified by the changing vision of E. A. Partridge, the Sage of Sintaluta, founder of the Grain Growers' Association, and a leader of early co-operative action. While he was from the beginning a more pragmatic secular thinker than other social reformers, Partridge nevertheless proved something of a contrarian with a utopian vision he articulated in 1925 of a state of western Canada, COALSAMAO, extending from the Pacific Ocean to Lake Superior.[49]

Entitled *A War on Poverty* (1925), it envisioned an alternative state or co-operative commonwealth, organized along different premises, much like a Wellsian state with a high court of control, and government or rather administration by experts. While neither specifically urban nor rural, this co-operative commonwealth would be organized into uniform "camps" of from 3,500 to 7,000 inhabitants, each one forming the basis of local and regional governments. With the elimination of the capitalist system and its reorganization into a state system of socialism, the way would be open for the elimination of private property, private debt, and taxation, and thereby the elimination of poverty, he believed. Since there would be no need to organize large pools of labour to serve capital interests, there need not be any cities. Instead the "camps" would be "all *suburban* with the same educational and recreational opportunities, and the same domestic conveniences for all." Standardization of every aspect of life from dress, housing, and technology was envisioned; even language would be standardized along phonetic lines. In sum, uniformity in all things was the order of life, right down to oleomargarine, since the Kingdom of Heaven would be a vegetarian commonwealth devoid of animal husbandry![50]

Little wonder then that Carl Berger calls Partridge's vision more of a dystopia – "an existence as joyless as that of the barracks" – than a utopia.[51] Yet in his own way, Partridge was offering what he thought was a real alternative social vision of (e)utopia, a good and real place, rather than an (o)utopia or "no place," with no working plans, nor real people.[52] A more telling contemporary criticism was offered by one of Partridge's correspondents, a businessman with the co-operative Wawanesa Mutual Insurance Company, who agreed on the real necessity of reform, but not the method or the extent Partridge's plan. He counselled that leaders should not get too far ahead of their supporters, just as he thought the prohibitionists had, and that the pendulum was now swinging the other way. He offered the practical view: "Until people become Utopians at heart, the Utopian form of government will not work. It might be possible to partially enforce Utopian laws if we have a sufficiently strong police force, but this would not make a Utopia."[53] The stark realism of the reader's response, a builder in the co-operative insurance field, in many ways matched the starkly realist vision of Partridge's own vision, which was a long way from the religious idealism of the social gospel a decade earlier.

The tension between the ideal and the real, the city of yes and the city of no, was in essence a binary, bipolar social construction. In the case of the City Beautiful and Garden City versus the real cities of western Canada, the former were metropolitan, imperial visions of an idealized heavenly city imposed upon the unplanned, organic urban growths that had taken hold on the treeless landscapes of the western Canadian prairies. The fate of Thomas Mawson's architectural drawings as insulation for a garage was not unlike the unhappy fate of the Stegner family volumes of Shakespeare loaned out to friends and discarded in the town dump, as described in Wallace Stegner's prairie memoir, *Wolf Willow*. The harshness of the frontier environment was unyielding, not only economically but also in mind and spirit. It was rather inimical to imported ideals and aesthetics. It would take another two generations before urban planning would take hold in the wealthier cities of the post-World War II period, and Mawson's plans dusted off and restored for discussion at a conference in 1978. Park planning, plus-15 walkways, glassed-in malls and atriums were all possible in the heady economic days of the late 1970s.

In essence then, the struggle over the birth of the western Canadian city was about total visions of a new order confronting old realities. Whether it would take as its expression a beautiful form combined with efficient function, as in Mawson's aesthetic vision, or the City of Salvation versus the City of Destruction, as in Salem Bland's view, it was dialectically expressed. Theirs was the planned paradise of a new world order of social perfection and regeneration versus a passive acceptance of the world as it was, of urban decay and degeneration. Their vision was also about inhabiting this brave new world with a new race of people via eugenics, the creation of a new Adam and Eve for the New Jerusalem. In that sense, the hard edge of struggle for the new earthly paradise might be won first in the city even before the country, since that was a more dramatic theatre of conflict, the sunshine and the shadow of labour-versus-capital confrontation. The potential of creating a modern paradise for the next generation also lay in the built environment of the parks and playgrounds. These quickening aspirations were summed up in Thomas Mawson's wish expressed above, to open "the gate of Paradise for a moment or draw the veil from Hades itself," for without parks and playgrounds "the child ... is father to the man without a job."

In the same sense, the urban social gospel and its vision of a civilized, progressive city was in a great hurry to construct a heavenly earthly paradise, an urban Kingdom of God in western Canada. For Woodsworth, the plan was to create a better world, particularly for the next generation. "My main line is the kiddies," he wrote. "We must make them good Christians and good Canadians, which is the same thing."[54] The dark side of that vision was its exclusivity as expressed in negative eugenics, and in the fearful view of less generous lights like J. W. Sparling, who wrote in the Introduction to *Strangers within Our Gates*: "We must see to it that the civilization and ideals of Southeastern Europe are not transplanted to and perpetuated on our virgin soil."[55] The social message was clear: the only way that Canada as the Promised Land could be saved was on the social battleground of the city, and that was by the total effort of all that God and Science combined would allow. Otherwise, "barbarians" would overrun the gates to the heavenly city, and Canada as a Christian paradise would be lost. Thus, the social gospellers were indeed poised between heaven and hell in the industrial city. To some extent, science offered a calmer objective voice, promising social salvation through science, education, and social action.

Yet, their legacy, despite the criticism that the reformers had gone too far, too fast, was impressive over the long haul, as the struggle still proved worth the candle. A co-operative commonwealth based on cooperation of both farm and labour was still possible and was taken much further by the political activities of the wheat pools, the co-operatives, and the political actions of the Ginger group, the Progressives, and the United Farmers in the 1920s. The co-operative ideals were further hardened in the crucible of the Great Depression into two resilient strands of pre- and post-millennial Christianity – Social Credit in Alberta and the

Co-operative Commonwealth in Saskatchewan. The search for an ideal new order, a city on the hill, proved to be a resilient ideology after all.

NOTES

1 Yevgeny Yevtushenko, *The City of the Yes, The City of the No* (Melbourne: Sun Books, 1966). This printed version differs somewhat in title, but is similar in spirit to the oral reading delivered in Calgary.

2 See Marie Louise Bernieri, *Journey through Utopia* (New York: Shocken, 1971); Robert S. Fogarty, *All Things New: American Communes and Utopian Movements, 1860–1914* (Chicago: University of Chicago Press, 1990); Carl J. Guarnieri, *The Utopian Alternative: Fourierism in Nineteenth Century America* (Ithaca, NY: Cornell University Press, 1991).

3 H. G. Wells, *A Modern Utopia* (London: Chapman & Hall, 1905). Huxley and Orwell are published in several editions since the original dates indicated in the text.

4 Fred Landon, *Lake Huron* (New York: Bobbs Merrill, 1944), 118–19.

5 A. W. Rasporich, "Utopian Ideals and Community Settlements in Western Canada," in *The Canadian West*, ed. H. C. Klassen (Calgary: Comprint, 1977), 37–62.

6 Ibid., 56–60.

7 Herbert B. Ames, *The City Below the Hill* (Toronto: University of Toronto Press, repr., 1972).

8 Peter J. Smith, "The Principle of the Utility and Origin of Planning Legislation in Alberta, 1912–75," in *The Usable Urban Past: Planning and Politics in the Modern Canadian City*, eds. Alan F. J. Artibise and Gilbert Stelter (Toronto: Macmillan, 1979), 200–202.

9 See Walter van Nus, "The Fate of the City Beautiful Thought in Canada, 1893–1930," in *The Canadian City: Essays in Canadian Urban History*, eds. Alan Artibise and Gilbert Stelter (Toronto: Macmillan, 1979), 167–86. Paul Rutherford, "Tomorrow's Metropolis: The Urban Reform Movement in Canada, 1880–1920," in P. Rutherford, ed., *Saving the Canadian City: The First Phase, 1880–1920. An Anthology of Early Articles on Urban Reform* (Toronto: University of Toronto Press, 1974). David Gordon, "Introducing a City Beautiful Plan for Canada's Capital: Edward Bennett's 1914 Speech to the Canadian Club," *Planning History Studies* 12, no. 1–2: 13–51.

10 Oiva Saarinen, "The Influence of Thomas Adams and the British New Towns Movement in the Planning of Canadian Resource Communities," in *The Usable Urban Past*, eds. Artibise and Stelter, 270–71.

11 Ibid., 274.

12 Cited in Thomas Gunton, "The Ideas and Policies of the Canadian Urban Planning Profession, 1909–31," in *The Usable Urban Past*, eds. Artibise and Stelter, 180.

13 Max Foran, *Calgary: An Illustrated History* (Toronto: James Lorimer, 1978), 98.

14 Calgary *Morning Albertan*, April 12, 1912. See also ibid., April 9 and 11, 1912.

15 Calgary *News Telegram*, January 21, 1913.

16 Thomas Mawson, *Calgary, Past, Present and Future* (Calgary: City Planning Commission, 1914), p. 78. The original title used by Mawson was *Calgary: A Preliminary Scheme for Controlling the Economic Growth of the City*. See also E. Joyce Morrow, *Calgary Many Years Hence: The Mawson Report in Perspective* (Calgary: City of Calgary/University of Calgary, 1979, 48pp. [unpaginated]), *passim*.

17 Trevor Boddy, *Modern Architecture in Alberta* (Regina: Canadian Plains Research Center/Alberta Culture and Multiculturalism, 1987), 29.

18 William Brennan, *Regina: An Illustrated History* (Toronto: James Lorimer, 1989), 84.

19 Ibid., 125.

20 Thomas Mawson, Regina: A Preliminary Report on the Development of the City, 4. Ms. Copy, Archives of Saskatchewan.

21 Ibid., 15–16.

22 Ibid., 23–24.

23 Ibid., 27–28.

24 Ibid., 32.

25 Ibid., 33, 35, 48.

26 William Brennan, *Regina*, 125. See also his article, "Visions of a City Beautiful: The Origin and Impact of the Mawson Plans for Regina," *Saskatchewan History* 46 (Fall 1994): 19–33.

27 Ramsay Cook, *The Regenerators: Social Criticism in Late Victorian English Canada* (Toronto: University of Toronto Press, 1985), 196–227.

28 J. S. Woodsworth, *Strangers within Our Gates* (Toronto: University of Toronto Press, reprint, 1972), 8. For the larger context, see Richard Allen, ed., *The Social Gospel in Canada*, (Ottawa: National Museums of Canada, 1975); Richard Allen, *The Social Passion: Religion and Social Reform in Canada, 1914–28*, (Toronto: University of Toronto Press, 1978).

29 J. S. Woodsworth, *My Neighbor* (Toronto: University of Toronto Press, reprint, 1972), 22–24.

30 Allen Mills, *Fool for Christ: The Political Thought of J. S. Woodsworth* (Toronto: University of Toronto Press, 1991), 48

31 J. S. Woodsworth, *My Neighbor*, 79.

32 Mills, *Fool for Christ*, 49.

33 Ibid., 43–44.

34 Lorry W. Felske, "Science and the Radical Social Gospel in Western Canada" (master's thesis, University of Calgary, 1975), 29–40. See also, for eugenics in the West and Canada: Ian H. Clarke, "Public Provisions for the Mentally Ill in Alberta, 1907–36" (master's thesis, University of Calgary, 1973); Angus McLaren, *Our Own Master Race: Eugenics in Canada* (Toronto: McClelland and Stewart, 1990); Allan Levine, "Perfect People, Perfect Country," *The Beaver* 85, no. 2 (April/May 2005): 26–31.

35 Ibid., 41.

36 J. S. Woodsworth, *My Neighbor*, 129–54.

37 Bryce M. Stewart, Report of a Preliminary and General Social Survey of Fort William, n.p.: The Department of Temperance and Moral Reform of the Methodist Church and The Board of Social Service and Evangelism of the Presbyterian Church, March, 1913, 12–20, *passim*.

38 Ibid., 32

39 Ibid., 8. The reference to "institutional completeness" of ethnic groups is to Raymond Breton, "Institutional completeness of ethnic communities and the personal relations of immigrants," *American Journal of Sociology* 70, no. 2 (September 1964): 193–205. For a further elaboration of this concept, see M. Kalbach and W. Kalbach, *Perspectives on Ethnicity in Canada* (Toronto: Harcourt Canada, 2000), 35–48.

40 See Richard Allen's introduction to Salem Bland, *The New Christianity, or the Religion of the New Age*, xvii. See also his "Salem Bland and the Spirituality of the Social Gospel: Winnipeg and the West, 1903–13," in *Prairie Spirit: Perspectives on the Heritage of the United Church of Canada in the West*, eds. D. Butcher et al. (Winnipeg: University of Manitoba Press, 1985), 218–32.

41 Vera Fast, "The Labor Church in Winnipeg," in ibid., 233–49.

42 *The Single Taxer*, July 1917, 7.

43 Felske, "Science and the Radical Social Gospel in western Canada," 53. He cites Regina *Morning Leader*, January 9, 1908.

44 United Church Archives, Box 5, no. 447, Salem Bland Papers. See also "Influence of Science on Xty," 18, Oct., 190–8 Box 1, ff.51.

45 Felske, "Science and the Radical Social Gospel," 54.

46 Bland, *The New Christianity*, 72–73.

47 See Mackenzie King, *Industry and Humanity: A Study in the Principles Underlying Reconstruction*, ed. D. J. Bercuson (Toronto: University of Toronto reprint, 1972); and his "Town Planning as the Premier Sees It," *Journal of the Town Planning Institute of Canada* 6 (1927): 1.

48 Cited in Felske, "Science and the Radical Social Gospel," 112. See also A. E. Smith, *All My Life l Rev. A. E. Smith, An Autobiography* (Toronto: Progress Books, 1977).

49 See E. A. Partridge, *A War on Poverty: The War that Can End War*, (Winnipeg: Wallingford Press, 1925), 129–30. COALSAMAO is a contraction of the provinces of British Columbia, Alberta, Saskatchewan, Manitoba and Ontario. See also Murray Knuttila, *"That Man Partridge": E. A. Partridge, His Thoughts and Times* (Regina: Canadian Plains Research Center, 1994), 95 pp.

50 Partridge, *A War on Poverty*, 131–56, *passim*.

51 Carl Berger, "A Canadian Utopia: The Cooperative Commonwealth of Edward Partridge," in Stephen Clarkson, *Visions 2020* (Edmonton: Hurtig, 1970), 262.

52 Partridge, *A War on Poverty*, 130.

53 Saskatchewan Archives, Paynter Family Papers, Anon. to E. A. Partridge, Regina, January 7, 1929.

54 J. E. Rea, " My main line is the kiddies … make them good Christians and good Canadians, which is the same thing," in Wsevolod Isajiw, *Identities: The Impact of Ethnicity on Canadian Society* (Toronto: Peter Martin, 1977), 3–10.

55 J. S. Woodsworth, *Strangers within Our Gates*, 8.

9

LAND OF THE SECOND CHANCE: NELLIE MCCLUNG'S VISION OF THE PRAIRIE WEST AS PROMISED LAND

Randi Warne

> In Canada we are developing a pattern of life and I know something about one block of that pattern. I know it for I helped to make it, and I know that I can say that now without any pretense or modesty, or danger of arrogance, for I know that we who make the pattern are not important, but the pattern is.[1]

This oft-cited reflection by Canadian bestselling author and social activist Nellie L. McClung does not explicitly detail the nature of the pattern she helped to work, but it is impossible to consider her many contributions to Canadian life without taking into account the centrality of prairie life to her activism and identity. A cursory reading of Nellie McClung's treatment of the Prairie West in her novels and in the speeches and essays that comprise *In Times Like These* would suggest she was a naively optimistic propagandist. The Canadian prairies were touted variously as "the Land of the Second Chance," and the "Land of Beginning Again." In light of utopian hopes such as these, there is some merit in considering McClung to be a staunch advocate of the redemptive, transformative power of prairie life. However, a closer reading reveals a position that is more nuanced and multi-faceted.

The essay that follows will focus primarily on McClung's four novels, *In Times Like These*, and her two-volume autobiography, in the hope that the complexity of her position may be better appreciated.[2] As I have argued elsewhere, Nellie McClung used her writing as a pulpit from which she could preach a gospel of feminist activism and social transformation.[3] She maintained those convictions throughout her life, but the context within which she advanced her cause changed over time, resulting in a change in mental landscape that is particularly underscored in her final novel, *Painted Fires*. The effect of McClung's own experience of moving from the sheltered life of a prairie pharmacist's wife to an internationally known writer, social activist, and public figure, along with the impact of the suffrage campaign and World War I and the aftermath of both of these socially dramatic events, will also be noted. In the end, this article will conclude that, while Nellie McClung did indeed hold high hopes for the Prairie West as Promised Land, she was neither as naïve nor as unconditionally optimistic as a superficial reading of her work might suggest. She was well aware of the harsh demands of building a new life in a less than hospitable climate[4] and she "preached her text" all the more enthusiastically as a result.

Prior to embarking on an exploration of McClung's writing, it is useful to consider the notion of the Promised Land itself. The story takes its origins in the Biblical book of Exodus. An oppressed and enslaved people, the Israelites, are led out of their Egyptian captivity by a divinely chosen leader, towards a new land "flowing with milk and honey" (Exodus 13:5), promised to them by God. This land is not empty – indeed, it is inhabited by any number of peoples, including "the Canaanites, the Hittites, the Amorites, the Hivites, and the Jebusites" (Exodus 13:5). Yet as God's Chosen, the Israelites', claim to the land supersedes those of its current inhabitants. The story of Exodus is thus a complex tale of unjust suffering and servitude eventually overcome through divine intervention and intent, a narrative of entitlement and reward.

The notion of a Promised Land has expanded beyond this narrative to include at least two divergent meanings. The first, more robust version, adheres closely to the Biblical narrative. It figures deeply in and indeed embodies the ideology of "American exceptionalism" that is foundational to the ideology and culture of the United States of America. From John Winthrop's "City on the Hill" to Woodrow Wilson's assertion of the United States as a "redeemer nation," to America's "manifest destiny" to expand its power and influence throughout the globe, the notion of America as a nation specially chosen by God permeates its self-understanding.[5] While undoubtedly a project of Empire, the European colonization of what eventually became Canada is inflected rather differently. Much could be written on this point, but for the purposes of this exploration, it is sufficient to state that Nellie McClung's notion of the "Promised Land" is not the salvific narrative of reward and entitlement found in the Exodus story and the ideology of American exceptionalism. Rather, to the degree that McClung does advocate a notion of a Promised Land, she does so in the second sense this term has come to embody, namely "promise" understood as hope and possibility. In particular, in much (if not all) of her writing, McClung accorded the Prairie West that status, seeing in its broad open vistas a land of opportunity and rich resources waiting only for energetic, hardworking effort to turn it into a welcoming, just, and life-affirming home.

McClung's most direct exposition of this position is found in "The Land of the Fair Deal," one of the culminating chapters of *In Times Like These*. This collection of speeches and essays was published shortly after McClung's move to Edmonton at the end of 1914 and comprises both "set pieces" she had given to advance political positions in Manitoba,[6] and reflections on social issues, such as the plight of the farmer in "As a Man Thinketh." *In Times Like These* currently enjoys pre-eminence in both the popular imagination and in scholarly treatments of her work, due in part to the groundbreaking initiative of Veronica Strong-Boag, who successfully recuperated the volume in 1972.[7] Lively, pithy, and well-adapted to inclusion in whole or in part in courses on Women's History, Canadian History and/or Women's Studies, *In Times Like These* has arguably been taken as representative of McClung's work as a whole. Its rhetorical status[8] is rarely acknowledged and it is worth noting that it definitely did not enjoy pride of place during McClung's lifetime. That it has become so is due in large measure to the preoccupations of the scholars who "rediscovered" McClung in the late 1960s and early 1970s, whose interests focused on "women's rights" in the public political arena.[9] This being said, *In Times Like These* also contains meditations of a different nature, within which the "pattern" McClung refers to in *The Stream Runs Fast* is given prominence.

Political issues such as pacifism, woman suffrage, and temperance[10] were part of this pattern, but their significance is integrated into a larger vision of Canada's role on the global stage. "The Land of the Fair Deal" addresses this within the context of the Great War and its anticipated aftermath. McClung opens her essay with a comment on national character, and the importance of developing Canada's in a distinct way.

While it is as large as Europe, Canada has the advantage of having "no precedents":

> We have no precedents to guide us and that is a glorious thing, for precedents, like other guides, are disposed to grow tyrannical, and refuse to let us do anything on our own initiative. Life grows wearisome in the countries where precedents and conventionalities rule, and nothing can happen unless it has happened before. Here we do not worry about precedents. We make our own![11]

While McClung is ostensibly talking about Canada as a whole, from her examples it is clear she is not referring to the Maritimes, or Quebec, both of which have histories going back to the 1600s, nor even to Ontario, with its somewhat later settlement. For McClung, the epitome of the open future she advocates is the prairies:

> Look out upon our rolling prairies, carpeted with wild flowers, and clotted over with poplar groves, where wild birds sing and chatter, and it does not seem too ideal or visionary that these broad sunlit spaces may be the homes of countless thousands of happy and contented people. The great wide uncultivated prairie seems to open its welcoming arms to the land-hungry, homeless dwellers of the cities, saying, "Come and try me. Forget the past if it makes you sad. Come to me, for I am the Land of the Second Chance. I am the Land of Beginning Again."[12]

In this open land of plenty and opportunity, true justice may be achieved, and a national character established for Canada as a whole:

> Among the people of the world in the years to come, we will ask no greater heritage for our country than to be known as the Land of the Fair Deal, where every race, color and creed will be given exactly the same chance; where no person can 'exert influence' to bring about his personal ends; where no man or woman's past can ever rise up to defeat them; where no crime goes unpunished; where every debt is paid; where no prejudice is allowed to masquerade as a reason; where honest toil will ensure an honest living; where the man who works receives the reward of his labor.[13]

This grand utopian vision is possible, McClung urges, but to do so it is necessary to reject the cultural practices of the past, exemplified by the Kaiser's Germany and embodied in the liquor traffic in Canada.

The complaint that "We have always had liquor drinking"[14] carried no weight with McClung:

> Social customs may change. They have changed. They will change when enough people want them to change. There is nothing about a social custom, anyway, that it should be preserved when we have decided it is of no use to us.[15]

The Canadian prairie, lacking centuries of custom, ostensibly open and unsettled, presented a perfect landscape upon which a new history might be built, one of justice, fairness, and fresh new beginnings.

It is this simple prairie life that forms the foundation for McClung's first two novels, *Sowing Seeds in Danny* (1908) and *The Second Chance* (1910). Set in the rural Manitoba that was McClung's own home, these successive installments in the life of the fictional Watson family radiate with a sense of optimism and ultimate good cheer, despite the family's poverty and the hard conditions under which they live. As the opening poem to *Sowing Seeds in Danny* observes:

> So many faiths – so many creeds, –
> So many paths that wind and wind
> While just the art of being kind, –
> Is what the old world needs![16]

The protagonist of the tales is young Pearlie Watson, a resourceful, quick-witted determined young woman just into her teens. Pearlie is distinguished by her passion to improve the lot of her "Shanty Irish" family, not out of desire for better social standing but because the possibility of doing so amply exists, if one simply applies oneself.[17] Indeed, this is one of the appealing aspects of the prairies – that the conventions and class distinctions of "the East" may be eschewed, however much characters may wish to re-establish them. In *Sowing Seeds in Danny*, McClung illustrates the folly of class pretense through the would-be politician, James Ducker, whose aspirations to be the Conservative nominee for the region are dashed when he mistakes a colleague's toddler son for a "McSorley … Low forehead, pug nose, bull-dog tendencies … surely a regular little Mickey."[18] In addition to skewering ethnic prejudice, McClung also takes a swipe at Conservatives in general, whose main purpose seems to be to try to maintain a static social order over which they rightfully rule.[19]

Small-mindedness – alternately, a lack of vision – is another favourite target for McClung. While she certainly believed that the prairie provided an excellent opportunity for people to work hard and "get ahead," a single-minded focus on the accumulation of material wealth is presented as soul-destroying. Mrs. Motherwell exemplifies how even a good-hearted person can be corrupted. She had been filled with grand dreams and high imagination as a girl, and

> [w]hen she had become the mistress of the big stone house, she had struggled hard against her husband's penuriousness, defiantly sometimes, and sometimes tearfully. But he had held her down with a heavy hand of unyielding determination. At last she grew weary of struggling, and settled down in sullen submission, a hopeless, heavy-eyed, spiritless woman, and as time went by she became greedier for money than her husband.[20]

The Motherwells' deadening influence infects their son, whose legitimate desire for some joy, or entertainment, or fun in life has been so thwarted by his parents' obsession that he becomes vulnerable to the blandishments of the bar-room:

> Tom had never heard any argument against intemperance, only that it was expensive. Now he hated all the petty meanness that he had been so carefully taught.
>
> The first evening that Tom went into the bar-room of the Millford hotel he was given a royal welcome. They were a jolly crowd! They knew how to enjoy life, Tom told himself. What's the good of money if you can't have a little fun with it? ... Thus the enemy sowed the tares.[21]

This perspective of alcohol (ab)use, as a form of "false exhilaration" when genuine entertainment was difficult to find, was held by McClung through most of her life, as was the belief that men were particularly vulnerable to its allure.[22]

There is no doubt that Nellie McClung considered alcohol to be one of the most serious threats to the establishment of the Land of the Fair Deal. She happily rejected the traditions of the past, particularly as they advantaged men and disadvantaged women and children. However, some rules were necessary to protect the "non-combatants" as she called women and children in the liquor battle.[23] McClung explains why temperance was such an important issue: "[T]he liquor traffic ... was corporeal and always present; it walked our streets; it threw its challenge in our faces!"[24] The ubiquity of liquor consumption is confirmed by writer James Gray:

> The universal practice of treating ... brought the problem of excessive drunkenness into the residential areas instead of confining it to the Main Street hotel strip. Grocery drinking with attendant rowdy behaviour, moreover, was done in full view of the women and children who were in and out of the stores on shopping excursions. Many a father who went down to the corner for a bag of potatoes returned listing badly to starboard from the alcoholic ballast he had taken aboard at the store.[25]

For the prairie to truly become the Promised Land, the evils of the liquor traffic needed to be expunged.

Given McClung's life-long advocacy of temperance,[26] it is interesting to consider how she apportions moral responsibility with regard to drinking. As we have seen, blind pursuit of material wealth, such as that found in joyless money-grubbers like the Motherwells, can drive their son to the stimulation of drink. The church is also responsible, as are unwelcoming, snobby Christians.[27] A certain responsibility lies with men as a class, who use the argument about personal liberty to defend their drinking, and McClung makes a telling point by comparing the attitude of these men to the Kaiser, with whose country Canada was currently at war.[28] The government, elected by and constituted by men, is further at fault, for in allowing the sale and consumption of liquor and collecting taxes on it, it is essentially serving the public as a drug-dealer, with unenfranchised women and children bearing the cost.

Given this harsh indictment, McClung's treatment of the alcoholic himself is much more nuanced than might be expected. Her rousing speeches in *In Times Like These* cite numerous violent characters similar to the horse-whipping wife-beater described by James Gray.[29] Yet in her most developed depiction of the drunkard, Bill Cavers, in *The Second Chance*, McClung is remarkably kind and forgiving, depicting him as a good man with a weakness he could not overcome. The practical effects of his drinking remained: a weather-beaten, constantly anxious wife, a depressed and deeply saddened child, a lost farm and lost future; but Bill Cavers himself is not charged with moral perfidy. That indictment belongs in part to the saloon-owner (in this story, Sandy Braden), but even more so to the bartender, who has direct control over service. Sandy

Braden's partner Bob Steele is harsh, venal, callous, and cruel. He joyously regales the patrons of the bar with how he seduced Bill into drinking, even though Bill initially refused. Appealing to personal liberty, he pours Bill drink after drink, despite the fact that Bill has given over all his money to his wife to forestall exactly this kind of circumstance.[30]

Thoroughly drunk, Bill Cavers wanders from the saloon towards the town picnic, where he passes out in the blazing sun and dies. The anger that might be directed towards the alcoholic is instead vented on the bartender, Bob Steele, when the Doctor lands "a smashing blow on the bar-tender's smirking face," drags him out of the bar by his collar, and kicks him into the muddy street.[31] Once again, the prairie Promised Land is compromised by selfish, money-grubbing people with no sense of community or social responsibility. Liquor is a dangerous substance, and its use and abuse a signal of unjust relations between women and men, but in the end the real sin lies in small-minded self-interest, informed by greed and legitimated by an appeal to individual liberty.

The bleak reality that frontier life draws such people to it is countered in McClung's fiction by a redemptive and transformative force mediated by the prophetic figure of Pearlie Watson. McClung's personal papers give no evidence that her own theological position was this transparent, but in both *Sowing Seeds in Danny* and *The Second Chance*, the trusting, uncomplicated faith of a child stands as a witness to God's love and active intervention in the people's lives.[32] When British settler Arthur Wemyss' life is threatened by appendicitis, and the Doctor is paralyzed for fear of killing another patient, it is Pearl's prayer that restores his confidence and allows him to save his patient's life. Similarly, Pearl counsels the discouraged young Bud Perkins who is chafing at the constraints of working on the farm to pray, and to rely on God to make life meaningful. She directs his attention to a cracked window in an old house:

> That old windy is all cracked and patched, but look how it shines when the sun gets a full blaze on it. That's like us, Bud. We're no good ourselves, we're cracked and patched, but when God's love gets a chance at us we can shine and glow.[33]

The trick says Pearl is "to keep turned broadside and catch all that's comin' [our] way."[34] This disposition ultimately serves as a form of insurance that allows people to weather the dark days that surely come.

Another strategy for survival is Pearl's optimistic vision of seeing things, not as they currently are, but as they might be in a finer future, whether that was "a weedy looking lot … [soon to be] aglow with fragrant bloom"[35] or an overworked farm daughter whose beauty had not yet been brought out. As Pearl observes:

> She's got hair … but she rolls it into such a hard little nub you'd never know. It needs to be all fluffed out. That nub of hair is just like Martha herself. It's all there, good stuff in it, but it needs to be fluffed out.[36]

A recurring theme in McClung's writing is the unnecessary and unjust sacrifice of women through overwork and male control of resources, when in reality "[t]here is enough for everyone, if we could get at it."[37] Inspirational figures like Pearl serve to shake people, humorously and encouragingly, out of "indifference and slothfulness," which rather than "real active wickedness" was for McClung the real sin of the world.[38] In sum, redemption is always possible. Nellie McClung's faith as expressed in her first two novels and in *In Times Like These* encouraged readers to adopt a persistent optimistic conviction in the possibility of a better world, the chief impediments to which were ignorance, laziness, and "hoggishness."[39] She is clear: "To bring this about – the even chance for everyone – is the plain and simple meaning of life."[40]

In the second volume of her autobiography, *The Stream Runs Fast*, McClung describes herself as follows:

> So far as I can see the truth, and I do try to see it, there was a queer streak of cheerful imbecility in me up to a certain period of my life. I believed easily, I trusted people; I grew sophisticated at last, but it came the hard way.[41]

She and her colleagues who were fighting for "the emancipation of women … were so sure that better home conditions, the extension of education, and equality of opportunity would develop a happy race of people who would not be dependent on spurious pleasures."[42] *Purple Springs*, the concluding volume of the Pearlie Watson trilogy, gives a fictionalized account of that time. While the theology is less heavy-handed, Pearl Watson remains God's agent on earth, standing by the outcast and working to bring about justice and social transformation. As with the earlier two novels, romantic subplots abound, with their requisite misunderstandings and secrets. The subject matter is more mature (Pearl defends a woman widely believed to be an unmarried mother, and seems unconcerned about her marital status so long as she is good to her child), and the class issues more starkly drawn,[43] but aside from a few twists and turns of plot, a happy conclusion is never in doubt. Pearl eventually wins her man, she enlightens a man who is about to purchase a saloon against his wife's wishes, she effects a reconciliation between the Premier and his estranged daughter-in-law (making him repent his previous injustice to all women in the process), she brings down the government, and she finds a cure for her soon-to-be-husband's wasting disease. Equally remarkable, Pearl takes the lead role in a "Woman's Parliament," a dramatic performance in men seeking enfranchisement from a government comprised of women. The play is a resounding success, putting a further nail in the coffin of a soon-to-be defeated Conservative government.[44] In reality, McClung played the role of the Premier, and the Conservative government was eventually brought down by the scandal surrounding the building of the Manitoba legislature rather than on the suffrage issue. However, the success of the Woman's Parliament in consolidating political sentiment in support of woman suffrage (and by extension, against the Conservatives) was undeniable.[45]

McClung devotes chapters thirteen through fifteen of *The Stream Runs Fast* to the battle for women's equality in Manitoba, and it is clear she considered this a high point of her life. It is worth considering these experiences in the context of the Prairie West as Promised Land. The fight for women's social and political equality was a longstanding enterprise, however the movement waxed and waned over time. Undoubtedly the activists who lobbied the government of Manitoba in the service of reform did so on the shoulders of those who came before, and benefited from the work of those fighting for the same goals elsewhere. At the same time, the influence and effectiveness of the small group of Manitoba women of which McClung was a part remains disproportional for their size and social standing. McClung described the circumstances under which they worked:

> We were only amateurs but we did find out a few things about how the "other half" lived. We made some other discoveries too. We found out that the Local Council of Women could not be our medium.[46] There were too many women in it who were afraid to be associated with any controversial subject. Their husbands would not let them "go active." It might imperil their jobs. The long tentacles of the political

> octopus reached far. So one night at Jane Hample's house on Wolsley Avene [*sic*] we organized the Political Equality League, with membership of about fifteen. We believed that fifteen good women who were not afraid to challenge public opinion could lay the foundations better than a thousand. Some good work had already been done by the Icelandic women of the city [Winnipeg], who had organized the first suffrage society many years before, and the W.C.T.U. could be counted on and the same was true of the Labor women.[47]

Political scientist Linda Trimble has written on the importance of attaining "critical mass" for women's political effectiveness.[48] While Trimble's focus is on female legislators rather than activists, the principle still holds. In McClung's day, Winnipeg was a small enough city that "a few good women" could make a direct and significant impact on the political scene. What is notable is the direct access social reformers seem to have had to the Premier, Sir Rodmond Roblin. An article entitled "Roblin Refuses Suffrage" outlines the fateful meeting of January 27, 1914, when a delegation "organized by the Political Equality League of Manitoba, includ[ing] also representatives from the W.C.T.U., the First Icelandic Woman's Suffrage Association, the Women's Civic League, the Mothers' Association, the Manitoba Grain Growers' Association and the Trades and Labor Council"[49] met with Sir Rodmond on the subject of woman suffrage. The delegation's composition, and its description, are significant, and are therefore worth outlining in some detail:

> The delegation was probably one of the most cosmopolitan companies that has ever approached a government in the interests of a single reform. It represented many nationalities: Anglo-Saxon, Icelandic, Hebrew, African, Polish, and it is difficult to say how many more. High browed professors were there shoulder to shoulder with plain working girls. Nurses, lawyers, business men, journalists, doctors and quiet little housewives whom the census describes as having no occupation. Slips of girls and old men leaning heavily on canes. It filled the legislative chamber and overflowed into the gallery and from the ladies' gallery into the press gallery. That it was a deadly earnest delegation the Premier was left in no doubt before he had concluded his decidedly ineffective reply to the avalanche of argument presented to him by the speakers.[50]

Roblin's reply to the delegation (as one article had it, that the "Home Will Be Ruined by Votes for Women"[51]) served as the basis of McClung's speech in the Woman's Parliament. As noted above, it was a devastating success. The *Montreal Herald* put it succinctly:

> The other evening Mrs. McClung spoke in Winnipeg in the Walker Theatre and long before the advertised hour of her address every seat in the large auditorium was filled. Last Thursday Sir Rodmond spoke here and on Monday his feminine tormentor made him look ridiculous. She has introduced into this campaign the most telling weapon which the bombastic Premier of Manitoba could be attacked and one which no person has ever wielded against him before so poignantly and effectively. All Manitoba has been made to laugh at Sir Rodmond Roblin by Mrs. McClung.[52]

The foregoing illustrates the notion of prairie Promised Land in two ways. The first reflects the relative newness, and small scale, of prairie settlement by non-aborigines. Social distinctions certainly exist in smaller centres, and McClung was adept at engaging these in her novels. At the same time, the fact that prairie culture was still "under construction" meant that questioning, challenging, and negotiating with those in power was an expected part of the mix. As McClung repeatedly described it, there is no need to reproduce worn-out social conventions in this new land. To do so is to be as foolish as lizards who walk into a campfire:

> It looks so warm and inviting, and, of course, there is a social custom among lizards to walk right in, and so they do. The first one goes boldly in, gives a start of surprise, and then shrivels, but the next one is a real good sport, and won't desert a friend, so he walks in and shrivels, and the next one is not a piker, so walks in, too. Who would be a stiff?[53]

The prairie provided open horizons socially as well as geographically. That frontier sensibility arguably served to empower McClung, Emily Murphy, Henrietta Muir Edwards, Louise McKinney, and Irene Parlby to petition for an interpretation of the *British North America Act* regarding women's full personhood under the law, positive resolution of which would allow Mrs. Murphy to be nominated to the Senate. As Murphy put it in a letter to McClung:

> I hear, though, that it has been a terrible shock to the Eastern women that 5 coal-heavers and plough-pushers from Alberta (Can anything good come out of Nazareth?) went over their heads to the

Supreme Court without ever saying, "Please ma'am can we do it?) [*sic*] We know now how to stir up interest in the East – just start it going ourselves."[54]

A second feature of the Prairie West as Promised Land is signalled by the composition of the delegation that met with Sir Rodmond Roblin. Its diversity in class, race, ethnicity, gender, and occupation is noteworthy and has not received the attention it should.[55]

McClung saw the overcoming of traditional cultural divisions as a particular gift offered by the West to those who settled there.[56] Her view is summed up in a short story fittingly entitled "The Way of the West."[57] The story centres around a "sorely, bitterly displeased … Irish Orangeman" named Thomas Shouldice.[58] Shouldice was incensed that "the American settlers who had been pouring in to the Souris valley" had staged a huge celebration of the Fourth of July. Seeing this as "a direct challenge to King Edward himself,"[59] Shouldice resolves to stage an Orange Parade on the Twelfth. Shouldice embodies the old order that McClung believed had to be left behind for the West to live up to its promise. He considered all those who were not like him to be "invaders"[60] against whose depredations witness must be borne, and further that "they should be intimidated to prevent trouble."[61] A motley crew is eventually assembled for "the walk," but enthusiasm for it is markedly lacking. The Methodist minister goes so far as to suggest that the speaker at the event be Father Flynn, as "there's no division of creed west of Winnipeg."[62] Shouldice's attempts to reinforce his own identity by rehearsing conflicts long past is poisonous; in Father Flynn's words, the Orange walk is "an institution of the Evil One to sow discord among brothers."[63]

The ludicrous walk begins, attended by Father Flynn and a large contingent of Americans who had no idea what an Orange walk signified but were happy to have a party.[64] Shortly, however, the drummer (who remembered the priest's kindness to his family and was deeply uncomfortable about the walk) changed the tune, and soon all were singing "Onward Christian Soldiers":

> Not a voice was silent, and unconsciously hand clasped hand, and the soft Afternoon air reverberated with the swelling cadence:
>
> "We are not divided,
> All one body we."[65]

"It is the Spirit of the Lord," Father Flynn murmurs; in McClung's words, "the spirit of the West was upon them, unifying, mellowing, harmonizing all conflicting emotions – the spirit of the West that calls on men everywhere to be brothers and lend a hand."[66]

The day ends with "a tired but happy and united company" bound together by a shared meal that is suggestive of communion.[67] McClung concludes with a great rhetorical flourish:

> Where could such a scene as this be enacted – a Twelfth of July celebration where a Roman Catholic priest was the principal speaker, where the company dispersed with the singing of "God Save the King," led by an American band? Nowhere, but in the Northwest of Canada, that illimitable land, with its great sunlit spaces, where the west wind, bearing on its bosom the spices of a million flowers, woos the heart of man with a magic spell and makes him kind and neighborly and brotherly![68]

To contemporary sensibilities, McClung's grand pronouncements on the promise of the Prairie West seem overblown, verging on the ridiculous. However, she was in keeping with much of the disposition of her own time.[69] It is also worth restating that her primary purpose in writing during this period of her life was to inspire and empower. Yet, as she herself acknowledged, she eventually lost the "cheerful imbecility" that marked her early forays into political life. In fact, she was deeply affected by her experiences, and her vision of the Prairie West darkened considerably as a result. McClung's final novel, *Painted Fires*, bears witness to that change, and it is worth asking how the change came about.

The Great War was shattering. Although she used it to rhetorical purpose in *In Times Like These*, 1915 was "early days yet," with many hoping, indeed expecting, that the conflict would be over shortly. A much more sombre mood is evident in *The Next of Kin: Those Who Wait and Wonder*, published in 1917.[70] Her Foreword states:

> Over the world to-day roll great billows of hatred and misunderstanding, which have darkened the whole face of the earth. We believe that there is a switch if we could get to it, but the smoke blinds us and we are choked with our tears.[71]

"Joining together" still is a remedy for life's discord, but here the "reaching out [is] of feeble human hands," and the linkage is a "great spiritual bond which unites all those whose hearts have grown more tender by sorrow."[72] Her son Jack's entry into the war was another blow for McClung, both because of her own ambivalent feelings towards the war itself and her concern for her first-born.[73] Equally difficult to bear was the evident change in Jack upon his return. He was impatient, and often depressed, and in seeing him McClung said:

> ... there was a wound in his heart – a sore place. That hurt look in his clear blue eyes tore at my heart strings and I did not know what to do. When a boy who has never had a gun in his hands, never desired anything but the good of his fellow men, is sent out to kill other boys like himself, even at the call of his country, something snaps in him, something which may not mend.[74]

This sense of helplessness is a far cry from the confident faith embodied in her earlier writing.

The Great War may have brought about another casualty for McClung, although this is more difficult to document in the absence of her diaries, which have been destroyed. During 1916 and 1917, at the behest of Carrie Chapman Catt, President of the National American Woman Suffrage Association, McClung undertook two tours of the United States in support of woman suffrage.[75] Her first tour, proposed for two weeks, quickly became a two-month marathon, with engagements in New York City, Buffalo, Toronto, Racine, Milwaukee, Superior, Muncie, Louisville, Nashville, Birmingham, New Orleans, Houston, San Antonio, Forth Worth, Dallas, Kansas City, Omaha, and Minneapolis, amongst others, all in a little over a month.[76] McClung was immensely popular, particularly in the southern states, and she was enthusiastically lobbied to return the following year. By that time, however, the United States had entered the war, and the American suffrage movement was deeply divided about whether or not to support it.[77] McClung's 1917 tour was abbreviated and, judging from newspaper reports of her speeches, often more subdued.[78] In addition, at one key event at which she spoke, a "loyalty vote" was passed against the Woman's Party,[79] shattering any notion that the woman's movement naturally transcended national boundaries. While it is not possible to determine precisely McClung's reasons for doing so, she declined further invitations to return to the United States to speak.

The attainment of woman suffrage was also not the unqualified success its supporters had anticipated. Although it is not the case that women's political involvement simply ground to a halt after the granting of the franchise to women,[80] it is certainly true that the complete social upheaval (either utopian or catastrophic) predicted by both its advocates and opponents did not occur. Instead, a variety of other social changes, many due to the after-effects of the war, led to a very different social climate than the one anticipated by McClung and her fellow activists. For one, women became social drinkers, something that filled McClung with "a withering sense of disappointment."[81] Women did vote, and some did enter politics, but the impact of these changes was not dramatic, and it soon became clear that formal equality was only one step in a much larger process of social transformation. Old prejudices against women remained, while at the same time many women rejected feminism as "old-fashioned" and irrelevant.[82] The war also resulted for many in a loss of faith, at least in the sunny, evangelical form in which it is expressed in McClung's earlier novels. In sum, the world of the 1920s was a darker, more complex, more troublesome place for a reformer like McClung. She was also in her 50s, no longer a young woman, with sons who did not follow in her abstemious ways.

McClung's faith in the transformative power of the Prairie West was thus considerably moderated by the time she wrote *Painted Fires*. By 1925, her inspirational altar call has been replaced by a different desire

> … to lay down a hard foundation of truth as to conditions in Canada. As a Canadian [McClung said] I blush with shame when I think of the false flattery which has been given to our country by immigration agencies in Europe, anxious to bring out settlers for the profit of steamship and railway companies. It's all fantastic now and seems so long ago and far away, but there was a dark tragedy in it for the deceived ones and Canada got a black eye, which in the minds of some people has lasted even until this time.[83]

Her protagonist has changed as well, from Pearl Watson, the evangelical/social activist prototypical McClung, to the hot-tempered, adventurous, beauty-loving Finlander, Helmi Milander.

The novel follows "the struggles of a young girl who found herself in Canada dependent upon her own resources with everything to learn, including the language."[84] Its plot and substance have been analyzed in depth elsewhere.[85] Briefly, Helmi Milander comes to North America to visit her exotic Aunt Lili, in part to escape the drudgery of an early marriage. She finds her once-lovely aunt dying from illness and heartbreak, the latter due to her callous husband's relief at the death of their newborn daughter. Helmi is warned against him, and against men generally, who are "queer and all for self."[86] After nearly being molested by Aunt Lili's husband, the cook sends Helmi by train from Minnesota to Winnipeg, to be cared for by the cook's sister. Eventually, Helmi is adopted by Miss Abbie, a spinster and church member. She introduces Helmi to the C.G.I.T. (Canadian Girls in Training) whose "Blue and Gold" book and motto serve as Helmi's guide throughout her ensuing troubles: "Cherish health; seek truth; know God; serve others."[87]

Helmi loves beauty and is seduced by the luxurious environment created by indolent Eva St. John, the doctor's wife. Bored and lazy, Eva St. John had become addicted to heroin, and when her supply is cut off, Helmi is sent to get more. Helmi is caught in a raid, and, abandoned by St. John, is incarcerated in the ironically named Girls' Friendly Home. Eventually, for reasons entirely due to self-interest, St. John manages to free Helmi from the Home, sending her on to Eagle Mines, Alberta.

In the past, this would have been the occasion for lauding the freedom of the open land, far away from the corrupting influence of the city. In *Painted Fires*, however, the city has its positive elements, such as Rev. Terry and Miss Abbie, while Eagle Mines is ugly, temporary, and dangerous.[88] Men and their wives may stay for many years, but the mentality is that of "getting rich quick." People work hard – indeed, endlessly – but the work is not redemptive. While working at the local boarding house, Helmi meets and falls in love with a young miner by the name of Jack Doran, but he leaves shortly after their marriage to stake a claim in the north. In his absence Helmi finds she is pregnant; she also finds that the money Jack has left for her has been stolen.

Betrayal and danger are constantly present in *Painted Fires*; almost no one can be trusted. Even "good" characters like Jack are subject to suspicion, doubt, and uncertainty. Many men are completely unscrupulous: the magistrate who pretended to marry Jack and Helmi, but failed to record it, thus rendering the marriage invalid. Jack's partner is another example. Both a thief and a seducer, he absconds with Jack's money and previously seduced a young girl with the promise of a stake in his mine. Assault, rape, seduction, racism, prostitution, presumed adultery, and drug addition, unthinkable topics in McClung's earlier writing, are fully consistent with the discordant world of *Painted Fires*. Hence, no cheerful helper intervenes when Jack returns from prospecting; Helmi has disappeared and their house is a shambles. Circumstances suggest that Helmi may have been unfaithful to him, and when he seeks further information of her whereabouts from the magistrate who first informed him of Helmi's incarceration in Winnipeg, he is told that she had moved to Edmonton and was working in a Chinese restaurant, the implication being that she was involved in drugs and/or prostitution. Seeing her there, Jack assumes the worst, and heads off to war. Graphically, Helmi's past *does* "rise up to defeat [her]," if not permanently, certainly significantly.

Jack is captured by the enemy and put in a prisoner of war camp from which he eventually escapes. After a number of twists and turns of plot, a happy ending is brought about. Jack and Helmi are reunited, and they build a good life for themselves on the shores of the English River near Eagle Mines. Yet the injuries have been more cruel, and the betrayals much more deep, than in any of McClung's other writing. The old dichotomies are disrupted. The city is not deceptive and the country restorative, as in "As A Man Thinketh" and in *In Times Like These*.[89] Beauty can be seductive rather than healing, as the dissolute character of Eva St. John amply illustrates. Selfishness reaches new depths, and male misogyny goes far beyond the general pomposity of *Purple Springs*' premier Graham. Instead there is the magistrate who believed foreign girls like Helmi were sexually loose, and therefore fair game for English men. Girl's clubs and women's groups who are working to change this situation are a particular target of men in power. As another character rants:

> Women and girls have too much liberty these days, and that's why they are going to the devil. They don't work any more – they just gad around to picture shows and get into trouble, and the women's organizations encourage them instead of trying to restrain them. The old-fashioned girl stayed at home and worked with her mother. But now the mothers are out reforming the world, and the girls are on the street or in their clubs.... I tell you, there's no religion in the homes anymore, no respect for law, – nothing but birth control clubs, political clubs, bridge clubs, while the young girls and boys steal cars, joy ride and snuff dope.[90]

McClung's darkened disposition is reflected in her treatment of theology. Helmi's initial understanding of God as "a terrible person, whom people only thought of when someone died, or in thunderstorms, floods, famine or sickness"[91] is presented as a superstition to be grown beyond, and the class-conscious, "repent your sins and maintain the status quo" theology of Old Sim, the church sexton[92] is debunked through humour.

Clearly, the position to be emulated is the Social Gospel stance of Reverend Terry who "comes boldly into public life without apology."[93] His job, however, is far beyond "being kind" – he is called upon to defend an innocent young woman like Helmi in a hostile court, and fails. There are no more easy victories, even for obvious heroes.

McClung's harshest judgment is reserved for the Wymuths, a couple from the east brought in to replace the young, progressive matron of the Girls' Friendly Home. The matron who was previously in charge of the Home was fired for her kind approach to the girls, and not least for her feminism. She objected to the board's description of girls as "fallen," instead citing "a double standard of morals which was made by men to shield men," leaving innocent young girls to fall "victims to men's lust and hypocrisy."[94] In contrast, the Wymuths blame the victims, believing their wills must be broken in repentance for what is obviously their sin. Cold and conservatively Christian, one of their favourite punishments for their charges is forcing them to listen to the screaming childbirth agonies of their fellow inmates. Patriarchal dominance is also sharply inscribed in their marriage. In contrast, the matron comes to share her home with one Miss de Forrest, who in an interesting stereotypical gesture is described approvingly by McClung as "a large woman, deep chested, deep voiced, dominant,"[95] and much less positively as "that big raw-boned valentine" by the character Eva St. John.[96] While it is hard to be certain, it may be that McClung was suggesting that a lesbian couple with appropriate ideas is preferable to a heterosexual couple with improper ideas.

McClung's liberalism continued into the 1920s. She believed women and men deserved the same rights and opportunities in the public sphere. She did not castigate unwed mothers and saw those who would judge these women as perpetuating a sexual double standard and a male-dominant status quo. She also continued to value hard work and to believe in its powers of moral purification, especially when that work gave back something to the community. For much of her life, she championed these values in the guise of a revivalist preacher, both in person and in print, linking them inextricably with the fresh and open Prairie West in which all things were possible. However, calling for the Kingdom of God on earth, and actually building it day by mundane day proved a more difficult task.

At the beginning of her career, Nellie McClung was utterly confident about people's essential goodness, however unfair or difficult circumstances might cause them to behave differently. Over time, these less desirable behaviours could become codified into convention, reinforced by a pre-judging that owed as much to laziness and "hoggishness" as it did to ignorance of a better way. For McClung, the Prairie West provided a perfect environment for what seemed to her at the time to be reasonably easily achievable remedies. In the place of ignorance, McClung offered a new social vision, the lineaments of which included temperance, fair treatment for women, and a willingness to put behind the habits of the past in order to build a fresh new world together. Laziness would be countered by inspiration and empowerment, as people began to see that new vision take shape. And finally, in a land where "there is enough for everyone," the fear and petty-mindedness that were the spur for selfishness would be overcome by the sheer richness of the bounty of the Canadian West.

Her vision was darkened by the horror of the Great War, and especially its effect on her eldest child. The exhilaration of winning the vote was followed by the reality of social compromise and mundane party politics, at which she fared poorly. The apparent solidarity of the movement for woman suffrage was shown to be riddled with fissures around issues of class, ethnicity, pacifism, and nationalism. Combined with a change in social mores that allowed and even encouraged women to be social drinkers, any notion that women would naturally and inevitably "clean things up"[97] in social and political life was no longer possible to sustain. In a passage comparing selfish, frivolous Eva St. John with her hardworking, religious, sweet-tempered mother-in-law, McClung's regret and profound disillusionment are palpable.[98] Misogyny also proved to be much more difficult to eradicate than McClung had earlier imagined. In the Pearlie Watson trilogy, a reasoned account of the wrongfulness of particular actions is received thoughtfully and with positive practical effect by the wrongdoers.[99] By *Painted Fires*, there is almost no point talking.[100] Uninformed acceptance of out-dated conventions cannot explain the vicious, spiteful rant against women's and girls' clubs, nor the deep anger against women evidenced thereby.

McClung's earlier vision of the Prairie West as Promised Land was consistent with the sunny optimism of Christian Perfectionism. If people are born sinless and learn to sin through the conditions into that they are born, what better place for achieving perfection than a place which was still in the process of construction? A new social order would produce better people, whose hard work and willing efforts would make the Promised Land a reality. Later, McClung would see this differently. It was not that she became convinced that people were inherently sinful, but rather that the wrongful, hurtful, damaging circumstances of life were much more difficult to eradicate than she originally imagined. Hard things can have permanent consequences, as her son's participation in the war and eventual suicide painfully bore out. Even the Prairie West with its freshness and open horizons could not transform harsh realities such as these.

If there is one constant to be found, Nellie McClung's autobiographies provide witness to one undeniable fact: Nellie McClung loved the prairies deeply. Her rich descriptions of the landscape encircle a narrative of prairie life that was demanding but ultimately could produce "great reward." While her initial enthusiasm was markedly curbed by her loss of cultural and political innocence, the fact remains that McClung herself embodied much of the promise of the Prairie West in her own life. Despite her unremarkable lower-class origins and relative lack of education,[101] McClung turned a natural talent for speaking and writing into a platform from which she was able to take on the great political issues of the day. She rocketed to international fame in less than a decade, as a representative of a new region with new ideas and a fresh energy to bring about a new world. The disillusionment that would eventually come notwithstanding, the fact remains that, for a number of years in a particular time and place, Nellie McClung was truly able to make a positive difference in the struggle to build "the Land of the Fair Deal." Her over-idealization of the Prairie West may best be understood in this context because, for her, even for a short time, the Promised Land had indeed been a reality.

NOTES

1 Nellie L. McClung, *The Stream Runs Fast* (Toronto: Thomas Allen, 1945), x.

2 Nellie L. McClung, *Sowing Seeds in Danny* (Toronto: William Briggs, 1908); *The Second Chance* (Toronto: William Briggs, 1910); *In Times Like These* (Toronto: University of Toronto Press, 1972, repr. Toronto: McLeod and Allen, 1915); *Purple Springs* (Toronto: University of Toronto Press, 1992, repr. Thomas Allen, 1921); *Painted Fires* (Toronto: Ryerson Press, 1925); *Clearing in the West* (Toronto: Thomas Allen, 1935); *The Stream Runs Fast* (Toronto: Thomas Allen, 1945).

3 Randi R. Warne, *Literature as Pulpit: The Christian Social Activism of Nellie L. McClung* (Waterloo: Wilfrid Laurier University Press, 1993).

4 See her descriptions of prairie life in both volumes of her autobiography, *Clearing in the West* and *The Stream Runs Fast.*

5 See, for example, JoAnne Jaffe, "With Us or With the Terrorists: American Hyperpatriotism as Fundamentalism," in *Contesting Fundamentalisms*, eds. Carol Schick et

al. (Halifax: Fernwood, 2004). God can also express his displeasure directly when America violates their holy covenant. For example, evangelist Pat Robertson claimed that the September 11 attacks on the United States occurred because "God Almighty is lifting his protection from us." Transcript of Pat Robertson's Interview with Jerry Falwell Broadcast on the *700 Club* , September 13, 2001, in Bruce Lincoln, *Holy Terrors: Thinking about Religion after September 11* (Chicago: University of Chicago Press, 2003), 104.

6 See Warne, *Literature as Pulpit*, 178, n. 21.

7 Nellie L. McClung, *In Times Like These* (Toronto: University of Toronto Press, 1972). Veronica Strong-Boag, Scholarly Introduction, vii–xxii.

8 That is, the purpose of the essays and speeches was to spur people into political action. As such, they were exhortative, encouraging, and unfailingly positive about the potential outcomes of social engagement.

9 For a critical assessment of these preoccupations, see Randi R. Warne, "Maternal Feminism: A Useful Category for Examining Women's Past?" in *Proceedings: Feminist Research Forum*, eds. Nola Erhardt and Pat Leginsky (Edmonton: Women's Program and Resource Centre, University of Alberta, 1989), 17–20.

10 See, for example, "'What Do Women think of War?,' The New Chivalry," and "Hardy Perennials," all in *In Times Like These*.

11 McClung, *In Times Like These*, 96.

12 Ibid., 97.

13 Ibid.

14 Ibid., 101.

15 Ibid.

16 McClung, *Sowing Seeds in Danny*, npg.

17 While "being kind" is obviously desirable, practical action in the face of material conditions is also required, as a poetic excerpt from Pearl's diary reveals: "The little lams are beautiful, There cotes are soft and nice, the little calves have ringworm, and the 2-year olds have lice! ... It must be very nasty, But to worrie, what's the use; Better be cam and cheerfull, And appli tobaka jooce [*sic*]." Ibid., 221.

18 Ibid., 110.

19 For example, see Mr. Steadman, Conservative member of the Chicken Hill district. As McClung describes him, "he was the centre of his own circle. There was a well-fed, complacent look about him too which left no doubt that he was satisfied with things as they were – and would be deeply resentful of change. There was still in his countenance some trace of his ancestor's belief in the Divine right of kings! It showed in his narrow, thought-proof forehead, and a certain indescribable attitude which he held towards others, and which separated him from his neighbors. Instinctively, the people who met him, knew he lacked human sympathy and understanding, but he had a hold on the people of his constituency, for through his hands went all the Government favors and patronage." McClung, *Purple Springs*, 93.

20 McClung, *Sowing Seeds in Danny*, 158. This is also a comment on men's inordinate legal power over family finances.

21 Ibid., 228–29.

22 "We did not believe that women would ever become drinkers. We argued, subconsciously, that women have more resources within themselves, more outlets for their energies, and so did not need this false exhilaration." McClung, *The Stream Runs Fast*, 62–63.

23 McClung, *In Times Like These*, 99.

24 McClung, *The Stream Runs Fast*, 62.

25 James Gray, *Booze* (Toronto: Signet, 1972), 13.

26 No social cause, even woman suffrage, animated McClung more than temperance. She got her first exposure to public speaking doing readings from *Sowing Seeds in*

Danny for the Woman's Christian Temperance Union, and she continued to witness centrally to the cause in *In Times Like These* and the novel *The Second Chance*. Her speeches as an Alberta MLA from 1921 to 1926 are distinguished by her passionate focus on this topic. Indeed, she believed that it was her steadfast commitment to temperance that caused her to lose her seat: "I might have known that the liquor interests do not forgive the people who oppose them. Temperance people will forget their friends and cheerfully forgive their enemies at election time, but the liquor people are more dependable." Nellie McClung, "How it Feels to be a Defeated Candidate," *Toronto Star Weekly*, October 2, 1926.

27 "When the church of God is cold and dark and silent, and the homes of Christ's followers are closed except to the chosen few, the bar-room throws out its evil welcome to the young man on the street." McClung, *The Stream Runs Fast*, 228.

28 McClung, *In Times Like These*, 102.

29 Gray, *Booze*, 40–41.

30 McClung, *The Second Chance*, 189–90.

31 Ibid., 191.

32 It is fair to assume that the more miraculous events that occur, such as the storm that blows the roof over Polly's poppies, thus protecting them, are simple plot devices rather than evidence that McClung believed in direct divine intervention in the material world, the chapter's title, "Faith Moveth Mountains" notwithstanding. See *Sowing Seeds in Danny*, 162–66. For McClung, a key agent of divine transformation is people of deep faith and active engagement like Pearl Watson.

33 Ibid., 158.

34 Ibid.

35 Ibid., 159.

36 Ibid., 137–38.

37 McClung, *In Times Like These*, 10.

38 Ibid.

39 McClung is reflecting a Protestant theological position that informed much religious social activism in the nineteenth and early twentieth centuries. Christian perfectionism, as it was known, held that persons are born sinless, but learn sin from their surroundings. The task, then, is to remove the occasion for sin (such as alcohol) to bring about a better society.

40 Ibid., 11.

41 McClung, *The Stream Runs Fast*, 145.

42 Ibid. 182.

43 McClung, *Purple Springs*, 149–51.

44 McClung, *The Stream Runs Fast*, 111–22.

45 "Women Score in Drama and Debate," *Manitoba Free Press*, January 29, 1914.

46 Greater attention to the class dynamics within women's activism of this time period would provide a welcome complement to scholarship that assumes the relative homogeneity of "elites."

47 McClung, *The Stream Runs Fast*, 106. For an account of the conditions of women in the early years of settlement in the Red River region, see W. J. Healy, *Women of Red River* (Winnipeg, Russell, Lang & Co., 1923). The book was "A tribute to the women of an earlier day by the Women's Canadian Club" (frontspiece). In 1923, the Secretary-Treasurer for the Women's Canadian Club was Mrs. Claude Nash, with whom McClung took Manitoba Premier Sir Rodmond Roblin to see the working conditions of women in Winnipeg's sweatshops. McClung, *The Stream Runs Fast*, 101–6.

48 Linda Trimble, "A Few Good Women: Female Legislators in Alberta, 1972–1991," in *Standing on New Ground: Women in Alberta*, eds. Catherine Cavanaugh and Randi R. Warne (Edmonton: University of Alberta Press, 1993), 87–118.

49 *The Grain Growers' Guide*, February 14, 1914.

50 Ibid.

51 *Manitoba Free Press*, January 28, 1914.

52 "Manitoba Tories Worried," McClung Papers, Provincial Archives of British Columbia, Add MSS 10, Vol. 35, cited in Randi R. Warne, Scholarly Introduction to McClung, *Purple Springs* (Toronto: University of Toronto Press, 1992), vi–vii.

53 McClung, *In Times Like These*, 101. The obvious reference is to drink.

54 Personal correspondence from Murphy to McClung, dated December 2, 1927. McClung Papers, Provincial Archives of British Columbia.

55 The tendency in scholarship over the last two decades has been to emphasize differences between social classes, and considerable ink has been shed on the topic of the classism and racism of the "elite" women who lobbied for woman suffrage. See, for example, Carol Lee Bacchi's ubiquitous, problematic, *Liberation Deferred? The Ideas of the English-Canadian Suffragists, 1877–1918* (Toronto: University of Toronto Press, 1983). While "oppositional politics" are important, a single-minded focus on that dynamic obscures the degree to which groups may work together to advance common aims, such as appears to be the case here.

56 McClung's position stands in stark contrast to renowned British scientist Sir Almwroth Wright, whom she takes on in *In Times Like These*, 70. Wright was aghast at the implications of granting woman suffrage, seeing in it the "goal of endeavour being that all distinctions depending upon natural endowment, sex, and race should be effaced." For Wright, this violation of the very order of nature "would make of every man and woman *in primus* a socialist; then a woman suffragist; then a philo-nature, negrophil, and an advocate of the political rights of natives and negroes; and then, by logical compulsion an anti-vivisectionist, who accounts it *unjust* to experiment on an animal; a vegetarian, who accounts it *unjust* to kill animals for food; and finally one who, like the Jains, account it *unjust* to take the life of even verminous insects." Sir Almwroth Wright, *An Unexpurgated Case against Woman Suffrage* (New York: Hoeber, 1913), 42.

57 Nellie L. McClung, "The Way of the West," in *The Black Creek Stopping-House* (Toronto: William Briggs, 1912), 209–24.

58 McClung's father's first wife was named Jane Shouldice; the surname echoes with the hierarchy and prejudice of "the Huron and the Bruce" counties of southern Ontario, where McClung was born.

59 Ibid., 210.

60 Ibid., 211.

61 Ibid. Note the contrast between this viewpoint and McClung's emphasis on new beginnings and common equality.

62 Ibid., 215. McClung reiterates this point in her address to the Fifth Ecumenical Methodist Conference held in London, England, in 1921: "In our preachers and workers we are not so strong on fine points of doctrine as we are on the spirit of service. Our W.M.S. women try to interpret the love of God to our people from distant lands; our new Canadians by building hospitals and boarding-schools for the children in the far distant districts. Linen sheets, loving and skilful hands, seem to be a good way to interpret God's love. It is effective. It works. It gets the message over. The people come to us so strange, so lonely, so homesick. It gives the opportunity for showing the spirit of love. Our workers are not so intent on making Methodists out of them as they are on interpreting God's love to them. Indeed, our Methodists working here forget that they are Methodists, so intent are they on their big work. Their theology might not get by the Ecumenical Conference, but it has vitality; it brings joy in heaven." *Proceedings* (London: n.p., 1921), 258.

63 Ibid., 220.

64 As Thomas Shouldice remarked to himself, "These Americans are a queer bunch … they're as ignorant as all get out, but, gosh! They're friendly." Ibid., 217.

65 Ibid., 222. Critics will be quick to note the presumption of Christian normativity enacted here.
66 Ibid.
67 Ibid., 223–24.
68 Ibid., 224.
69 For example, consider the conclusion to *Women of Red River*, published in 1923: "There spoke the true Winnipeg spirit, the true Western spirit, foreseeing the whole panorama of Western Canadian progress to be unfolded in the decades to come – the inflow of immigration, the spreading of the prairie wheatfields that stretch to the circling skyline, the tall, red, high-shouldered elevators rising where settlements clustered into villages, the appearance of towns and cities linked by a network of railways radiating from the city which had grown out of the little muddy hamlet at the Forks," 261.
70 Nellie L. McClung, *The Next of Kin: Those Who Wait and Wonder* (Toronto: Thomas Allen; Boston and New York: Houghton Mifflin, 1917).
71 Ibid., 20.
72 Ibid.
73 For a fuller discussion of McClung's position on the Great War, see Randi R. Warne, "Nellie McClung and Peace," in *Up and Doing: Canadian Women and Peace*, eds. Deborah Gorham and Janice Williamson (Toronto: The Women's Press, 1989), 35–47.
74 McClung, *The Stream Runs Fast*, 195. Jack committed suicide in 1944, causing a full year's delay in this volume's completion. It may be that McClung was trying to give a partial explanation for "the reeling blow" of the loss of her eldest child. Ibid., 311.
75 Mary E. Hallett and Marilyn I. Davis, *Firing the Heather* (Saskatoon: Fifth House, 1993), 156–57, refer to the tentative itinerary found in McClung's papers. A detailed assessment of McClung's tours, including a corrected itinerary, may be found in Randi R. Warne, "Crossing the Line: Nellie McClung in America," an unpublished paper presented at the Northern Great Plains History Conference in Brandon, Manitoba, September 28–30, 1995.
76 These engagements were corroborated through local newspaper articles on McClung. See "Crossing the Line," 17 n. 47, and Appendix. [Copies available from the author.]
77 For example, the Woman's Party believed it was hypocritical to try to "make the world safe for democracy" when women were denied the democratic right to vote. Members of the National American Woman Suffrage Association and its affiliates claimed, in contrast, that not supporting the war was unpatriotic, and ultimately contrary to women's advancement. See Warne, "Crossing the Line," 19–20.
78 For example, she concluded one of her speeches with: "what the women in Canada, as a whole, have found in this great war [is] power; power over themselves, power over loss and misery and death, power in the face of trial and struggle and tribulation; it is something to have achieved that!" "Things Have Changed for the Better…," *Birmingham Age-Herald*, Tuesday, November 27, 1917, cited in Warne, "Crossing the Line," 23, nn. 62 and 63.
79 Ibid., 22–23.
80 See, for example, Nancy Langford, "All that Glitters: The Political Apprenticeship of Alberta Women, 1916–1930," in *Standing on New Ground*, eds. Cavanaugh and Warne, 71–85.
81 McClung, *The Stream Runs Fast*, 181.
82 See, for example, Dorothy L. Sayers, *Are Women Human?* (Grand Rapids: Eerdmans, 1971), 17.
83 McClung, *The Stream Runs Fast*, 241.
84 Ibid., 237.
85 See Warne, *Literature as Pulpit*, chap. 2, "The Importance of Discernment."
86 McClung, *Painted Fires*, 5.
87 Ibid., 168.

88 McClung describes it: "The sun poured down with a pitiless glare on the confirmed ugliness of the little box-like houses. The kindly white snow which had covered the littered backyards, was gone, and now there came in full view the piles of cans, discarded clothing, old boxes, old boots, which the snow had mercifully hidden. Water stood in puddles on the one little street where the general store, the hotel, postoffice, mine office and boarding-house, sat side by side all looking at the station, which, because it belonged to a system and was not dependent on local caprice, had walls of stone grey and a red roof. So far as could be seen, not another tin of pain had ever gained a foothold in Eagle Mines. Helmi shuddered at the ugliness of it all." Ibid., 131.

89 "... the city is a careless nurse and teacher, who thinks more of a cut of a coat than of the habit of mind; who feeds her children on colored candy and popcorn, despising the more wholesome porridge and milk; a slatternly nurse, who would rather buy perfume than soap ... and fills their ears with blatant music, until their eyes are too dull to see the pastel beauty of common thing ... who lures her children on with many glittering promises of ease and wealth, which she never intends to keep, and all the time whispers to them that this is life. The good old country nurse is stern but kind, and gives her children hard lessons, which tax body and brain, but never fail to bring a great reward.... Happy is the child who learns earth's wisdom from the good old country nurse, who does better than she promises, and always 'makes her children mind'!" McClung, *In Times Like These*, 119.

90 McClung, *Painted Fires*, 76.

91 Ibid., 49.

92 Ibid., 42–44.

93 McClung, *Painted Fires*, 76.

94 Ibid., 81.

95 Ibid., 109.

96 Ibid., 110.

97 "Women have cleaned things up since time began; and if women ever get into politics there will be a cleaning-out of pigeon-holes and forgotten corners, on which the dust of the years has fallen, and the sound of the political carpet-beater will be heard in the land." McClung, *In Times Like These*, 48.

98 McClung, *Painted Fires*, 287–88.

99 This is particularly true in *Purple Springs*, McClung's novel about Manitoba politics. For example, in addition to Premier Graham, noted above, Mr. Paine is turned from his goal of selling the farm and buying a saloon by Pearl's intervention (chap. 13, "The Storm," 165–88).

100 As Miss de Forrest observes to a crowd of Eva St. John's friends, "Some of you women should be on the Board and try to get some sense into its wooden head. I now know the origin of the word "Board." McClung, *Painted Fires*, 110.

101 McClung learned to read at age nine and was a country schoolteacher by the age of fifteen.

10

THE KINGDOM OF GOD ON THE PRAIRIES: J. S. WOODSWORTH'S VISION OF THE PRAIRIE WEST AS PROMISED LAND

R. Douglas Francis

Analysts of J. S. Woodworth's ideas and religious beliefs have rightly identified him as an exemplary social gospeller.[1] Central to social gospel thinking was the belief in establishing the Kingdom of God on earth. Social gospellers argued that religion should not be so much concerned with individual salvation in the afterlife but instead should work towards social salvation in this life. J. S. Woodsworth certainly expounded such a position. For some social gospellers, this belief in the establishment of God's heavenly kingdom on earth was only an ideal to strive for, some vision to guide social reformers, rather than a possibility to achieve in reality. But for J. S. Woodsworth, the belief in the establishment of the Kingdom of God on earth had realism and imminence to it, something that could be achieved here and now. For Woodsworth, the "here" was in the Prairie West and the "now" was the first two decades of the twentieth century.

Woodsworth believed implicitly that the fertile soil of the Canadian prairies nurtured the right conditions for the growth of God's heavenly kingdom on earth – the Promised Land, and that the fertile conditions were at their best in the era of optimism in the early twentieth century, thus making it possible to achieve this vision in his own lifetime. This conviction of the Prairie West as the Promised Land sustained Woodsworth's social reform impulse.

In an article of reflection on his religious beliefs, Woodsworth maintained that abstract questions about "first causes or final causes" held little meaning for him. It was sufficient simply to accept where he was and to deal with his immediate surroundings in an effort to make them better. "Our primary interest is with the present life," he wrote. "And we are none the less spiritual for that."[2] He explained what such a perspective meant to him: "The very heart of the teaching of Jesus was the setting up of the Kingdom of God on earth. The vision splendid has sent forth an increasing group to attempt the task of 'Christianizing the Social Order.' Some of us whose study of history and economies and social conditions has driven us to the socialist position find it easy to associate the Ideal Kingdom of Jesus with the co-operative commonwealth of socialism."[3] In a speech given in 1913 in which he urged westerners to be concerned about the social problems in their midst, Woodsworth was more explicit: "Thy kingdom come as in Heaven, so in Regina and Moose Jaw, Saskatoon and Winnipeg."[4] In an article of analysis of the Lord's Prayer, Woodsworth explained more fully what the phrase "Thy kingdom come on earth as it is in heaven" meant to him: "'Thy kingdom come' not in some future state in some far off world, and not in some vague way all over the universe, but thy kingdom come right here in Canada, in Manitoba, in Winnipeg, in Brownsville, in my own township."[5]

Thus to present Woodsworth's social gospel perspective without discussing his vision of the Prairie West where he believed God's kingdom on earth would be achieved in the heyday of the Canadian West in the early twentieth century is to present only half of his social gospel beliefs, and the half that makes Woodsworth appear to be an idealistic, impractical, and aloof social reformer out of touch with reality. Such a perspective fails to take into account the importance of Woodsworth's immediate environment in shaping his social gospel thinking. For Woodsworth, his social gospel vision and his vision of the Prairie West were inextricably linked.

Woodsworth's vision of the Prairie West as Promised Land had two components to it: the *physical* west and the *social* west. His vision of the *physical* west, the land itself, with its wide open spaces and its landscape of earth and sky, as the ideal setting for establishing God's kingdom on earth never wavered throughout his life. He believed implicitly that the prairies were indeed the Promised Land, a veritable land of milk and honey. And Woodsworth upheld the belief of his age in environmental determinism, that environment shaped character. Thus this ideal prairie land had the magic quality to transform the right people into perfect moral beings, those worthy of living in the Promised Land. In 1913, he wrote, for example: "Transplanted into our rich new soil and under our sunny skies and watered with the rains of heaven, many of these immigrants stunted and dwarfed in their old-world environment develop at a rate and to an extent and along lines that are almost incredible. After a few years, they are literally new creatures, new creations, so much so that the more thoughtful look back at their old world self as at an altogether different personality. The new land often means intellectually and morally a new birth."[6]

Woodworth's vision of the *social* west changed during his formative years up to 1920. He was enough of a pragmatist to realize that not everyone who came to the prairies could be transformed into perfect citizens for God's earthly kingdom. Like the biblical Israelites, only certain people were chosen by God to dwell in the Promised Land. What altered in Woodworth's vision of the social west were the groups that he identified as the "chosen people." In his earlier writings, such as *Strangers within Our Gates* (1908) and *My Neighbor* (1911), he presented a nativistic perspective towards "foreigners" coming into the prairies. He maintained that their presence, with beliefs that were "foreign" to Canadian values, undermined the unity of the region and lessened the reform impulse so necessary to achieve God's earthly kingdom on the prairies. As a result, he advocated the assimilation of "foreigners" into the Anglo-Protestant norm. God's earthly kingdom had to have only one voice – English – and one culture – Anglo-Canadian. In his writings after 1913, however, he presented a more tolerant view of "foreigners" in the West, arguing now that their different beliefs and values enriched the region rather than detracted from it. Now he envisioned the ideal Prairie West – the Promised Land – as a mosaic in which each group made a positive contribution to, and enriched, the region as a whole.

Analysts of Woodsworth's ideas have noted this change in perspective but have failed to give an explanation for the shift. The altered perspective is the result of Woodsworth's leaving the Methodist Church in 1913 to work for secular institutions such as the Welfare League and the Bureau of Research for the governments of Manitoba, Saskatchewan, and Alberta. Although Woodsworth had tendered his resignation from the Methodist Church as early as 1907 on the grounds that his beliefs were not compatible with those of the mainline church, his resignation was turned down and he continued within the pale of the church. His first two publications, *Strangers within Our Gates* and *My Neighbor*, were both published by the Young People's Forward Movement Department of the Methodist Church. They reflected the prevailing official view of the Methodist Church at the time.[7] After 1913, when he was no longer writing under the watchful eye of the church, Woodsworth was able to present his own views more in keeping with his particular social gospel perspective. Ironically, then, Woodsworth presented a more tolerant vision of the West and a viewpoint more in tune with his religious convictions only *after* he left the Methodist Church.

This article examines J. S. Woodsworth's vision of the Prairie West in the context of his social gospel beliefs to argue that he saw his vision of the Kingdom of God on earth being fulfilled in the specific locale of the Prairie West during the heyday of prosperity that spanned the first two decades of the twentieth century. This vision Woodsworth presented most forcefully only after he severed his ties to the Methodist Church and no longer wrote under the auspices of the mainline church. Once freed from the restraints of the church doctrine, Woodsworth presented an idealistic vision of the Prairie West as a mosaic of ethnic groups living in harmony and working together to achieve the Kingdom of God on earth.

James Shaver Woodsworth was his father's son in his formative years in terms of his perspective on the West.[8] And his father, James Woodsworth, was the pillar of the Methodist Church on the prairies in that he held the highest position in the region as superintendent of missions for the Manitoba and North-West Conference of the Methodist Church (1885–1915). J. S. inherited from his Methodist father not only his missionary zeal, his reform impulse, and his compassion for the less fortunate, but also his initial ambivalent perspective on the region. James Woodsworth had tremendous faith in the potential of the prairies for material and spiritual growth, but he also emphasized the limiting ability of the region so long as "foreign immigrants" weakened its Protestant (which for James Woodsworth meant Methodist) and Anglo-Canadian nature. James Woodsworth's memoirs, *Thirty Years in the Canadian North-West*, presents his ambivalent perspective, one that is reflective of the Methodist Church itself. But equally and significantly *Thirty Years in the Canadian North-West* also presents and reflects J. S. Woodsworth's early views, since J. S. edited the volume for his father and admitted to adding his own views in the process.[9]

Thirty Years in the Canadian North-West emphasizes the great potential of the West in terms of its economic growth and material prosperity. Indeed, at times it reads like one of the numerous immigration pamphlets issued by the Canadian government or the Canadian Pacific Railway Company to lure immigrants to the West in terms of its upbeat tone, its promise of unlimited prosperity, its numerous statistics recording population growth, and its booster mentality. It presents the West as a veritable Promised Land. On one occasion, for example, the book proclaims: "The future is bright with promise.… Thirty years ago the territory now comprising the three prairie provinces contained a population of less than ninety thousand. This same territory now contains a population of approximately one million four hundred thousand.… So much has been written on the great extent and marvellous resources of the Canadian West that the subject might seem to be exhausted. But her future defies anticipation."[10] James hoped that this economic growth and material prosperity would result in spiritual growth too. What was needed, he believed, were institutions, like the Methodist Church, that could bring that spiritual growth to fruition. Thus he saw the Prairie West in its formative years as a *tabula rasa* to be shaped according to the wishes and beliefs of the early Christian settlers, of which the Methodists were a prominent group.

Despite such potential, however, the West had two obstacles that prevented the region from reaching that potential and thus becoming God's kingdom on earth, according to James Woodsworth. One obstacle was, ironically, the region's great economic wealth. He feared that a "spirit of materialism" was taking hold of the region that would deter the growth of a "spirit of Christ," resulting in westerners focusing only on their material well-being at the expense of their spiritual growth. The other obstacle was the "immigrant problem" – the inability or unwillingness of certain immigrant groups on the prairies to assimilate into prairie society or to display good Christian values. In *Thirty Years in the Canadian North-West*, James singled out two groups in particular: Mormons and Galicians. With regard to the former group, he acknowledged that they were "good settlers, in the sense of being good producers and consumers." But this was also one of the group's weaknesses. "Is such material consideration sufficient justification for tolerating, much less encouraging, these people to come to Canada?" he asked rhetorically.

"As a country we may pay dearly for our love of the Almighty Dollar."[11] He also noted that "the principles professed by them [Mormons] are subversive of sound morals and good government,"[12] although he failed to elaborate on how this was the case. With regard to the latter groups, the Galicians, James expressed a concern in his memoirs as to the lack of education among their children: "thousands of children are growing up in ignorance," he pointed out in discussing the impact of the Galicians on the region. "They are almost equally destitute of any provision for their religious and spiritual training."[13]

In setting out his concerns for the region, James also set out his vision for the Prairie West, a vision that J.S. would have agreed with at that point in time:

> I am not convinced that the principal object in view should be so much the rapid filling up of this great country, as the securing of such a quality of material that a type of national life may be produced equal in its intelligence, as well as in its moral and religious fibre to any on the face of the earth; a nation whose foundations are laid in righteousness, whose people are the Lord's, and whose pre-eminence because of righteous principles and conduct will ensure its prosperity and long-continued existence. Such a realization will largely depend upon:
>
> 1st The character of the material to be incorporated in the national edifice; and
>
> 2nd The skill, fidelity, and industry of the builders – upon the work of those who are here in the initial stages of our country's history and development.
>
> It is but early in the day in Manitoba and the North-West.[14]

In the end, James emphasized that if the two limitations of the region – its "spirit of materialism" and its "immigrant problem" – could be overcome then the Prairie West had the potential of becoming the Promised Land. But he left the distinct impression in *Thirty Years in the Canadian North-West* that these challenges were formidable ones, thus leaving the hope of achieving the Promised Land well into the future.

Early on in his own writings, J.S. Woodsworth realized the importance of the prairie social environment in shaping the quality of the region. In a series of articles under the general topic "Sketches of Western Life," J. S. Woodsworth noted some of the ways that the social environment of the prairies dictated and shaped a preacher's life:

> The successful prairie preacher may claim, with Paul, 'I am become all things to all men that I may by all means win some.' His college theology is greatly modified, as it is adapted for the needs of hard-working men and lonely women. His set notions of church order and discipline are rudely disturbed by the exigencies of a new and rapidly developing country. His dignified bearing and conventional etiquette vanishes as he learns to ride his 'broncho,' or eats his dinner in a settler's 'shack'.... It is under such conditions and by such means that the church in the west is endeavoring to fulfil her mission. It is thus that she takes her part in laying the foundations of our national life. The labor is arduous and slow and unnoticed, but posterity will recognize the faithful work of the prairie preacher.[15]

J. S. Woodsworth presented his initial reflections on the West with regard to the impact of "foreign" immigration on the region in his first major publication, *Strangers within Our Gates*, published under the auspices of the Methodist Church, as noted earlier. As the title indicates, the book examines the impact of the "motley crowd of immigrants"[16] who were coming to Canada and predominantly to the prairies in large numbers. He focused on the impact immigrants had on the moral and spiritual life of the region, and thus he geared the study to the role of the churches. At one point, he noted: "The churches to whom has been granted a vision of the Kingdom of God cannot ignore the presence of such large numbers of foreigners."[17] And he ended the book with a chapter on "A challenge [of immigrants] to the church," in which he opened with a quotation from the *North-West Baptist*, which read in part:

> [T]here is cause for some alarm when we consider that as these peoples come to us we take them for better for worse, for richer for poorer, in sickness and in health. And, as we view their uncouth ways, their laxity of morals, their alien ideals, the ignorance and superstition of many of them, we sometimes have reason to fear that to us is coming a tremendous contribution of the worse – a contribution against which we will have cause to measure our highest ideals of manhood, our noblest conceptions of womanhood sanctified by faith in the God of the nations and a knowledge of the Gospel of His Son.[18]

According to Woodsworth, immigrants were coming for one major reason: "that of escaping from evils which have made existence intolerable, and of reaching the free air of countries where conditions are better shaped to the welfare of the masses of the people."[19] Thus already Woodsworth was presenting an image of the Prairie West as a land of freedom and unlimited opportunity. He linked the idyllic image of the prairies to that of America in general. Using phrases reminiscent of Frederick Jackson Turner's image of America coming out of the great American West at that time, Woodsworth noted: "Why do these people come to Canada? America, generally, has had a time of wonderful prosperity. It is a new land – almost an unoccupied land – of vast extent and wonderful resources. It is a land of freedom – of democratic government; a land where every man has a chance; a land without a past to darken the glowing colors of the ideal future. It appears to offer the immigrant just that which he has not had."[20]

Nowhere was this promise more imminent than in the Prairie West, J. S. Woodsworth believed, as had his father in *Thirty Years in the Canadian North-West*. But he also stressed even more than his father had done in his memoirs the obstacles in the way of the West achieving its potential, most notably the "immigrant problem." His introductory chapter to *Strangers within Our Gates* is entitled "Immigration – a world problem." Here he presents a litany of "problems" that immigrants posed for the Prairie West: too many undesirable groups entering the region, too many of them ending up lowering the overall quality of life on the prairies, some becoming the criminal element in the region, and too many of them having undesirable values and unacceptable beliefs that detracted from the good Christian values of the host society. J.S., like his father, singled out two groups in particular as problematic: Mormons and Galicians, and then added a few of his own, namely Poles and Blacks. With regard to the Poles, he wrote: "Most of the Poles who reach this country are peasants, or workingmen from the cities and towns – far from the best class. They are poor, illiterate, and with a code of morals none too high."[21] To be sure, Woodsworth emphasized the need for Canadians to realize that behind the immigration figures and reports lay human beings with hopes and fears, aspirations and disappointments, successes and failures. But in the end, he judged these various groups by the way they either aided or deterred the region from becoming God's kingdom on earth. On this question, Woodsworth gave the clear impression that until these groups were exorcised or else made into "loyal British subjects," this ideal would never become a reality. At this point in his thinking, Woodsworth believed that many could enter God's earthly kingdom on the prairies, but they could only truly be citizens of this "kingdom" if they adopted the values and religious beliefs of the dominant white Anglo-Saxon Protestant (especially Methodist) (WASP) majority who were the "prophets" leading the people to this Promised Land. This meant a policy of assimilation. As he wrote: "Essentially non-assimilable elements are clearly detrimental to our highest national development, and hence should be vigorously excluded."[22]

In *My Neighbor*, Woodsworth's second publication under the auspices of the Methodist Church, he focused on the problem that fast-growing cities posed to the West, especially when these cities became havens for poor immigrants who crowded into ethnic slums that became warrens of disease and crime. Now, however, he saw immigration and fast-growing cities as part of a larger problem facing the prairie region: the entrenchment of the capitalist system in the West. He believed that the capitalist system was responsible for fuelling large-scale growth and dictating the way immigrants were integrated into society. Woodsworth saw the capitalist society as being highly competitive, and competition was premised on the belief that a few people should naturally succeed while the majority would fail. He advocated instead a system of socialism for the prairies based on the spirit of co-operation as more in keeping with true Christian values and as a means of transforming the region into God's earthly kingdom.

Woodsworth noted the ways that the Prairie West had both limitations and promise in achieving such an objective. In terms of limitations, the region's sheer size and limited population meant that people lived in isolation, especially in rural areas. Compounding the problem were the 160-acre farms. While they allowed an individual farmer a sizeable plot of land to farm, they also left farm families far from neighbours. Thus, the physical size and the layout of the prairie region militated against a spirit of co-operation. On the positive side, however, the prairies were a newer society, and thus more willing to challenge established beliefs and entrenched economic systems than the traditional society of the East. As well, a spirit of co-operation already prevailed in the West coming out of the settlement experience and the willingness of westerners to help one another to get started. He ended *My Neighbor* on an optimistic note with regard to the Prairie West's potential by quoting from Dr. Frank Mason's book, *The Christian City*: "One Christian city, one city in any part of the earth, where citizens, from the greatest to the humblest, lived to the spirit of Christ, where religion had overflowed the churches, and passed into the streets, inundating every house and workshop and permeating the whole social and commercial life – one such Christian city would seal the redemption of the world."[23] While Mason's "Christian city" could have been any city, by quoting him in the context of the Prairie West, Woodsworth implied that the "one Christian city" would ultimately be a prairie city.

J. S. Woodsworth's perspective on the immigrant and urban problems confronting the Prairie West in his early writings reflected that of the Methodist Church at the time under whose auspice he was writing. In his study, *The Methodist Church on the Prairies, 1896–1914*, historian George Emery sketches out the prevailing attitude. He notes that the "Methodists perceived the non-Anglo-Saxon immigrants as posing a problem with many dimensions"[24]: posing a moral threat with their "strange beliefs"; undermining working-class living standards by accepting low wages and crowded unsanitary housing; a political threat by being eligible to vote but manipulated by corrupt political bosses; and threatening to balkanize Canadian society. Emery then goes on to note the ways that the Methodist Church attempted to deal with these problems: demanding the Canadian government adopt a selective immigrant policy; pressing governments at all levels to implement "moral legislation," such as prohibition and Sunday observance; insisting that provincial governments bring in compulsory English-language instruction in public schools; and finally establishing missions among the "foreigners" whether abroad or in Canada.[25] Without these necessary reforms, Methodist Church leaders warned, the Prairie West was in danger of losing its Christian values. The Reverend John Maclean, a reporter for the *Christian Guardian*, the Methodist Church's newspaper in the West, expressed the prevailing attitude of the church towards "foreign" immigrants when he wrote: "The general opinion of the people in this country is that we do not want any more of these people in the west. The quality of the immigrants is more important to us than the quantity. We cannot afford to have the refuse of Europe dumped into our western country, as an ignorant foreign population can work a great deal of harm"[26] In the years from 1907 to 1913, J. S. Woodsworth would have concurred wholeheartedly with Maclean's opinion while also expressing similar complaints about immigrants and proposing many of the same solutions as that of the leaders of the Methodist Church. J. S. Woodsworth's early vision of the West and that of the Methodist Church remained one and the same.

In 1913, J. S. Woodsworth resigned from his position as superintendent of All Peoples' Mission in Winnipeg and severed his connection with the Methodist Church in regard to church-related work. Instead, he worked for secular organizations, first as secretary of the Canadian Welfare League from 1913 to 1916, and then as director of the Bureau of Social Research for the governments of Manitoba, Saskatchewan and Alberta in 1916–17, at which time he was forced out of the position due to his criticism of the Canadian government's implementation of conscription. He tendered another letter of resignation to the Methodist Church in 1918, which was accepted this time. But his letter of resignation, I would argue, was the final act of years of distancing himself from the Methodist Church rather than the initial move in that direction. Clearly his resignation from All Peoples' Mission and his decision to seek a job in the public sector reflected his alienation from the church and the views it espoused. Woodsworth's letter of resignation encapsulated his feelings about the Methodist Church at the time:

> The Church, as many other institutions, was becoming increasingly commercialized. This meant the control of the policies of the Church by men of wealth, and, in many cases, the temptation for the minister to become a financial agent rather than a moral and spiritual leader. It meant, also, that anything like a radical programme of social reform became in practice almost impossible. In my own particular work among the immigrant peoples, I felt that I, at least, could give more effective service outside denominational lines. Intellectual freedom was not sufficient – I must be free to work.[27]

Thus by the time Woodsworth left the church and pursued employment outside the confines of Methodism, he realized that one of the greatest obstacles to achieving the Kingdom of God on the prairies was, ironically, the Methodist Church itself with its nativistic attitudes, its intolerance of people outside of the church, and its narrow vision of the ideal society in prairie Canada. Woodsworth had come to realize that the church's vision was not his vision, nor was it in keeping with his social gospel beliefs. Woodsworth was now free to expound his own vision of the West.

His new vision of the Prairie West focused on its *potential* to be God's heavenly kingdom on earth rather than on the problems and obstacles that stood in the way of achieving this end. His altered perspective is evident in a series of fourteen articles he wrote for the *Winnipeg Free Press* in 1913 under the general title "Canadians of Tomorrow." In one of the articles, he began: "The coming of the immigrants is fraught with dangers, but it is also full of promise. From every country in

Europe are flowing streams bearing rich deposits which unite, mingle their waters, and then spread out over our wide plains, enriching and fruitifying the hitherto uninhabitable wastes."[28] In another article in the series, he reminded his readers "the immigrants are coming Canadians, their children Canadian-born."[29] Rather than a "problem," they are a promise for the future, a contribution to making the Prairie West a "Promised Land."

For those immigrants who did not fit in, the blame, Woodsworth now argued, lay neither with them nor with the land, as he argued earlier, but with the host society that did not accept them as one of their own. He blamed mainstream Canadians who were indifferent, if not downright hostile, towards immigrants, with the result, Woodsworth maintained, that immigrants had a low opinion of themselves. The term "foreigner" had become an identity that ethnic immigrants loathed. So now Woodsworth saw not only the Methodist Church but the dominant Anglo-Protestant majority as the barriers to the Prairie West becoming the Kingdom of God on earth.

He even went further to argue that the immigrants were the true means to transform the West into the Promised Land. For he now believed that God's earthly kingdom must consist of a richly diverse mix of people, each ethnic group adding to the richness of the whole. Using the metaphor of a garden, reminiscent of the Garden of Eden, Woodsworth noted: "In our Canadian garden under the shelter of the maple, there will flourish not only the rose, the shamrock, the thistle, and the fleur-de-lis, but a score more flowers of which as yet we hardly know the names."[30] On another occasion, he used the metaphor of the garden again to reinforce the diversity of ethnic groups that went into the cultivation of a beautiful and harmonious whole.

> 'God has many bests,' as a wise teacher once put the truth which we are emphasizing. In the garden of Allah grow many varieties of flowers – each perfect after its kind. All cannot be judged according to one standard. If ever we in Canada attain a national ideal, it must be big enough – Catholic enough – to give a place to the highest and best which each class of immigrant brings to this country.[31]

Now Woodsworth looked to social workers rather than church leaders to prepare the West to be God's kingdom on earth. The latter were too narrow-minded in their view of immigrants to lead this new multicultural society he saw emerging in the new West. What was required was the ability to create a sense of brotherhood. "Last century made the world a neighbourhood; this century must make it a brotherhood,"[32] he proclaimed in an article on "Nation Building" in 1917. Here too, immigrants had a role to play, since they brought "a reverence and a patriotism which we need in this new and commercialized country of ours."[33] Thus, Woodsworth had come to appreciate that non-Methodist, even non-Christian, immigrants brought spiritual and moral values to the Prairie West that offset the North American obsession with materialism so evident in the region.

In his article "Thy Kingdom Come," in which he showed the relevance of the Lord's Prayer for everyday living in prairie communities, Woodsworth set out what Christ's message meant for transforming the Prairie West into God's kingdom on earth. "The plague-spots must be cleaned out; the dark places must be made light; the crooked places straight and the rough places smooth."[34] He cited the example of how science had discovered the cause of malaria in the Panama Canal district and transformed it into a healthy living environment. The same could be done in the Prairie West, he argued, once people realized that their social problems resulted from poor social conditions that science could eliminate. He used an example familiar to prairie residents. He had officiated at a funeral of a child in the poor district of Winnipeg. The scripture chosen bespoke of the child's death as being God's will with the biblical passage: "For as much as it hath pleased Almighty God, in His wise Providence, to take out of the world the soul of the deceased."[35] Woodsworth recalled thinking at the time that it was wrong to blame God for something that was the fault of human error. The child had died from contaminated milk in an unclean environment that could have been prevented with the application of scientific knowledge. Thus, he concluded that true religion had to concern itself with these social problems. "To really save *one* man you must transform the community in which he lives," Woodsworth emphasized. What did this require?: "The making of good roads; the getting rid of weeds; the improvement of stock; the providing of a ball ground; the higher education of the young people; a square deal for the stranger; better laws and better administration of law – all these are essentially religious, all are surely part of the work of bringing in the kingdom of God in your home district."[36]

Woodsworth frequently used scenes of funerals and death as the means to convey his message of hope and transformation of the Prairie West. Death, particularly premature death, was an ever-present reality on the prairies at the turn of the century. But also etched in the minds of prairie inhabitants was the promise of new life in the afterlife through the Christian message. The metaphor of death and resurrection conveyed his message of new life before death in a world transformed into the Kingdom of God on earth. Rebirth and new life could admonish death in a world concerned with the well being of all citizens. This message Woodsworth conveyed while present at the funeral of the son of his close friend William Ivens. He noted the incongruity of Ivens attending his son's funeral, while being considered a "criminal" due to his participation in the Winnipeg General Strike, and "accompanied by a jail guard."[37] Out of that experience came the conviction of Woodsworth and others to begin a Labour Church that would be devoted to servicing the needs of the working class. As Woodsworth described the experience: "By the open graveside we pledged ourselves to be true to our comrades, and in our hearts there came a deeper determination to continue the fight until every man and woman and child had a chance in life and this cruel competitive system had been replaced by an era of co-operation and brotherhood."[38] It was this fusion of social gospel beliefs with his experiences living on the prairies that formed the basis of Woodsworth's conviction that here on the prairies the conditions were right for the creation of the Kingdom of God on earth in his own lifetime.

The two – his social gospel belief in the Kingdom of God on earth, and his conviction that the Prairie West would be the place where God's heavenly kingdom would be fulfilled – came together most poignantly in yet another scene of a burial of a child. Entitled "Eventide on the Prairies," Woodsworth described the consecration of a child's grave. The child was clearly of immigrant parents, the family of a non-Protestant denomination, recent arrivals on the prairies, anxious to make a new beginning, a new life. It was a scene of tragedy and hope, death and life, land and sky, a fusion of heaven and earth.

> Headed by the crucifix, the little procession moved slowly from the church to the grave – rough sunburned men, kerchiefed women and little children. The grave – it was only the third in "God's acre" – was marked by a rude wooden cross. The priest read the service and sprinkled the grave, then all knelt in a little group and chanted a hymn. It was a most touching scene – the little grave, the reverent spirit of the kneeling group, the subdued grief of the parents. A tiny child, escaped from his mother, patted gleefully the wooden cross.... The wind stirred the long prairie grasses, a meadow-lark's note rang

> across the fields and the Western sun bathed the whole in a golden glow. It was the hour when the mystery of the prairie casts its spell upon its true sons. All heads were bowed low to receive the blessing. The great, rude tree with its cross-beam had been planted in the prairie soil. Death and Life were both there! Their spirits subdued, their faith strengthened, the little company departed quietly in the stillness of the evening.[39]

Woodsworth's vision of the Prairie West as the Kingdom of God on earth was most poignantly presented in the decade from 1907 to 1917 when Woodsworth lived on the prairies and was involved in social work there. This faith in the Prairie West as the Promised Land was the source and sustenance of his social reform impulse. After 1917, he briefly worked as a minister in Gibson's Landing on the west coast and then as a longshoreman in Vancouver. He returned to Winnipeg in 1919 at the time of the Winnipeg General Strike to become editor of the *Labor Paper*, resulting in his arrest as an alleged contributor to the strike. From 1921 to 1942, he was the member of Parliament for Winnipeg North Centre, during which time, in 1932, he founded and became the first leader of the new Co-operative Commonwealth Federation (CCF) party. His social reform impulse and his vision of the Prairie West as the Promised Land continued to guide him in these subsequent years, but they never became the focus of his thoughts and writings after 1917. His involvement in national politics, his hope for the CCF to become a national party, and his concern with national and international affairs, especially as the threat of another world war loomed on the horizon in the 1930s, all shifted his focus and concern from regional to national issues. But Woodsworth never lost his spirit of reform or his faith in the Prairie West as the seedbed for establishing the Kingdom of God on earth. His roots were in prairie soil, and his vision shaped by his formative years as a social worker in prairie society. His vision of the Kingdom of God on earth *and* his vision of the Prairie West as the Promised Land together guided and sustained him throughout his life.

NOTES

1 For a discussion of J. S. Woodsworth's social gospel ideas, see Allen Mills, *Fool for Christ: The Political Thought of J. S. Woodsworth* (Toronto: University of Toronto Press, 1991); Kenneth McNaught, *A Prophet in Politics: A Biography of J. S. Woodsworth* (Toronto: University of Toronto Press, 1959); Ramsay Cook, *The Regenerators: Social Criticism in Late Victorian English Canada* (Toronto: University of Toronto Press, 1985); and Richard Allen, *The Social Passion: Religion and Social Reform in Canada, 1914–28* (Toronto: University of Toronto Press, 1971).

2 J. S. Woodsworth, "My Religion," in *"Following the Gleam": A Modern Pilgrim's Progress – to date!* (n.p., 1926), 17.

3 Ibid., 18.

4 "The Kingdom of Heaven in Regina," Regina *Leader*, May 5, 1913.

5 "J. S. Woodsworth: Thy Kingdom Come," from 'Sermons for the Unsatisfied,' *Grain Growers' Guide* (June 30, 1915); reprinted in H. D. Forbes, ed., *Canadian Political Thought* (Toronto: Oxford University Press, 1985), 224.

6 Woodsworth, "Canadians of Tomorrow: More Danger Signals: The Effect of Canada upon the Immigrant," *Winnipeg Free Press*, June 2, 1913.

7 For the official Methodist Church perspective on the prairies at the turn of the century, see George Emery, *The Methodist Church on the Prairies, 1896–1914* (Montreal and Kingston: McGill-Queen's University Press, 2001). I am not suggesting that the mainline Methodist Church did not have within it a social gospel perspective; I am arguing, however, that the Methodist Church's social gospel perspective in the early twentieth century was incompatible with Woodsworth's after 1913, particularly with regards to the place of "foreign" immigrants in Canadian society. Whether he had already moved away from the Methodist Church's perspective by 1913 or was drawn away from the Church's position as a result of beliefs after 1913 that he no longer could accept is a moot point. What is significant is that Woodsworth had distanced himself from the beliefs of the prominent members of the Methodist Church by 1913 to present a position that he felt was more in keeping with his vision of the social gospel.

8 For an interesting comparison of James Woodsworth and J. S. Woodsworth, see Benjamin Smillie, "The Woodsworths: James and J.S. – father and son," in *Prairie Spirit: Perspectives on the Heritage of the United Church of Canada in the West*, eds. Dennis L. Butcher et al. (Winnipeg: University of Manitoba Press, 1985), 100–121.

9 In a letter from J. S. Woodsworth to his cousin, C. B. Sissons, January 21, 1917, he informed Sissons that he "handled the final editing of his father's book and claimed to have altered it in ways that he believed improved it." Quote is from Mills, *Fool for Christ*, 5. Therefore, in my discussion of Rev. Woodsworth's *Thirty Years in the Canadian North-West* (Toronto: McClelland, Goodchild & Stewart, 1917), I am assuming that the ideas presented reflected both James and J. S. Woodsworth's views.

10 Woodsworth, *Thirty Years*, xii–xiii.

11 Ibid., 229.

12 Ibid., 236–37.

13 Ibid., 235.

14 Ibid., 232–33.

15 James S. Woodsworth, "Sketches of Western Life: II. The Prairie Preacher," *The Christian Guardian*, April 18, 1906. Copy in PAC, J. S. Woodsworth Papers, Vol. 18, Scrapbook, 1906–1910.

16 J. S. Woodsworth, *Strangers within Our Gates: or, Coming Canadians* (1909). Reprint with an Introduction by Marilyn Barber (Toronto: University of Toronto Press, 1972), 9.

17 Ibid., 240.

18 Ibid., 244.

19 Ibid., 12.

20 Ibid., 172.
21 Ibid., 115.
22 Ibid., 232.
23 Ibid., 177.
24 Emery, *The Methodist Church on the Prairies, 1896–1914*, 10.
25 Ibid., 10ff.
26 Quoted in ibid.,127.
27 Woodsworth, "Why I Resigned from the Christian Ministry," in *"Following the Gleam,"* 9.
28 J. S. Woodsworth, "Canadians of Tomorrow: The Assets which the Immigrant Brings," *Winnipeg Free Press*, May 31, 1913.
29 Woodsworth, "Canadians of Tomorrow: More Danger Signals: The Effect of Canada upon the Immigrant," *Winnipeg Free Press*, June 2, 1913.
30 J. S. Woodsworth, "Canadians of Tomorrow: How to Make True Canadians," *Winnipeg Free Press*, June 3, 1913.
31 J. S. Woodsworth, "Nation Building," *The University Magazine* 16, no. 1 (February 1917), 90–91.
32 Ibid., 85.
33 Ibid., 89.
34 "J. S. Woodsworth: Thy Kingdom Come," in Forbes, *Canadian Political Thought*, 225.
35 Ibid.
36 Ibid., 226.
37 J. S. Woodsworth, *The First Story of the Labor Church and Some Things for Which It Stands* (Winnipeg: Labor Church, 1920), 5.
38 Ibid.
39 Woodsworth Papers, vol. 15, File: Personal Papers – J. S. Woodsworth – Twenty Years, 1908–1929. J. S. Woodsworth, *Hours that Stand Apart* (n.d.), 5.

11

"A FAR GREEN COUNTRY UNTO A SWIFT SUNRISE": THE UTOPIANISM OF THE ALBERTA FARM MOVEMENT, 1909–1923

Bradford J. Rennie

Migrations to new worlds or new frontiers frequently spawn utopian hopes. When people leave their homes, communities, or countries to settle in a distant, sparsely populated, undeveloped place, they need to believe it is the Promised Land. If it is not, the decision to move was foolish and possibly disastrous. Who would want to think that?

So it was with pioneers of the Canadian West, the "last, best West." Whether middling or poor, and whatever their place of origin – the United States, Ontario, eastern Canada, or Europe – all felt a poignant blend of anxiety and optimism. What would the future hold? Milk and honey, surely?

To the newcomers, the Canadian West was a blank slate. Untainted by the evils of so-called civilization, an ideal society could be fashioned on the riffling short grass or amid the aspen copses. Here, in the late nineteenth and early twentieth centuries, a plethora of small, mostly ephemeral, utopian communities sprang up. They were of all sorts: aristocratic, democratic, socialist, sectarian, and pastoral; one was a temperance colony.[1] All sought to create a social order of harmony, community, and collaboration.

So did the early Alberta farm movement, but its impact was much greater. By spawning a new economic institution (the wheat pool), and supporting an astonishingly successful political movement, the farm movement literally changed the face of Alberta and, to some extent, Canada. Previously studied as a class, populist, or western protest movement,[2] or as an occupational or educational movement,[3] the Alberta farm movement was also, as this paper shows, a utopian movement – with a shining vision of a Promised Land. Just as Robert Owen could perceive happy, self-governing communes emerging in industrial Britain, beneath the soot-filled skies, so Alberta farmers could see, always before them on the distant, clear-blue horizon, a socially just, co-operative, truly democratic order. Forged by frontier expectations, religious impulses, and a congeries of reform and other ideas, the farm movement's utopianism attracted thousands. How could a farmer *not* join a movement that would further her or his interests *and* create a new heaven and a new earth?

Like other North American farm organizations, the Alberta farm movement was a response to perceived economic and political inequalities. Discriminatory freight rates, tariff protectionism, high interest rates, a monopolistic meat industry, and an oligarchic grain trade packed with speculators – these were the key obstacles, farmers felt. They believed the cards were stacked in favour of parasitic middlemen, big industrialists, and financiers. The worst part was, these "plutocrats" controlled the political parties. What was the solution? Agrarian organization. By collective action, farmers could solve some problems themselves – by creating co-operatives, for example – and force governments to solve others. Then and only then could the Promised Land of Alberta be fully realized.

Initially, the Alberta farm movement consisted of several short-lived organizations: first the Patrons of Industry, then the Farmers' Association of Alberta, and then the Alberta Farmers' Association and the Society of Equity, the latter an American offshoot. None left a profound impression, but the Alberta Society of Equity, established in 1904, was tinged with utopianism. The Society promised to organize all farmers of the world. Then it would dictate to governments and control agricultural markets. Never again would monopolists manipulate farm product prices. The result would be "justice and equity to all." According to the white-bearded, ex-American Populist R. C. Owens – who looked like an Old Testament prophet – the Society of Equity was "the greatest movement on behalf of humanity that had been inaugurated since the birth of Christ."[4] Bold and hopeful words these were.

Alas, the promise of the Society of Equity would not be fulfilled. The Alberta Society was only a shadow of its American parent, and in 1909 it amalgamated with its rival, the Alberta Farmers' Association, to become the United Farmers of Alberta (UFA). The UFA forthwith went from strength to strength, forming a women's section, the United Farm Women of Alberta (UFWA), and spurting from 5,000 to almost 38,000 members by 1921. Meekly responding to this goliath, the provincial Liberal government supported co-ops and rural hospitals, enacted prohibition, suffrage, women's property rights, and introduced democratic reform. Responding to all Canadian farmers, Ottawa curbed abuses in the grain business, reigned in patronage, and taxed those rich corporations. These were significant accomplishments that gave farmers a sense of collective power and possibility. But when the Reciprocity Agreement, a semi-free trade deal, went down to defeat in 1911, tariffs and freight rates were increased during the war, and the old political parties – and even the non-partisan federal Union government – seemed increasingly unresponsive to farmers, if not corrupt, many farmers, especially in Alberta, resolved that independent political action alone could solve their problems and realize their ideals.

UFA/UFWA supporters were sure those ideals were realizable because they believed, with almost unshakable faith, that Alberta was the Promised Land. Almost never did they question the agricultural productivity of the province; when their aspirations for material comfort were thwarted, some human agency was to blame. The country was not at fault; it was bountiful. "We have here a country of great possibilities with natural conditions as nearly ideal as possible, but with many artificial conditions that do not make for the welfare of the people," proclaimed the UFA's first president, James Bower. It was the task of the UFA to right the man-made wrongs so the garden could bloom. "We are in the formative stage now," Bower told a convention of farmers, "and are laying the foundation of the future weal or woe of our own later years and of the generations that are to follow."[5]

That Alberta *was* the land of milk and honey was not a matter of opinion; farmers were convinced it was fact. After all, they had won more than their share of trophies from the Dry Farming Congresses of the prewar years. In 1911 the Alberta delegates to the Congress returned "proud of their province and more than ever convinced that it is by a long way the best portion of the American continent," noted the UFA's first secretary, E. J. Fream. Indeed, Alberta's farmland was so productive that even the parasites could not steal all the wealth. "We are reaping unthinkable sums of money from the farms of this country," related UFA vice-president W. J. Tregillus, a future UFA president, "and notwithstanding the exploitation of trusts and combines, the excessive tariffs, market and transportation difficulties, we are rapidly making for a condition unsurpassed by any other class of citizenship."[6] If only farmers could throw off their shackles, their prosperity would be incalculable!

Even after years of post-war recession and drought in the deep South, most farmers' utopian lenses remained unscratched. Agriculture was suffering, but the inherent goodness of the land was not doubted. In 1923 Donald Cameron, a UFA member of the Legislature, told the House that, despite difficult conditions, "he had not lost any portion of his faith in the province. It was still the land of promise for the man who desired to establish himself in peace and prosperity." There was an element of hyperbole to such rhetoric, but deep down Cameron, and others like him, truly did feel Alberta was the best place be. "The province was blessed with a wealth of natural possibilities," he elaborated, "and its settlers were a hardy and determined people." They would succeed, even thrive, if governments did their "part to help restore economic conditions."[7]

And certainly they deserved to thrive. Echoing the French physiocrats, W. J. Tregillus insisted that "the farmer alone, of all the occupations known to man, adds to the common wealth." Like Atlas, the world rested on his shoulders; without him civilization would crumble. For that reason agriculture should be given every encouragement. In their political platform, farmers unabashedly declared that farming must not be "hampered by tariff restrictions," since every other occupation was "so dependent on its success."[8] Only if farmers received their rightful share from the Promised Land – only if unjust, human-imposed conditions were eliminated – could everyone prosper.

Not only was farming the source of all wealth, but it was the wellspring of happiness and virtue. Tregillus preached that farming was "the most natural and healthful life we can live"; moreover, farmers were "not subject to the temptation to rob and ruin their fellows, as in so many other lines of endeavour, for in agriculture integrity and absolute honesty must be observed."[9] Here was the Jeffersonian ideal of the honest, contented yeoman – the moral fabric of the nation – tilling an Edenic paradise.

Tregillus's idealized yeoman was outstandingly masculine. He was gritty, tenacious, principled, a man of faith and action. He epitomized "thorough-going manliness." On the other hand, the soil had feminine, nurturing qualities. Quoting Thomas Carlyle, Tregillus wrote:

> The land is the mother of us all, nourishes, shelters, gladdens, lovingly enriches us all; in how many ways from our awakening to our last sleep on her blessed mother-bosom does she, as with blessed mother arms, enfold us all.[10]

If the land was kind and gentle and a fountain of morality and wealth, cities were harsh, parasitic, and degenerate. They were blight on human society. Alberta farmers' utopian ideal, like that of Jefferson, was an agrarian one. "We don't want to build up large cities," intoned F. W. Godsal, a UFA supporter. "They have done enough harm already." Bert Huffman, another well-known UFA man, eloquently contrasted the peace and liberty of country living with the stress, frustrations, and vice of city life:

> The city's stifled throngs go by
> With empty heart and aching eye:
> The burning street, the maddening roar,
> The killing routine, o'er and o'er.
> What cramped and narrow life it seems –
> Its fevered conflicts, fruitless dreams;
> Its barren walls, its dust and dins;
> Its licence, lust, and haunting sin!
>
> But, O, so near that surging tide
> There lies the restful countryside:
> Untrodden paths in miles of green,
> The beckoning fields in Autumn sheen;
> The glory set in land and sky,
> A feast for heart and soul and eye,
> A velvet carpet for your tread,
> A grassy pillow for your head –
> A freer life, a higher view,
> A wider outlook calling you –
> And health and life and gladness wait
> Inside the country's open gate![11]

UFA leaders called for reforms that would set agriculture "on the plane that it should occupy"; otherwise, cities might spread like cancer, and paradise would be lost. F. W. Godsal exhorted farmers to make farming "the most honourable, attractive, and respected business of Canada ... for country life produces more and healthier ... children than does city life."[12]

The farmers' utopian vision was not only pastoral; it was infused with the social gospel overtones of the era. Whether liberal or conservative in theology, farmers like Alice M. Hart, a UFWA leader, felt they must "build on earth the kingdom of the Lord," a society shaped by Christian humanitarian ethics. There was too much self-centredness, too much materialism in the world. "How many individuals," asked Bert Huffman, "give a serious thought to another's gain or pleasure or welfare? How many of our 'great' banking syndicates, railroad syndicates, commercial syndicates have anything but the coldest, cruellest, narrowest, selfishness for their sole creed?"[13]

For Huffman, the solution to this situation was fundamentally spiritual. "How easily might wrongs be righted, might poverty be removed, might failure and hatred and ignorance be eradicated, if this Heavenly Spirit – this Spirit of Brotherhood – could be instilled as the working creed of the world." The prairies desperately needed this regeneration. "Try to conceive, if you can," he went on to say, "how little of this Spirit of Brotherhood is found in our new and boasted land of the West. How much of it enters into our systems of land selling, of transportation, of marketing, of trading and trafficking and dealing?" "There is truly a marvellous mission" for the "farmers' organizations to perform," he concluded.[14]

After the war, it seemed that mission might be fulfilled. Farmers desperately wanted to believe the soldiers had not died in vain – surely their shed blood would bring social and economic redemption? Alluding to the rise of agrarian agitation and labour strife, an anonymous UFA member reflected:

> Why this state of affairs? Is it because our age has lost faith in the Divine? Have doubt and scepticism burned the divine dew off the grass and left it sere and brown? Nay, a thousand times, nay. Is it not rather that the Divine has been revealed as never before – a new vision of the earth as a possible paradise?

In the mind of one UFA writer and many other UFA/UFWA followers, there was no doubt the prairie farm movement would usher in that utopia; it was "the most powerful agent for the furtherance of the kingdom of God on earth."[15]

That kingdom would provide equality of opportunity, a notion captured by the UFA motto "equity" and the oft-repeated Jacksonian slogan: "Equal rights for all, special privileges for none." No longer would bloated plutocrats be lavished with high tariffs, government bonuses, and patronage. Markets would be free, and corruption and handouts for the wealthy would end. "When this longed-for epoch arrives," opined UFA president James Bower, "all unnatural inequalities, all artificial obstructions ... and all unfairly acquired wealth will be eliminated." "Every man, woman, and child" will have a chance for his or her "highest development – physical, mental, spiritual."[16]

But the UFA/UFWA vision went beyond Gladstonian liberalism. Influenced by the European co-operative movement, Fabian socialism, British labourism, North American agrarianism, positive liberalism,[17] and a host of thinkers ranging from Karl Marx to Henry George, Alberta farmers wanted "a fairer division of the wealth that is created," a measure of economic equality, and not just for farmers. Implementation of the Canadian Farmers' Platform, calling for tariff and electoral reform, state-owned railways, government ownership or supervision of major industries and utilities, progressive taxation, and modest social welfare measures, would reduce, if not eliminate, the hardship of many occupational groups. "Economic justice, as it is understood by the farm people," insisted Irene Parlby, president of the UFWA and a future UFA member of the Legislature, "will tend to lift the burden from the shoulders of every struggling class: the artisan, the clerk, the minister, every man and woman working on a salary will benefit as much or even more than the farm people."[18]

For W. J. Tregillus, the single tax – the taxation of land values alone, a nostrum adopted in Alberta and around the world before the Great War – would literally inaugurate the millennium. It would

> ... do away with fraud, corruption, and gross inequality inseparable from our present methods of taxation, which allow the rich to escape while they grind the poor ... and would throw open to labour the illimitable field of employment, which the earth offers to man, thereby solving the labour problem, doing away with involuntary poverty, raise wages to the full earnings of labour, make overproduction impossible

> until all human wants are satisfied, render labour savings inventions a blessing to all, and cause such an enormous production and such an equitable distribution of wealth as would give to all comfort, leisure, and participation in the advantage of an advancing civilization.[19]

Thus, the farmers' utopia would touch everyone. It would be anchored in the countryside, but its beneficence would extend into the towns and, yes, even into the cities. And though its epicentre would be in Alberta and the West, it would radiate beyond – to "a far green country under a swift sunrise."[20] "A brilliant light spreads forth its rays, o'er all our fair domain,"[21] proclaimed a UFA song. Unlike most prairie utopian movements, which sought escape from the evils, dangers, and exploitation of the world, UFA/UFWA members, like the American pilgrims, conceived of themselves as a city on the hill, a beacon in the darkness, pointing to a Promised Land.

Alberta farmers hoped Canada would follow that "light" and embrace the Farmers' Platform, recast and reforged in 1918 as the "New National Policy," a policy for the people, unlike the old national policy, a policy for the few. Then the UFA/UFWA, in concert with other farmers and reformers, would transform the world. "I feel a power which if rightly directed must mean the dawn of a brighter tomorrow," mused Mrs. Charles Bruels, "a tomorrow when the social evils, under which we writhe and which are a disgrace to our civilization, are banished – a tomorrow when, instead of being selfishly wrapped up in our own affairs, we reach out our hands to all humanity, feeling that they are all our own." Embracing the same idealistic, universal outlook, Anna M. Archibald, a UFWA leader, told her readers:

> Now I believe that this is a great movement for reform, greater than we imagine, though we ourselves are making it. And isn't it fine to think that every one of us linked up with this movement has an unsurpassed opportunity of giving to the work the best of our thought and efforts, of going forward ... to make this world of ours a better place to live in?[22]

That world would be co-operative. Shaped by the social gospel and the ideology of the co-operative movement, inspired by the writings of Edward Bellamy, with his shining vision of a future co-operative commonwealth, and melded together by a sense of mutuality in the farm movement, Alberta farmers believed that co-operation must replace competition in all human relations – between individuals, organizations, the sexes, ethnic and racial groups, social classes, and countries. Susan Gunn, a prominent UFWA leader, later reminisced: We "visualized society in all its ramifications across national boundaries, creeds, and tongues being transformed through the substitution of co-operative endeavour instead of competition as the dominating factor in society."[23] Once humanity embraced the co-operative spirit, wars, selfishness, and social evils would cease.

The Promised Land of Alberta, Canada, and beyond would be truly democratic as well as co-operative. "Our ideal for ourselves and for the world," pronounced UFA secretary P. P. Woodbridge before the 1918 UFA convention, "is a great democracy; and while many of our members are taking active part in the fight overseas to make the world safe for democracy, the call is no less urgent for us to make the democracy at home safe for the world. We, on our part, cannot afford to be content with the mere form of democracy, but we must learn to understand and exercise the real spirit of democracy."[24] Direct legislation – the initiative, the referendum, and the recall – which Alberta enacted in 1913, proportional representation, and Senate reform would put power into the hands of the people, farmers believed.

But more was needed, declared Henry Wise Wood, the UFA's prophet, priest, philosopher-king, and greatest president. Imbued with civic republicanism, an ideology committed to community, citizenship responsibility, and political virtue,[25] Wood lamented that plutocracy – powerful manufacturing and financial interests – controlled politics and the economy. He believed ordinary people must organize themselves into economic groups and take collective industrial and political action against plutocracy. If they did not, a truly democratic and co-operative order would be impossible, because the plutocrats would continue to exploit the masses and manipulate governments. And international economic competition would keep on driving the machine of war.[26]

But there was hope, Wood assured farmers. Soon the various economic groups of the people – farmers, labour, and others – would federate their groups into a great democratic force to confront plutocracy in an apocalyptic "showdown."[27] "When these forces are finally thus marshalled," Wood predicted, "the irrepressible conflict will be on. The conflict between democracy and plutocracy, between civilization and barbarism, between man and money, between co-operation and competition, between God and Mammon." Who would win? Of course, the democratic side, because it was guided by "immutable" natural and social laws:

> To say that democracy will fail will be to say that the design of nature in creating a social being and bringing him into obedience to social laws has failed.... It will not fail ... because the Supreme Power that flung the numberless hosts of worlds into infinite space ... has this work in hand and will not let it fail.[28]

There was no doubt: the people would destroy the power of plutocracy and inaugurate an era of democracy, co-operation, justice, and peace. They would achieve victory, not by force of arms or violence, but by concerted economic co-operation and, to a lesser extent, through politics. Initially, Wood counselled farmers to work through the existing political parties, but in 1919 he proposed one of the most utopian political schemes ever concocted.

The party system, Wood now stated, must go. It was inherently corrupt and undemocratic – it did not give voice to the people. It must be replaced by group government, a government in which each economic group would elect, to the legislatures and parliament, its own occupational representatives. These representatives, in close consultation with their constituents, would meet and come to a consensus on legislation. If any group member tried to selfishly force through a law, the other members would block that effort. The representatives would be forced to co-operate, and government decisions would reflect the input of all group members. There would be no party whip, no toeing the party line, no kowtowing to the cabinet, no corporate political influence, no deceit – just fair legislation. No more political plutocracy; no more exploitation. A political utopia, quite literally.

Excited by that possibility, farmers elected Alex Moore, the UFA candidate, in the Cochrane provincial by-election of 1919. "No force in Canada, except bayonets, could have stopped the farmers exercising their franchise" in the way they had wished, Wood commented. The election demonstrated "that our hope of developing a real democracy is not a vain one," that "the political party system is passing away." It seemed Alberta farmers had crossed the Red Sea. Referring to the stunning victory of the United Farmers of Ontario in the 1919 provincial election, an anonymous Alberta farmer enthused: "We feel a sense of victory and triumph ... and we trust a new and more equitable order is being established."

"If old Ontario," he surmised, "dear to the hearts of so many Albertans who claim it as their birthplace, can with one stroke level those walls of protected iniquities, how much better should Alberta do when next we get a chance to case our ballots for democracy?"[29]

The belief that a new heaven and a new earth were descending on the foothills province rose to new heights after the UFA standard bearer, Robert Gardiner, won the Medicine Hat federal by-election of 1921. "SCENES OF ENTHUSIASM PROBABLY WITHOUT PARALLEL IN ANY PREVIOUS ELECTORAL CONTEST IN THIS CITY FOLLOWED THE ANNOUNCEMENT OF THE VICTORY OF THE UFA CANDIDATE BY STUPENDOUS MAJORITY OVER THE GOVERNMENT CANDIDATE," broadcasted one report. At the scene, Charles Harris, a long-standing UFA battle horse, testified, with tears in his eyes and a smile from ear to ear: "This is the happiest day of my life." Said Herbert Greenfield, soon-to-be UFA Premier of Alberta:

> The result in Medicine Hat is an expression of the new democracy which I believe has been born in Canada. It is the unmistakable demand of the people that there be a better and cleaner political life. The old partisan shibboleths are outworn and discredited.[30]

Such beliefs seemed all the truer when the UFA, to its own astonishment, won thirty-eight seats in the subsequent provincial election of 1921 – enough for a majority government. Then, equally shocking and amazing, all ten UFA federal candidates and sixty-five candidates of the Progressive party, a national agrarian party, were elected in the federal election of 1921, held in December. "I believe we are entering the dawn of a new era,"[31] declared W. T. Lucas, just before becoming the UFA member of Parliament for Victoria. Alberta farmers believed they had entered the political Promised Land. And they would show everyone else the way; other groups would follow suit. They, too, would elect their occupational representatives, and the political parties would fall into the abyss. The age of political righteousness would ensue.

But as Henry Wise Wood, aptly called the "Moses of Alberta," reminded farmers, politics could not solve all problems. When, in 1923, the UFA government, the UFA members of Parliament, and other farm leaders and organizations failed, despite their best efforts, to reinstate a federal wheat board, a government grain-marketing agency, farmers looked to a producer-owned and operated wheat pool for economic salvation. This time the prophet was not Wood, but an outsider: that renowned American pool organizer and propagandist, Aaron Sapiro, brought to Alberta in 1923 by the *Calgary Herald*. A spell-binding orator with the platform presence of a fiery evangelist, Sapiro held packed audiences in rapt attention. What did he tell them? Farmers could organize a pool in a few short weeks. "I am not telling you guesswork," he promised. "I have seen these movements in co-operation and it will go. I never saw a province so ripe for it. Do this, men, and you are making the greatest contribution toward world freedom and in the right handling of the greatest commodity that has ever been!" What would a pool do? It "will make for a finer citizenship ... it means real independence. Why, it means a sweeter and finer life for the boys and girls on the farms." A pool would create economic stability and prosperity. Here was a message of great hope – a piercing light in dark economic times. No wonder there were "scenes of wild enthusiasm." No wonder an Edmonton reporter, using the often-repeated image of a breaking sunrise, concluded that the meetings "bid fair to mark the dawn of a new era in the province of Alberta."[32]

He was right. A literal groundswell of enthusiasm swept rural Alberta, and the campaign to sign up farmers to supply half the province's wheat acreage to the pool for five years was a success;[33] Alberta Pool opened its doors in October 1923. Inspired by this accomplishment, Saskatchewan and Manitoba created pools in 1924. In a few short years, the three pools would be the largest co-operative of their kind in the world. It seemed the dream – a longstanding agrarian dream – of bypassing the private grain trade had been fulfilled. Some farmers believed they were in sight of the co-operative commonwealth, a truly co-operative economic order. Perhaps the age of exploitation and competition was over. Perhaps farmers were leading the country and the world out of Egypt – economic slavery – and into Canaan. Indeed, the pools went from strength to strength – until they were sideswiped by the Great Depression.

The depression would hit the UFA government even harder, and in the meantime the farmer government failed to transform the political system. As early as 1922, the ideal of group government, with its call for free votes and consensual decision-making, had largely evaporated, blown away by the winds of political reality – the need for caucus discipline to keep the party in power. On the other hand, most of the UFA members of Parliament, not burdened with the responsibilities of governing, manfully struggled to follow the utopian precepts of group government, voting in the interests of their constituents and occupational group, paying little heed to the impact of their actions on the old-line parties. Almost self-righteously, they avoided the deals and strategies of party politics, believing their stance would inaugurate a perfect political system. Yet in 1935 they, along with the UFA government, were utterly swept away by the Social Credit party, headed by a new saviour, William Aberhart, who pledged to bring Albertans out of the desert of economic depression. He would take them into the Promised Land on a sea of state-issued monthly dividends. But by the early 1940s, the Social Credit party was shedding its promises of peace and prosperity; it was undergoing a metamorphosis into a staid, free-enterprise party. Utopian politics in Alberta was dead.

Most Alberta farmers failed to reach any Promised Land. The first to taste the bitterness of defeat were the tens of thousands who had settled in the dry belt of southeastern Alberta after 1909. It was tragic: they had faithfully practised the principles of dry farming, the so-called "ten commandments of the dry farmer,"[34] which the agricultural experts had promised would make the land bloom; but instead of milk and honey, they had discovered a desert without water. An exodus of Biblical proportions left this forsaken place in the decade after 1916. For them the dream quickly shattered.

For others, the dream lingered into the 1930s. Indeed, many parts of Alberta did not forsake farmers in that decade: low product prices rather than environmental disaster were primarily responsible for the sad plight of most producers. But the elusive land of wealth – of cups running over – remained beyond the grasp of almost all, and some hopes are not eternal. Most farmers, the ones that remained, would enter the war and post-war years with their feet firmly planted on the ground and their heads beneath the clouds.

So what, then, was the impact of agrarian utopianism in Alberta? That it built up the early farm movement there can be no doubt. Thousands joined the UFA/UFWA and the wheat pool not only for the economic benefit but also because they literally thought these organizations could create an ideal society. The Alberta farm movement was more than a bread-and-butter conglomeration of farmers, seeking a reform here, a few extra dollars there. With its western and Ontario counterparts, though to a greater extent than they, it sought fundamental social, economic, and political change – and actually believed it was within reach. Certainly, the incredible success of the Alberta Wheat Pool owes much to the idealism of the farm movement. Farmers were convinced this new non-capitalistic means of marketing grain would pave the way for other forms of co-operative buying and selling and forever destroy the exploitative power of the old speculative system, thus inaugurating an age of prosperity. And the fact that the UFA government remained in power from 1921 to 1935, and that UFA federal candidates were elected in most rural ridings in that period – long after the independent farmer political movement had fizzled elsewhere in the country – can be attributed to Alberta farmers' steadfast determination, which most other Canadian farmers did not share, to introduce a radically new and superior kind of politics.

So why was utopianism so strong in Alberta? Perhaps because Alberta *was* the last, best West, the last frontier of North American settlement, the last place for a Promised Land. Equally important, Alberta was blessed with a host of idealistic agrarian leaders. Finally, it was intoxicating for farmers to believe that by pursuing their own agenda they were building an earthly kingdom of heaven. Who would not want to think *that!*

They came to Alberta seeking a "far green country unto a swift sunrise." Through the farm movement, they would drive out the Canaanites – end social, economic, and political exploitation – and take the land of milk and honey and enjoy its bounty. They dreamt of building an Arcadian paradise, but also the kingdom of God on earth, a truly Christian society. They aspired to lead Canada and the world "out of Egypt" and into the dawn of a new era, an age of equal opportunity, social justice, co-operation in all human relations, and grassroots democracy. The Farmers' Platform, along with group government and the wheat pools, would bring in the day of contentment and prosperity.

But the far green country was not so green in the Great Depression. And the rising sun was too swift to be grasped; it parched the dreams of a Promised Land.

NOTES

1 See A. W. Rasporich, "Utopian Ideals and Community Settlements in Western Canada, 1880–1914," in *The Prairie West: Historical Readings*, 2nd ed., eds. R. Douglas Francis and Howard Palmer (Edmonton: Pica Pica Press, 1991), 352–77.

2 Analyses of the Alberta and prairie farm movements as movements of the "petit-bourgeois" class include C. B. Macpherson's *Democracy in Alberta: Social Credit and the Party System*, 2nd ed. (Toronto: University of Toronto Press, 1962, 1968 reprint) and John F. Conway's "Populism in the United States, Russia, and Canada: Explaining the Roots of Canada's Third Parties," *Canadian Journal of Political Science* 2, no. 1 (Spring 1984): 137–44. The best analysis of the prairie farm movement as an expression of populism is David Laycock's *Populism and Democratic Thought in the Canadian Prairies, 1910–1945* (Toronto: University of Toronto Press, 1990). The best analysis of the western farm movement as a western protest movement is W. L. Morton's *The Progressive Party in Canada* (Toronto: University of Toronto Press, 1950).

3 Analyses of the farm movement as an occupational movement include Paul F. Sharp's *The Agrarian Revolt in Western Canada: A Survey Showing American Parallels*, with introductions by William Pratt and Lorne Brown (Regina: Canadian Plains Research Center, 1997, originally published by the University of Minnesota Press, Minneapolis, 1948) and Bradford J. Rennie's *The Rise of Agrarian Democracy: The United Farmers and Farm Women of Alberta, 1909–1921* (Toronto: University of Toronto Press, 2000). Analyses of the movement as an educational movement include Carrol L. Jaques, "The United Farmers of Alberta: A Social and Educational Movement" (master's thesis, University of Calgary, 1991), and John LeRoy Wilson, "The Education of the Farmer: The Educational Objectives and Activities of the United Farmers of Alberta and the Saskatchewan Grain Growers' Association, 1920–1930" (PhD diss., University of Alberta, 1975).

4 *Edmonton Bulletin*, March 1, 1905, 7; David Embree, "The Rise of the United Farmers of Alberta" (master's thesis, University of Alberta, 1956), 176.

5 *Grain Growers' Guide*, December 28, 1910, 24.

6 Ibid., November 1, 1911, 20; December 21, 1910, 13.

7 Scrapbook Hansard, 1923, p. 16, *Edmonton Journal*, February 6.

8 *Guide*, December 21, 1910, 12, 4.

9 Ibid., December 21, 1910, 12.

10 Ibid.

11 Ibid., July 15, 1915, 11; October 18, 1911, 12.

12 Ibid., June 29, 1910, p. 16; March 27, 1918, 17.

13 Glenbow Archives, Minutes and Reports of Annual UFA Convention, 1919, 90; *Guide*, July 3, 1912, 8.

14 *Guide*, July 3, 1912, 8.

15 Ibid., November 19, 1919, 25; October 5, 1921, 14.

16 Minutes and Reports, 1913, 5.

17 This was the liberalism of British thinkers like Thomas Hill Green who believed state intervention was necessary to promote the individual liberty of the marginalized of society. For an analysis of this positive liberalism in Canada, see Barry Ferguson, *Remaking Liberalism: The Intellectual Legacy of Adam Shortt, O.D. Skelton, and W. A. Mackintosh, 1890–1925* (Montreal and Kingston: McGill-Queen's University Press, 1993).

18 *Guide*, April 2, 1919, 10; Minutes and Reports, 1919, 77. The Farmers' Platform, endorsed by the major provincial farm organizations, including the UFA, was introduced in 1910, expanded in 1916, and revised in 1918 and 1921.

19 Minutes and Reports, 1913, 9.

20 This phrase, which appears in the title of this article, are the words of Gandalf to Pippin in the movie *The Lord of the Rings: The Return of the King*, Alliance Atlantis, New Line Productions, Inc., 2003.

21 *Guide*, December 28, 1921, 9.

22 Ibid., July 31, 1918, 35; December 31, 1919, 29.

23 Provincial Archives of Alberta, Susan M. Gunn Letters, Acc. 83.507, Gunn to Robinson, n.d., 1.

24 Minutes and Reports, 1918, 62–63.

25 For an analysis of civic republicanism in Canadian history, see Janet Ajzenstat and Peter J. Smith, eds., *Canada's Origins: Liberal, Tory, or Republican?* (Ottawa: Carleton University Press, 1995), esp. chap. 1.

26 For a detailed analysis of Wood's philosophy, which he began preaching at the end of the war, see Bradford J. Rennie, *The Rise of Agrarian Democracy*, chap. 9.

27 *The U.F.A.*, April 15, 1922, 25; *Canadian Forum*, December 1922, 73.

28 *The U.F.A.*, April 15, 1922, 25, 27.

29 *Guide*, November 12, 1919; *Western Independent*, November 5, 1919, 15.

30 Glenbow Archives, M1157, Walter Norman and Amelia Turner Smith Fonds, file 50, sheet beginning with, "THE OVERWHELMING VICTORY"; *Guide*, July 6, 1921, 4.

31 *Guide*, November 16, 1921, 15.

32 Robert Collins, "An idea whose time had arrived; the Wheat Pool burst into being," in Ted Byfield, ed., *Alberta in the Twentieth Century*, vol. 5, *Brownlee and the Triumph of Populism* (Edmonton: United Western Communication, 1994), 40; *Edmonton Journal*, August 7, 1923, 11, 6; August 4, 1923, 1.

33 Forty-five per cent of the wheat acreage was committed by contract to the pool that Fall – enough for the pool to go ahead.

34 Cited in David C. Jones, *Empire of Dust: Settling and Abandoning the Prairie Dry Belt* (Calgary: University of Calgary Press, 2002), 137.

IV

A PROMISED LAND FOR THE "CHOSEN PEOPLE"

12

"NO PLACE FOR A WOMAN": ENGENDERING WESTERN CANADIAN SETTLEMENT

Catherine A. Cavanaugh

The gender tensions alive in the idea of the Prairie West as Promised Land were brought into sharp relief in March 1996 when Madeleine Gould's nine-year quest for recognition as a Yukon pioneer was quashed by the Supreme Court of Canada's decision to uphold the right of the territory's fraternal Order of Pioneers to exclude women from its ranks.[1] In their majority decision, the seven male justices in the nine-member highest court noted the long history of the all-male organization, "formed in 1894 by the Forty Mile community … for the purposes of establishing a police force" and providing mutual support and protection to its members: "male persons of integrity and good character who met a ten-year residency requirement."[2] By the early 1900s, the order's policing activities were no longer necessary, and it became a social organization primarily concerned with preserving local history. Noting this shift in activities, Mister Justice La Forest upheld the order's right to exclude women on the basis that it was a private organization dedicated to "preserving the moral values, male camaraderie and mutual respect, traditions and secret rites that were engendered by and formed the fabric of a Klondike brotherhood of the 1890s."[3]

The court's two female justices disagreed, stressing both the order's public function to preserve history and its private function to maintain the status and prestige bestowed on its members. Noting a range of public benefits membership conferred, including "a respect in the community" as a "'modern' pioneer, part of the select society of past pioneers,"

Madame Justice Beverley McLachlin pointed out that "[t]he order has assumed an important role in defining the pioneers of the Yukon, and that recognition as a member of the order and recognition of a person as a Yukon pioneer are largely synonymous in the mind of the public." "Can it be right then," she asked, "that [membership] is denied to one-half of the Yukon population, its women?"[4] Siding with the Yukon Human Rights Commission in its original decision, Madame Justice Claire L'Heureux-Dubé also rejected the "male camaraderie" argument, adding that the exclusion of women from the order distorted the history it created because it left women out. Quoting from the evidence presented in the case, L'Heureux-Dubé concluded that as a result "[t]oday, these women have been all but forgotten, with not even their names recorded."[5]

In *Gould v. Yukon Order of Pioneers*, the court was asked to rule on a narrow question of Canadian human rights legislation regarding sex discrimination, but the case is also a sharp reminder of the ways in which the "promise" of the West was circumscribed by social discourse, establishing a deep and persistent legacy. In particular, the issues before the court highlight the uses of gender ideology – in this instance, "male camaraderie" and "Yukon brotherhood" – to naturalize male privilege as founding fathers, while excluding women from settlement history.

This paper argues that the gender divisions the case reflects were established early in expansionist and settlement discourse and perpetuated in both the official and popular mind, with far-reaching implications. It begins with an exploration of the ways in which Victorian gender ideology was used to provide the conceptual framework, or mental map, upon which European colonization and settlement took place.[6] The contradiction at the heart of this discourse was the notion of the promise of the Prairie West as simultaneously open to all comers but also the special preserve of Anglo-Canadian male elites. In constructing and reconstructing the promise of the West – from wilderness wasteland to economic hinterland to agrarian paradise – expansionist discourse perpetuated the myth of the West as a "manly" space, assigning to it a moral and political force that underwrote élite Anglo-Canadian men's hegemony in the territories.[7] Finally, the implications for women of this masculinist cultural context are considered using three examples.

The first example is taken from the so-called Foss-Pelly scandal that gripped the Red River colony in 1850. It examines the role of Sarah Ballenden, a Métis daughter of the fur trade, in the events surrounding the scandal to show how gender was used to construct categories of race in the new West. The second example explores the campaigns to extend married women's property rights in the three prairie provinces in the 1910s and 1920s. Women won important legislative changes, but the cultural assumptions that underwrote men's control of land, and therefore wealth, in the new provinces remained intact. The third example considers women's engagement with electoral politics in the years immediately following the extension of provincial suffrage in 1916–17. It illustrates how the legacy of settlement continued to shape prairie women's political opportunities during the interwar period.

This analysis shows that during the settlement period gender ideology was integral to cultural constructions of the West. It underwrote institutional practices and conventions ranging from the sexual division of labour, economic opportunity, and political rights to what Sarah Carter terms "the categories and terrains of exclusion" constructed along racial and class lines.[8] This study suggests that, while the possibilities for women (and men) were shaped by a masculinist cultural context, in the shifting realities of the turn-of-the-century, Euro-Canadian women's responses to cultural constructions of the West as a manly space were neither inevitable nor always predictable.

Studies of settlement discourse focus primarily on the American settlement frontiers and the place of the West as a dominant symbol of nation-building and the opportunity for conquest.[9] As Richard Slotkin so expertly argues, for the United States, the "this myth-historiography" of frontier was variously used to underwrite American colonialism and to explain the nation's distinctive culture and emergence as a world power.[10] Within this tradition, the significance of "wilderness-going" as a source of individual and national regeneration owes much to Frederick Jackson Turner and his disciples, who argued that American democracy was forest-born, emerging out of the individual (male) pioneer's struggle to subdue the wilderness – and its native inhabitants – and wrest a living from the land.[11] But, as Slotkin points out, while Turner assigned to "yeoman farmers" the leading role in American development, it was Theodore Roosevelt in *The Winning of the West* (New York, 1897) who elevated the frontiersman to the legendary hunter/Indian-fighter, representing him as the ideal of American manhood.[12]

North of the forty-ninth parallel, the American frontiersman's Canadian counterpart laboured in comparative obscurity. Historians of the Canadian West tended to minimize the symbolic role of the frontier in nation-building, favouring instead explanations of national differences between the countries. In Canada, patterns of western settlement are taken as further evidence of the development of a unique political culture, characterized by peace, order, and good government. Even when Canadian scholars document similar perceptions of the significance of western settlement to national identity – even national destiny – the uses of masculinity in constructing a mythical West remain largely unexplored.[13]

To be sure, Canadian dreams of empire fell far short of the American achievement of world power status, but a brief examination of the contemporary Canadian literature reveals striking parallels with American expansionist discourse. Canadians too saw the West as a source of national regeneration and spiritual renewal through a reinvigorated manhood. Consider, for example, what popular writer Ralph Connor says about the West and the men who settled it.[14] Connor's early novels, *Black Rock* (Toronto, 1896) and *The Sky Pilot* (Toronto, 1899), were both run-away bestsellers based on his experiences as a Presbyterian missionary in western Canada during the mid-1890s.[15] In his novels, Connor's frontiersmen stand as the salvation of a "worn-out civilization."[16] Having turned away from what was widely perceived at the time as the moral decline of urban, industrial society, he explains that these "hardy soul[s] … pitched their camp, and there, in lonely, lordly independence, took rich toll of prairie, lake, and stream as they needed for their living."[17] For Connor, the "untrammelled, unconventional mode of life" of the frontier had transformative power: "Freed from the restraints of custom and surrounding," even the most "high bred … young lads … soon shed all that was superficial in their make-up and stood forth in the naked simplicity of their native manhood. The West discovered and revealed the man in them."[18]

By assigning masculinity to the expansionist enterprise, settlement discourse employed gender ideology to support Euro-Canadian nation-building and buttress the claims of competing white male élites in the political and economic skirmishes for dominance in the territories following the annexation of the Hudson's Bay Company lands in 1870. Expansionists touted the manly West as more democratic than the East, uncorrupted by the influences of industrialization and urbanization, or the emasculating effects of "overcivilized" domesticity, casting the West's wide open spaces and bracing climate as sources of moral and spiritual uplift. In the West, a man was thought to be freed from the oppressive gentility of the urban East and the alienating influences of modern bureaucratization and industrial capitalism's wage labour. In his physical struggle in an alien and hostile environment, the frontiersman/farmer/rancher supposedly reasserted his "natural" independence and manly dignity. So, in 1873, George M. Grant, an advocate of western settlement, could claim that in the West, "a man feels like a young giant," and "cannot help indulging in a little tall talk, and in displays of his big limbs." Thomas Spence (1880) could confidently predict that the only capital a homesteader needed to succeed in the West was "brawny arms and a brave heart," and Nicholas Flood Davin (1891) readily asserted that just "three years" in the Northwest would raise a prairie farmer "higher on the scale of manhood." Emily Murphy shared these views, but in a clear attempt to include women in the expansionist project, she attributed the physical and moral qualities of the pioneer to both men and women. "It is a great place, the Canadian West," she boasted as Janey Canuck, "the country of strong men, strong women, straight living and hard riding."[19]

In the discourse of western expansion, Murphy is an exception. Typically, women are represented as existing outside of the masculine enterprise of settlement. When women do appear, it is more often as "civilizers" or "gentle tamers."[20] Created in opposition to the middle-class ideal of active, conquering manhood, civilizing womanhood is made passive and disembodied, thereby guaranteeing representations of men's dominance. This relationship is captured in the following newspaper account published in 1891. Assuming that western settlement was an exclusively male experience, the author explains that as European men travelled West:

> … all that was independent and self-assured in them was developed.… Men weak and impractical were hardened into sterner stuff.… Sentiment and weakness were discarded; laziness fled utterly. Each was anxious to rifle nature, and that, too, as quickly as possible. Caste and social distinction were blotted out. All men were equal in that strange pilgrimage. Strength was capital then.… Women's part in this strange existence was an influence for the good. Rough and godless as were these men, woman was still enshrined in their hearts, in the tender memory of mother, sister, sweetheart. And so they idolized and worshipped faraway woman … good or bad she saved those wicked men from a hardness scarcely less than that of the rocks they crushed.[21]

Or, consider Ralph Connor's introduction to *The Sky Pilot*, "a story," he writes:

> … of the people of the Foothill Country … those men of adventurous spirit, who left homes of comfort, often of luxury, because of the stirring in them to be and to do some worthy thing … freed from all the restraints of social law, denied the gentler influences of home and the sweet uplift of a good woman's face.[22]

Literary constructions of the West as a "manly" space often contradicted the reality of settlement and were primarily intended for eastern audiences. But they also worked to shape newcomers' responses to their new environment and give meaning to the settlement enterprise. For example, after spending his first winter homesteading in the Buffalo Lake district of the Northwest Territories (east of present-day Lacombe, Alberta) in 1893–94, John Wilcox associated himself with the hearty band of pioneers at the centre of Connor's stories. In a letter to his cousin Jack in Ontario, Wilcox praises the exceptional beauty and abundant resources of western Canada. The West, he reports, is truly a land of promise: it is "the best country for stock I have seen … there is everything here a man wants, plenty of hay, water, wood and mountains of coal … [t]he lakes and creeks are full of fish … this is the home for geese and ducks … I have a splendid good gun. I tell you it is great fun hunting here." "[B]ut God help it for lonesomeness," Wilcox added, "It is so lonesome I don't know how to live … it is no place for a woman." "Dear Jack," he continues, "I wish you lived here so I could have an old friend to talk to." But ending his letter on a melancholy note, Wilcox recognizes that his cousin probably would not want "to leave civilization" to come West.[23]

Wilcox's letter echoes expansionist literature in the way he uses gender to make meaning of space. On first reading, his approach seems contradictory. He admits that he is alone and isolated – "10 miles to … [the] nearest white bachelor," and "27 miles to a white woman" – but concludes that the West is "all right for a man to come [to] … to make money." His cousin is a man, but Wilcox assumes Jack would prefer the comforts of the developed East. While confessing that he does not "know how to live" beyond the reach of "civilization," Wilcox asserts that in the West there is "all that a *man* wants." His own feelings of isolation and loneliness lead him to conclude that the West "is no place for a *woman*/there is no Sundays here."[24] In part at least, these contradictions were reconciled by symbolic constructions of the West as a place of mythical masculine renewal.

Indeed, Connor and Wilcox are engaged in a similar project. By staking his claim to the future in the West, Wilcox is imaginatively joined to the manly struggle for survival in the harsh prairie wilderness. Framed as a masculine enterprise, the promise of the West is much more than the making of money. The search for wealth becomes a struggle for essential manhood. In both the official and popular mind, this idea was fundamental to the way in which the West was conceived, organized, and incorporated into the national dream. For example, when two of the largest areas of the Northwest Territories were joined to confederation as the provinces of Alberta and Saskatchewan, prime minister Wilfrid Laurier considered it a symbolic coming of age. Self-government, he told the nation, reflected the West's "state of manhood" in 1905.[25]

The antecedents of the manly West of colonization and settlement are found in the imaginary landscapes of the fur trade. In popular literature, this mythical country is populated by gentlemen adventurers, staunch missionaries, hardy traders, and backwoodsmen whose exploits served symbolically to underwrite imperial masculinity. Abjuring the comforts of European civilization was as crucial to the heroic test of their masculine mettle as was their mastery over the "barbarous" conditions of Indian country and its indigenous peoples.[26] Over time, the boundary between these two worlds shifted, but to the Euro-Canadian mind, the characteristics that separated them remained clear. When Frances Simpson, the English wife of governor George Simpson, first encountered the "boundless Wilderness" of the Northwest in 1830, she thought that "the boundary between the Civilized and the Savage Worlds" lay roughly two days by canoe from Montreal. Her journals capture her mounting sense of danger as she travelled deeper into the territories, although she seems uncertain as to whether the greater threat lay with "Nature in her grand, but Savage and uncultivated state," or in the "wild & savage habits of the Aborigines."[27]

Simpson's trepidation underscores the political significance of European constructions of the West as simultaneously "alien" and "manly." While his western odyssey was thought to be the making of British manhood, entering this "wild & savage" land was assumed to have the opposite effect on genteel women. As recent studies argue, the "Frail Flower" of Victorian womanhood, assumed to be physically and emotionally weak, was supposedly more vulnerable then her male counterpart to the dangers of the "untamed" West. Seen as powerless and unable to adapt to this alien environment, she was considered to be entirely dependent on the protection of European men.[28] This uncritical view of sex difference has persisted in the historical literature so that the arrival of European women in the West is seen to disrupt two hundred years of relatively peaceful relations based on marital alliances between European men and Aboriginal women. In this analysis, the events surrounding the Foss-Pelly trial, which began in Red River on July 16, 1850, mark a racial divide in the history of the Canadian West, precipitated by the appearance of white women in the colony.[29]

The Foss-Pelly sex scandal has been described in detail by historian Sylvia Van Kirk and need be outlined only briefly here.[30] The case involved Captain Christopher Foss, a British army officer newly arrived in Red River, and Sarah Ballenden, the Métis wife of the Hudson's Bay Company's chief factor, John Ballenden.[31] For about a year, rumour had circulated throughout the colony that Ballenden and Foss were involved in a relationship "of such a character as to entitle Mr. B(allenden) to a divorce."[32] Hoping to put an end to the gossip, Foss sued three company employees and their wives, including the clerk, A. E. Pelly, and his wife Anne Clouson Pelly, for instigating a defamatory conspiracy. The ensuing trial focused on Sarah Ballenden's moral character and sexual behaviour. Much of the testimony consisted of suspicion and innuendo and the jury quickly found no basis for the charges of sexual misconduct. Ballenden was completely exonerated and heavy damages were found against the defendants. But, as Van Kirk points out, this did not end the matter. The trial and its aftermath divided the colony along racial lines. Ballenden's supporters, largely drawn from the Indian and Métis population, continued to assert her innocence, while her accusers and their supporters, predominantly white Protestants backed by the local clergy, persisted in their attacks on her character and standing in the community. Vilified as a fallen woman and suffering ill health, Ballenden was ultimately driven from the colony in social disgrace. She died of consumption three years later at the age of thirty-five.

Van Kirk's argument that Sarah Ballenden was the victim of white women's racism rests on the role of two British women, both recently arrived in the colony, Anne Clouson Pelly and the sister of Reverend David Anderson, Anglican Bishop of Rupert's Land, Margaret Anderson, who Van Kirk describes as "the epitome of the strait-laced, sharp-tongued spinster."[33] Van Kirk identifies Pelly and Anderson as Bellenden's chief accusers, arguing that they were motivated by a sense of racial superiority and a perception that inter-racial marriages threatened the future welfare of white women. Viewed as agents of empire, but limited to a narrowly defined competition as the preferred wives of white men, the actions of these newcomer women appear petty and vindictive.

There can be little doubt that white women were often just as Eurocentric as their male counterparts. Indeed, it would be unusual if they were not equally embedded in the cultural assumptions of nineteenth-century imperialism. Moreover, as wives, sisters, and daughters of imperial officers and company officials, the work of enforcing social hierarchies often fell to colonizing women, making them more visible in that process.[34] But, as Margaret Strobel has pointed out, the tendency in imperial histories to interpret white women's actions as more aggressively racist than those of white men, perpetuates Victorian gender ideology. The myth of the destructive female preserves nineteenth-century assumptions of a dependent femininity and white women's moral superiority, while exaggerating their social power.[35] Blaming Anglo-Canadian women for the deterioration of race relations at Red River may be convenient, but it obscures the reality of gender roles in the colony and misses their political significance. In large part, white women's influence in colonial settings was derived from their marital status to imperial men. Circumscribed by official opinion, their influence could not be exercised directly or independently.[36] As white settlement increased, political and economic power at Red River became concentrated in the governing class of élite Euro-Canadian men. Ultimately, Sarah Ballenden's position in the colony – and, as it turned out, her life – depended upon the goodwill of the newly appointed associate governor of the territories, Eden Colvile. Colvile and his British wife protected Ballenden for a short time, but when the governor withdrew his patronage in the winter of 1850, the ailing Ballenden was left to her unhappy fate.

Characterizing the Foss-Pelly scandal as a struggle between two groups of women for status as the preferred brides of European men distracts us from the crucial question of social formation during a critical period in the development of western Canada. The scandal offers compelling evidence that a shift in favour of white institutions and conventions occurred in the Northwest as early as 1850. Understanding the nature of this change requires a fuller appreciation of the ways in which gender was used to construct relationships of power between men and women, but also between classes and races.

The question of rank was alive in the events at Red River, serving to further inflame the racial attacks aimed at Ballenden, wife of the chief factor, and the highest ranking woman in the colony at the time. But rank failed to protect her from imperial and patriarchal goals that rested on complementary assumptions of British racial superiority and white male dominance. If Sarah Ballenden had been the wife of a rank-and-file trader, it is quite likely that she would have avoided censure altogether or at least managed to negotiate the crisis more successfully. As it was, her social status, which devolved from her family relationships to two white men, was doubtless a contributing factor in the effort to discredit her. But once her reputation as a respectable woman was called into question, even her husband's loyal support proved insufficient protection. This suggests that in the shifting interests of Euro-Canadian expansion, some men (notably those married to aboriginal or Métis women) also experienced a sharp decline in status and power.

Ballenden's mixed-race heritage was central to the charges of sexual misconduct, which formed the basis of the attack on her respectability. Fraternization with aboriginal (or Métis) women could be tolerated, even advocated, within the context of the fur trade, on the grounds that it enhanced company profits. But, the collapse of the Hudson's Bay Company trade monopoly in the territories in the 1840s, combined with a rapidly expanding American frontier to the south (the neighbouring Minnesota Territory was established in 1849), presaged great changes in the established order at Red River. Western expansion held the promise that great fortunes might be made. Indeed, the success of the colony itself, which boasted a population of 172,000 by 1860, more than that of the entire Hudson's Bay territories, only fuelled expansionists' dreams. A realignment of political and economic forces dictated a shift in the social order, one that would ensure élite Euro-Canadian men's hegemony in the new West.

The Foss-Pelly scandal illustrates the ways in which imperial and patriarchal goals were joined in the cause of establishing a new Euro-Canadian male élite in western Canada. After about 1850, when there was the prospect of more wealth to be had, élite men had greater concern to marry women of their own race and class whose children would be their legitimate heirs.[37] Under the conditions of colonization and settlement, Métis women who, like Sarah Ballenden, had successfully adapted to European culture in the context of fur trade society, were made especially vulnerable to these new imperatives. In the European drive to clearly demarcate social categories, these women were caught in an ambiguous – and, to the official mind, socially disruptive – space defined by newcomers as neither white nor Indian. Thus, the charge of sexual misconduct levied against Ballenden served a dual purpose. Underwritten by the widely held Euro-Canadian belief that Indian women were, by nature, promiscuous and therefore a social danger, it attempted to resolve Ballenden's racial ambiguity by denying her élite or respectable status. This had the effect of insisting upon her Indian identity.[38] In the new order, which increasingly defined the West from the mid-nineteenth century, acculturated Métis women would be forced to choose between their heritages. This point is underscored by the fact that Ballenden's younger sisters resolved the dilemma by settling among the English in Quebec.

Imperialists' constructions of aboriginal peoples as the "uncivilized" other were interwoven with representations of the West as a vast, untamed wilderness, unsuited to white settlement and to white women in particular. As the geographic frontier continued to push inland during the closing decades of the nineteenth century, the well-established divide between Canada and the territories remained intact. By 1870, William Francis Butler, a British army officer, drew this imaginary line between the civilized and uncivilized world in the prairie grassland immediately west of Winnipeg. Setting out to investigate the western territories for the federal government, Butler wrote:

> [on] the 24th of October I quitted Fort Garry at ten o'clock at night, and, turning out into the level prairie, commenced a long journey towards the West.... Behind me lay friends and news of friends, civilization, tidings of a terrible war, firesides, and houses; before me lay unknown savage tribes, long days of saddle-travel, long nights of chilling bivouac, silence, separation, and space.[39]

Expansionists saw this widespread perception of an uninhabitable West as a serious impediment to their purposes and set out to reconstruct the western prairies of the fur trade as a commercial and agricultural Eden. As outlined above, the ideological uses of gender reached a high point in the excesses of their booster literature, which took as a central theme the reconfiguration of the ideal frontiersman from social renegade to domesticated man, head of the farm family.

Connor's hardy band of ranchers and cowboys now stood in opposition to successful settlement, which dictated that Western man accept limitations on his freedom. In exchange, expansionists held out a new promise: "free land ... and the prospect of a competence acquired through industry."[40] In their vision of a new, agricultural West, manly virtue was preserved in the enterprising farmer who was willing to trade on his wit and brawn to "make good." As one official from the department of the interior put it: "the men of good muscle ... are willing to hustle."[41] In these new masculinist definitions of the ideal settler, women's exclusion continues to be so taken for granted that it seems to be less an idea than the natural order of things. On the question of preferred immigration, the first man in charge of populating Butler's "great lone land," minister of the interior Clifford Sifton, was emphatic: "[w]e do not want anything but agricultural labourers and farmers or people who are coming for the purpose of engaging in agriculture, either as farmers or labourers."[42] When pressed in the House of Commons on whether or not the government would grant homesteads to women, Sifton's successor, Frank Oliver, was equally unequivocal, noting that "the department does not recognize the right of a woman to take up homesteads."[43] The only exception to this rule was in the case of a widow with dependent children, but this regulation was given the narrowest interpretation, making it difficult, even impossible, for women to qualify. Elaborating on his position five years later, Oliver explained that "the object in giving homesteads is to make the land productive, and this would not be the case if [they were] held by women."[44] When Cora Hind, Manitoba journalist and wheat crop forecaster, objected to the decision, Oliver protested that "to admit [women] to the opportunities of the land-grant would be to make them more independent of marriage than ever." And Oliver felt this would defeat the government's purpose of recreating the middle-class domestic ideal on the prairies. As Hind explained: "[by] granting a land-gift to men," the minister intended "to induce them to make home on the prairie – home in the centre of their agricultural pursuit."[45]

The push to domesticate the West meant that official attitudes toward women settlers were contradictory. On one hand, Ottawa recognized that its vision of placing "a large producing population upon the Western prairies ... to wholly transform the financial difficulties of the country" would not be achieved without women's productive and reproductive labour.[46] Indeed, the government implicitly recognized what was obvious when it established a fee of two dollars paid to immigration agents for each woman who settled in the West.[47] On the other hand, the assumption that agriculture was an exclusively male enterprise had the effect of making women's work invisible. Women, of course, did "make the land productive," but the ground they tilled was not a *tabula rasa*. Just as a masculinist cultural context sharply narrowed the possibilities for aboriginal women in the new West, it also shaped the contours of the lives of newcomer women. By inscribing the West with meaning that relied on Victorian gender ideology, settlement discourse worked simultaneously to include aboriginal women as the exotic "other" and exclude them as "uncivilized" and therefore unwomanly. It had a similar, if opposite, effect on Euro-Canadian women. Cast as civilizers, Anglo-Canadian women in particular were assigned the privileges that were assumed to accrue to their race, but race privilege rested on sex difference and was hedged around by dominant notions of ideal femininity.[48]

Evidence of the power of masculinist conventions to exclude Euro-Canadian women on the basis of their sex is apparent in the attenuated voices of newcomers. The high-born Frances Simpson, for example, found the myth of the manly West so compelling that she failed to count herself among those European influences making themselves felt in the Northwest from the mid-nineteenth century. Only where European men were present at "a Trading Post of the Honourable Hudson's Bay Company ... [or] small [American] Garrison" was she "reminded ... of the enterprise of Europeans ... providing employment for thousands, taming the ferocious lives of the Indians, and gradually introducing the peaceful occupation of husbandry; the first step towards civilization."[49] Years later, when another genteel Englishwoman, Irene Parlby, minister without portfolio in the United Farmers' Government of Alberta, was asked to recall her pioneering experiences for *The Canadian Magazine*, she wrote instead of the "clear-eyed man the real pioneer type ... content to travel with a good stout axe, and make his road as he went along."[50] Elizabeth Hanson remembered that when she arrived in Alberta in 1911, it was a "wild country ... nothing was completed. It was a raw, man's world, not for women."[51]

For other Anglo-Canadians, just being a woman in the West seemed to disrupt old gender conventions, making new ones possible. Like Emily Murphy, Agnes Higginson Skrine included herself in the settlement project on the same basis as men. Writing in 1898, she asserted that "[s]peaking as a ... female, I like the country ... I like the simplicity, the informality of the life.... I like both the work and the play here, the time out of doors and time for coming home, I like the summer and the winter, the monotony and change. Besides, I like a flannel shirt, and liberty."[52] For Anglo-Canadian women, the private sense of sex-defiance that came with being a woman in a manly country provided a critical counter-narrative to the myth of the womanless West. In the early decades of the twentieth-century West, the "girl of the new day" adopted the stand of the sex renegade, not because she had entered manly work in the factory or professions, but because she stood in a new, more equitable relationship to man as his partner in the settlement enterprise. But when the idea of a pioneering partnership was used to underwrite Western women's bid for public authority in the new West, it had the effect of reinforcing dominant gender conventions, despite reformers' implicit challenge to élite men's arbitrary privilege.

Like their male counterparts, women reformers in western Canada drew upon settlement discourse to advance their political aims. As partners in nation-building, they accepted their mission to clean up society, but their vision of the future West differed sharply from men's. They sought to reconcile the contradictions inherent in social and symbolic constructions of the West as a manly country that ignored women's contribution to settlement while assuming that they would willingly populate the land and make it productive. They began by demanding legal recognition of the value of their labour in the home and on the farm. Their approach was twofold: to gain access to homesteads on the same basis as men and to win legal recognition of their economic contribution to the family farm. Questions of citizenship and constitutional status became the focus of reform only after initial efforts to renegotiate the social relationship between men and women failed.

On the question of homesteads for women, male legislators stood their ground and used their power to say no. The issue remained largely dormant for twenty-five years, as a result of federal-provincial disputes over jurisdiction of crown land, but women did continue to press forward on their demands for parental rights and homestead dower.[53] The dower campaign began modestly. Initially, Western women sought what Eastern women already had: the right of the wife to a portion of her husband's estate following his death.[54] When this was denied, they took the more radical step of insisting that the law guarantee the wife ownership during the husband's lifetime. This became the principle distinguishing feature of homestead/dower legislation once it was enacted.[55]

By 1920, all three prairie provinces had introduced a dower law, but the legislation was subsequently seriously eroded by judicial interpretation. Specifically, the decisions of the male court put in question the wife's ownership when it upheld the right of the husband to sell, mortgage, or otherwise encumber the homestead without his wife's consent. This was a disappointing setback for prairie women, who sought to protect their home and livelihood against speculation and sale during a period of rapidly escalating land prices. Recognizing that the new law did not give them and their children the security they sought, reformers began to see dower itself as a stumbling block to women's economic independence. As one commentator put it: women were no longer content to accept "little bits of favouritism in legislation" in the form of "relief provisions" to the wife and insisted that the "interests of the two home builders … [be] fully recognized in law."[56] The ensuing debate, public and within the ranks of organized women, underscored male intransigence on the question of a pioneering partnership, moving organized women to claim an equal share in property they had helped to build up. In 1925, Irene Parlby introduced a matrimonial property bill that anticipated joint ownership by both husband and wife.[57]

Matrimonial property on the basis of joint ownership marked a dramatic shift in women's demands. Coupled with a call for equal custody rights for the mother, it attacked the age-old principle of male authority in the family by asserting the legal personality of the wife. In Alberta, organized farm women played a crucial role in guiding the matrimonial property bill to the floor of the provincial legislature. The bill was turned over to a legislative committee charged with investigating married women's property rights and recommending appropriate legislative changes.[58] Parlby headed the committee of two men and four women, including Henrietta Muir Edwards, Emily Murphy, and Gwendolyn Duff (committee secretary and a lawyer). Parlby, Edwards, and Murphy were already active in lobbying for legal reforms for women. Edwards published an account of the legal status of women in Canada in 1908 and a review of Alberta law as it affected women and children in 1917.[59]

Murphy was a magistrate of the provincial court and was actively pursuing the question of Canadian women's constitutional status as persons under the *British North America Act*. As president of the United Farm Women of Alberta from 1916 to 1920, Parlby took a lead in provincial debates on women's legal status. She personally promoted changes to the Alberta law along the lines of the then existing Swedish legislation, which recognized the economic value of women's domestic labour and provided for mediation in the event of a dispute between husband and wife.[60] But, following extensive enquiry into Canadian and European law as it affected women during marriage, the committee recommended against substantive changes.

That the committee's final report fell so far short of the actions and public statements of three of its leading members suggests that its authorship lay elsewhere. No record exists of the committee's deliberations, but there is every reason to believe that the members reported privately to the government, which was responsible for the document as it appeared in its final form. Indeed, it is entirely likely that Premier John E. Brownlee had a direct role in writing the report. Certainly such an action would be consistent, not only with Brownlee's reputedly heavy-handed approach to governing, but also with his past relationship with the United Farm Women of Alberta.[61] As legal advisor to the United Farmers, Brownlee frequently attended United Farmers of Alberta (UFA) conventions, where he participated in discussions on the legal reform resolutions brought by the women. He worked closely on early drafts of the Farm Women's proposals for matrimonial property legislation. For example, when the convention members failed to agree on the women's 1920 resolution calling for "Equal Custody and Equal Property Rights," the resolution was tabled – along with delegates' instructions that the UFA executive, together "with Mr. Brownlee, could deal with [it] more deliberately."[62] When it reappeared at the 1922 meetings, additions included a legal definition of community of property similar to that in the matrimonial property bill of 1925, and an entirely new clause that established the husband as "head of the community" with the sole right to manage the family property but "restricted as to selling or mortgaging real estate, or leasing it for more than one year, without the concurrence of his wife."[63] This provision also appeared in Parlby's bill. Brownlee again made his position clear when, under his direction as attorney general in 1923, the department issued a statement opposed to joint ownership. Government lawyers explained that, despite the "inequality" and "apparent injustice" in the law as it affected married women, any remedy would require "community practically on the basis of partnership" (which was the essence of women's demands), and this would be too costly, too radical, inconvenient, unjustifiable, as well as generally too disruptive to the economy and therefore bad for business.[64] This was Brownlee's opinion in 1927 when his government submitted its final report.

Taken together, the campaigns for homesteads for women, custody, and dower struck at the very heart of the manly West. They challenged men's control of land, and therefore wealth, in the predominantly agricultural West, and men's sole authority as *paterfamilias*, or head of the prairie household as Minister of the Interior Oliver envisioned it.[65] Having breached the masculinist convention of the West, women began to make themselves visible by contesting male authority and intervening in public discourse on their own behalf. But, because women had no vote or power to initiate change, male legislators could readily refuse their demands. The limited success of their early reform campaigns led directly to prairie women's call for suffrage. Emily Murphy, suffragist, novelist, and social reformer, put the need succinctly when she explained that "because women had no votes their going to the Legislature was not taken seriously ... all that was considered necessary [by provincial legislators] was respectful treatment."[66] As events would show, formal recognition of women's citizenship also proved inadequate to curb males acting on their own interest.[67]

Winning the vote did open the door to a second manly space: the territory of high politics. During the years immediately following the extension of the provincial franchise in 1916, women eagerly took up the challenge of elected office, although their representation among sitting members of western legislatures remained small.[68] By the 1930s, women had all but disappeared from the ranks of prairie legislators. Understanding how a masculinist culture shaped the conditions of women's entry into public life in western Canada also illuminates the contours of their exclusion from political power.

On the prairies, women's organized reform was closely linked to the "farm revolt." The Alberta Non-Partisan League gave Canada its first woman legislator when Louise McKinney was elected to that province's legislature in 1917. And, in the run-up to the Alberta provincial election of 1921, all political parties actively recruited female candidates, hoping to win the support of the new woman voter. That year, eight women candidates, representing six political parties, entered the field; two were elected.[69] On the day before the election, one of the capital city's leading newspapers proudly boasted that "Thirty-One Thousand Voters ... Will Elect Five Men to Legislature."[70] Following the headline, the paper printed a list of the candidates running in the constituency of Edmonton. They included four men and one woman, the popular novelist, temperance activist, and social reformer, Nellie McClung. What McClung thought of the editors' assumption that politics was an exclusively male domain we do not know. The paper's view, however, was widely shared.

Critics claimed that the new woman voter took little interest in politics and lacked the independence necessary for the responsibility of citizenship. The editorial opinion of the *Calgary Western Standard* was typical, declaring "women in politics are a failure." According to the editors:

> … [v]ery few of the women voters understood who and what they were voting for. They were in most cases biased in their opinions being persuaded entirely by the opinions of their husbands or sweethearts.… The Standard will also wager that a majority of these women voters were disgusted with their time spent in the booths and would much have preferred to be down town shopping.… It is all very well and highly complimentary to give the lady-folk the right to vote but seriously politics is a man's game and it is just as easy to make a woman a politician as it is to make a lady's hat-maker out of the average man. It isn't in the calibre of the being.[71]

This was not the official view of organized farmers who were among the earliest supporters of women's suffrage. Farm men argued that women's moral leadership in public life was crucial to social improvement. William Irvine, a leading spokesman of the UFA and author of *The Farmers in Politics*, explained that on the social question, farm women were "in the van[guard] … in education, health, home life, the development of the young … and in raising the moral standard" of the community. Moreover, when he urged that the "farmer and his partner stand shoulder to shoulder in the great political and economic struggle that is ahead," the agrarian leader, Henry Wise Wood, instructed his members that women should be seen as "an active, necessary part" of the farm movement and not "merely … [as] lending their silent moral support" to the men.[72] Irvine credited women with broadening the social vision of the UFA, explaining that:

> … the farmer's organization was primarily economic in origin and aim. In the earlier stage, it did not see much beyond the price of wheat, the lowering of freight rates, and the abolition of the tariff. But men, in their struggle against the evils of commercialism have been commercialized.… Plutocratic organizations are dominated by the desire for higher profit, labor organizations concentrate on higher wages, and farmer organizations, too, began by seeking higher prices.… [But] the United Farm women have helped greatly to save the United Farmers' movement from the usual fate of male movements. The male mind, during the individualistic system of society, went to

> seed on commercialism; and the human values … have been choked out.… To remedy this state of affairs was the work which the United Farm Women undertook first.

According to Irvine, the women's campaigns revitalized the farm movement, taking it into a "larger world of thought and action."[73]

As a political manifesto, *The Farmers in Politics* was intended to present the movement as a united front in the battle against eastern interests. Published in 1920 at the height of the agrarian revolt, it also sought to establish the UFA as the official voice of reform in the western provinces. By invoking conventional notions of women's moral authority, Irvine hoped to buttress the UFA's political claims. But the alliance between farm men and women was never as smooth as Irvine suggested. Based on the politics of separate spheres, which positioned women as the moral guardians of national life, it confined women to a narrow sphere of influence – what Irvine called the "spiritual side of life."[74] This delicate alliance was also subject to the political settlement that signalled the collapse of western progressives as a national force by 1925. Having won major concessions from Ottawa, including guaranteed transportation rates and control of wheat marketing, organized farmers retreated from electoral politics. Only the UFA continued in government until the mid-1930s. Still, the skirmishes for political ascendancy that marked the early decades of the twentieth century did open a space for organized farm women to intervene directly in political life. They used this opportunity to press for social and legal reforms that would see newcomer women share in the dividends of settlement. In much the same way as an earlier generation of Anglo-Canadian women had taken up their assigned civilizing mission, a political generation of prairie women accepted the social question as their special mandate.

When they responded to the call for social improvement, prairie women took hope and inspiration from the settlement project. For example, Irene Parlby saw women's settlement work as the basis of their claim to a voice in the future of the West. She argued that just as women had been prepared to "follow their men into the wilderness, to share with them its privations, so they were prepared to take their part actively, in the new work to be done" to build up prairie society.[75] In her view, questions of social and economic justice arose naturally from settlement and the "cultivation of the land must be followed by the cultivation of a worthy social and economic system of living."[76]

By drawing on settlement discourse, women reformers sought to establish their authority to share in determining the future direction of the country and make government accountable to them. They argued that women's contribution to settlement, specifically their farm and domestic labour, entitled them to look to public institutions to ameliorate the harsh conditions they faced on western homesteads; to in effect include women in the promise of the Prairie West. They called on legislators to "consider the real value of the human being, particularly women and children, in equal degree to that of property."[77] The Saskatchewan feminist, Violet McNaughton, pointed to the link between women's private concerns and public campaigns when she explained the origin of her long-held commitment to improving public health care on the prairies. While recuperating from surgery in a Saskatoon hospital in 1911, she heard "the echoes of the real estate boom" in the city and thought of "the only solid thing back of the boom, the homesteads of Saskatchewan. Back of these homesteads were the frozen noses, long travail on the trail, the grain in the bedrooms" (a reference to her first bedroom in Canada, which doubled as a granary). "Here was I," she wrote, "a part of this one solid thing – and I had to come 65 miles for medical treatment." As unnecessary deaths of rural mothers and their infants mounted, McNaughton redoubled her resolve to see nursing care established in every rural district. "I am going right after this medical aid question," she declared in 1916, "I am going to make it my subject."[78]

Prairie women sought to relieve the hardships farm families faced by redressing the economic inequalities between urban and rural populations, but they also pointed out that farm women and their children suffered disproportionately compared with men. As Parlby put it: "no group of women [worked] so hard, so ungrudgingly and so unselfishly. And yet we know for a fact that in many instances, not even the produce that they raise by their own labour, can be sold and claimed as their own."[79] Parlby argued that any economic improvements brought about by what she described as "the dollars and cents side" of the Farmers' platform should not sit as increased profits in the pockets of individual farmers, but must benefit rural families generally through improved services, education, and health care.

The problem, as organized farm women saw it, was that they were excluded from a share in the benefits of settlement. Vulnerable to arbitrary male power, they sought to curb men's authority and win greater autonomy by urging that benefits should be more broadly distributed.

Parlby thought that the "socially minded man and woman will think almost identical thoughts," but counted progressive men in the minority. As she saw it: "male selfishness" and "drive to dominate" were the main obstacles to social equality. For Parlby and others, evidence of the failure of male authority to govern lay in the death and destruction of the war of 1914–18. They concluded that "in the interest of civilization the future centre of power must rest not in the fighting male of the race but in woman."[80]

For these reformers, the promise of the West was manifest in the social experiment taking place on the prairies with their "many races, many tongues, many creeds." Particularly in the midst of the Great War and its immediate aftermath, they pointed to this cultural and ethnic diversity as proof of the possibilities for bridging "human barriers," including those that divided men and women, and for building a safer, more tolerant, more just society.[81] They were not so naive as to believe that social harmony was a simple matter of sympathetic understanding, rather, they argued that understanding was a necessary precondition for achieving their goal. Anglo-Canadian women activists did not always live up to their own ideals. Moreover, there was no inevitable trajectory from women's reform activities to equality for all women. By demanding greater equality with men, middle-class women intended to extend their own authority. This had the effect of excluding other women on the basis of race, class, and ethnicity or because they were relative latecomers to the West and therefore not part of a select group of founders.[82] Still, women's challenge to the idea of the West as an exclusively male space did shift political discourse, offering a broader social vision than masculinist conventions alone would allow.

When women put their social vision to the test in the years immediately following suffrage, becoming pioneers in a second gendered space – that of "high" politics – they understood what was at stake. McClung went to the heart of the matter when she summed up the challenge confronting women in the 1920s: "I knew the whole situation was fraught with danger," she wrote. If a woman "failed, it would be a blow to women everywhere." If she "succeeded, her success would belong to her as an individual. People would say she was an exceptional woman. She has a 'masculine' mind."[83] This was indeed what happened to the Saskatchewan reformer Violet McNaughton. Describing McNaughton's ability to hold a convention floor, one reporter observed that she "fights as a man fights. There have been rare moments on the floor of a convention when [McNaughton] has argued her case against that of a masculine opponent with a wit so subtle that he has turned, half expecting to see her exercise that prerogative of her sex and duck under his elbow, but he finds her standing in her place."[84] According to Parlby, women entering politics faced a hostile environment. "To-day women are on trial in the political field," she explained, "[e]very false step they take, every little remark which may sound foolish, is eagerly discussed, and widely heralded abroad with the cynical sneer: 'What else can you expect of a woman?!'"[85]

Parlby entered public life because she believed that prairie society needed women's "intuition, their idealism, their willingness to sacrifice their individual interests, their willingness to give service without thought of personal gain."[86] McClung also saw women as "cleaning up politics," but in her view, corruption in public life was not the central question for the future. Rather, it was "the problem of living together." Any effective solution must include women at all levels of society since, in McClung's view, "the world has suffered long from too much masculinity and not enough humanity."[87] McNaughton looked to the day when "an army of women workers ... women on every executive and every committee ... women organizers and women speakers" would transform prairie politics.[88] But when McNaughton's efforts to penetrate the ranks of the male-dominated Progressive Party collapsed, along with the party, in the interwar years, she retreated from high politics, focusing on her work as an editor writing in the pages of *The Western Producer.*[89]

For this generation of activists, the formal political field remained a manly preserve. Even McClung, who was especially skilled at the political joust, had surprisingly little to say about her legislative career.[90] Her silence speaks loudly of her frustrations and disappointments in public life. Five years after entering the Alberta legislature, she welcomed the defeat that allowed her to return to her first love. Writing and publishing provided a degree of independence, freedom, and authority denied her as a woman in politics. Parlby was the more reluctant politician, but she remained in office for thirteen years.[91] Her election in 1921 was greeted with widespread speculation that she would be appointed minister of health.[92] Instead, she was named minister without portfolio, with no salary, no budget, and no department of her own.[93] Publicly, she accepted her appointment with grace, but complained privately that "Minister without Portfolio is a stupid position."[94] She was right. In the absence of any specific government initiatives on social reform, her mandate to inform ministers on issues of particular concern to women and children could bring few concrete results. Her position as the "Women's Minister" was more symbolic than real, giving her influence at the table but no direct power to set the government's legislative agenda.

Historians explain the slim record of achievements for prairie women reformers in the early decades of the twentieth century as conservative middle-class women's betrayal of an earlier generation of more radical feminists or as the result of deep disillusionment following the high expectations that marked the votes-for-women campaign.[95] Having exaggerated the power of a few newcomer women to act in the interests of their class and race during the early period of colonization and settlement, scholars then subordinated a later generation of political activists to class interests or fractious feminist politics. This paper suggests that the contours of prairie women's politics were shaped more broadly by the ways in which gender was used to inscribe meaning on the West as social space. While settlement stimulated new debates (such as how to live in the West), by demarcating and privileging a mythical pioneering brotherhood, and the values it represented, expansionist discourse circumscribed the possibilities for change.

By intentionally foregrounding gender as a primary way in which social relationships were organized under the conditions of western expansion, we begin to see the ways in which women were both bound and freed by colonization and settlement even as they were divided from each other by race and class. The cultural construction of the West as "no place for a woman" represented aboriginal women as a threat to the social order Europeans deemed necessary to their imperialist project, positioning them outside the boundaries of "civilized" society. It had a similar, if opposite, effect on Euro-Canadian women. By casting newcomer women as gentle tamers, it positioned them as the antithesis of a rough and ready, independent West that underpinned capitalist expansion. In settlement discourse, middle-class white women embodied everything that the frontiersman had rebelled against. Men, like John Wilcox, might lament the loss of Sundays and all that they represented of the comfort and society of home, but their self-assigned task of manly conquest and regeneration relied upon the absence of the very thing they most urgently sought.

The difficulty for women reformers in the West was that by definition, *they* were the social problem. Opposition to women's full inclusion in the civic life of the country was not unique to western Canada. But in the West, where gendered categories and terrains of exclusion were a legacy of recent settlement, women activists continued to be seen as interlopers in a manly country and a drag on western man. Moreover, by transforming the search for wealth into a quest for manhood, settlement discourse marginalized the social question of how to live in the harsh reality that was the turn-of-the-century West. Cast as an individual problem, the social question remained beyond the reach of political reform. Attempts by agrarian reformers like William Irvine to unite the two in the 1920s failed because the political debate was bound by masculinist conventions that placed individual independence above social community. But claims to independence rested on gender asymmetry that mediated race and class hierarchy. Despite Agnes Higginson Skrine's bid for freedom in the wide open spaces of the prairies, that place was culturally inscribed in ways that worked to frustrate her expectation. A manly West dictated that "a flannel shirt and liberty" remain the exclusive rallying cry of a specific prairie manhood.

While some women saw the West as liberating them from conventional femininity, their assertions of equal status with the frontiersman had the opposite effect. By denying the differences sex difference made, women were drawn further into dominant gender conventions. Those who attempted to transcend the boundaries of middle-class femininity found themselves adopting a masculine stance, which, implicitly at least, denigrated their femaleness. On the other hand, when women like Parlby and McClung insisted upon their female specificity (and the values that were assumed to accrue thereto), they were barred from an autonomous political authority on the grounds of that very specificity. By focusing on the ways in which a gendered West constructed relationships of power by hierarchically organizing access to wealth and opportunity, we begin to see the history of western Canadian settlement more fully, revealing the contradictions and tensions at the heart of the notion of the Prairie West as a Promised Land.

NOTES

1 This paper was originally published in *Western Historical Quarterly* 27, no. 4 (Winter 1997): 493–520. I have made minor revisions for publication in this volume.

2 Gould first applied for membership in 1987 but was turned down because she was a woman. She then took her case to the Yukon Human Rights Commission and won. That decision was overturned by the Supreme Court of the Yukon Territory. After failing to convince the Court of Appeal to reverse the lower court's decision, Gould turned to the Supreme Court of Canada. See *Gould v. Yukon Order of Pioneers*, 133 *Dominion Law Reports* (4th), 449.

3 Ibid., 460.

4 Ibid., 511.

5 Ibid., 504.

6 "Gender ideology" refers to that set of Euro-Canadian beliefs which underwrote social relations and institutions in the nineteenth century by "specifying difference as binary opposites that turned on sex" — what Mary Povey, *Uneven Developments: The Ideological Work of Gender In Mid-Victorian England* (Chicago: University of Chicago Press, 1988), describes as "the characteristic feature of the mid-Victorian symbolic economy."

7 Karen Dubinsky, *Improper Advances* (Chicago: University of Chicago Press, 1993) makes a similar point for northern Ontario.

8 Sarah Carter, "Categories and Terrains of Exclusion: Constructing the 'Indian Woman' in the Early Settlement Era in Western Canada," *Great Plains Quarterly* 13 (Summer 1993): 147–61.

9 Jane Tompkins, *West of Everything: The Inner Life of Westerns* (New York: Oxford University Press, 1992), 4. See also, Patricia Nelson Limerick, *The Legacy of Conquest: The Unbroken Past of the American West* (New York: Norton, 1987), and Richard Slotkin, *Regeneration through Violence: The Mythology of the American Frontier, 1600–1860* (Norman, OK: University of Oklahoma Press, 1973).

10 Richard Slotkin, *Gunfighter Nation: The Myth of the Frontier in Twentieth-Century America* (Norman, OK: University of Oklahoma Press, 1992), 10.

11 See Ray Allen Billington, *Frederick Jackson Turner: Historian, Scholar, Teacher* (New York: Oxford University Press, 1973). For another example of the creation of this myth, see Kim Townsend, "Francis Parkman and the Male Tradition," *American Quarterly* 38 (Spring 1986): 97–113.

12 Slotkin, *Gunfighter Nation*, 29–61.

13 The antimodernist sentiments of settlement discourse coexisted with faith in the benefits of modern industrial capitalism. Indeed, it represented wilderness going as restoring individual initiative and enterprise by offering a "real life" or "authentic" experience as described T. J. Jackson Lears, *No Place of Grace: Antimodernism and the Transformation of American Culture, 1880–1920* (New York: Pantheon Books, 1981), esp. 4–58.

14 "Ralph Connor" is the pseudonym of Reverend Charles W. Gordon. Connor's novels were among the most popular of the period and are reputed to have sold over five million copies. See Edward McCourt, *The Canadian West in Fiction*, rev. ed. (Toronto: Ryerson, 1970), 24–41; J. Lee Thompson and John H. Thompson, "Ralph Connor and the Canadian Identity," *Queen's Quarterly* 79 (Summer 1972): 159–70; and F. W. Watt, "Western Myth: The World of Ralph Connor," *Canadian Literature* 1 (Summer 1959): 26–36. I am grateful to Jeremy Mouat, who first urged me to read Connor's novels.

15 According to one source, *The Sky Pilot* sold thousands of copies "almost overnight" and the total sales of Gordon's books exceeded five million copies, making him one of the most popular writers of his day. See Edward A. McCourt, *The Canadian West in Fiction* (Toronto: Ryerson, 1970), 24–25. Other Connor novels set in western Canada

are: *The Prospector* (1904), *The Settler: A Tale of Saskatchewan* (1909) and *The Doctor: A Tale of the Rockies* (1906).

16 Connor, *The Settler*, 227

17 Ibid., 147.

18 Connor, *The Sky Pilot*, 27.

19 See R. Douglas Francis, *Images of the West: Responses to the Canadian Prairies, 1690–1960* (Saskatoon: Western Producer Prairie Books, 1989), 103, 121, 125, 124.

20 For a critical discussion of "gentle tamers," see Joan Jensen and Darlis Miller, "The Gentle Tamers Revisited: New Approaches to the History of Women in the American West," *Pacific Historical Review* 49 (May 1980): 173–214; Paula Petrik, "The Gentle Tamers in Transition: Women in the Trans-Mississippi West," *Feminist Studies* 11 (Fall 1985): 678–94; and Elizabeth Jameson, "Women as Workers, Women as Civilizers: True Womanhood in the American West," in Susan Armitage and Elizabeth Jameson, eds., *The Women's West* (Norman, OK: University of Oklahoma Press, 1987), 145–64.

21 Quoted in Jeremy Mouat, *Roaring Days Rossland's Mines and the History of British Columbia* (Vancouver: UBC Press, 1995), 112.

22 Connor, *Sky Pilot*, preface.

23 See *Land of the Lake: A Story of the Settlement and Development of the Country West of Buffalo Lake* (Lacombe, AB: Lamberton Historical Society, 1974), 43–44.

24 Ibid. Author's emphasis.

25 Quoted in Lewis G. Thomas, ed. *The Prairie West to 1905* (Toronto: Oxford University Press, 1975), 128.

26 On British imperialism and masculinity, see Graham Dawson, "The Blond Bedouin: Lawrence of Arabia, Imperial Adventure, and the Imagining of English-British Masculinity," and other essays in Michael Roper and John Tosh, eds., *Manful Assertions: Masculinities in Britain since 1800* (New York: Routledge, 1991), 113–44; J. A. Managan and James Walvin, eds., *Manliness and Morality: Middle-Class Masculinity in Britain and America, 1800–1940* (New York: St. Martin Press, 1987). Also suggestive is Elizabeth Vibert, "'Real Men Hunt Buffalo': Masculinity, Race and Class in British Fur Traders' Narratives," in Joy Parr and Mark Rosenfeld, eds., *Gender and History in Canada* (Toronto: Copp Clark, 1996), 50–67.

27 Quoted in Germaine Warkentin, ed., *Canadian Exploration Literature* (Toronto: Oxford University Press, 1993), 384–95.

28 For a critical exploration of this idea, see in particular Sarah Carter, "The Exploitation and Narration of the Captivity of Theresa Delaney and Theresa Gowanlock, 1885," in Catherine Cavanaugh and Jeremy Mouat, eds., *Making Western Canada* (Toronto: Garmond Press, 1996), 31–61; and Carroll Smith-Rosenberg, "Captured Subjects/Savage Others: Violently Engendering the New American," *Gender and History* 5 (Summer 1993): 177–95.

29 Sylvia Van Kirk, *"Many Tender Ties": Women in Fur-Trade Society, 1670–1870* (Winnipeg: Watson & Dyer, 1980) does much to recover the history of Aboriginal women in the trade, but her analysis of the role of European women falls within this traditional interpretation. According to Van Kirk, male racism remained dormant until the arrival of European women when "the question of colour became an issue for the first time" (p. 201). Jennifer S. H. Brown, *Strangers in Blood* (Vancouver: UBC Press, 1980), also points to familial relations relatively free of racial tensions, arguing that change occurred during the years leading up to and immediately following the merger of the North-West and Hudson's Bay Companies in 1821, which "were conspicuous for the rise of racial categorization and discrimination and for the economic and sexual marginality of native born sons and daughters to the new order," 205.

30 Van Kirk, *"Many Tender Ties,"* 220–30. See also her article "'The Reputation of a Lady': Sarah Ballenden and the Foss-Pelly Scandal," *Manitoba History* 11 (Spring 1986): 4–11.

31 Ballenden was the eldest daughter of chief trader Alexander Roderick McLeod and his Indian wife. European trained and educated, her three younger sisters resided in Canada (Quebec) following their father's death in 1840. See Brown, *Strangers in Blood*, 183–84, 215.

32 Van Kirk, *"Many Tender Ties,"* 220.

33 Ibid., 221.

34 Studies of European women in colonial settings focus on Asia and Africa. See especially Jane Hunter, *The Gospel of Gentility: American Women Missionaries in Turn-of-the-Century China* (New Haven, CT: Yale University Press, 1984); Anne Laura Stoler, "Carnal Knowledge and Imperial Power: Gender, Race and Morality in Colonial Asia," in Micaela di Leonardo, ed., *Gender at the Crossroads of Knowledge: Feminist Anthropology in the Postmodern Era* (Berkeley: University of California Press, 1991): 51–101; and Stoler, "Rethinking Colonial Categories: European Communities and the Boundaries of Rule," in Nicholas B. Dirks, ed., *Colonialism and Culture* (Ann Arbor: University of Michigan Press, 1992): 319–52. For a thoughtful consideration of the issues raised by women and imperialism see Jane Haggis, "Gendering Colonialism or Colonising Gender?" *Women's Studies International Forum* 13, no. 1/2 (1990): 105–15.

35 See Margaret Strobel, *European Women and the Second British Empire* (Bloomington, IN: Indiana University Press, 1991).

36 Hilary Callan and Shirley Ardener, eds., *The Incorporated Wife* (London: Croom Helm, 1984), 1–25. See also Helen Callaway, *Gender, Culture and Empire: European Women in Colonial Nigeria* (Urbana, IL: University of Illinois Press, 1987).

37 I am grateful to Sarah Carter for discussion of this point.

38 For further discussion on the ways gender constructed respectability, see Erica Smith, "'Gentlemen, This is no Ordinary Trial': Sexual Narratives in the Trial of the Reverend Corbett, Red River, 1863," in Jennifer S. H. Brown and Elizabeth Vibert, eds., *Reading Beyond Words: Contexts for Native History* (Peterborough, ON: Broadview Press, 1996), 364–80.

39 William Francis Butler, *The Great Lone Land: A Narrative of Travel and Adventure in the North-West of America* (1910), 200–201.

40 Quoted in D. J. Hall, "Clifford Sifton: Immigration and Settlement Policy," in Howard Palmer, ed., *The Settlement of the West* (Calgary: University of Calgary Comprint Publishing, 1977), 74.

41 Ibid., 71.

42 Quoted in D. J. Hall, *Clifford Sifton* (Vancouver: University of British Columbia Press, 1985), 69.

43 *Debates*, House of Commons, Canada, cols. 9271–72, July 11, 1905. Homestead law granted heads of households, or any man over eighteen years of age, "free" access to one hundred and sixty acres of land, subject to an entry fee, residence, and improvements. In practice, this meant any man over eighteen.

44 Georgina Binnie-Clark, *Wheat and Woman* (Toronto: University of Toronto Press, 1979), xxvi.

45 Ibid., 308.

46 Quoted in Hall, *Clifford Sifton*, 2:81.

47 This policy also stipulated that an agent would be paid three dollars for every man and one dollar for every child who settled in Canada as a direct result of his efforts. See Hall, "Sifton: Immigration and Settlement Policy," 70.

48 Much has been written on the double disadvantage imposed by gender as a system that constructs "woman" as the "Other" over and against shifting notions of "man" and "human." But see in particular Simone de Beauvoir, trans. H. M. Parshley, *The Second Sex* (New York: Knopf, 1949; reprint, New York: Knopf, 1953), xvii–xxv; Denis Riley, *"Am I That Name?": Feminism and the Category of Women in History* (Minneapolis,

MN: University of Minnesota Press, 1988), esp. 18–43; Joan Wallach Scott, *Gender and the Politics of History* (New York: Columbia University Press, 1988), 42–43.

49 Francis, *Images of the West*, 389–90.

50 Irene Parlby, "The Milestones of My Life," *The Canadian Magazine*, June 1928, 14. Parlby arrived in the North West in 1896.

51 Eliane Leslau Silverman, *The Last Best West* (Saskatoon: Fifth House Publishing, 1984), 7.

52 *A Flannel Shirt and Liberty*, Susan Jackel, ed. (Vancouver: University of British Columbia Press, 1982), 100.

53 On the homestead legislation in Canada, see Catherine Cavanaugh, "The Women's Movement In Alberta as Seen through the Campaign for Dower Rights, 1909–1928" (master's thesis, University of Alberta, 1986); and "The Limitations of the Pioneering Partnership: The Alberta Campaign for Homestead Dower, 1909–25," *Canadian Historical Review* 74 (1993): 198–225; Susan Jackel, "Introduction," in Binnie-Clark, *Wheat and Woman*, xx–xxxi; and Margaret McCallum, "Prairie Women and the Struggle for Dower Law, 1905–1920," *Prairie Forum* 18 (Spring 1993): 19–34; and *The Matrimonial Home*, Alberta Law Reform Institute Report for Discussion no. 14, March 1995.

54 Common law dower, long established in English Canada, was abolished in the West in 1886 when the federal government introduced the *Territories Real Property Act* as part of its settlement policy. As a result, married women who moved from central and eastern Canada lost the limited protection available to them in their home provinces. Similarly, women immigrants from the western United States lost the homesteading privileges available to them under the American legislation. This partly explains why the issue was raised at the time.

55 The precedent for Canadian homestead dower was American legislation, which originated in the state of Texas in 1839, where it was intended to protect the home against financial misfortune. See the Manitoba Law Reform Commission, *Report on an Examination of "The Dower Act"* (Winnipeg: Manitoba Law Reform Commission, 1984), 160.

56 Cavanaugh, "The Women's Movement in Alberta," 67.

57 Ibid., esp. 50–52, 58–65. The bill was an important move toward a positive right of the wife in the "common estate" of the marriage. This broke with the inchoate right of dower, which remained dormant during the husband's lifetime and had proved a stumbling block for the courts. The bill was limited in that it established the husband as "head of the community," giving the wife what was in effect a veto over his power to encumber or dispose of community property. Nevertheless, the bill represented a break from the old common law principle of coverture, which subsumed the wife's legal personality in that of her husband. In addition to securing family property during marriage, the bill opened the door to equal division of family assets in the event of marriage breakdown or the death of a spouse.

58 Ibid., 86.

59 Henrietta Muir Edwards, *Legal Status of Canadian Women as shown by extracts from dominion and provincial laws relating to women and children* (Calgary: National Council of Women in Canada, 1908), and *Legal Status of Women of Alberta as shown by extracts from dominion and provincial laws* (Edmonton, University of Alberta, 1917).

60 The committee's final report did recommend establishing a provincial mediation service to assist in the event of domestic disputes and marriage breakdown but no action was taken.

61 Carl Frederick Betke, "The United Farmers of Alberta, 1921–1935: The Relationship between the Agricultural Organization and the Government of Alberta" (master's thesis, University of Alberta, 1971), describes Brownlee as the "strong man in the party," who "exercised such amazing influence over U.F.A. votes" (p. 79). Betke's is still the

most complete treatment of the Farmer's in government. He attributes the UFA retreat from radical politics to Brownlee's influence as premier and head of the party from 1925 until he resigned under a cloud of scandal in 1934.

62 Ibid., 71.

63 Ibid.

64 Cavanaugh, "The Women's Movement in Alberta," 75.

65 The married mothers' custody rights developed unevenly in statute and in case law. In Manitoba, the 1922 *Child Welfare Act*, Statutes of Manitoba, c. 2, ss.122–147, asserted the mother's equal custody right; Saskatchewan passed similar legislation in 1919–20 as *The Infants' Act*, c. 77, s. 2, which applied to children age 14 and under; and Alberta introduced its *Domestic Relations Act* in 1927, s. 61 (1). Along with custody rights, the mother was also made equally liable with the father for the maintenance of the child.

66 Edmonton *Bulletin*, October 28, 1912: 3.

67 Western women were the first to win the vote in Canada. Manitoba passed suffrage legislation in 1916, followed by Saskatchewan, Alberta, and British Columbia in 1917. Catherine Lyle Cleverdon, *The Woman Suffrage Movement in Canada* (Toronto: University of Toronto Press,1950) provides a detailed but dated account of the votes-for-women campaigns in Canada. See also Deborah Gorham, "Singing Up the Hill," *Canadian Dimension* 10 (June 1975): 26–38. For a further discussion of the effects of suffrage on women's participation in politics, see the essays in Linda Kealey and Joan Sangster, eds., *Beyond the Vote: Canadian Women and Politics* (Toronto: University of Toronto Press, 1989). For prairie women, see Veronica Strong-Boag, "Pulling in Double Harness or Hauling a Double Load: Women, Work, Feminism on the Canadian Prairie," *Journal of Canadian Studies* 1 (Fall 1986): 95–106. The federal franchise was proclaimed in 1919.

68 For a further discussion of women in Alberta politics in the immediate post-suffrage era see Nancy Langford, "'All That Glitters:' The Political Apprenticeship of Alberta Women, 1916–1930" in Catherine A. Cavanaugh and Randi R. Warne, eds., *Standing on New Ground* (Edmonton: University of Alberta Press, 1993), 71–85.

69 In Calgary, Mrs. Langford and Mrs. A. Gale ran as Liberal and Independent Liberal candidates, respectively; Louise McKinney and Irene Parlby ran under the UFA banner; and in Edmonton, Mrs. E. Ferris ran as a Conservative, Mary Cantin was an Independent Labour candidate, Marie Mellard, Labour Socialist, and Nellie McClung, ran for the governing Liberals. See Edmonton *Bulletin*, July 13, 1921: 3. The UFA landslide victory swept the Liberals from office so that, while McClung was victorious, she served her term on the opposition side of the House. Parlby won her riding of Lacombe. She was re-elected twice and served in the UFA cabinet until her retirement in 1934. McKinney was defeated.

70 Edmonton, *The Morning Bulletin*, July 18, 1921, 1.

71 Calgary, *Western Standard*, June 11, 1917, 1.

72 UFA Bulletin No. 5 A (Calgary, 1918) in Violet MacNaughton Personal Papers Saskatchewan Archives Board (hereafter VMNP), G 291.7.

73 William Irvine, *The Farmers in Politics* (1920 repr., Toronto: McClelland and Stewart, 1976), 123–24.

74 Ibid., 118.

75 Irene Parlby, "Awhile Ago – And To-day," *The Canadian Magazine* (July 1928): 26.

76 Irene Parlby, "The Great Adventure," *Grain Growers' Guide* (April 1927): 5.

77 Shielah Stier, "The Beliefs of Violet McNaughton" (master's thesis, University of Saskatchewan, 1979), 92.

78 Georgina M. Taylor, "A personal tragedy shapes the future," *Western Producer* (Saskatoon) January 10, 1991: 11.

79 Quoted in Linda Rasmussen et al., *A Harvest Yet to Reap: A History of Prairie Women* (Toronto: Women's Press, 1976), 170.

80 Parlby, "The Great Adventure," 5.
81 Ibid.
82 Scholars disagree on the extent to which women's reform activities reinforced existing social divisions. For example, Mariana Valverde, "'When the Mother of the Race is Free': Race, Reproduction, and Sexuality in First-Wave Feminism," in Franca Iacovetta and Mariana Valverde, eds., *Gender Conflicts* (Toronto: University of Toronto Press, 1992), 3–26, argues that women were inevitably divided by race and class. Carol Bacchi takes a similar approach in "Race Regeneration and Social Purity: A Study of the Social Attitudes of Canada's English-Speaking Suffragists," *Historie sociale/Social History* 11 (November 1978): 460–74. Nancy M. Sheehan, "Women Helping Women: The WCTU and the Foreign Population in the West, 1905–1930," *International Journal of Women's Studies* 6 (November/December 1983): 396–411, argues that patterns varied depending upon local circumstances. For a positive interpretation of middle-class-led reform in English Canada, see Christina Simmons, "'Helping the Poorer Sisters': The Women of the Joist Mission, Halifax, 1905–1945," *Acadiensis* 14 (Autumn 1984): 3–27, and Mariana Valverde, *The Age of Light, Soap, and Water: Moral Reform in English Canada, 1885–1925* (Toronto: McClelland and Stewart, 1991).
83 Nellie L. McClung, *The Stream Runs Fast* (Toronto: Allen, 1945), 175.
84 Myrtle Hayes Wright, "Mothering the Prairie," *MacLean's Magazine* 39 (April 1, 1926): 22.
85 Irene Parlby, "What Business Have Women In Politics," notes for a 1928 speech, Irene Parlby's Papers, Glenbow Museum and Archives, Calgary, Alberta.
86 Parlby, "The Great Adventure," 5.
87 Nellie McClung, *In Times Like These* (Toronto: McLeod & Allen,1915), 153.
88 Stier "The Beliefs of Violet McNaughton," 115.
89 See Georgina Taylor, "Violet begins her career with the Western Producer," *Western Producer* (Saskatoon), January 31, 1991: 12–13, and "Violet's life as a journalist," *Western Producer*, February 7, 1991: 10–11.
90 In her biography, *The Stream Runs Fast*, McClung notes that she "enjoyed" politics but felt women's efforts had left little lasting impact. Beyond this cryptic comment, she offers few details of her time in office. Her biographers, Mary Hallett and Marilyn Davis, *Firing the Heather* (Saskatoon: Fifth House , 1993), shed little light on McClung's silence.
91 Catherine Anne Cavanaugh, "In Search of a Useful Life: Irene Marryat Parlby, 1868–1965," (PhD diss., University of Alberta, 1994).
92 The rumours were based on the UFA's emphasis on health care during the 1921 campaign and their promise to establish a minister of health. Farm women had led the debate on health care so that Parlby's appointment would have made a logical choice. Once in office, the Farmer's followed their Liberal predecessors on the question of health care, focusing on building hospitals in urban areas.
93 The issue of a salary was resolved by an order-in-council, granting ministers without portfolio an allowance of fifteen dollars "for attendance at each and every meeting of the Executive Council" in addition to the travel and living allowance available to all ministers. See "Memo: Orders in Council Re Subsistence Allowance of Members of Executive Council," 88.553/15, The Attorney General's Papers, Provincial Archives of Alberta, Edmonton, Alberta.
94 Irene Parlby letter to Violet McNaughton, October 13, 1921, A1 D.54, VMNP.
95 See in particular Carol Bacchi, *Liberation Deferred? The Ideas of the English-Canadian Suffragists, 1877–1918* (Toronto: University of Toronto Press, 1983) and John Herd Thompson and Allen Seager, *Canada 1922–1939: Decades of Discord* (Toronto: McClelland and Stewart, 1985). For a reconsideration of prairie women's politics in this period, see Veronica Strong-Boag, "Pulling in Double Harness or Hauling a Double Load: Women, Work and Feminism on the Canadian Prairies," in *Journal of Canadian Studies* 1 (Fall 1986): 35–52.

13

PREACHING PURITY IN THE PROMISED LAND: BISHOP LLOYD AND THE IMMIGRATION DEBATE

Chris Kitzan

> I have faced the rifles of rebels on these prairies and endured every conceivable hardship imposed by climactic extremes to help keep this country British and I'm not going to be deterred at this late date by mere words or any other consideration from doing my duty as I see it.[1]
> – Bishop G. E. Lloyd, 1928

For more than four decades, George Exton Lloyd engaged in a personal, unwavering struggle to realize a British prairie Promised Land populated by loyal citizens possessing "the same language, the same ideals, the same character, the same King, the same flag, and the same old Mother Church of England."[2] The crusade began in 1885 when, as a young soldier and clergyman, Lloyd first marched west to defend the region and its potential from "disloyal" Métis insurgents; and it ended in 1931 when, exhausted from a lifetime of battling, he resigned his office as Anglican Bishop of Saskatchewan and retired to warmer climes. Though weary, he left confident in the belief that he had yet again helped avert another major threat to the ideal, this time from "unpreferred" immigrants arriving from central and eastern Europe under the auspices of the Railways Agreement. Such dutiful consistency was important to Lloyd. Whether defending the West from without or from within, as soldier or bishop, his faith and conviction never wavered – in the British Empire, which he accepted as "a God given instrument for the good of the whole world," in its citizens, His chosen race, and in the prairie Promised Land.[3] It was on the prairies that Lloyd believed that the British, modelling themselves after the Israelites, could fulfill God's plan and realize its promise so long as they kept "themselves clear from contamination with other nations."[4] Answering "God's call to the British race," Lloyd contended that the English were fulfilling the promises of the Old Testament, not "because we have any of the blood of the tribes of Israel. Not because we are White or Black but because, as far as I can see, we are the most Christian nation."[5] With the British as his model nation, the Prairie West his Canaan, the "Fighting Bishop" would use his passion, prestigious position, and the press to rally public opinion in a successful campaign against the federal government and its open immigration policies.

The West that Lloyd entered for the first time in 1885 was more virtual than real – an eastern Canadian vision of a Promised Land that was born of practical necessity but that was nurtured and raised on rhetoric and hyperbole. Recognizing that most of the good land in Upper Canada was under cultivation, and that there was nowhere left for future farmers to settle, a small group of eastern Canadian expansionists had begun to take an interest in the vast, largely uninhabited, region in the middle of the nineteenth century. Rejecting the existing, widely held belief that the North West was a barren wasteland suited only for fur traders, first nations, and missionaries, they soon began constructing a new, more romantic vision of the West as an agricultural Eden. Not only would the region serve as a bountiful agricultural and economic frontier, expansionists contended, it would also eventually become the lynchpin of a great nation and an even stronger empire. This interest in promoting both nation and empire was not, according to historian Doug Owram, contradictory:

> The Canadian sense of duty in the North West had as its initial determinant the sense of membership in the Imperial community. From Isbister through A. Morris and Charles Mair, expansionists had always seen the west not only within the national but within the imperial context; the North West was important to the role of Canada within the Empire and, possibly, the Empire within the world.[6]

The role Owram's eastern generals of Canadian imperialism, such as Alexander Isbister, Alexander Morris, and Charles Mair, played in developing a unique national vision for western Canada before the turn of the century has been well covered. These expansionists, while they would help establish a vision of the ideal Anglo-Saxon society they hoped to create in the West, were more interested in speculating on the economic and political implications of westward expansion on the nation and the empire.

While George Exton Lloyd followed in the footsteps of his expansionist predecessors, his regional perspective and imperial focus would eventually differentiate his vision of the West from theirs. Like them, he was considered both a patriot and an imperialist. But, while he too could be found, from time to time, dreaming of a future in which Canada would eventually become the "centre of the British Empire,"[7] his efforts were concentrated more singularly on promoting and defending the creation of an ideal society within the British prairie Promised Land. Moreover, although in his own way an expansionist and a prairie booster, Lloyd was rarely given to promoting fanciful and exaggerated descriptions of the West as a land of milk and honey; his promised land had its roots in the nature of the population, not the soil, in the pure stock of nations, not hybrid grains. The support he received demonstrated that he was not alone in his dedication to keeping the West British.

Considering the zeal with which he would promote all things British, it is unfortunate that little is known about Lloyd's formative years in England. He was born in Bethnal Green on January 6, 1861, to Anne and William Lloyd. His mother died when he was young, and it was left to his father, a teacher and teetotaller, to instruct and shape the young man's mind and morals. In his teens, George enrolled in St. John's College in London, and enlisted with a volunteer regiment, the West Middlesex Rifles. Despite a promotion to sergeant in 1880, he temporarily abandoned his military career after meeting the bishop of Rupert's Land, who was visiting England to promote Canadian missionary work. Inspired, the young man decided to set sail for the New World to do God's work.

Arriving in Canada on Good Friday, 1881, Lloyd spent his first year teaching and providing church services under less than ideal circumstances near Maynooth, Ontario. In 1882, he decided to complete his divinity training at Wycliffe College in Toronto before enlisting again, this time with the Queen's Own Rifles militia unit. When the Northwest Rebellion broke out in 1885, Lloyd was one of many who travelled patriotically west to defend British authority, law, and order. During the battle of Cut Knife Hill, while attempting to protect comrades trapped under heavy fire, Lloyd was shot in the back and seriously wounded. His recovery would be both slow and painful.

Ordained as an Anglican priest in 1887, Lloyd spent the next decade serving in a variety of positions in Canada, the United States, and Jamaica before returning to England in 1900 to become deputation secretary for the Colonial and Continental Church Society (C.C.C.S.). Centred in London, this evangelical society was dedicated to providing for the spiritual welfare of British emigrants. Armed with his own immigrant experience, Lloyd was hired to promote missionary work in Canada. He addressed more than seven hundred meetings on the topic of the "Expansion of Canada," and his popular speaking style generated enough interest that it inspired him to publish a letter in the London *Times* exhorting "British blood to settle upon these fine farming lands."[8] Reprinted in a number of newspapers, it not only captured the imagination of the general public but also impressed Reverend Isaac Barr, a Canadian clergyman who was independently devising his own scheme to bring a group of British settlers to the Canadian prairies.

Lloyd's role in helping convince twenty-five hundred emigrants to set out for western Canada, his replacement of Barr as their leader en route, and his efforts at piloting the moral conduct of their newly established community that became known as the Barr Colony have become the stuff of prairie legend. Amongst the colonists, his attempts to restrict their interaction with non-British settlers and to ban liquor received mixed reviews. Loved by many, reviled by others, Lloyd's strong personality was aptly summed up by one colonist who recalled that: "we liked Lloyd very, very much, but he was a dictator with very strong ideas. He was under the impression that progress was entirely with his Church. He was above Barr, you understand, he was a representative of God."[9] Outside the colony, perceptions of Lloyd as a divine agent were less ambivalent. Labelling Lloyd the colony's Joshua, one clerical contemporary praised him as the most "outstanding missionary" in the employ of the C.C.C.S.[10] Exaggerated or not, Lloyd's reputation attracted the attention of those guiding Anglican work in the Saskatchewan diocese.

The Anglican Church, although a leader in missionary work among the First Nations of Canada at the turn of the century, had not proven to be as well prepared as its rival denominations to minister to the country's immigrant settlers. As a result, it had by that time seen its comparative number of adherents slip to fourth behind the Catholics, Methodists, and Presbyterians. In 1905, the bishop of Saskatchewan asked Lloyd as the new archdeacon of Prince Albert and general superintendent of all white missions in the diocese of Saskatchewan to help address this deficiency. Lloyd quickly set to work. Believing that it was "by looking after the ten today" that the church would "gain possession of the field by and by,"[11] he travelled to Britain in 1906 to successfully recruit fifty-six catechists, known in lore as "the Sixty of Saskatchewan."[12] In addition to pursuing divinity studies at Prince Albert's Emmanuel College, these young men were expected to spend two thirds of the year preaching in remote areas of the province to Britons and foreigners. Their arrival contributed to Lloyd's growing reputation as one of the "master builders" of empire and church.[13]

"Keep Canada British and Christian" was the motto that guided Lloyd throughout his career. Achieving the successful Anglicization and Anglicanization of the Canadian West required that the number of British settlers remained proportionately large. While he recognized that there was a difference between Englishmen "of grit, tone, force and bulldog stick-at-it-ness" and those "toast and butter, warm slipper, return to Liverpool with a weary smile men,"[14] Lloyd considered even second-rate settlers from the Isles as preferable to most others. They at least were representatives of a great race and a model empire. Their very presence, he maintained, ensured the moral, religious, and social standards of the developing West. At the turn of the century, these standards, in Lloyd's estimation, were in danger of being diluted by the arrival of large numbers of non-British settlers.

Lloyd, like many other Canadians during that period, believed implicitly in a moral and intellectual hierarchy of nations. At the top stood Great Britain, followed by western and northern European nations; at the bottom were the countries of central, eastern, and southern Europe, along with those of Asia and Africa. In western Canada, however, the newcomers that caused the most consternation for Lloyd were the immigrants from central and eastern Europe – the "Continentals,"[15] not because they were at the bottom of his list but because they made up the largest percentage of non-British immigrants. While acknowledging that these "stalwart peasants in sheepskin coats" might make reasonable farmers, Lloyd argued that their value had to be weighed against other, more meaningful, criteria. For example, he viewed such immigrants as "illiterate" and "uneducated," and therefore morally and intellectually inferior. Thus, while he willingly conceded on one occasion that the Doukhobors in their first year in western Canada were more productive than their English counterparts, he contended that the gap closed by the second year and that "by three or four years the Doukhobor is nowhere in comparison, so far as his general usefulness as a citizen goes."[16] Lloyd's definition of "usefulness" was selective. It can be gleaned from a comparison he made between Englishmen and another non-preferred group, the Galicians. If all Canada wanted was hog-raisers and cow-punchers, he argued, then the Galician might indeed prove preferable. But if "citizenship is measured by a clean, law-abiding, respectable, Church-going community, with some culture and a larger outlook upon life," as he contended it should be judged, "then these Englishmen have it by a very long way."[17]

While Lloyd could be dismissive of non-British immigrants, he did believe that they were capable of being assimilated so long as the numbers that arrived remained relatively manageable.[18] During a canoe trip down the North Saskatchewan River in 1914 to take stock of how the Anglican church was faring, Lloyd praised members of a Buchavarian community as "clean, wholesome and anxious to be polite."[19] They appeared "eager to learn English and anxious never to return to their country."[20] Groups like this, with the proper tutelage, he believed, had the potential to become, if not ideal Canadians, at least dependable citizens. Lloyd proposed that the best way to "mould these foreigners" was to bring into the West, as quickly as possible, a large number of "really Christian teachers" from the British Isles, and to "let them do what they can by individual conversation until the law provides for something more in the schools themselves."[21] When his attempts to win support for his idea from the C.C.C.S. failed, he went back to Britain to pursue it on his own initiative. Soon thereafter, the Fellowship of the Maple Leaf (F.M.L.) was born.

Five hundred teachers travelled to the West under the aegis of the F.M.L. between 1916 and 1928 to aid Lloyd in his fight to "Keep Canada British." Referring to one settlement served by an F.M.L. teacher, Lloyd said: "fifty mles [*sic*] from anywhere, very few visitors, no church nearby, twenty-eight children, eight Germans, seven Austrians, five Servians [*sic*], five Scandinavians, three English. Could they all speak English? They can now. They all stood up and repeated a Psalm and sang a hymn from memory and then answered all kinds of questions – flag – homes – religion."[22] Such successes did not go unnoticed by Lloyd's former diocese. Although not living in Canada at the time, in 1921 George Exton Lloyd was elected bishop of Saskatchewan.

Older, more experienced, and wielding greater authority, Lloyd returned to Canada determined to help create and train a "New Nation" made up predominantly of British Christian subjects.[23] To realize his new mission, Lloyd worked to expand his catechist and teacher schemes while at the same time rigorously campaigning to restrict further foreign immigration. To that end, he advocated completely suspending continental immigration for a period of ten years to allow the Canadian government the opportunity to increase the proportionate number of British settlers while properly educating those foreigners that were already there.[24]

Lloyd's advice went unheeded by the government and largely unheralded by the public. It is easy to understand why. The number of immigrants arriving during the early twenties was relatively small. In fact, the numbers were so modest that the two major railway companies, the Canadian Pacific Railway (CPR) and the Canadian National Railway (CNR), complained to the government that more immigrants were needed to bolster the western Canadian economy. The railway companies, of course, recognized the benefits increased immigration would bring to them. New farmers would travel by rail, transport their goods by rail, likely settle on railway land, and provide a market for eastern Canadian goods. With the number of British immigrants to the West dwindling – despite the best efforts of Canada's immigration officials – the companies' successful appeals motivated the government to initiate a gradual softening of the restrictions imposed on continental immigration.

Such action only intensified Lloyd's efforts – and rhetoric – to stop immigration from continental European countries. On his 1923 annual confirmation tour, he warned that the numbers of non-English speaking immigrants were rising, and expressed his fear that "ultimately Canadians will not hold their own."[25] At the 1924 Diocesan Synod, he further cautioned that if "we have the land filled with little Asias and little Russias and little Balkans, it is going to make our Church work ten times harder, and in many cases impossible."[26] In 1925, Lloyd's worst fears were realized. Responding to mounting pressures from the CPR and CNR, the federal government passed the Railways Agreement that allowed the railways to recruit agricultural labourers directly from eastern and central Europe.

Lloyd could not ignore the serious threat the Railways Agreement posed to his prairie Promised Land. While living in Canada between 1902 and 1914, he had already, at different times and with varied vigour, challenged Canada's immigration policies. But though passionate, he was above all practical; his fears were always magnified more by relative percentages and disturbing trends that threatened British predominance than by absolute numbers. As early as 1902, when numbers from both the United States and "other" countries outstripped the number of immigrants arriving from the United Kingdom, Lloyd had begun calling on Britons to fill the vast tracts of empty land. If they did not, he warned, Canada within five years would be overflowing with "Americans and foreigners."[27] Conversely, despite the fact that the annual numbers for both groups were approximately double that of 1902, Lloyd's attitude towards immigration trends in 1906 had been more tempered, largely because of the corresponding meteoric rise of British immigration. He even went so far as to applaud the government and its minister of the interior, Frank Oliver, for "concentrat[ing] all his efforts to bring in English-speaking and Scandinavian immigrants."[28] In 1909 and 1910, when the number of American immigrants once again surpassed those from the United Kingdom, Lloyd wrote a letter to the archbishop of Rupert's Land and the House of Bishops, warning that the heart of the nation, between Lake Superior and the Rocky Mountains, was becoming "predominantly American." He hoped the church would react to counter this trend, which he insinuated would negatively affect the "motives, the characteristics, and the religious tone" of the region.[29]

This threat was soon replaced by the more dangerous rise of continental European immigration. Between 1911 and 1914, the number of arrivals from Britain increased only marginally, the number from America actually decreased, while that from "other" countries more than doubled.[30] In 1913, Lloyd tried to take a concrete step towards altering this flow when he unsuccessfully presented a motion at the provincial synod to cap foreign immigration "to at least such proportions as can be easily assimilated into the body of the nation without lowering the general tone of the Canadian language, law, character, and religious life."[31] In sum, Lloyd had tried a number of times, often through the church, to bring to the attention of Canadians and the Canadian government the threat the non-British immigrant posed to the West.

Given Lloyd's earlier actions, it was no wonder he would end up leading the attack against the Railways Agreement. At no other point during the twentieth century was the threat to his ideal so obvious. Statistics published in the 1926 *Regina Leader* that listed the number of immigrants who arrived in Canada between January and September clearly indicated the danger – 16,776 from the United States, 54,640 from "other countries" compared to only 41,419 from the British Isles.[32] In Lloyd's opinion, the federal government had sold out to two railway corporations more concerned with profit than with issues of nationhood, with cheap labour than with British blood.

This time, others agreed. When Reverend Sweeney, Bishop of Toronto, innocently proposed at the 1927 General Synod that Anglican ministers officially congratulate the Canadian government on its immigration policy, he did not foresee the antagonistic response his suggestion would engender. Many ministers, using "as strong language as it was possible for clergy to use in public,"[33] censored Reverend Sweeney and denounced the government's policy as threatening the British makeup of the country. Prominent among those who expressed concern were ministers from Lloyd's own diocese of Saskatchewan. Together the dissenters succeeded in having a motion passed calling for a quota on non-British immigration.[34]

The Anglican resolution lent authority, and public credibility, to Lloyd's campaign against Canada's immigration policies. Canadians, one editor from the *Western Producer* noted, found in the Anglican debate "the crystallization of complaints and rumours that have been current in some circles in Canada for a long time."[35] *The Sentinel*, the Orange Order's newspaper, argued that the debate "awakened" the general populace to the claims they had been making for some time, with less success.[36] Even the Ku Klux Klan, a rising force in Saskatchewan in the late 1920s, suggested that "when the stalwarts of the Anglican Synod cast the bomb into the Immigration Department ... denials excuses and contradictions were poured into the press" and "a special committee was appointed by the House to investigate the charges."[37] When the Report of the Select Committee on Agriculture and Colonization, submitted in June 1928, failed to address the major concerns outlined by the Anglican synod, Lloyd set out on a personal campaign to incite the public to action.

In July, Lloyd spoke before the Grand Orange Lodge of British America on the subject of "The Building of the Nation." Keeping the views of his audience in mind, Lloyd began by decrying the nefarious Catholic alliance of French and foreigner, a theme he would repeat over the next few years when it benefited his cause. Once his audience had been aroused, he then focused on what he considered to be the major threat to "building the nation" – the railway interests and the immigration officials. The presidents of the CPR and the CNR, Edward Beatty and Henry Thornton, he maintained, were responsible for knowingly "prostituting" the blood of the Canadian nation. To make matters worse, they were also filling the cities with "Continentals who will sleep 20 on the floor in a room," and who would eventually force the Canadian worker, who was not used to living under such conditions, out of the workforce.[38] He had numbers to prove his point. Since the agreement began, 2,098 settlers had been brought to Winnipeg under the direction of the CNR. Of these, 1,785 were foreigners, while only 300 were British. The CPR was equally culpable; during three weeks in early April, it brought in 1,680 "aliens" to 170 British settlers.[39] In an earlier speech he had made that spring, Lloyd had clearly identified those he held ultimately accountable for these trends. "I do not blame Sir H. Thornton or Dr. Black," the European manager of the CNR's department of colonization and development, Lloyd argued, "their business is to make the railway pay. But I do blame the [prime minister] and the minister of immigration for selling this nation's blood, character and future to make a railway dividend."[40] Now speaking before the Order, Lloyd warned Prime Minister William Lyon Mackenzie King that if he did not have "the courage to withdraw this Iniquitous Order in Council" then the general public would make it clear to the prime minister and the railway officials that they "exercise this ill-gotten franchise in opposition to the will of the people of this country."[41] He ended his passionate speech with twelve resolutions aimed at solving Canada's immigration problem, none of which were novel or complex. Together, however, they provided a detailed, coherent blueprint for Lloyd's vigorous campaign aimed at ending the Railways Agreement, dramatically reducing immigration from "unpreferred" countries, and bolstering British immigration.

Seventy thousand! – that was the number of letters of protest that the Fellowship of the Maple Leaf estimated Lloyd sent out during the summer of 1928 to promote his cause.[42] Published in newspapers across the country, they included copies of his nation-building speech, articles on immigration, open letters to government and railway officials, and individual responses to supporters and detractors. While the general message of these letters was always the same – increase British while restricting continental immigration – the language of each one varied. Few could ignore headlines like the one that blared: "British Australia, Mongrel Canada." In the article, Lloyd reminded his readers of the dangers facing the country when too many different races were mixed.[43] When chastised for using the term "mongrel," he replied that he did not intend to target any particular ethnic group but rather to show "what this nation will become if the 'melting pot,' 'open door' policy continued. It will be a 'Mongrel' Canada in comparison with a 'British New Zealand.'" Likening Canada to a bulldog, he argued that the influx of foreigners would eventually result in a mixed breed:

> Fifty per cent is going to be bull dog. The two hind legs will be French poodle. One fore leg will be Austrian wolf hound and the other leg is sure to be German, for they are coming in by thousands. The tail will be Ukrainian, as that uses up 100% of the population, the poor Canadian dog will have no inside. As the British Tommy in the trenches would say, "nice dawg that, he ain't got no guts."[44]

If Lloyd's "Mongrel" article created a stir, it was nothing compared to the reaction generated by an inflammatory letter he wrote that summer warning Winnipeg clergymen of the problems Canada would face if the current flood of un-preferred, "dirty, ignorant, garlic-smelling Continentals" continued.[45] Soon after the letter appeared in the newspapers, the press was swamped with responses from individuals and organizations denouncing Lloyd's harsh language. Their feelings were summed up by one "dirty continental," who suggested that "it ill becomes a church dignitary to expose his ignorant venom, hatred, prejudice and bigotry."[46]

To the dismay of his detractors, Lloyd, church dignitary and "Canadian patriot,"[47] was widely accepted as a credible authority. Even many of those who disagreed with the language he used supported his message. Writing to the Saskatoon *Star Phoenix*, John C. Mortimer summed up these commonly shared attitudes when he said:

> It is not suggested that the man on the street is opposed to Dr. Lloyd in the mere matter of immigration. As far as that goes, thousands of average men are undoubtedly sympathetic. It may even be that the Bishop speaks for the majority. But that, for the present, is not the point. The point is this: that even those who agree with the Bishop regarding immigration are more or less conscious of the fact that his lardship's [*sic*?] attitude and language are not the attitude and language that would be adopted by Christ.[48]

Even the *Star Phoenix*, which attacked Lloyd on a number of occasions, agreed to publish his articles and letters, because the "Right Rev. George Exton Lloyd, as bishop of Saskatchewan, holds a position of great prominence in the life of this province," and because he has "strong views on the immigration question which others may share."[49]

Its letterbox justified their decision. From the middle of May to the middle of September 1928, 203 letters were published in the Saskatoon periodical, of which approximately 83 dealt in some form or fashion with immigration. Of these, ten were by Lloyd, nineteen by his supporters, and twenty by his opponents. In other words, more than one third of all the letters focused on immigration, and almost one quarter of the total number of letters printed were either written by, or alluded to, Lloyd.

Not every newspaper opposed to Lloyd was as magnanimous as the *Star Phoenix*. The editor of the *Prince Albert Herald*, whose dislike of the bishop was unparalleled, gleefully censured Lloyd's submissions. When the editor continued, however, to print letters and editorials that disparaged the Saskatchewan bishop, public pressure, critical of the imbalance, forced him to desist.[50] At the other extreme were newspapers like the *Unity Courier* and the *North Battleford Optimist*, which published glowing reports of Lloyd's contribution to the West. They noted Lloyd's heroic actions in 1885, and maintained that his current campaign was simply a more recent example of the bishop's strength and courage.[51] Not surprisingly, the Orange Order's newspaper, *The Sentinel*, alluded to Lloyd's courage and patriotism: "Bishop Lloyd is a remarkable man. That has been known widely for a long time, but the fight he is putting up at the present time is for a man of his age proof of courage and determination such as few men possess, or would be able to carry out."[52] Similarly, a number of British-based organizations came to Lloyd's defence, including the Canadian Legion, the Empire Club, the Canadian Club, the Sons of England, the Ladies Imperial Club, as well as rotary clubs and various local, provincial, and national chapters of the Orange Order, and the Imperial Order Daughters of the Empire (I.O.D.E.).

Buoyed by such support, Lloyd was determined to co-ordinate these various patriotic organizations into "a single force devoted to retaining in Canada the supremacy of British language, law, traditions, blood characteristics … and loyalty to the crown as the king pin of Empire."[53] From this idea, the National Association of Canada (N.A.C.) was born in 1927. Little is known about the N.A.C. or its membership. While Lloyd authored letters and gave numerous speeches under its auspices, few other members identified themselves by name. This lack of available data makes it difficult to draw conclusions about the association's influence on public opinion. The organization, did, however, clearly influence the immigration debate. Between April 1928 and early 1929, dozens of letters were sent by members of the N.A.C. to the federal authorities questioning and challenging the government's immigration policies.[54] Rather than signing their names, they used their organizational titles as identification: master, chaplain, secretary, or member of council. In September, the N.A.C. sponsored a meeting in Saskatoon at which Lloyd spoke on the topic of immigration. Over three hundred attended. Lloyd followed this meeting up with a tour of small towns throughout the province, where he was well received. The editor of the *Unity Courier*, describing one of these stops, noted that "the fact that Chautaqua was in full swing" did not stop a large group from listening to Lloyd speak on immigration. The editor further informed his readers that Lloyd, "[o]n his return to Prince Albert … will send your editor particulars and membership cards of this Association. We shall then seek to gain as many members as we possibly can get to help in reaching the ideals of the National Association."[55] It must be assumed, with this pattern repeated across Saskatchewan, that the association's ranks increased during many of these stops. This fact could not have been lost on the federal government, particularly when even prominent westerners, like Grande Prairie MP D. M. Kennedy, felt compelled to write the government to ask whether the N.A.C.'s claims against the government were true.[56]

Whether or not the federal government feared the influence of Lloyd and his association, it was clear that many non-British immigrants were concerned about the impact the bishop and his organization were having. Christian Smith, the leader of the Netherlands's Colonization Board, summed up the fears shared by many Canadians of foreign extraction when he wrote:

> Reading of Bishop Lloyd's latest attempts to upset Canadian unity, I am tempted to exclaim, as did an English King, "will no one rid me of this insolent priest?." … In conclusion, I would say that I consider Bishop Lloyd a menace to the public peace and I think it is a pity he was ever let into this country. However, the bishop is sowing his seed and as he sows he will probably reap.[57]

Reverend P. Oleksiew, administrator of the Ukrainian Greek-Catholic diocese in Canada, prayed that Lloyd might stop "creating unnecessary hatred between the Ukrainians and English speaking population," while Reverend S. W. Savchuk, head of the consistory of the Ukrainian Orthodox Church and pastor of the cathedral in Winnipeg, questioned why Lloyd – who he contended had a good reputation amongst the Ukrainian settlers in his diocese – would try to turn people against them.[58]

German, French, and Jewish associations and newspapers were equally critical of the Saskatchewan bishop and his message.[59]

The most publicized attack against Lloyd came at the hands of Canada's first Ukrainian MP, Michael Luchkovich, when he rose to speak in the House of Commons in May 1929. He judged it

> … a crime against Christianity, against civilization and against Canadian unity when a bishop, who should be following in the footsteps of the Prince of Peace and preaching the gospel of eternal love and the brotherhood of man, can see nothing better in Central Europeans than a class of dirty, ignorant, garlic-smelling, unpreferred continentals.[60]

Angrily challenging the "false apostle of the Prince of Peace," Luchkovich contended that the Saskatchewan bishop and the National Association were behind the "frame-up against the central European."[61] Waging war on Lloyd's terms, Luchkovich subsequently sent 4,000 copies of this speech to interested individuals across the country.

Lloyd was unfazed by the personal attacks. Reading Luchkovich's speech, he was reported to have said with a smile "the more of this the better."[62] Perhaps, as one letter writer suggested, there was method to Lloyd's intemperate language:

> Bishop Lloyd, I firmly believe, has no intention in the world of inflaming public opinion against any race, religion or individual now resident in Canada. I am sure he must be very much amused at some of the criticism hurled at his head. But he realizes that national problems are constantly being made the football of politicians of both parties and that united public opinion can rouse the government to action. The bishop, I believe, has deliberately provoked criticism in order that the matter be brought to a focal point in the mind of every thinking Canadian.[63]

A major concern shared by Luchkovich and Lloyd's other opponents was the fact that the Anglican bishop spoke not only as an individual, but also on behalf of the church. One contributor to the *Manitoba Free Press* wrote: "I would suggest that if the reverend gentleman wishes to imply that any particular race will prostitute the blood of this nation, he take off his frock before he speaks, then there would be no misunderstanding as to whether it is the church speaking through its bishop, or just plain George Exton Lloyd giving us his quaint, if unflattering, views."[64]

In August 1928, the Church of England issued a stern warning to Bishop Lloyd, threatening to take action if he continued his vituperative attacks against the foreigner.[65] Although Lloyd's opponents could take some satisfaction from the verbal spanking meted out by the English church, they were disappointed that its Canadian counterpart did not follow its lead. Canon Vernon, the general secretary of the council of social service of the church in Canada, made it clear that "Bishop Lloyd's views are definitely not those of the Church of England in Canada,"[66] but neither Vernon nor any other prominent members of the cloth made much of an attempt to silence him. Indeed, many prominent Anglican figures, particularly in the West, vocally supported Lloyd's stance. Even those who publicly opposed him often betrayed their own nativist sentiments. Bishop Gray of Edmonton, portrayed by some newspapers as the voice of reason, expressed his concern that the West was threatening to become a "tower of babel."[67] Similarly, Canon Nelson Smith of Minnedosa, although objecting to Lloyd's "abusive language," believed that it was "an outrage that this British country should be overwhelmed with undesirable settlers" and agreed that "any united effort to convince the government that the western provinces are finding the immigration policy of the last few years intolerable is worthy of support."[68]

The attitude of the other churches towards Lloyd remains largely a mystery. Most religious leaders did not challenge him, at least publicly. A report by a United Church committee, selected to study the position of non-Anglo-Saxons (1930–31) in the West, indicated how some members of the United Church felt towards Lloyd. One question asked members of the church community: "Is the attitude of the Anglican Church towards these people [the foreigner], better than that of the United Church?" One of the responses the committee printed was a not-so-subtle stab at Bishop Lloyd's description of the continental European: "The answer is 'No,' and such phrases as 'garlic smelling continentals' would never be used by United Churchmen."[69] Still, the United Church, which had more known members in the Ku Klux Klan than any other denomination, was hardly one to throw stones.[70]

By the end of 1928, growing unemployment, combined with rising nativist fears, ensured that Canadians were becoming increasingly vocal in their opposition towards Canada's immigration policy. Led by Lloyd, the pressure they exerted on the government forced it to initiate change. The first move was taken in December 1928, when the immigration department made public its new plan to attract more British immigrants to the country by reducing passage fares from the British Isles and improving medical inspection facilities.[71] Then, acknowledging the "very strong feeling against the unduly large proportion of foreign, as compared with British immigrants" entering the country, the deputy minister of immigration, W. J. Egan, issued a public statement in January of 1929 promising that "[o]nly thirty per cent of the number of agricultural labourers from non-preferred countries, who came to this Dominion during 1928 will be allowed to enter Canada during 1929."[72]

Lloyd praised the minister of immigration for the government's new immigration initiatives. And when the CPR and the CNR challenged the government's decision to curtail foreign immigration, the ever-alert bishop was quick to respond. In an open letter addressed to Mackenzie King, Lloyd reminded the prime minister:

> The railways have dominated Canada to such an extent that the Department of Immigration cannot stand by its decision unless they are strongly supported by public opinion. I believe that opinion has been steadily forming in the Dominion during the year 1928 and is now ready to support the Department on the two steps they have taken recently (1) to open the ways from the British Isles and (2) to curtail the irrational privileges granted to the railway companies commonly known as 'the railway agreement.'[73]

Lloyd need not have worried. Instead of giving in to railway pressure as it had done in 1925, the government reduced the railway quota by another 25 per cent in the fall of 1929, and, in October 1930, cancelled the Railways Agreement altogether. The bishop's campaign had been successful – a point that was not lost on supporters and detractors alike. Soon after the government's decision to increase British immigration in 1928 was publicized, the *Regina Morning Leader* found it noteworthy that the federal government had "received the indorsation [*sic*] of Bishop Lloyd, who, to date, has been one of the most vigorous critics of the Canadian immigration policy."[74] Other newspapers, including the *Manitoba Free Press*, the *Toronto Daily Star*, and the *Star Phoenix*, also acknowledged Lloyd's role,[75] while the *Winnipeg Tribune* went so far as to refer to the new government policies as "approximating the quota system that Bishop Lloyd of Saskatchewan, the Canadian Legion and other individuals and organizations have been advocating."[76] A writer to the *Western Jewish News*, and an opponent of Lloyd's anti-immigrant campaign, ruefully summed up his impact:

> The Bishop of Saskatchewan has left his footprints, not only through the West where the mark takes the form of bitter animosity and race-resentment, but also in the sands of policy in the Department of Immigration. His influence has carried weight, and we now see that the innovations and changes of immigration policy, if they do not exactly follow the pattern of Bishop Lloyd's recommendations, are at least noticeably colored by them.[77]

Lloyd's heavy trodding left him exhausted. In early 1929 he attempted to turn his sights on the premier of Saskatchewan, James Gardiner, and his "pro-Catholic" and "pro-immigrant" provincial Liberal government. Lloyd's promise in March of 1929 to publicly campaign against Gardiner in the upcoming provincial election must have concerned the premier,[78] who was aware of the bishop's persuasive abilities. Just as he had monitored the Ku Klux Klan and the danger it posed to his government, Gardiner had kept a similarly wary eye trained on the bishop. The thick files of newspaper articles he collected on both were testament to his fears.[79] But while the Klan was able to lend itself vigorously to supporting Gardiner's opponents during the election campaign of 1929, Lloyd was never able to personally fulfill his promise. In April of the same year, suffering from complications of his old war wound, the bishop was forced to leave the country to recuperate, returning only in time to deliver one parting shot at the Liberal regime before its election defeat in June.[80]

Gardiner's loss, followed in 1930 by the cancellation of the Railways Agreement and the fall of the federal Liberal government, gave Lloyd the satisfaction of knowing that the enemies he had identified as threats to his ideal were no longer in positions of authority. His contribution to their downfall was interpreted by the Orange *Sentinel:*

> [I]t is high time that some concerted action be taken to publicly acknowledge the great work done by the Bishop of Saskatchewan to focus the attention of the people on the great issue at stake and the dangerous position into which this country was drifting. Above all party considerations Bishop Lloyd has been the means of welding public opinion on the side of the maintenance of British ideals and British institutions in this country.[81]

Lloyd and his supporters had reason to congratulate themselves. The abolition of the Railways Agreement, combined with increasing restrictions placed on Canada's immigration policies as a result of the depression, meant that Lloyd's prairie Promised Land, though increasingly dusty and wan, faced no further threat to its British stock and standards during the thirties. For those who, like Lloyd, believed that the ideal West would be revealed in the nature of its populace, not the fertility of its soil, this must have given them some comfort during a lean decade that forced many to go without either "milk or honey."

In 1931, at the urgings of his doctor, Lloyd left the demanding life of a diocesan bishop and retreated to warmer climes on Vancouver Island, British Columbia. Although retired, he remained vigilant. When CPR president Edward Beatty suggested in a speech that Canada try to implement "controlled immigration," Lloyd fired off a letter to Beatty warning him that any attempt to revive the Railways Agreement would meet with stiff opposition.[82] Even in his seventies and far from the main battlefield in the Prairie West, Lloyd was still prepared to lead the troops. But his age and his deteriorating health finally caught up to him. On December 8, 1940, less than a month away from his eightieth birthday, Lloyd passed away. His battle to bring about a British populated Promised Land on the prairies had ended.

The prairie Promised Land Lloyd tried to maintain was an exclusive club. Reserved for the well-bred of British stock, it reluctantly opened its doors to small numbers of others, so long as they tended willingly to its gardens, conformed to its standards, and assimilated to its values. Dedicated members of the club were many, but it was Lloyd in his dual role as club promoter and gatekeeper who rallied its constituents in support of various plans and schemes aimed at furthering the ideal. Buttressed by his reputation and his influential position, and armed with a tireless determination, he successfully stirred many western Canadians to support his cause.

NOTES

1 Anglican Church General Synod Archives (ACGSA), Lloyd (George Exton) Papers, Periodicals and Clippings, *Toronto Telegram*, August 29, 1928.

2 *Canadian Churchman*, July 2, 1925.

3 *Canadian Churchman*, July 2, 1925.

4 Lloyd's "plan for Canada" was captured by an editor of the *Lloydminster Times* after hearing the Bishop speak. *Lloydminster Times*, October 18, 1928.

5 ACGSA, Lloyd, Barr Colony Celebrations, Lloyd to Hall, October 12, 1938.

6 Doug Owram, *The Promise of Eden: The Canadian Expansionist Movement and the Idea of the West 1856–1900* (Toronto: University of Toronto Press, 1980), 125–26.

7 Saskatoon *Star Phoenix*, January 30, 1920.

8 Bruce Peel Special Collections Library (BPSC), Lyle Files, Vol. 59, George Exton Lloyd to unknown, February 1, 1904, and Barr Colony Heritage Centre, Lloydminster File, Lloyd, G. E. *The Canadian Wheat Belt*, September 22, 1902.

9 Helen Evans Reid, *All Silent, All Damned: The Search for Isaac Barr* (Toronto: Ryerson Press, 1969), 107.

10 Reverend Norman Tucker, *From Sea to Sea: The Dominion* (Toronto: Prayer and Study Union of the M.S.C.C., 1911), 46.

11 *New Era* 4, no. 12, December 1906.

12 BPSC, Lyle Files, Vol. 57, Lloyd, G. E., "White Settlers in Canada," *The Churches Missions in Christendom: Official Report of the Pan-Anglican Congress*, Vol. VI, 1908, 5.

13 *New Era* 5, no. 10, October 1907.

14 Quoted in Lynne Bowen, *Muddling Through: The Remarkable Story of the Barr Colonists* (Vancouver: Douglas & McIntyre, 1992), 125.

15 Those immigrants arriving from a list of countries that included Russia, Czechoslovakia, Austria, Lithuania, Hungary, Romania, Poland, Yugoslavia, and the Ukraine.

16 BPSC, Lyle Files, Newspapers and Periodicals Vol. 40, *Edmonton Bulletin*, July 30, 1906.

17 *Canadian Churchman*, August 13, 1914.

18 Indeed, comparing Lloyd's various public attacks over the years with annual foreign immigration statistics, reveals that he was inspired to action more by relative percentages (in 1902, 1909, and 1913) and disturbing trends that threatened British predominance than by absolute numbers. Thus, for example, he publicly criticized the arrival in Canada of large numbers of Americans and "foreigners" in 1902. Conversely, despite the fact that the annual numbers for both groups were approximately double in 1906, Lloyd's attitude towards immigration trends in 1906 was actually positive, largely because of the corresponding meteoric rise of British immigration.

19 *Canadian Churchman*, July 30, 1914.

20 Ibid., July 23, 1914.

21 Ibid., July 23, 1914, and August 6, 1914.

22 *Saskatchewan Synod Journal*, June 18, 1921.

23 Ibid., 1923.

24 *Saskatoon Star*, October 18, 1922.

25 *Prince Albert Herald*, October 13, 1923.

26 *Saskatchewan Synod Journal*, June 1924.

27 Barr Colony Archives (BCHCC), Lloydminster File, "The Canadian Wheat Belt." September 23, 1902. In 1902, the numbers were United Kingdom 17,259, United States 26, 388 and "Other" Countries 23,732. In contrast, the British had made up more than 50 per cent of all arrivals in 1897. Canada Dominion Bureau of Statistics, *The Canada Year Book*, 1927–28 (Ottawa: F. A. Acland, 1928), 190.

28 *New Era* 4, no. 12, December 1906. Lloyd was pleased to report that in October of that year the number of British immigrants had increased by 21,000, while the

number of "foreigners" had only gone up by 7,000. The total numbers for 1906 were 86,796 from the United Kingdom, 57,796 from the United States and 44,472 from "Other." *Canada Year Book*, 190.

29 ACGSA, Lloyd, G. E. "The New Nation: A letter addressed to His Grace the Archbishop of Rupertsland and to their Lordships the Members of the House of Bishops" (Prince Albert, Saskatchewan, 1909). In 1908 the numbers from the United Kingdom were 120,182, from the United States 58,312, and from "Other" 83,975. In 1909 and 1910, the disturbing American trend, as opposed to the dramatic drop in British immigration, was obvious: **1909:** 52,901, 59,832, 34,175; **1910:** 59,790, 103,798 and 45,206. *Canada Year Book*, 190.

30 The numbers were: United Kingdom, 123,013 to 142,622; the United States, 121,451 to 107,530; and "Other," 66,620 to 134,726. *Canada Year Book*, 190.

31 *Saskatchewan Synod Journal*, 1913. In the 1911 fiscal year, 123,013 immigrants arrived from the United Kingdom, 121,451 from the United States and 66,620 from "other countries." In 1914 these numbers were 142,622, 107,530 and 134,726. W. G. Smith, *A Study in Canadian Immigration* (Toronto: Ryerson Press, 1920), 14.

32 During that year the number of immigrants were: United Kingdom, 49,784; United States, 21,025; "Other," 73,182. *Canada Year Book*, 190.

33 *Sentinel*, September 29, 1927.

34 The quota was to "limit the number of certain classes of foreign-born immigrants admitted during any year to not more than 50 per cent of the British born admitted during the previous year." Ibid.

35 *Western Producer*, September 29, 1927.

36 *Sentinel*, November 17, 1927.

37 Ibid.

38 ACGSA, Lloyd, G. E., *The Building of the Nation, Natural Increase and Immigration: a paper read before the Grand Orange Lodge of British America at Edmonton Alberta, July 26, 1928* (Toronto: Ontario Press, 1928), 7, 8, 18.

39 *Western Producer*, May 3, 1928.

40 Saskatoon *Star Phoenix*, June 30, 1928.

41 ACGSA, Lloyd, *Building the Nation*, 7.

42 John E. Lyons, "George Saskatchewan," *Vitae Scholasticae* 7 (1988): 432.

43 *Western Producer*, May 3, 1928.

44 ACGSA, Lloyd, *Building the Nation*, 5.

45 SAB, Gardiner, Newspaper, *Manitoba Free Press*, July 18, 1928.

46 Saskatoon *Star Phoenix*, July 23, 1928.

47 In the Saskatoon *Star Phoenix*, for example, one man wrote of Lloyd: "His work in Canada as a teacher, a soldier, a colonizer and a missionary in western Canada entitle him to first rank as a Canadian patriot" and consequently, these deeds "quite apart from his important position in the church of England, entitles him to a serious hearing for his views," September 22, 1928. There were many others who shared these sentiments, including J. A. Horsely (June 23, 1928), V. J. Ferguson (August 11, 1928) and S. A. Barker (August 25, 1928). See also Geo H. Lord in *Western Producer*, August 16, 1928.

48 Saskatoon *Star Phoenix*, October 13, 1928.

49 Ibid., August 15, 1928.

50 In May 1928, he referred to one of Lloyd's letters as "not only inaccurate but offensive," and in June he delivered a scathing attack when he suggested that the bishop, facing a plight similar to that experienced by Mother Goose's Humpty Dumpty, was cracking up. *Prince Albert Herald*, May 5, 1928; June 27, 1928.

51 Ibid., *The Unity Courier*, October 3, 1928. Similarly positive articles could be found in other newspapers including: *Indian Head News*, November 15, 1928; *Sintaluta Times*, May 24, 1928; *Melfort Journal*, May 29, 1928; *Banff Crag and Canyon*, August 17,

1928; *The Toronto Globe*, May 10, 1928; *Ottawa Citizen*, October 8, 1928; *Ottawa Journal*, November 16, 1928, and ACGSA, Lloyd (George Exton) Papers, Clippings and Periodicals, *Toronto Telegram*, August 29, 1928.

52 *Sentinel*, September 27, 1928.

53 ACGSA, Lloyd, *Building the Nation*, 4, 18.

54 See Library and Archives Canada (LAC), RG 76, Immigration Papers, National Association of Canada, vol. 335.

55 SAB, Gardiner, Newspaper, *Unity Courier*, November 7, 1928.

56 Ibid., D. M. Kennedy to W. J. Egan, May 28, 1928.

57 Saskatoon *Star Phoenix*, August 4, 1928.

58 SAB, Gardiner, Newspaper, *Manitoba Free Press*, July 23, 1928.

59 *Der Herold*, as quoted in, *Manitoba Free Press*, October 6, 1928; position of the Regina Catholic Association published in *Regina Daily Post*, October 1, 1928; ACGSA, Lloyd (George Exton) Papers, Clippings and Periodicals, *Le Patriote*, August 8, 1928; *Western Jewish News*, September 27, 1928; *Israelite Press* as quoted in *Toronto Globe*, July 23, 1928.

60 Quoted in the Appendix of Michael Luchkovich, *A Ukrainian Canadian in Parliament: Memoirs of Michael Luchkovich* (Toronto: Ukrainian Canadian Research Foundation, 1965), 61.

61 Ibid., 65.

62 Saskatoon *Star Phoenix*, May 31, 1929.

63 Ibid., July 7, 1928.

64 Ibid., *Manitoba Free Press*, June 26, 1928.

65 Ibid., *Regina Leader*, August 1, 1928.

66 Ibid., *Regina Daily Post*, October 3, 1928.

67 Saskatoon *Star Phoenix*, September 24, 1928.

68 *Manitoba Free Press*, July 14, 1928.

69 SAB, The Records of the United Church of Canada, Committee to Study Non-Anglo-Saxons, 1930–1931, XI.C.5.

70 William Calderwood, "The Rise and Fall of the Ku Klux Klan in Saskatchewan" (master's thesis, University of Saskatchewan, Regina Campus, 1968), 180.

71 *Regina Morning Leader*, December 21, 1928.

72 Saskatoon *Star Phoenix*, January 10, 1929.

73 LAC, King Papers, MG26 JI, Vol. 164, 139381. Open letter from Bishop Lloyd to Mackenzie King. January 31, 1929.

74 *Regina Daily Post*, December 20, 1928.

75 For example: Saskatoon *Star Phoenix*, January 11, 1929; SAB, Gardiner, Newspaper, *Manitoba Free Press*, February 5, 1929, and *Toronto Daily Star*, January 17, 1929.

76 SAB, Gardiner, Newspaper, *Winnipeg Tribune*, January 11, 1929.

77 SAB, Gardiner, Newspaper, *Western Jewish News*, January 31, 1929.

78 *Sentinel*, March 28, 1929.

79 SAB, Gardiner, Newspaper. There are 139 clippings in this file, all of which mention Lloyd.

80 Saskatoon *Star Phoenix*, June 5, 1929.

81 *Sentinel*, September 4, 1930.

82 LAC, Mackenzie King Papers, MG 26 JI, Vol. 236, Open Letter from Reverend George Exton Lloyd to Sir Edward Beatty, February 9, 1937, 203036.

14

POLICING THE PROMISED LAND: THE RCMP AND NEGATIVE NATION-BUILDING IN ALBERTA AND SASKATCHEWAN IN THE INTERWAR PERIOD

Steve Hewitt

> During the war … all foreigners received the most considerate treatment as long as they obeyed the laws of the country and pursued their ordinary avocations. The returned soldiers found them filling their jobs and enjoying prosperity. In Winnipeg, Calgary, Medicine Hat and other points, the resentment of the soldiers found expression in small disturbances provoked by the indiscreet acts and words of these people, who, as a body, have shown little appreciation of the just and fair treatment meted out to them by the people of this country. They have shown themselves ready to follow and support the extremists who play upon their ignorance and appeal to their national prejudices and sympathy for the central powers. Bolshevism finds a fertile field among them and is assiduously cultivated by the ardent agitator.
>
> The assimilation of our large alien population is of the greatest importance and it demands wise and sympathetic action and constant attention.[1]

The idea of the "Promised Land" is as old as the Bible. For many immigrants to Canada, the new provinces of Alberta and Saskatchewan appeared to offer just such a vision: plenty of cheap land and the freedom to pursue their chosen life, particularly in terms of religious practice. Only ability would determine success or failure. The reality, however, was far from the ideal. In fact, as with the biblical "Promised Land," the Prairie West was considered by many to be a land reserved for the "chosen people." This specifically consisted of those deemed to be nearest to the Anglo-Canadian norm, a category that evolved depending on external events and changing tastes. This had been true since 1896 when, under the direction of cabinet minister Clifford Sifton, the Laurier Liberals sought the rapid expansion of the West through immigration. Famous for his desire to attract the "men in sheepskin coats," Sifton also had in mind those whom he did not want: the urban proletarian, African Americans, Asians, and southern Europeans. His successor, Frank Oliver, who did not share Sifton's appreciation for immigrants from central and eastern Europe, would also seek to exclude them once he became minister of the interior in 1905.[2] Extensive efforts before 1914 were made to keep out the long list of "unwanted."[3]

World War I, and the radicalized Canada that emerged from it, made citizenship, particularly on the prairies where large immigrant communities existed, an even more pressing issue. The presence of certain groups, far from being a nuisance, seemed to threaten the Canadian state and Anglo-Canadian hegemony. This threat, as socially constructed by the state, became divided along ethnic, racial, religious, and, in the aftermath of the Russian Revolution, ideological lines.[4]

The increasingly exclusionary prairie "Promised Land" required a body to patrol its boundaries. Enter its official police force: the Royal Canadian Mounted Police (RCMP). Ironically, the quote advocating vigilantism against "foreigners" across the West, which opened this paper, came from the leader of the Mounted Police. The words of Canada's top policeman, Commissioner A. B. Perry, head of the Royal North West Mounted Police (RNWMP), did not emerge spontaneously; they appeared in the force's annual report for a period that included the end of World War I and the Winnipeg General Strike. Perry's targeting of "foreigners" is instructive, both for revealing the extent of prejudice in Canadian society but equally for providing an indication of the perceived top threat for the interwar period: his force would be in position to exclude and remove those individuals that the Anglo-Canadian elite deemed to be undesirable citizens of the "Promised Land."

The experiences of the war were crucial to this new and negative approach to nation-building. Traditionally, the war has been identified positively as a key period in Canada's development as a nation. Pierre Berton, in his book *Vimy*, popularizes the view that the conflict made Canada a country.[5] More recently, Jonathan Vance, the author of *Death So Noble*, took issue with those who have challenged this perspective: "The First World War was the catalyst that transformed Canada into a nation. It was the seminal event in the lives of countless Canadians, an experience that, perhaps for the first time, made them feel distinct from Britain. To suggest otherwise simply because it also produced discord is to employ a crude reductionism."[6]

Vance's book is more balanced in its assessment of the war than Berton's in that he recognizes the many divisions that the war engendered.[7] These included French-English divisions over participation in the war and then over conscription, and rural/regional divisions, as farmers, despite being promised that their sons would be exempt from conscription, found the exact opposite. Several thousand travelled to Ottawa in the spring of 1918 to protest the government's failure to keep its promise. Many of these farmers would be among those who cast their ballots for the Progressive Party, which, in 1921, smashed the monopoly the Liberals and Conservatives had held over Canada's political system. The country was also divided along ethnic lines – eight thousand people, including about five thousand of Ukrainian background, spent part of the war in internment camps. Tens of thousands of others were forced to register on a regular basis with the RNWMP. Finally, a general strike in Winnipeg and a series of other sympathy strikes across the nation demonstrated the strong class divisions present in Canada and the importance to the state of the mounted police.

World War I did not create these fractures in the Canadian nation. All had existed prior to the beginning of the conflict in 1914. It did, however, widen them and clearly worked against the positive nation-building vision being put forward in the wartime propaganda.[8] Furthermore, there was a perception among the Anglo-Canadian elite that these divisions represented a threat. Nowhere were these fault lines more prevalent than across the prairies, where a majority of the Ukrainians interned lived, and where urban-rural and ethnic splits over the war festered.

One response of the state was to ignore or downplay the differences. The war and its interpretation in this sense proved useful, according to Vance: "[It] came to be the answer to Canada's problems, be they social, economic, political, or racial. It was at once an object lesson, a source of inspiration, and a focus for unity; it was the magic elixir that could cure the country of any ill."[9] The Saskatchewan government made an attempt at encouraging consensus when it employed the latest technology to create: "Nation-Building in Saskatchewan: The Ukrainians." The film was designed to encourage Ukrainians to assimilate to the Anglo-Canadian ideal. It also implicitly reassured other Saskatchewanians that the provincial education system was doing its job, in the terminology of the day, by "Canadianizing" the newcomers.[10] In neighbouring Manitoba, an effort was also underway to strengthen dominant constructs of Canadian citizenship. A few months after the Winnipeg General Strike, the local business community organized the National Conference on Character Education in Relation to Canadian Citizenship. English-speaking Canada sent 1,500 delegates, including businessmen, teachers, academics, and religious leaders, to the Winnipeg conference. Among the decisions taken was to recommend the use of teachers in a direct effort to "Canadianize" immigrants and to express support for the assimilationist activities of organizations such as the Boy Scouts, Cadet Corps, YMCA, and other related groups.[11]

These measures, particularly the widespread belief in the need for newcomers to be "Canadianized," represent positive nation-building since they were directed at groups which, to use Benedict Anderson's concept, were "imagined" to still have a role to play in the Canadian nation.[12] The imagined Canadian nation at the time consisted of an Anglo-Celtic, Christian ideal that fully subscribed to the tenets of liberal democracy, the capitalist system, and Canada's entrenched position within the British Empire. This perspective was particularly strong among the Anglo-Celtic elite on the prairies, because of the perceived threat from the large ethnic population there.

Clearly, however, not everyone on the prairies was seen as representative of this ideal. What about the fate of those who did not meet these criteria? What about those whom Anglo-Canadian society viewed as not fitting into imagined notions of nation because they resisted being assimilated, were believed to be unassimilable, or were considered to be too radical to be worthy of entry? In fact, their very presence imperilled the fulfillment of the Promised Land, so they could not be ignored, members of the host society believed.

Dealing with the perceived problem was the Royal Canadian Mounted Police. Performing such a task was a fitting role since the RCMP had historically played the dual role of being a national and regional institution and symbol, particularly in Saskatchewan, where the force's training barracks and museum, and until the end of the war, the force's headquarters were located.

Although a version of the force had existed in 1873, its modern incarnation came into existence in 1920 when it officially merged with the Dominion Police, Canada's secret service, to form the RCMP. With the exception of the north, the RCMP's role in this period consisted of enforcing federal statutes in the provinces and performing other duties on behalf of the government. This shift in duties had occurred in 1917 when Alberta and Saskatchewan created their own police forces. In 1928, Saskatchewan replaced its provincial police with the Mounties, and Alberta and several other provinces did the same in 1932. Among the duties performed on behalf of the government in the 1920s was surveillance as the RCMP became Canada's intelligence agency. The force used undercover officers to spy on groups and individuals, to recruit informants, and to infiltrate suspicious organizations. It had done such work during the war, largely among ethnic minorities, but it was in 1920 that these functions were officially codified. Both the RCMP's regular policing and its intelligence work helped to preserve the exclusivity of the Promised Land on the prairies.

There was another reason why the mounted police found itself in such a leading role: its members resembled the dominant elites. At the start of the war, 79 per cent of the members of the mounted police had been born in the United Kingdom.[13] A detailed study of 797 obituaries of Mounties who served in either Alberta or Saskatchewan at some point between 1914 and 1939 found that 31 per cent were Anglo-Celtic by birth. It is safe to assume that many of the 65 per cent of the Canadian-born Mounties in the same period were of Anglo-Canadian background.[14]

Then there were the activities performed by the Anglo-Canadian RCMP. Mounted policeman monitored the activities of those who were perceived as a threat to the status quo on the prairies. At the end of the war this involved a wide cast of characters. Among them were politicians, such as J. S. Woodsworth and William Irvine, who had their activities secretly observed by the RCMP.[15] Eventually, however, the police focused their attention on the revolutionary left, principally the Communist Party of Canada, formed in 1921. Across Alberta and Saskatchewan, the Mounties monitored communist activities, in part by infiltrating the fledgling party with police officers and others recruited as informants. Indeed, the most famous mounted policeman of the interwar period was John Leopold, an unnaturalized immigrant from eastern Europe who, speaking with accented English and using the pseudonym Jack Esselwein, joined the Regina chapter of the CPC and moved up the party ranks by acting as an informant.[16]

The real reason for targeting communists for surveillance, beyond their linkage (both real and imagined) to the wider communist movement,[17] was the potential that their message would find resonance with immigrant and ethnic communities and working-class people. There was an accepted belief among the Anglo-Canadians that radicalism was synonymous with certain ethnic groups. Ethnicity, and to a lesser extent class, were important factors in determining who might be a threat to the security of the nation. Such long-standing views were reinforced by the war. Long-time Conservative loyalist and Ottawa lawyer C. H. Cahan, for example, warned the federal government in September 1918 that the real threat to Canada no longer lay with the heinous Huns but with the "Russians, Ukrainians and Finns, employed in the mines, factories and other industries." They represented the real danger because they were "thoroughly saturated with the Socialistic doctrines which have been proclaimed by the Bolsheviki [*sic*] faction of Russia."[18] The involvement of "enemy aliens" in the Winnipeg General Strike confirmed this reality in the minds of many who conveniently ignored the predominance of Anglo-Canadians in the strike leadership. Since Alberta and Saskatchewan had a large number of "foreign immigrants," they were on the frontline of such concerns about the potential threat posed by the non-preferred.

Ukrainians on the prairies, who since the nineteenth century had resisted assimilation, were a prime target for police surveillance. A 1920 RCMP report described a large meeting of Ukrainians in Alberta, where "speakers did not refer to the assimilation with the Canadian race or the fostering of Canadian ideas in the educating of their children, advocating only Ukrainian Nationalism." The refusal by Ukrainian school children in Drumheller to salute the flag and carry on other nationalist trappings ended up in an RCMP report as well.[19] Also receiving RCMP attention in 1920 was a Ukrainian boarding school in Saskatoon, the Peter Mohyla Institute, affiliated with the University of Saskatchewan. Of equal concern was the establishment in Saskatchewan of a Ukrainian Greek Orthodox theological seminary. The report noted that the priest of the seminary had earlier been involved in a dispute with younger men who were keen on maintaining Ukrainian cultural traditions, such as schools, the language, and the flag.[20]

In 1923 Cortlandt Starnes, Perry's successor as commissioner, wrote to Herbert Greenfield, the premier of Alberta, to warn of the danger of Ukrainian schools to his province:

> The principal subjects to be taught are the Ukrainian language, folk-songs, and revolutionary songs and music. Every effort is made to induce the children to hate religion, patriotism, and the government and social and economic system of Canada, and to desire and expect revolution, with its accompanying horrors. Great use is made of concerts; the elders are encouraged to attend entertainment at which the children furnish the programme, most of the recitations, songs etc. having revolutionary tendencies. Sometimes the children act revolutionary plays. The evidence is that these are attractive to the parents. Great hostility is shown to the public schools, which are incessantly denounced as designed to darken the understandings of the children, to teach militarism and religions, and to bolster up capitalism. Bitterness is shown towards those Ukrainians who imbibe Canadian ideals.[21]

In the memo, Starnes added that other "nationalities dabble in this activity from time to time, but not in so organized and systematic a manner as the Ukrainians" who, in his opinion, consistently resisted "Canadianization."[22] The commissioner advised against outright repression, observing that the schools operated outside public school hours, thus not affecting attendance, which was governed by law.[23] Instead, demonstrating his support for the ultimate solution for those who refused to be assimilated, he advocated the deportation of the teachers who worked at the schools, a course of action taken with at least one such individual as a result of evidence supplied by the RCMP.[24]

The wider cultural activities of Ukrainians additionally concerned the RCMP because they demonstrated an unwillingness to be assimilated, or, in the words of the police, were "averse to being Canadianized."[25] Even the activities of an all-female Ukrainian mandolin orchestra touring western Canada during the 1920s found its way into a police intelligence report.[26] At each stop in the West, reports or, more accurately, concert reviews of the orchestra, flooded in from RCMP informants and secret agents. One noted that while "O Canada" was sung at the beginning of the concert, it was skipped at the end.[27] An Edmonton-area Mountie undercover agent was assigned to report on a Ukrainian concert in that city despite not being able to speak the language. The agent clearly set out what he did not like about the concert:

> The whole sentiment of the Concert was anti-Canadian and revolutionary in the extreme, dangerous to the peace of the country in as much as it was inciting the workers to revolution.
>
> One deplorable and striking feature of the whole affair was the number of small children that took part and entered wholeheartedly into the seditious programme, their enthusiasm only being excelled by that of the younger members of the audience, who cheered and applauded in the wildest manner, the Chairman having to ask them to modify their applause. Most of the children present are all Canadian born, and speak English with no trace of a foreign accent, but the appalling fact as demonstrated above, is that they are being trained as REVOLUTIONISTS....
>
> The Concert was brought to a conclusion by the Ukrainian Mixed Choir singing the "RED FLAG," the audience rising. The Theatre was filled to capacity, about eight hundred being present; over ninety percent of who were foreigners, mostly Ukrainians. The audience was orderly throughout, and paid the closest attention to all parts of the programme, but after certain red seditious songs, etc., applauded in the wildest manner, showing the spirit of the audience was revolutionary.[28]

The RCMP's handling of immigrants, and of ethnic and racial minorities on behalf of the state, extended beyond surveillance and the accumulation of material on files. As John Torpey notes in *The Invention of the Passport*, World War I marked the beginning of an era of more restrictive control of movement across national boundaries.[29] In Canada during the interwar period, the RCMP played an increasingly important role on behalf of the Canadian state and the provinces by helping determine who became citizens and who did not. Naturalization investigations by the police helped reassure Anglo-Canadians that not only would they alone be admitted to the Promised Land but also that the land would be cleansed of the "undesirables" already present.[30]

At the behest of the Canadian government, the RCMP investigated the background of thousands of potential citizens, forwarding the information to government authorities who would make the final decision.[31] In his first annual report in 1923, commissioner Starnes reiterated the force's "close relation with the immigration authorities," a number of members of the force acting as special immigration officers. In addition, "special inquiries are made, and a certain amount of detective work is done. Many undesirables are refused admission as a result of our activities."[32] In Alberta and Saskatchewan between 1919 and 1939, the RCMP conducted more naturalization investigations than criminal ones.[33]

Part of this work targeted those of Chinese background, both those who had been naturalized and those who had not yet attained citizenship. Under the auspices of the 1923 *Chinese Immigration Act*, which required the registration of all Chinese residents in Canada,[34] the RCMP registered some 1,125 Chinese in 1924 in southern Saskatchewan, with "each registration occupying approximately three-quarters of an hour," one senior Mountie reported. He went on to note: "This was not the finish of it, as the certificates were returned to be handed back to the Chinamen, and also in several cases further information was asked for by the Chief Comptroller, when the Chinamen had to be interviewed again."[35] That the police force focused on the Chinese is not surprising. It, along with the Anglo-Canadian elite, firmly believed that the Chinese were not able to be assimilated.[36]

Underlying such intolerance was fear on the part of some social reformers, such as Emily Murphy (one of the members of Alberta's "Famous Five" who fought for women's equality) that the Chinese posed a serious threat to "white" society and especially "white" women.[37] Murphy and other women reformers feared the Chinese. As historian Madge Pon notes: the myth of the yellow peril was distinctly tailored to fit the western construction of Chinese men as cunningly deceitful, morally dangerous, and peculiarly feminine. Co-existing with the idea of "yellow" and "unmanly" Chinese men was the contradictory belief that they posed a moral and sexual threat to "white" women.[38]

The use of drugs by the Chinese, particularly opium, was seen as a serious threat because of its perceived use in luring "innocent" Anglo-Celtic women.[39] Drugs became a symbol of assault upon the purity of the white race and therefore a justification for restricting Chinese immigration and for harassing those already in the country. According to social historian Mariana Valverde: underlying the work of reformers was an attempt "to legitimize certain institutions and discourses – [such as] the patriarchal nuclear family, and racist immigration policies – from the point of view of morality."[40]

It was no coincidence that illicit drugs received so much attention at the end of the war. Rumours of returning veterans hooked on narcotics were commonplace. Prohibition of alcohol was also in place in the United States and in parts of Canada, and the drug threat provided a new crusade for both supporters and opponents of alcohol prohibition.[41] The fact that the drug trade seemed dominated by "foreigners" complemented the growing fears, especially in the aftermath of the Winnipeg General Strike, about the threat of immigration and the activities of ethnic minorities.[42] Drug use, like radicalism, became one more form of "deviance" from the perspective of the dominant society.

The mounted police's enforcement of the *Opium and Narcotic Drug Act* (ONDA) across the prairies left little doubt as to the racialized nature of the legislation. The law's separation of opium, accurately viewed as a narcotic predominantly used by those of Chinese background, from other illicit drugs reflected its racialized nature. The equivalent of the ONDA for the Anglo-Canadian population would have been, according to criminologist Neil Boyd, a law targeting saloons.[43]

In the annual RCMP reports, enforcement of the ONDA was the only area that identified race for those arrested: "Chinese, White, Colored, and Japanese."[44] In 1924, for example, 55 per cent of those arrested by the RCMP under the ONDA across Canada were Chinese.[45] Examples from that period in Saskatchewan included W. J. Morrison of Mossback, arrested for possessing "tablets alleged to be half grain tablets of morphine sulphate"; Mack Hoy of Birch Hills, picked up for possession of an "opium pipe"; Katie Hooper of Viceroy, arrested for possession of "one small glass vial containing morphine"; Yu Lung Chuny of Swift Current, charged for possessing "one tin of opium"; and Lu Bnos of Kindersley, arrested for opium possession.[46]

Arresting the "undesirables" under the ONDA was the initial way the legislation could be used by the police to regulate the Anglo-Canadian vision of the Promised Land. In this respect it was one part of an increasingly preferred solution for dealing with those who it was believed could not be naturalized and assimilated or who were unwilling to do so. Deportation was the ultimate tool for dealing with the unwanted Chinese, the troublemaking radical, and those unwilling to be assimilated. Again, the police had a part to play.

In the case of the Chinese, the *Opium and Narcotic Drug Act* was designed not to imprison Canada's unassimilable Asians but to get rid of them. Under ONDA, those non-naturalized individuals who were found guilty could be deported, a point superintendent Christen Junget of "K" Division in southern Alberta understood clearly when he noted in his contribution to the commissioner's annual report for 1925 that of the twenty-eight people convicted in his district under ONDA, twenty-six were aliens.[47] The mounted police turned over the names of the Chinese convicted to the chief commissioner of Chinese immigration, thus playing an important role in a system that the Canadian minister of health boasted in the House of Commons was "deporting Chinamen as fast as we can."[48] Between 1923 and 1932, nearly 2 per cent of the Chinese population in Canada were deported, their average time in Canada having been seventeen years.[49]

As early as 1919, deportation became the state's ultimate weapon in the war against the undesirable born outside of Canada. It was a simple method for getting rid of the problem for good. Parliament recognized this reality when it passed amendments to the *Immigration Act* in June 1919, which allowed for the detention and deportation, without trial, of everyone, except naturalized Canadians, who advocated the violent overthrow of the Canadian government.[50]

The mounted police in Alberta and Saskatchewan enthusiastically enforced the new rules. At the same time as the government changed immigration laws, it appointed several senior mounted police officers, including Perry and Starnes, as immigration officers to provide them with the necessary power to make arrests under the new amendments. An immigration official made it clear that it would not be difficult to appoint additional policemen in this capacity.[51]

The effect of the amendment to the *Immigration Act* was immediately obvious in southern Alberta's "K" Division. The monthly reports that Superintendent P. W. Pennefather filed detailed operations against immigrants and ethnic minorities. The first reference to the use of the new law appeared in July 1919:

> On the 18th of the month we made our first arrest under the new Immigration Act, that of Romeo Albo charged under section 41 of the Act, with attempting to create public disorder by word or act. The Minister gave his sanction for the arrest and prosecution of this man, and much good work was done in securing evidence against him. Being a man of some education he was prone to writing letters for the public press, most of them of a very inflammatory nature, and these were heavy evidence against him. In addition to this we were able to produce witnesses of statements he had made. Altogether a most interesting case was brought to a most satisfactory conclusion by the order of the Board of Inquiry for his internment and deportation to Italy.[52]

Pennefather moved against another perceived troublemaker the following year. The police arrested Sanna Kannasto, a Finnish Socialist, because of her political activities. Pennefather wanted her tried under section 98 but was instead ordered to turn her over to immigration authorities who held a board of inquiry, apparently to have her deported.[53]

Such powers gave the mounted police a great deal of control over the lives of immigrants. "I am of the opinion," wrote Superintendent Pennefather, himself an Irish immigrant, "that the majority of these agitators have a deadly fear of being sent back to the countries they came from. The worst agitators in my District came from the slums and that is where they should be sent back to."[54] Commissioner Starnes reiterated this point in 1929, when he forwarded a police report to the department of immigration. Spelled out in the report was the police interpretation that the majority of immigrants "are sympathetic towards Communism, but they are afraid to join ... [since] they may be deported."[55]

Deportation became less important in the mid-1920s as the economy improved. The Liberals, a party more sympathetic to immigrants and less favourably inclined to infringements on civil liberties, took power in 1921 and, except for a brief interregnum in 1925, held power for the rest of the decade. Still, much of Anglo-Canadian society was displeased with the 1925 Railways Agreement passed by the Liberal government, which once more opened Canada's doors to those considered undesirable. The agreement allowed railway companies to enact their own immigration policy. They sought a cheap supply of labour and, as a result, thousands of previously "non-preferred" immigrants began once again to enter Canada; many ended up in Alberta and Saskatchewan.[56] As for the Mounties, they continued to worry about those who somehow violated the dominant norms surrounding ethnicity, politics, and cultural habits. Certainly deportation remained a weapon of choice – Starnes' recommendations that Ukrainian teachers and Doukhobors be deported being evidence of this.[57] In 1930, the Conservatives, a party that was ideologically closer to the perspective of the police, gained power. The arrival of both the Tories and the Great Depression made deportation a popular option once again.

Some Mounties wanted to make it even easier to deport undesirables. In 1933, S. T. Wood, at the time in charge of Saskatchewan's "F" Division, urgently recommended to Commissioner MacBrien that sections 40 and 41 of the *Immigration Act* be revised to simplify deportation. Wood specifically objected to the fact that naturalized Canadians of at least five years were exempt from deportation and that it was up to the state to prove that an individual was an active communist, not merely a member, before he or she could be deported. Wood wanted amended laws because "deportation is the one effective weapon against foreign agitators and one of which they are in continual fear. Communist Party directives stress the necessity of protecting foreign agitators by assuming English names and by other means."[58]

Commissioner MacBrien had publicly called for the removal of radicals of foreign birth in a 1932 speech. His reference to expulsion as a solution to Canada's internal problems was not a rhetorical flourish; he worked to ensure that it became common practice. On October 13, 1931, for example, MacBrien met in Ottawa with major-general McNaughton, chief of the general staff, W. A. Gordon, the acting minister of justice, the minister of national defence, and the commissioner of immigration. The topic of discussion was the deportation of unnaturalized communists. It was decided that a military barracks in eastern Canada would be given to the RCMP for the creation of an "Emigration Station."[59]

RCMP work for the department of immigration and colonization had long involved collecting material in order to deport an individual, a process acknowledged by Commissioner Starnes in 1923: "we have obtained the evidence upon which a number of deportations have been made."[60] The initiative for some deportations came directly from the RCMP. In 1919, a Mountie detective in Calgary reported on two American labour organizers whom he said should be arrested and deported.[61] In 1931, superintendent T. S. Belcher wrote to the commander of "K" Division in southern Alberta to inquire how long a particularly troublesome communist had been in Canada. "If he has been here five years he cannot be deported," the superintendent added.[62] A year later, the head of the mounted police detachment in Saskatoon wrote to his superior to report that "of the 750 single unemployed receiving relief from the City, not more than 20% are residents of Saskatoon, the remainder are transients, a great number of which are foreigners, many of them not yet having established Canadian domicile." The clear message to his superior was that these unemployed men, who were beginning to challenge authority in the Saskatchewan city, were an exportable commodity.[63]

The RCMP viewed deportation as a preventive measure, as punishment, or both. A violent riot occurred in Estevan, Saskatchewan, on September 29, 1931, two weeks before MacBrien met in Ottawa with other officials to discuss deportation. A local Mountie believed that non-British locals caused the violence: "The rioters consisted largely of Foreigners as very few English speaking people took an aggressive part in the riot." As a response, he recommended "discriminate deportation of the radical foreign element."[64] Two months later, Superintendent J. W. Spalding, commander of the southern Saskatchewan district, expanded on this idea when he supplied the officer in charge of the Estevan area with a list of names of possible communists or at least men with "'Red' tendencies." He asked that the names on the list be "investigated with a view to their possible deportation."[65]

The force was intricately involved in deportation operations in western Canada. John Sembay (Symbay), a Ukrainian involved in the ULFTA in Edmonton, and mentioned in security bulletins in the 1920s because of his connection with Ukrainian schools, was ordered deported under section 41 on May 10, 1932. The decision was based on the evidence of RCMP secret agent 125 (Jacob Tatko). Tatko specifically linked Sembay with "revolutionary utterances looking to the overthrow of our economic and governmental structure in Canada by the use of force or violence." The final blow was testimony from Mountie Sergeant John Leopold, a famous infiltrator of the Canadian Communist Party, that the ULFTA was connected with the Communist Party.[66] Gottfried Zurcher, on the other hand, was found to have contravened section 41 of the *Immigration Act* based on the evidence of RCMP constables – although in this case they neglected to find out the man's nationality.[67] Another faced deportation in 1933 because of the evidence supplied by Leopold that the Finnish organization the man belonged to was a "subsidiary organization of the Communist Party."[68]

Ultimately, the deportation of radicals and those convicted under ONDA paled in comparison to the number of people deported during the Depression because they had become unemployed or were on relief.[69] Here again, the mounted police played a significant role. They arrested vagrants and others who could be deported because they had not been naturalized and thus lacked the protection of citizenship. Regardless of the reasons for removal, the common belief was that as people they were expendable and that the provinces of Alberta and Saskatchewan, where the Depression struck hardest, were better off without them.

There was another example from the interwar period of the RCMP's work that in some ways echoed the agenda of others, specifically groups on the far right of the political spectrum in Alberta and Saskatchewan, who sought to ensure the exclusionary nature of the Promised

Land. A myth would later develop that the mounted police treated the far right and far left equally. In fact, the police did not view the radical right as posing the same level of threat to Anglo-Canadian hegemony as the revolutionary left. If anything, the far right addressed issues of concern to the police. The best example of this relates to the Ku Klux Klan, with thousands of members in Saskatchewan. The RCMP began investigating the Klan in Saskatchewan as early as 1924 and references appear elsewhere over the subsequent years, often after left-wing radicals under police surveillance made reference to the Klan and its activities. In 1927, reports to Lucien Cannon, the acting minister of justice, described the spread of the Klan from southern Saskatchewan to the north.[70] A Mountie officer reassured the King government in June 1927 that "the agitation now in progress in Southern Saskatchewan probably is one of the dying flickers of this movement." Although he based his judgment on the incompetence of some of the initial organizers, superintendent Worsley's judgment was premature. The Klan did not simply disappear in 1927. In fact, with new organizers it grew in strength over the next three years to the point where 25,000 people belonged to the KKK, a membership comparable with other Saskatchewan organizations, such as the Grain Growers' Association. It also had ties to the Conservative party, which won the 1930 provincial election in Saskatchewan.[71] These developments appear to have been irrelevant to the RCMP after 1927, since monitoring the Klan was no longer considered a priority. When premier James Gardiner sought details on the KKK, he did so through private detectives and sources in other provinces.[72]

There is a more revealing reason, however, why the RCMP did not take a greater interest in the activities of the Klan. When it railed against "foreigners," the Klan represented the opinion of many in Saskatchewan, even though not every person who held these views joined the KKK. Klan leaders skilfully tailored their message and traditional values, such as law and order, to pre-existing prejudices.[73] Many mounted policemen shared such nativist sentiments as evidenced by Commissioner Perry's quote that opened this paper, in which he defended vigilante attacks on "enemy aliens" and called for an all-out government effort to assimilate ethnic minorities.[74] The fact that members of the KKK shared similar backgrounds to those in the RCMP meant that, from the perspective of the police, the KKK did not challenge Anglo-Canadian traditions and institutions to the same degree as the Communist Party of Canada did.[75]

Its continual work at ensuring Anglo-Canadian hegemony made the RCMP indispensable in the struggle to ensure a "Canadianized" and ordered Promised Land. The latter purpose of the police was evident in 1930 when Premier J. E. Brownlee wrote to the Saskatchewan attorney general to ask about the willingness of the RCMP to deal with challenges to order, specifically those posed by labour and the unemployed.[76] "Police have co-operated in every way with us and ... I am satisfied will do everything they can to help us" came the reply.[77]

This, and the other functions performed by the RCMP on behalf of various levels of government, represented a form of nation-building in Canada during the interwar period. The nature of the police work reflected the degree of tension that existed in Canada, particularly across the prairies in the 1920s. Tolerance toward deviations from the dominant norms had never been great. The war with its high cost in lost and damaged lives and widespread turmoil on the home front, particularly in 1918 and 1919, pushed forward intolerance as a preferred course of action. The chosen and most effective tool for the state to enforce conformity in a rapidly developing region like the prairies was the RCMP. It had the presence, the status, and the power to pursue the state's campaign of conformity against those who either resisted being "Canadianized" or who were unsuitable candidates for such a fate in the first place. Equally significant was the fact that Mounties themselves, predominantly drawn from the dominant Anglo-Canadian population, believed in the importance of the work they performed. After all, what could be more crucial than ensuring that a promised land lived up to its promise. The RCMP's vision of themselves as guardians of the Promised Land is captured in a stanza from Robert Thompson and E. Brown's collection of poems entitled *The Old Timer, and Other Poems*, published in 1909:

> This to us is the chosen land,
> And the land of Promise fair,
> And we will ride the prairie wide
> And breathe Alberta air,
> And swear that never was a land
> More free than this our own
> And we take our place with the men that stand
> For the power of Britain's throne[78]

NOTES

1 "Report of the Royal North West Mounted Police for the Year Ended September 30, 1919," *Sessional Papers*, 14.

2 Robert Craig Brown and Ramsay Cook, Canada, *1896–1921: A Nation Transformed* (Toronto: McClelland & Stewart, 1991 [1974]), 50–64; Donald Avery, *"Dangerous Foreigners": European Immigrant Workers and Labour Radicalism in Canada, 1896–1932* (Toronto: McClelland and Stewart, 1979), 9.

3 R. Bruce Shepard, *Deemed Unsuitable* (Toronto: Umbrella Press, 1996).

4 These definitions are complex. "Race" here is defined as "a group of human beings socially defined on the basis of physical characteristics." Stephen E. Cornell and Stephen Ellicott, *Ethnicity and Race: Making Identities in a Changing World* (London: Pine Forge, 1998), 24. "Ethnicity" is defined as cultural activities. More complex is that in this era race was applied to represent both so that, for example, Ukrainians, who in the present would be referred to as an ethnic group, were labelled a race at the time.

5 Pierre Berton, *Vimy* (Toronto: Anchor Canada, 2001).

6 Jonathan Vance, "Turning Point of a Nation," *National Post*, February 11, 2000.

7 Jonathan Vance, *Death So Noble: Memory, Meaning, and the First World War* (Vancouver: UBC Press, 1997).

8 Vance, "Turning Point of a Nation."

9 Vance, *Death So Noble*, 229. See also 241–56.

10 *Nation Building in Saskatchewan: The Ukrainians*, Government of Saskatchewan, 1921.

11 Tom Mitchell, "'The Manufacture of Souls of Good Quality': Winnipeg's 1919 National Conference on Canadian Citizenship, English-Canadian Nationalism, and the New Order After the Great War," *Journal of Canadian Studies* 31, no. 4 (Winter 1996–97): 7, 20–22.

12 Benedict Anderson, *Imagined Communities: Reflections on the Origin and Spread of Nationalism* (London: Verso, 1991).

13 Canada. House of Commons' *Debates*, February 12, 1914: 710.

14 Steven Roy Hewitt, "'Old Myths Die Hard': The Mounted Police in Alberta and Saskatchewan, 1914–1939," (PhD diss., University of Saskatchewan, 1997), 71.

15 Ibid., 193–98.

16 Steve Hewitt, "Royal Canadian Mounted Spy: The Secret Life of John Leopold/Jack Esselwein," *Intelligence and National Security* 15, no. 1 (Spring 2000): 144–68.

17 Steve Hewitt, *Spying 101: The RCMP's Secret Activities at Canadian Universities, 1917–1997* (Toronto: University of Toronto Press, 2002), 3-30.

18 Cahan to Borden, September 14, 1918, and October 21, 1918, as quoted in Donald Avery, *"Dangerous Foreigners*, 75.

19 CSIS Records, Spalding to O.C., "K" Div, Doc. No. 57, file 88-A-75, January 23, 1925.

20 Security Bulletin No. 44, October 7, 1920, in *R.C.M.P. Security Bulletins: 1919–1929*, 196.

21 Ibid., "Revolutionary Schools" – Memo prepared by Starnes for Gouin, December 30, 1922.

22 Ibid.

23 Ibid.

24 Carl Betke and S. W. Horrall, *Canada's Security Service: An Historical Outline, 1864–1966, Volume 1* (Ottawa: RCMP Historical Section, 1978), 429–30.

25 Security Bulletin No. 9, January 29, 1920, in *R.C.M.P. Security Bulletins: 1919–1929*, 30.

26 Security Bulletin No. 332, August 19, 1926, in *R.C.M.P. Security Bulletins: 1919–1929*, 337.

27 Security Bulletin No. 331, August 12, 1926, in *R.C.M.P. Security Bulletins: 1919–1929*, 331.

28 CSIS, RCMP Records Related to the Communist Party of Canada in Edmonton, vol. 22, file No. 88-A-61, Doc. No. 22, pt. 7, Report of [deleted], "G" Division, April 3, 1923.

29 John Torpey, *The Invention of the Passport: Surveillance, Citizenship and the State* (London: Cambridge University Press, 2000), 111–21.

30 "Report of the RCMP for the Year Ended September 30, 1927," 28.

31 "Report of the RCMP for the Year Ended September 30, 1925," 16.

32 "Report of the RCMP for the Year Ended September 30, 1923," 21.

33 Source: RCMP Annual Reports.

34 Barbara Roberts, *Whence They Came: Deportation from Canada, 1900–1935* (Ottawa: University of Ottawa Press, 1988), 108.

35 Allard as quoted in "Report of the RCMP for the Year Ended September 30, 1924," 27.

36 W. Peter Ward, *White Canada Forever: Popular Attitudes and Public Policy Toward Orientals in British Columbia* (Montreal and Kingston: McGill-Queen's University Press, 1978), 12. J. S. Woodsworth stated bluntly that the "Orientals cannot be assimilated." Several negative characteristics such as disease, prostitution, gambling, and the aforementioned drugs were attributed to them. J. S. Woodsworth, *Strangers Within Our Gates: or, Coming Canadians* (Toronto: University of Toronto Press, 1972 [1909]), 155.

37 Emily Murphy, *The Black Candle* (Toronto: Thomas Allen, 1922). "White" represented a socially constructed designation with changing membership over time. For more on the social construction of this category, see Matthew Frye Jacobson, *Whiteness of a Different Color: European Immigrants and the Alchemy of Race* (Cambridge, Mass: Harvard University Press, 1998), 1–7.

38 Madge Pon, "Like a Chinese Puzzle: The Construction of Chinese Masculinity in Jack Canuck," in Joy Parr and Mark Rosenfeld, eds., *Gender and History in Canada* (Toronto: Copp Clark, 1996), 88.

39 Steve Hewitt, "'While Unpleasant It Is a Service to Humanity': The RCMP's War on Drugs in the Interwar Period," *Journal of Canadian Studies* 38, no. 2 (Spring 2004): 80–104.

40 Mariana Valverde, *The Age of Light, Soap, and Water* (Toronto: McClelland and Stewart, 1991), 167.

41 David F. Musto, *The American Disease: Origins of Narcotic Control* (New York: Oxford University Press, 1999), 115; Carstairs, "Innocent Addicts, Dope Fiends and Nefarious Traffickers: Illegal Drug Use in 1920s Canada," 33, no. 3 (Fall 1998), 146–47; Desmond Manderson, *From Mr Sin to Mr Big: A History of Australian Drug Laws* (New York: Oxford University Press, 1994), 95.

42 Tom Mitchell and James Naylor, "The Prairies: In the Eye of the Storm," in *The Workers' Revolt in Canada, 1917–1925*, ed. Craig Heron (Toronto: University of Toronto Press, 1998), 211–14.

43 Neil Boyd, "The Origins of Canadian Narcotics Legislation," in R.C. Macleod, ed., *Lawful Authority: Readings on the History of Criminal Justice in Canada* (Toronto: Copp Clark Pittman, 1988), 203.

44 RCMP Annual Reports. This category ended in 1938.

45 Hewitt, "'While Unpleasant It Is a Service to Humanity'," 89.

46 Library and Archives Canada (LAC), RG 18, Reel T-4511, 'Arrests Under the Opium and Narcotic Drug Act,' 270–332.

47 "Report of the RCMP for the Year Ended September 30, 1925," 25–29.

48 As quoted in Robert Montserin, "Criminalization of Drug Activity in Canada," (M.A. thesis, University of Ottawa, 1981), 58.

49 Catherine Carstairs, "Deporting 'Ah Sin' to Save the White Race: Moral Panic, Racialization and the Creation of Canada's Drug Laws," *Canadian Bulletin of Medical Health* 16, no. 1 (1999): 32.

50 F. A. Blair, an official with the Immigration Department, wrote in 1920 that many of the "'Reds' floating about this country ... should be picked up and deported." LAC, Department of Immigration, RG 76, vol. 627, file 961162, reel c-10443, Blair to Under Secretary of State, January 9, 1920. Blair gained greater notoriety in the 1930s. See Irving Abella and Harold Troper, *None Is Too Many: Canada and the Jews of Europe, 1933–1948* (Toronto: Lester & Orpen Dennys, 1982).

51 LAC, RG 76, Department of Immigration Records, vol. 29, file 653, pt. 2, F. C. Blair to A. L. Jolliffe, March 11, 1920.

52 LAC, RG 18, vol. 1933, file G-57-9-1, "K" Division, Lethbridge, Confidential Monthly report for July 1919. Pennefather was overly optimistic in his conclusion to the case. It is not clear if the individual was ever expelled from Canada.

53 Ibid., "K" Division, Lethbridge, Confidential Monthly report for February 1920.

54 Ibid., "K" Division Confidential Monthly Report for June 1919.

55 CSIS, RCMP Records Related to the Communist Party of Canada in Edmonton, vol. 7, file 88-A-61, Starnes to Department of Immigration, Department of Insurance, January 9, 1929.

56 Avery, *"Dangerous Foreigners,"* 100–101.

57 John McLaren, "Wrestling Spirits: The Strange Case of Peter Verigin II," *Canadian Ethnic Studies* 27, no. 3 (1995): 101.

58 LAC, RG 76, vol. 738, file 513057, Wood to MacBrien, March 3, 1933.

59 LAC, A.G.L. McNaughton Papers, Manuscript Group (MG) 30, E133, Series II, vol. 10, file 46, Memorandum, October 13, 1931.

60 "Report of the RCMP for the Year Ended September 30, 1923," 21.

61 LAC, RG 146, RCMP Records Related to the Winnipeg General Strike, vol. 1, file 1025-9-9028, pt.12, Report of Detective S. R. Waugh, May 27, 1919.

62 LAC, RG 146, RCMP Records Related to the National Association of Unemployed, vol. 21, file 92-A-00099, part 1, T. S. Belcher to O.C. "K" Division, October 29, 1931.

63 LAC, RG 146, vol. 27, file 92-A-00123, pt. 2, Walter Munday, O.C. Saskatoon, to Superintendent J. W. Spalding, O.C. "F" Division, November 5, 1932.

64 LAC, RG 146, vol. 6, file 1025-9-91093, pt. 3, Insp. Moorhead to M. A. MacPherson, Attorney General of Saskatchewan, October 15, 1931.

65 Ibid., Spalding to O.C., Weyburn Sub-District, December 15, 1931.

66 LAC, RG 76, vol. 738, file 513057, Assistant Commissioner of Immigration, R. L. Munroe to Jolliffe, Commissioner of Immigration, May 10, 1932.

67 Ibid., Memo from Munroe, May 25, 1932.

68 Ibid., Memo for Commissioner of Immigration, May 26, 1933.

69 Roberts, *Whence They Came*, 45.

70 Gregory S. Kealey and Reg Whitaker, eds., *R.C.M.P. Security Bulletins: The Early Years, 1919–1929* (St. John's: Canadian Committee on Labour History, 1994), 622, 305-6. CSIS, RCMP Records related to threats to the security of Canada by Right-Wing Extremists, vol. 109, file 88-a-34, pt. 1, Superintendent G. S. Worsley to Lucien Cannon, Acting Minister of Justice, June 25, 1927.

71 Martin Robin, *Shades of Right: Nativist and Fascist Politics in Canada, 1920–1940* (Toronto: University of Toronto Press, 1992), 61–84.

72 Ibid., Worsley to Under Secretary of State, June 20, 1927; Robin, *Shades of Right*, 34–35, 44, 62–63, 15–16.

73 Robin, *Shades of Right*, 50–52; David E. Smith, *Prairie Liberalism: The Liberal Party in Saskatchewan, 1905–71* (Toronto: University of Toronto Press, 1975), 144.

74 Commissioner A. B. Perry, RNWMP Annual Report for 1919. For more on Mountie attitudes toward ethnic minorities, see Hewitt, "'Old Myths Die Hard'," 89–146. There is a parallel with the sympathetic attitudes of the FBI toward the Ku Klux Klan in the southern United States in the 1960s. See David Cunningham, *There's Something*

Happening Here: The New Left, The Klan, and FBI Counterintelligence (London: University of California Press, 2004), 12.

75 Robin, *Shades of Right*, 56, 61–84.

76 Public Archives of Alberta (PAA), Premier Papers, Access No. 69.289, file 77A, Brownlee to MacPherson, November 5, 1930; ibid., file 108, Brownlee to MacPherson, November 12, 1930.

77 Ibid., MacPherson to Brownlee, November 8, 1930.

78 Robert Thompson Anderson, *The Old Timer and Other Poems* (Edmonton: Edmonton Printing & Publishing Co., 1909), 16.

V

READADJUSTING THE VISION OF THE PROMISED LAND IN THE MODERN ERA

15

UNCERTAIN PROMISE: THE PRAIRIE FARMER AND THE POST-WAR ERA

Doug Owram

> There was land – lots of it. There were immigrants – lots of them. There was wheat – lots of it. And markets seemed limitless. But few drink this wine of self-assurance now. – H. H. Kritzwiser, Regina *Leader-Post*, November 27, 1945

So much of the mythology of the West is wrapped up in agriculture. From the first settlements forward, the notion of prosperity through agricultural development has been integral to the character and identity of the region. It has also been the centre of its great promise to the nation and to those who would go there. Much has been written on this subject and those themes will be reviewed in this paper. However, the real purpose is to look at the promise of agriculture from a different perspective. By the middle of the twentieth century, the promise of Canada was no longer the promise of agriculture. Even in the less urbanized West, forces were changing the nature of the economy and society. Farmers and farm communities, emerging from the disaster of the Great Depression and the volatile war years, remained as committed as ever to their land and way of life. The world in which they lived, however, was one in which the promise of the West and the nation was focused elsewhere.

There is much rhetoric around agriculture in Canadian history. The vastness of the land, and the reality of a pre-industrial immigrant society meant that the promise of the West and the promise of agriculture were inseparable.[1] In the 1850s when British North America began to look westward, it first had to convince itself that this was a fertile land suitable for agriculture. It was thus not surprising that both the British and the Canadian governments sent scientific expeditions west to assess the region in a new light. The result was a specific link between the region's future and its agricultural potential. "It is a physical reality of the highest importance," wrote Henry Youle Hind, the leader of the scientific expedition for the government of the Canadas in 1858, "that this continuous belt can be settled and cultivated from a few miles west of the Lake of the Woods to the passes of the Rocky Mountains."[2] It was one of the earliest definitive statements linking the future of the West to the promise of agriculture.

Through the next decade such comments multiplied, from the informed to the merely enthused. "There is in truth, a prospective poetry in the soil here. The poetry of comfort and independence,"[3] wrote Charles Mair, a Canadian expansionist, in the Toronto *Globe*. In the 1870s and 1880s, after Canada had annexed the West, the rhetoric multiplied. Government pamphlets, newspaper articles, and political speeches all linked Canada's destiny, western development, and agricultural promise. There might be minerals, cities, and even some ongoing furs in the West's future, but by now the region had become linked above all to the promise of agriculture. Here was a soil capable "of raising anything," as George Grant put it in 1873.[4]

Of all the things that could be grown, however, one crop came to dominate – wheat. The prairies were to be the breadbasket of the world. They contained lands considered "probably more favourable for the growth of wheat in greater abundance and perfection than those of any other country in the world."[5] The imagery, once established, was persistent. From Thomas Spence's *Manitoba and the North West of the Dominion* (1871) to *Winning Through: Stories of Life on a Canadian Farm told by new British Settlers* (1929), the promise of the West was the promise of the farmer and, above all, the wheat farmer. "In the olden days all roads led to Rome, but today they all lead to the Empire where wheat is King – the Prize Wheat Belt of Western Canada."[6]

The pattern thus established in the settlement years involved the development of three basic national mythologies about the promise of the West. First, the vast western prairies had tremendous potential that had been missed or misunderstood in the fur trade era. It was to be the new frontier and the destination of immigrants. It had the resources to provide wealth and abundance for both the individual and the nation as a whole. Second, the destiny of the West was agricultural. There would be cities and towns but the heart of the region was its agriculture. Third, those who tilled the soil – the farmers – would dominate the region. A pamphlet, published during the boom of the early twentieth century, nicely captured the chain of logic. "As a producer of the world's breadstuff, the farmer ranks first among all others in the importance of his labor." Waves of immigration in the late nineteenth century had begun the settlement of the West in both Canada and the United States and made western farmers "the most prosperous class of people in the world." The American lands were now filled, however, and the future lay in Canada. "It is but natural that the future 20 years will see development here even greater than that which occurred in the Western States during a like period."[7] Tied up with the importance of the farmer was the belief in his inherent moral superiority over the urban dweller. The West was to be based on "a great, a comfortable and therefore contented yeomanry."[8] If that was done, the success of the region, not just materially but morally, was assured.

Together these three assumptions created incredible promise. The West was not to be just another region opened to settlement. It was, instead, Canada's means to material and moral greatness. Once fully developed, "there is no reason why Canada should not, as a portion of the British Empire, become as powerful as any other country upon the American continent."[9]

The reality was never as simple as the utopian dreams spun by realtors, governments, and local writers.[10] Nonetheless, at any time before the Great Depression, the promise of the West seemed to be agriculturally centred and to be moving, if bumpily, towards fulfillment. The agricultural vision was vital because, for all the exaggeration of the literature, the farm and especially the western farm was a central part of the Canadian economy. By the later 1920s the total agricultural output in Canada was close to $2 billion. The Dominion Bureau of Statistics reported that agricultural output made up some 38 per cent of total national production, more than any other category including manufacturing.[11] Within agriculture, wheat was indeed king. It led all categories of exports and, along with wheat flour, accounted for more than a third of total Canadian exports. Add as well those other grain crops of barley, rye, and oats and more than 40 per cent of all Canadian exports were included.[12]

In spite of such growth, there were many who failed on the frontier. As E. B. Osborn complained at the turn of the century, the writers of Canadian government pamphlets that were "full inside of glowing testimonies to the phenomenal fertility of the country," had obviously never sat down to talk to potential farmer immigrants.[13] Some explanation, he claimed, was needed for the tales of failure and hardship that drifted eastward and overseas. How could one explain the gap between the promise of western agriculture and the day-to-day realities for many farmers?

Throughout most of the development of the West, this gap was explained by pointing to external and malevolent agencies. The list of these obstacles evolved through time. The Canadian Pacific Railway, high tariffs, eastern politicians, the banks, and inappropriate immigrants, all helped explain why the promise of the region was as yet only partly fulfilled. The important thing about such demonization, though, is twofold: that it created the possibility of action to remedy the situation, and that it failed to challenge the essential premise underlying the vision. "The Western farmer premised his fight against the East, big business, and urban encroachments on the image that 'God made the country, Man made the Town' – that farmers were God's chosen people and that the family farm was the ideal social unit."[14]

The response, whether in the formation of the co-operative movements at the turn of the century or the Progressive Party after World War I, was to seek to remove these impediments by linking the clout of the farmer with the growing political power of the region.[15] Whatever the challenges, the West was an agricultural region and its promise would rise or fall with the farmer. Farmers were "the apostles of co-operation; they have captured the imagination of the nation by combining true radicalism with scientific moderation, and it is safe to say they are the most hopeful factor in Canadian national life today,"[16] wrote William Irvine, a leader of the farmers' revolt in Alberta, in his tract, *The Farmers in Politics* (1920).

By the end of World War II, the mood was very different. Changes in social and economic structures worked to undermine the link between the West, the nation, and the farmer. This time, however, it was not so easy to turn on malevolent external forces for an explanation. Something more fundamental was happening, and for the farmers and small towns of the West, the one thing that had never been in doubt – their centrality to the future of the West – was now a threatening question.

During the previous generation, everything had seemed to conspire to push the farmer to the margins of society. First the Great Depression

IMMIGRANT ARRIVALS IN CANADA, 1921-39

YEAR	NUMBER
1921	91,728
1922	64,224
1923	133,729
1924	124,164
1925	84,907
1926	135,902
1927	158,886
1928	166,783
1929	164,993
1930	104,806
1931	27,530
1932	20,591
1933	14,382
1934	12,476
1935	11,277
1936	11,643
1937	15,101
1938	17,244
1939	16,994

had ravaged western agriculture. Low commodity prices internationally and drought at home meant that the great land of promise and the prize wheat belt of the world was impoverished. Farm capital on the prairies decreased by nearly 30 per cent in the early 1930s. The province of Saskatchewan, the largest and most prosperous of the prairie provinces in the 1920s, saw personal income drop by almost two thirds between 1928 and 1933.

Given such conditions, it is not surprising that the life-blood of all those promotional pamphlets – the immigrant – ceased coming to Canada. The average number of immigrants arriving in Canada in the mid-1930s was less than 10 per cent of the number of only a few years earlier. Enthusiastic pamphlets on the "Last Best West" gave way to such publications as *The Drought Areas of Western Canada and Some Measures to Meet the Problem* or *The Canadian Desert: An Attempt to Stop the Loss of the West.* When the cumbersomely named Saskatchewan Immigration and Settlement Convention Committee sought to appeal to immigrants, many of the statements were not all likely to encourage people to gamble their future on the prairies. "It is too early to conclude that the vast and hitherto fertile plains of this continent are about to be reduced to a desert."[17]

If there were few new arrivals, there were many who left. All three prairie provinces saw significant rural depopulation between 1931 and 1946. Thousands of farms were abandoned with a majority of the migrants from the area going to Ontario and British Columbia. Even for those who stayed on the prairies, drought and low commodity prices led to significant movement within the region. In general terms, people moved from the south, the main agricultural area in the region, to the north and to the west. They also moved from farms into the towns and cities. They were fleeing from the centre of the drought, the old Palliser's Triangle, and as well from the lack of opportunity, the hardships, and the uncertainty of marginal farming.

Alberta, a province that was used to growth and immigration, saw some 60,000 people leave in the 1930s and early 1940s. Every census district east of Highway 2 and south of Edmonton saw depopulation. Every census district south of Red Deer, except for Calgary, lost population or remained stagnant. Even in the patterns of urbanization there was a preference for the north. Edmonton grew significantly faster than Calgary over this twenty-year period and was, by 1951, the province's largest city.[18] By the 1950s, therefore, the population of Alberta was arrayed very differently than twenty years earlier.

The only possible consolation for Albertans was that Saskatchewan was even worse off. Vast areas of southern Saskatchewan experienced some of the driest conditions suffered during the 1930s. Census districts one through four, running across the south of the province, all lost more than a third of their population in these years. For the province as a whole, rural population declined by more than 14 per cent.[19] Such movement spelled the end of Saskatchewan's dominance on the prairies. The province was still the centre of Canada's wheat production, but that title now contained a degree of ambivalence.

Two other major changes occurred as a by-product of the Depression. First, "king" wheat was at least partly dethroned. In some cases, as in the driest lands of southern Alberta and Saskatchewan, wheat land was simply abandoned or converted to cattle grazing. More generally, however, scientific advice, local talk in the coffee shops, and government policy all encouraged a shift to other crops.[20] Overall in the Canadian economy, although wheat remained important, it was not as important as it had been. By the 1950s, newsprint exports were well over one and a half times the value of wheat, while wheat and flour accounted for just over 10 per cent of total exports.[21]

The other dramatic change occurred in numerous small towns across the prairies, especially in the south. As farms were abandoned, the centres that served those farms declined as well. Farmers were the customer base for the seed stores, the grocers, and others. Communities across the prairies that only a decade before had boasted of a future that rivalled Chicago, or at least Winnipeg, found themselves struggling to remain in existence. In 1911, Alameda, Saskatchewan, had published a glowing brochure asking, "did it occur to you that very few people living in Pennsylvania fifty years ago had the least idea that the lands of Illinois would be worth as much as Pennsylvania?" The message was clear. Alamaeda, with its "fine new brick school house, government centre and a local telephone line," would be the next region to replicate such growth.[22] The reality was somewhat different. By 1946, Alameda had shrunk to a mere 246 people.[23] Across the southern prairies – and even in the parkland – the story was much the same. Towns like Souris, Gladstone, and Emerson in Manitoba, or Ardath, Broadview, Wolseley, and Shaunavon in Saskatchewan all saw buildings boarded up and businesses close as people left the region. Depression and war had reshaped the face of the prairies.

What of the future? The war years had brought a rebound in both production and prices for wheat. However, as farmers emerged from the war, they faced more uncertainty. Complex trade arrangements with Britain, a combination of starving populations in Europe and uncertain grain prices, along with debates about marketing controls versus free enterprise echoed through the press, especially in the later 1940s. As Alberta's deputy minister of agriculture concluded in 1947: "the transition from war to peace" led to a "noticeable attitude of frustration and indecision among farmers as they awaited the outcome of the changes."[24]

True, volatility had been a fact of farm life from the first agricultural settlements. Massive drought in 1919 had caused dislocation and hardship for parts of the region, only to see faith restored in the 1920s.[25] The fact was, however, that the temporary dislocations of the later 1940s, though frustrating, were not fundamental to what was happening. Instead, farmers came to realize in the post-war years that what they faced was not another cyclical variation. This was a permanent change. Over the first decade after the war, rural areas of the prairies and the small towns that serviced these areas had to come to grips with a new West.

In its most basic form, the change concerned the relative role of the farmer in society. Even if crop prices remained good and yields constant, there was a widespread recognition that the place of the farmer in the future was not what it had been in the past. A few statistics illustrate the point. First, the farm population of the country and the region was in decline and the recovery of the war and post-war years did not change that fact. Between 1931 and 1956, the total farm population of Canada decreased from 3.3 million to 2.7 million. Most importantly perhaps, farm population was declining as overall population soared. In the same period of time, the Canadian population increased from 10.3 million to 16 million. To put it another way, the farm population in these years decreased from 32 to 17 per cent of the population. Even on the prairies, the farmer was now in a minority. Every one of the prairie provinces saw a decline in the absolute number of farmers and, by the mid-fifties, all had a greater non-farm than farm population.[26]

The High River *Times* complained in 1949 that the trend needed to be reversed. "The need was never greater. Hundreds of thousands of acres of cleared land are neglected or improperly cultivated. Canada's agriculture can expand internally all across the continent."[27] The Sylvan Lake *News* reported a discussion in Parliament on housing shortages. The answer, it was said, was clear: "A movement back to the land would … alleviate the housing shortage in the cities."[28] A farmer in Elgin, Manitoba, complained that "there is only one place where wealth can come from and that is the earth.… That's why you have to stop all these people going to the city and get more people on the farms."[29]

However, in contrast to the post-World War I era, neither the government nor any other agencies attempted to revive the notion of massive land settlement. For one thing, aside from specific areas like the Peace River, there was not a great deal of good farmland left to open. Further, the strong memories of the Depression provided ample warning of what happened if marginal lands were settled. Indeed, the results of one such program only emphasized the dangers. In what might seem a rather dubious policy, Alberta decided, at the height of the dust bowl and low wheat prices, to institute a plan to settle relief families on farms. By 1947, with the abandonment rate under the program running at 70 per cent, the government quietly concluded that the farm was no longer a safety valve for problems of unemployment.[30]

At the federal level, the Veterans Charter of 1944–45 did provide support for returning armed service members who could qualify as "veterans who have practical experience in farm operation." However, this was not a revival of the older vision of the settlement frontier. Even within the *Veterans Land Act* there was as much emphasis on providing support for those returning to existing farms as for those who wanted to buy a farm. Within the overall package of veterans' benefits, the land settlement provisions were just one small section of a package that really focused on urban employment and education.[31] As the Department of Veterans Affairs itself noted: "land settlement cannot be expected to meet the needs of the majority of veterans in becoming reinstated in civilian life."[32] Second, the provisions in the new act brought reminders from those veterans settled on land after the last war; they were, they argued, the ones who needed attention. Farming had left them impoverished by large mortgages and inadequate income.[33] It was hardly the base on which to build a new "back-to-the-land" movement. Both for new immigrants and for veterans, the future lay in the booming cities. The department of reconstruction acknowledged as much. Future growth, it stated publicly at war's end, would be in the metropolitan areas in central Canada rather than in "the distant regions."[34]

Even in the "distant regions" though, urbanization was a post-war fact of life. Nowhere was that truer than in Alberta. The discovery of oil at Leduc in 1947 and at Redwater the following year transformed the economy of the province. The discoveries created thousands of new jobs and pumped money into the coffers of government and citizen alike. As Social Credit politicians always reminded the voters, these new streams of revenue were not as great as the output of the agricultural sector. It hardly mattered though. The new money and the new jobs were in oil and gas. Edmonton and Calgary were Canada's two fastest growing cities, often drawing on the rural areas of their own province and others across the prairies.

The contrast between such growth and the situation of the farmer only highlighted the changed circumstances. In the face of rhetoric about Alberta's wealth, the High River *Times* commented: "the average individual [in High River] … does not feel very much 'in the money' as a consequence of the rich strikes."[35] The Calgary *Herald* summed it up best, though, when it lamented that this province "has been so wound up in its oil discoveries, its new refineries, its pipelines, its population figures and its big oil salaries that many people have tended to forget the importance of farming."[36] The reality was that, whatever the concerns, the department of reconstruction was right: growth would be in the cities and would remain there.

What made this all the more significant was that it was not a cyclical phenomenon. As farmers themselves well knew, structural changes within their industry were largely responsible for the trend. Especially on the prairies, efficiency demanded mechanization. Mechanization, in turn, enabled larger farms. Larger farms meant fewer farmers and a lack of opportunity for a new generation to be absorbed. The Saskatchewan Royal Commission on Agriculture and Rural Life summed it up in 1955: "As industry becomes more and more specialized so did the farmer. As industrial specialization resulted in a reduction of the number of firms, so did agricultural specialization reduce the number of farms."[37] All the available data underlines this point. The number of trucks on Saskatchewan farms increased from about 3000 in 1926 to some 55,000 by 1951. Some 80 per cent of farms had tractors. All three prairie provinces had more invested in farm machinery than any other province.[38]

Such an investment made large farms not only possible but necessary. Only massive economies of scale could justify the overhead involved. If abandonment had been the pattern of the thirties, consolidation was the order of the day in the decade after the war. Between 1921 and 1961 the average farm size in southwest Saskatchewan more than doubled, going from 663 to 1386 acres. A study of farms in southern Alberta found the same pattern, with an increase in size from an average of 605 acres in 1931 to over 1400 by 1951. At the same time and partly as a result of this trend, the population had decreased by almost 50 per cent.[39] The magnitude here reflected the changing nature of the drier southern areas, but throughout the prairies farm size increased substantially.

Most government advisory bodies, politicians, and economists argued that mechanization was to be the means by which the farmer could cope with a fast-changing world. Not surprisingly, companies like Massey-Harris promoted the idea with such slogans as "mechanization leads the way to a better future." The accompanying picture of a very prosperous farm family, with a modern house and a shiny new tractor drove home the point.[40] Yet to the post-war farmer, the massive investment created a paradox. The investment was necessary but its effects were questionable. When the Saskatchewan minister of agriculture complained in 1946 that the machine age had not helped the farmer, he was criticized by urban papers but found resonance among farm publications. Machinery had not protected the farmer in the depression, argued the

Western Producer. Indeed, the large scale investment in machinery only made the farmer more vulnerable to cyclical forces. Once you bought an expensive machine you were stuck with the investment in good times and bad. In contrast, farm labour could be hired only as necessary.[41] Almost a decade later the Saskatchewan Royal Commission took a similar position. Investment was fine "in a period of buoyant returns but may create a problem when the farmer feels he cannot justify the cash outlay."[42] The real beneficiary of the investment in machinery, complained the *Western Producer*, was the "community that consumed the product. Cheap food was demanded and was produced at the expense of the farmer and at the expense of the fertility of the soil."[43]

Given such circumstances, the prairie farm organizations and individual farmers waged an occasionally bitter debate as to the solutions to their problems. The role of co-operatives, the Winnipeg grain exchange, and international wheat agreements all produced endless articles and letters to the editor in the press in the immediate post-war years. The complex and often desperate discussions are beyond the scope of this article but underlying them all was the desire to be sheltered from the turbulence. As one article noted: "For farmers, the great problem for the coming years is the establishment of a permanent system which will assure to them as good a standard of living as that of any other body of wealth creators in the national economy. We need some authoritative pronouncement on the technique for such a system."[44]

The most dramatic attempt to reverse events came in a short-lived farmers strike in 1946. The United Farmers of Canada called the strike but it was supported primarily by smaller producers and those most vulnerable to the increasingly large, machine-based operations. For the strikers the action was in the grand tradition of prairie politics. Rhetoric recalled the bankers that had charged the farmer extortionate interest rates in pioneer days and the grain handlers who "marketed the farmers' dearly won golden grain and the grower was gypped on dockage, grade, weight and price." The strike recalled the farmer heroes of days past, "Patridge of Sintaluta, Motherwell of Abernethy, Peter Dray of Indian Head" and so on. "These were men who gave strong and sane leaderships [*sic*] in trying to find solutions to the farmers' mounting economic problems."[45]

The problem was that farmers in 1946 had neither the clout nor the unity of those earlier generations. Nor were the same external agents clearly at fault for what was happening. As many farmers themselves recognized, the economic forces were much more impersonal than demonological. The very efficiencies of the modern world meant that fewer, larger, and more capital intensive farms were needed. As a result there were going to be fewer farmers. What followed was the realization that farmers had less political clout than a generation earlier. It was no wonder, as one analyst put it, that "many prairie farmers and others concerned with Prairie rural life feel betrayed, confused or powerless in the face of these impersonal economic forces."[46]

Farming was an economic activity, but the importance of farming was inseparable from a set of values. From the first settlements, part of the "promise" of the West had been in the way of life in an open land.[47] As W. B. Baker, director of the School of Agriculture at the University of Saskatchewan, put it in 1955: "the intangibles of rural life must be considered" for the "importance of the spiritual, social and cultural values" could not be over-estimated.[48] Not surprisingly farm and small town papers agreed. "Farming is sturdy work and sturdy work develops sturdy characters," concluded the Strathmore *Herald*.[49] The farm, said the Rocky Mountain House *Mountaineer* "is a great place for kids" and "a farm background is a very handsome thing to have."[50]

In contrast, life in the city was far less rewarding and much more dangerous. "When one reads of the atrocious crimes, [and] acts of wantonness and cruelty committed by teen age gangs in the cities," concluded the High River *Times*, "this town and district must take great pride in the general caliber of the young people."[51] The *Weyburn Review* added "congestion and the tendency to tuberculosis" to the risks for the urban youth.[52] It was also a matter of independence. "Instead of this crazy movement to the towns and cities we should have a back-to-the-land movement.... Town life is artificial, in housing, eating and recreation. He [the town dweller] can't have anything of the gifts of nature." Most of all, the farmer "could get up in the morning and feel like a free man instead of just being a cog in a wheel."[53]

It was especially gratifying to relate stories of those who had left the town to find true happiness in the country. The Stettler *Independent* ran a long and somewhat cumbersome story about a city woman who married a farmer. She knew nothing about rural life but found it so attractive that when her husband died, she remained and ran the farm.[54] The Red Deer *Advocate* reprinted a story of the many reasons why experienced teachers preferred rural schools and the orderly, intelligent children found in them![55]

The celebration of rural life was formalized when the Alberta government acted to recognize those who demonstrated the benefits of farming. Under the slogan, "Good Farming, Right Living, Clear Thinking," the "Master Farm Family" program solicited nominations from across the province for farm families that "embody all those basic qualities upon which people have built this country."[56] The winners had their stories published and received a cash prize. There was no doubt that many of the stories were truly ones of success. The underlying message was also clear though. Across the bottom of each page ran various phrases, such as "unstable is the future of the country which has lost the taste for Agriculture," and "farming is the most honorable of professions and unquestionably a romantic and inspiring one."[57]

The stories themselves hearkened back to the promise of the pioneer era and the qualities of the people who believed in it. One of the stories recounted: "When Charlie Conrad walked into the Peace River area via the historic Edson trail in 1913, he brought only a packsack, a willingness to work and a faith in that pioneer land. Now, 41 years later, that faith is vindicated by his family being declared a Master Farm Family."[58]

By mid-century, however, the notion that farming was "a romantic and inspiring" life, as the Master Farm Family program had put it, was increasingly under challenge. In many ways the gap in quality of life between the city and the small village or rural area was growing all the greater. It was a matter of heresy when one farm wife advised her daughters to marry a city man. Yet she got support. One commentator mused about the farm woman feeding pigs and chickens and doing all the cooking and washing "without the modern conveniences" while the urban woman went downstairs in the morning and could "turn on the thermostat, the electric range and toaster … turn a tap for the hot water and then an electric button to start the washer and finally pull a plug when the washing is done."[59]

Such comments reflected real differences that were emerging by mid-century between rural and urban living. Across the prairies in 1955, for example, only 9 per cent of farm families had inside running water compared to some 81 per cent of urban families while only 24 per cent had a furnace compared to 74 per cent.[60] As post-war urban cities sprouted modern, if homogeneous, rows of new houses, the romance of fresh air and outdoor toilets had ambivalent appeal to many.

To counter this, the Manitoba Canore *Courier* argued that "the average farm home ought to be a 'town' home in the country."[61] There were many attempts to catch up but it was easier said than done. Numerous rural electrification schemes were launched by local communities. Small towns sought central water and sewer services in order to attract newcomers and retain a younger generation.[62] Yet the very appeals for such developments also underlined the gap between city and rural life. As the *Albertan* noted in 1946, life on the farms without electricity "is hard and lonely." Change was also difficult. The cost was a classic example of economies of scale, however. It was prohibitive for a small number of farmers to join up. Yet convincing large numbers to make such an investment in the face of the needs was also difficult.[63] Even a decade after the war, less than one third of prairie farms had electricity compared to almost universal coverage in urban areas.[64]

The gap in conveniences between farm and city simply emphasized the broad social impact of rural depopulation and farm consolidation. It was not just access to electricity but to all services. Western Canada had always faced the tyranny of distance given the large-scale nature of farming. However, as farms grew larger and populations smaller, a chain effect set in. The local community lost population and services because there were fewer farmers to purchase goods. The farmers who did remain then found themselves with longer and longer drives for access to equipment repair, restaurants, or church services. In a forewarning of what was to happen in the next twenty years, the immediate post-war period saw railways begin to shut down local spur lines and grain companies begin to consolidate their elevators.[65] As well, in all three prairie provinces a number of local agricultural societies and the small, local "Class C Fairs" were abandoned. A Saskatchewan task force attributed the problem to mechanization and rural depopulation.[66] It was no different in Manitoba. James Giffen, writing in 1946, noted that the "annual agricultural fair in Elgin, which was the climax of the events in the community calendar, has become defunct, in common with a number of other small fairs in the province."[67]

The relationship between the attractions of the towns and the impact on the countryside were well summed up by a rural minister. In a long article in Winnipeg's venerable *Country Guide*, Gerald Hutchison lamented that the "rural church, long the backbone of both church and nation, is languishing, and in some communities practically dead." The problem, he believed, was directly related to "the confusion and weakness" that had overcome the rural community. Rural depopulation and access to urban centres due to the spread of vehicles weakened the local infrastructure. Underlying it all were the very real attractions of the town:

> Goods, services and entertainment are to be found in town. The advantages of town life are proclaimed constantly and with effect. New homes are built in towns. Lights and plumbing offer a convenience and comfort that appeal strongly. There is no point in deploring the attraction of the town but the effect on the rural community, and upon the attitudes of people who remain on the farm, is often unfortunate.[68]

Perhaps the change that caused the most anguish was the consolidation of rural schools. By the post-war years, it was apparent that the old structure of highly localized, multi-grade schools was not able to continue. "Inadequate salaries, poor accommodation, the isolation of rural teaching and the lack of social life, inadequate facilities and equipment, [and] ungraded classrooms" all meant that rural districts could not keep teachers. By 1955, Saskatchewan found that almost one third of its 5000 school districts were not operational and another 500 were struggling along with fewer than 10 students![69] Clearly things could not continue as they were. The decrease in the rural population meant that it was simply impossible, as with many other services, to maintain even the most rudimentary local school. Yet, for many farm families, sending children to some relatively distant "town school" only emphasized the uncertain future of rural life for the next generation.

By mid-century, some even challenged the most basic claim for country life – its moral and social values. In a series of letters to the Calgary *Herald*, a "young RCAF veteran" went on the attack against those who propagated the myth that – whatever the challenges – there was something to be gained by living in small communities or rural areas. He was unrelenting. After discussing all the "gossip and interference," he noted how many still believed that "life in the country is often very pleasant. Many people prefer to live away from the city because they say that only in the country do they find true friendliness." Even that was a delusion, he claimed, for it was sheer loneliness that made for so-called friendships. "It is no joke to be isolated for weeks at a time with not a soul outside the family with whom to pass the time. After a very little while of this kind of detachment, almost any neighbour is better than no neighbour at all."[70] If you did find somebody with whom to pass the time, he went on to argue, it certainly would not be much of a conversation, for "the rural dweller's taste in music, literature and art is execrable."[71]

At about the same time that the young RCAF veteran was attacking rural life and values, a Toronto sociologist was doing field work in the Hannah area of south-eastern Alberta for a book that was published three years later. *Next Year Country*, by Jean Burnet, took the criticism of small town and rural life from the level of disgruntled individuals to the realm of "scientific inquiry." Her book was almost the antithesis of all the glowing pamphlets and articles of earlier years. The end result was a picture of bleakness and "failure to adjust" that left little room for the older utopian visions of the West.

What made Burnet's commentary especially harsh was that she fully accepted the mythology of pioneer days. In a passage worthy of any prairie booster, she recounted the community that went with the challenging task of building a pioneer society:

> On the informal level there was a wealth of activity – visiting, bees, plays, concerts, dances, picnics, and charivaris. Gatherings, which people sometimes endured great hardship to attend, lasted a long time and were very hilarious. They created the possibility among the dry-belt farmers of accepting a common purpose, of communicating, and of attaining a state of mind under which there is a willingness to co-operate. Out of them grew formal structures, which in turn strengthened the formal relations. Prominent among the formal structures were self-government, educational and religious organizations, and most important, farmers groups which came to dominate almost every area of rural life.[72]

All that was now gone, however. Like others, she pointed to the impoverishment of drought, the rural depopulation, and the resultant impact on services. If she had stopped there, her comments would have been unexceptional. However, she went much further. The "old patterns of rural living have failed in the Hanna area" with disastrous results, she wrote. There was distrust between the town and farmers. There was excessive drinking and gambling. Family life seemed a very long way from the enthusiastic rhetoric of the settlement era. "Running away from home is common among teen-age boys. There are many cases of sex irregularities within the family group. Incestuous relations between father and daughter or stepfather and daughter are frequently and circumstantially discussed. Adulterous relationships are talked of enough to seem frequent in occurrence. Divorce and separation are also not rare." There was even a species of "prairie madness" or "mental disease" inherent in the rural communities,[73] she argued. In Burnet's hands, the promise of the "last best west" had turned decidedly dystopian.[74] Though local papers reacted with outrage, the publication summed up the disappearance of traditional mythologies and the impossibility of holding to earlier utopian promises of the West as an agrarian Eden.

The opening of the West had always been inseparable from its agricultural promise. For three generations of Canadians, the belief in a utopian future and the centrality of the farmer to that future had been preserved. In cases where the reality did not meet the vision there were always explanations. The external enemy would be overcome, or next year's crop would return the farm community to its rightful place in Canadian life. The promise of the West, the promise of the farmer, and the promise of Canada, in other words, had remained intact. The post-war years, however, marked the end of both an era and this unified vision. The nation that was to rest on a vast agricultural empire was now an urban and industrial nation. This structural change was vastly different than the old cycles of prairie successes and hardship. Now these three integrated mythologies had fragmented. Neither the West, nor certainly Canada, looked to the future with a vision of an agrarian utopia.

Of course, agriculture remained a vital part of the western economy and Canadian agriculture has remained one of the most efficient food production systems in the world. Whatever the absolute importance of the western farm, the important thing is that its relative importance, economically, politically and in terms of its impact on the national imagination, was in decline after 1945. Even on a regional basis, the farmer had increasingly to compete with a "new west," one based on the majority non-farm population. This was most dramatically expressed in Alberta where energy came to dominate the promise of the future. Across the prairies, however, there was a similar trend underway, albeit at a slower rate. Farms continued to mechanize and consolidate. The younger population looked increasingly to an urban future and local villages stagnated or withered. For three quarters of a century the promise of Canada, the promise of the West and the promise of the farm were intertwined. By the latter half of the twentieth century that was no longer the case.

NOTES

1. On the image of the West, see Doug Owram, *Promise of Eden: The Canadian Expansionist Movement and the Idea of the West, 1856–1900* (Toronto: University of Toronto Press, 1980) and R. Douglas Francis, *Images of the West: Changing Perceptions of the Prairies, 1690–1960* (Saskatoon: Western Producer Prairie Books, 1989).
2. Henry Youle Hind, *Narrative of the Canadian Red River Exploring Expedition of 1857 and of the Assiniboine and Saskatchewan Exploring Expedition of 1858* (London, 1860), II, 234.
3. Toronto *Globe*, January 20, 1869, Letter from Charles Mair.
4. On the emphasis on the agricultural empire, see Owram, *Promise of Eden*, 107–9.
5. Canada. *Annual Report of the Department of Agriculture*, 1872, 8.
6. Department of the Interior, *Western Canada: The Prize Wheat Belt of the World* (Ottawa, 1915), 4.
7. Tracksell, Andeson and Company, *Western Canada Lands* (Regina, 1906), n.p.
8. Cited in Owram, *Promise of Eden*, 136.
9. Department of the Interior, *Facts Relating to the West* (Ottawa, 1902), 21.
10. See, on the idealization of the West, Owram, *Promise of Eden*, and Francis, *Images of the West*.
11. Canada. Dominion Bureau of Statistics, *Canada Year Book*, 1930, 190, 205 (statistics are for 1927).
12. Ibid., 1930, 477.
13. Edward Bolland Osborn, *Greater Canada: The Past, Present and Future of the Canadian North-West* (London: Chatto and Windus, 1900), 67.
14. R. Douglas Francis, "Changing Images of the West," in *The Prairie West: Historical Readings*. 2nd ed., eds. R. Douglas Francis and Howard Palmer (Edmonton: Pica Pica Press, 1992), 717–39, 726.
15. On the sense of grievance and regionalism, the classic article is W. L. Morton, "The Bias of Prairie Politics," *Transactions of the Royal Society of Canada*, Series III, XLIX (1955): 57–66.
16. William Irvine, *The Farmers in Politics* [1920] (Toronto: University of Toronto Press, 1976), 102.
17. Saskatchewan Immigration and Settlement Convention Committee, *British Family Settlement in Canada: Saskatchewan's stand-point as set out in four addresses* (Saskatoon: n.p. 1937), address by W. W. Swanson "Colonization and Economic Progress of Saskatchewan," 5. See also Samuel Penter, *The Drought Areas of Western Canada and Some Measures to Meet the Problem* (Montreal, 1938); and Duncan Stuart, *The Canadian Desert: An Attempt to Stop the Loss of the West* (Toronto: 1938).
18. Dominion Bureau of Statistics (henceforth DBS), *Census of Canada. 1951*, Vol. 1, "Population," Table 6.
19. DBS, *Census of Canada*, 1946, Saskatchewan, Table 1.
20. See, for example, "Agricultural Diversification," Red Deer *Advocate*, editorial, April 4, 1951, 2. *The Economic Annalist*, 26 (August 1956) has a series of articles on the changes in crop production in the western provinces.
21. *Canada Year Book, 1959*, 1004–1011.
22. Canada, *Arcola-Alameda Districts Saskatchewan* (Ottawa, 1906), 5.
23. *Census of Canada*, 1946, Saskatchewan, Table 1.
24. Province of Alberta, *Annual Report of the Department of Agriculture for 1947*, 6.
25. David Jones, *We'll all be Buried Down Here: The Prairie Dryland Disaster, 1917–1926* (Calgary: Alberta Records Publication Board, 1986).
26. M. C. Urquhart and K.A.H. Buckley, *Historical Statistics of Canada*, 2nd ed. (Ottawa: Supply and Services, 1983), Table M1-11.
27. "Farms Need Young Men," [editorial] High River *Times*, April 7, 1949, 2.

28 "Many Vacant Farm Homes," Sylvan Lake *News*, April 7, 1948, 7.
29 P. James Giffen, *Rural Life: Portraits of the Prairie Town, 1946*. Edited with an afterword by Gerald Friesen (Winnipeg: University of Manitoba Press, 2004), 30.
30 Province of Alberta, *Annual Report of the Department of Agriculture for 1947*, 150.
31 "Back to Civil Life," Section 118 in Peter Neary and J. L. Granatstein, eds., *The Veterans Charter and Post-World War II Canada* (Montreal and Kingston: McGill-Queen's University Press, 1998), Appendix 2, 268.
32 Department of Veterans Affairs, *Annual Report*, 1945 (Ottawa, 1946), 46.
33 "The Soldier Settler," *Western Producer*, July 11, 1946, 6.
34 "Predicts Drift Toward Cities Will Continue to Drain Farms," ibid., December 27, 1945, 2.
35 "Educational Trends," High River *Times*, January 25, 1951, 2.
36 "The Farmers' State Concerns Us All," Calgary *Herald*, September 11, 1951, 4. See also "Importance of Alberta Farms to City Industry Stressed," *Edmonton Journal*, December 11, 1951, 5.
37 Province of Saskatchewan, *Reports of the Royal Commission on Agriculture and Rural Life*, Report 2, "Mechanization and Farm Costs," 12.
38 Ibid., 17, 59.
39 Alexander Paul, "Depopulation and Spatial Change in Southern Saskatchewan," in *Regina Geographical Studies*, No. 1 (1977) (Regina: University of Regina, 1977): 65–85. 71. Canada, Department of Agriculture, *Appraisal of Dryland Farming in the Special Areas of Alberta* (Ottawa, 1954), 3–4.
40 This advertisement or similar ones were common in the small town newspapers after the war. This particular citation is from the Strathmore *Standard*, April 10, 1947, 7.
41 "Farm Machinery," *Western Producer*, March 14, 1946, 6.
42 Saskatchewan, *Royal Commission on Agricultural and Rural Life*, Report 2, 99.
43 "Farm Machinery," *Western Producer*, March 14, 1946, 6.
44 "A Guarantee for Farmers," ibid, November 22, 1948, 21. See also the advertisement by Alberta Pool Elevators in Strathmore *Standard*, September 21, 1944, 4.
45 United Farmers of Canada, *Rural Romance: A Story of the Saskatchewan Farm Movement and its Objectives* (Saskatoon, 1948), 4–5. On the legacy of the strike see Rocky Mountain House *Mountaineer*, July 2, 1947, Letters to the Editor.
46 William J Carlyle, "Rural Change in the Prairies," in *A Social Geography of Canada. Essays in Honour of J Wreford Watson*, ed. Guy Robinson (Edinburgh: North British Publishing, 1988), 243–67, 252.
47 See David Jones, "'There is Some Power About the Land,' – The Western Agrarian Press and Country Life Ideology," *Journal of Canadian Studies* 17, no. 3 (Fall 1982): 96–108.
48 Saskatchewan, *Royal Commission on Agricultural and Rural Life*, Report 3, 12.
49 "Agricultural Week," [editorial] Strathmore *Herald*, June 20, 1946, 4.
50 "Farming is Big Business," Rocky Mountain House *Mountaineer*, November 26, 1947, 2.
51 High River *Times*, September 1, 1955. Cited in Paul Voisey, *High River and the Times* (Edmonton: University of Alberta Press, 2003), 170.
52 Cited in the Regina *Leader-Post*, September 10, 1945, 11.
53 Henry Willner, letter to the editor, *Western Producer*, January 24, 1946, 21.
54 "A True Life Story," *Stettler Independent*, reprinted in Red Deer *Advocate*, February 15, 1950, 5.
55 "Experienced Teachers Prefer the Challenge of Rural Schools," Red Deer *Advocate*, March 8, 1950, 6.
56 Province of Alberta, Department of Agriculture, *Master Farm Families*, 1954.
57 Ibid., 1956, 6.
58 Ibid., 1954, 6.

59 Letter to Editor, *Western Producer*, January 24, 1946, 21.
60 Dominion Bureau of Statistics, *Handbook of Agricultural Statistics*, August 1955, Table 5.
61 Cited in Regina *Leader-Post*, September 4, 1945, 11.
62 See, for example, "Strathmore's Opportunity," [Editorial] *Strathmore Standard*, September 28, 1944, 4.
63 Province of Alberta, *Annual Report of the Department of Agriculture for 1947*, 95.
64 Dominion Bureau of Statistics, *Handbook of Agricultural Statistics*, August 1955, Table 5.
65 See for example, Rocky Mountain House *Mountaineer*, September 3, 1947, 1.
66 B. Y. Card, "Perspectives on Rural Western Canada in the 1950s," in *The Making of the Modern West: Western Canada Since 1945*, ed. A. W. Rasporich (Calgary: University of Calgary Press, 1984), 145–66, 157.
67 Giffen, *Rural Life*, 17.
68 Gerald Hutchison, "The Challenge to the Rural Church," *Country Guide: The Farm Magazine* (March 1953), 7. See similar comments in Giffen, *Rural Life*, 19.
69 Saskatchewan, Royal Commission, *Rural Education: A Summary*, 3. See also "Rural Education is a Many Sided Problem," *Western Producer*, August 1, 1946, 14.
70 "Small Town Life in Alberta," Calgary *Herald*, December 28, 1948, 4.
71 "Small Town Life in Alberta," Calgary *Herald*, December 30, 1948, 4.
72 Jean Burnet, *Next Year Country: A Study of Rural Social Organization in Alberta* (Toronto: University of Toronto Press, 1951), 122.
73 Ibid., 33, 122, 148.
74 Local papers reacted against Burnet. See, for example, High River *Times*, December 20, 1951.

16

THE ARTIST'S EYE: MODERNIST AND POSTMODERNIST VISUALIZATIONS OF THE PRAIRIE WEST

George Melnyk

The colonizing settlement of the Canadian West after the construction of the railroad in the 1880s left a reasonable body of photographic material. Of course the corporate and state photography of the period emphasized the agricultural bounty of the region, while the documentary record provided alternative views, such as the now famous photo of Doukhobor women hitched to a plough breaking the virgin prairie. But the painterly record of the creation and consolidation of the agrarian economy is less fulsome because fine art was a rarefied cultural commodity. In dealing specifically with the dominance of the agrarian period in the West, one can think of the era as displaying a modernist spirit, which celebrated the overt achievements of agrarianism and their importance for regional identity. In the post-agrarian phase, one discovers a curious blending of continuity and contrast in prairie art – continuity with the images proffered by the agrarian myth and discontinuity with its purported values.

While the modernist spirit in art generally embraced the concept of the Prairie West as a Promised Land, the artistic values of the post-agrarian period are explicitly postmodernist in that they are critically self-reflective when dealing with the legacy of the agrarian society. This postmodernism is supported by the transformation of the political economy of western

Canadian society into a non-agrarian, urban-dominated, post-industrial society. While the immigrant artists of the modernist/agrarian period shared in the cultural gaze of their society, which, at least, up to the Great Depression was generally positive about the region, the postmodernist prairie artist has learned to play with the symbols and icons of regional identity once sacred to agrarian culture. Contemporary readers or interpreters of modernist prairie art, formed as they are by the cultural modalities of postmodernism, are essentially critical of the older art forms, finding that they do not express current sensibilities. This means that they necessarily look upon them with an alien eye. As postmodernists we are outsiders to modernism.

The earliest Euro-Canadian art was done in the 1800 to 1850 fur-trade period and therefore is pre-modernist. A good example may be found in the watercolour and ink works of Peter Rindisbacher (1806–1834), who arrived with Swiss settlers brought to the Red River in 1821 by Lord Selkirk. These were most frequently images of First Nations' figures or landscapes.[1] Toward the end of this period, Paul Kane (1910–1871) became famous with his portraits of First Nations' persons and scenes from western life. His images were well-received in his day and now comprise an irreplaceable cultural legacy of colonial Victorian romanticism.[2] It was about this time that the photograph began to compete with original art as a form of documentation. Whether in lithographic reproduction or simply photo-imitative illustrations in journals of the day, the audience demanded to "see" the region as it was. The *London Illustrated News* was a vital expression of this form of ersatz photojournalism.[3] The result was an emphasis on representational realism as the only mode of recording and visualizing the West artistically This approach carried over to the pioneer culture in which the recording and documenting of this kind of physicality expressed an attachment to the land as a site of both human triumph – the sodbuster – and nurture – the bountiful harvest. The agrarian sensibility found the land as either beautiful or fruitful or a complementary presence in human enterprise. The artist and his society saw the westerner in an essential agrarian partnership with the land.

The context of the modernist impulse in western Canadian art in the first half of the twentieth century reflected the artistic values imported by the immigrant artists who were its first regional practitioners. These artists were Euro-Canadians, usually from Great Britain, for whom the imperial project was natural and of intrinsic value. They shared in the general enthusiasm for settlement, for creating a Europeanized society in the West, and they believed, as did the majority of their contemporaries, that the region was to serve as a vast breadbasket for Europe and even the world. The immensity of the land and its supposed fertility were viewed as essential features that required a spirit of enterprise, determination, and nobility. The myth of the English yeoman farmer as the quintessence of English cultural and economic values was transferred to the western prairie with enthusiasm. The non-English peoples who immigrated to the region were praised if they emulated this model.

The agrarian period itself had two phases that attracted artistic interest: the *pioneering* period from 1880 to 1919 and the *mature* period from 1920 to 1969. These two phases constitute the total modernist era with each phase having a distinct art style. How the political realities of the time intersected with the artistic spirit was reflected in the movement from utopianism to alienation, especially during the 1930s, when the region's agrarian productivity was ravaged by depression and drought. The postmodernist era begins in 1970 and extends to the present. It, likewise, has two phases: the *post-agrarian* phase from 1970 to 1988, when the Free Trade Agreement was signed between Canada and the United States and the *continentalist* phase that followed that signing.[4] This makes a total of four periods during 125 years – two in the agrarian phase and two in the post-agrarian phase. During this time numerous artists, both residents of the region and travellers, painted the West in oil and watercolour, as well as producing pen and ink drawings and charcoal sketches. After 1970, western artists appropriated other forms such as clay or bronze sculpture and art installations to this repertoire.[5] This study will deal solely with artists who made the region their home at one point or other in their lives. One of the key features of the transition from modernism to postmodernism in prairie art was the development of new genres of artistic expression to make statements about the West. It was a way of breaking the confines of the modernist vision, which was single-mindedly confident in its colonizing paradigm and Caucasian dominance.

A seminal study of the visualization and representation of the region is R. Douglas Francis, *Images of the West: Changing Perceptions of the Prairies, 1690–1960.* Written at the height of the post-agrarian phase of postmodernism, the book explained the transition from the modernist phase to postmodernism in this way: "the image of the West in literature, art and historical writing shifted from that of an actual physical landscape … to a mental landscape, a 'region of the mind' shaped by its own mythology."[6] Francis points out how then-contemporary prairie artists found "earlier depictions of the West as unrepresentative of their perception of the region."[7] This dissatisfaction was rooted in the historical evolution of artistic styles, such as abstraction, and in a new socio-economic configuration of the region with urbanization and rural depopulation that made the agrarian identity nostalgic rather than real. Postmodern prairie art is formed equally by a multi-faceted re-evaluation of agrarianism as *history* and by a new context provided by energy-rich Alberta and the wider movement toward a post-industrial first world economy in North America that constituted *contemporary reality*. Agrarianism as history rather than reality creates an automatic distancing, which allowed postmodern artists to reject the presuppositions of prairie modernism. They were living in the same place but in a different world.

This paper will deal with three artists that exemplify the art of the agrarian period and its two phases. The first is Alexander J. Musgrove (1882–1952), who was born in Edinburgh, then came to Winnipeg in 1913 and lived there until his death. The second is Henry George Glyde (1906–1998), who was born in England, trained at the Royal Academy in London, and came to Alberta in 1935. He taught at the University of Alberta until his retirement and died in Victoria. The third is Illingworth Holey Kerr (1905–1989), who was born in Lumsden, Saskatchewan. He studied in eastern Canada and London. Eventually he settled in Calgary where he headed the Provincial Institute of Technology and Art's art department, precursor of the Alberta College of Art and Design.

Musgrove was also a teacher. He came to Winnipeg to serve as principal of the School of Art. He later founded the Winnipeg Sketch Club and served as president of the Manitoba Society of Artists from 1931 to 1935. As a former student and one-time instructor at the Glasgow School of Art, his work reflected the school's emphasis on "blended colour and decorative quality."[8] An untitled watercolour, most likely from the early 1920s, presents a quintessential prairie agrarian scene. Executed in a post-impressionist style, the work portrays a barn, hidden by a stand of trees in the far left of the horizon line, while a man and a team of horses cut wheat or hay on a parallel plane to the right of the work. It is definitely the fall and the painting consists of a series of four parallel planes leading to the back of the picture. In the foreground is a small slough surrounded by natural prairie vegetation of varied colours. In the mid-ground is the yellow field that is being harvested. Then there is the blurred horizon-line and finally,

Alec J. Musgrove. *Prairie Harvest*, circa 1920.
Courtesy of the author.

the near-cloudless sky that occupies slightly more than half the work. It is painted a purple-blue shade.[9] This watercolour is just one small example of a whole tradition of prairie imagery that seeks to emphasize the importance of the land to regional identity.[10]

Because the modernist sensibility in prairie art is both realistic in execution and decorative in its intent, this work is meant to hang in a prairie home, express the social values of its day, omit controversy, and not challenge artistic taste or social propriety. It represents a colonial mentality that is assured of its place in the imperial universe and whose agrarian identity is both sociologically real and economically triumphant. Its documentary aspects are celebratory. And it is precisely this celebratory tone that later becomes an object of contention for postmodernist western artists.

A later work by H. G. Glyde moves away from this scene of agrarian idyll to a more contested sense of prairie identity because it was realized after the trauma of the Great Depression and executed at the

Henry G. Glyde, *The Exodus,* 1941.
Courtesy of the Alberta Foundation for the Arts, Edmonton.

beginning of World War II. *The Exodus* (1941) is a very powerful allegorical image based on biblical themes that alludes to Adam and Eve being driven from the Garden of Eden and to the exodus of the Jews from Egypt on the way to the Promised Land. Painted with an expressionistic emphasis and formed by the populist and proletarian interests of the 1930s, best expressed by the Mexican muralists, this painting shows a ragtag column of men and women escaping from tumbledown wooden rural buildings threatened by a burst dam, while struggling to reach the higher ground of concrete towers that symbolize the city.[11] On the far horizon are the Rocky Mountains. Another interpretation may be linked with war refugees being displaced by the floodgate of history bursting upon them.[12] In contrast to Musgrove's bucolic scene, Glyde fills his art with a touching poignancy that harks back to the despair and suffering of the dustbowl of the 1930s that engulfed the region and impoverished its inhabitants.

This painting is part of the high modernism of the 1940s and 1950s that represents the mature phase of agrarianism. This maturity is reflected in a balance between praise and condemnation, an adult acceptance of negativity as part of prairie life. The whole atmosphere of the time undermined thoughts of the West as a peaceable kingdom or as having the promise of a utopian "New Jerusalem," where all would live in equality and productive happiness.[13] In Glyde's painting, the human figure is out of harmony with the landscape, which has become revengeful, unmanageable, and a source of pain. Patricia Bovey in her study of prairie art in the 1930s alluded to this when she described the art of the period as "successful, mature, and varied portrayals of the difficult landscape."[14] The art of high modernism contained the essential motif of the figure in the landscape, but Glyde replaced the romanticism of Musgrove's watercolour with his own sense of dark realism. Because the earlier era of hope had weathered a time of despair, high modernism lacked the optimism of the *pioneering* phase. It had been forced by circumstance to become more anguished.

The Canadian West, while embraced by a myth of agrarian bounty, had had to participate in two world wars and the dislocations – economic, social, and political – of the Dirty Thirties. The myth had to be modified because of these changes and events. The political upheavals of the 1930s that brought protest politics to the West with the upstart, radical governments of Social Credit in Alberta and the Co-operative Commonwealth Federation in Saskatchewan were part of Glyde's reality and were reflected in his art. While also producing war art propaganda during World War II that glorified service men and women, Glyde was sufficiently insightful to balance this work with more challenging pieces such as this one. World War II served as a transition point for western agriculture. While the Depression had broken the spirit of optimism of individual farmers and bank foreclosures constructed a new path to farm consolidation and rural depopulation, the war augmented these trends with the increased mechanization of prairie agriculture. Only those who wanted to ignore these historical trends or were antithetical to them were available to embrace the agrarian nostalgia that came later on.

Illingworth Kerr's *Prairie Winter Road* (1968) is an oil painting of the late modernist period.[15] It depicts a prairie scene of a road stretching up through the middle of the painting over rolling countryside toward a distant horizon, whose sky is contained by a chinook arch. The brush strokes are thick and bold, reminiscent of the paintings of the Group of

Seven. Human presence is represented by the road cut into the landscape and the string of telephone poles that line it. It is not a great or original work, but it captures the essential element of modernism – the celebration of a landscape partially transformed by human effort. Although Kerr did go through a period of abstraction in the 1950s and early 1960s, his return to landscape showed how the modernist spirit had stayed with him. It also provided his contemporaries with a pristine vision that was land-oriented and agrarian-sensitive. This pro-agrarian vision was now moving in the direction of an imagined world rather than one of a dominant reality.

The postmodernist impulse that followed after 1970 aimed to take the imaginative even further by actually fictionalizing the documentary mode. It wanted to take what was "really there" in a physical sense and transform it into an imagined place. It contextualized the documentary outside reality. It was able to do this by creating historical distance, so that everything inherited from the past is no longer real. It is irrelevant. The juxtaposition of the real and the unreal results in a spirit of hybridity, which is defined as the inseparability of the real and the imaginary.[16] It is this play of opposites that defines postmodernist art in the West, especially when it deals specifically with agrarian themes.

Three artists of the postmodernist period have been chosen from each of the prairie provinces – Don Proch, Victor Cicansky, and Joan Nourry-Barry. Don Proch (1944–) was born in rural Manitoba of Ukrainian descent, graduated with his MFA from the University of Manitoba in 1966, and has been a practising artist in Winnipeg ever since. Victor Cicansky (1935–) was born in Regina, took his MFA from the University of California (1970), and has lived in the Qu'Appelle Valley north of Regina since the mid-1970s. Joan Nourry-Barry (1928–) lives in Sherwood Park, a suburb of Edmonton.

Each of these artists has expressed a postmodern sensibility in their treatment of the West as an agrarian homeland. Don Proch has consistently turned agrarianism upside down. Early in his career, he was making prints like *Luke's Cultivator* or *3 Furrows*. In the former he portrays an ugly steel tractor wheel cutting deep into the earth in a kind of assault, while in the latter he turns the prairie landscape into an eyeball with furrows like tears, blending the human perspective with objective reality.[17] About the same time Proch created sculpture that reflected the same agrarian-critical themes, a series of three-dimensional human heads imprinted with surreal prairie landscapes.[18] Again the emphasis is

Don Proch, *Grainscape*, ceramic and mixed media sculpture. Courtesy of the artist. Photo: Ernst Mayer

on the nature of interpretation and the how the eye sees. Proch seems to be saying that, while the landscape does imprint itself on the human psyche, it is the human psyche that creates its own picture of that objective reality.

In 1998, the Ukrainian Cultural and Educational Centre in Winnipeg held a show of his sculpture. The poster advertising the show carried an illustration of one of the works. It was a clay piece representing an old-fashioned, red-painted wood grain elevator of that kind that once dotted the prairie region but which had become increasingly obsolete and destined for demolition. This once ubiquitous form, which had come to symbolize the success of the agrarian culture and economy, was being replaced in the 1980s by a much smaller number of huge, concrete silos. This ongoing rationalization of the grain trade went hand in hand with the death of small towns and resulting rural depopulation. Fewer and larger farms meant the inevitable end of a way of life created during the period of pioneering settlement. Proch has attached a skyscape to the grain elevator, overpowering it. Unlike the blue prairie sky of Musgrove's world, this sky is grey like the concrete silos. If the skyscape is only the sky, then the future of the old grain elevator is grey indeed. If it also represents the new grain terminals, then agrarianism is overshadowed in the same way that a house in the city is overshadowed by a high rise. In the bottom there is a small landscape that crosses over from the skyscape to the grain elevator. The whole structure stands on a rug-imitative base, which has yellow wheat-like roots growing underground, like a grass skirt.

It is obvious that Proch is playing with a prairie icon and reflecting on its contemporary status. In the age of corporate globalization, this once almighty symbol of western agrarianism has now been rationalized into near oblivion like the agrarian world it represents. Here it is a piece of nostalgia. However, because it is wooden and lovingly painted, it reflects the spirit of community that once lived here. The new inland terminals as grain collection points have no spirit. They are functional economic and corporate entities that lack a human identity of the kind derived from local life and epitomized by the grain elevator. In having the wheat grow underground rather than above, Proch makes a historicizing reference to the roots of prairie society but also to the underground nature of agrarian life and values.

While one might smile at this perverse presentation, one can be impressed with the work's symbolic commentary. The agrarian is now

Vic Cicansky, *Singing the Joys of the Agrarian Society* (1970) and *Mixed Farming* (1970). Clay. Courtesy of the artist.

something not to be revered but to be played with. It has become a toy of consciousness, where the artist can play aesthetic games. It has been superseded by more powerful elements and its practical worth diminished into an internalized *nonscape*, which may be commemorated but definitely relegated to the past. The old land/sky integration of modernism is now simply a platform to be danced upon by the artist. In this case, what was once so idealized and romanticized can now be either fancifully eroticized or condemned by new ideologies such as ecological environmentalism.

Vic Cicansky takes up the playful and makes the modernist image of the virginal fecund earth into something erotic. In the medium of clay he has created voluminous, colourful imitations of canning jars filled with preserves that a prairie farmwife would have put up for the winter, whose shapes tend to burst out of their shapes. He has sculpted, pun-titled books on gardening that hold the eye with their thick shapes. Even his death-symbolic buffalo skulls painted in vibrant rainbow of contrasting colours with bright yellow or Indian red corn-on-the-cob for horns lift the natural world out of its ordinary shades to make one feel one is seeing the artificial shiny sheen of a polished automobile. He is quick to juxtapose the sombre black of a grand piano, symbolizing high-brow culture with the cultivation of vegetables that fill it in a work titled *Gardenmusic.*[19] Here we have the piano used like a fruit bowl with the value for humans of the organic contrasted to the inorganic.

The eroticisation of agrarian life, only suggested in these varied pieces, is explicit in two of his earlier works: *Singing the Joys of the Agrarian Society* (1970) and *Mixed Farming* (1973). Both are of outhouse-shaped, decrepit shacks with a cartoon-like, doorway-size veranda on which are placed two figures. In the former it is a cherubic, baroque-era figure, now most commonly associated with a baby cupid, who sports an oversized penis. In the latter a golden-haired nude of the kind one would have seen in a men's-only calendar sits provocatively cradling an erect phallic green pickle. In a sense each piece is a kind of temple with a god or goddess in the doorway. The juxtaposition of artful images, represented by the ceramic figures, with the collapsing structures that "house" them, contrast the crumbling reality of agrarian society with the life force of art. Although kitsch-like in its execution, each piece carries a powerful message about the disjunction between the myth of the agrarian West that seems so essential to regional identity and its diminished reality in the post-agrarian period. The de-sacralization and re-sacralization in a secularized paganism of the temple of agrarian myth achieved in these pieces is clearly an attack on the seriousness that underlay the modernist view of agrarian society. Only when the institutions of agrarianism, such as the wheat pools and even the Wheat Board, begin their decline into increasing irrelevance can the artist feel free to comment on the new situation.

The blending of the secular and the religious is also evident in a politicized commentary found in Joan Nourry-Berry's *Time Expired* (1973), which was first exhibited in the 1973 *For an Independent Hairy Hill* travelling exhibit organized by the National Gallery of Canada. It served as a showcase of Alberta artists from the Edmonton area. The show was explicit in its denunciatory attitude toward the disappearance of agrarian society. Hairy Hill is the name of a village in central Alberta, which the exhibit held up as a symbol of the slow and inevitable death of rural culture in the region. The documentary filmmaker Tom Radford wrote an essay in the catalogue titled "A Disappearing West" in which he bemoaned the passing of a way of life. "Each year in the area around Hairy Hill," he states, "one can find more abandoned farms and more boarded-up buildings."[20] He then denounces the economic trends that are depopulating the rural West. This *cri de coeur* was made thirty years ago, and in the intervening years the heritage of the family farm created by innumerable homesteaders a century ago has been almost erased. The grain co-ops that were its greatest socio-economic achievements have all but faded away and the family farm is now viewed as purely small business enterprise.

Time Expired is a fascinating and sophisticated commentary on the post-agrarian reality painted at a time when it was first recognized. It is a large painting on masonite that uses the motif found in Illingworth Kerr's *Prairie Winter Road* – a road stretching vertically from the middle of the painting toward the horizon line. The area is the rolling hills of the parkland terrain of central Alberta. The road is a muddy, furrowed farm road in early winter or spring. Dominating the image is a large Ukrainian grave marker in the shape of a cross at the top of which is a parking meter, whose red Time Expired marker has popped up. Red means stop. Along the bottom of the window in the meter is the inscription: "Ottawa will not turn handle." On the body of the meter is a picture of a deceased pioneer. Situated behind this surreal mix of the spiritual and the secular are several more gravestones of ethnic origin. Together they create a kind of crucifixion scene with the crosses of the nameless thieves on either side of the Christ figure that dominates the painting like one sees in a Station of the Cross. Painted in a pointillist style, the work expresses an angry sadness about the death of a way of life and its people.[21] It does so with a kind of in-your-face militancy that was common in the western regionalism and Canadian cultural nationalism of the early post-agrarian period.[22] In the later continentalist phase of postmodernism, issues of economic integration with the United States, rather than differentiation, tended to dominate both economics and politics.[23]

One can consider *Time Expired* as a kind of Byzantine icon. It sanctifies the agrarian pioneer, who is portrayed as one who has sacrificed his life for agrarian society. The figure-in-the-landscape that is so strong in the modernist period remains in this painting but is turned into the new reality of a granite gravestone. The figure is dead. The meaning of his life is now questioned because of its being turned to biblical dust. A minor, yet significant aspect of this painting is the contrast between the yellow stop sign in the right-hand lower corner of the painting and the

Joan Nourry-Barry, *Time Expired*, 1973.
Courtesy of the author and the artist.

red Time Expired marker at the top. The artist contrasts the fact that time, i.e., history, cannot be turned back but gives it a political slant with the comment about Ottawa as having the power to slow down the process. This red flag that states that agrarian society has stopped is different from the aging yellow stop sign by the road. The older stop signs were yellow and not red. They were put up by the society of the day. Today, yellow means slow down. It is a warning sign. So what is contrasted is the meaning of red and the meaning of yellow in terms of stopping. There is an indigenous, now defunct, sense of stopping and an external one that is authoritarian.

The road itself is symbolic of the passing of time, of the fullness of the road at the front of the painting, which is the present, and the smallness of the road at the back of the painting, which is the past where our perspective narrows and eventually is lost. We cannot see the distant past as memory shrinks toward the disappearance of actual events that blend into the eternalness of the horizon and the sky. *Time Expired* is elegiac and commemorative, but with a hint of sacrilege as the gravestone turns into a parking meter. The religious is overcome by the secular, political economy of the present.

Whether one is discussing Proch or Cicansky or Nourry-Barry, the main feature of the postmodernist approach to agrarianism is profound ambiguity. These postmodernist artists of the West are simultaneously critical of the agrarian myth and genuinely attached to it. This results in a sense of conundrum that artistic ingenuity must solve. The artistic statements found in their art are open to a wide range of interpretation, which is not possible with the more obvious statements in modernist western Canadian art. The question of who is a westerner and what is the region results in a disquieting sense of disorientation in postmodernism. There was a level of comfort found in modernist art, which has been replaced with a certain discomfort, a feeling of being not quite *at home* in the postmodernist. This is also true of political developments in the region, which in the post-agrarian phase have developed negative images such as the "blue-eyed sheiks" of Alberta in the 1970s. The loss of agrarian regional homogeneity and its replacement with a diversified political economy that distinguishes the provinces from each other is part of the transition to multiplicity that postmodernism is very good at capturing.

In comparing the agrarian and post-agrarian periods, one can see the link between the socio-economic evolution of western Canadian society or what one might call its political economy and the changes in artistic expression. For the artist who wished to express the life of the region in the modernist period when agrarianism was dominant, the range of possibilities was limited by social conformity and artistic convention. For the postmodernist artist, modernist limits provide an opportunity for going beyond in a significant way. Art that reflects the region is tied to historical evolution over which it has no control. It does not make history other than art history. Instead it is formed by the events and trends that transform societies. Early Euro-Canadian artists who had been witness to, or reared by, the agrarian myth as the fundamental identity of the region had to work within the dominant paradigm. It was not until the Group of Seven became recognized in the 1920s for their pioneering cultural nationalism that Canada could say it had an artistic identity that was struggling to distinguish itself from its European sources. Only later on did those who sought to reject modernism as irrelevant to their artistic concerns such as the abstractionists (The Regina Five) escape the agrarian paradigm. It must be noted that First Nations artists, who gained prominence in the post-agrarian period, did not refer to this myth in their work.[24] Instead they turned to aboriginal traditions, First Nation-specific cultural imagery and stories for their inspiration. The transformation of agrarian society was not important to them since their world had been marginalized by it. Likewise, those prairie artists who turned totally to abstraction found their identity in the current art styles of the day. The contribution of these elements increased the overall complexity of postmodern western Canadian art, as did folk art and traditional landscape painting.[25]

A comparison of the work of the agrarian and post-agrarian periods that deals specifically with the agrarian myth results in four general points of difference. The first was the immigrant nature of agrarian artists compared to their postmodern successors. Both Musgrove and Glyde were from the United Kingdom. While Kerr was born in Saskatchewan, his artistic values were formed by the same forces that influenced his immigrant contemporaries. This coming-to-a-new-land that characterizes the immigrant artist results in what may be termed as coming to grips with "the shock of the new." There is a cultural disorientation of sorts in settler society, which encourages taking possession of the new landscape visually. This appropriation combines the new content – the landscape – with the old form – European aesthetics. The result is a distinctly western Canadian regional expression.

In contrast, the western Canadian-born postmodernists were acclimatized to the regional environment from birth. It was their society from the start and they matured as it evolved. As something internal, rather than external, to their cultural formation, the region and its identity was already integral to them. Its contradictions and anomalies were inherent so that the artist could focus on de-mythologizing rather than the earlier work of mythologizing the West.

Second, modernist art tended toward reverence in its realistic representation, while postmodern art was more irreverent in its symbolism. Even if we take Glyde's highly allegoric *Exodus*, which is filled with biblical allusion, and compare it with Nourry Barry's *Time Expired*, which is also highly religious, we find that there is a major difference. The biblical allegory in Glyde is commensurate with the unchallenged Christian culture of his day, while Nourry-Barry is prepared to mix symbols like the cross and a parking meter that no modernist would dare integrate.

Third, modernist art was strongly documentarian and utilitarian in its orientation. The presentation of "what is" had a realistic underpinning that was meant to celebrate achievement in its actuality. Postmodern art, in contrast, was dealing with a reality that was disappearing before the artist's eye. It was becoming a mirage, a memory, a nostalgic presence that had to be presented in a different non-documentary way. Postmodern art fictionalized the agrarian West, mixing various elements of historical and mythological knowing into a story of what *no longer existed*. That is why postmodern art is so playful. The artist need no longer take agrarianism seriously but have fun with the former reality. Neither Cicansky's books nor jars are functional. Their use is purely aesthetic and imaginary. If Kerr celebrates the prairie road as a quintessential statement of rural landscape that is readily visible in any rural outing, Nourry-Barry can take the same road and turn it into a fantasy landscape that becomes a symbolic graveyard.

Fourth, the modernist aesthetic was unified and singular, when dealing with the topic of agrarian life, while the postmodern aesthetic was diverse. The male Anglo artists of the agrarian period were part of the British imperial mindset and its dominance of English-Canadian society. The non-aboriginal artists of the postmodern period were diverse in gender and ethnicity, though Euro-Canadian. Urban, feminist, and ethnic cultures came to the forefront after 1970. They represented the first sign of the postcolonialism that is such a crucial fact in postmodernist ideology. While the Prairie West was relatively late in racial diversification in terms of non-white immigrants, the vacuum was filled with aboriginal artists of the region, whose aesthetic was non-European.

These differences are dialectical in that the postmodern art of the West subsumes the originating modernist thesis into itself. Postmodern art about agrarianism retains the earlier representational quality, its celebratory and honorific echoes, the documentary impulse, and its populist orientation and Euro-Canadian cultural roots. But it makes these features into postcards from a distant past. The present of postmodern art cannot treat the agrarian world as anything more than an object of demythologization. In this way, it combines continuity and discontinuity in a seamless new synthesis that provides a thesis to be challenged by the next generation that must take on the consequences of contemporary demythologization.

When the *For an Independent Hairy Hill* exhibit premiered in Edmonton, I was so taken by it that I wrote an article analyzing it for *White Pelican*, a quarterly founded by Sheila and Wilfred Watson.[26] The article was then reprinted in *Radical Regionalism* (1981). After that I gradually evolved away from my commitment to a region-wide identity encompassing the three prairie provinces and toward a more Alberta-centric viewpoint (*The Literary History of Alberta*), which argued that in the post-agrarian and continentalist phase of western Canadian identity Alberta's economy was becoming more closely tied to that of British Columbia than Saskatchewan and Manitoba.[27] Regionalism had shifted and the old agrarian verities had divided into a *have* province based on energy income and two *have-not* provinces. The strong base of the rightwing federal Reform Party in the two provinces, the post-1970 oil and gas linkages in production and exploration, the increased air links between Calgary and Vancouver that eventually surpassed those between Calgary and Edmonton, the booming population of the two most westerly provinces compared to dowager Winnipeg and the stagnant population of Saskatchewan, the sizeable new Asian immigration to Vancouver and Calgary in the 1990s – all contributed to a newly evolving world of common interests and associations. When a neo-conservative government was elected in British Columbia in the new century, it was heralded by Alberta's neo-con government as its brother, while at the same time both Saskatchewan and Manitoba had NDP governments. This shift in my thinking was based on a post-agrarian, energy-resource-driven economic paradigm that was also creating a new cultural imperative. I had to ask myself if the *figure-in-the-landscape* theory of prairie populist art that I had articulated three decades ago had become part of history like agrarianism or did it still have relevance?

Western agrarianism in its contemporary form (huge cattle feedlots, 10,000 acre-farms, continentalist agri-business corporate power) is a fundamental part of the economy of the West and remains even in Alberta the second-most-important sector. Is the art of the new agrarianism *figure-in-the-landscape* dominated? From the examples I have provided, it may be claimed that for that sector of the art community that is interested in the issue of agrarian identity and is politically populist, the theory still holds true though it has become postmodernist in its sensibility. However, one can also claim that the new urbane sophistication of cities like Calgary and Edmonton, with populations of one million each, orients artistic culture toward a more continentalist and international artistic aesthetic in which digital art production and dynamic, provocative art installations are the norm.

One example of how the new regionalism of Alberta and British Columbia may be influencing art may be found in the work of Norman Yates (1923–), an artist who participated in the *For an Independent Hairy Hill* exhibit, taught art at the University of Alberta, and retired to British Columbia. Yates was born in Calgary but grew up in Regina. Yates's *Regina Riot 1935* series of drawings is a perfect example of the theory in its heyday. The series was exhibited at the Edmonton Art Gallery in 1973.[28] Later on, while still living in Edmonton, Yates moved toward figureless, abstract landscapes or what he termed "landspaces" of the prairies.[29] These works paralleled those of Takao Tanabe from the same period.[30] When Yates began painting on Vancouver Island, he retained his wide, horizontal abstract landscape format but filled it with vibrantly coloured abstract seascapes, which were much more about motion than light.[31] The stillness of his prairie world was replaced by a dynamism that came from a new form of geography or better still hydrography. He retained his wide horizon perspective and his distillation of the natural using abstract forms and powerful colours that he had developed in the post-agrarian period but changed the content of the paintings to reflect his new natural environment. His migration paralleled what happened to the artists of the United Kingdom in the pioneering phase of agrarianism, when they became prairie artists by bringing new content and a new light to their previous training. The strong presence of the land that Yates experienced in Alberta, and earlier in Saskatchewan, was replaced with the equally strong presence of the sea. Yet, he did not put a figure

Norman Yates. *Farm Drawing No. 7*, 1977.
Courtesy of the artist and the author.

into this environment, as he had in his prairie birthplace. He excused the human from his art to acknowledge his strangeness to the place.

The evolution of Norman Yates from prairie populist to prairie abstractionist to west coast maritime colourist is highly indicative of the tensions in the new regionalism of Alberta and British Columbia. There are links and there are differences – geographic differences and economic links. I suspect that if Yates had settled in the interior of British Columbia with its dominant mountainscape his prairie populist roots would have been more influential. But then he would have had to decide if forests were figures-in-the-landscape or the landscape itself.

The birth of this new regionalism has not invalidated the artistic theory as such, only shrunk the area to which it may be applied, and opened it to broader, more elastic interpretations. At some point the influence of agrarian populism in art may fade completely as prairie agriculture becomes more and more corporatized. In *Hiding the Audience*, Frances W. Kaye alludes to this issue when she states that "a regional culture must have a self rooted in a community or it is simply tumbled about by the metropolitan cultures."[32] As that community changes, so does its art. The move from modernist to postmodernist perspectives is an acknowledgment of that historic change in the character of the prairie region. Kaye also points out that "regional culture and identity" display a tension between indigenous and settler audiences.[33] Nevertheless, the western Canadian's artist's eye, whether aboriginal or Euro-Canadian or Asian-influenced, continues to contribute to the discussion of an evolving regional identity.

In the related field of postmodern prairie literature, the crossing of once rigid modernist boundaries by linking the dominant with the formerly marginalized occurred as early as Andrew Suknaski's *Wood Mountain Poems* (1976) when the poet wrote in his "Western Prayer":

> time to unsaddle
> this lame horse ridden
> into ancestral dust
> and cease living like an indian
> of old.[34]

It has continued in the work of Trevor Herriot, whose *River in a Dry Land* (2000) brought the aboriginal and the white worlds of the Qu'Appelle river and valley together. In his next book, *Jacob's Wound: A Search for the Spirit of Wildness* (2004), Herriot considers the aboriginal sweat lodge "a place of accommodation between the indigenous and non-indigenous peoples of the Great Plains."[35] These writers indicate that a new blending may be occurring. If this is the case, then it could lead to a new, third stage for postmodernist prairie populist art, a post-continentalist phase in which the settler audience naturalizes itself by incorporating the indigenous worldview into regional identity rather than relying simply on the agrarian myth. In this way the former dichotomy between the indigene and the colonizer is overcome. Of course, this is an old, pre-agrarian western dream, first articulated by Louis Riel and now re-visioned for the twenty-first century. It is part of the region's ongoing artistic diversity, as Kaye terms it.[36] At some point in regional history. the *métisization* of art may very well become an accepted orthodoxy.

One of the key elements that may influence western Canadian art in the future is a restatement of ocularity. Seeing is supposedly about space rather than time. But it is clear from this study of postmodernist examples that the presentation of regional agrarian space is currently dominated by a sense of history or time. The art gives us an overpowering sense of the passage of time, especially in a work like *Time Expired.* For postmodernists, the sense of the local involves a rewriting of the meaning of location and locality. The site of their art is not so much spatial as it is temporal. Time takes us out of place by making us sensitive to its demands rather than the physicality of space. These are works of art about the history of the region but in a non-documentary way. They are works of dis-location. They are not historic art in the sense of the genre of historic novels that seek to recreate the past. Instead they are art that takes visual space and binds it to time and historical change. This self-consciousness results in a rewriting of the space-consciousness of the modernist for whom prairie space was the great value. That space is *now* irrelevant because the agricultural economy and the farmer are not what they once were. And with that irrelevance is also the space-oriented irrelevance of landscape art so dear to the modernists. Instead, what is relevant is a sense of time, of the region's history. History allows a re-imagining in which other possibilities exist. Only when the future is uncertain or novel is the past embraced with energy.

The artist's eye plays to our belief in the truth of what we see, while that ocularity is undermined by the fanciful images that the artist puts in the postmodernist work of art. We are made to think, to reflect on what was and is, rather than simply acknowledge and accept. The documentary mode of the modernist offered a reality that often went unchallenged, while the surrealist mode of the postmodernist offers a new West that is being defined in relationship to its past, a past that was mythologized but which is now demythologized, along with the transformation of the region's political economy as it integrates into the continentalist project. Regional distinctness is passing as the identity of the region is influenced by continentalism and the economics of a new westerly regionalism. Now, and in the near future, it is time that is of the essence rather than space, but eventually it may very well be that the new regionalism, based on the division of the West, will proffer a new space, a new regional identity or identities. For now the postmodernist artist has made time a priority in his art and brought an awareness of historical change to western Canadian art. But like all art this is only a phase. Where once we had the art of the Promised Land we now have the promise of a post-industrial society's landless art.

NOTES

1 For a brief discussion of Rindisbacher in a western context and examples of his art, see Virginia G. Berry, *A Boundless Horizon: Visual Records of Exploration and Settlement in the Manitoba Region, 1624–1874* (Winnipeg: Winnipeg Art Gallery, 1983), 15–20. For a wider context of Canadian exploration art, see Michael Bell, *Painters in a New Land: From Annapolis Royal to the Klondike* (Toronto: McClelland and Stewart, 1973), 188–89.

2 A great deal has been written on Paul Kane. The most lavish summary of his work is J. Russell Harper, *Paul Kane's Frontier* (Toronto: University of Toronto Press, 1971).

3 A particular illustration would be described as "a correct reproduction" or "from a sketch by."

4 The original statement describing the post-agrarian and continentalist phases was used in regard to the evolution of different forms of western regionalism. See George Melnyk, "The West as Protest: The Cycles of Regional Discontent," in George Melnyk, ed., *Riel to Reform: A History of Protest in Western Canada* (Saskatoon: Fifth House, 1992), 1–11. The use of political or socio-economic landmarks for distinguishing artistic periods is not an unusual approach in art history. The association of movements like Dadaist art with the trauma of World War I or German Expressionism with post-war economic despair is fairly common.

5 An important example of the struggle of modernism and postmodernism in the period around 1970 was the commissioning, and subsequent decommissioning, of a statute of Louis Riel, the controversial leader of the Metis rebellion, that led to the formation of the province of Manitoba. With the centennial of the province in 1970, the New Democratic government of the day unveiled an expressionistic interpretation of Riel as the father of the province on the legislative grounds. The nude figure in a contorted pose suggesting the pain of birth was rejected by the Metis community, whose leaders considered it inappropriate and offensive. It was later replaced by a work in monumental style of an enthroned figure clearly identifiable as Riel. The symbolism of birth was replaced by the more acceptable symbolism of statesmanship, the father of his people. For a detailed discussion and insightful interpretation of this event, see Francis W. Kaye, *Hiding the Audience: Viewing Arts and Arts Institutions on the Prairies* (Edmonton: University of Alberta Press, 2003), 185–226.

6 R. Douglas Francis, *Images of the West: Changing Perceptions of the Prairies, 1690–1960* (Saskatoon: Western Producer Prairie Books, 1989), 193.

7 Ibid., 203.

8 Berry, *Vistas of Promise*, 61.

9 Collection of the author. For other examples of the same period by the same artist and discussion, see Berry, *Vistas of Promise*, 63.

10 A retrospective study of Musgrove's place in prairie art may be found in Nancy E. Dillow, *The Forgotten Innovator: Alexander J. Musgrove* (Winnipeg: Winnipeg Art Gallery, 1986).

11 This work appears on the cover of Dan Ring, Guy Vanderhaeghe, and George Melnyk, *The Urban Prairie* (Saskatoon: Fifth House, 1993).

12 For an assessment of Glyde, see Patricia Ainslie, *A Lifelong Journey: The Art and Teaching of H. G. Glyde* (Calgary: Glenbow Museum, 1987).

13 See Benjamin G. Smillie, ed., *Visions of the New Jerusalem: Religious Settlement on the Prairies* (Edmonton: NeWest Press, 1983). and David Laycock, *Populism and Democratic Thought in the Canadian Prairies 1910–1945* (Toronto: University of Toronto Press, 1990).

14 Patricia Bovey, "Prairie painting in the Thirties," in *The Dirty Thirties in Prairie Canada*, eds. D. Francis and H. Ganzevoort (Vancouver: Tantalus Research, 1980), 121.

15 The work is reproduced in Illingworth Kerr, *Paint and Circumstance* (Calgary: Jules and Maureen Poscente, 1987), 136.

16 Dawne McCance, "Introduction," *Mosaic* 37, no. 4 (December 2004): xi.

17 See the catalogue for "Don Proch's Asessippi Clouds" (WAG, 1975) for illustrations of these prints.

18 The first of these sculptured three-dimensional drawing-on-masks was circulated in a travelling exhibition by the Winnipeg Art Gallery in 1977.

19 For a recent discussion of Cicansky and his work, see Don Kerr, *The Garden of Art: Vic Cicansky Sculptor* (Calgary: University of Calgary Press, 2004).

20 Tom Radford, "A Disappearing West," in *For an Independent Hairy Hill* (Ottawa: National Gallery of Canada, 1973).

21 For a discussion of the artists and art in the show, see George Melnyk, *Radical Regionalism* (Edmonton: NeWest Press, 1981), 27–34.

22 Examples of this kind of cultural regionalism and nationalism of the 1970s range from Margaret Atwood's *Survival* (1972) and Northrop Frye's *Bush Garden* (1973) to George Melnyk's *Radical Regionalism* (1981).

23 The best example of this trend was the formation of the pro-American Reform Party by Preston Manning of Alberta. The party went through several transformations before absorbing the Progressive Conservative Party to become the Conservative Party of Canada. During this decade and a half process, the rural West was a strong supporter.

24 In Alberta Alex Janvier and in Manitoba Jackson Beardy were among the pioneers. They were followed by Joanne Cardinal-Schubert and George Littlechild, among others.

25 William Kurelek was the most famous of the region's folk artists. Roland Gissing was a typical landscape painter. See Max Foran and Nonie Houlton, *Roland Gissing: The Peoples' Painter* (Calgary: University of Calgary Press, 1988).

26 *White Pelican* 5, no. 1 (1975): 13–25.

27 See "On Being a Self-styled Guru of Western Regionalism," in George Melnyk, *New Moon at Batoche: Reflections on the Urban Prairie* (Banff: Banff Centre Press, 1999).

28 March 25–April 24, 1975.

29 For examples of the transition out of the figure-in-the-landscape motif, see the catalogue for his nationally toured exhibit *Norman Yates: Drawings and Paintings* (Edmonton: Edmonton Art Gallery, 1976).

30 See Nancy Dillow, *Takao Tanabe 1972–1976: The Land* (Regina: Norman Mackenzie Art Gallery, 1976).

31 See the catalogue for his show.

32 Kaye, *Hiding the Audience*, 259.

33 Ibid., 258–60.

34 Andrew Suknaski, *Wood Mountain Poems* (Toronto: Macmillan, 1976), 122.

35 Trevor Harriet, *Jacob's Wound: A Search for the Spirit of Wildness* (Toronto: McClelland and Stewart, 2004), 318.

36 Kaye, *Hiding the Audience*, 259.

17

THE DREAM STILL LIVES: PROMISED LAND NARRATIVES DURING THE SASKATCHEWAN GOLDEN JUBILEE

Michael Fedyk

In 1952, during the second reading debate on legislation outlining government plans for the 1955 Saskatchewan Golden Jubilee, Woodrow Lloyd, one of the celebration's chief architects, spoke passionately about the meaning of the upcoming commemorations: "this is the assurance which we ought, on this occasion, as we are talking today, give to the pioneers.... And we ought also to give the younger people of Saskatchewan, 'the dream still lives, it lives, it lives, and shall not die!'" The "dream" Lloyd alluded to drew on hopes for a Promised Land, but more than just an idyllic future; it suggested a narrative that included an escape from the past as well as the trials and hardships that the early pioneers experienced. Concepts of pioneers and progress, past and future, dominated the Saskatchewan Jubilee. The integration of these two themes combined historical and contemporary influences that captured both the optimistic expectations of the 1950s and the lingering fears left over from the Great Depression. Lloyd's dream, like many aspects of the Jubilee, allayed insecurities left from the past by projecting confidence in the future.

Few, if any, people used the term "Promised Land" during the Golden Jubilee. Despite this, "Promised Land narratives" were evident throughout the celebrations.[1] The use of the term "narrative" here draws upon the ideas of Paul Ricoeur and Hayden White. They define narrative as any organization of factual and/or descriptive information (what White calls "content") that provides "meaning" by shaping the past.[2] Ricoeur argues that narratives create meaning by accessing the universal human experience, which "promises a future because it finds a 'sense' in every relationship between past and present."[3] Narratives express meanings based on the perspectives and/or the purposes of the person or people who create the narrative. There are many types of narrative structures that can be applied to the same or similar content. Stories about the same event or person, therefore, will vary depending on what type of narrative structure the storyteller chooses. The purpose of narratives rests primarily on the lessons they teach. Thus narratives relay information only as a secondary function, and never in a purely objective manner.

While some historians use the term rather generically to describe any kind of hope for a utopian future, the Promised Land alludes to the *Old Testament* narratives. These relate how the Israelites as the chosen people escaped slavery in Egypt and underwent trials and hardships while wandering for forty years in the desert before finally reaching the Promised Land. Further, the Bible does not end when the Israelites reach Israel, as they continue to face challenges for hundreds of years afterwards.[4] In a general way, then, Promised Land narratives typically feature a significant break with an unpleasant past and focus on the achievement of a better future. This future requires struggle and frequently can only be maintained through vigilant adherence to values often handed down by past generations. Therefore, in this article, Promised Land does not indicate a simplistic, naive, or impractical vision of an idealistic future, but rather represents a more nuanced optimism grounded in a belief that a positive future is possible but that to achieve it will exact a price.

Studies that focus on the idea of the Canadian West as a Promised Land often emphasize what appears, at least in hindsight, to have been unrealistic expectations that Euro-Canadian expansionists and settlers held before arriving in the West. In *Promise of Eden*, Doug Owram points out the complexities underlying exaggerated claims about the potential of the West. "The expansionist campaign was effective," states Owram, "only because it appealed to widespread hopes and fears within the Canadian community."[5] Concerns about American intentions and limitations on commercial activities in the East influenced perceptions of the West as much as economic prosperity and faith in technology.

Expansionists often had to debunk previously popular notions about the Canadian West that discouraged development or had to compete with ideas about the opportunities available in the American West. Such cases suggest that insecurity underlay some of the bravado of expansionist rhetoric.

Regardless of the extent to which settlers accepted expansionist propaganda prior to their arrival, once in the West, they soon became aware of the difference between advertising and reality. Owram contends that "the great strength of the expansionists was their ability to evoke an image of the future, their great failure was their inability to maintain any sort of relationship between the myth and the much harsher and more prosaic reality of frontier life."[6] He indicates that, despite this gulf, as the West developed, it appropriated both expansionist spirit and rhetoric. "Faith in the future," says Owram, "is an essential part of the farmer's character if he is to persevere in his precarious livelihood. In its outlook such an attitude is strikingly similar to the tendency of the expansionist to look not at the actual state of things but at the potential of the land for the future."[7]

By the 1950s, a more sophisticated version of expansionism had developed. While retaining much of the optimistic language of its earlier champions, it also incorporated a sense of the realities and hardships of the settlement era and, in particular, of the Great Depression of the 1930s. There were numerous versions of Promised Land narratives, but ideas about pioneers or progress defined the most common types and frequently provided the basis for single narratives combining both themes. The provincial government naturally identified honouring the pioneers and celebrating progress as the Jubilee's principal themes because both concepts enjoyed widespread popular acceptance long before the Jubilee.[8]

The government's Jubilee agenda initially focussed on a massive public relations campaign designed to build Saskatchewan's tourism industry, convince potential outside investors the province had a healthy business climate, and enhance cultural and educational resources. However, it was pioneers and progress that account for the massive participation of Saskatchewan citizens in Jubilee activities. These themes were front and centre at 475 local Jubilee celebrations that attracted approximately three million people, in thousands of articles and stories in Jubilee edition weekly newspapers and local histories, and through numerous other vehicles such as literature and art contests, historical pageants, and school activities. Prominent individuals such as premier

Tommy Douglas, Woodrow Lloyd, Lieutenant-Governor William Patterson, Jubilee chairperson Edward Culliton, Jubilee executive director Fred McGuinness, and Legislative librarian John Archer also used these themes in their speeches, as did small town mayors, local business people, and men and women from all major ethnic groups and many different occupations. Such individuals fashioned narratives that used pioneers and progress to teach lessons about the past that they believed would help create a brighter future – a Promised Land.

Progress had been a major aspect of western Canadian perspectives of the future long before the Jubilee. Historian Gerald Friesen, for instance, asserts that: "Nowhere [other than the Canadian west] was that central tenet of the nineteenth century gospel [progress] to mean more. Faith in western development was part of the philosophy of Confederation, and the West itself was founded upon local expectations of growth, prosperity and power."[9] Although faith in progress diminished during the Great Depression, it re-emerged after World War II with startling strength due in no small measure to the social and economic conditions of the time.[10] The massive disruptions of the Depression and the war made many members of the postwar generation anxious to make up for lost time. John Archer's comments in a 1954 speech accurately reflected such feelings: "Theirs [his generation] was the victory [of World War II].... Saskatchewan since the war, burst out in new strength and new vigour ... we are young and strong and eager to meet the future."[11] Almost identical sentiments appeared at Jubilee celebrations in Battleford, where one speaker stated:

> [Battleford] stands at the cross roads of the old and the new.... With the cessation of hostilities [World War II], came a resurgence of hope for the old town. A younger generation is now at the helm in every sphere of community activity. A new day is dawning for the community that has given so freely of its best in peace and war, to the upbuilding of Western Canada.[12]

The economic conditions and technological innovations of the 1950s seemed custom-made for the optimism of Saskatchewan's postwar generation. Following the war, farmers enjoyed fairly stable commodity prices and good crops.[13] Net income for the province's farmers was $201,403,000 in 1950, and increased every year until 1953 when it reached $437,744,000.[14] It declined in 1954 due to damage caused by excessive moisture, but the exceptional crops of 1952 and 1953 provided a cushion that supported farm incomes over these rough years.[15] Farm mechanization also contributed to rural prosperity. The number of combines on Saskatchewan farms increased from 42,997 to 61,861 between 1951 and 1956.[16] Various types of improved and affordable farm equipment made it possible to farm more land with fewer workers.[17]

During the 1950s, governments steadily built highways and improved the grid road system. Between 1949 and 1955, the number of vehicles registered in Saskatchewan increased from 185,027 to 274,950.[18] Growing vehicle ownership and road building alleviated much of the sense of isolation among rural people. As A. W. Johnson suggests in *Dream No Little Dreams*, during the 1950s "the automobile made distances of twenty-five to fifty miles insignificant on Saskatchewan's plains."[19]

Rural electrification was also in full swing by the start of the 1950s. Between 1949 and 1958, the government added between two thousand and sixty-five hundred farms to the rural grid annually, and by the end of the 1950s almost complete rural electrification was achieved. Rural electrification boosted the economy by increasing consumer demand for electrical appliances, but most importantly it made farm life considerably more comfortable. As Clint White points out in *Power for a Province*: "Farmers were definite in their opinion that power had made farm life more pleasant and had improved living conditions, having done more than any other recent technological development to make such conditions comparable with urban centers."[20]

Urban prosperity and growth accompanied the improvements to rural life. In 1952, the Saskatchewan Industrial Development Office stated that the Saskatchewan residents had a personal income 20 per cent higher than the national average,[21] and predicted even more prosperity in 1953.[22] In addition, during the 1950s both the federal and provincial governments built large new buildings in Regina and Saskatoon. As well, large numbers of new multi-grade and multi-purpose schools replaced the province's system of one-room schools.[23] Between 1946 and 1956, the province's urban population grew from 208,872 to 322,003, and even after factoring in rural depopulation, the province gained 47,977 new citizens.[24]

Economic diversification was one of the most significant factors in the province's growing prosperity. As Johnson shows, while agriculture remained the province's most dominant industry, diversification into petroleum, natural gas, mining, tourism, and forestry increased during the 1950s.[25] In his 1955 budget address, provincial treasurer Clarence Fines enthusiastically described the expansion of some of these new industries:

> The most spectacular gains were recorded, as everyone knows in the mineral industries. Total value of production jumped some 19 per cent – from $48 million in 1953 to $57 million in 1954, and again I note that these figures exclude the increasing value of production of radio-active substances. In petroleum, both value and volume of output were doubled, while that of natural gas was tripled.... All told the investment in exploration, drilling, pipelines and refineries in 1954 is estimated at about $86.4 million, and the Department of Mineral Resources officially designated as new discoveries during the year a total of nineteen new oil fields.... Sharing the spotlight with oil in 1954 was the rapid development of the Athabaska [*sic*] uranium fields.... In regard to potash, not only was actual development work pushed ahead by two companies, but at least two other internationally known firms entered the province to take up exploration and development rights.[26]

Not surprisingly, progress commonly found expression in the Jubilee through celebrations of the 1950s by emphasizing these positive economic conditions and technological innovations. The following poem from the *Touchwood Times*, for example, glorified modern technology:

> We've left the oxen behind us, the buggie, and brave old Bill,
> The separators hum, and the engines wild-west shrill,
> And come to the Fords, and Cadillacs all, and combines and
> Tractors too,
> From wireless to radio, phone and T.V. and Jet Planes
> Speeding high in the blue
> So, here's to SASKATCHEWAN'S *Golden Grain*, shipped
> Out to every part,
> Carried by up-to-date diesel train, down to the shipping port.[27]

The extent of progress in Saskatchewan often engendered a source of pride. An advertisement for the Arcola Co-operative Association stated:

> Few regions on the earth have witnessed such a transformation in the short space of fifty years and those of us who now reside here should have some realization of the effort, fortitude and resolve which went into building of prairie prosperity. The Co-operative movement has progressed from the ox-cart stage to the oil well age in step with the progress and development of the Saskatchewan economy.[28]

Symbols of technology, rural electrification, highway construction, modern schools and buses, along with the north, which came to symbolize both natural resource development and tourism, were used to project the province's promising economic future and appeared throughout the Jubilee. "Parades of Progress" that became a standard component of local celebrations contrasted settlement era with 1950s technologies. The presence of combines in Jubilee edition advertising, and in Jubilee paintings and movies, made it one of the most ubiquitous symbols of progress. In some advertisements, splendid, even science fiction-like, graphics depicted progress.[29] A historical pageant enacted by students at Regina's Central Collegiate traced Saskatchewan history from pre-contact times to the 1950s and concluded with a scene set in the future. The scene was entitled "Land of Promise," and starred "Mr. Success," an urban big-business figure.[30]

Predictions that Saskatchewan's future would be even more prosperous were common. Premier T. C. (Tommy) Douglas was the province's chief booster. Douglas's speeches typically included lengthy lists that outlined the potential of Saskatchewan's oil, gas, uranium, and other mineral deposits. In a provincial radio address during the Jubilee's closing banquet, the premier concluded that while Saskatchewan was once regarded as "the poor country cousin of Confederation, [it is now in the 1950s considered] ... a lady of considerable means and excellent prospects. Saskatchewan continues to surprise the people of the rest of Canada with her achievements for no province in Canada is more richly endowed than ours."[31]

Douglas's vision of the future was widely shared, as symbols of economic expectations appeared almost everywhere during the Jubilee. In the Jubilee movie, *Face of Saskatchewan*, for example, images of oil drilling, gas pipelines, modern highways, and northern mineral development accompanied by the following narration communicated the message that Saskatchewan possessed a growing diversified economy:

They are drilling for more oil near Kindersley
Pipelines cross her prairies
Oil for Saskatchewan refineries
Here working together is a way of life
Federated Co-op is a nerve centre of community endeavor
New services link prairie town to prairie town, in spite of weather
Now all-weather roads cross her plains
She stretches high to the north
Here she has traded flat plains for pine and lake
This is the land where minerals and lumber have broadened the
base of Saskatchewan's one crop economy[32]

To emphasize the increasing diversification of the Saskatchewan economy, depictions of oil derricks along with wheat sheaves were evident on Jubilee publications, and in local histories, special Jubilee editions and local historical pageants.[33] An editorial in the *Shaunavon Standard* related the significance of such symbols: "The discovery of oil in the Shaunavon district has been the highlight of the past half-century and may be termed as a link between the past and the future, the culmination of an era of pioneering and development and an indication of a coming era of vast mechanism, the beginning of which has been evident in recent years."[34] During the Jubilee, such symbols of progress anticipated a future even more prosperous and secure than the present and much better than the past.

The optimism of the progress theme, however, was tempered by the memories of the 1930s, which remained very powerful in the Saskatchewan of the 1950s. The Depression had hit Saskatchewan especially hard because of its dependence on agriculture, and this countered any feelings of security the relative strength of the agricultural economy may have created. The tendency of many Saskatchewan people in the 1950s was not to place faith in prosperity because they feared it would eventually end. This tendency was especially prevalent in the province's dominant agricultural sector.[35] As John Archer aptly noted in his history of Saskatchewan: "[during the 1950s] the memory [of the 1930s] yet rode with the younger generation on their tractors."[36]

Such feelings support Doug Owram's argument in *Born at the Right Time* that a major characteristic of the postwar period was a sense of insecurity caused by the Depression and the disruptions of the war. According to Owram, because insecurity was associated with a past full of hardship and difficulty, people despised the old and embraced "faith in technology."[37] During the 1950s, people allayed their insecurities with symbols of technology, which came to symbolize the present and the future. Advertising during the Jubilee period reflected such sentiments by stressing the advantages of farm mechanization over older technology. A 1955 advertisement in the *Assiniboia Times* proclaimed a new tractor, "SO NEW SO BIG SO POWERFUL," and urged readers to: "[s]ee it today … Own one … and forget the troubles of yesterday."[38] The advertisement promoted technology as an antidote to the insecurities embodied by Depression memories.

The link between fears of another depression and perceptions of weakness in the agricultural economy also accounted for why growth in other areas became important symbols. Economic diversification held the promise of a future economy not dependent on the vagaries of weather or unstable agricultural commodity prices. Economic diversification addressed the lingering anxieties left by a depression that in the West was the result of an over-emphasis on agriculture, and also provided a balance to concerns generated by rural depopulation, which threatened the future of family farms and the small communities.[39] As John Archer explained in the Jubilee speakers' guidebook: "Today Saskatchewan prospers, but even the prospect of the biggest harvest on record does not entirely stifle the poignant undertones of anxiety born of the instabilities of the past. These may well be muted in a future of oil and industry."[40] The language of progress may have appeared little more than naive bravado, but it also spoke to a deep insecurity born from the reality of hardship in a recent past.

What most strongly grounded the idea of progress in reality, even more than the undercurrent of insecurity, was its association throughout the Jubilee with pioneers. Ideas about pioneers incorporated a long line of oral and folk traditions, as well as influences such as settlement-era propaganda, but they were not merely a regurgitation of past beliefs. The theme was adapted to fit a 1950s perspective. One influence on such a perspective was the continuing presence in the 1950s of the living members of the pioneer generation. The government deliberately chose not to provide a definition for who was considered a pioneer, preferring to leave this entirely to each community.[41] Few communities developed any type of criteria but generally recognized their oldest citizens as pioneers, which in most communities meant every non-Aboriginal person over seventy years of age, including both men and women and members of every large ethnic group. In addition to early agricultural settlers, most

Local Jubilee celebrations most frequently centred on recognizing the living members of the pioneer generation. Groups like these from Rush Lake (top) and Moosomin (bottom) were typical.

cities and towns acknowledged any early residents regardless of occupation as pioneers.[42]

Pioneers represented a significant portion of Saskatchewan's people. In 1951, there were 100,953 people, nearly one eighth of the population, who had been between the ages of 14 and 44 in 1905, and of these 45,903 had been at least four years old in 1885. These numbers declined to 78,651 and 27,811 respectively by 1956, but this still represented a significant number of individuals.[43] The pioneers were the parents, grandparents, friends, and neighbours of the postwar generation, and they provided what the *Kindersley Clarion* called "the link of living memory," a tangible connection to the settlement era.[44] Virtually every local celebration centred on honouring the pioneers. Local committees honoured them with banquets, gifts, mementos, free entry to events, and special seating. The pioneers' successors dedicated local histories, plaques, parks, buildings, and innumerable speeches to them.[45]

The personal connection between generations reverberated throughout local celebrations. Many people stressed the importance of recognizing the pioneers' contributions before they passed on.[46] Expressing appreciation to senior citizens motivated many local organizers as shown by comments from several organizers that emphasized how happy pioneers appeared when they received even small tokens of recognition.[47] The Jubilee chairwoman from Kelstern expressed the feelings of many people concerning the purpose of local celebrations: "When the evening ended an oldtimer stood up, and on behalf of all the guests thanked those who had thought enough of the old Folks to do what we had done for them. They enjoyed everything, banquet, music and all the work and worry was forgotten."[48] In several communities, local committees arranged special presentations for pioneers bedridden at home or in a hospital. In a radio speech, premier Douglas described the emotion such presentations engendered:

> I cannot begin to describe the pleasure on the faces of these old people at knowing that they had not been forgotten by their community. I remember one old man who was 91 who showed me his lovely bouquet of flowers and then said with tears in his eyes, 'They haven't forgotten me.' That was the spirit which characterized the Golden Jubilee – the people of this province showed the pioneers in a hundred little ways that we hadn't forgotten them and that we are deeply indebted to them.[49]

The sense of debt successor generations felt to the pioneers owed much to their perceptions of the settlement era. They seldom romanticized the past, and their tributes to the pioneers typically included long lists of hardships such as blizzards, prairie fires, droughts, grasshopper infestations, floods, and hail. One Blaine Lake Jubilee organizer wrote: "Provisions were scarce, livestock few and implements crude and scarce. Prairie fires, mosquitoes and harsh winters added further to the difficulties of the early years."[50] An equally negative passage in the history of Semans and District discussed the lone weary journeys endured by the homesteaders, the plagues of mosquitoes in summer, and severe frosts and raging blizzards during the winter.[51] Descriptions of the settlement era invariably used words like "privations," "sorrow," "loneliness," "arduous," "suffering," and "hard times" that left little doubt that few people found the so-called "good old days" appealing. As a Co-operative Creamery advertisement placed in numerous Jubilee editions pointed out: while some might have looked back to the past with affection, "few would like to go back to horses, or open cars … [or the] hard times, severe setbacks and calamities of one kind or another."[52]

Successor generations expressed their attitude towards the settlement era through unflattering comparisons between the technology used by the pioneers and that of the 1950s. This contrast was particularly evident in the "Parades of Progress." These started with examples of farm equipment, vehicles, and other technologies from earlier decades and concluded with 1950s machinery. Some parades included floats contrasting sod shacks with modern homes. Others compared conveniences, such as running water, with settlement-era technology like washing boards.[53] The use of words like "ancient"[54] and "primitive"[55] to describe pioneer farm machinery and agricultural practices emphasized the contrast between the 1950s and the settlement era. In similar representations used throughout the Jubilee, the past always appeared more difficult, less developed, less convenient, and less comfortable compared to the 1950s.[56]

The feelings of successor generations towards the settlement era owed much to their Depression experiences. They had shared hardships comparable, if not worse, to what the pioneers experienced during the settlement era, and this allowed them to empathize with their parents and grandparents. For this reason, discussions of the Depression were often linked to the hardships endured during the settlement era.[57] K. F. Cleall, the mayor of Unity, for example, penned an article for the local newspaper that reflected on the development of his community in relation to the significance of the provincial anniversary. When he discussed the Depression, he philosophically acknowledged that the experience, although very difficult, steeled his generation and helped them to appreciate the values of their forebears, the pioneers. "After all," he stated, "the actual hardships [of the Depression] were not as great as what the pioneers endured but they looked always to the future and not to at [*sic*] the past."[58] The Depression sequence of the provincial historical pageant expressed similar sentiments. The script called for the narrator to state that "out of the drifting dust and tumbling Russian thistle grew again the old, indomitable spirit of the pioneers."[59] The members of the successor generations involved in the Jubilee associated the pioneers' hardships with their own experiences. While they respected the pioneers, they did not want to recreate pioneer times. The Jubilee celebrated pioneers, but not the settlement era.

The fact that pioneers had endured the hardships of the settlement era without the advantages of 1950s technology made them natural heroes to their successors. The writers of the community of Hudson Bay's local history marvelled that the pioneers had "with their bare hands … carved homes from the reluctant wilderness."[60] An editorial from a Yorkton paper said the pioneers were heroes because not only did they survive the "tests of nature" but also "the hardships of an undeveloped country – no roads, no adequate tools, no medical or educational facilities."[61] Not surprisingly, some members of successor generations, such as the daughter of one pioneer at the Elrose Jubilee, expressed feelings of humility in the presence of the pioneers.[62] For an age group that associated modern technology with success, comfort, and ease, they saw the pioneers' achievements without this technology as nothing less than heroic.

The perceived prosperity of the 1950s added purpose to the pioneers' experiences. They had endured because they had the vision of the future that had become reality. These comments in an editorial from the *Saltcoats Star* captured this belief:

> We of this modern generation are enjoying all these privileges, advantages, and luxuries and taking them more or less as a matter of course, should never lose sight of the fact that they were bought for us with a price. That price being the struggles, privations and toil of our forefathers, who with *foresight* and faith laid the foundations of this province.[63]

Woodrow Lloyd's comments during the introduction of the Jubilee legislation expressed similar sentiments:

> It seems to me that we do get faith for the future by adding up the accomplishments of the past [using history] we can develop the proudness required in our province.... We do stand looking backwards to get strength from our history, and we stand looking to the future, with a faith that comes from the assurance of a past of which we can be proud ... that, it seems, to me, is the assurance which we ought, on such an occasion as we are talking today, give to the pioneers ... and we ought also to give the younger people of Saskatchewan, "the dream still lives, it lives, it lives, and shall not die!"[64]

Lloyd's declaration was a promise to younger people that his generation would continue the work of the pioneers. Numerous speakers exhorted their audiences with similar rhetoric. Jubilee chairman Ted Culliton declared the Jubilee represented confidence and pride, which was "something to display, something the pioneers had."[65] "Pioneers set a high mark," asserted lieutenant-governor William Patterson. "We have their record and tradition to emulate."[66] A United Church minister in Estevan told his parishioners that future generations must "build upon the foundation laid by our forefathers."[67] The mayor of Herbert wrote: "Fifty years ago they [the pioneers] accomplished many impossible looking tasks"; "we can do the same today."[68] Numerous slogans such as "Building the Future on a Pioneer Foundation," which appeared on a 4-H float in the Senlac Jubilee parade, also promoted this idea.[69]

The use of pioneers as symbols of inspiration did not conjure up an image of a golden past but rather challenged the youth of the 1950s to face the future with the same courage as their predecessors. Pioneer symbols throughout the Jubilee, therefore, were primarily inspirational in nature. One of the best examples was the dedication sculpted at the entrance of the Museum of Natural History in Regina. It portrayed a pioneer family consisting of a man, a woman, and a female child standing on swathed wheat with the accompanying inscription:

> THIS MUSEUM OF NATURAL HISTORY IS DEDICATED TO THE HONOUR OF ALL THE PIONEERS WHO CAME FROM MANY LANDS TO SETTLE THIS PART OF CANADA A TRIBUTE TO THEIR VISION TOIL AND COURAGE WHICH GAVE SO MUCH TO SASKATCHEWAN AND THIS NATION[70]

The dedication of the Museum of Natural History in 1956. The unveiling of the dedication in 1955 by Governor General Vincent Massey officially launched the Jubilee and signified the centrality of Promised Land narratives to the anniversary celebrations.

Although this dedication was more expensive and formalized than most portrayals of the pioneer theme, the text and sculpture contained meanings found in other acknowledgments to pioneers. The dedication communicated a powerful sense of generational debt and provided a heroic model for future generations. "VISION" and the family's reverential gaze skyward expressed the pioneers' faith in the future. "TOIL" represented their work ethic that, along with the scythe by the man's feet, symbolized the hardships of the settlement era. "COURAGE," along with the male figure's lack of a shirt, projected heroism and vitality. The wheat suggested the pioneers' economic contributions, while the child figure acknowledged women's specific contributions as well as the link to successor generations.

The inspirational power of these symbols was not lost on a radio reporter covering the opening of the museum on May 16, 1955. A week

Messages like the one on this 4-H float in the Senlac Jubilee parade were very common. They linked Promised Land hopes of the pioneers to the similar aspirations of the 1950s generation.

prior to the opening, Saskatchewan suffered from torrential rains that caused some of the heaviest flooding and crop damage in provincial history. Newspaper reports gloomily dashed all hopes for a good crop, and the weather on the day of the museum's opening was foreboding.[71] The reporter commented that the cold, windy day, with its driving rain, felt more like March than May, but then added: "The rain crushed many farmers hopes but has not broken their spirit. Which is so reminiscent of the pioneers who are commemorated with the opening of this museum."[72] The reporter in effect stated: "we can survive this because we are cut from the same cloth as the pioneers and they survived."

The pioneer theme suggested that a brighter future was probable but also taught the lesson that it was neither guaranteed nor easy to attain. This notion coloured the 1950s optimism expressed in the progress theme as the two concepts were frequently linked. During the debate introducing the Jubilee legislation, the member of the Legislative Assembly for Melville put the connection succinctly when he said: "We [current generations] … are pioneers in the progress of Saskatchewan."[73] The government of Saskatchewan's advertisement that appeared in every Jubilee edition contained a written message from Douglas, which emphasized the pioneer theme but surrounded it with graphics depicting modern Saskatchewan's economic development.[74] Jubilee advertisements from local, provincial, national, and international companies contained similar juxtapositions. Imperial Oil's advertisement featured oil derricks and modern combines with a text that boasted that the company "pioneered in the oil exploration … which is today bringing new prosperity to Saskatchewan's citizens."[75] A 1955 editorial in the *Star City Echo* made similar linkages: "During the course of the year, much emphasis has been placed on the progress of the province as a grain producer. Rapid development is also being witnessed since the war in the industrial arena, and in the development of natural resources.… For blessings of material progress we give thanks to God, and we pay tribute to those hardy men and women who pioneered, and made the sacrifices, so essential to the development of the land to its present state of productivity."[76]

Such integration of pioneers and progress allowed younger people to take on the mantle of the pioneers. Successor generations drew parallels between the progress of the 1950s and the goals of the pioneers. Therefore, as an advertisement for the North Battleford co-op centre explained, people building their lives during the postwar period were pioneers:

> It took courage and cooperation by our early pioneers to carve a rich land out of a wilderness. Community minded people have pioneered their own co-operative business and have built a modern shopping centre to supply themselves with services at fair prices and honest quality. Share in the benefits of co-operation by joining your local Co-op and be a pioneer of progress by assuring a better future for all.[77]

In a similar vein, a Regina *Leader-Post* editorial concerning the opening of the water treatment plant at Buffalo Pound Lake associated the progress of the 1950s with the work of the pioneers:

> That the primitive prairie town which became the province's capital 50 years ago has progressed to where virtually on its own it financed and built the $7,000,000 project to bring water 40 miles to the city, in itself is symbolical of the giant forward strides the province

has made in its first half century. That this is an undertaking by the new generation who have followed in the footsteps of the pioneers is a happy augury for the future; it is outward manifestation of the fact that the vicissitudes of the cruel and harsh thirties left un-impaired the initiative, the enterprise, and the high hopes for the future for the people of Regina, and of Saskatchewan.[78]

Such comparisons filled Jubilee speeches and publications. The radio program, "A Salute to Saskatchewan Women," compared the lives of early settlers with the lives of oil rig workers in Saskatchewan in the 1950s. "The new pioneers of Saskatchewan," it stated, "are the oil men and their wives."[79] An advertisement from the local kinsman club in the *Wadena News* linked their activities to the pioneers by stating: "Much of the service work that is carried on in Wadena today by the Kinsmen Club of Wadena, is a protégé [*sic*] of their [the pioneers] wishes."[80] An article from the *Weyburn Review* reported: "When Saskatchewan observes its 100th birthday, the mayor said he was quite certain that tribute would be paid not only to the pioneers of 1905 but also to the pioneers of 1955."[81]

One of the best examples of ideas of progress transforming pioneers into symbols of the future was an advertisement from a local shoe store in the *Swift Current Sun*. A text and graphics featuring a settlement-era cowboy in front of a futuristic city proclaimed:

> Today … in the era of Jet flight and the Atomic bomb … We're Pioneering the Future!
>
> In this Jubilee Year, when we stand on the door step of a era, we must accept that torch passed on by our pioneers, and carry it forward into the future. Let us remember that 50 years from now we will be included in that great company of pioneers we are memorializing today, for the Age of the Pioneer never passes. And so we must fashion from the conference tables of the world and the new atomic power a glorious new and a more secure and peaceful world.[82]

Such futuristic qualities bestowed pioneer symbols with modern relevance. The Red River cart, for instance, like the log cabin in American frontier iconography, came to symbolize great achievements from small beginnings.[83] The government built replicas of these carts to mark Red River cart trails where they intersected with modern highways, which linked the hardships of the pioneers to the challenges. As the text of one of the markers stated: "It [the trail] was the first 'highway' through these

The use of Red River carts, such as this one in the Perdue Jubilee parade, linked the Promised Land narratives of the settlement era with those of the 1950s.

plains and hills."[84] The *Hamilton Spectator* commented on this connection in a business column: "the thought was driven home that this cumbersome, two-wheeled cart was just as much a challenge to future generations as it was a monument to the past. It symbolized transportation – the link between east and west upon which Canada's defence and economy depends – whether it be aeroplanes, railways or steamers, oil pipelines or gas pipelines."[85] Local committees inundated the Jubilee office with requests to borrow Red River carts for parades and some communities reconstructed carts themselves.[86] Important guests and local leaders often rode in them in parades, indicating that the cart bestowed status on its passengers.[87]

Such combinations of the two themes were highly significant because the pioneer always symbolized overcoming hardship. As a result, various Jubilee celebrations of progress consistently qualified themselves with reminders, as the Jubilee movie stated that "any kind of progress means work, hard work usually." Like many Jubilee conveyances, *The Face of Saskatchewan* was filled with symbols of prosperity and technology, but it also included cattle frozen to death in blizzards, roads washed out by torrential rain, and several references to the Depression. The movie ended on a positive note as the sun emerges from clouds but only after a violent thunderstorm and allusions to the 1930s drought and the anxieties of being at the mercy of the weather.[88]

The pioneer theme also qualified the materialism of the progress theme. During his speech at the Jubilee's closing banquet, Premier Douglas immediately followed his remarks about economic development with this statement: "But the balance sheet of a province is not measured in material terms alone. The pioneers did more than build a province they left us a heritage of courage and determination, of good neighborliness, and service to one's fellow man, and qualities like that will make any province strong and prosperous."[89] In a radio address prior to the final banquet, Douglas summarized what he considered the most important aspects of the Jubilee. While he made numerous references to economic development and progress, his most poignant remarks centred on community values rather than material success:

> A few days ago a farmer in southern Saskatchewan lost his hand while applying a belt dressing on his combine. Neighbors from far and near gathered with their power machinery and in a single day took off his entire crop. I visited this young farmer in the hospital the other evening and he told me how much it meant to have neighbors like that. This is the sort of thing that makes Saskatchewan a wonderful place in which to live. It is something our forefathers learned in time of adversity; let us never lose it in times of prosperity.[90]

These types of sentiments were more than a product of Douglas's personal convictions. William Patterson, lieutenant governor, former Liberal premier, and political rival of Douglas, frequently expressed very similar ideas. Patterson spoke extensively at Jubilee events, where he described Saskatchewan's material and technological advances, but he always asserted that while these were useful it was the qualities such as tolerance, embodied by the pioneers, that were really important.[91] Patterson argued that, without spiritual progress, material progress was "nothing." According to Patterson, the Jubilee was important because it reinforced spiritual values, and "[n]o matter what progress [was made] in the next fifty years – without these [the spiritual qualities – progress will be of] little importance."[92]

Accompanying many celebrations of material progress and prosperity were suggestions to keep these in their proper perspective. The editor of the *Bruno Banner* reminded his readers that, while there are few millionaires in Saskatchewan, "neither do our people die for want of bread or meat or drink. And all can learn to read and write and worship God. And all are free to live, to speak, to plan a life, to think."[93] In a message to his constituents, the member of the legislature for Elrose argued that financial success was not the "true index of people's greatness … [because] only as we lose ourselves in the fulfillment of our nobler ambitions can we make any contribution to our day and generation."[94] In a message predicting that an upcoming oil boom would double the population of Unity, the town's mayor commented: "However all this may be, may I be pardoned for saying once again that the size of the population is not all that counts, but, what is important, is the spirit of tolerance and co-operativeness of the people."[95]

Each time Saskatchewan people called on pioneer and progress themes they were alluding to Promised Land narratives, even if they were not conscious of doing so. They hoped for a better future – that they might reach the Promised Land – but acknowledged that, like the pioneers, they would face challenges along the way. In some cases, however, these symbols were used to construct complete narratives. Such was the case with the winning entry in the one-act play division of the Saskatchewan Art Board's Jubilee literature competition. It included all the principal pioneer and progress elements that made Promised Land narratives so potent. "Magic Lake," by Anne Flavell of Saskatoon, used a story about generational relationships to address the underlying anxieties caused by memories of the Depression. The plot concerns a young man who wishes to invest in a tourism venture in northern Saskatchewan. Lacking sufficient capital, he recruits a curling team in order to win a large cash prize at a local tournament. His mother, due to her strong memories of the Depression, forbids him to enter the draw because she wants him to take a safe job at a local bank. The son (Ken) challenges his mother (Mrs. Robertson), arguing that investment in northern Saskatchewan is too good an opportunity to miss.[96]

Mrs. Robertson: I do understand, but I still have to think of your future.

Ken: [Jumping up again] That's just it. It's my future. So why not let me decide what to do with it? Maybe my plan doesn't sound very sensible to you. But your parents came out here before the railroad, when there were no roads, no telephone, no hospitals. That wasn't very safe or sensible, was it?

Mrs. Robertson: But, that was different. They …

Ken: How was it different? I'll bet their parents were sitting back in Ontario, shaking their heads. But they came anyway. And look at the country they opened up. There aren't half as many chances for us kids today, but some of us still want to be pioneers while there's pioneering left to do! …

Mrs. Robertson: It's a beautiful dream, Kenneth, but that's all it is.

Ken: OK, so it's a dream. What would happen to this world if no one ever dreamed? They'd never have climbed Mount Everest, or flown the Atlantic, or invented television sets. If nobody dreamed what a dull world it would be.

Mrs. Robertson: I know security sounds dull to you, but you haven't lived through the Depression like I have.

Ken: Just because there was a Depression once, does that mean we have to go pussy-footing around for the rest of our lives?

One of the members of Ken's curling team then explains that his life is miserable because his wife squashed his dreams and forced him to take a secure job instead. Shortly after this, that man's wife bursts in and berates him for his irresponsibility and blames Ken for leading him astray. This ultimately wins Mrs. Robertson over to Ken's position because she wants her son to have a better future than being trapped in a job that he hates. She rises to Ken's defence stating:

Mrs. Robertson: Mrs. McGregor [the friend's wife], my son earned that money with his own two hands, and I'm thinking he has a right to spend it as he wills. It takes courage to go up there and risk your money – and maybe even your life – to open up the north country of ours. It's men like him, Mrs. McGregor, who made this country what it is today. And if my son has what it takes to set out and be a pioneer, then all I can say is "The more power to him!"[97]

Narratives like "Magic Lake" were used to demonstrate that the dream of the expansionists and early settlers, as Woodrow Lloyd said, still lived. They were dreams, however, that faced the reality of the challenges and hardships of living in the West. These dreams were Promised Land narratives that assuaged fears aroused by memories of the Depression by celebrating the prosperity and technology of the 1950s. Individuals who embraced such narratives did not look into the future with rose-coloured glasses. Their vision was sharp and their expectations realistic. Among the countless speeches and articles that captured the appeal of Promised Land narratives, Premier Douglas, not surprisingly, provided one of the best examples. In a radio address on September 1, he called on his generation to pioneer the future:

> I believe destiny is knocking at our door and if we seize our opportunities with the same faith and determination as the pioneers did theirs we to shall leave the generations that come after us forever in our debt. Therefore let us dedicate ourselves to the tasks that lie before us. Let us resolve to so conduct ourselves that fifty years from now another generation which has entered into its inheritance will be able to say of us that we were worthy of the pioneers and that we met the challenge of the times in which we lived.[98]

NOTES

1 While there were many references to a brighter future during the Jubilee, the actual phrase "Promised Land" never appeared aside from a student play that had a scene entitled "The Land of Promise" (see note 30).

2 Paul Ricoeur, quoted in Hayden White, *The Content of the Form: Narrative Discourse and Historical Representation* (Baltimore: Johns Hopkins University Press, 1987), 174–211. White, *The Content of the Form*, 2, 14–24.

3 Ricoeur, quoted in White, *The Content of the Form*, 53.

4 P. S. Minear, "Promise," *The Interpreter's Dictionary of the Bible: An Illustrated Encyclopedia* (New York: Abingdon Press, 1962), 893–94. "Pre-eminent among *Old Testament* promises is that which God gave to Abraham. He swore to this patriarch that he would give to him a son and would make of him a mighty nation.... This promise is directly linked to God's later call of Moses to lead his people from Egypt toward the Promised Land. Declared to all the people at Horeb, and affirmed by them as their charter, this promise guided them throughout their weary pilgrimage, providing the source of their endurance and the object of their rebellions. As celebrated in song and saga, this promise to Abraham and Moses was proof of God's steadfast love, his readiness to forgive, and his determination to bring them to a good end. After they settled the Land of Promise, their history received its continuity through the same promise.... Discontent with God's promise was the root sin of Israel; confidence in it was the essence of HOPE. Reliance on the promise sustained the individual in his daily obedience to the law."

5 Douglas Owram, *Promise of Eden: The Canadian Expansionist Movement and the Idea of the West 1856–1900* (Toronto: University of Toronto Press, 1980), 41.

6 Ibid., 218.

7 Ibid., 222.

8 T. C. Douglas, *Hansard*, March 26, 1952, Volume 34, 5th Session of the Legislative Assembly of Saskatchewan. Saskatchewan Archives Board [SAB], R-230, I.14-1.

9 Gerald Friesen, "The Western Canadian Identity," *Canadian Historical Association Annual Report* (1973), 15.
10 Michael Kammen, *Mystic Chords of Memory: The Transformation of Tradition in American Culture* (New York: Alfred A. Knopf, 1991), 41.
11 John Archer, Speech to Business and Professional Women's Club, January 18, 1954. SAB, R-230, I.55.
12 Official Program: Battleford Jubilee Program, July 17, 1955, Battlefords. SAB, R-230, I.50a.
13 John Archer, *Saskatchewan: A History* (Saskatoon: Western Producer Prairie Books, 1980), 268–70.
14 F. H. Leacy, ed., *Historical Statistics of Canada* (Ottawa: Statistics Canada, 1983) 2nd ed., Series M 109–18.
15 Clarence Fines, "Budget Speech," *Hansard*, March 2, 1955 14–15, SAB, R-230, I.18.
16 "Table X: Grain Combines on Farms 1951–56," *Census of Canada Analytical Report 1956* (Ottawa: Queen's Press, 1959), Bulletin 3–8, 8–16.
17 Archer, *Saskatchewan: A History*, 269–70.
18 Leacy, *Historical Statistics*, T-142-94.
19 A. W. Johnson, *Dream No Little Dreams: A Biography of the Douglas Government of Saskatchewan, 1944–1961* (Toronto: University of Toronto Press, 2004), 182.
20 Clinton White, *Power for a Province: A History of Saskatchewan Power* (Regina: Canadian Plains Research Centre, 1976), 281–89.
21 Industrial Development Office, "Industrial Expansion in Saskatchewan 1953," Government Report, 1953, 5. SAB, R-230 I.15.3.
22 Ibid., 1.
23 Johnson, *Dream No Little Dreams*, 205–15.
24 Archer, *Saskatchewan: A History*, 360.
25 Johnson, *Dream No Little Dreams*, 181–84.
26 Fines, "Budget Speech," 15–16.
27 W. J. Boyer, "A Dream," *Touchwood Times*, December 7, 1955, 15.
28 Arcola Co-operative Association, *Moose Mountain Star-Standard*, July 6, 1955, B-1.
29 *Assiniboia Times*, June 15, 1955, B-6 and B-7. *Swift Current Sun*, June 22, 1955, p. C-12.
30 "Saskatchewan's Jubilee Journal." SAB, R-230, I.15-3, File #6.
31 T. C. Douglas, "Golden Jubilee Banquet, September 5, 1955." SAB, CBC R-5982 and R-5983.
32 W. O. Mitchell, *The Face of Saskatchewan* (Regina: Saskatchewan Golden Jubilee Committee, 1955).
33 "Drake," SAB, R-230, I.50a.
34 Glen Kruger, "Oil Recovery Highlights of Past Half-Century," *Shaunavon Standard*, July 20, 1955, 2 and 9.
35 Paula Rein, "These Changing Conditions: A Study of the Saskatchewan Royal Commission on Agriculture and Rural Life" (Master's thesis, University of Regina, November 1994), 49–50.
36 Archer, *Saskatchewan: A History*, 293.
37 Douglas Owram, *Born at the Right Time: A History of the Baby-Boom Generation* (Toronto: University of Toronto Press, 1996), 71.
38 "Fifty Years of Agricultural Progress," *Assiniboia Times*, June 15, 1955, 6.
39 Rein, "These Changing Conditions," 49–50.
40 John Archer, "Introduction," *A Speaker's Handbook about Saskatchewan and Its Jubilee* (Regina: Golden Jubilee Committee, 1954), 4.
41 Letter to Ruby Stevenson from Fred McGuinness, February 22, 1955. SAB, R-230, I.15-1. Letter to George Cooper from Fred McGuinness, July 13, 1955. SAB, R-230, I.15-1.

42 SAB, R-230, 50a.
43 *Census of Canada 1951, Volume 1 – Population: General Characteristics* (Ottawa: Dominion Bureau of Statistics, 1951), Table 19-5. *Census of Canada 1956 Bulletin 1-10 Single Years of Age* (Ottawa: Dominion Bureau of Statistics, 1956), Table 21-1.
44 No title, text on cover page, *Kindersley Clarion*, May 12, 1955, 1.
45 SAB, R-230, 50a. SAB, R-230, 58-38.
46 T. C. Douglas, *Hansard*. W. Russell, letter from Russell to Norah McCullough (no date). SAB, R-230, I.19-3.
47 SAB, R-230, 1.50a. See particularly Round Plain.
48 Kelstern, SAB, R-230, I.50a.
49 T. C. Douglas, "CBC Golden Jubilee Tribute," September 1, 1955. SAB, R 33-1 T. C. Douglas Papers, l.952e (138) CXXIII.
50 "Blaine Lake Celebrates Golden Jubilee," *Prince Albert Daily Herald*, July 4, 1955, 6–7. "Blaine Lake," SAB, R-230, I.58a.
51 "The History of Semans and District," *Semans Gazette*, June 29, 1955, 2.
52 "Saskatchewan Co-operative Creamery Association Limited," *The Aneroid News Magnet*, May 19, 1955, 7.
53 SAB, R-230, 50a.
54 "Golden Jubilee Fair Memorable Event," *The Craik Weekly*, December 22, 1955, 9.
55 "Pioneer Agricultural Methods were Primitive," *Estevan Mercury*, June 30, 1955, 5.
56 "Provincial Supplement," *Broadview Advance*, May 12, 1955, 2–7.
57 "The Homesteader's Reverie," *Kindersley Clarion*, May 12, 1955, p. C-3. "Some years sweat was might cheap," *Kipling Citizen*, October 20, 1955, p. B-18. K. F. Cleall, "Predicts Town will soon be more than Double in Size," *Unity Courier-Herald*, July 14, 1955, p. B-2. A. C. Stewart, "New Good Times," *Unity Courier-Herald*, July 14, 1955, p. C-3.
58 K. F. Cleall.
59 Muriel Clements, *Saskatchewan: The 50th Year* (Regina: Queen's Press, 1955), 12. SAB, R-230, I.58-16-17-18.
60 *The Hudson Bay Story*, 1955. SAB. Local Histories File.
61 "Our Heroes," article clipped from unidentified newspaper, no date. Yorkton, SAB, R-230, 58a.
62 "Elrose Celebrates with Grand Birthday Party," *The Elrose Review*, June 20, 1955, 1-B.
63 "Introduction," *Saltcoats Star*, June 29, 1955, 12.
64 Woodrow Lloyd, *Hansard*, p. 13.
65 Ted Culliton, untitled speech, no date. SAB, R-824, Files of E. M. Culliton, 74.
66 Carlyle Jubilee Observances, June 14, 1955, William J. Patterson Papers, SAB, R-79.7.
67 E. A. King, quoted in "United Church Services Mark Golden Jubilee," *The Estevan Mercury*, June 30, 1955.
68 T. F. Cornelson, "Message from Mayor T. F. Cornelson," *The Herbert Herald*, July 7, 1955, 1.
69 Senlac, SAB, R-230, I.50a.
70 SAB, Photograph collection. Photograph No. R-B4760.
71 "Bumper Crop hope in 55 washed out," and "50 Families Flee Flood," *Leader-Post*, May 5, 1955, 1. "Sask. Asks Aid to Drain 2,000,000 Flooded Acres," *Leader-Post*, May 16, 1955, 1.
72 "Opening of the Museum of Natural History, May 16, 1955." SAB, CBC R-5989.
73 V. P. Deshaye, *Hansard*.
74 T. C. Douglas, "Saskatchewan's Golden Jubilee," Government of Saskatchewan advertisement, *The Broadview Advance*, May 12, 1955, 6.
75 Untitled Esso advertisement, *Broadview Advance*, May 12, 1955, 12.
76 "Our Heritage," *Star City Echo*, August 24, 1955, 1.

77 "PIONEERS of PROGRESS," *The News-Optimist*, June 15, 1955, 8.
78 "An Historic Date," *Leader-Post*, June 3, 1955. SAB, R-230, I.56.
79 Jean Hinds, "A Salute to Saskatchewan Women," SAB, CBC 331-R-6334.
80 Advertisement for Wadena Kinsmen Club, *Wadena News*, September 29, 1955, 3.
81 "Record Crowds Gather for Opening of Park," *Weyburn Review*, no date. SAB, R-230, IV. File 17.
82 "The Age of the Pioneer Never Passes." *The Swift Current Sun*, June 22, 1955, p. c-12.
83 Richard White, "Frederick Jackson Turner and Buffalo Bill," James Grossman, ed., *The Frontier in American Culture* (Berkeley: University of California Press, 1994), 21.
84 Inscription-Fort Walsh-Wood Mountain Trail, Historic Marker, from J. D. Herbert, *Guide to the Historic Sites of Saskatchewan* (Regina: Saskatchewan Golden Jubilee Committee, 1955), 11.
85 Milford Smith, "Look at Business, Red River Cart Challenges Canadians to Master Natural Barriers to Growth," *Hamilton Spectator*, June 25, 1955. SAB, R-230, I.56.
86 SAB, R-230, IV. File 1.
87 Perdue, SAB, R-230, 50a. "Gardiner Speaks at Celebration," *Leader-Post*, July 6, 1955. SAB, R-230, IV. File 17.
88 Mitchell, *Face of Saskatchewan*.
89 T. C. Douglas, "Golden Jubilee Banquet, Sept. 5, 1955." SAB, CBC R-5982 and R-5983.
90 T. C. Douglas, CBC Golden Jubilee Tribute, Saskatchewan Network, September 1, 1955. SAB, R-33-1, T. C. Douglas Papers, CXXXIII.952e (138). Saskatchewan's Golden Jubilee.
91 William Patterson, "Carlyle Jubilee Observances," June 14, 1955. SAB, R-79 William J. Patterson Papers, 7. Speeches.
92 William Patterson, Speech to Kisbey Men's Club, October 14, 1955. SAB, R-79, 7.
93 Bud Daigle, "The Golden Milestone," *The Bruno Banner*, June 1955, 1.
94 M. J. Willis, "Message from MJ Willis-Elrose MLA," *The Elrose Review*, June 20, 1955, 4.
95 K. F. Cleall, "Predicts Town will soon be more than Double in Size," *The Unity Courier-Herald*, July 14, 1955, B-2.
96 Anne B. Flavell, "Magic Lake-A Play in One Act." SAB, R-230, I.53.
97 Ibid., 10–29.
98 T. C. Douglas, "CBC Golden Jubilee Tribute."

18

FROM FARM TO COMMUNITY: CO-OPERATIVES IN ALBERTA AND SASKATCHEWAN, 1905–2005

Brett Fairbairn

This essay is about the cultural importance of locality and social cohesion in two sister Canadian provinces, as evidenced in a set of social movements that overlapped the provincial boundary and helped shape both provinces in different ways. These movements engaged the reality of the Prairie West as a land that did not live up to its promise. By engaging transformatively with the social and economic realities of development, people in the two provinces developed new, more practical visions of the kind of Promised Land they could actually hope to create. What they discovered might be summed up in a phrase: community as a source of creativity in an age of ongoing, global change. This article concentrates on the formative period up to 1955, which is when the movements in the two provinces were most agrarian and most similar, and concludes with a look back over the most recent fifty years.

What the movements considered here had in common was their focus on co-operative economic activity. A co-operative is an "autonomous association of persons united voluntarily to meet their common … needs and aspirations through a jointly owned and democratically controlled enterprise."[1] Arising in connection with agrarian movements of early settler society, co-operatives developed into significant parts of the economies of both provinces. But while co-operatives continued to form and exist throughout the period 1905–2005, their shape and meaning changed dramatically. Important early co-operatives were driven by politicized agrarian sectional interests, but most of the ones that survived became rooted as co-operatives primarily of place. The local roles of co-operatives were and are similar in the two provinces, even though economic co-operation came to be articulated differently in political cultures.

Prairie co-operatives had their origins in one of the great social engineering projects of the Canadian state: the effort to settle the vast expanses with farmers who would become rational producers and model citizens. The utopian visions, the conceptual simplifications, and the uneven implementation are paradigmatic of "development" projects of the twentieth century.[2] The project in what became Alberta and Saskatchewan required re-creating the prairies as a kind of *tabula rasa* on which a modern society could be sketched, the outlines to be filled in by immigrants from Europe, other parts of Canada, and the United States. The prairies were re-created conceptually by imagining the First Nations and Métis inhabitants as absent and past, and also physically, by removing Aboriginal people to reserves and surveying the great expanses of land. In the emptiness so constructed, settlers hoped to build desirable societies.

A few of them were determined, from the outset, to create societies characterized by high degrees of social integration, co-operation, and harmony. Two examples of this were the brothers, Ed. and Will Paynter, who created the Harmony Industrial Association in the Qu'Appelle Valley (1895–1900).[3] But the rareness of such intentional communities testifies to the extent to which the settlement project for most of its participants was one based on the individual.

The land-survey system itself epitomized the vision for a new society. Land was parcelled in a relentless geometric grid, adapted as little as possible to topography. Settler-families were to live independently on their separately owned and operated, equally sized farmsteads. Self-reliance was to shape autonomous, rational citizens – a British answer to Jeffersonian agrarian democracy. It is true that there were block settlements of non-British ethnic groups within this framework. But the settlement pattern, together with the kind of citizens it was intended to create, was an ideological artifact of the age.

There were alternatives. South of the border, American surveyor John Wesley Powell had proposed in the 1870s that settlers should learn from the sparseness of the Aboriginal population and settle lightly on the dry lands. Powell recommended towns fronting on rivers, around which more intensive agriculture could occur on small farms, with the lands between such towns given over to more extensive grazing. He developed his recommendations in part by learning from the Métis and First Nations inhabitants of the region; but his recommendations were ignored, and Canada followed the United States in implementing the rational, Jeffersonian geometric grid of settlement.[4]

Without real consideration of such alternatives, the settlers' Promised Land began as a promised land for the sturdy, self-reliant individual, who might be a good neighbour and a good citizen but who was responsible for his (in the ideology, rarely her) family's success. But many settlers could not succeed on their own merits, on equal-sized plots of unequal land, subject to fluctuations of weather and markets, and dependent on a rudimentary infrastructure of companies, services, and transportation. A majority failed, in those first attempts, and those who made it often discovered that they needed more than individual effort. It was, primarily, the circumstances of settler society itself – the collision of the utopian project with prairie realities – that gave rise to co-operative movements. Co-operatives resulted from a mismatch between an imagined society and a real environment, and from gritty internal conflicts of interests within the new societies. Albert Memmi has mentioned how colonization projects involve tensions between big colonizers and little ones, and it was out of such tensions that co-operatives sprang: coping mechanisms of little colonizers.[5]

Co-operatives arose early in the settlement of both provinces and multiplied in conjunction with growing grievances. Early co-ops are little-documented but included scattered buying clubs and creamery co-operatives in the 1890s.[6] The real "first wave" of co-operative organizations developed from 1900 to 1920 and paralleled the growing political mobilization of producers.[7] The big agrarian organizations of the day – the United Farmers of Alberta (UFA) and the Saskatchewan Grain Growers' Association (SGGA, later United Farmers of Canada, Saskatchewan Section or UFC) – were based on local "lodges" of farmers, and these local groups launched many of the first wave of co-operatives.[8] These co-operative activities emerged with apparent spontaneity, likely facilitated by shared experience of a harsh physical and economic environment, informal co-operation among neighbours, a sense of agrarian common interest, and in many cases settlers' familiarity with co-operative ideas from their previous lives in the United States, central and eastern Canada, Britain, or Scandinavia.[9]

Mrs Nellie Peterson of Mayerthorpe, Alberta, recalled many years later: "people didn't come into the co-operative movement on a theory, but they went into it as an answer to a problem. When you found you had been hooked for your groceries … or your coal, or anything, you said, let's get together and bring a carload of coal in…. We brought in a carload of apples and a carload of coal, unloaded right at the station…. People were meeting an immediate need."[10]

The Orangeville, Saskatchewan, local of the SGGA launched co-operative buying in February, 1913, when it opened its business meeting by asking attendees to place orders for flour and feed; later meetings of the local were called specifically to organize carload purchases of apples and flour. The Grain Growers also ordered barbed wire, fence posts, bran, rolled oats, and sugar.[11] The co-operative buying club in Lewvan, Saskatchewan, (near Regina) was formed in 1914 by twenty-five farmers who were outraged that the local barber was charging $1.50 a bushel for potatoes. They sent a member, C. C. Downs, to Fargo, North Dakota, to bring back a boxcar load for all of them. Some co-operatives continued in this mode for decades, building no facilities of their own and instead using boxcars as "rolling stores."[12] A few developed into full-fledged co-operative country stores in scattered places like Ponoka, Killam, Lloydminster, and Davidson.

A group of UFA locals in the Wetaskiwin area were the basis for what became the Wetaskiwin U.F.A. Co-operative Association Limited, organized in 1917, one of the early successful co-op stores in the province. British and Scandinavian farmers in the area collaborated to form the co-op, which began with group buying of salt, flour, binder twine, apples, feed, and seed grains. Seven locals of the United Farm Women of Alberta assisted in the development of the store and provided educational, health, and recreational activities associated with it, an early example of how women built co-operatives of place.[13]

Three important points stand out in these early accounts. First, co-operative action was based on the experience and perception of need, and it was often pragmatic and material in its focus. As Mrs. Peterson said, it was about apples, not theories. But second, solving economic problems through mutual action changed the character of the economic transaction: it was about apples, but apples purchased and unloaded by co-operative labour, which embodied and reinforced a sense of community and of relationships among local farmers. Third, economic action occurred within a framework of agrarian politics, of farmer identity-building, and friction between farmers as a group on one hand and town and commercial interests on the other. It is likely no coincidence that Mrs. Peterson referred to the motivating force of feeling she had been "hooked" for her groceries, and that the Lewvan farmers were reacting to the high prices charged by the local barber.

This co-operative activity did not come easily. Many settler co-operatives failed. Buying clubs often dwindled into inactivity. The first association registered under Alberta's 1913 *Co-operative Associations Act* was the Farmers' Co-operative Association of Huxley, Ltd. It did not survive.[14] In fact, of the sixteen co-operatives registered in 1913–14, only one existed a generation later. This was the Killam District co-operative led by Englishman William Halsall, which played a critical role in the Alberta co-operative movement in the 1920s and 1930s. The first association registered under Saskatchewan's 1913 act was the Juniata Co-operative Association Limited, formed by eight shareholders in the district thirty-five miles west of Saskatoon.[15] At first, progress was promising, but a terminal decline began when the wholesale supplier cut the co-operative loose. That wholesaler was the newly created Trading Department of the SGGA. In an early development that foreshadowed two decades of conflict, a local farmer co-operative was put out of business by a centralized farmer-driven enterprise.[16]

Lack of sufficient interest and commitment by farmers was a problem identified by volunteers in the Landis, Saskatchewan, area, who commented that early co-ops met "apathy," "skepticism," and "ridicule" from farmers as well as hostility from merchants and townsfolk.[17] An organizer of the failed Saskatchewan Purchasing Company wrote: "I am forced to the conclusion that the average Western farmer (there are glorious exceptions) is only a co-operator to the extent that co-operation becomes an aid to his worship of the almighty dollar.... [He has] many commendable traits ... yet when he enters the arena of ordinary commercial life he becomes singularly suspicious and selfish.... His regard for practical co-operation is measured only by his ability to purchase [at] a co-operative store five cents cheaper than he can elsewhere."[18]

Under such circumstances, co-ops "died like flies" in the post-World War I recession, recalled a co-operative manager.[19] A 1941 study by the Saskatchewan government noted that more than half of co-operatives incorporated prior to 1938 had ended up being dissolved, with the chief reasons given as "mismanagement" (such as overextended credit to members) and "lack of interest."[20] George Keen, general secretary from 1909–45 of the Co-operative Union of Canada, recalled that his first trip to Saskatchewan was "not flattering" to the co-operatives. It did not surprise him that many failed. "The main causes … were a lack of real co-operative interest and understanding" among the members, as well as "ignorance" by directors and "incompetent administration" by managers.[21]

Contrary to popular opinion, prairie settlers were not inherently co-operative. The aboriginal peoples who preceded them were more advanced in co-operation. Prairie farmers who settled on their separate parcels of land within a competitive economic system and a moral framework of individual self-reliance co-operated because they had to, not because they had a genius for it. But necessity started them on a multigenerational process of discovery, of trial and error, at the other end of which lay resilient co-operative institutions.

For a generation after 1905, province-building dominated the public agenda as an infrastructure of government and politics, towns and cities, transportation, and education was constructed throughout the agricultural areas of the two provinces. Farmers organized as a class to engage the politics and economics of the new provincial states. This agrarian collectivism was only in certain respects a repudiation of individualism. The abstraction of producer roles and identities at the provincial level did not negate the self-reliance of farms and farmers; organizations aggregated the rational self-interest of producers, disembedded from local community relationships. The individualism of landownership and farming and the collectivism of the early agrarian movement were less than opposites and more like two sides of a coin.

The history of the big agrarian co-operatives has been better documented than the histories of other aspects of the co-operative movement. The first of these large organizations was the Grain Growers' Grain Company (GGGC) organized in 1905–6 on the basis of a famous trip by E. A. Partridge, a Sintaluta, Saskatchewan, area farmer and visionary, to observe the activities of the Winnipeg Grain Exchange. Partridge concluded that farmers should own their own trading company so that the profits from trading activity could be returned to them instead of going to others. The GGGC took a seat on the exchange, traded grain, and began branching out into building an elevator network and handling other commodities. It was the oldest ancestor of the later (1917) United Grain Growers (UGG) and present-day (2005) Agricore United.[22]

But farmers showed little patience when the companies they created turned out to be conservative. The GGGC was slow to build its own elevator network, and it rankled farmers to deliver their grain through for-profit local handlers. Partridge proposed that grain elevators be owned and operated by governments as a nonprofit service, and in 1910 the Manitoba government experimented with this approach. The Saskatchewan and Alberta governments went a different route and instead backed the creation of government-financed but farmer-controlled elevator co-operatives. The Saskatchewan Co-operative Elevator Company was established by an act of the legislature in 1911, and the Alberta Farmers' Co-operative Elevator Company (AFCEC) followed in 1913.[23]

Farmers' aspirations kept expanding, and the elevator co-ops were soon criticized in their turn. Their leadership elite was too intermingled with the Grain Growers' and United Farmers' executives, too cozy with the provincial governments, and too limited in their vision. The new interest of farmers after 1918 was pooling. The experience of the wartime Canadian Wheat Board excited many farmers, as they saw an orderly way to sell wheat directly to overseas customers with every farmer receiving the same price for the same grade and no one taking a profit. The growing strength of the pooling movement in the United States was also an inspiration. When governments failed to re-establish the wheat board, farmers looked for ways to pool on a voluntary basis.[24]

The UFA was the first (in July 1923) to decide to launch a voluntary, contractual wheat pool. The SGGA followed shortly thereafter. A splinter group in Saskatchewan, the Farmers' Union of Canada, issued an invitation to American pooling guru Aaron Sapiro to speak to prairie farmers. The Edmonton *Journal* and Calgary *Herald* reinforced this call with invitations of their own. Sapiro came first to Calgary where, on August 2, 1923, he addressed some 3,500 people. At that meeting, and at eight subsequent meetings over three days in Calgary, Edmonton, Lacombe, and Camrose, he laid out an optimistic but precise, clear, and simple vision of how pooling should work.[25] Alberta Co-operative Wheat Producers Ltd. was incorporated within two weeks of his visit, and started operations in October with nearly 50 per cent of the province's wheat acreage signed up.[26]

Saskatchewan was more complicated, despite the excitement generated by Sapiro's speeches. The province fell far short of its 50 per cent pooling target that fall and had to try again in the spring of 1924. The greater scale of the province's wheat acreage (requiring a larger logistical effort) may have been a factor, but there were also reservations expressed by farm leaders in the SGGA, the elevator co-op, and the Liberal government. Their cautionary remarks, combined with the intimidating nature of the five-year, "ironclad" pooling contracts, may have scared off some farmers. But by 1924, a huge publicity campaign was underway, supported by what is now *The Western Producer* weekly newspaper and created specially to support pooling. Pooling had become a community cause that the Saskatchewan government, municipal governments, and urban daily newspapers now supported with enthusiasm. Many town councils declared Pool sign-up day, on June 10, 1924, a civic holiday. This time, the pool met its target, was declared operational, and in late July met with representatives of the Alberta and Manitoba pools to create a common central selling agency.

The pools were the crowning achievement of the mass agrarian mobilization of prairie farmers. As a group, they were among the largest businesses in Canada; companies democratically controlled by farmers sold a majority of Canada's greatest export. After facing initial opposition from elevator companies, the pools built their own elevators, soon becoming the largest elevator operators in the region as well. The Saskatchewan pool absorbed the co-op elevator company's network over the resistance of the SCEC directors in 1926. In Alberta, the co-op elevators had by this point become part of UGG, but that farmer-controlled company was supportive of pooling.

Despite the impressive successes, advocates of local, gradualist, and multiple forms of co-operatives were skeptical of the brash, uniform organizations of the 1920s. George Keen of the Co-operative Union wrote to his correspondents in Saskatchewan and Alberta to compare producers' co-operatives to trade unions – by which Keen, not unsympathetic to unions, meant that they had a narrow and self-interested view, mere "agrarian class consciousness," not a genuine, social-improvement-orientated co-operative spirit.[27] Some years later, he explained to Halsall of Killam Co-op: "producers' co-operatives are only 'co-operative' in a limited sense. They serve the interests of group, or of a class," even sometimes "at the expense of society as a whole."[28] While this might be desirable in a context where farmers had genuine grievances, it was not ideal.

The dispute was not only philosophical. Practical conflicts of interest became evident when the UGG began competing with the smaller co-ops in selling farm supplies. Then in the mid-1920s, the United Farmers organizations entered into direct competition with the local co-operatives across a full range of mail-order goods. Flush with confidence, the UFC in Saskatchewan revitalized the old SGGA Trading Department in 1926, offering mail-order goods to its farmer-members, encouraging them to form their own member-only associations, and meanwhile undercutting existing buying clubs and co-operative stores. The ambitions of the big agrarian organizations threatened to wipe out smaller and alternative forms of co-operation. Keen deplored the "spirit of institutional competition." "Underneath the whole thing is a poverty of real Co-operative spirit.... I feel much discouraged."[29] Yet Alberta and Saskatchewan co-operators sympathized with, and believed in, the larger producers' movement, leaving them in an awkward and subservient position when the agrarian organizations' interests or decisions conflicted with their own.

It seemed as though the centralized, class-interest form of agricultural co-operation was going to define both provinces. It also appeared that there was little to choose between Alberta and Saskatchewan in their political culture or their farm and co-operative movements. Alberta was, if anything, the more agrarian of the two with its UFA government, but though in Saskatchewan the Liberals held power, the United Farmers and the wheat pool wielded tremendous influence. These mass agrarian-interest organizations were projections of the economic identities of individual producers. The provinces had been defined as agrarian political communities based upon the power and prosperity of commodity organization.

The trauma of the Great Depression of the 1930s remade the co-operative movements in the two provinces. Both the idea of the sturdy individual and the mass agrarian projects of the 1920s largely collapsed. As seen through the lens of co-operative movements, the Depression meant a return to the local as a site for cohesion and for action; and it meant an expansion of the hard-edged idea of the co-operative producer into a more rounded notion of the co-operative person. By the time it was done, the co-operative movement was barely recognizable: it was larger, more diversified, and more community-based. For many who lived through those times, co-operatives became not just an economic interest but also something essential to their way of life. In the process, co-operators raised what amounted to a vision of a new kind of Promised Land: a society based on community and articulated through economic democracy, pursuing the best possible quality of life within the environmental and economic limits they faced. This was in one sense a narrowing of the original, utopian-individualist dream to something more practical. And yet, in another sense, it was a broadening and development of the idea of people-in-community as the basis for society and economy.

In institutional terms, the Depression hastened a resolution to the conflict between centralized and federated forms of co-operation, where centralized forms reflected mass occupational identities and federated forms expressed local engagement. The resolution of this tension was slightly different in the two provinces.

In Alberta, consumer co-operatives had formed an Alberta Co-operative Wholesale Association (ACWA) in 1928. As manager A. P. Moan explained to a general meeting in February 1929, the new wholesale was "looking for support from the UFA locals."[30] Encouraged by the UFA and the provincial government (since 1921, also UFA), and with a loan from the latter, the wholesale tried to expand to service the producers' movement. There was a distinct sense in these meetings that the co-op wholesale was the junior partner desperate for the favour of the big partners – the UFA and the government. When things went south, it was the junior partner left holding the bag. The ACWA had bought a large amount of lumber in 1929 on speculation that it might be sold through UFA locals. With the onset of the Depression, sales plummeted and the underfinanced wholesale was nearly bankrupted.

While the consumer co-ops were crippled by their ill-timed speculation, the UFA at first marched onward. Indeed, during the 1930s, the UFA blended co-operation and politics in a way that was unique in Canadian history. It organized its own co-operative purchasing associations on a constituency-by-constituency basis, for UFA members only. According to one observer, the main impulse behind the UFA purchasing scheme was MLA and speaker of the Alberta legislature, George Johnson.[31] The provincial government's supervisor of co-operative activities, D. M. Malin, attended the founding meetings of the Coronation constituency co-op association in 1929–30, which may have been the first, and he seems to have supported the blending of party politics and co-operation. Symbolically, the Coronation UFA party constituency association and the co-op kept their minutes in the same book.[32]

The co-ops were desperate that the UFA not launch a central wholesale business competing with their own to supply its constituency co-ops, but matters were evidently tending in that direction. Premier

Brownlee of the UFA government personally called together the representatives of the UFA and the consumer co-operatives in 1931 to try to resolve their differences and appears to have criticized the UFA organization for competing with the co-ops – but to little effect.[33] The UFA preferred to work together with the UGG and the wheat pools to have large-scale purchasing of farm inputs to supply to their members, with no involvement from other co-operatives. In 1931–32, the UFA organized its own UFA Central Co-operative Association for bulk purchasing and ceased working with the rump co-op wholesale. The UFA Co-op outlived the collapse of its parent political organization and still exists today as a farm-supply co-operative, active throughout Alberta and even over the border into Saskatchewan.[34]

The speeches of Norman F. Priestley from the 1930s illustrate the centralist thinking of the Alberta farm movement. Priestley dismissed local consumer co-operatives by saying: "this particular chapter in co-operation is not a happy one. About five out of every six of these stores have failed." The conclusion he drew was that agriculture "must organize on the basis of occupation" such as the UFA was doing.[35] Priestley's ideas were consistent with those of Henry Wise Wood, the immensely influential UFA leader who developed ideas of group government and class unity.[36] In 1928, when Wood was both president of the UFA and chairman of the Alberta Wheat Pool, he stated boldly: "You cannot organize all the consumers in one big organization. Everybody is a consumer and you cannot organize them.... We have to have a common interest and it is that common interest [as producers] that makes it possible for us to organize."[37]

By contrast, the Liberal government in Saskatchewan hired co-operative officials who were champions of conventional forms of co-operation as these were understood in Europe and other parts of Canada. The Saskatchewan government invited George Keen from Ontario and paid his expenses to meet with, and discuss, co-operative principles and approaches with local leaders in the 1920s.[38] While agrarian-centralist points of view were also very influential in Saskatchewan, there was a nucleus of government officials who worked with leaders of the local consumer co-operatives, ultimately contributing to a different kind of co-operative movement.

In Saskatchewan, too, the consumer co-ops faced a threat and a competitor in the form of the UFC's trading department. The co-ops wanted to take over the wholesaling function through their own federated organization, but the UFC and the trading department investors resisted. The best the co-ops could achieve was one-third control of a hybrid UFC/co-op enterprise. But then a fraud scandal in 1929 discredited the trading department management, leading to a Saskatchewan co-operative wholesale society under 100 per cent co-operative control.[39] Saskatchewan ended up with a relatively healthy federated co-operative controlled by local associations, while Alberta ended up with a movement divided between the centralized, producer-driven UFA co-op and a weakened wholesale based on a federation of the local stores. The divergence was partly the result of chance – the Saskatchewan scandal – and partly because of the greater political strength of the UFA.

The Depression also meant that first the pools, and then the United Farmers, were laid low. The pools were virtually bankrupted by falling grain prices in late 1929, and in 1931 were rescued by the federal government. The price of the rescue was that they give up pooling, concentrate on running elevators – since that time wheat pools have not pooled wheat – and repay their debts. Pooling as such ultimately became the business of the Canadian Wheat Board in the 1940s. (Ironically, prairie farmers got, by the failure of the pools, what their organizations had first demanded: a mandatory government wheat board.) And it wasn't only the wheat pools: other commodity pools created for milk, poultry, eggs, livestock, and other commodities also went under or had to be reorganized. The "parent" organizations – the United Farmers groups – suffered as well, their finances collapsing as farmers were unable to pay dues during the Depression. The proud agrarian organizations of the 1920s were virtually swept away.

From the GGGC of 1905–6 to the failures of the 1930s was a generation-long roller-coaster ride for prairie producers. They had built some of the biggest, most powerful, and most centralized enterprises in the world, and lost them. Long in their shadow, the smaller-scale community co-operatives began to flourish. In fact, the harsh economic conditions of the Depression seemed almost more conducive to their success.

A turning point came when the different co-operatives began to work together more effectively, and when they began to emphasize educational work among their members. Saskatchewan Wheat Pool led the way by rededicating its field staff to general rural education, turning them into what Ian MacPherson has called "missionaries of rural development."[40] Under an "affiliate plan" in 1933–34, the pool organized its members at local points into buying clubs to buy from the provincial co-op wholesale. The intention was that the buying clubs would retain savings and be converted into free-standing, autonomous co-operative associations. It was, really, what co-operative leaders had asked for in the 1920s: that the producer organizations put their energies behind helping and promoting local co-operatives, instead of competing with them. The success of the affiliate plan was followed in the 1940s by the "associated stores" concept, a mechanism for co-operatives to buy out established local merchants who were planning to retire, convert the stores to brand-new co-ops, and hire the merchants back as managers for the first few years. By this point, the co-op movement was growing by leaps and bounds.[41]

Farmers also launched some unprecedented new ventures. The most striking was the decision of twelve farmers in 1934 to control transnational petroleum supplies. They decided to organize a consumer-owned oil refinery. In the midst of the Depression, they raised $34,000 in share capital from farmers, working with, and through, existing co-ops in southern Saskatchewan that handled petroleum products. This sum is amazing, both as a huge amount to raise from impoverished farmers, and as a tiny amount with which to start a refinery. The start-up was so strapped for cash that one of the directors, unknown to his colleagues, pledged his farm as collateral to persuade the railway to release a tank car of crude oil to the refinery. Despite the small scale, the refinery was an instant success, earning $34,000 in surplus (profit) in its first year. Repeated investments by co-ops led to the present-day co-op refinery complex on the north edge of Regina, the only full petroleum refinery left in the prairies outside Alberta.[42]

The mid-1930s were a turning point in another way as well, as they revealed a growing divergence of political cultures in Alberta and Saskatchewan, even though the new political forces in the two provinces drew from the common populist and co-operative well. Alberta elected its second rural-based populist government with the Social Credit victory of 1935. Social Credit, like the UFA before it, built on the ideas and language of the co-operative movement, representing its provincial policy as a kind of co-operation writ large.[43] Co-op leaders were wary. Halsall feared becoming "entangled" with the new government: "we had enough of that with the U.F.A. Government."[44] The fear was justified, since the Social Credit movement organized its own constituency co-operative associations in answer to the UFA ones, and there was friction in some co-ops like Wetaskiwin where, by one report, Socreds tried to take a majority on the local board.[45] While people and ideas from the co-operatives contributed to the new political movements, that doesn't mean the co-ops themselves fit easily into the new parties or regimes.

Community-level co-operation received an additional boost with the introduction of credit unions in the two provinces under new legislation in 1937 in Saskatchewan and in 1938 in Alberta. This legislation was the result of ideas seeping into the two provinces from outside as well as the facilitation of government officials and leaders in existing co-operatives who had come to believe that credit unions were a needed and practical idea. The initial concept of credit unions was strongly influenced by the American model, under which they were understood as largely urban institutions for groups of depositors and borrowers who shared a "common bond" of a strong shared identity such as occupation, place of work, or religious/ethnic affiliation. Thus the first six credit unions in Saskatchewan were all urban, including the Regina Hebrew Savings and Credit (which helped finance Jewish refugees), and the Pioneer Credit Union for railroad workers in Moose Jaw.[46] Alberta was similar: the first three were all in Edmonton and included Mangan Credit Union, Provincial Civil Servants Credit Union, and Edmonton Transit Employees in the fall of 1938.[47]

For about the first ten years after the introduction of credit unions, Alberta's Social Credit government was quite supportive of them, at least rhetorically. The idea of people banding together to solve their credit problems and to boost their economic activity seemed to be an example of Social Credit macroeconomic theories being put into practice. However, an alternative view eventually won out, which saw small, autonomous credit unions as too fragmented for the large-scale ambitions of Social Credit planners. The result was the development in the 1950s of Alberta's Treasury Branch state banking system, which caught on particularly in rural areas where Social Credit had many supporters. The Treasury Branches undoubtedly did more to limit the growth of credit unions than Social Credit encouragement had ever done to promote them and provide an explanation for why credit unions in Alberta remained more urban and more closed than the Saskatchewan movement became.[48]

Rural credit unions were slow to develop for a variety of reasons, including needs in agriculture for long-term credit, and the perception of banking as a mysterious and difficult business. But there were early examples. Alberta had credit societies with municipal and provincial government participation, beginning with one formed in the Sibbald-Alsask area on the Alberta-Saskatchewan border in 1918. It took the name Bertawan Society.[49] William Halsall's small-town Killam co-op store also started a co-operative bank in the 1920s as a way to enable farmers and local residents to put their savings to work in an institution that would support local co-operative enterprise. But these early experiments in Alberta were not emulated widely.

The turning point for rural credit unions came with T. H. Bourassa, a small-town businessman in Lafleche, Saskatchewan, who was critical of the established banks. Bourassa saw that some local people had savings and others needed credit. What was needed was an institution to circulate capital locally. But the banks, he observed, were happy to take deposits and reluctant to make loans locally, with the effect that local capital was siphoned away. He conceived of credit unions as a tool for putting rural capital to work, leading to the creation of the Lafleche Credit Union in 1938. Credit unions spread widely in rural Saskatchewan in the 1940s. In the process, they moved away from the idea of requiring an occupational or religious common bond and became open-bond or community credit unions for all local residents.[50]

By 1944, Saskatchewan struck off in another different direction by electing the Co-operative Commonwealth Federation (CCF) into government. George Keen claimed that the CCF name was "an embarrassment to us.... A misnomer, and an awkward title."[51] And yet, it appears many members and activists did not share these reservations. Like Social Credit, or even more so, the CCF drew activism and energy from the co-operative movement. At the grassroots level, a large majority of the CCF's delegates and local organizers were people who had experience in the co-operative movement.[52] The party praised co-operatives and used the co-operative idea of working together as a metaphor for state planning, crown corporations, and other collectivist public projects. Once in power, the CCF devoted more attention to state projects than co-operative ones, for the most part leaving the established co-ops alone. But it did create a new department of co-operation and co-operative development, which undertook some significant developments in the 1940s to 1960s, such as creating co-operative farms for returning war veterans, promoting new agricultural production co-operatives of various types, and developing the first aboriginal co-operatives in the province's north.[53]

Developments in the two provinces were remarkably similar, but differences were visible. The UFA more strongly pursued agrarian-centralist ideas and hindered the development of consumer co-operatives in the

1920s and early 1930s, while the Social Credit government subsequently hindered the development of credit unions by its concentration on Treasury branches. In other words, the movements diverged at least in part because Alberta's governments were more centralist and interventionist. The history of co-operatives to mid-century implies that community-based social movements developed more strongly in Saskatchewan because governments left communities more to their own devices; these movements, in turn, helped influence the political culture and public policy.

The year 1955 marks the midpoint of Alberta's and Saskatchewan's first century, and a symbolic moment to take stock of what the co-operative social movements in the two provinces had accomplished. From 1905 to 1955, ordinary people in prairie communities – farmers, consumers, and borrowers – had acquired important ownership stakes in their society through co-operatives. The popular economic institutions they had created were experiencing their most dramatic spread at mid-century. They were larger later in members and volumes of business, but there was never more energy, optimism, and institutional innovation than in the postwar generation. This gave co-operatives at mid-century a heightened sense of being a co-operative "movement."

The optimism of the late war years gave a tremendous boost to co-operation. The Allied victory in the war was interpreted and represented as a victory of co-operation and democracy over tyranny and dictatorship. After the trauma of the Depression and the war, better prices for producers did not seem to be enough – a better society was called for. The first report to shareholders by the new Saskatchewan Federated Co-operatives Limited, formed in 1944 by the amalgamation of the province's successful co-op wholesale and oil refinery, stressed that "[m]an has solved the problem of production, and the problem of equitable distribution can also be solved if the peoples of the world determine to no longer tolerate poverty in the midst of plenty, and resolve to banish greed and selfishness in dealing with one another." The directors went on: "Future wars can be prevented by the practical application of co-operative principles, for our movement is a peaceful one.... We can assist in developing a better way of life by practicing co-operation in our everyday lives."[54]

A prolific publicist who came into his own in this era was J. Russell Love, a former UFA member of the legislature in the 1921–35 governments who ended as treasurer in the provincial cabinet. With the collapse of the UFA political movement, Love found a new cause in co-operatives. For many years he had edited farm co-operative magazines: the dairy co-ops' *Cowbell* and then the broader *Co-operative News.*[55] His rhetoric was without match.

> In a very short time, hundreds of thousands of Canadians will be returning to civilian life. What will the post-war world have in store for them? Will it mean jobs, homes, security, and a good living? The co-operative movement maintains that the promise of a new world is within our reach if we are prepared to build for it.
>
> ... The rugged individualism of pre-war days with its wasteful economic strife and its ruthless competition, and its fear of insecurity and unemployment, must give way to a new order of mutual understanding and co-operation designed to substitute peace for violence, construction for destruction, and abundance for scarcity.[56]

As Love put it in a later editorial during the Cold War: "I believe in co-ops because I disbelieve in dictatorship and fascism, whether in government or in economic life." Issues of democracy and fascism were expressed, he argued, in ordinary purchasing decisions: "I believe that every time I spend a dime in chain stores and their kind that might have passed through my co-op, I am feeding a monster that ignores human values because its primary goal is profit."[57]

While the optimism came from the 1940s, the underlying commitment often came from having lived through the 1930s. Typical of co-operative leaders of this generation was one I interviewed in 1988, an Alberta farmer who, during his career, rose to the highest levels of leadership in national-level co-operatives. When I asked him why he became involved, he said: "the prime reason was, I was growing up during the depression. I thought certainly there must be an alternative to the misery I saw around me."[58] The people who responded to the optimistic co-operative ideology of the 1940s–50s were, by and large, people who had lived through the life-changing experience of the Depression.

Premier T. C. Douglas (who at the time was also minister of co-operation and co-operative development) succinctly wrapped together many of these themes when he summarized the significance of co-operatives as follows in 1956:

> The history of the co-operative movement in Saskatchewan is the story of our struggle for economic democracy....
>
> Visitors ... often ask why the co-operative movement is so much stronger in Saskatchewan.... The answer is to be found in economic

> necessity. Climate, geography and the vulnerability of a one-crop economy have all combined to make living on these prairies a hazardous undertaking....
>
> Under the pressure of sheer necessity our people have turned to co-operation as offering the best means of survival in a highly monopolistic economy. During the past quarter of a century our people have proven that co-operation not only means their economic salvation but also a finer and more democratic way of life.[59]

Co-operatives may, indeed, have helped people achieve a finer and more democratic way of life, and yet it was not the idyllic future people foresaw in the 1940s. They had to build their new ways of life within a rapidly and inexorably changing world, in which it soon became apparent that the rural communities of the 1940s were being undermined and destroyed.

The height of the most intense "movement" phase of co-operation was also the time when co-operatives began to perceive an unpalatable, but for the most part unavoidable, future. They had become large organizations with thousands of volunteers and employees, widespread networks into most rural communities, and strong capacities to communicate and educate. This strength was enough to enable them to see what was happening as prairie society urbanized, but not enough for them to change many of the parameters. Under the circumstances of the post-1945 global economy and culture, the settlement project of the early twentieth century proved to have been overextended. Co-operatives in remote rural areas were now called upon to help manage the reduction of settlement.

This was an era in which co-operatives hung on in rural communities when competitors shut their doors and business relocated into larger centres. Often the co-ops were the last local stores, banks, and agricultural services in struggling villages and towns, or provided the only competition in slightly larger towns where a private merchant remained. Almost unnoticed, co-ops went from being "the farmers' store," whose threshold townsfolk would not cross, to being linchpins of community commerce. Co-operatives took on new significance as focal points for interaction and exchange without which the communities themselves might cease to exist. They learned to speak more and more for, and to, consumers and women and others, as provincial society became more complex and prosperous. Meanwhile, in the growing urban centres, new co-ops and new kinds of co-ops were quietly emerging, transforming the formerly rural movement in numbers if not in perception.

This is an era that continues to the present day. In Saskatchewan, the Royal Commission on Agriculture and Rural Life (1952–57) marked a turning point. It shone a spotlight on rural problems and raised for the public the prospect that rural decline might be long-term and structural. The six commissioners included leaders drawn from the co-operative movement, notably T. H. Bourassa, the originator of the Lafleche credit union, and Harry Fowler, the key organizer of the co-op refinery. Local co-operatives and women's guilds were active in the commission process, presenting briefs and participating in discussions in a large-scale process of citizen engagement. Research and adult education were important parts of the process. The commission chair, W. B. Baker, went on to head a new centre for community studies at the University of Saskatchewan, and staff member Harold Chapman was the founding principal of a new Co-operative College of Canada.[60] The commission realistically diagnosed key social-economic changes such as increasing farm sizes, urbanization, the need for improved rural services, and so on; and it prescribed things like improved knowledge, techniques, and efficiency as responses. People were no longer dreaming so much of new social orders. They were looking at ways to preserve what they could and adapt in the face of massive change.

While there was certainly a renewed pragmatism and utilitarianism among co-operatives, there was also a new communitarianism. Rather than being sectional organizations of the agrarian community in particular, many co-operatives were striving to assume public roles in local and regional networks. One writer on the subject argued in Alberta's *Co-operative News* in 1955 that co-operatives should grow beyond their "protest" roots, build bridges to local private merchants and other former opponents, and take "a more active part in the life of the community as a whole."[61] They needed to be seen as part of a web of church, educational, municipal, patriotic, fraternal, recreational, social, service, health, and occupational organizations that make up communities. Educational events, sponsorship of local activities, advertising, the activities of women's guilds, volunteer engagement, media relations, and fraternal connection with parallel organizations would help them perform this role. This 1955 vision captures in many ways the local role that co-operatives have in fact pursued.

The pressures on communities meant that it was increasingly difficult for local co-operatives to get by on local resources alone. Despite powerful traditions of democratic autonomy, co-operatives gradually (though never universally) began to work together more effectively. For the consumer co-ops and credit unions, this meant three interrelated trends: improved marketing and management at all levels, amalgamations or co-operative arrangements between small neighbouring co-ops, and development of strong central organizations with attendant central services and subsidiaries.

The strongest illustration of these trends was among the retail co-operatives. A landmark was the amalgamation of the Alberta and Saskatchewan wholesales in 1961. J. Russell Love of Alberta explained the logic as follows. First, the prairie provinces comprise "a natural trading area" – Manitoba had already joined Federated Co-ops in 1955, and British Columbia was added later, in 1970.[62] Second, "the co-operative movement can only be completely successful by being big itself" to compete with increasing concentration in the private retail trade. For the local societies to remain viable, their central wholesaler had to become larger and achieve economies of scale. Third, "one strong prairie wide co-op can hasten expansion" by undertaking development efforts, and, fourth, it could raise capital from co-op members for this purpose.

The retail co-ops developed the idea of becoming "one system" in the 1960s with all co-ops and their central wholesaling and manufacturing operations tightly integrated with each other in their operations. This vision has been pursued, in different stages, to the present day, with Federated Co-operatives Limited and its member local co-operatives conceptualizing themselves as "The Co-operative Retailing System" of western Canada.[63] While local co-ops remain autonomous, separately incorporated and governed by their own locally elected boards, their operations have been increasingly interlinked by common merchandising, training, signage, advertising, and policies, even across provincial borders.

The credit unions in both provinces followed a similar path, a little less obviously. From the 1940s to the 1970s, credit union centrals emerged in both provinces as central banks, trade associations, and developers or providers of services to the local credit unions. Deposit-guarantee arrangements and national insurance and trust companies, developed in the 1940s and 1950s, have grown and have become important institutions for the credit-union sector. These lines of development reached new levels in the early twenty-first century with amalgamations and restructuring among the central organizations. Saskatchewan and Alberta credit unions today share many back-room central functions, so that a statement for a Saskatchewan credit-union member may arrive from an Alberta office. In 2004, Co-operative Trust Company amalgamated with the financial functions of Credit Union Central of Saskatchewan to create Concentra Financial Services, a credit-union-owned company positioned for a more integrated and regional/national role. This is unlikely to be the last such change. The development of the central organizations is now an important part of the success of many of the local credit unions.

Parallel to the changes among the central co-operatives, local credit unions diversified over the last half of the twentieth century. The changes are remarkable, yet taken for granted as credit unions have developed into more or less full-service community banks. They began as simple savings and loan companies, adding chequing services and mortgages in the early years, then expanding, in many cases into agricultural and business lending. In many communities today, credit unions are important lenders to local businesses and play critical roles in local economic development. Automated banking machines were introduced in the 1970s, telephone, and then Internet banking became common, and – through separate companies because of legal restrictions – credit union members were also able to access co-operative insurance, investment services, ethical mutual funds, and other products. Credit unions have paralleled, that is to say, the evolution of Canada's banking system, but providing local and nonprofit services; and in so doing have acquired a niche as locally and regionally orientated banks. This role was implicitly recognized when credit unions purchased small-town bank branches in the 1990s and 2000s from major banks that were shifting their attention to global markets

Along the way, credit unions and other co-operatives, which in Saskatchewan and Alberta usually think of themselves as having rural roots, have become urban institutions as well. This process has occurred almost by the back door because popular perceptions and, often, the representative structures of the co-operative sectors still privilege the rural areas.

The history of the Calgary Co-operative Association dramatically encapsulates the rural-to-urban migration of the co-operative idea. The Calgary Co-op began as part of the UFA's 1940s foray into urban stores, which it saw as places for farmers to shop when they were in the cities. In 1951, the UFA Co-op sold its store at 11th Avenue and 1st Street SE in

Calgary to the Alberta Co-op Wholesale. A dynamic duo of co-operators campaigned for the store to become a locally directed co-op. John Suits was the manager and Gordon Barker a promoter and organizer who achieved this objective in 1956; Barker became the first president. From there Calgary Co-op embarked on over four decades of rapid expansion, strategically locating stores in new neighbourhoods, growing to become the largest locally owned consumer co-operative in North America.[64] Currently the co-operative counts over twenty locations, including in the nearby communities of Airdrie and Strathmore, and over three hundred thousand active members. It is an urban retailing success that handles no significant agricultural or farm supplies; rather, it is a leading and innovative retailer of groceries and petroleum to primarily urban people.

Even in cities, most co-ops remain locally orientated. As Calgary Co-op's elected board chair told me in 1988: "It's a community co-op." Unlike competitors, it is tied to the community for the long term: "we can't run. We've got no place to run – we're part of the community," in Calgary the same as in a smaller community. As an expression of this, the co-op supported the Calgary Stampede, the chuckwagon races, the Stampeders football team, and so on. While private companies are relatively free to donate to such causes, for a co-op "that's members' money," and the decision has to be made accountably and responsibly. Nevertheless, many co-ops choose to donate large sums to community causes. "I think that's been one of our strengths."[65]

In 2003, then-CEO Milford Sorensen put it in similar terms. Sorensen came to Calgary Co-op from Atlantic Canada and discovered that "there's a huge commitment to local business.... Part of the reason we're successful in Calgary is because we're a strong local business, and we happen to be a co-operative.... Albertans like to support their own. They don't like the profits taking off to the United States of America or to Toronto."[66] His board chair, Barry Ashton, elaborated the same message. "It's become an integral part of the fabric of this city," he told me.[67] Like most co-op presidents and managers, he stressed the co-op's community sponsorships and investments. "Corporate social responsibility has become a sort of a fashionable term in business parlance today, and co-operatives ... have always been corporately, socially responsible."

Calgary is a special case, and yet, it is different only in scale, not in the basic relationship of co-ops and local community. In many communities across Alberta and Saskatchewan, it is just understood that part of the role of the co-op is to support every possible local initiative. This is a consequence and demonstration of the fact that the co-ops are locally owned and locally orientated. In this and other ways, the co-operatives in the two provinces have probably become more alike, and certainly more interconnected, than they ever were before.

When Alexander Fraser Laidlaw of the Co-operative Union of Canada addressed the Federated Co-operatives delegates in 1960, he told them their transborder co-operative federation represented "perhaps the most unifying force on the Prairies. It represents the rural area, the town, the city; it is based on agriculture and on urban industry too; it crosses provincial boundaries, and other boundaries too."[68] It gives pause for thought: is there any other common organization, any at all, that brings together so many Alberta and Saskatchewan people? Of course, as Mrs. Peterson of Mayerthorpe might have said, all they're doing together is "buying apples." But Laidlaw went on to say: "I remember an old Scottish professor who used to say, 'The thing itself is not the thing – it's the thing behind the thing that's the thing.'"

The history of co-operatives in Alberta and Saskatchewan is surprisingly rich and under-examined. This essay has attempted only to follow selected themes with respect to the largest and historically most familiar co-operatives in the two provinces: agricultural handling and marketing co-ops, consumer or retail co-ops, and credit unions. These large and widespread forms provided platforms from which many other kinds of co-operatives were developed. Sometimes the older co-ops provided a kind of general inspiration and legitimation, serving by their existence to remind people that co-ops are a viable model when community entrepreneurs wanted to create something new. Existing co-ops also have helped secure legislation or policies supportive of new ones, much like the 1930s when credit-union legislation was introduced. But sometimes the connections between generations of co-operatives have been direct, as in the case of the Saskatoon community clinic. The co-operative clinic was organized in the 1960s and led by people experienced in co-operation, including long-time president Smokey Robson who had been a field agent for Federated Co-operatives Limited. Its first building was financed by Co-op Trust (now Concentra Financial Services). In ways like these, the human, social, and financial capital built up through co-operatives has continued to be put to work in creating new social enterprises.

Co-operatives now exist in fields from childcare to natural-gas distribution, from cable television networks to worker co-ops, from housing to film editing. A few large and centralized co-ops also operate in the two provinces, like UFA Co-op or the Vancouver-based Mountain Equipment Co-op, but for the most part the thousands of co-operatives in the two provinces are local and embedded in urban neighbourhoods and small towns. Such co-operatives have found ways to prosper by tapping and reinforcing the social cohesion of rural and urban communities. Centralized co-operatives succeeded for a long time, especially in agricultural handling and marketing, but when they encountered difficulty the results were catastrophic. This has again become evident in recent years with losses, failures, and conversions among the grain and dairy co-ops.

Saskatchewan Wheat Pool forecasted in the mid-1990s that the grain trade was going to be rationalized and that only a few companies would survive. Acting to prepare for that eventuality, the company arguably hastened it. In 1996–97, the company improved its borrowing capacity by converting its existing co-operative stock, owned by farmers, almost wholly to stock tradeable on the Toronto Stock Exchange; the equity conversion enabled farmers to cash in their shares without the company having to pay them out. SWP was able to issue some new shares and raise a certain amount of capital from the stock exchange, but it also went heavily into debt to finance the ambitious redevelopment of its far-flung network of wooden rural elevators into larger, more regionalized, and much more expensive concrete elevators; and, at the same time, a buying and investment spree to acquire a wide range of trading, processing, and food subsidiaries. Market share fell; some of the investments produced spectacular losses; and the company grew more and more beholden to its creditors, bondholders, and investors until, in February 2005, delegates voted effectively to let them take over the company, ending its co-operative character almost completely.[69]

The Alberta Wheat Pool tried to stave off financial collapse by merging in 1998 with the Manitoba Wheat Pool to make a new multi-province agrarian co-operative, Agricore, but it was likely too late. Agricore was taken over in 2001 by UGG, which had long since ceased itself to be a co-operative. The new company, Agricore United, is still significantly farmer-directed, a tribute to the co-operative roots of the enterprise, but in essence it is orientated towards its investors.

These changes in the grain co-ops were paralleled by others: the interprovincial amalgamation of the dairy co-ops to form Dairyworld, which subsequently sold its processing facilities to transnational Saputo. Such changes amount to the completion of the process begun in the 1930s by which the proud agrarian co-operatives have been dismantled.

While many co-operatives remain in agriculture – machinery co-operatives, co-operative pastures, artificial-insemination co-operatives, processing of particular commodities, not to mention related co-operatives such as for rural irrigation and utilities – the sector of large agrarian commodity-marketing and -handling co-operatives has been eliminated by the interplay of federal policy, international markets, and producers' own decisions. What remains of this heritage are government-mandated marketing boards like the Canadian Wheat Board, and primarily investor-driven entities like Agricore United and the new SWP.

The disappearance of the big commodity co-operatives is the complement of another process, not so negative, in which the co-operatives that have survived on the prairies have mostly been the ones that made the transition from agrarian sectionalism to local communitarianism, from centralized producer mentalities to locally orientated community service. Co-operatives, for a time, seemed to be about building regional, sectional, and provincial identities. Perhaps paradoxically, in an age of globalization – or perhaps it is no paradox at all – they have become tied once again to localities, as they were in the beginning.

NOTES

1 "The ICA Statement on the Co-operative Identity," in Ian MacPherson, *Co-operative Principles for the 21st Century* (Geneva: International Co-operative Alliance, 1996).

2 Compare James C. Scott, *Seeing Like a State: How Certain Schemes to Improve the Human Condition Have Failed* (New Haven, CT: Yale University Press, 1998).

3 Alex MacDonald, *Practical Utopians: The Lives and Writings of Saskatchewan Co-operative Pioneers Ed and Will Paynter* (Regina: Canadian Plains Research Center, 2004).

4 On Powell, see the biographies by Wallace Stegner, *Beyond the Hundredth Meridian: John Wesley Powell and the Second Opening of the West* (Lincoln: University of Nebraska Press, 1954), and Donald Worster, *A River Running West: The Life of John Wesley Powell* (Oxford: Oxford University Press, 2001). I have so far not come across a Canadian equivalent to Powell.

5 Albert Memmi, *The Colonizer and the Colonized*, expanded edition (Boston: Beacon Press, 1991; original French edition 1957), 10. I am indebted to Georgina Taylor for showing me this way of reading this text.

6 Ian MacPherson, *The Co-operative Movement on the Prairies, 1900–1955*, Canadian Historical Association Booklet No. 33 (Ottawa, 1979), 3–4. MacPherson notes that early agrarian organizations like the Patrons of Husbandry (Grange) beginning in the

1870s, and Patrons of Industry in the 1890s, promoted co-operatives and motivated the Territorial government to encourage farmer-owned creameries in 1890.

7 Ibid. On the early history of the UFA, see Bradford James Rennie, *The Rise of Agrarian Democracy: The United Farmers and Farm Women of Alberta, 1909–1921* (Toronto: University of Toronto Press, 2000).

8 Provincial farmers' associations were formed in 1905 when Alberta and Saskatchewan were created; previously, the Territorial Grain Growers' Association of 1901 represented Territorial farmers. In Alberta, the Farmers' Union of Alberta and the Society of Equity joined in 1909 to form the United Farmers of Alberta. In Saskatchewan, the SGGA merged with the Farmers' Union of Canada to form the UFC in 1926.

9 MacPherson, *Co-operative Movement on the Prairies*, 4, makes these points, but in respect to Alberta and Saskatchewan may not sufficiently stress the degree of American influence. Scandinavian countries mostly developed co-operative movements after 1900 (only Denmark did earlier). One of few works to stress the similarities to the United States remains Paul F. Sharp, *The Agrarian Revolt in Western Canada: A Survey Showing American Parallels* (Minneapolis: University of Minnesota Press, 1948; repr. Regina: Canadian Plains Research Center, 1997).

10 Taped interview by J. E. Cook and F. Johnson on February 28, 1970, in Provincial Archives of Alberta [hereafter: PAA] 70.282.

11 As recounted in J.F.C. Wright, *Prairie Progress: Consumer Co-operation in Saskatchewan* (Saskatoon: Modern Press, 1956), 37.

12 "Big Things Done in Little Lewvan," *The Co-operative Consumer* June 19, 1964, 4; "Boxcars were 'Rolling Stores' in Lemberg Co-op's Early Years," ibid., 10.

13 Ed Peterson, *Wetaskiwin Co-op: Fifty Years of Progress, 1917–1967* (n.p., n.d.), . 10–13. I found this in the Provincial Archives of British Columbia.

14 F. J. Fitzpatrick, Supervisor Co-operative Activities and Credit Unions, Province of Alberta, "Co-op History," *The Canadian Credit Institute Bulletin* No. 179 (April 1948), 3.

15 *First Annual Report of the Co-operative Organization Branch, Department of Agriculture, Saskatchewan, 1914* (Regina, 1915), 7.

16 Wright, *Prairie Progress*, 56ff. The Trading Department was not a co-operative, but a company run in connection with the SGGA, loosely controlled by it, and with individual investors.

17 Wright, *Prairie Progress*, 89. Wright lived in the Landis area and based these comments on his talks with local pioneers.

18 John Archer, "An Early Co-operative: The Saskatchewan Purchasing Company," *Saskatchewan History* 5 (Spring 1953): 55–56.

19 Robert McKay, later manager of the Saskatchewan Co-operative Wholesale Society, quoted by Wright, *Prairie Progress*, 58.

20 W. J. Hansen and A. H. Turner, *Some Facts Concerning the Dissolution of Co-operative Purchasing Associations in the Province of Saskatchewan 1914–1938*, in Saskatchewan Archives Board [hereafter: SAB] R261 f. 1.

21 G. Keen, *The Birth of a Movement: Reminiscences of a Co-operator* (n.p., n.d. [c. 1949]), 9.

22 On Partridge, see Murray Knuttila, *"That Man Partridge": E. A. Partridge, His Thoughts and Times* (Regina: Canadian Plains Research Center, 1994); On the early history of UGG, see R. D. Colquette, *The First Fifty Years* (Winnipeg: The Public Press, 1957).

23 On the elevator issue, see Robert Irwin, "'The Better Sense of the Farm Population': The Partridge Plan and Grain Marketing in Saskatchewan," *Prairie Forum* 18, no. 1 (Spring 1993): 35–52.

24 Louis Aubrey Wood, *A History of Farmers' Movements in Canada* (Toronto: Ryerson Press, 1924), 323ff.

25 G. Fairbairn, *From Prairie Roots: The Remarkable Story of Saskatchewan Wheat Pool* (Saskatoon: Western Producer Prairie Books, 1984), 22 (and ff for the following).

26 On the history of Alberta Wheat Pool, see Leonard D. Nesbitt, *Tides in the West* (Saskatoon: Modern Press, ca. 1962),

27 Keen to Waldron, March 16 and 23, 1926, in Library and Archives Canada, Co-operative Union of Canada box 37 [hereafter: LAC CUC-37].

28 Keen to Halsall, January 7, 1936, in LAC CUC-167.

29 Keen to Waldron, February 10, 1926 ("competition"), and February 23, 1926 ("discouraged"), in LAC CUC-37.

30 "General Meeting of the Managers and Directors of Co-operative Associations held in the ball room at the Palliser Hotel, Calgary, February 26, 1929," in Alberta Co-operative Wholesale Association (ACWA) minute book 1929– (corporate records of Federated Co-operatives Limited, Saskatoon).

31 William Halsall to Keen, August 16, 1932, in LAC CUC 156.

32 PAA 74.353 – 1 contains the minute book from 1929–43. Malin was appointed to this office in 1928, coming from Mannville Co-op, but was unfriendly to consumer co-operation generally, according to George Keen (Keen to Waldron, September 28, 1928, in LAC CUC 44). On the constituency co-ops, see *The U.F.A.* 10, 9 (May 1, 1931), 4.

33 Special meeting of CWS and UFA, May 25, 1931, in ACWA minutes 1929–.

34 Brett Fairbairn, *Building a Dream: The Co-operative Retailing System in Western Canada, 1928–1988* (Saskatoon: Western Producer Prairie Books, 1989), chap. 5. The UFA's educational and political functions were merged into the new Farmers' Union of Alberta in 1948, leaving the supply co-operative as the only organization remaining with the UFA name.

35 See 1934–39 speeches, notes for speeches, and drafts in Glenbow Alberta Institute, M1003, Priestley papers, f. 2. It isn't clear which speeches and articles were actually delivered. In the 1940s Priestley was general manager of the UFA Central Co-op.

36 On Wood, see William Kirby Rolph, *Henry Wise Wood of Alberta* (Toronto: University of Toronto Press, 1950).

37 Remarks to 1928 Alberta Institute of Co-operation, in PAA 86.307.

38 Keen described this arrangement to T. Swindlehurst of the Alberta Co-operative League, April 12, 1927, in LAC CUC – 40. He also noted that government funding was two-edged, since it led co-operators to regard him "as if I were a Government Official" – that is, they disregarded him. Although he accepted the government's support, he preferred that local co-ops pay his expenses.

39 Ibid., chap. 6.

40 Ian MacPherson, "Missionaries of Rural Development: The Fieldmen of the Saskatchewan Wheat Pool, 1925–1965," *Agricultural History* 60, no. 2 (Spring 1986): 73–96.

41 Fairbairn, *Building a Dream*, 61ff and 101ff.

42 Fairbairn, *Building a Dream*, chap. 8.

43 On the connections between the co-operative movement and the democratic ideas of the agrarian organizations, Social Credit, and the CCF, see David Laycock, *Populism and Democratic Thought in the Canadian Prairies, 1910 to 1945* (Toronto: University of Toronto Press, 1990).

44 Halsall to Keen September 14, 1935, in LAC CUC 161.

45 Halsall to Keen, December 29, 1936, in LAC CUC 167.

46 Muriel Clements, *By Their Bootstraps: A History of the Credit Union Movement in Saskatchewan* (Toronto/Vancouver: Clark Irwin, 1965), 51–53.

47 Arthur E. Turner, *Forging the Alternative: A History of the Alberta Credit Union Idea* (Calgary: Credit Union Central of Alberta, 1984), 99.

48 Turner, esp. chaps. 8 and 12.

49 Turner, 28.

50 Clements, 59–65 and ff.

51 Halsall to Keen, August 23, 1932, in ibid.

52 See S. M. Lipset, *Agrarian Socialism: The Co-operative Commonwealth Federation in Saskatchewan. A Study in Political Sociology*, rev. and exp. ed. (Berkeley: University of California Press, 1971), 222.

53 On the somewhat distant relationship with government, see Ian MacPherson, "The CCF and the Co-operative Movement in the Douglas Years: An Uneasy Alliance," in J. William Brennan (ed.), *"Building the Co-operative Commonwealth": Essays on the Democratic Socialist Tradition in Canada* (Regina: Canadian Plains Research Center, 1984).

54 SFCL *Report to Shareholders* for special general meeting in Saskatoon, June 13–15, 1945, 3.

55 See J. Russell Love, *Our Changing Economy: A Review of Factors and Conditions Affecting our Economy from 1900 to the Present Time* (Edmonton: Co-operative Union of Canada, [1946]), esp. biographical preface by A. B. MacDonald.

56 Comments as president of Interprovincial Co-operatives Limited in *Alberta Co-operative Leaders* (Alberta Livestock Co-operative: n.p., c. 1946), 30. I found this in PAA 86.307. The contributions were originally radio broadcasts promoting Victory Bonds.

57 "Believe Co-op … And You Will Buy Co-op," editorial, *Co-operative News* 28, no. 5 (May 1954).

58 Interview of Morris Jevne with Brett Fairbairn, January 16, 1988.

59 Douglas, Foreword to Wright, *Prairie Progress.*

60 On Baker, the Royal Commission, the Co-op College, the Centre for Community Studies, and other initiatives of this era, see Harold Baker, James Draper, and Brett Fairbairn, eds., *Dignity and Growth: Citizen Participation in Social Change. Essays in Honour of Bill Baker* (Calgary: Detselig Enterprises, 1991).

61 Eric Hopkins, "The Place of the Co-op Store in the Community," *Co-op News* 29, no. 8 (August 1955): 1 and 6–7.

62 As summarized by R. A. Findlay in memo to A. T. Baker, February 3, 1960, in Glenbow M2369 (Alberta Wheat Pool papers).

63 See Fairbairn, *Building a Dream*, esp. chaps. 13, 16, and 20.

64 See Fairbairn, *Building a Dream*, chap. 18; also Rob and Nancy Millar, *A History of the Calgary Co-op* (Saskatoon: Modern Press, ca. 1981). Calgary Co-op is said to be working on a new history. It is fair to say that the organization has attracted less than its share of attention from academics.

65 Interview of Bruno Friesen by Brett Fairbairn, 1988.

66 Brett Fairbairn, *Living the Dream: Membership and Marketing in the Co-operative Retailing System* (Saskatoon: Centre for the Study of Co-operatives, 2003), 87.

67 Interview of Barry Ashton by Brett Fairbairn, May 5, 2003.

68 "Address of Dr. A. F. Laidlaw National Secretary, Co-operative Union of Canada to the Delegates attending the 31st Annual Meeting January 21, 1960," in Saskatchewan Archives R110 file 70e.

69 These dramatic events remain to be analyzed by academic researchers. My colleague Murray Fulton is investigating changes in agricultural co-operatives as part of current SSHRC-funded research. In the meantime, apart from newspaper sources, see (for an overview) the entry on SWP in *The Encyclopedia of Saskatchewan* (2005), and (on the share conversion) Brett Fairbairn, "Principles of Organizational Restructuring in Rural Organizations: Co-operatives," in *Changing Rural Institutions: A Canadian Perspective*, ed. R. C. Rounds (Brandon: Canadian Rural Restructuring Foundation, 1997), 105–25.

NOTES ON CONTRIBUTORS

SARAH CARTER is Henry Marshall Tory Chair in the Department of History and Classics, and Faculty of Native Studies, University of Alberta. Her publications include *Lost Harvests: Prairie Indian Reserve Farmers and Government Policy*; *Capturing Women: The Manipulation of Cultural Imagery in Canada's Prairie West*; *Aboriginal People and Colonizers of Western Canada*; the co-authored book *The True Spirit and Original Intent of Treaty 7*, with Treaty 7 Elders and Tribal Council, Dorothy First Rider and Walter Hildebrandt; and the co-edited collection *Unsettled Pasts: Reconceiving the West through Women's History*, with Lesley Erickson, Patricia Roome, and Char Smith. Her present research project is a comparative and borderlands study of gender, race, and land policy in the North American West.

CATHERINE CAVANAUGH is an Associate Professor at Athabasca University, where she teaches history and women's studies. She is co-editor of *Standing on New Ground: Women in Alberta*; *Making Western Canada: Essays on European Colonization and Settlement*; and *Telling Tales: Essays in Western Women's History*. Most recently, she co-edited (with Michael Payne and Donald Wetherell) *Alberta Formed, Alberta Transformed*, a two-volume collection of essays on Alberta history. Her article "'No Place for a Woman:' Engendering Western Canadian Settlement" was awarded the O.O. Winther Prize and the Joan Jenson-Darlis Miller Prize.

BRETT FAIRBAIRN is Professor and Head of the Department of History, University of Saskatchewan, and Fellow in Co-operative Thought and Ideas at the Centre for the Study of Co-operatives. His research and teaching concern the history and interdisciplinary study of democracy, social movements, and co-operative enterprises in Canada and around the world. He has more than eighty publications, including his two most recent books, *Co-operative Membership and Globalization* (co-edited with Nora Russell) and *Living the Dream: Membership and Marketing in the Co-operative Retailing System*. In recognition of his public and scholarly contributions, Brett was awarded the Queen's Golden Jubilee Medal by the Lieutenant Governor of Saskatchewan in 2002.

MICHAEL (MIKE) FEDYK holds a master's degree in History from the University of Regina (2005). He has developed and produced a number of historical re-enactments as part of tourism and commemorative projects. The most notable was a recreation of the famous 1957 debate between Tommy Douglas and Ross Thatcher (2003). An enthusiastic and passionate speaker, he is committed to making history accessible to popular audiences.

R. DOUGLAS FRANCIS is a Professor of History at the University of Calgary, where he specializes in Canadian intellectual history and Western Canadian history. He is the author of *Frank H. Underhill: Intellectual Provocateur* and *Images of the West: Changing Perceptions of the Prairies, 1690–1960*, and co-author (with Richard Jones and Donald B. Smith) of *Origins: Canadian History to Confederation*, 5th ed., *Destinies: Canadian History since Confederation*, 5th ed., and *Journeys: A History of Canada*. He has edited a number of volumes and has published numerous articles in his areas of specialty.

DAVID HALL is Professor Emeritus of the Department of History and Classics, University of Alberta, and is author of a two-volume biography of Clifford Sifton: *Clifford Sifton: Vol. 1, The Young Napoleon, 1861–1900*; and *Clifford Sifton: Vol. 2, A Lonely Eminence, 1901–1926*. His current interests involve the history of territorial Alberta to 1905 and the life of Hon. Frank Oliver.

STEVE HEWITT is a Lecturer in American and Canadian Studies at the University of Birmingham in the United Kingdom. He is the author of *Riding to the Rescue: The Transformation of the RCMP in Alberta and Saskatchewan, 1914–1939*; with Reg Whitaker, *Canada and the Cold War*; and *Spying 101: The RCMP's Secret Activities at Canadian Universities, 1917–1997*. His personal webpage is www.spying101.com.

Western Canadian historian **CHRIS KITZAN** currently manages content creation for the Web Content and Services Division of Library and Archives Canada. Formerly a curator at the Canadian Museum of Civilization, Chris has more than fifteen years' experience authoring historical productions, exhibitions, and publications for both academic and popular audiences.

LAURENCE KITZAN is Professor Emeritus in the Department of History at the University of Saskatchewan, where he taught from 1963 to 2004. He did his PhD at the University of Toronto and is a specialist in British imperial history. He has published on such topics as the London Missionary Society, the First Burmese War, and Winston Churchill. His book in British imperial history is titled *Imperial Writers and the Image of Empire: The Rose-Colored Vision*. He is currently researching British travellers and explorers in the eighteenth and nineteenth centuries.

GEORGE MELNYK is Associate Professor, Faculty of Communication and Culture, University of Calgary. He is the author of the two-volume *Literary History of Alberta* (1999), and co-editor (with Tamara Palmer Seiler) of *The Wild Rose Anthology of Alberta Prose*. He has written extensively on western Canadian culture and society in four collections of essays. He has just finished co-editing a manuscript on Alberta writing titled *Wild Words: Essays on Alberta Writers*.

DOUG OWRAM is Deputy Vice Chancellor and Professor of History at the University of British Columbia Okanagan. He is also a Professor Emeritus of the University of Alberta in Edmonton. He is the author of some eight books and over twenty research articles on Canadian history. Professor Owram is a member of the Royal Society of Canada and the recipient of the University of Alberta's highest award for research, the Kaplan award. Dr. Owram was Provost and Vice-President Academic of the University of Alberta from 1998 to 2003 and from 2003 to 2005 served as President of the Canadian Federation of Humanities and Social Sciences.

A.W. RASPORICH is Professor Emeritus of History at the University of Calgary. His long-term research interests have included ethnic and utopian communities in western Canada. He was co-editor of the national journal *Canadian Ethnic Studies/Etudes Ethniques au Canada* from 1980 to 2003. His most recent books include a co-edited collection of historical essays entitled *Harm's Way: Disasters in Western Canada*, and *Make No Small Plans: The University of Calgary at Forty.*

BRADFORD J. RENNIE received his PhD at the University of Victoria. He has taught at the University of Alberta, the University of Calgary, the University of Victoria, and Mount Royal College. He is the author of *The Rise of Agrarian Democracy: The United Farmers and Farm Women of Alberta, 1909–1921*, and the editor of *Alberta Premiers of the Twentieth Century.*

A specialist in western and northern Canadian history, **BILL WAISER** has been a member of the Department of History at the University of Saskatchewan since 1984. He is the author of ten books, including the award-winning *Saskatchewan: A New History.* In November 2006, Bill was awarded the Saskatchewan Order of Merit, the province's highest honour.

MATTHEW WANGLER is the Head of Alberta's Historic Places Designation Program. His program is responsible for identifying and protecting the province's most significant heritage properties. He is currently in the final stages of completing his master's degree in history at the University of Alberta. His research interests include Canadian intellectual and religious history, and the relationship between nature and culture in Western Canada.

RANDI R. WARNE is Coordinator of Cultural Studies and Chair of the Department of Philosophy/Religious Studies at Mount Saint Vincent University in Halifax, Nova Scotia. She has written extensively on Canadian feminist, social activist, and writer Nellie L. McClung and is co-editor (with Catherine Cavanaugh) of *Standing on New Ground: Women in Alberta*; and *Telling Tales: Essays in Western Women's History.* She also publishes in the area of gender theory.

INDEX

D

E

F

I

L

M

P

S

Y

Z